INTRODUCTION TO M

# INTRODUCTION TO MATHEMATICAL ECONOMICS

Anthony L. Ostrosky, Jr.
*Illinois State University*
James V. Koch
*Ball State University*

WAVELAND PRESS, INC.
Prospect Heights, Illinois

For information about this book, write or call:
Waveland Press, Inc.
P.O. Box 400
Prospect Heights, Illinois 60070
(312) 634-0081


1986 reissued with changes by Waveland Press, Inc.

ISBN 0-88133-236-4



Printed in the United States of America

7 6 5 4 3 2

*To Dad and Mom Ostrosky, Dad and Mom Koch,*
*the Pittsburgh Steelers, and the St. Louis Cardinals*

# CONTENTS

# PREFACE

*"The age of chivalry is gone; that of sophisters, economists, and calculators has succeeded."*
EDMUND BURKE

The discipline of economics has experienced very few periods of prosperity such as it has known in the 1970s. Economists are called on with increasing frequency to apply their logic and tools to a variety of societal problems: pollution; depletion of natural resources; crime; urban sprawl; taxation; food production; the depreciating dollar—the list swells daily. The ability of the economist to speak to these problems reflects a well-developed body of theory, modes of analysis that emphasize logic, and sophisticated quantitative tools. The comparative poverty of the other social sciences can be traced directly to their deficiencies in one or all of these areas.

Mathematics has played a central role in enabling economists to rigorously state their theorems, with emphasis on logical inference, and in enabling them to go far beyond other social sciences in testing the empirical validity of their theories. The primary aim of this book is to show fledgling students how, where, when, and why they can appropriately utilize mathematics in economics and business. The student who masters the mathematical tools presented in this book will not only be able to read and apply most of the "language" that modern economic theory uses, but also he or she will learn (and perhaps for the first time understand) a great deal of economic theory. If the readers of this book are similar to the students at Illinois State University, then one can expect that this combination of mathematics and economics will turn on lights, open doors, and yield deeper understandings. Many are the "math econ" students who have suddenly exclaimed, "Now I see what my Econ 100 instructor really meant!"

We do not claim to present all the many applications of mathematics to economics and business in this book. This book is a well-defined one-semester introductory approach to the use of mathematics in economics and business. Undergraduate economics majors at Illinois State University are required to take a course entitled "Introduction to Mathematical Economics" that very closely parallels the topics and the level of difficulty of this book. Despite being a demanding course, Introduction to Mathematical Economics is a popular course that attracts numerous students from other departments, such as Business Administration, Finance, Marketing, Management, Mathematics, and Accounting. We entertain similar hopes for this book of the same name, and feel that it may appropriately be used in courses in all the above departments, in addition to the Economics department.

The outstanding feature of this book is the plentiful use of examples and applications. Each chapter contains a large section that is entirely devoted to applications of the mathematical tools; one entire chapter is devoted to specific applications of matrix algebra. Several examples, such as Stigler's famous "diet problem," are used on a number of occasions in order to demonstrate the power of applied mathematics. The book also contains "danger flags" that identify material and concepts that often tend to be confused by students, and that therefore need to be clearly identified and learned.

The organization of the book is based on the view that a thorough review of basic precalculus mathematics and algebra is the correct place to start. The differential calculus, with its many applications, is then introduced. Maximization and minimization techniques are plentifully used and illustrated. The integral calculus is the next major topic; two chapters are devoted to its exposition and application. Finally we cover matrix algebra, and devote an entire chapter to linear programming and input-output analysis in a matrix-algebra context. The overall organization of the book stresses a building-block approach, whereby each newly introduced topic depends on the topics previously covered.

Although we alone are responsible for any errors of omission or commission that appear in this book, we gratefully acknowledge the helpful comments of Professor Thomas Shilgalis of Illinois State University, Professor David Finifter of the College of William and Mary, Professor Howard Taylor of the University of Akron, Professor Charles Mott of Bowling Green State University, and Professor James Kenkel of the University of Pittsburgh, who reviewed several chapters of the manuscript and made many positive contributions. Susan Gintner excelled as our typist. All these individuals have our thanks.

Anthony L. Ostrosky, Jr.
James V. Koch

# THE ROLE AND POWER OF MATHEMATICS

# 1

Mathematics is a rigorous and well-defined study of the structures, configurations, and interrelationships that characterize the world in which human beings live. Mathematics functions as an exacting language that articulates the essential characteristics of a wide range of situations so that the key aspects of those situations can be dispassionately examined. Modern mathematics is "economical" in the very best sense of the word, in that: (1) It clearly states the bare-bones assumptions that underpin a relationship. (2) It highlights the logical processes that characterize the relationship. (3) It states any conclusions that are implied by the relationship in a clear and concise form.

The modern fields of business and economics are filled with topics that are amenable to mathematical analysis. Relationships can be specified relating production cost to output, output to inputs, wages to worker productivity, and so forth. Further, the decision-maker is often interested in minimizing the cost of achieving a certain objective, or maximizing the output of a particular productive process. In still other circumstances, a business person may wish to know how much change will occur in sales when the firm alters the amount of advertising it is undertaking.

Fortunately nearly all the concepts that business executives, accountants, economists, and marketing and finance experts deal with are susceptible to quantification. Costs of production, wage rates, sales, and output can all be represented in a quantitative fashion. To this list, however, we might also add the concept of *utility*, which preoccupies economists. *Utility* is a number that is assigned to an alternative for purposes of choice-making. Utility is often given an interpretation such as "satisfaction." It is a highly abstract concept that is assigned characteristics that can be represented by mathematical analysis.

The relevant point is that mathematics is capable of dealing with a wide range of relationships that confront decision-makers in the business and economic arenas. Some of these relationships involve obviously physical magnitudes, such as tons of fertilizer and bushels of corn. Other relationships—such as that describing the conditions that must hold for a consumer to maximize utility—are high-level abstractions.

The versatility of mathematics is apparent. Equally important is the power of mathematics. With the help of mathematics, the decision-maker can attack and solve problems that can be given only a cursory glance with a strictly verbal analysis. Indeed, one can make certain statements mathematically that with verbal language either cannot be made at all or that must be made only in an awkward fashion. Since mathematics is a specialized language, it can open doors that were previously closed. The student who ignores the contributions of mathematics to the study of business and economics not only bucks a strong trend in these areas, but also cannot take advantage of tools and a mode of analysis that have greatly enhanced the power and ability of decision-makers in those areas.

## STIGLER'S DIET PROBLEM: AN EXAMPLE

The previous paragraphs make strong claims concerning the usefulness and power of mathematics as a means of formulating and solving problems in business and economics. It is appropriate that we support these claims with an example.

In 1945, George Stigler specified and attempted to solve the so-called "diet problem."[1] The crux of the diet problem is easily understood. What is the least expensive combination of foods available to consumers that will enable them to satisfy the recommended daily dietary allowances established by the Food and Nutrition Board of the National Academy of Sciences? That is, what is the cheapest way to obtain the protein, calories, vitamin $B_1$, and so forth, that individuals need to sustain life? The diet problem is an extremely significant subject, since at least 80% of the world's population fails to satisfy the recommended dietary allowances in a given year.[2] The looming specter of worldwide malnutrition speaks strongly in favor of the need to solve the diet problem.

The diet problem reduces to what we shall in future chapters refer to as a "constrained minimization problem." This means that we wish to find the minimum value of something (in this case, the cost of a particular diet), given that we must at the same time satisfy various constraints (in this case, the constraints are the dietary requirements).

Let the letter $X$ represent the quantity of a food consumed by an individual. $X_1$ is then the quantity of a particular food, say peanut butter, that the individual can choose to consume. Stigler allowed the consumer to choose among 80 different foods. Therefore we can represent the quantity of these foods by the variables $X_1, X_2, X_3, \ldots, X_{80}$.

Each of the 80 different foods has a price. We shall represent the 80 different prices by the variables $P_1, P_2, P_3, \ldots, P_{80}$. For example, $P_1$ might be equal to $0.02 and represent the price per ounce of peanut butter.

Our task is to minimize the amount of money we spend on the 80 foods. Hence we wish to minimize Equation (1.1),

$$C = P_1X_1 + P_2X_2 + P_3X_3 + \cdots + P_{80}X_{80} \tag{1.1}$$

Note that $P_1$ times $X_1$ is the price of peanut butter times the amount of peanut

[1] George J. Stigler, "The Cost of Subsistence," *Journal of Farm Economics*, 27 (May 1945), pp. 303–314.

[2] See Sohan L. Monocha, *Nutrition and Our Overpopulated Planet*, (Charles C Thomas, Springfield, Illinois, 1975), Chapter 1.

butter purchased. This means that $P_1 X_1$ represents the total amount of money the consumer spends on peanut butter. Similarly, $P_2 X_2$ represents the total amount of money the consumer spends on food $X_2$, and so forth. The capital letter $C$ denotes the sum of all these expenditures. It is $C$ that we seek to minimize (make as small as possible).

The obvious way to minimize $C$ is to not spend any money on food. This, however, is not permissible, since we must also satisfy the recommended daily dietary allowances. Let $R$ symbolize a dietary requirement. Thus $R_1$ might represent the recommended intake of calories per individual per day. $R_1$ was 3000 in Stigler's example. We can represent the nine different dietary requirements utilized by Stigler by the variables $R_1, R_2, R_3, \ldots, R_9$.

The diet problem is inherently challenging because two different foods seldom yield the same amount of a nutrient per ounce of that food. For example, 1 ounce of uncooked bacon yields 186 calories, whereas 1 ounce of uncooked sirloin steak yields only 88 calories. Let the symbol $a_{ij}$ represent the number of units of nutrient $i$ that are satisfied by 1 ounce of food $j$. Hence the $a_{ij}$ for uncooked bacon is 186, whereas it is only 88 for uncooked sirloin steak.

A nutrient requirement can be satisfied by eating many different foods. The term $a_{ij} X_j$ represents the total number of units of nutrient $i$ that are obtained when one consumes a given number of ounces of food $j$. For example, if one consumes 6 ounces of uncooked bacon, then $X_j = 6$; given $a_{ij} = 186$, this means that $a_{ij} X_j = (186)(6) = 1116$ calories.

We have previously noted that Stigler assumed that an individual must obtain at least 3000 calories per day from the foods consumed. The consumer could choose among 80 different foods to satisfy the requirement. Thus the constraint or requirement is that the sum of all the calories the consumer derives from consuming various foods must be 3000 or greater. That is,

$$a_{11}X_1 + a_{12}X_2 + a_{13}X_3 + \cdots + a_{1,80}X_{80} \geq 3000 \tag{1.2}$$

Equation (1.2) expresses the fact that the total calories derived from the consumption of the 80 possible foods must be greater than or equal to 3000 calories. The symbol $\geq$ expresses the meaning "greater than or equal to."

Stigler, in his diet problem, imposed nine different dietary requirements on the consumer (see Table 1.1). This means that there are nine constraints, of which Equation (1.2) is one, that the consumer must satisfy in his or her purchases. In addition to the constraint requiring the consumer to obtain at least 3000 calories daily, Table 1.1 reveals additional constraints. For example, it is required that the consumer's purchases yield at least 70 grams of protein and 12 milligrams of iron per day. These nine constraints are represented by Equations (1.3).

$$\begin{array}{l} a_{11}X_1 + a_{12}X_2 + a_{13}X_3 + \cdots + a_{1,80}X_{80} \geq R_1 \\ a_{21}X_1 + a_{22}X_2 + a_{23}X_3 + \cdots + a_{2,80}X_{80} \geq R_2 \\ a_{31}X_1 + a_{32}X_2 + a_{33}X_3 + \cdots + a_{3,80}X_{80} \geq R_3 \\ \quad\vdots \qquad\quad \vdots \qquad\quad \vdots \qquad\qquad\quad \vdots \\ a_{91}X_1 + a_{92}X_2 + a_{93}X_3 + \cdots + a_{9,80}X_{80} \geq R_9 \end{array} \tag{1.3}$$

We can now state the diet problem directly. We wish to minimize the value of Equation (1.1) subject to the nine nutrient constraints given in Equation (1.3). Today mathematical tools are available that enable one to find the solution to this type of problem with relative ease. Unfortunately for Stigler, these tools were not commonplace in 1945. Hence, Stigler noted that his approach to solving the problem was "...experimental because there does not appear to be a direct method of finding the minimum of a linear function subject to linear conditions."[3] That is, Stigler was forced to find a solution by hit-or-miss methods.

The application of modern constrained-maximization techniques to Stigler's diet problem results in the diet recorded in Table 1.2. Note that this 1945 application of a 1944-vintage minimum-cost diet required an expenditure of only 16.41 cents per day, or $59.88 per year.

Since 1944, food prices have risen more rapidly than the Consumer Price Index as a whole.[4] There are also many foods available today (for example, frozen foods) that did not appear in the grocery stores in 1944. Most importantly, there are seven additional nutrient requirements that became quantifiable by 1975, and six nutrient requirements have changed in amount since 1944. Hence the situation has changed profoundly since 1944.

Table 1.2 records the solution to a 1975-vintage diet problem in which the consumer can choose among 117 different foods and must satisfy 16 different nutrient constraints. The daily cost of the minimum-cost diet in 1975 is 43.72 cents, and the annual cost is $159.58.[5] The solution was generated by resorting to the simplex linear-programming algorithm, a constrained-maximization technique of the type we shall develop in this book.

Table 1.1 The nine daily nutritional requirements used by Stigler

| *Nutrient* | *Daily required allowance* |
|---|---|
| 1. Calories | 3000 calories |
| 2. Protein | 70 grams |
| 3. Calcium | 800 milligrams |
| 4. Iron | 12 milligrams |
| 5. Vitamin A | 5000 International Units |
| 6. Vitamin $B_1$ (thiamine) | 1.8 milligrams |
| 7. Riboflavin | 2.7 milligrams |
| 8. Niacin | 18 milligrams |
| 9. Ascorbic acid | 75 milligrams |

*Source:* George J. Stigler, "The Cost of Subsistence," *Journal of Farm Economics*, 27 (May 1945), pp. 303–314, at p. 305. Reprinted with permission.

[3] Stigler, p. 310.

[4] The price index for food (1967 = 100.0) was 50.7 in 1945 and 171.2 in April 1975. The Consumer Price Index for all items was 53.9 in 1945 and 158.6 in April 1975. Therefore the food price index increased 237.7% during that time period, while the Consumer Price Index increased only 194.2% in the same time period.

[5] This 1975-vintage solution may be found in L. J. Bassi, "The Diet Problem Revisited," *The American Economist*, 20 (Fall 1976), pp. 35–39.

The lessons to be drawn from the diet-problem example are several. First, mathematics is a powerful tool that can assist the decision-maker in solving important problems. The diet problem is one example among many that you will encounter in this book.

Second, many powerful mathematical tools (such as the simplex linear-programming algorithm) can be acquired and mastered by students who are not professional mathematicians. You need not be a mathematics major or minor to be able to solve problems such as the diet problem.

Third, the great advances that have occurred in applied mathematics in recent decades make it possible for decision-makers in the business and economics arenas to deal with problems that were previously extremely tedious or impossible to solve. Stigler, for example, was forced to admit (in 1945) that there was no general way to solve the diet problem. That is no longer the case. We shall develop tools in this book that will enable us to solve the diet problem.

The development and use of mathematical tools to solve business and economic problems has expanded very rapidly in recent years. A course covering the materials presented in this book is now required of business administration, accounting, marketing, and economics majors in most colleges and

Table 1.2 Diet problem solutions

| *Stigler's August 1944 solution* | *Cost* |
|---|---|
| 80 foods | Daily cost: 16.41¢ |
| 9 nutrient constraints | Annual cost: $59.88 |
| 1. Flour, wheat (23.45 ounces daily) | |
| 2. Cabbage (4.69 ounces daily) | |
| 3. Spinach (.57 ounce daily) | |
| 4. Flour, pancake (5.87 ounces daily) | |
| 5. Liver, pork (1.10 ounces daily) | |
| *1975-vintage problem* | |
| 117 foods | Daily cost: 43.72¢ |
| 16 nutrient constraints | Annual cost: $159.58 |
| 1. Kidneys, beef (0.40 ounce daily) | |
| 2. Milk, nonfat solid (1.07 ounces daily) | |
| 3. Beans, red (4.73 ounces daily) | |
| 4. Cabbage (2.30 ounces daily) | |
| 5. Spinach (2.14 ounces daily) | |
| 6. Flour, all-purpose (11.59 ounces daily) | |
| 7. Flour, whole wheat (9.78 ounces daily) | |

*Sources*: Stigler's August 1944 solution is adapted from George J. Stigler, "The Cost of Subsistence," *Journal of Farm Economics*, 27 (May 1945), pp. 303–314, at p. 311. Reprinted with permission. The 1975-vintage problem is taken from L. J. Bassi, "The Diet Problem Revisited," *The American Economist*, 20 (Fall 1976), pp. 35–39, at p. 37. Reprinted with permission.

universities. It behooves the student who wishes to be well prepared and efficient to master the mathematics that we shall present in the following chapters. Given the multifold applications of mathematics to business and economic problems, not only should our studies in the following chapters prove to be interesting, but also they should open new and exciting doors to you.

## PROBLEMS

1. Mathematics can clearly be used in very useful ways in solving business and economics problems. This has led some enthusiasts, who are labeled extreme logical positivists, to contend that "If you can't measure it, it isn't worth knowing about," or "If you can't measure it, it doesn't exist." Write a critique of these statements.
2. Many historians claim that they do not use models in writing history and in arriving at conclusions about historical phenomena. Is it possible to analyze something without having an underlying model? Will hard work produce insights and generalizations if you do not have a model?
3. Those who use mathematical tools in the analysis of business and economics problems frequently contend that it is possible to say things with mathematics that could not be said verbally. Is this true? Can the reverse be true?
4. A frequent criticism of business and economics models is that they do not fit the real world with precision. The real world nearly always seems to be somewhat different from the world outlined in the model. Is this a valid criticism? Can we construct models that precisely relate to a particular situation, or to all situations?
5. Business and economic models that employ mathematics are occasionally criticized on the grounds that they employ unrealistic assumptions. For example, economists assume that individuals maximize utility. Some criticize this assumption as being unrealistic. Are realistic assumptions necessary when one is using mathematical models?

# REVIEW OF BASIC CONCEPTS

# 2

In Chapter 1 we used Stigler's diet problem to demonstrate that the appropriate use of mathematics can enable a decision-maker to deal with a wide range of problems that might otherwise receive only a cursory glance. Mathematics enables us to isolate and examine the crucial forces operating in an increasingly complex world.

It is the complexity of the world, however, that bedevils the mathematician, accountant, or economist who must make decisions. The endless variety of possible experiences and circumstances that one finds in society means that no decision-maker can usefully attempt to make decisions by considering *all* the factors that might influence that decision. It is humanly impossible for any individual to provide a complete description of the richness, complexity, and variety that characterize the world. Consider the multitude of writers who have unsuccessfully tried to provide a complete description of the complicated role and activities of the modern American corporation.

Realistic, successful analysis of a typical problem that faces a decision-maker requires that the decision-maker isolate the key aspects of reality in that problem. That is, the analyst must abstract and simplify, always taking care to retain in his or her decision-making those factors that are crucial to the situation at hand. For example, the availability of iron ore is a crucial factor in the production of steel, whereas the religious affiliations of steel workers is an irrelevant factor. The skillful analysis of a problem results in a *theory*.

DEFINITION A theory is an abstract set of relationships from which we can derive meaningful propositions about the world.

A good theory clearly delineates the crucial forces that are at work in a situation, the circumstances under which those forces are related, and the probable result of the interaction of those forces. You have doubtless learned over time to have considerable (though not complete) confidence in theories that indicate that students who are more intelligent, and who study more, will generally earn higher grades than others not as well equipped or prepared. Such a theory forthrightly states two of the most important factors that determine student grades, and also indicates the relationship between these two factors and grades. On the other hand, as stated here, this theory tells us little about the interrelationships and tradeoffs between intelligence and hours of study in terms of the end product, grades.

The language and component parts of theories deserve further examination, for it is our ability to construct and use abstract theoretical relationships that in the end determines our ability to make intelligent choices and decisions.

In the analysis of economic and business problems, it is common to combine several theories into a *model.* We can express an economic model as a series of mathematical equations, but we need not do so. Many models are developed verbally, although such models often suffer from lack of precision. A model identifies the factors and influences that are thought to be important in a situation, and delineates the relationships among those factors and influences. A model is best thought of as a systematic presentation of interrelated theories.

## VARIABLES

Mathematics is a specialized language that can be used with great success to describe a wide range of relationships. A foundation stone of any relationship is the concept of a *variable.*

DEFINITION A *variable* is something that can assume different values at different points of observation.

The magnitude of a variable can assume various values. For example, the gross national product (GNP) of the United States could be 100, 1000, 1500, or, indeed, any positive magnitude. Because a variable's magnitude can assume various different values, a variable must be represented by a general symbol. Hence the price of a pizza might be represented by the symbol $p$, while the tax rate might be represented by the symbol $t$. In the diet problem presented in Chapter 1, the magnitudes of the 80 different foods were represented by the symbols $X_1, X_2, X_3, \cdots, X_{80}$. It is customary to use the letters at the end of the alphabet, such as $u, v, w, x, y,$ and $z$, to symbolize the magnitudes of variables used in mathematical relationships. This, however, is a matter of convention rather than of necessity.

We may also classify variables as being either *continuous* or *discrete* in terms of the magnitudes that are permissible for those variables.

DEFINITION A *continuous variable* is one that can assume any value within a given interval of values.

DEFINITION A *discrete variable* is one that can assume at most a limited number of values within a given interval of values.

Consider the number of gallons of gasoline that can be pumped into the 12-gallon tank of a Ford Escort. An infinite number of possibilities exist within the interval between and including 0 and 12. For example, 4.5 gallons of gasoline might be pumped into the tank. Or 11.6 is another possibility, as are 11.61, 11.612, 11.6123, and so forth. An infinite (noncountable) number of values exist within a given interval when a variable such as gasoline is continuous in nature.

By way of contrast, assume that the gasoline station has a policy that forbids the sale of fractional gallons. Thus 2.0 gallons of gasoline may be pumped, but not 2.01 or 2.63. Within the interval 0 to 12, the number of possibilities is now finite and countable. The only possibilities are 0, 1, 2, ..., 12. In terms of the language that we shall later develop, the magnitudes of gasoline that can be pumped are limited to *integer* values such as 5, 6, or 7.

EXAMPLES

1. Gross national product (GNP) is a continuous variable in that it can assume any magnitude between 0 and an infinitely large positive number. Hence 1,543.324 billion dollars is one possible magnitude. In actual practice, however, the actual reports and computations of GNP are typically restricted to integer values. 1,543.324 becomes 1,543 when GNP is regarded as a discrete variable.
2. Assume that we repeatedly flip a coin and observe, after each flip, whether a head or a tail has resulted. Excluding the exceedingly small possibility of a coin landing on its edge, there are only two possibilities that can occur: a head or a tail.

   Suppose that we choose to represent the appearance of a head by a 0 and the appearance of a tail by a 1. This is a *discrete* variable, because values such as .50 or .75 can never appear; 0 and 1 are the only permissible values. Observe, however, that the mean or average of such values is a *continuous* variable that is defined on the interval between 0 and 1. If the coin is "fair," then the mean value of the discrete variable will approach .50 as the number of coin flips becomes large. On the other hand, if the coin is bent and a tail appears more often as a result, then a mean of .75 is a distinct possibility.
3. Some variables that are reported in discrete form are sometimes assumed to be continuous when a large number of observations or instances of that variable are available. For example, many professors report examination scores of students on a scale that ranges from 0 to 100. Noninteger values, such as 58.372, are not generally reported and may actually be impossible to achieve on this examination. However, when a large number of different scores are involved, it is often assumed that the distribution of scores is continuous. Any score in the interval 0 to 100 is permissible. The "normal distribution" is one such example; many professors use it for grading purposes. The normal distribution is continuous in that any score, integer or otherwise, is possible.

Variables may also be classified as to whether or not they are *endogenous* or *exogenous* in nature.

DEFINITION An *endogenous variable* is one whose value is to be determined by the model or theory.

DEFINITION An *exogenous variable* is one whose value is taken as given; its value is determined by forces that are external to the model or theory.

The magnitude of endogenous variables is explicitly examined and determined by the model or theory. Simple supply-and-demand analysis explicitly determines the price of goods and services. Price is the focus of the analysis, and the magnitude of price is determined by supply-and-demand analysis. Price is an endogenous variable in such a case. However, should the Organization of Petroleum Exporting Countries (OPEC) dictate that the price of a barrel of oil will be $35, then price becomes an exogenous variable given to the market.

EXAMPLES

1. A simple marketing theory might relate the sales of a given item such as Corn Flakes to the size of a tax rebate received by consumers. The tax rebates given the consumers are exogenous and external to the model.
2. The $Y = C + I + G$ equation (where $Y$ = national income, $C$ = private consumption expenditures, $I$ = business investment expenditures, $G$ = governmental purchase of goods and services) has often been used to explain national income determination. In the simplest models, $C$ is considered to be endogenous, while $I$ and $G$ are considered to be exogenous. That is, the value of $C$ is determined inside the model, whereas the values of $I$ and $G$ are exogenous, already known, and taken as given.

## EQUATIONS, ROOTS, AND CONSTANTS

Mathematical models are usually expressed in the form of equations.

DEFINITION An *equation* is a statement that asserts the equality or equivalence of two (or more) mathematical expressions.

There must be at least one variable in each equation.[1] For example, it is possible to assert that $2X = 10$. $X$ is the variable whose magnitude is initially unknown. The statement that $2X = 10$, however, asserts that $2X$ is equivalent to (" is the same as ") 10. By inspection, we can see that $X$ must be 5 in order for the statement to be true.

In the previous example, $2X$ is equal to 10 when $X$ is equal to 5. By way of contrast, $2X$ is *not* equal to 10 when $X$ is equal to 4. $X = 5$ is a critical root or solution value of the equation $2X = 10$, whereas $X = 4$ is not.

DEFINITION *Critical root*(s) or *solution value*(s) is (are) the value(s) of the variable(s) of an equation that cause(s) the equation to hold true.

There are many examples of critical roots (solution values) in the field of economics. The equilibrium price that clears the market; the magnitudes of inputs and outputs that maximize profits; and the dollar value of the consumption of private individuals that leads to an equilibrium level of GNP—are all examples of critical roots. We shall have frequent opportunity to work with these particular cases involving critical roots in future chapters.

Some equations are characterized by mathematical terms that never change in value. You are undoubtedly aware that the value of Π (pi) is a constant that is equal to 3.14159 ... . The value of Π never changes. Another example of a constant is $e$, the base of the system of natural logarithms, which is equal to 2.71828 ... .

[1]Some equations contain more than one variable. The statement that $2X = Y$ is one such example.

DEFINITION A *numerical constant* is a magnitude that is fixed and does not change in value.

You may plumb your memory of plane geometry for the equation $A = \Pi r^2$, which describes how to find the area $A$ of a circle. In this case, the radius $r$ is a variable whose magnitude changes as the radius of the circle in question changes. $\Pi$, however, is a constant that we can approximate by the value 3.14159, and this never changes.

Many equations include parameters that act as numerical constants in a limited fashion.

DEFINITION A *parametric constant* or *parameter* acts as a constant only within the context of a particular equation or problem, but may assume a different constant value in other equations or problems.

The difference between numerical constants and parametric constants can be sharpened by means of an example. Assume that the demand for seats at a St. Louis Cardinal baseball game is given by the equation $Q = 50{,}000 - bP = 50{,}000 - 6000P$, where $Q$ is the number of seats demanded, and $P$ is the price of the seat. The term 50,000 is a numerical constant and never changes. As it happens, it represents the number of seats available in the ballpark, which is fixed. The term $b = 6000$ is a parametric constant that is fixed only for this particular situation.[2] It expresses the relationship between baseball attendance and the price of baseball tickets in St. Louis at one point in time.

This relationship might well change in the future, thus necessitating a change in the parameter. You will recognize in the above equation that if the price of a seat were \$5, then 20,000 fans would buy a seat and attend the baseball game. Should the St. Louis area be hit by an economic slowdown, then the parameter $b$ might well change, perhaps to 8000, so that $Q = 50{,}000 - 8000P$. If the ticket price were held at \$5, attendance would then fall to 10,000 fans.

It is customary to use letters at the beginning of the alphabet (for example, $a$, $b$, $c$, and $d$) to symbolize parameters in a particular equation.

EXAMPLE We shall now utilize a simplified Keynesian national-income model to illustrate the various terms and definitions that we have developed in this subsection. We begin with four equations:

$$Y = C + I + G \tag{2.1}$$

$$C = a + bY = 150 + 0.75Y \tag{2.2}$$

$$I = 25 \tag{2.3}$$

$$G = 20 \tag{2.4}$$

where $Y$ = national income, $C$ = private consumption, $I$ = private investment, and $G$ = government spending.

[2] When a constant is joined to a variable, that constant is often referred to as the *coefficient* of that variable.

The above four-equation model has two endogenous variables ($Y$ and $C$) and two exogenous variables ($I$ and $G$). The values of the exogenous variables ($I$ and $G$) are assumed to be determined outside this model. The consumption function, given by Equation (2.2), illustrates the use of two parameters ($a = 150$ and $b = 0.75$).[3] The values of the exogenous variables ($I$ and $G$) are also numerical constants.

The solution values of $Y$ and $C$ that are consistent with the above four equations may not seem readily apparent. We can find the solution values by substituting Equations (2.2), (2.3), and (2.4) into Equation (2.1). This results in

$$Y = C + I + G$$

$$Y = (150 + 0.75Y) + 25 + 20 = 0.75Y + 195$$

$$0.25Y = 195$$

$$Y = \frac{195}{0.25} = 780 \tag{2.5}$$

When $Y = 780$, $C = 150 + 0.75(780) = 735$. We may label $Y = 780$ and $C = 735$ as critical roots (solution values) of the system of four equations described above.

## REAL NUMBER SYSTEM

A variety of mathematical relationships and terms are used to express business and economic phenomena. The theories that make up the body of knowledge in these areas are made up of equations that variously contain variables, constants, and parameters. These variables, constants, and parameters usually take on numeric values. It is possible to classify numeric values in terms of their position on the real number line.

Consider the *positive integers* (1, 2, 3, ...), the *negative integers* (−1, −2, −3, ...), and *zero*. All these values may be found on the *real number line* portrayed in Figure 2.1.

A real number line has the following characteristics: (1) The origin (location of zero) on the real number line is arbitrarily chosen. (2) The units of measurement on the real number line are arbitrarily chosen. (3) A positive or negative direction along the real number line is indicated by the sign of the number; this sign reflects the location of a particular point relative to the origin. (4) The ordering relation among the numbers on the real number line is that, if $x < y$, then the point $x$ lies to the left of point $y$ on the real number line.

Figure 2.1 Real number line

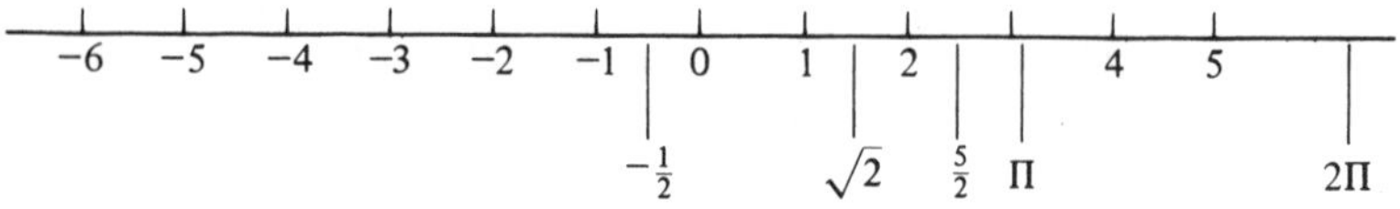


[3] $b = 0.75$ is also the coefficient of variable $Y$.

The origin of the real number line in Figure 2.1 is at zero. However, zero could well have been located anywhere on the page instead of where it is. The unit of measurement on this particular real number line is $\frac{1}{2}$ inch, which is equal to one unit. All negative numbers appear to the left of the origin on the real number line. All positive numbers appear to the right of the origin on the real number line. Any number $y$ that is larger than number $x$ will be to the right of number $x$ on the real number line. Hence $-2$ is to the right of $-4$, 0 is to the right of $-2$, and $+97$ is to the right of 0.

The gaps between the whole, integer values found on the real number line in Figure 2.1 may be partially filled with *rational numbers*. A rational number results from the division of one integer by another, provided that the denominator is not equal to zero. For example, the number one-half may be expressed as the quotient of two integers, 1/2, and is more commonly known as a *fraction*. Any integer may be expressed as the quotient of some two integers. Therefore every integer is a rational number. For example, $4 = 8/2$.

The remaining gaps on the real number line are filled by *irrational numbers*. Irrational numbers cannot be expressed as the quotient of two integers. An example is the value of $\Pi$ (pi), which is 3.14159 .... The square root of two ($\sqrt{2}$) is another example of an irrational number, because $\sqrt{2} = 1.4142$ ....

DEFINITION A *rational number* is the quotient of two integers, the denominator not being equal to zero.

DEFINITION An *irrational number* cannot be expressed as the quotient of two integers.

DEFINITION A *fraction* is a rational number that is not an integer.

The rational and irrational numbers together form the *real number system*. The one-to-one relationship between the real number system and the *real number line* means that we may use the terms "real number" and "point" interchangeably. A real number is a point on the real number line.

The relationship among real numbers, rational and irrational numbers, integers, and fractions is visually summarized in Figure 2.2.

Figure 2.2 The real number system

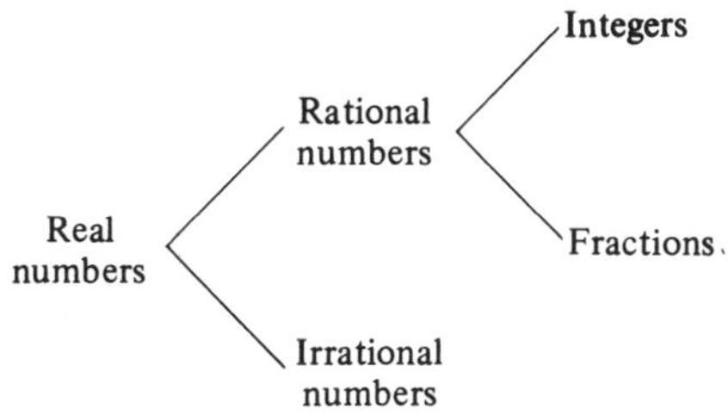

## SET THEORY

The theory of sets, as developed in the latter part of the nineteenth century, forms the foundation of much of modern mathematics. A thorough treatment of set theory would require an enormous and exhaustive amount of work. However, you can acquire a working knowledge of the basic concepts of set theory with considerably less effort.

DEFINITION A *set* is a collection of distinct, well-defined objects.

The individual objects belonging to a set are referred to as the *elements* or *members* of the set. Capital letters such as $A$, $B$, and $C$ are generally used to denote sets, while lower-case letters such as $a$, $b$, and $c$ are typically used to represent the elements of a set. It is customary to enclose the elements of a set by braces. For example, the set $S$ that contains elements 1, 2, and 3 is symbolized as follows: $S = \{1, 2, 3\}$.

There are two major alternative means of identifying the elements of a set. The first is the *enumeration* or *roster* method, which involves the actual listing of each and every element in the set. The second is the *definition* method, in which a rule is specified that delineates whether or not any specific element does or does not belong to the set.

EXAMPLES

1. If the possible grades that a student can earn in mathematics are A, B, C, D, and F, then the set $G$ of all possible grades that a student can earn can be enumerated as $G = \{\text{A, B, C, D, F}\}$.
2. When a die is rolled, the set of all possible outcomes $D$ can be enumerated as $D = \{1, 2, 3, 4, 5, 6\}$.
3. The set consisting of all positive integers $P$ is infinite in size, and it is impossible to enumerate all its elements. Instead a defining rule is used: $P = \{x \mid x \text{ is a positive integer}\}$. This is read as "the set $P$ of all $x$ such that $x$ is a positive integer."
4. The set $I$ consisting of all real numbers greater than 0 but less than 100 can be written as: $I = \{x \mid 0 < x < 100\}$.

### Set Membership

Membership in a particular set is usually signified by the symbol $\in$, which is read as "is an element of" or "belongs to." Thus, in Example 1 above, $\text{A} \in G$; $\text{B} \in G$; $\text{C} \in G$; $\text{D} \in G$; and $\text{F} \in G$. When an element does not belong to a particular set, we use the symbol $\notin$. Thus, in Example 1 above, $\text{E} \notin G$.

### The Null Set

A set that contains no elements at all is referred to as the *null set,* or the *empty set,* and is denoted by the symbol $\varnothing$. The set of all basketball players in the National Basketball Association whose height is less than 5 feet is the null set $\varnothing$.

**Set Algebra**

There are many different ways in which sets can be related to one another. We shall consider the following relationships: (1) equality, (2) subsets, (3) union, (4) intersection, (5) difference, (6) universality, and (7) complementarity.

*Equality of sets*

DEFINITION Two sets $S_1$ and $S_2$ are said to be equal or identical if and only if $S_1$ and $S_2$ have exactly the same elements.

EXAMPLES

1. Consider the sets $S_1 = \{1, 2, 3\}$, $S_2 = \{3, 2, 1\}$, and $S_3 = \{1, 2\}$. Sets $S_1$ and $S_2$ are identical and equal, whereas set $S_3$ is not equal to either set $S_1$ or set $S_2$.
2. Given $S_1 = \{a, b, c\}$ and $S_2 = \{a, b, b, c, c, c\}$. $S_1 = S_2$, and the two sets are equal because they contain the same elements. The fact that elements $b$ and $c$ appear repeatedly in $S_2$ is irrelevant. In fact, it is customary to enumerate each member of a set only once.

*Subsets*

DEFINITION A set $S_1$ is said to be a subset of a set $S_2$ if and only if every element of $S_1$ also belongs to $S_2$. That is, if $x \in S_1$, then $x \in S_2$.

The symbol used to designate a subset relationship is $\subset$. $S_1 \subset S_2$ is read as "$S_1$ is a subset of $S_2$" or "$S_1$ is contained in $S_2$." The statement $S_1 \not\subset S_2$ is read as "$S_1$ is not a subset of $S_2$."

EXAMPLE Given the following four sets: $S_1 = \{2, 4, 6, 8\}$, $S_2 = \{x \mid x \text{ is an even integer}\}$, $S_3 = \{x \mid x \text{ is an even positive single-digit integer}\}$, and $S_4 = \{1, 2, 3, 4, 5, 6\}$. The following set-theoretic relationships hold: $S_1 \subset S_2$, $S_3 \subset S_2$, $S_1 = S_3$, $S_1 \not\subset S_4$, and $S_4 \not\subset S_2$.

When $S_1 \subset S_2$ and $S_2 \subset S_1$, then it follows that $S_1$ and $S_2$ are subsets of each other. Therefore $S_1 = S_2$.

*Union*

A new set may be formed by taking the union of two sets.

DEFINITION Let $S_1$ and $S_2$ be any two arbitrary sets. The union of $S_1$ and $S_2$ consists of the elements that are in $S_1$, in $S_2$, or in both $S_1$ and $S_2$.

The union of two sets $S_1$ and $S_2$ is denoted by $S_1 \cup S_2$, and is read as "$S_1$ union $S_2$." Formally, $S_1 \cup S_2 = \{x \mid x \in S_1 \text{ and/or } x \in S_2\}$.

EXAMPLES

1. Given $S_1 = \{1, 3, 5\}$ and $S_2 = \{1, 2, 3, 4, 5, 6\}$. Then $S_1 \cup S_2 = \{1, 2, 3, 4, 5, 6\}$.
2. Given $S_3 = \{2, 4, 6, 8\}$ and $S_4 = \{1, 3, 5, 7, 9\}$. Then $S_3 \cup S_4 = \{1, 2, 3, 4, 5, 6, 7, 8, 9\}$.

*Intersection*

A new set may be formed by finding the intersection of two sets.

DEFINITION Let $S_1$ and $S_2$ be any two arbitrary sets. The intersection of $S_1$ and $S_2$ consists of the elements that are in both $S_1$ and $S_2$.

The intersection of two sets $S_1$ and $S_2$ is symbolized by $S_1 \cap S_2$, and is read as "$S_1$ intersection $S_2$." Formally, $S_1 \cap S_2 = \{x \mid x \in S_1 \text{ and } x \in S_2\}$.

EXAMPLE Given $S_1 = \{1, 3, 5\}$, $S_2 = \{1, 2, 3, 4, 5, 6\}$, $S_3 = \{2, 4, 6, 8\}$, and $S_4 = \{1, 3, 5, 7\}$. Then we can state that $S_1 \cap S_2 = \{1, 3, 5\}$, $S_3 \cap S_4 = \varnothing$, $S_2 \cap S_4 = \{1, 3, 5\}$.

When the intersection of two sets results in the empty set $\varnothing$, then the two sets are said to be *disjoint*. For example, when $S_1 = \{1, 2\}$ and $S_2 = \{3, 4\}$, then $S_1 \cap S_2 = \varnothing$ and $S_1$ and $S_2$ are said to be disjoint.

*Set difference*

It is frequently the case that some elements of one set are not found in another set.

DEFINITION Given any two arbitrary sets $S_1$ and $S_2$. The *set difference* of $S_1$ and $S_2$ consists of the set of all elements that belong to $S_1$ but not to $S_2$.

The set difference between $S_1$ and $S_2$ is denoted by $S_1 - S_2$. This set difference can be written formally as $S_1 - S_2 = \{x \mid x \in S_1 \text{ and } x \notin S_2\}$.

EXAMPLE If $S_1 = \{1, 2, 3, 4, 5\}$ and $S_2 = \{1, 3, 5\}$, then $S_1 - S_2 = \{2, 4\}$ and $S_2 - S_1 = \varnothing$.

*Universality*

In certain games or activities, only a well-defined and limited number of outcomes are possible. For example, when a coin is flipped, either a head or a tail must result (unless the coin balances on its edge). Similarly, when a die is rolled, the possible outcomes include the numbers 1, 2, 3, 4, 5, and 6.

DEFINITION The *universal set* is a complete listing of all elements or outcomes that can be associated with a particular situation or action.

It is customary to indicate the existence of a universal set by means of the capital letter $U$. In the case of the rolled die, $U = \{1, 2, 3, 4, 5, 6\}$. No other outcomes are possible, and all possible outcomes are included in this universal set.

*Complementarity*

When a die is rolled, we have seen that the universal set is given by $U = \{1, 2, 3, 4, 5, 6\}$. Assume that the die is rolled three times and that these three rolls produce a result that we shall term set $S = \{1, 2, 4\}$. We can readily observe that the remaining elements in the universal set are 3, 5, and 6. These remaining elements in the universal set are referred to as the *complement* of set $S$.

DEFINITION If $U$ denotes the universal set in a particular situation, and if $S \subset U$, then there exists another set $S'$, the complement of $S$, which is the set of elements that do not belong to $S$.

Stated rigorously, the complementary set $S' = \{x \mid x \in U \text{ and } x \notin S\}$.

## SET GEOMETRY: VENN DIAGRAMS

The algebraic relationships between sets that we have outlined above can be illustrated visually by means of *Venn diagrams*, as shown in Figure 2.3. In part

Figure 2.3 Set geometry: Venn diagrams

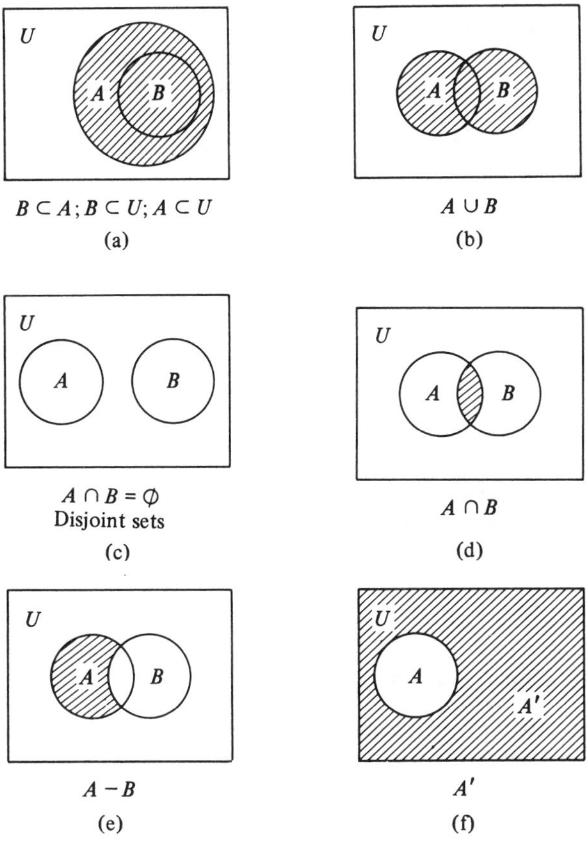

(a), it is apparent that set $B$ is entirely inside set $A$; hence set $B$ is a subset of set $A$. Similarly, sets $A$ and $B$ are both subsets of the universal set $U$. Part (b) illustrates the union of sets $A$ and $B$. The hatched area here consists of all the area found in $A$ or $B$, or both. Sets $A$ and $B$ in part (c) neither overlap nor are tangent to each other. Their intersection, therefore, results in the null set because they are disjoint.

Part (d) depicts the intersection of two sets, $A$ and $B$, that are not disjoint. The hatched area in part (d) is $A \cap B$. Part (e) illustrates the difference between two sets. The hatched area contains all those elements that are in set $A$, but are not in set $B$. Finally, part (f) demonstrates the concept of complementarity. Given set $A$, there exists a set $A'$ [hatched in part (f)] that consists of all the elements in the universal set $U$ that are not in set $A$. The hatched area represents $A'$, the complement of $A$.

**EXERCISE 2.1**

1. Using set notation, specify each of the following.
   (a) The set of all integers greater than $-5$ but less than 5.
   (b) The set of all prime numbers from 0 to 25.
   (c) The set of all real numbers greater than 0.
   (d) The set of all even numbers that are also "prime" numbers, in the sense that they cannot be divided by any integer to obtain another integer.
2. Let $S = \{1, 2, 3\}$, $T = \{3, 4, 5\}$, $V = \{3, 2, 1\}$, and the universal set $U = \{1, 2, 3, 4, 5\}$. Which of the following statements are correct? If a statement is incorrect, correct it.
   (a) $S = T$ (b) $S = V$ (c) $3 \in S$
   (d) $4 \in V$ (e) $S \subset V$ (f) $T \subset S$
   (g) $V \not\subset T$ (h) $S \cup T \neq U$ (i) $S \cap T = U$
   (j) $V \cap T = \varnothing$ (k) $S \cup V = S$ (l) $U - S = T$
   (m) $V' = T$ (n) $U - S = U - V$ (o) $S \cup V \cup T = U$
3. Let $A = \{1, 2, 3\}$, $B = \{2, 3, 4, 5\}$, and $C = \{1, 3, 5\}$, verify that:
   (a) $A \cap (B \cup C) = (A \cap B) \cup (A \cap C)$
   (b) $A \cup (B \cap C) = (A \cup B) \cap (A \cup C)$
4. Using Venn diagrams, verify 3(a) and (b).
5. If $A \subset B$ and $C \subset D$, does this mean that $A \cup B \subset C \cup D$?
6. If $A \subset B$ and $C \subset D$, does this mean that $A \cap B \subset C \cap D$?
7. Using Venn diagrams, show when the following operations hold.
   (a) $A \cup B \cup C = C$ (b) $A \cap B \cap C = C$
   (c) $A \cap B \cap C = \varnothing$

## *SET THEORY: THE FORMAL ALGEBRA

We can formally translate the Venn-diagram analysis of the previous section into a series of laws that define the algebra of sets. These laws perhaps lack the

* This section contains material that can be omitted without loss of continuity.

intuitive appeal of the Venn diagrams. However, the fact that they are algebraic rather than graphical in character is advantageous in certain circumstances. Throughout, we shall assume the existence of three sets—$A$, $B$, and $C$—that are subsets of the universal set $U$.

1. *Commutative laws*
   (a) $A \cup B = B \cup A$ (b) $A \cap B = B \cap A$
2. *Associative laws*
   (a) $A \cup (B \cup C) = (A \cup B) \cup C$ (b) $A \cap (B \cap C) = (A \cap B) \cap C$
3. *Distributive laws*
   (a) $A \cap (B \cup C) = (A \cap B) \cup (A \cap C)$
   (b) $A \cup (B \cap C) = (A \cup B) \cap (A \cup C)$
4. *Idempotent laws*
   (a) $A \cup A = A$ (b) $A \cap A = A$
5. *Identity laws*
   (a) $A \cup \varnothing = A$ (b) $A \cup U = U$
   (c) $A \cap U = A$ (d) $A \cap \varnothing = \varnothing$
6. *Complement laws*
   (a) $A \cup A' = U$ (b) $A \cap A' = \varnothing$
   (c) $(A')' = A$ (d) $U' = \varnothing$
   (e) $\varnothing' = U$
7. *DeMorgan's laws*
   (a) $(A \cup B)' = A' \cap B'$ (b) $(A \cap B)' = A' \cup B'$

## ORDERED AND UNORDERED PAIRS

In our study of set theory, we found that the two-element set $\{x, y\}$ was equal to the two-element set $\{y,x\}$. That is $\{x,y\} = \{y,x\}$. The pair $\{x,y\}$ is therefore said to be an *unordered pair,* in that the ordering is irrelevant. Contrast this to an *ordered pair*, in which $(x, y) \neq (y, x)$ and the ordering of elements $x$ and $y$ is crucial.

DEFINITION Given two elements $x$ and $y$, a pair $(x, y)$ is said to be an *ordered pair* if $(x, y) \neq (y, x)$ unless $x = y$.

We can extend the concept of ordered pairs in order to distinguish between ordered and unordered triples, quadruples, and so forth.

When ordering is unimportant, it is customary to use set notation $\{x, y\}$. When an ordered pair exists, we use the conventional parenthesis notation $(x, y)$.

EXAMPLES

1. Assume that we are dealing with ordered pairs consisting of the wins followed by the losses of professional football teams. For example, the ordered pair (2, 12) would represent the 2-win, 12-loss record of the Chicago Bears in 1975. Note that this ordered pair $(2, 12) \neq (12, 2)$.
2. A complete listing of the individuals who occupied the position of President of the United States during the time period 1960–1970 is given by the

unordered quadruplet {Eisenhower, Kennedy, Johnson, Nixon}, which is equivalent to the listing given by the unordered quadruplet {Nixon, Johnson, Kennedy, Eisenhower}.

## RELATIONS

All ordered pairs constitute a relation.

DEFINITION Given the ordered pair $(x, y)$, for every value of $x$, there is a *relation* that specifies one or more values of $y$.

Many relations are not unique in the sense that many ordered pairs might be consistent with that relationship.

EXAMPLES

1. The set $\{(x, y) | y = x^2\}$ constitutes a relation that includes the following ordered pairs: (0, 0), (1, 1), (2, 4), and so forth.
2. The set $\{(x, y) | y^2 = x\}$ also constitutes a relation of ordered pairs, including (1, 1), (1, −1), (4, 2), (4, −2), and so forth.

## OPEN AND CLOSED INTERVALS

Many of the problems that confront a decision-maker require that he or she be aware of the maximum and minimum values that particular variables can assume. It is necessary, therefore, to be able to distinguish between the intervals of values that include the maximum or minimum points (endpoints) and those intervals that do not include them.

DEFINITION Given points $a$ and $b$ on the real number line, where $a < b$, the *closed interval* from $a$ to $b$ is denoted by $[a, b]$ and refers to the collection of all values of $x$ that satisfy the weak inequality $a \leq x \leq b$.

The closed interval $[a, b]$ includes the endpoints $a$ and $b$. If we exclude the endpoints, then we have an *open interval* from $a$ to $b$, which is denoted by $(a, b)$ and which satisfies the strong inequality $a < x < b$.

There is also the possibility that an interval may be *half-open* (or *half-closed*). The interval $(a, b]$ is open at point $a$, but closed at point $b$. The interval $[a, b)$ is closed at point $a$, but open at point $b$. The interval $(a, b]$ satisfies the inequality $a < x \leq b$, whereas the interval $[a, b)$ satisfies the inequality $a \leq x < b$.

We shall have several occasions to utilize the concept of open and closed intervals in future chapters.

## RECTANGULAR COORDINATES

The concepts of the real number line and ordered pairs enable us to develop and utilize what is commonly referred to as the rectangular (or Cartesian) coordinate system. We begin by assuming that we have two real number lines that are perpendicular to each other. Straight lines $XX'$ and $YY'$ in Figure 2.4 are suitable examples. The intersection of these two real number lines is

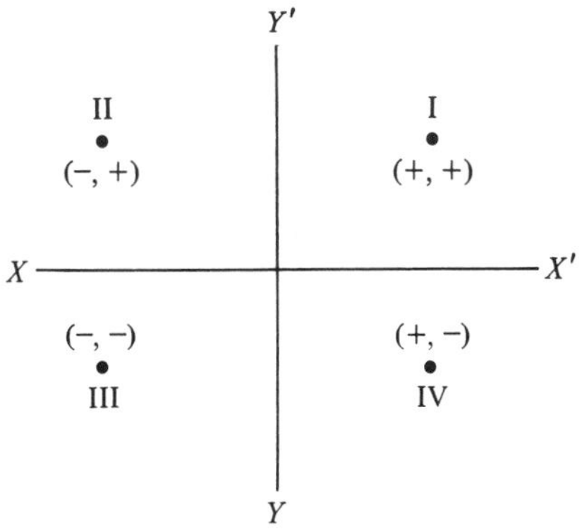


Figure 2.4 Quadrants

designated the *origin* of our coordinate system. The horizontal line $XX'$ (called the $x$ axis) and the vertical line $YY'$ (called the $y$ axis) together form the coordinate axes, or $xy$ axes.

Both of the coordinate axes in Figure 2.4 have the basic properties of any real number line. Points to the right of the origin on the $x$ axis and upward on the $y$ axis indicate positive values; points to the left of the origin on the $x$ axis and downward on the $y$ axis represent negative values.

Each ordered pair of real numbers is represented by a unique point on the plane that is formed by the $x$ and $y$ axes. Given the ordered pair $(a, b)$, the $x$ coordinate, or *abscissa* of the variable $x$ on the $x$ axis, is always the first element in the ordered pair. The second element of the ordered pair is the $y$ coordinate, or *ordinate* of the variable $y$ on the $y$ axis. This means that the point given by the ordered pair $(a, b)$ is not the same as the point given by the ordered pair $(b, a)$ unless $a = b$.

The $x$ and $y$ coordinates that comprise an ordered pair indicate the location of the point given by that ordered pair. As Figure 2.4 demonstrates, when the elements of ordered pair $(a, b)$ are both positive, then the point that corresponds to this ordered pair lies in the *first quadrant*, that is, the area of the coordinate system that lies to the right of the $y$ axis and above the $x$ axis.

When the signs of the ordered pair $(a, b)$ are $(-, +)$, then the point in question lies in the *second quadrant*, which is to the left of the $y$ axis and above the $x$ axis.

When the signs of the ordered pair $(a, b)$ are both negative, then the point lies in the *third quadrant*, which is to the left of the $y$ axis and below the $x$ axis.

Finally, when the signs of the ordered pair $(a, b)$ are $(+, -)$, the point lies in the *fourth quadrant*, to the right of the $y$ axis and below the $x$ axis.

It is apparent from Figure 2.4 that the coordinate system is divided into four quadrants that are numbered with Roman numerals I through IV in a counterclockwise direction. We can use these quadrants to locate any point or to describe the location of a particular graph.

The two real number lines in Figure 2.4 that form the coordinate system illustrated there *need not have* the same units of measurement. That is, their scales of measurement need not be the same. One axis might measure profit and the other axis number of units sold. Or one axis might measure price in terms of dollars and the other axis quantity in terms of physical units. This latter example describes the coordinate axes that we use when we engage in supply-and-demand analysis.

## FUNCTIONS

There is an important difference between the equations $y = x^2$ and $y^2 = x$, which we used in a previous section. There exists *only one* $y$ value corresponding to any given $x$ value in the equation $y = x^2$. That is, given an $x$ value, there is one and only one $y$ value that corresponds to that particular $x$ value. Such is not the case when $y^2 = x$, for in that case a particular $x$ value is not uniquely related to a particular $y$ value. For example, when $x = 1$, $y$ might be either $-1$ or 1.

DEFINITION A *function* is a relation (a set of ordered pairs) such that no two ordered pairs have the same first element.

A function is denoted by $y = f(x)$, which is read "$y$ is a function of $x$" (*not* "$y$ equals $f$ times $x$"). Other functional notations that are frequently used include $g(x)$, $h(x)$, and $F(x)$.

A function is nothing more than a special case of a relation. A function exists when no two ordered pairs have the same value for $x$, but different values for $y$. The definition of a function implies that it *must* be a relation. The reverse, however, is not true. Not every relation is a function, since in a relation there may be several ordered pairs that exhibit the same value of $x$, but different values of $y$. Functions are therefore a subset of relations.

A different letter must be used to denote each function used in a particular problem. For example, if quantity demanded $q_d$ and quantity supplied $q_s$ are different functions of price $p$, then the functional notation used must reflect the fact that two different functions exist. Hence one might write $q_d = f(p)$ and $q_s = g(p)$. This indicates that the two functions are not equivalent, that is, that $f(p) \neq g(p)$.

Given the functional relationship $y = f(x)$, the value of variable $y$ depends on the value of variable $x$. Once variable $x$ takes on a particular value, only then can we determine the value of $y$. Variable $y$ therefore depends on $x$, and is referred to as the *dependent variable*, whereas variable $x$ is the *independent variable*.

Often only certain values are permissible for both the independent and dependent variables. For example, let $m = f(g)$, where $m$ is miles traveled per tank of gasoline in an automobile, and $g$ is the gallons of gasoline in the tank. Negative gallons of gasoline in a tank make no sense whatsoever. Hence the values that $g$ can assume are effectively limited to positive real numbers and zero. This is another way of stating that the *domain* of variable $g$ is limited.

DEFINITION Given $y = f(x)$, the set of all values that variable $x$ may assume is referred to as the *domain* of the function.

The individual elements of the domain of a dependent variable are labeled *arguments* of the functional relationship, or arguments relating to the dependent variable. If, for example, we are given the function $y = 2x$, then, when $x = 3$, $y = 6$. The value $x = 3$ is the argument of the function $y = 2x$.

Analogously, it is sometimes true that only certain values are permissible for the dependent variable. Let $y = x^2$. Then, regardless of what real number value the independent variable $x$ assumes, the value of $y$ cannot be negative. The *range* of variable $y$ is prescribed and limited.

DEFINITION Given $y = f(x)$, the set of all values that variable $y$ may assume is referred to as the *range* of the function.

The elements that constitute the range of a function are often referred to as the *value* of that function. In the case above, where $y = x^2$, the value of the function must fall between zero and positive infinity.

It is standard procedure to place the dependent variable on the left-hand side of a functional relationship, and the independent variable(s) on the right-hand side of the functional relationship. Hence $q_d = 5 - 0.5p$ explicitly states that $q_d = f(p)$. It is *not* customary to write this functional relationship as $5 - 0.5p = q_d$.

**EXERCISE 2.2**

1. Determine the range and domain for each of the following relations and indicate which constitute functions.
   (a) $A = \{(1, 1), (2, 2), (3, 3), (4, 4)\}$
   (b) $B = \{(9, -1), (8, -2), (7, -3), (6, -4), (5, -5)\}$
   (c) $C = \{(1, 5), (2, 5), (3, 5), (4, 5), (5, 5)\}$
   (d) $D = \{(-5, 0), (5, 0), (-3, 1), (3, 1), (0, 4)\}$
   (e) $E = \{(3, 1), (3, 2), (3, 3)\}$
2. For each of the following, determine the range of the dependent variable $y$ and the domain of the independent variable $x$.
   (a) $y = 8 + x$ (b) $y = \sqrt{x}$ (c) $y = \sqrt{4 - x}$
   (d) $y = \dfrac{1}{x^2 - 1}$ (e) $y = \dfrac{1}{8 - x}$
3. Write out a few of the elements that are in the set $\{(x, y)\}$ of ordered pairs of real numbers formed from the following rules. Indicate which rules constitute a function.
   (a) $y = x^3$ (b) $y = x^4$ (c) $y^2 = x$ (d) $y^3 = x$
   (e) $y^4 = x$ (f) $y \leq x$ (g) $y = \sqrt{x}$ (h) $y = 1/x$
   (i) $y = \Pi x^2$ (j) $y^2 + x^2 = 4$ (k) $y + x^2 = 1$
   (l) $y^2 + x = 9$ (m) $x = 3$ (n) $y = 1/2$
4. The total revenue, which is defined as $TR = P \cdot Q$, of a firm per day is a function of its daily sales $Q$. Assume that the firm's output capacity is

$Q = 10$ units per day. What are the domain and range if the total-revenue function is given as $TR = 5Q - \frac{1}{2}Q^2$?

5. A supply curve is a functional relationship between quantity supplied and price. Graph the following supply schedule. Be careful when you label your axes.

| $Q_s$/week | \$$P$ |
|---|---|
| 1,000 | 5 |
| 2,000 | 6 |
| 4,000 | 7 |
| 7,000 | 8 |
| 11,000 | 9 |

## COMPOSITE FUNCTIONS

Given two functions $f(x)$ and $g(z)$, it may be possible to create a new function by means of an operation known as *composition.*

DEFINITION Given $y = f(x)$ and $x = g(z)$, the *composite function* or *composition* of $f(x)$ and $g(z)$ is the function $h(z)$ for which $y = f[g(z)] = h(z)$.

The functional relationship $y = f[g(z)]$ is read as "the function $f$, of a function $g$, of $z$," and indicates that variable $y$ is a function of variable $x$, which itself is a function of variable $z$. To evaluate the function $h(z)$, one must first compute $g(z)$ and then evaluate $f(x)$ at the point $g(z)$. The function $h(z)$ is defined only at those points $z$ for which $g(z)$ is in the domain of $f(x)$.

EXAMPLE Given that $y = f(x) = \sqrt{x}$ and $x = g(z) = z + 1$, the composite function is given by $y = f[g(z)] = \sqrt{z + 1}$. Note that the function $g(z)$ is defined for all real values of $z$, whereas the function $f(x)$ is defined only for those values such that $x \geq 0$. This means that the composite function $f[g(z)]$ can be satisfied only when $(z + 1) \geq 0$. (The symbol $\geq$ means "greater than or equal to," while the symbol $\leq$ means "less than or equal to.")

■ One must be careful in reading the composite function notation. $f[g(z)]$ is read "$f$ of $g$ of $z$." It is *not* considered to be the product $f(x) \cdot g(z)$. Thus, given $y = \sqrt{x}$ and $g(z) = z + 1$, $f[g(z)] = \sqrt{z + 1}$ and *not* $[(\sqrt{x})(z + 1)]$.

### EXERCISE 2.3

1. Given that $f(x) = 100 + 7x$, find (a) $f(0)$; (b) $f(5)$; (c) $f(-10)$.
2. Given that $f(x) = 10 - 4x$, find (a) $f(1)$; (b) $f(10)$; (c) $f(a + h)$.
3. Given that $f(x) = x^2 + 4x - 6$, find (a) $f(0)$; (b) $f(-2)$; (c) $f(10)$.
4. Given that $f(x) = 1/x^2$, find (a) $f(2)$; (b) $f(-4)$; (c) $f(x + h)$.
5. Given that $f(x) = 2^x$, find (a) $f(0)$; (b) $f(3)$; (c) $f(-3)$.
6. Given that $f(x) = x^2 - 2x + 2$, show that $f(-2) \neq -f(2)$.
7. Given that $f(x) = x^2$, show that $f(x + h) - f(x) = h(2x + h)$.

8. Given that $f(x) = (1 + x)/(1 - x)$, show that $f(1/x) = -f(x)$ and $f(-1/x) = -1/f(x)$.
9. Given that $f(x) = x(x - 1)$, show that $f(x + 1) = f(-x)$.
10. Given that $f(x) = x^2 + 8x - 3$ and $g(z) = 2$, find $f[g(z)]$.
11. Given that $f(x) = 4x - x^2$ and $g(z) = 1/z$, show that $f[g(z)] \neq g[f(x)]$.
12. Given that $f(x) = \sqrt{x}$ and $g(z) = (z+4)^2$, find $f[g(z)]$.
13. Given that $f(x) = 1/(1 + x)$, show that $f(x) + f(-x) = 2f(-x^2)$.
14. Given that $f(x) = 1/(1 - x)$, show that $f(x) + f(-x) = 2f(x^2)$.

## FUNCTIONAL FORMS

In this section we shall discuss specific functional forms that are of use to decision-makers in the area of business and economics. We shall limit the discussion to functions of two variables, typically of the form $y = f(x)$.

### Polynomial Functions

A polynomial is a very general functional form that is capable of representing a large number of relationships.

DEFINITION A *polynomial function* $y = f(x)$ is defined for all real values of $x$ by an equation of the form

$$y = f(x) = a_0 x^0 + a_1 x^1 + a_2 x^2 + \cdots + a_n x^n$$

Since $x^0$ is by definition equal to 1, and $x^1 = x$, we can rewrite the definition of a polynomial as

$$y = f(x) = a_0 + a_1 x + a_2 x^2 + \cdots + a_n x^n$$

Using summation notation, this becomes

$$y = f(x) = \sum_{i=0}^{n} a_i x^i$$

The symbols $a_0, a_1, a_2, \ldots, a_n$ are the coefficients of the polynomial.
It is possible to differentiate polynomials in terms of their degree.

DEFINITION The *degree* of a polynomial function is the highest nonnegative integer power of any independent variable in the polynomial.

EXAMPLES

1. $y = 5x$ is a first-degree polynomial.
2. $y = 5x^2$ is a second-degree polynomial.
3. $y = 5x + 5x^2$ is a second-degree polynomial.
4. $y = 5x + 5x^2 + 5x^5$ is a fifth-degree polynomial.

*Exponents: A digression*
In our consideration of polynomial functions, we introduced the concept of the degree, or highest power, of a polynomial. The power to which a variable (or a number) is raised is referred to as the *exponent* of that variable or number.

DEFINITION The expression $x \cdot x \cdot x \cdots x \equiv x^n$ represents the product of $n$ $x$'s. The variable $x$ is referred to as the *base* of the term $x^n$, and the letter $n$ is called the *exponent* of variable $x$.

The base of a function that incorporates an exponent need not be a variable; it may instead be a number. An example of this is the term $5^2$, which means the number 5 raised to the second power, or $5^2 = 5 \cdot 5 = 25$. In general, any function that is characterized by a base raised to a constant exponent is referred to as a *power function.*

Table 2.1 states the laws that govern the use of exponents and gives an example of each of these laws in operation.

*Specific Polynomial Functions*

We can immediately utilize our brief study and review of the laws governing the use of exponents to help us interpret polynomial functions. Table 2.2 contains information concerning several specific polynomial functions that are often used in situations that confront decision-makers. We shall discuss each of these polynomial functions in turn.

1. *Constant functions*

When the degree of a function is zero, the value of the function remains fixed (constant), regardless of the value of the independent variable of that function. If $y = f(x) = k$, where $k$ is a constant, then $y$ remains a constant value $k$, no matter what value of $x$ we choose. The graph of this function is a line that is parallel to the horizontal axis on the coordinate plane. Figure 2.5(a) contains an example of a constant function where $y = f(x) = 5$.

Situations also arise in which the domain is a constant, that is, in which $x = c$, where $c$ is a constant. In this case, the value of $x$ stays fixed for all values of $y$. You should be aware that a function does not exist in this case. Instead, a

Table 2.1 Laws governing the use of exponents and examples of these laws in operation.

| *Law* | *Example* |
|---|---|
| 1. $x^0 = 1$ | $8^0 = 1$ |
| 2. $x^m x^n = x^{m+n}$ | $x^2 x^5 = x^7$ |
| 3. $(x^m)^n = x^{mn}$ | $(x^2)^5 = x^{10}$ |
| 4. $(xy)^n = x^n y^n$ | $(xy)^5 = x^5 y^5$ |
| 5. $x^{-n} = 1/x^n$ | $x^{-5} = 1/x^5$ |
| 6. $x^m/x^n = x^{m-n}$ | $x^2/x^5 = x^{-3}$ |
| 7. $(x/y)^n = x^n/y^n$ | $(x/y)^5 = x^5/y^5$ |
| 8. $x^n/x^n = x^{n-n} = 1$ | $x^5/x^5 = 1$ |
| 9. $x^{1/n} = \sqrt[n]{x}$ | $x^{1/5} = \sqrt[5]{x}$ |
| 10. $(xy)^{1/n} = x^{1/n}y^{1/n} = \sqrt[n]{x}\sqrt[n]{y} = \sqrt[n]{xy}$ | $(xy)^{1/5} = \sqrt[5]{xy}$ |
| 11. $x^{1/n}/y^{1/n} = \sqrt[n]{x}/\sqrt[n]{y} = \sqrt[n]{x/y}$ | $x^{1/5}/y^{1/5} = \sqrt[5]{x/y}$ |
| 12. $x^{m/n} = \sqrt[n]{x^m} = (\sqrt[n]{x})^m$ | $x^{2/5} = \sqrt[5]{x^2} = (\sqrt[5]{x})^2$ |

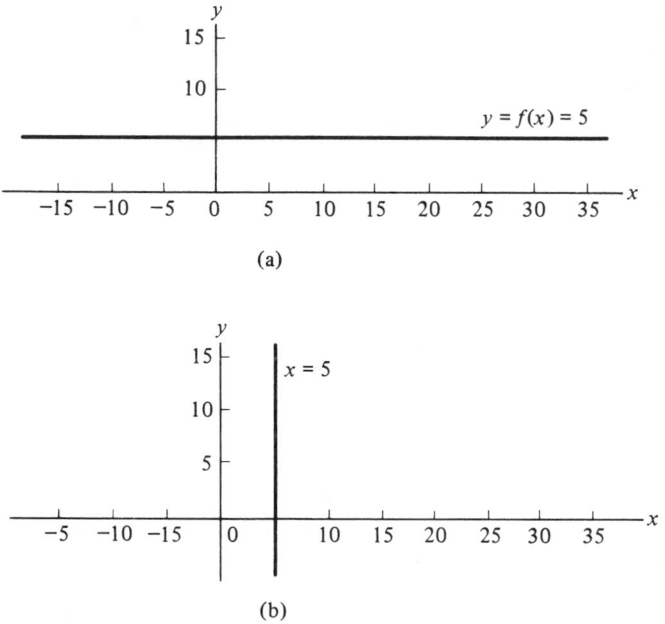


Figure 2.5 Graphs of a constant function and a constant relation. (a) Constant range, constant function. (b) Constant domain, constant relation

relation exists. The graph of this relation is a straight line parallel to the vertical axis (ordinate) and perpendicular to the abscissa. Figure 2.5(b) illustrates the graph of the relation $x = 5$.

*Examples of constant functions*

1. Given $Y = C + I + G$ in national income analysis. In many models, it is assumed that $I = I_0$, that is, that investment expenditures are determined exogenously and are constant. If, for example, $I = 50$, then investment remains constant at 50 regardless of the values of $Y$, $C$, and $G$. The graph of this investment function is a straight line that is parallel to the abscissa at all points where $I = 50$.

Table 2.2 Specific polynomial functions

| *Functional form* | *Degree* | *Name of function* |
|---|---|---|
| $y = a_0$ | 0 | Constant function |
| $y = a_0 + a_1 x$ | 1 | Linear function |
| $y = a_0 + a_1 x + a_2 x^2$ | 2 | Quadratic function |
| $y = a_0 + a_1 x + a_2 x^2 + a_3 x^3$ | 3 | Cubic function |

2. Some resources are virtually or totally nonreproducible, in the sense that their supply is fixed and unresponsive to price. Land is a good example. The frontage area facing on Wilshire Boulevard in Los Angeles, the number of corners at State and Madison Streets in Chicago, and the total size of Manhattan Island in New York City are effectively fixed. The supply curve for such land is a straight line that is parallel to the ordinate (vertical axis) at $x = c$, where $c$ is the fixed amount of land available.

2. *Linear functions*

A two-variable equation in which both variables are of the first degree, and in which the two variables never appear together in the same term, is a *linear function.*

DEFINITION Given $y = f(x) = mx + b$, where $m$ and $b$ are real numbers. Such a function is termed a *linear function* and is represented graphically by a straight line.

The general equation of a linear function contains two parameters, $m$ and $b$, that have a very definite influence on the graph of the linear function. In order to define a straight line, we need either two points on that line, or one point on that line and the slope of the line.

An easy way to draw the graph of a linear function is often to find the $x$ and $y$ intercepts of that graph. That is, we must find the point at which the graph crosses the $x$ axis and the point at which the graph crosses the $y$ axis. The $x$ intercept (abscissa) is that point at which $y = 0$. Since we know that $y = mx + b$, we set $y = 0$, and solve for $x$:[4]

$$y = mx + b, \qquad 0 = mx + b,$$

$$x = \frac{-b}{m} \tag{2.6}$$

Equation (2.6) tells us that the straight line crosses the $x$ axis at the point given by the ordered pair $(-b/m, 0)$. Similarly, we can find the $y$ intercept (ordinate) of any straight line by setting $x = 0$ and solving for $y$:

$$y = mx + b, \qquad y = m(0) + b$$

$$y = b \tag{2.7}$$

Hence, when $x = 0$ and $y = b$, $b$ is said to be the $y$ intercept or ordinate of the linear equation. The ordered pair $(0, b)$ is a point on this straight line. We can construct the graph of a linear function by connecting the two ordered pairs $(-b/m, 0)$ and $(0, b)$. The linear function illustrated in Figure 2.6 is given by the equation $y = f(x) = 5 + 0.5x$, where the ordered pair $(-b/m, 0) = (-10, 0)$ and the ordered pair $(0, b) = (0, 5)$.

An alternative method of graphing a linear equation uses the slope of the linear function, $m$. Intuitively, the slope of a function is nothing more than the

[4] The functional form $y = mx + b$ is equivalent to the functional form $y = a_0 + a_1 x$.

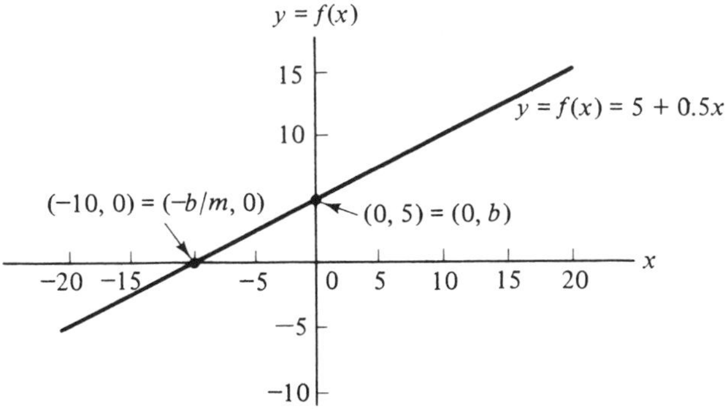


Figure 2.6 Graph of a linear function

steepness of the graph of that function. The larger the absolute value[5] of the slope, the steeper that line. Hence, when $y = 5 + 2x$, the slope is not as steep as it is when $y = 5 + 4x$.

DEFINITION Let $(x_1, y_1)$ and $(x_2, y_2)$ be any two ordered pairs that lie on the line $y = mx + b$. The slope of this line is given by

$$\frac{\Delta y}{\Delta x} = \frac{y_2 - y_1}{x_2 - x_1} = \frac{mx_2 + b - (mx_1 + b)}{x_2 - x_1} = \frac{mx_2 + b - mx_1 - b}{x_2 - x_1}$$

$$= \frac{m(x_2 - x_1)}{x_2 - x_1} = m \tag{2.8}$$

where $x_2 \neq x_1$ and $\Delta y$ is read as "delta $y$" and means "change in $y$."

*Example of a linear function*

Figure 2.7 contains two points, each of which is an ordered pair. Both of these points (both of these ordered pairs) are on the straight line labeled $LL'$. The slope of straight line $LL'$ is labeled $m$, and is equal to $(y_2 - y_1)/(x_2 - x_1)$. If you have some knowledge of trigonometry, you can verify that the slope of line $LL'$ is also equal to the tangent of angle $\alpha$. That is, the tangent of angle $\alpha$ is equal to the opposite side of the right triangle divided by the adjacent side of the right triangle. The right angle of the right triangle is formed by the two dashed-line perpendiculars; the hypotenuse of the right triangle is straight line $LL'$.

[5] For any real number $n$, the absolute value of $n$ is defined as

$$|n| \equiv \begin{cases} n & \text{if } n > 0 \\ -n & \text{if } n < 0 \\ 0 & \text{if } n = 0 \end{cases}$$

Hence, if $n = 15$, then $|15| = 15$; however, if $n = -15$, then $|-15| = -(-15) = 15$. In effect, the absolute value of any real number is the numerical value of that real number after the sign has been removed. For this reason, it follows that $|n| = |-n|$.

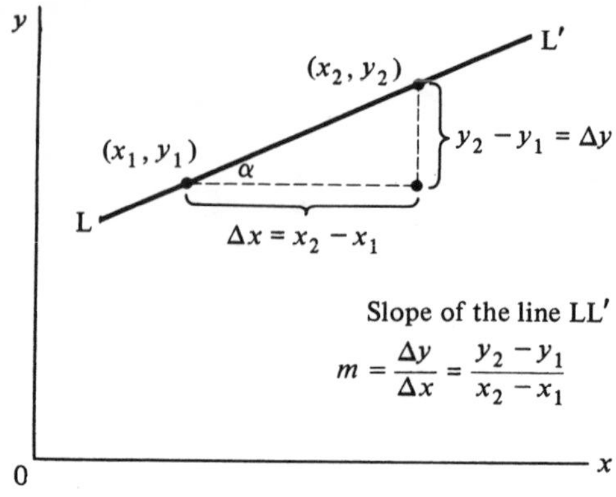


Figure 2.7 Slope of a straight line

The slope of a straight line has the unique property of being a constant equal to $m$, which is a parameter. Any two points that lie on that straight line can be used, as in Figure 2.7, to define the slope $m$ of that straight line. Indeed, the slope of a line is independent of whether we initiate our measurement of $\Delta y/\Delta x$ from one ordered pair or another. That is,

$$m = \frac{\Delta y}{\Delta x} = \frac{y_2 - y_1}{x_2 - x_1} = \frac{y_1 - y_2}{x_1 - x_2} \tag{2.9}$$

As long as we are consistent with respect to the ordering of subscripts for both the ordered pairs in the numerator and denominator of Equation (2.9), the computed slope will be the same regardless of whether we subtract ordered pair $(x_1, y_1)$ from ordered pair $(x_2, y_2)$, or vice versa.

Regardless of which of the two methods outlined in Equation (2.9) we utilize to find the slope of a straight line, the slope of an upward-sloping straight line (from left to right) such as line $LL'$ in Figure 2.7 will have a positive sign. The sign of the slope of a downward-sloping straight line, however, is always negative. This follows from the definition of slope as expressed in Equations (2.8) and (2.9).

Figure 2.8(a) and (b) demonstrates this visually. In part (a), the line $y = 5 + 0.5x$ is upward-sloping from left to right and

$$\frac{\Delta y}{\Delta x} = \frac{y_2 - y_1}{x_2 - x_1} = +0.5$$

In part (b), the line $y = 20 - 0.5x$ is downward-sloping (from left to right) and

$$\frac{\Delta y}{\Delta x} = \frac{y_2 - y_1}{x_2 - x_1} = -0.5$$

Hence the line in part (a) has a positive slope, and the line in part (b) has a negative slope.

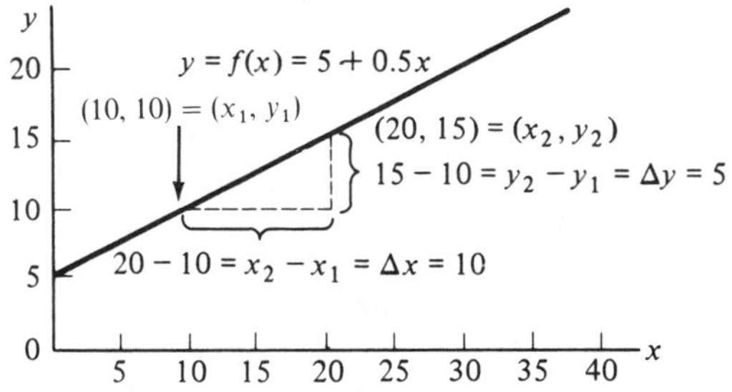


(a) Slope of the line $= \dfrac{\Delta y}{\Delta x} = \dfrac{5}{10} = 0.5$

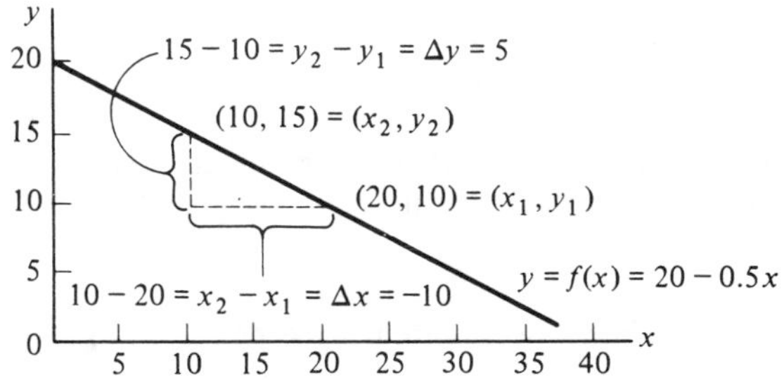


(b) Slope of the line $= \dfrac{\Delta y}{\Delta x} = \dfrac{5}{-10} = -0.5$

Figure 2.8 Linear functions: (a) Positive slope. (b) Negative slope

Two special cases involving the slopes of straight lines often confuse students. In the first case, when the line is parallel to the $x$ axis [as in Figure 2.5(a), where $y = f(x) = 5$], $x_1 \neq x_2$ and $y_1 = y_2$, so that the slope of the line is

$$m = \frac{y_2 - y_1}{x_2 - x_1} = \frac{0}{\Delta x} = 0$$

In general, the slope of any line that is horizontal (that is, parallel to the $x$ axis) is zero. In the second case, the line is parallel to the ordinate [as in Figure 2.5(b), which shows the relation $x = 5$], $x_1 = x_2$ and $y_1 \neq y_2$. The slope

$$m = \frac{y_2 - y_1}{x_2 - x_1} = \frac{\Delta y}{0}$$

which is undefined and is not a number. In general, when a line is parallel to the $y$ axis, the slope of that line is undefined. Note well, however, that it is customary in business and economic analyses to refer to such a slope as being *infinite*. Although the notion of the slope of a vertical line being "infinite" is not mathematically correct, it is nonetheless frequently encountered and has intuitive appeal.

Having found the slope of a straight line, we need only one additional point that is also on that straight line in order to be able to graph that straight-line function. In Figure 2.8(b), for example, if we know that the $y$ intercept of a line is 20 and the slope of that line is $-0.5$, then we can draw the graph of that line with ease. The fact that the slope of the line is $-0.5$ tells us that a one-unit increase in variable $x$ will bring about a one-half-unit decrease in variable $y$. Similarly, a two-unit increase in $x$ will evoke a one-unit decrease in $y$. Proceeding from the $y$ intercept at $y = 20$, we therefore know that the ordered pair $(x, y) = (1, 19.5)$ is a point on this straight line. Similarly, the ordered pair (2, 19) is also a point on the line. We can find the graph of this function by connecting the point representing the abscissa intercept (0, 20) and one other point, for example, (2, 19). The two points define the straight line given by the functional relationship $y = f(x) = 20 - 0.5x$. This straight line extends infinitely in both directions.

To find the equation of a linear function that has already been graphed, we reverse the process outlined above. The graph of the line is known, but its equation is not. Hence we must either find the coordinates of two points on that graph or find the slope of the straight line on the graph and one other point on that graph in order to determine what the equation of that line is.[6]

*Examples of finding the equation of a straight line*

1. Find the slope of a straight line passing through the points (2, 8) and (4, 20).

[6] There are five major methods used to determine the equation of a straight line whose graph is already known.

(1) *Two-point method*: Find two ordered pairs $(x_1, y_1)$ and $(x_2, y_2)$ that are on the graph of the straight line. Connect these points by a straight line that is extended to the ordinate axis. The $y$ intercept is thus identified. You can find the slope of the function by extending perpendiculars from each of the points and determining the slope in the fashion of Figures 2.4 and 2.5.

(2) *Point-slope method*: When you already know the slope of the function, then you need find only one other point on that linear function. For example, if you know that the slope of the function is 1, and you find that the point (5, 6) is on the graph of the function, then the equation of the function is $y = 1 + x$.

(3) *Slope-intercept method*: When you already know the slope of the function, and you find that the ordered pair, as in method (2), is the $y$ intercept, then you need only write the equation. For example, if $m = -1$ and $b = 5$, then the equation of the function is $y = 5 - x$.

(4) *Intercept method*: In this case, you know both the intercepts of the function, but not the slope of the function. Since two points define a straight line, you can connect these two intercepts and infer the slope of the function by means of these two points. Assume that the $y$ intercept of a particular function is given by the ordered pair (0, 10), while the $x$ intercept of the same function is given by (20, 0). Then you can see that a 20-unit increase in variable $x$ brings about a 10-unit decrease in variable $y$. Hence the slope of the function is $-10/20 = -0.5$, and the equation of this function is $y = 10 - 0.5x$.

(5) *Family-of-lines method*: Situations may arise in which you know the slope of the function because you are dealing with a family of functions, each of which has the same slope. You do not know the intercept of the function, however. For example, consider a budget line in the theory of consumer choice, in which $y = 10 - 2x_1$. An increase in this consumer's income will not change the prices of goods $x$ and $y$. Only the $x$ and $y$ intercepts will be changed by an increase in the consumer's income. Suppose that the consumer's income doubles. Then the $y$ intercept becomes 20 and the $x$ intercept rises from 5 to 10.

Let $(2, 8) = (x_1, y_1)$ and $(4, 20) = (x_2, y_2)$. Then

$$m = \frac{y_2 - y_1}{x_2 - x_1} = \frac{20 - 8}{4 - 2} = 6 \qquad \text{or} \qquad m = \frac{y_1 - y_2}{x_1 - x_2} = \frac{8 - 20}{2 - 4} = 6$$

Note that, had we let $(2, 8) = (x_2, y_2)$ and $(4, 20) = (x_1, y_1)$, we would also have gotten a slope of 6:

$$m = \frac{y_2 - y_1}{x_2 - x_1} = \frac{8 - 20}{2 - 4} = 6$$

2. Find the equation of the line passing through the points (2, 8) and (4, 20).

   Let $(2, 8) = (x_1, y_1)$ and $(4, 20) = (x_2, y_2)$. Then, using the two-point form, we have:

$$y - y_1 = \left(\frac{y_2 - y_1}{x_2 - x_1}\right)(x - x_1), \qquad y - 8 = \left(\frac{20 - 8}{4 - 2}\right)(x - 2)$$

$$y - 8 = 6(x - 2) = 6x - 12$$

$$y = 6x - 4$$

3. Find the equation of the line passing through the point (2, 8) and having a slope of 6.
   Using the point-slope method, we have

$$y - y_1 = m(x - x_1), \qquad y - 8 = 6(x - 2) = 6x - 12$$

$$y = 6x - 4$$

4. Find the equation of the line having an $x$ intercept of $(a, 0)$ and a $y$ intercept of $(0, b)$.
   Using the two-point method, we can find a general intercept method:

$$y - y_1 = \left(\frac{y_2 - y_1}{x_2 - x_1}\right)(x - x_1)$$

$$y - 0 = \left(\frac{b - 0}{0 - a}\right)(x - a)$$

$$y = -\frac{b}{a}(x - a) = -\frac{b}{a}x + b$$

   Therefore, in the specific example in which the $x$ intercept is $(a, 0) = (5, 0)$ and the $y$ intercept is $(0, b) = (0, 10)$, the equation would be

$$y = b - \frac{b}{a}x = 10 - \frac{10}{5}x$$

$$y = 10 - 2x$$

Table 2.3 states the general properties of linear functions involving two variables.

Table 2.3 Linear functions of two variables: Summary

General form: $y = f(x) = mx + b$
$y$ intercept (ordinate) $(0, b)$
$x$ intercept (abscissa) $(-b/m, 0)$

Slope: $m = \dfrac{\Delta y}{\Delta x} = \dfrac{y_2 - y_1}{x_2 - x_1} = \dfrac{y_1 - y_2}{x_1 - x_2}$

**EXERCISE 2.4**

1. Graph the following functions and determine the slope and the $x$ and $y$ intercepts.
   (a) $x - 20y - 100 = 0$ (b) $5y - 15x = 5$ (c) $y = 10 + 0.5x$
2. Determine the slope of a straight line passing through the points (2, 4), (4, 3).
3. Determine the slope of a straight line passing through the points (5, 70), (4, 55).
4. In each of the following, determine a general linear equation of a straight line, using the given information.
   (a) Passes through the points (2, 2) and $(-1, -7)$
   (b) Passes through the points (1, 16) and $(-2, -2)$
   (c) Passes through the points (1, 1) and $(-1, 3)$
   (d) Passes through the point $(-3, 18)$ and has slope $-5$
   (e) Passes through the point (2, 4) and has slope $-\frac{1}{2}$
   (f) Has $x$ and $y$ intercepts of (1, 0) and (0, 4)
   (g) Has $x$ and $y$ intercepts of $(0, -2)$ and (2, 0)
   (h) Has $y$ intercept of (0, 4) and slope $\frac{1}{2}$
   (i) Has $y$ intercept of (0, 10) and slope $-\frac{1}{5}$
   (j) Passes through the points (3, 0) and (3, 10)
   (k) Passes through the point $(-5, 5)$ and has slope 0

3. *Quadratic functions*

Many relationships and functions that decision-makers in business and economics deal with are also nonlinear, that is, are not characterized by straight lines. One of the most common nonlinear functions is the quadratic function.

DEFINITION A polynomial function $y = f(x)$ is said to be *nonlinear* if the degree of the function is greater than 1. A *quadratic function* is a nonlinear function of the second degree whose equation is given by the form $y = f(x) = ax^2 + bx + c$, where $a$, $b$, and $c$ are parameters.[7]

The difference between a linear function and a quadratic function lies in the term $ax^2$. When $a = 0$, the term $ax^2$ disappears and we are left with a linear function, $y = bx + c$. Hence, in order for a quadratic function to exist, $a \neq 0$.

For a specific value of $y$ (usually $y = 0$), we are interested in knowing the

[7] The functional form $ax^2 + bx + c = 0$ is equivalent to the functional form $y = a_0 + a_1 x + a_2 x^2$ when $y = 0$.

particular values of variable $x$ that make the equation hold true. We usually find these values, which we have already termed *solution values* or *critical roots*, by using one of the following methods: (a) factoring, or (b) the quadratic formula.

*Factoring* as a method of solving a quadratic equation relies on the fact that if the product of two or more real quantities is equal to zero, then at least one of those quantities must also be equal to zero. That is, given two real quantities $A$ and $B$, with $AB = 0$, then either $A = 0$ or $B = 0$. When one finds the value of $x$ in a two-term multiplicative equation that makes the value of either term equal to zero, then not only must the product of the two terms be equal to zero, but also this value of $x$ satisfies the original equation. As applied to quadratic equations, this knowledge suggests that we should factor the equation into the form $AB = 0$. Then, if we find the value(s) of $x$ for which either of the quantities $A$ and $B$ is equal to zero, these values also satisfy the original unfactored equation and are considered to be solution values.

EXAMPLES

1. $y = f(x) = x^2 + 2x + 1 = 0$
   Factor: $(x + 1)(x + 1) = 0$

   Set each factor equal to zero:

   $$\left.\begin{aligned} x + 1 = 0;\ x &= -1 \\ x + 1 = 0;\ x &= -1 \end{aligned}\right\}\ \text{Solution values}$$

2. $y = f(x) = 2x^2 - 4x - 6 = 0$
   Factor: $(2x + 2)(x - 3) = 0$

   Set each factor equal to zero:

   $$\left.\begin{aligned} 2x + 2 = 0;\ x &= -1 \\ x - 3 = 0;\ x &= 3 \end{aligned}\right\}\ \text{Solution values}$$

We can solve many quadratic equations by factoring. However, this sometimes involves long and tedious work. A more general approach to the solution of a quadratic equation is to use the *quadratic formula*.

THEOREM 2.1 Given the quadratic equation $ax^2 + bx + c = 0$. The solution values or critical roots of this equation are given by the formula

$$x = \frac{-b \pm \sqrt{b^2 - 4ac}}{2a}$$

*Proof* Given $ax^2 + bx + c = 0$, where $a \neq 0$. Dividing both sides of the equation by $a$, we obtain

$$x^2 + \frac{b}{a}(x) + \frac{c}{a} = 0 \tag{2.10}$$

Subtracting $c/a$ from both sides gives

$$x^2 + \frac{b}{a}(x) = -\frac{c}{a} \tag{2.11}$$

Completing the square on the left-hand side of Equation (2.11) involves adding the term $(b/2a)^2$ to both sides of the equation, giving

$$x^2 + \frac{b}{a}(x) + \left(\frac{b}{2a}\right)^2 = \left(\frac{b}{2a}\right)^2 - \frac{c}{a} \tag{2.12}$$

Factoring gives

$$\left(x + \frac{b}{2a}\right)^2 = \frac{b^2 - 4ac}{4a^2} \tag{2.13}$$

Taking the square root of both sides of Equation (2.13) yields

$$x + \frac{b}{2a} = \pm\frac{\sqrt{b^2 - 4ac}}{2a} \tag{2.14}$$

Subtracting the term $b/2a$ from both sides of Equation (2.14) results in

$$x = -\frac{b}{2a} \pm \frac{\sqrt{b^2 - 4ac}}{2a} \tag{2.15}$$

Or

$$x = \frac{-b \pm \sqrt{b^2 - 4ac}}{2a} \tag{2.16}$$

Q.E.D.

As both the theorem and the proof assert, two values of variable $x$,

$$x = \frac{-b + \sqrt{b^2 - 4ac}}{2a} \quad \text{and} \quad x = \frac{-b - \sqrt{b^2 - 4ac}}{2a}$$

satisfy any quadratic equation of the form $ax^2 + bx + c = 0$.

In our work with linear functions, we found that there is *only one* critical root or solution value for each linear equation. By contrast, a quadratic equation may have *two*, but *never more* than two, critical roots (solution values). We can use a simple technique to determine whether the critical roots of a quadratic equation are real or imaginary, equal or unequal. The numeric value of the numerator of the term under the radical sign in Equation (2.16) is the key. This term, $b^2 - 4ac$, is referred to as the *discriminant* of the quadratic equation. When $b^2 - 4ac > 0$, then the roots of the quadratic equation are real numbers and unequal to each other. When $b^2 - 4ac = 0$, then the roots are again real, but are equal to each other in value. When $b^2 - 4ac < 0$, then the roots are imaginary numbers and are unequal to each other.

EXAMPLES

1. Let $5x^2 + 2x + 6 = 0$. Then

$$x = \frac{-2 \pm \sqrt{(2)^2 - 4 \cdot 5 \cdot 6}}{2 \cdot 5} = \frac{-2 + \sqrt{-116}}{10}$$

and

$$x = \frac{-2 - \sqrt{-116}}{10}$$

The roots are imaginary numbers and unequal.

2. Let $x^2 + 9x + 1 = 0$. Then

$$x = \frac{-9 \pm \sqrt{(9)^2 - 4 \cdot 1 \cdot 1}}{2 \cdot 1} = \frac{-9 + \sqrt{77}}{2} \quad \text{and} \quad x = \frac{-9 - \sqrt{77}}{2}$$

Hence the two roots are $x \simeq -0.11$ and $-8.89$, which are real and unequal.

3. Let $x^2 - 2x + 1 = 0$. Then

$$x = \frac{+2 \pm \sqrt{4 - 4}}{2} = 1$$

Hence the two roots are real and equal; $x = 1$.

Whatever method you choose to solve quadratic equations, it is quite certain that you will find many examples of them in business and economic situations. Sales functions, total utility functions, production functions, depreciation as a function of time, the ability of management to control and effectively supervise organizations of increasing size—all these relationships are potentially characterized by quadratic functions.

Figure 2.9(a) presents the graph of one particular quadratic function, $y = f(x) = 5 + 5x - 0.1x^2$. Note that quadratic functions often exhibit posi-

Figure 2.9 Graphs of two polynomials. (a) Quadratic function. (b) Cubic function

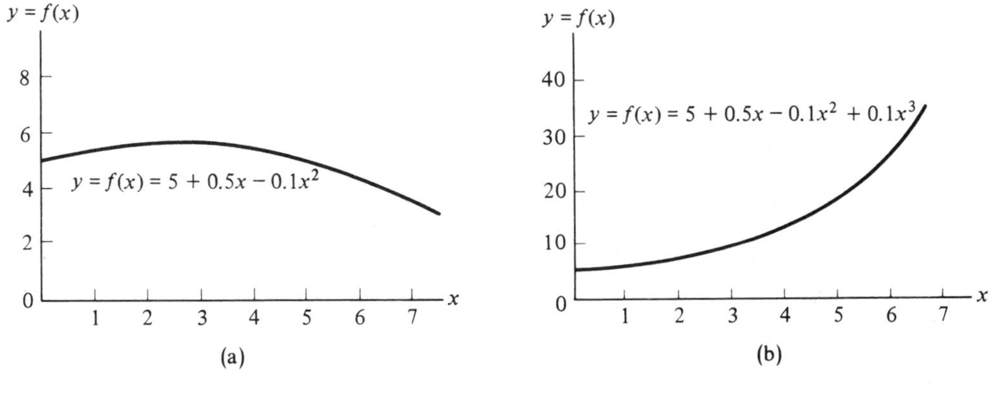

tive slopes at some values of the independent variable, but negative slopes at other values of the independent variable. This gives them a desired flexibility that is absent in linear functions.

**EXERCISE 2.5**

Solve the following functions for the critical values of $x$.

1. $x^2 - x - 6 = 0$
2. $x^2 - 25 = 0$
3. $x^2 + 6x + 8 = 0$
4. $3x^2 + 7x - 3 = 0$
5. $x^2 - 4x + 4 = 0$
6. $x^2 + x - 12 = 0$
7. $x^2 - 5x + 3 = 0$

4. *Cubic functions*

DEFINITION A *cubic function* is a nonlinear function of the third degree whose equation is given by the form $y = f(x) = a_0 + a_1 x + a_2 x^2 + a_3 x^3$, where $a_0$, $a_1$, $a_2$, and $a_3$ are parameters.

The difference between a quadratic function and a cubic function lies in the $a_3 x^3$ term. When $a_3 = 0$, the term $a_3 x^3$ disappears and the function is in fact a quadratic rather than a cubic one. Hence, for a cubic function to exist, $a_3 \neq 0$. Like quadratic functions, cubic functions can also exhibit positive slopes at some values of the independent variable, but negative slopes at other values of the independent variable. The addition of the $a_3 x^3$ term in the cubic equation allows for the possibility of a slope that, for example, is initially positive, then negative, and finally once again positive.

EXAMPLE F. M. Scherer has made an interesting and relatively simple use of a cubic equation in his studies of the output of patents by the largest firms in the American economy.[8] Scherer investigated the relationship between the size of firms (as measured by their sales) and their output of patented inventions. He estimated the following cubic equation for 448 firms from *Fortune Magazine*'s list of the 500 largest firms in 1955:

$$P_i = -3.79 + 144.42S_i - 23.86S_i^2 + 1.457S_i^3 \qquad (2.17)$$

where $P_i$ = patent output of the $i$th firm, $S_i$ = sales in dollars of the $i$th firm, and $i = 1, 2, \ldots, 448$.[9]

A function such as that estimated by Scherer in Equation (2.17) takes the general form of the graph found in Figure 2.10. The output of patents increases as firm size increases, but does so at a *decreasing* rate. (We shall elaborate the concept of a function increasing or decreasing at an increasing rate considerably in the next few chapters.) In Scherer's words, ". . . we find diminishing returns dominating." However, when firms of the very largest sizes are considered, increasing returns are noted. This is that area of the graph in Figure 2.10 that is enclosed and shaded. This increase in patenting activity among the very few largest firms is reflected in the positive sign on the cubic

[8] F. M. Scherer, "Firm Size, Market Structure, Opportunity, and the Output of Patented Inventions," *American Economic Review*, 55 (December 1965), pp. 1097–1125.
[9] Scherer, p. 1106.

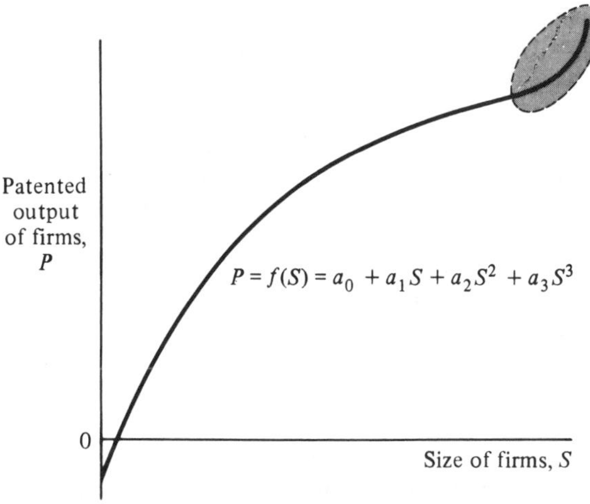


Figure 2.10 A Scherer-type cubic patent equation

term $S_i^3$ in Equation (2.17). Most important, a quadratic equation is incapable of accurately portraying this particular idiosyncrasy of patenting, since there is no cubic term in a quadratic equation.

Figure 2.9(b) contains the graph of still another cubic equation. This one has a positive slope throughout, a slope that is continuously increasing. This demonstrates the flexibility of a cubic functional form in representing a wide range of real-world phenomena.

**Nonpolynomial Functional Forms: Exponential and Logarithmic Functions**

*Exponential functions:* $y = b^x$

Not all functional forms need be polynomials of the form $y = f(x) = a_0 + a_1 x + a_2 x^2 + \cdots + a_n x^n$. Earlier in this chapter, we introduced the concept of a power function, which we defined as a variable raised to a constant power, for example, $y = x^5$ or $y = x^{1/5}$. We shall now extend our use of exponents to the case in which the exponent itself may be a variable, for example, $y = 3^x$ or $y = 3^{1/x}$. In such cases, the base (which is 3) is fixed and the exponent contains the variable.

DEFINITION An *exponential function* is given by the form $y = f(x) = b^x$, where $b$ = a fixed base such that $b > 0$ and $b \neq 1$, and $x$ = an independent variable that is any real number.

In any exponential function, important restrictions are placed on both the base $b$ and the domain and range of the function itself. First, the independent variable $x$ has a domain consisting of the set of all real numbers. Hence $x = -5$ or $x = 1/3$ or $x = 3.7486$ are all possibilities. Second, the fixed base $b$ can be any real $n$ number such that $b > 0$ and $b \neq 1$. The $b > 0$ restriction ensures that one will never need to take the root of a negative number. The

$b \neq 1$ restriction prevents a situation in which $b = 1$ such that $1^x = 1$. If $b = 1$, then the function reduces to the value of 1, and is no longer exponential in nature. Third, the domain of an exponential function is the set of all real numbers.

The graph of an exponential function typically assumes one of two basic shapes, depending on whether $0 < b < 1$ or $b > 1$. When $0 < b < 1$, as in Figure 2.11(a), the graph of the exponential function decreases from left to right.[10] This means that when the variable $x$ increases, the variable $y$ decreases steadily. However, when $b > 1$ [as in Figure 2.11(b)], the exponential function increases from left to right. This means that when variable $x$ increases, variable $y$ steadily increases. In both parts (a) and (b), the $y$ intercept is (0, 1). Also it is apparent that both graphs approach, but never touch, the $x$ axis. This is formally stated as follows: "The function asymptotically approaches the $x$ axis."

Finally, negative values of variable $x$ are permissible. Formally, this means that the graph of either exponential function lies in both quadrants I and II. This implies that the range of variable $y$ is positive.

Although any positive value of $b$ (other than $b = 1$) is permissible in an exponential function of the form $y = b^x$, there is one particular value of $b$ that is used far more than any other. It is the constant number $e$, which we have encountered previously.[11] When $b = e$, the value of $b$ is approximated by 2.718281828 .... The value of $e$ is generated by considering the following function:

$$y = f(x) = \left(1 + \frac{1}{x}\right)^x \tag{2.18}$$

Figure 2.11 Exponential functions for various values of the base $b$. (a) $y = f(x) = b^x$, where $0 < b < 1$; (b) $y = f(x) = b^x$, where $b > 1$. (Note: Roman numerals I, II, III, and IV are numbered quadrants of a graph)

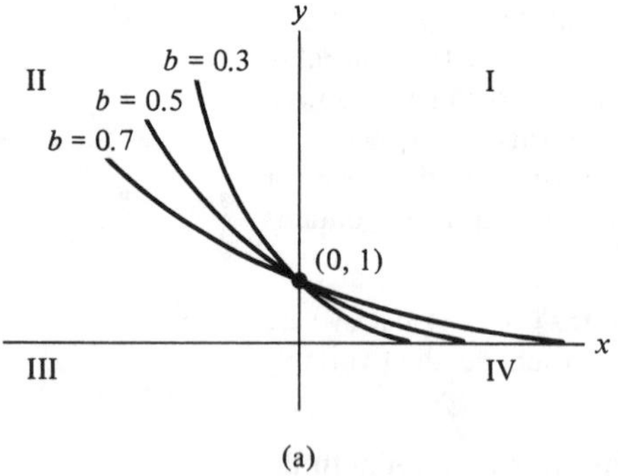


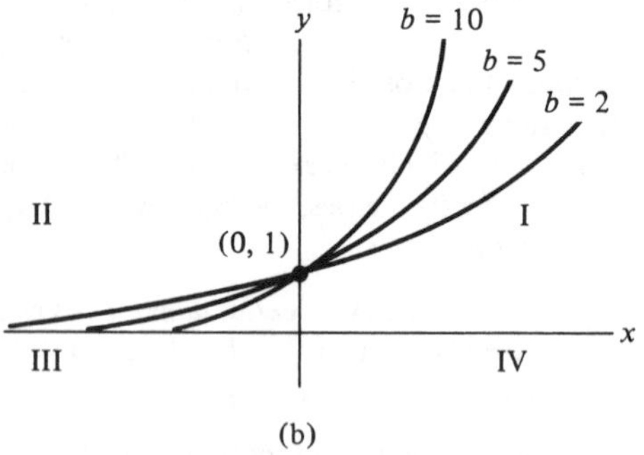


[10] In the language of later chapters, the exponential function decreases monotonically when $0 < b < 1$.

[11] $e$ is also an irrational number, in the sense that it is not the quotient of two integers, whereas any rational number *is* the quotient of two integers. There are no two integers that can be divided one by the other to produce $e$.

As the values of variable $x$ increase, we can see that $(1 + 1/x)^x$ takes on larger values that asymptotically approach 2.718281828 . . . . Specifically, we find that

$$
\begin{aligned}
f(1) &= (1 + 1/1)^1 &&= 2.00 \\
f(2) &= (1 + 1/2)^2 &&= 2.25 \\
f(3) &= (1 + 1/3)^3 &&= 2.37 \ldots \\
&\vdots && \vdots \\
f(20) &= (1 + 1/20)^{20} &&= 2.65 \ldots \\
&\vdots && \vdots \\
f(100) &= (1 + 1/100)^{100} &&= 2.70 \ldots
\end{aligned}
$$

If the process of letting $x$ increase in value were allowed to go on indefinitely,[12] then the function $y = f(x) = (1 + 1/x)^x$ would converge to the number 2.718281828 . . . .

EXAMPLE Consider the following particular exponential function, which is known as the "logistic" function:

$$y(t) = \frac{K}{1 + e^{-0.2t}}$$

where $y(t)$ is the percentage of households that have purchased color television sets in time period $t$, $K$ is a constant that expresses the expected upper limit to the percentage of households that might acquire color television sets, $e = 2.718 \ldots$, and $t$ is a variable representing years, $t \geq 1$. Let $K = 0.8$ for purposes of this example. As $t$ becomes increasingly large, the following pattern emerges:

$$
\begin{aligned}
y(1) &= \frac{0.8}{1 + e^{-0.2}} = 0.44 \\
y(2) &= \frac{0.8}{1 + e^{-0.2(2)}} = 0.48 \\
y(3) &= \frac{0.8}{1 + e^{-0.2(3)}} = 0.52 \\
&\vdots \qquad \vdots \qquad\qquad \vdots \\
y(10) &= \frac{0.8}{1 + e^{-0.2(10)}} = 0.70 \\
&\vdots \qquad \vdots \qquad\qquad \vdots \\
y(20) &= \frac{0.8}{1 + e^{-0.2(20)}} = 0.78
\end{aligned}
\tag{2.19}
$$

[12] This process involves the concept of a limit, which we discuss in Chapter 3.

Hence, within one year after the introduction of color television sets in this market, 44% of all households have purchased a color television set. This percentage rises to 70% after 10 years, and to 78% after 20 years. It will asymptotically approach a limit of 80%. (We shall deal with the concept of a *limit* in Chapter 3.)

*Exponential functions:* $y = ab^{cx}$
A more general exponential functional form than $y = f(x) = b^x$ does exist. It is $y = f(x) = ab^{cx}$. When $a$ and $c$ are equal to 1, then $y = ab^{cx} = b^x$. The function $y = b^x$ is therefore a special case of the function $y = ab^{cx}$.

There are four interesting cases involving the values assumed by $a$ and $c$ that are worthy of further examination: (a) $a > 1$; (b) $0 < a < 1$; (c) $c > 1$; (d) $0 < c < 1$.

(a) $a > 1$
The parameter $a$ determines the ordinate intercept of the exponential function. Consider Figure 2.12(a) and (b). In (a), the exponential functions $y = b^x$ and $y = 2b^x$ are graphed. (The value of parameter $c$ is implicitly equal to 1.) The ordinate intercept is shifted upward from point (0, 1) to (0, 2) when the value of $a$ changes from 1 to 2.

(b) $0 < a < 1$
Figure 2.12(b) has graphed the exponential functions $y = b^x$ and $y = 0.5b^x$. The effect of changing the value of parameter $a$ from 1 to 1/2 shifts the ordinate intercept of the exponential function from point (0, 1) to (0, 0.5). While the particular case in which $a < 0$ is not illustrated, it is a possibility.[13] When $a < 0$, the graph of the exponential function begins in the third quadrant.

(c) $c > 1$
The parameter $c$ in the general exponential function $y = ab^{cx}$ determines how rapidly the graph of the exponential function increases. Figure 2.13(a) graphs

Figure 2.12 Parameter $a$ and the exponential function $y = ab^{cx}$. (a) $a \geq 1$, $c = 1$; (b) $0 < a \leq 1$, $c = 1$

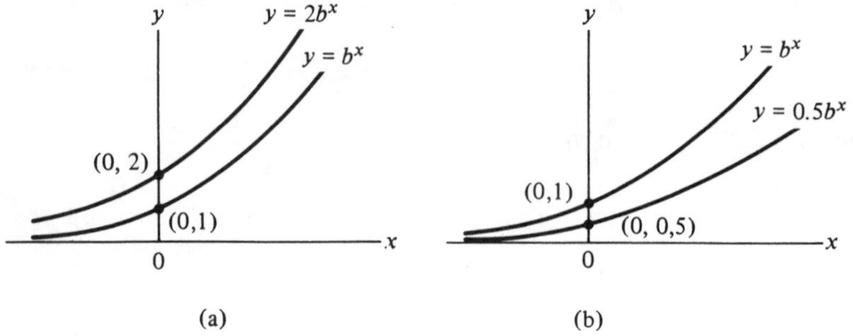


[13] The case of $a < 0$ is considered in Exercise Set 7 in this chapter.

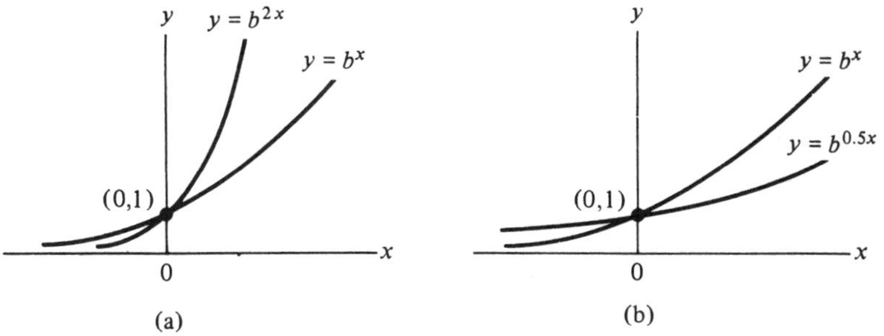


Figure 2.13 Parameter c and the exponential function $y = ab^{cx}$. (a) $c \geq 1$, $a = 1$, (b) $0 < c \leq 1$, $a = 1$

the exponential functions $y = b^x$ and $y = b^{2x}$. It is apparent that increasing the value of the parameter $c$ from 1 to 2 causes the exponential function to rise more rapidly. More precisely, doubling the parameter $c$ causes the graph of the exponential function to increase twice as fast.

(d) $0 < c < 1$
Figure 2.13(b) graphs the exponential functions $y = b^x$ and $y = b^{0.5x}$. The decrease in the value of parameter $c$ from 1 to 1/2 causes the graph of $y = b^{0.5x}$ to increase less rapidly than the graph of $y = b^x$. The intercept of an exponential function is unaffected by changes in the value of parameter $c$. Hence, since $y = b^x = ab^x$ when $a = 1$, the $y$ intercept in both (a) and (b) is given by the point (0, 1).

**EXERCISE 2.6**

1. Sketch on the same set of axes the graphs of the exponential functions $y = b^x$ for $b = 4$, 8, and 12.
2. Sketch on the same set of axes the graphs of the exponential functions $y = ab^x$ for $a = 0.3$, 1, and 7; $c = 1$.
3. Sketch on the same set of axes the graphs of the exponential functions $y = b^{cx}$ for $c = 0.3$, 1, and 7; $a = 1$.
4. Sketch on the same set of axes the graphs of the exponential functions $y = 7^x$, $y = 7^{3x}$, and $y = 4(7^x)$.
5. Sketch on the same set of axes the graphs of the exponential functions $y = 0.8^x$, $y = 0.8^{0.7x}$, and $y = 0.3(0.8)^{0.7x}$.

*Logarithmic functions*
Exponential functions and logarithmic functions are closely related. An exponential function of the form $y = f(x) = b^x$ is a "one-to-one" function in the sense that for each particular value of variable $x$ there is one and only one value of variable $y$. Any function that exhibits a one-to-one relationship also has associated with it an *inverse function*.[14]

[14] We deal with the concept of an inverse function later in this chapter.

DEFINITION Given $x = b^y$, where $b > 0$ and $b \neq 1$, we refer to $y = \log_b x$ as the logarithmic function of $x$ to the base $b$.

This definition implies that the logarithm of a number is the *exponent* to which a base must be raised in order to yield the original number. In general, it is true that

$$x = b^y \Leftrightarrow \log_b x = y \tag{2.20}$$

Stated once again, the preceding definitions and Equation (2.20) tell us that the log of some variable $x$ to the base $b$ is in fact the power to which we must raise the base $b$ in order to yield the value $x$.

EXAMPLES

1. The following common logarithms are used frequently.
   Since $10^0 = 1$, then $\log_{10} 1 = 0$.
   Since $10^1 = 10$, then $\log_{10} 10 = 1$.
   Since $10^2 = 100$, then $\log_{10} 100 = 2$.
   Since $10^3 = 1000$, then $\log_{10} 1000 = 3$.
   Since $10^{-3} = 0.001$, then $\log_{10} 0.001 = -3$.
   Since $10^{-2} = 0.01$, then $\log_{10} 0.01 = -2$.
   Since $10^{-1} = 0.1$, then $\log_{10} 0.1 = -1$.
2. The expression $5^2 = 25$ can also be written in logarithmic form as $\log_5 25 = 2$.
3. Since $2^{-3} = \frac{1}{8}$, then $\log_2 \frac{1}{8} = -3$.

The two preceding definitions and Equation (2.20) imply a prohibition against negative or zero logarithms. We already know that an exponential function is defined by $y = f(x) = b^x$ and that by definition $\log_b y = x$, where $x$ is the log of $y$ to the base $b$. In our study of exponential functions, however, we restricted the value of $y$ to any positive real number. The domain of the function $\log_b y = x$ is the set of all positive real numbers; the range of this function is all real numbers. This means that we shall not deal with zero or negative logarithms.

Given the logarithmic function $\log_b y = x$, any positive real number is permissible as the base $b$. However, the two most popular choices for the base $b$ are $b = 10$ and $b = e = 2.718\ldots$. When we use the logarithmic function $\log_{10} y = x$, we refer to the value of variable $x$ as a "common logarithm." You will probably remember that your first contact with logarithms in junior or senior high school involved common logarithms. Indeed, when a logarithmic function is written *without* a specific base, the base is *assumed to be* 10. Thus $\log_{10} y = x = \log y$.

DEFINITION Given the logarithmic function $\log_{10} y = x$, the value of variable $x$ is the common logarithm of variable $y$ to base 10.

By contrast, when we use the logarithmic function $\log_e y = x$, we refer to the value of $x$ as the *natural* or *Naperian logarithm.* It is customary to denote

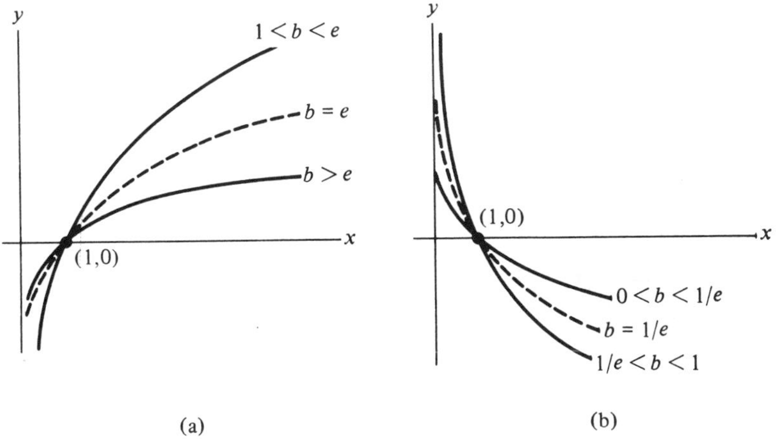


Figure 2.14 Logarithmic functions for various values of the base $b$. (a) $y = \log_b x$, where $b > 1$; (b) $y = \log_b x$, where $0 < b < 1$

natural logarithms by the abbreviation "ln" rather than "$\log_e$." That is, $\log_e y = x = \ln y$. The use of ln instead of $\log_e y$ is predominant and growing.

DEFINITION Given the logarithmic function $\log_e y = x$, the value of variable $x$ is the Naperian or natural logarithm of variable $y$ to base $e$.

As with exponential functions, there are several laws pertaining to the use and manipulation of logarithmic functions that must be followed. These laws, which are stated along with examples in Table 2.4, are valid for both common logarithms and natural logarithms.

Figure 2.14(a) and (b) illustrates the graphs of several logarithmic functions of the general form

$$y = f(x) = \log_b x, \qquad \text{where } b > 0 \text{ and } b \neq 1$$

As is the case with exponential functions, the parameter $b$ determines the curvature of logarithmic functions. When $b > 1$, as in (a), the logarithmic

Table 2.4 Laws concerning the use of logarithms

| *Law* | *Example* |
|---|---|
| 1. $\ln e^x = x = e^{\ln x}$ | $\ln e^{x^2} = x^2 = e^{\ln x^2}$ |
| 2. $\log_b (xy) = \log_b x + \log_b y$ | $\log_b 5A = \log_b 5 + \log_b A$ |
| $\ln xy = \ln x + \ln y$ | $\ln 5A = \ln 5 + \ln A$ |
| 3. $\log_b (x/y) = \log_b x - \log_b y$ | $\log_{10} (13/3) = \log_{10} 13 - \log_{10} 3$ |
| $\ln (x/y) = \ln x - \ln y$ | $\ln (13/3) = \ln 13 - \ln 3$ |
| 4. $\log_b x^n = n \log_b x$ | $\log_7 5^{0.4} = 0.4 \log_7 5$ |
| $\ln x^n = n \ln x$ | $\ln 5^{0.4} = 0.4 \ln 5$ |
| 5. $\log_b A = 1/\log_A b$ | $\log_b 5 = 1/\log_5 b$ |

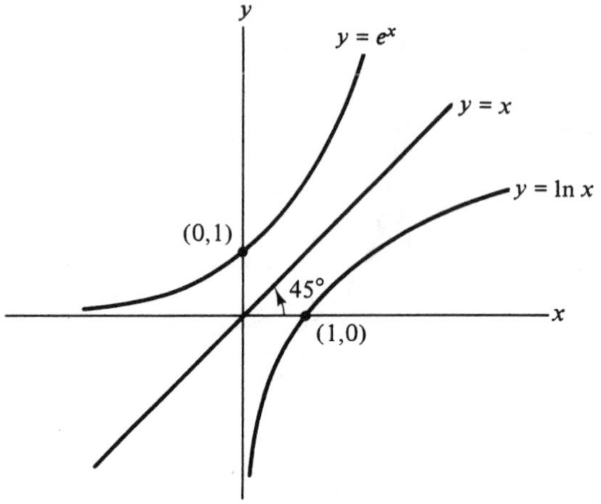


Figure 2.15 The function $y = e^x$ and its inverse function, $y = \ln x$

function is positively sloped and increases continuously (that is, the logarithmic function increases monotonically). When $0 < b < 1$, as in (b), the logarithmic function is negatively sloped and decreases continuously (that is, it decreases monotonically).

In both (a) and (b), the $x$ intercept is the point (1,0), and the logarithmic functions are asymptotic to the $y$ axis. The two graphs lie entirely within the first and fourth quadrants. This means that the domain of variable $x$ is restricted to positive values.

The relationship between the graph of an exponential function such as $y = b^x$ and its inverse function, $y = \log_b x$, is symmetric with respect to the line $y = x$.

Similarly, there is a symmetry between the graph of the exponential function $y = e^x$ and its inverse function, $y = \ln x$. Figure 2.15 illustrates the symmetry between the latter two functions, and Table 2.5 indicates the key aspects of that symmetry. The symmetry in question relates to the 45° line given by $y = x$. The two graphs are mirror images of each other.

**EXERCISE 2.7**

1. Express the following logarithmic functions exponentially and the exponential functions logarithmically.

Table 2.5 The function $y = e^x$ and its inverse, $y = \ln x$

| *Characteristics of the graph* | $y = e^x$ | $y = \ln x$ |
|---|---|---|
| Intercept | (0, 1) ordinate | (1, 0) abscissa |
| Quadrants | I, II | I, IV |
| Asymptotically approaches | $x$ axis | $y$ axis |

(a) $6^2 = 36$ (b) $10^4 = 10{,}000$
(c) $\log_{10} 0.0001 = -4$ (d) $\log_2 8 = 3$
(e) $4^3 = 64$ (f) $\log_3 27 = 3$
(g) $\log_2 x = 9$ (h) $8^{1/3} = 2$
(i) $5^{-2} = 1/25$ (j) $\log_2 64 = x$

2. Determine the range of values $x$ can have so that the following functions will be defined.
(a) $y = \ln (x + 8)$ (b) $y = \ln (8 - x)$
(c) $y = \ln (x^2 - 4)$ (d) $y = \ln (25 - x^2)$
(e) $y = \ln (x - 9)$ (f) $y = \ln (x^3 + 8)$
3. Using the laws concerning the use of logarithms found in Table 2.4, express each of the following as a single logarithm.
(a) $\ln x + \ln y + \ln z$ (b) $\ln (x + y - 25)$
(c) $\frac{1}{2} \ln (x + y) - 2$ (d) $\dfrac{1}{\log_b 5} + \log_5 x$
4. The first law given in Table 2.4 states that $\ln x$ and $e^x$ are inverse functions of each other. That is, $\ln e^x = x = e^{\ln x}$ for all $x > 0$. Using this relationship, simplify the following.
(a) $e^{\ln x3}$ (b) $e^{\ln 5x2}$
(c) $\ln \dfrac{x^2}{e^2}$ (d) $\ln e^{x2}$
(e) $e^{2 \ln 5x}$ (f) $e^{-\ln x2}$
(g) $\ln 4x^3 \cdot e^{x5}$ (h) $e^{x3 + 3 \ln x2}$
5. Pareto's law of the distribution of incomes says that the number of individuals $N$ from a given population whose incomes exceed $x$ dollars is given by $N = a/x^b$. Pareto suggested that the value of $b$ was approximately 1.50. If $a = 10{,}000$, what is the number of individuals whose incomes exceed \$20,000?
6. Given the general exponential form $y = f(x) = ab^{cx}$, graph (and compare) the shapes of the curves found in Figures 2.12 and 2.13 when (a) $a < -1$; (b) $-1 < a < 0$; (c) $c < -1$; and (d) $-1 < c < 0$. Note that the graphs of the exponential functions found in Figures 2.12 and 2.13 are restricted to the cases in which $a, c > 0$. How do the shapes of these graphs change when $a, c$ can be less than zero, as in (a) through (d) above?

### *Inverse functions*

In the previous sections, we have talked about a function that is the *inverse* of another function. It is time to refine our notion of the character of an inverse function.

Consider a function $y = f(x)$ that is strictly increasing or decreasing for all values of $x$ from some point $a$ to another point $b$. A strictly increasing function is a monotonically increasing function.

DEFINITION A function $f(x)$ is said to be increasing if $f(x_i) > f(x_j)$ for all values of $x_i > x_j$.

When a function $f(x)$ is monotonically increasing, this means that, as we increase the value of variable $x$, the function $f(x)$ also increases in value. Similarly, a strictly decreasing function is known as a monotonically decreasing function.

DEFINITION A function $f(x)$ is said to be decreasing if $f(x_i) < f(x_j)$ for all values of $x_i > x_j$.

When a function $f(x)$ is monotonically decreasing, this means that, as we increase the value of variable $x$, the value of the function $f(x)$ also decreases.

Consider a function $y = f(x)$ that is strictly increasing for all values of $x$ from $a$ to $b$, as in Figure 2.16(a). Consider also a function $y = f(x)$ that is strictly decreasing for all values of $x$ from $a$ to $b$, as in Figure 2.16(b). Each of the functions illustrated in parts (a) and (b) is a "one-to-one mapping." That is, for every value of $x$ in the interval $(a, b)$, there is one and only one value of $y$ in the interval $(c, d)$ such that $y = f(x)$. Hence a change in the value of $x$ always yields a unique and different value of $y$, and vice versa. The mathematical notation for this relationship is the following: $x = f^{-1}(y) = g(y)$. This is read, "$x$ is an *inverse function* of $y$." This new function, $x = f^{-1}(y) = g(y)$ is called an *inverse function*. Its domain is the interval $(c, d)$.

An inverse function $(f^{-1})$ exists for both of the functions illustrated in Figure 2.16(a) and (b). In general, for an inverse of a function to exist, the original function must be monotonic. This follows from the fact that both the original function and the monotonic function are one-to-one correspondences between the points of the two intervals $(a, b)$ and $(c, d)$. Further, if $f$ is the original function, and $f^{-1}$ is the inverse of function $f$, then the original function $f$ must also be the inverse of function $f^{-1}$. That is, if a function $f$ has an inverse function $f^{-1}$, then it is also true that function $f$ is the inverse of function $f^{-1}$. Functions $f$ and $f^{-1}$ are inverses of each other.

Figure 2.17 shows the graphical relationship between a function $f$ and its inverse function. We can obtain the graph of one from the graph of the other

Figure 2.16 Increasing and decreasing functions: one-to-one mappings. (a) Increasing function, (b) decreasing function

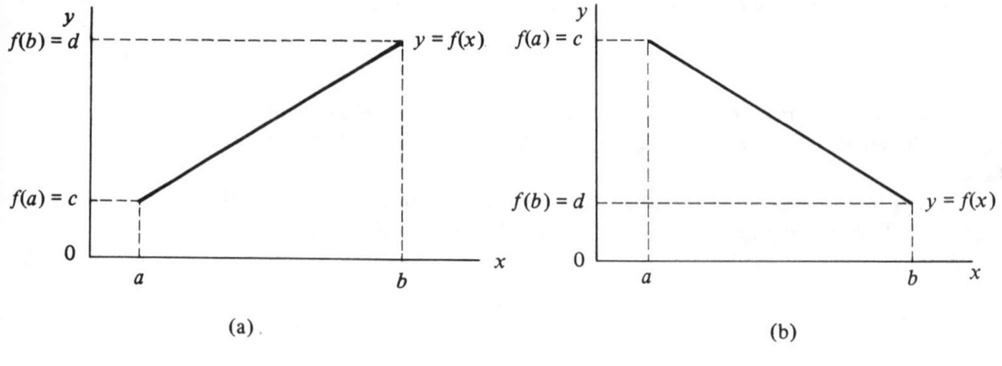

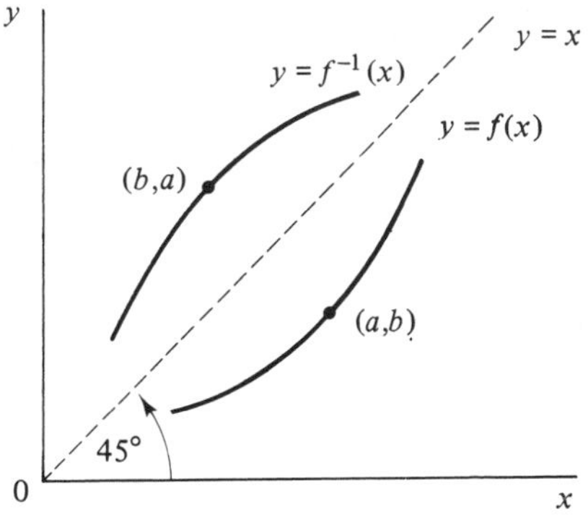


Figure 2.17 The function $y = f(x)$ and its inverse, $y = f^{-1}(x)$

because each graph is a mirror image of the other graph with respect to a 45° line drawn from the origin. This must be so because a point $(a, b)$ is on the graph $f(x)$ if and only if the point $(b, a)$ lies on the graph $f^{-1}(x)$.

■ One must avoid the error of assuming that the inverse function notation $(f^{-1})$ means that this is some function $f$ raised to the $-1$ power. $f^{-1} \neq 1/f$.

EXAMPLE If

$$y = f(x) = 4x - 5$$

then the inverse function $f^{-1}$ is given by

$$x = \tfrac{1}{4}(y + 5)$$

However, $[f(x)]^{-1}$ implies that the function $f(x)$ is raised to the $-1$ power. Thus, if

$$y = f(x) = 4x - 5$$

then

$$[f(x)]^{-1} = (4x - 5)^{-1} = \frac{1}{4x - 5}$$

This implies that

$$(f)^{-1} = \frac{1}{f}$$

## SUMMATION NOTATION

In many business and economic problems, one is required to sum a large number of terms (numbers, variables, parameters, coefficients, and so forth). A shorthand notation that makes use of the Greek letter sigma ($\sum$) enables us to write such lengthy sums in a more compact form. For example, using summation notation, we can express the sum of the first ten positive integers as follows:

$$1 + 2 + 3 + \cdots + 10 = \sum_{i=1}^{10} i = 55 \tag{2.21}$$

Equation (2.21) is read, "The sum of $i$ for all consecutive integers from 1 to 10, inclusive." The symbol $i$ represents each integer.

Similarly we can use the summation symbol $\sum$ to represent the summation of a sequence of variables:

$$x_1 + x_2 + x_3 + x_4 = \sum_{j=1}^{4} x_j \tag{2.22}$$

The letter $j$ in Equation (2.22) serves the same purpose as the letter $i$ in Equation (2.21). They each serve as an *index of summation* and are arbitrary or dummy indices. Summation indices are commonly denoted by letters such as $i$, $j$, or $k$. This summation,

$$\sum_{j=1}^{4} x_j \quad \text{could also be written} \quad \sum_{j=1}^{4} x_j = \sum_{i=1}^{4} x_i = \sum_{k=1}^{4} x_k \tag{2.23}$$

Table 2.6 Rules governing the use of summation notation and examples of the rules in use

| *Rule* | *Example* |
| --- | --- |
| $\sum_{i=1}^{n} (a_i + b_i) = \sum_{i=1}^{n} a_i + \sum_{i=1}^{n} b_i$ (Additive property) | Let $x_i = i + i^2$ <br> $\sum_{i=1}^{3} (i + i^2) = \sum_{i=1}^{3} i + \sum_{i=1}^{3} i^2$ <br> $= (1 + 2 + 3) + (1^2 + 2^2 + 3^2) = 20$ |
| $\sum_{i=1}^{n} kx_i = k \sum_{i=1}^{n} x_i$ (Homogeneous property) | Let $x_i = i$ <br> $\sum_{i=1}^{3} 4i = 4\sum_{i=1}^{3} i$ <br> $= 4 \cdot 1 + 4 \cdot 2 + 4 \cdot 3 = 24$ |
| $\sum_{k=1}^{n} (a_k - a_{k-1}) = a_n - a_0$ (Telescoping property) | Let $x_j = 2j + 3$ for $j = 1, \ldots, 4$ <br> $\sum_{j=1}^{4} x_j - x_{j-1}$ <br> $= (x_1 - x_0) + (x_2 - x_1)$ <br> $+ (x_3 - x_2) + (x_4 - x_3)$ <br> $= x_4 - x_0 = 11 - 3 = 8$ |

By now, it should be apparent that expressions such as $i = 1$, $j = 1$, and $k = 1$ delimit the range of values that the index is allowed to assume. For example, in Equation (2.22), $j = 1$ is the lower limit or first value that $j$ assumes. Similarly the number 4 above the symbol $\sum$ in Equations (2.22) and (2.23) indicates the upper limit or last value of the sequence.[15]

Table 2.6 summarizes the use of summation notation.

## PRODUCT NOTATION

Another useful shorthand mathematical notation relates to the multiplying of a large number of terms (numbers, variables, parameters, coefficients, and so forth). The Greek capital letter pi, $\prod$, is used to denote the product of several terms. For example, using product notation, one can express the product of the first ten positive integers as

$$1 \cdot 2 \cdot 3 \cdot \ldots \cdot 10 = \prod_{i=1}^{10} i = 3{,}628{,}000 \tag{2.24}$$

Equation (2.24) is read, "The product of $i$ for all consecutive integers from 1 to

Table 2.7 Rules governing the use of product notation and examples of the rules in use

| *Rule* | *Example* |
|---|---|
| $\prod_{i=1}^{n}(a_i b_i) = \left(\prod_{i=1}^{n} a_i\right)\left(\prod_{i=1}^{n} b_i\right)$ (Multiplicative property) | $\prod_{i=1}^{3}(i+1)(i+2)$ $\left[\prod_{i=1}^{3}(i+1)\right]\left[\prod_{i=1}^{3}(i+2)\right]$ $= (2 \cdot 3 \cdot 4)(3 \cdot 4 \cdot 5) = 1440$ |
| $\prod_{j=1}^{n}(ca_j) = c^n \prod_{j=1}^{n} a_j$ (Homogeneous property) | $\prod_{i=1}^{3} 2i^2 = 2^3 \prod_{i=1}^{3} i^2$ $= 8(1 \cdot 4 \cdot 9) = 288$ |
| $\prod_{k=1}^{n}(a_k/a_{k-1}) = (a_n/a_0)$, where $a_0 \neq 0$ (Telescoping property) | Let $x_i = \dfrac{i+1}{i^2+2}$ as $i = 0, \ldots, 3$ $\prod_{i=1}^{3} \dfrac{x_i}{x_{i-1}} = \left(\dfrac{x_1}{x_0}\right)\left(\dfrac{x_2}{x_1}\right)\left(\dfrac{x_3}{x_2}\right) = \dfrac{x_3}{x_0}$ $= \dfrac{(3+1)/(9+2)}{(0+1)/(0+2)} = \dfrac{8}{11}$ |

[15] It is usually wise to avoid using the letter $n$ as an index of summation. The letter $n$ is an extremely popular upper bound limit for summations. "$n$ people," "$n$ goods," and the like are often assumed. Hence the letter $n$ should not ordinarily be used as the index of summation.

10, inclusive." In general, the product of any $n$ real numbers $a_1, a_2, a_3, \ldots, a_n$ is given by

$$a_1 \cdot a_2 \cdot a_3 \cdot \ldots \cdot a_n = \prod_{i=1}^{n} a_i \tag{2.25}$$

Analogous to the summation notation, the letter $i$ in Equations (2.24) and (2.25) is referred to as the *product index* and is an arbitrary or dummy index. Once again, the range of values that the index may assume is indicated below and above the symbol $\prod$.

Table 2.7 lists three important properties associated with the use of product notation and gives examples of each.

### EXERCISE 2.8

For each of the following functions, sketch the graphs of $f$ and $f^{-1}$ and determine the range and domain for both the function and its inverse.

1. $y = 5 + 4x$
2. $y = 3 - 2x$
3. $y = \sqrt{2x + 8}$
4. $y = \dfrac{x}{x + 1}$
5. $y = x$
6. $y = 2x - 3$

Evaluate each of the following sums.

7. $\sum_{j=40}^{44} j$
8. $\sum_{k=1}^{4} 2^{k-1}$
9. $\sum_{i=0}^{5} (-1)^i$
10. $\sum_{k=1}^{4} \dfrac{k-1}{k+1}$
11. $\sum_{i=5}^{8} (3i + 5)$

Rewrite the following in summation notation.

12. $1 + x + x^2 + x^3 + x^4$
13. $1 + 2 + 4 + 8 + 16 + 32$
14. $1 + \dfrac{a}{x} + \dfrac{a^2}{x^2} + \dfrac{a^3}{x^3} + \cdots + \dfrac{a^n}{x^n} \qquad x \neq 0$

Evaluate each of the following products.

15. $\prod_{j=40}^{42} j$
16. $\prod_{j=2}^{5} x^j$
17. $\prod_{i=1}^{5} i^2$
18. $\prod_{i=1}^{4} (3i + a)$

### PROBLEMS

1. Solve the equation $x^2 + 5x + 6 = 0$ for $x$ using the quadratic formula.
2. Indicate whether the sets of numbers below can be properly described as

being any or all of the following: integers, fractions, rational numbers, real numbers, irrational numbers.

(a) $\{-5, -1, 2, 4\}$ (b) $\{\frac{4}{3}, \frac{1}{2}, -\frac{3}{8}, \frac{11}{12}\}$
(c) $\{\sqrt{2}, \sqrt{3}, \Pi, \sqrt{11}\}$

3. Given the equation $y = 4x - 5$. (a) Find the values taken on by the dependent variable $y$ when independent variable $x$ takes on integer values between 1 and 3. (b) Graph the function $y = 4x - 5$.
4. Graph the equation $y = x^2 - 2x + 1$. What kind of functional form is this? What is the range of this function?
5. Given the following price and quantity demanded data for pizza.

| *Quantity demanded* | *Price per pizza* |
|---|---|
| 50 | \$5 |
| 60 | \$4 |
| 70 | \$3 |
| 80 | \$2 |
| 90 | \$1 |

(a) Find the equation of the demand function for pizza such that $Q = f(P)$.
(b) What are the slope and the ordinate (intercept) of the demand function?

6. The manager of the Tampa Gas and Electric Company must frequently communicate with some or all of the employees. The manager can do this by either: (a) typing a letter, then inserting it into a photocopying machine in order to make additional copies, or (b) typing a letter on a ditto, then producing the needed copies on a ditto machine. The mean cost of typing a letter or stencil is \$3.00; a stencil costs \$0.25; a sheet of paper for a letter, the photocopying machine, or the ditto machine costs \$0.01; the cost of using the copy machine (excluding paper) is \$0.02 per copy.

What is the least expensive way for the manager to send a communication to 5 employees? to 25 employees? to 50 employees? to 100 employees?

The least expensive way of communicating depends on the number of copies of the communication that are needed. Find the number of copies for which the total cost of the two methods is identical. Demonstrate this solution both algebraically and graphically.
7. Indicate which of the following equations are functions, relations, or both.

(a) $x = f(y)$ (b) $y = f(x)$ (c) $x = y^2$
(d) $y = 6x^3$ (e) $y = 4x/y^3$

8. The gross national product (GNP) of Nuevo Laredo, a relatively less developed country, was valued at 100 billion pesetas in the year 1978. The leaders of the country feel that a realistic growth target is for GNP to grow to 220 within seven years (the year 1985). Consider GNP as a function of time $t$. Which of the following functional relationships most

accurately portrays such a growth path? (a) $\mathrm{GNP} = 99 + 2^t$; (b) $\mathrm{GNP} = 100 + t^2$; (c) $\mathrm{GNP} = 100 + 2t$. Identify each of these three functional forms and indicate why one in particular is preferred to the others in describing the growth path of Nuevo Laredo GNP.

9. The demand function for carpenters in Portland is given by $Q = 100{,}000W^{-2}$, where $Q$ = quantity of carpenters employed and $W$ = wage rate of carpenters per hour. How many carpenters will be employed if they insist on receiving a wage of \$15 per hour? What kind of functional form is this demand function?

10. Profit maximization requires that a firm equate marginal cost (MC) with marginal revenue (MR). The marginal cost curve for the production of mathematical economics textbooks is given by

$$\mathrm{MC} = 8 + 0.01Q$$

where $Q$ is the number of textbooks produced. The marginal revenue realized from the sale of textbooks is given by

$$\mathrm{MR} = 100 - 0.05Q$$

Find the profit-maximizing output and sales of the firm.

11. The Numerical Control Company produces numerical control units that are attached to machine tools. The units automatically control the speed and operation of the machine tools far more efficiently than could be accomplished by hand. Numerical Control has developed a new and more efficient control unit, the DX-3. A total of 10,000 firms could ultimately purchase one DX-3 each. Numerical Control feels that the DX-3 will be profitable if 70% of these firms adopt the DX-3 within five years of the beginning of its production and distribution. The adoption function for the DX-3 is given by:

$$p(t) = \frac{k}{1 + e^{-0.2t}}$$

where $p(t)$ = cumulative percentage of firms that have adopted the DX-3 in year $t$

$t$ = time in years from beginning of initial production

$k$ = a constant that represents the maximum percentage of firms that could adopt the DX-3, and which therefore is equal to 100 in this problem

Will 70% of the firms adopt the DX-3 within five years? How many years will it take for 100% of the firms, or arbitrarily close thereto, to adopt the DX-3? What kind of functional form is represented by the adoption function?

12. Given the production function $Q = f(L, K)$, where $Q$ = output of the firm in units, and $L$ and $K$ are the number of units of labor and capital, respectively, that the firm chooses to hire. The specific form of the production function of the firm is $Q = 3\sqrt{L} + 5\sqrt{K}$. The marginal production of labor $\mathrm{MP}_L$ and the marginal product of capital $\mathrm{MP}_K$ are

respectively equal to $1.5/\sqrt{L}$ and $3.0\sqrt{K}$. The wage that must be paid to a unit of labor is symbolized by $w$ and is equal to \$1 per unit. The price of capital per unit, $r$, is \$2. The price of the output is symbolized by $P$ and is \$4 per unit. Profit maximization requires that the firm equate the price of its output to the value of the marginal product of each input. That is, the firm must satisfy $w = \text{VMP}_L$ and $r = \text{VMP}_K$, where $\text{VMP}_L = P \cdot \text{MP}_L$ and $\text{VMP}_K = P \cdot \text{MP}_K$.
(a) What are profit-maximizing magnitudes of $L$, $K$, and $Q$?
(b) How much profit will the firm earn?

13. The total cost TC of producing output $X$ is given by the equation $\text{TC} = 100 + 7x - 3x^2 + x^3$. (a) Find TC for integer values of $x$ ranging from 1 to 10. (b) Find average cost (AC), where $\text{AC} = \text{TC}/x$, for the same levels of output. (c) What kind of functional form is represented by the total cost function? (d) Explain intuitively what effects the signs of each coefficient in the total cost function have on the shape and configuration of the graph of the total cost function.
14. Numerous studies that have attempted to predict the salaries of college professors have used some form of the equation $\ln Y = f(X)$, where $Y$ = the professor's salary and $X$ = various characteristics of the professor, for example, degree status, publications, age, and so forth.[16] Suppose that $\ln Y = 9.5 + 0.023x$, where $x$ = the experience of the professor in years. (a) Find the predicted salary for a professor who has 20 years' experience; 40 years' experience. (b) Does this particular specification of the relationship between salary and experience tend to overstate or understate the effect of experience on professors' salaries? (c) How does this "semilog" type of specification value initial years of experience vis-a-vis later years of experience?
15. We can approximate the value of $X$ dollars left undisturbed to earn compound interest at a simple annual rate of interest $r$ for $t$ years by the following formula:

$$\text{Future value} = Xe^{rt}$$

What will the value of \$100 be if the interest is left to compound at a simple annual rate of interest of 6% (0.06) for 20 years? The present value of $X$ dollars, which will not be received until $t$ years have passed, can be expressed as

$$\text{Present value} = \frac{X}{e^{rt}}$$

What is the present value of \$100 that will not be received until 20 years have passed?
16. The "common" logarithm of a number $X$ is defined as

$$\log_b X = n \quad \text{or} \quad b^n = X, \qquad \text{where } b = 10$$

[16] See, for example, George E. Johnson and Frank P. Stafford, "The Earnings and Promotion of Women Faculty," *American Economic Review*, 64 (December 1974), 419–427.

The "natural" logarithm of the same number $X$ is defined as

$$\ln_b X = n, \qquad \text{where } b = e = 2.718 \ldots$$

The natural logarithm of any number may be approximated by multiplying the common (base 10) logarithm of the number by 2.3026. That is, $\ln X = 2.3026(\log X)$. (a) Find ln 89; ln 356; ln 6. (b) Demonstrate that the following statement is true: "We can approximate the common logarithm of the number 1000 by the natural logarithm of the number 1000 divided by 2.3026."

# LIMITS, CONTINUITY, AND DIFFERENTIABILITY

# 3

We are now ready to begin our formal exploration of the calculus. The calculus has traditionally been divided into two parts: differential calculus and integral calculus. As we shall see, the operations of differentiation and integration are the inverse of each other, just as addition and subtraction, and multiplication and division, are the inverse of each other.

We can view *differentiation* intuitively as the rate of change of a particular function. This rate of change is actually the slope of the tangent to the graph of that function. *Integration*, on the other hand, is intuitively the process of determining what function corresponds to a particular rate of change. One of the major practical uses of an integral is related to the fact that we can use an integral to find the area under a particular curve or function.

We are by now accustomed to expressing the relationship between two variables in a functional form. In many situations, however, it is not sufficient merely to know the identity of the independent and dependent variables. What we need is information concerning how the dependent variable changes in response to changes in the independent variable.

The supply-and-demand analysis of introductory economics provides a good example both of functional relationships and of the need to know how the dependent variable changes when the independent variable changes. Quantity demanded $Q_D$ and quantity supplied $Q_S$ are both a function of market price $P$.

$$Q_D = f(P) \tag{3.1}$$

$$Q_S = g(P) \tag{3.2}$$

Given a change in price, both quantity demanded and quantity supplied will change. In what direction will, for example, the change in quantity demanded be? What will be the magnitude of this change? The simple functional relationship outlined in Equation (3.1) does not answer either of these questions. However, introductory economics tells us that there is an inverse relationship between price and quantity demanded. When price decreases (increases), quantity demanded increases (decreases).

The second question above, which deals with the magnitude of change in quantity demanded, is not answered so easily. Where certain goods are concerned, a given change in price elicits a large change in quantity demanded, whereas for other goods a given change in price elicits only a negligible change in quantity demanded. For example, a \$1 rise in the price of a hamburger seriously reduces the quantity of hamburgers demanded, whereas a \$1 rise in the price of Cadillacs scarcely affects the quantity of Cadillacs demanded. We need, therefore, to be able to make a more definitive statement about the change that occurs in quantity demanded as a result of changes in market price.

We can view the rate of change between an independent variable and a dependent variable either qualitatively or quantitatively. If we are interested in the direction of change that the dependent variable takes when there is a change in the independent variable, then we are analyzing *qualitative* or *directional* change. Thus the direction of change in the example concerning quantity demanded was negative. As we have already seen, however, the magnitude of change (*quantitative* change) is also important. We want to know how much quantity demanded changes when price changes.

Differential calculus is an invaluable tool in determining both qualitative and quantitative change. The first derivative of a function (we shall define the first derivative later) tells us not only the direction of change in the dependent variable when there is a change in the independent variable, but also the magnitude of that change. We can use the differential calculus to generate precise information concerning both the direction and magnitude of change in quantity demanded (or quantity supplied) when market price changes. In general, we can find the direction and magnitude of change in any variable that we believe to have been brought about by a change in another variable. A very brief listing of relationships that we might examine by means of the differential calculus includes cost and output, depreciation and investment, the size of the firm and its profitability, advertising and sales, debt leverage and firm growth, and so forth.

We shall also see that we can use the differential calculus to find the maximum and minimum points of a function. For example, what is the most profitable output that the firm can produce? What is the cheapest combination of inputs that will produce a given level of output? What is the greatest amount of sales that can be generated from a territory? These are but a few of the many maximum and minimum problems that we can attack by means of the differential calculus.

Chapters 3 through 6 discuss the differential calculus and its applications. We shall reserve consideration of the integral calculus to Chapter 7. We shall begin our study of the calculus by familiarizing ourselves with the concepts of limits, continuity, and differentiability.

## LIMITS

The concept of a limit is one with which most students are intuitively familiar. Assume that a person is holding a 10-ounce glass under a water faucet. As the glass fills with water, the amount of water in the glass approaches an obvious limit, which in this case is 10 ounces. The glass can hold no more than 10 ounces of water; hence 10 ounces could be said to be a limit in this case.

In the same fashion, we might seek to determine the maximum (limiting) profits that a firm can earn in a given situation, if this is not already known, or we might try to determine the minimum (limiting) cost method of maintaining an inventory of a particular good. In sum, we deal intuitively with the concept of a limit in business and economics, as well as in our daily lives.

We shall initially define the limit of a function as follows.

DEFINITION Given $y = f(x)$. Let $x_0$ be a specific number. If, as $x$ approaches $x_0$, the values of $f(x)$ approach some number $A$, then $A$ is said to be the limit of $f(x)$ as $x$ approaches $x_0$.

Limit notation such as

$$\lim_{x \to x_0} f(x) = A$$

is read, "The limit of $f(x)$, as $x$ approaches a finite number $x_0$, is another finite number $A$." That is, $f(x)$ approaches $A$ as $x$ approaches $x_0$.

EXAMPLES

1. Consider the function $y = f(x) = x^2$. What value does the dependent variable $y$ approach as the value of the independent variable $x$ approaches 3? Table 3.1 summarizes the approach of this function to the value of 9 as the value of $x$ approaches 3. We can easily see that regardless of whether $x$ approaches the number 3 from above or from below, the corresponding value of the dependent variable $y$ becomes closer and closer to 9. Hence 9 is said to be the limit of $y = f(x) = x^2$ as the value of $x$ approaches 3.
2. Consider the function $y = f(x) = (x^2 - 1)/(x - 1)$. This function has a restricted domain in that it is defined for all values of $x$ except $x = 1$. Following the procedure outlined in Example 1, we analyze what happens to dependent variable $y$ when independent variable $x$ approaches a value of 1 from either direction. Table 3.2 illustrates that as $x$ approaches a value of 1, the value of $y$ approaches 2.
3. An interesting example of a limit is contained in an ancient problem

Table 3.1 The limiting process of $v = f(x) = x^2$ as $x$ approaches 3

| $y = f(x) = x^2$ | | | |
|---|---|---|---|
| *When* $x < 3$ | | *When* $x > 3$ | |
| $f(1)$ | $= 1$ | $f(5)$ | $= 25$ |
| $f(2)$ | $= 4$ | $f(4)$ | $= 16$ |
| $f(2.5)$ | $= 6.25$ | $f(3.5)$ | $= 12.25$ |
| $f(2.7)$ | $= 7.29$ | $f(3.3)$ | $= 10.89$ |
| $f(2.9)$ | $= 8.41$ | $f(3.1)$ | $= 9.61$ |
| $f(2.99)$ | $= 8.94$ | $f(3.01)$ | $= 9.06$ |
| $f(2.999)$ | $= 8.994$ | $f(3.001)$ | $= 9.006$ |

Table 3.2 The limiting process of $y = f(x) = (x^2 - 1)/(x - 1)$ as $x$ approaches 1

$$y = f(x) = \frac{x^2 - 1}{x - 1}$$

| *When* $x < 1$ | | *When* $x > 1$ | |
|---|---|---|---|
| $f(0)$ | $= 1$ | $f(2)$ | $= 3$ |
| $f(0.5)$ | $= 1.50$ | $f(1.5)$ | $= 2.50$ |
| $f(0.7)$ | $= 1.70$ | $f(1.3)$ | $= 2.30$ |
| $f(0.9)$ | $= 1.90$ | $f(1.1)$ | $= 2.10$ |
| $f(0.99)$ | $= 1.99$ | $f(1.01)$ | $= 2.01$ |
| $f(0.999)$ | $= 1.999$ | $f(1.001)$ | $= 2.001$ |

known as Zeno's Paradox.[1] Consider the following sequence of numbers: $2, 1 + \frac{1}{2}, 1 + \frac{1}{4}, 1 + \frac{1}{8}, 1 + \frac{1}{16}, 1 + \frac{1}{32}, \ldots, 1 + 1/2^x$, as $x$ becomes very large. Visually, this sequence of numbers is represented in Figure 3.1. Given the numbers 1 and 2 on a number scale, each succeeding number is one-half the distance between the number 1 and the preceding number. Thus the number $1 + 1/2$ bisects the distance between the numbers 1 and 2. Similarly, the number $1 + 1/4$ bisects the distance between the numbers 1 and $1 + 1/2$. As the bisecting process continues, we can observe that we come arbitrarily close to the number 1. We can confirm this by writing the underlying function algebraically: $y = f(x) = 1 + (1/2)^x$. As $x$ becomes very large, the value of the fraction $(1/2)^x$ approaches 0. For example, when $x = 10$, $(1/2)^{10} = 0.001$, and the value of $1 + (1/2)^{10} = 1.001$. We can therefore state that "as $x$ gets large without bound," the function $y = 1 + (1/2)^x$ approaches the value of 1. The "paradox" is contained in the fact that we never actually reach the number 1 by this process.

## *The Concept of a Limit: A More Rigorous Definition

The previous three examples demonstrate intuitively the concept of a limit. However, language such as "approaches" or "gets closer and closer" is hardly

Figure 3.1 Zeno's paradox and the number line

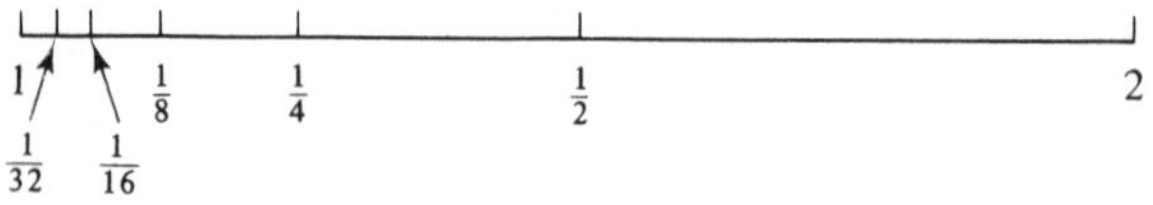


[1] See Carl B. Boyer, *The History of the Calculus and Its Conceptual Development*, Dover Publications, New York, 1959, p. 13.

* This section contains more difficult material that may be bypassed without loss of continuity. However, you should master the material in this section if you want a formal and more rigorous grounding in mathematics.

precise. We must now add rigor and substance to the definition of a limit that we developed earlier.

DEFINITION Given $y = f(x)$. Let $x_0$ be such that $f$ is defined for all $x$ near $x_0$, that is, for $0 < |x - x_0| < a$, where $a$ is a number. If there is some number $A$ such that, for each $\varepsilon > 0$, there is a number $\delta > 0$ which satisfies $|f(x) - A| < \varepsilon$ whenever $0 < |x - x_0| < \delta$, then $A$ is said to be the limit of $f(x)$ as $x$ approaches $A$.

Limit notation such as

$$\lim_{x \to x_0} f(x) = A$$

is read, "The limit of $f(x)$, as $x$ approaches a finite number $x_0$, approaches another finite number $A$." The limit notation $f(x) \to A$ as $x \to x_0$ is read: "$f(x)$ approaches $A$ as $x$ approaches $x_0$."

The preceding definition formally and precisely defines what we mean when we talk about "getting closer and closer." It introduces the absolute values $|f(x) - A|$ and $|x - x_0|$. They measure, respectively, the distance that separates $f(x)$ and $A$ from each other and the distance separating $x$ from $x_0$. Since a limit involves making $f(x)$ arbitrarily close to $A$, and since we have also specified that the value of $x$ must be arbitrarily close to $x_0$, we have rigorously delineated the concept of a limit. However, let us now introduce a graphical demonstration of this definition in order to solidify our understanding of the concept of a limit.

Consider Figure 3.2, which graphs the function $y = f(x)$. Notice, however, that there exists a small interval in the graph of function $y = f(x)$, and that this interval contains the point that has the ordinate $A$. We must demonstrate that in the arbitrarily small interval containing $A$, there is an interval ($x_0 - \delta$,

Figure 3.2 Geometric interpretation of a limit

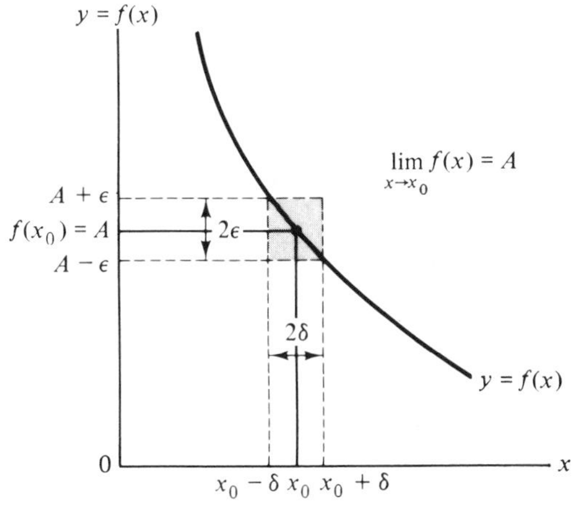

$x_0 + \delta$) containing points of the domain of $f$ (with the exception that $x$ cannot be equal to $x_0$).

Figure 3.2 contains two horizontal dashed lines with ordinates $(A + \varepsilon)$ and $(A - \varepsilon)$. This vertical distance about point $A$ is $2\varepsilon$ in length and represents any arbitrarily chosen small interval[2] about the ordinate $y = A$.

Figure 3.2 also contains an interval measuring $2\delta$ around point $x_0$. This interval is given by points $(x_0 - \delta)$ and $(x_0 + \delta)$ on the abscissa. The horizontal and vertical intervals, when extended into the first quadrant, form a rectangle, which is shaded in Figure 3.2. We can see that for every value of $x$ that is in the interval $(x_0 - \delta, x_0 + \delta)$, the entire graph of $f(x)$ lies within the shaded rectangle and the interval $(A - \varepsilon, A + \varepsilon)$. We must understand that no matter how small we wish the interval around $A$ to be, we can find some positive $\delta$ that forms an interval around $x_0$. That is, regardless of how small the interval around $A$, $x_0$ is included in the corresponding interval on the $x$ axis.

Consider the function $y = f(x) = x^2$, which we have dealt with before in our study of limits. Figure 3.3 contains the graph of the function $y = x^2$ as well as a series of intervals. Using the $\varepsilon$, $\delta$ definition of a limit, we see that no matter how small $\varepsilon$ might be, as long as it is greater than 0, we can find a value of $\delta$ such that the following relationships hold:

$$4 - \varepsilon < x^2 < 4 + \varepsilon \qquad \text{or} \qquad |x^2 - 4| < \varepsilon \tag{3.3}$$

[2] In Figure 3.2, $\varepsilon$ is assumed to be arbitrarily small. The distances $2\varepsilon$ and $2\delta$ are exaggerated for purposes of graphical representation. They are actually so small that they could not be usefully graphed.

Figure 3.3 Intervals around the point (2, 4)

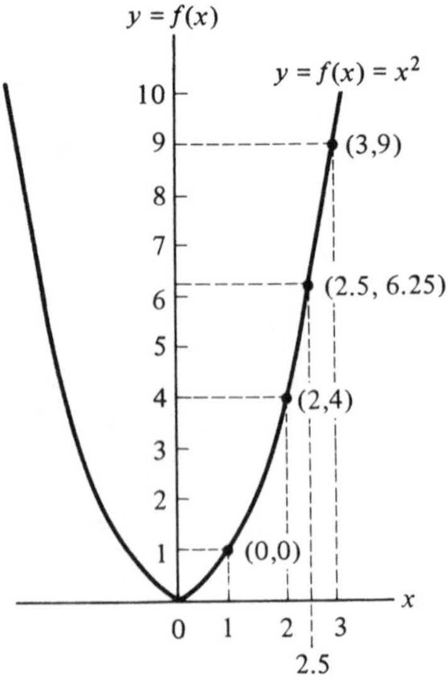

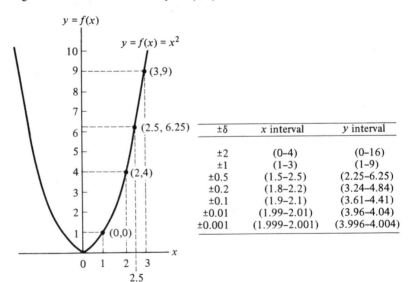

| $\pm\delta$ | $x$ interval | $y$ interval |
|---|---|---|
| ±2 | (0–4) | (0–16) |
| ±1 | (1–3) | (1–9) |
| ±0.5 | (1.5–2.5) | (2.25–6.25) |
| ±0.2 | (1.8–2.2) | (3.24–4.84) |
| ±0.1 | (1.9–2.1) | (3.61–4.41) |
| ±0.01 | (1.99–2.01) | (3.96–4.04) |
| ±0.001 | (1.999–2.001) | (3.996–4.004) |

whenever

$$2 - \delta < x < 2 + \delta \qquad \text{or} \qquad 0 < |x - 2| < \delta \tag{3.4}$$

Equation (3.3) can be factored into

$$|x^2 - 4| = |x - 2| \cdot |x + 2| < \varepsilon \tag{3.5}$$

Suppose that we decide to choose $\delta \leq 1$ if possible; then we need a $\delta$ such that $0 < \delta \leq 1$ and such that $|x - 2| < \delta$. Clearly,

$$|x + 2|\,|x - 2| < |x + 2|\delta \tag{3.6}$$

and

$$|x - 2| < \delta \leq 1 \qquad \text{or} \qquad |x - 2| < 1$$

which is equivalent to $-1 < x - 2 < 1$, or $1 < x < 3$. Therefore

$$|x + 2| < 5 \qquad \text{and} \qquad |x + 2|\,|x - 2| < 5\delta \tag{3.7}$$

Thus

$$|x + 2|\,|x - 2| < \varepsilon \qquad \text{if and only if} \qquad 5\delta \leq \varepsilon$$

which means that

$$\delta \leq \varepsilon/5$$

Thus $|x^2 - 4| < \varepsilon$ whenever $0 < |x - 2| < \delta$ if we let

$$\delta = \min\left(1, \frac{\varepsilon}{5}\right) \tag{3.8}$$

A review of our definition of a limit and a glance at Figure 3.2 reveals that neither the definition nor the graph makes an assertion about what happens to the function at the point $x_0$ itself. The interval around $x_0$ refers to points that are very "close" or "near" to $x_0$, but distinct from $x_0$ itself. Hence it is *not* proper to obtain the limit of $y = f(x) = x^2$ by setting $x = x_0$; that is, by setting $x = 2$ when $x$ is allowed to approach 2. Such a procedure can lead to problems. Consider the function

$$y = f(x) = \frac{x^2 - 1}{x - 1} \qquad \text{where } f(x) \to 2 \text{ as } x \to 1$$

It is improper to insert the value $x = 1$ into the equation in order to determine the limit. This is because the denominator is then equal to zero. Nonetheless, the function $y = (x^2 - 1)/(x - 1)$ does have a limit of 2 as $x$ approaches 1 (see Table 3.2). Our definition of a limit does not require that the underlying function be defined at $x = x_0$.

### The Basic Limit Theorems

Our definition of a limit would be quite difficult to use in many situations. There are, however, certain fundamental limit theorems (summarized in Table 3.3) that we can use to simplify the task of evaluating the limit of a function. These limit theorems are consistent with our definition, and may be used instead of the definition.

Assume that $K$ is a constant, that

$$\lim_{x \to x_0} f(x) = A \qquad \text{and that} \qquad \lim_{x \to x_0} g(x) = B$$

The following theorems[3] apply.

THEOREM 3.1 $\lim_{x \to x_0} K = K$

*Discussion* When a function $y = f(x)$ is a constant for all values of $x$, then the limit of this function is equal to that constant.

EXAMPLES

1. Given that $y = f(x) = 100$, then $\lim_{x \to x_0} 100 = 100$
2. Given that $y = f(x) = Z$, then $\lim_{x \to x_0} Z = Z$

[3] Proof of the limit theorems may be found in Thomas Apostol, *Calculus*, Volume I, Blaisdell Publishing Company, A Division of Random House, Inc., New York, 1961, pp. 165–168ff.

Table 3.3 Summary of the basic limit theorems

| | |
|---|---|
| Given: | (1) $K$ is a constant<br>(2) $\lim_{x \to x_0} f(x) = A$<br>(3) $\lim_{x \to x_0} g(x) = B$ |
| *Theorem 3.1* | $\lim_{x \to x_0} K = K$ |
| *Theorem 3.2* | $\lim_{x \to x_0} Kf(x) = KA$ |
| *Theorem 3.3* | $\lim_{x \to x_0} [f(x) \pm g(x)] = A \pm B$ |
| *Theorem 3.4* | $\lim_{x \to x_0} \sum_{i=1}^{n} f_i(x) = \sum_{i=1}^{n} A_i$ |
| *Theorem 3.5* | $\lim_{x \to A} 2f(x) = \lim_{x \to A} [f(x) + f(x)] = 2A$ |
| *Theorem 3.6* | $\lim_{x \to x_0} f(x) \cdot g(x) = A \cdot B$ |
| *Theorem 3.7* | $\lim_{x \to x_0} \prod_{i=1}^{n} f_i(x) = \prod_{i=1}^{n} A_i$ |
| *Theorem 3.8* | $\lim_{x \to x_0} \frac{f(x)}{g(x)} = \frac{A}{B}$ |
| *Theorem 3.9* | $\lim_{x \to x_0} [f(x)]^j = A^j$ |
| *Theorem 3.10* | $\lim_{x \to x_0} f(x) \cdot f(x) = A^2$ |

THEOREM 3.2 $\lim_{x \to x_0} Kf(x) = K \lim_{x \to x_0} f(x) = KA$

*Discussion* The limit of a constant times a function is equal to the constant times the limit of the function.

EXAMPLES

1. Given that $y = 5x^2$, then $\lim_{x \to x_0} 5x^2 = 5 \lim_{x \to x_0} x^2 = 5x_0^2$
2. Given that $y = 2x^2$, then $\lim_{x \to 2} 2x^2 = 2 \lim_{x \to 2} x^2 = 2 \cdot 4 = 8$

THEOREM 3.3 $\lim_{x \to x_0} [f(x) \pm g(x)] = \lim_{x \to x_0} f(x) \pm \lim_{x \to x_0} g(x) = A \pm B$

*Discussion* The limit of a sum (difference) of two functions is equal to the sum (difference) of their respective limits.

EXAMPLES

1. $\lim_{x \to x_0} (2x + 3x^2) = 2 \lim_{x \to x_0} x + 3 \lim_{x \to x_0} x^2 = 2x_0 + 3x_0^2$
2. $\lim_{x \to 3} (2x + 3x^2) = 2 \lim_{x \to 3} x + 3 \lim_{x \to 3} x^2 = 2 \cdot 3 + 3 \cdot 9 = 6 + 27 = 33$
3. $\lim_{x \to 1} (x^2 - 4x) = \lim_{x \to 1} x^2 - 4 \lim_{x \to 1} x = 1 - 4 = -3$

THEOREM 3.4 Given that $\lim_{x \to x_0} f_i(x) = A_i$, for all $i = 1, 2, \ldots, n$, then

$$\lim_{x \to x_0} \sum_{i=1}^{n} f_i(x) = \sum_{i=1}^{n} \lim_{x \to x_0} f_i(x) = \sum_{i=1}^{n} A_i$$

*Discussion* Theorem 3.3 is a special case of Theorem 3.4. When a finite number of functions are summed (subtracted), the limit of that summation (difference) is the sum (difference) of the limits of the individual functions.

EXAMPLES

1. $\lim_{x \to 2} (2x^3 - 3x^2 + 3x - 4) = 2 \lim_{x \to 2} x^3 - 3 \lim_{x \to 2} x^2 + 3 \lim_{x \to 2} x$
   $- \lim_{x \to 2} 4 = 2 \cdot 8 - 3 \cdot 4 + 3 \cdot 2 - 4 = 6$
2. $\lim_{x \to 4} (\tfrac{1}{2}x^3 - 8x + 3\sqrt{x}) = 6$

THEOREM 3.5 Given that $\lim_{x \to x_0} f(x) = A$, then

$$\lim_{x \to x_0} 2f(x) = \lim_{x \to x_0} [f(x) + f(x)] = \lim_{x \to x_0} f(x) + \lim_{x \to x_0} f(x) = A + A = 2A$$

*Discussion* This is a special case of Theorem 3.2.

EXAMPLES

1. $\lim_{x\to -2} (x^2 + x^2) = \lim_{x\to -2} 2x^2 = 2 \lim_{x\to -2} x^2 = 8$

2. $\lim_{x\to a} (\sqrt{x} + \sqrt{x} + \sqrt{x}) = \lim_{x\to a} 3\sqrt{x} = 3 \lim_{x\to a} \sqrt{x} = 3\sqrt{a}$

THEOREM 3.6 $\lim_{x\to x_0} f(x) \cdot g(x) = \lim_{x\to x_0} f(x) \cdot \lim_{x\to x_0} g(x) = A \cdot B$

*Discussion* This is the product limit theorem. It says that the limit of the product of two functions is the limit of the first function times the limit of the second function.

EXAMPLES

1. $\lim_{x\to 1} e^x = 2.718$ and $\lim_{x\to 2} e^{x^2} = 54.598$. Therefore

$$\lim_{x\to 1} e^x \cdot \lim_{x\to 2} e^{x^2} = (2.718)(54.598) = 148.413$$

2. $\lim_{x\to 2} x^2 = 4$ and $\lim_{x\to 2} x^3 = 8$. Therefore

$$\lim_{x\to 2} x^2 \cdot \lim_{x\to 2} x^3 = \lim_{x\to 2} x^5 = 4 \cdot 8 = 32$$

■ Note that it is not permissible to perform the multiplication $x^2 \cdot x^3 = x^5$, and then to take the limit of $x^5$ as $x$ approaches 2, *unless* the limit of both functions is taken as the function approaches 2. A glance at Example 1 reveals that such was not the case there. The limit of one function was taken as $x$ approached 1, while the limit of the other function was taken as $x$ approached 2.

THEOREM 3.7 If $\lim_{x\to x_0} f_i(x) = A_i$, for all $i = 1, 2, \ldots, n$, then

$$\lim_{x\to x_0} \prod_{i=1}^{n} f_i(x) = \prod_{i=1}^{n} \lim_{x\to x_0} f_i(x) = \prod_{i=1}^{n} A_i$$

*Discussion* This is an extension of Theorem 3.6 in which we seek to take the limit of a finite number of functions multiplied by one another.

EXAMPLES

1. Given that $\lim_{x\to x_0} f_1(x) = A_i$, $\lim_{x\to x_0} f_2(x) = A_2$, and $\lim_{x\to x_0} f_3(x) = A_3$, then

$$\lim \prod_{i=1}^{N} f_i(x) = \prod_{i=1}^{3} A_i = A_1 \cdot A_2 \cdot A_3$$

2. Let $\lim_{x\to x_0} f_1(x) = 1$, $\lim_{x\to x_0} f_2(x) = 2$, ..., $\lim_{x\to x_0} f_6(x) = 6$. Then

$$\lim_{x\to x_0} \prod_{i=1}^{6} f_i(x) = 1 \cdot 2 \cdot 3 \cdot 4 \cdot 5 \cdot 6 = 720$$

THEOREM 3.8 $\lim_{x \to x_0} \frac{f(x)}{g(x)} = \frac{\lim_{x \to x_0} f(x)}{\lim_{x \to x_0} g(x)} = \frac{A}{B} \qquad B \neq 0$

*Discussion* This is the quotient-limit theorem. The limit of the quotient of two functions is equal to the quotient of their limits.

EXAMPLES

1. $\lim_{x \to 2} x^3 = 8$ and $\lim_{x \to 2} x^2 = 4$. Then,

$$\frac{\lim_{x \to 2} x^3}{\lim_{x \to 2} x^2} = \lim_{x \to 2} \left(\frac{x^3}{x^2}\right) = \frac{8}{4} = 2 \qquad \text{or} \qquad \lim_{x \to 2} \frac{x^3}{x^2} = \lim_{x \to 2} x = 2$$

2. $\lim_{x \to 3} x^3 = 27$ and $\lim_{x \to 2} x^2 = 4$. Then

$$\frac{\lim_{x \to 3} x^3}{\lim_{x \to 2} x^2} = \frac{27}{4} = 6.75$$

■ Note that it is *not* appropriate to reduce the quotient $x^3/x^2$ to $x$ and then find the limit of $x$, because the limit of one function is being taken as $x$ approaches 3, while the limit of the other function is being taken as $x$ approaches 2.

THEOREM 3.9 $\lim_{x \to x_0} [f(x)]^j = \left[\lim_{x \to x_0} f(x)\right]^j = A^j$

*Discussion* This is the power-limit theorem. The limit of the $j$th power of a function is equal to the $j$th power of the limit of that function.

EXAMPLES

1. $\lim_{x \to 2} x^2 = 4$; $\lim_{x \to 2} [x^2]^3 = \lim_{x \to 2} 4^3 = 64$ or $\lim_{x \to 2} x^6 = 2^6 = 64$
2. $\lim_{x \to 2} e^x = 7.389$; $\lim_{x \to 2} [e^x]^2 = [7.389]^2 = 54.598$

THEOREM 3.10 $\lim_{x \to x_0} f(x) \cdot f(x) = \lim_{x \to x_0} [f(x)]^2 = A^2$

*Discussion* This is a special case of Theorems 3.6, 3.7, and 3.9.

EXAMPLES

1. $\lim_{x \to 2} x^2 = 4$; hence $\lim_{x \to 2} [x^2 \cdot x^2] = \lim_{x \to 2} [x^2]^2 = \lim_{x \to 2} x^4 = 16$
2. $\lim_{x \to 2} e^x = 7.389$; hence $\lim_{x \to 2} [e^x \cdot e^x] = [7.389]^2 = 54.598$

**EXERCISE 3.1**

In each of Exercises 1 through 15, evaluate the limits.

1. $\lim_{x \to 2} (2x - 1)$
2. $\lim_{x \to 4} (x^2 + 4x)$
3. $\lim_{x \to -1} (3x^3 - 2x^2 + x + 10)$
4. $\lim_{x \to 0} \dfrac{x^2 - 8}{x^2 + 2x + 1}$
5. $\lim_{x \to 2} \dfrac{x^2 - 4}{x^2 + 4}$
6. $\lim_{x \to -1} \dfrac{x^2 - 3x^3}{2x + 1}$
7. $\lim_{x \to 3} (x^2 - 5)^2$
8. $\lim_{x \to 0} (x^2 - 4)(x^3 + 4x - 3)(4x + 7)$
9. $\lim_{x \to 0} \dfrac{x + 4}{x - 4}$
10. $\lim_{x \to 2} \left(2 - \dfrac{x^2}{4}\right)$
11. $\lim_{x \to 0} 8^x$
12. $\lim_{x \to 1} 10^{-x}$
13. $\lim_{x \to 3} \dfrac{x^3 - 2x^2 + 3x - 24}{x - 6}$
14. $\lim_{x \to -2} 10^x$
15. $\lim_{x \to 0} \dfrac{x^2 + 2e^{x^2}}{e^{x^3}}$

## EXTENSIONS OF THE LIMIT CONCEPT

Our definition of a limit states that as variable $x$ approaches some finite number $x_0$ in the limit, the value of function $f(x)$ approaches some finite number $A$. That is, $\lim_{x \to x_0} f(x) = A$. You can reflect on the fact, however, that variable $x$ can approach the value of $x_0$ either from values greater than $x_0$, that is, from values "above" $x_0$, or from values less than $x_0$, that is, from values "below" $x_0$. Situations exist in which a function may approach a limit from either above or below. The limit of a function from above may be the same as the limit taken from below. As we shall see, however, that need not be the case.

DEFINITION A right-hand limit exists when $f(x) \to A$ as $x \to x_0$ through decreasing values (from the right on the real number line). This is indicated by

$$\lim_{x \to x_0^+} f(x) = A$$

DEFINITION A left-hand limit exists when $f(x) \to A$ as $x \to x_0$ through increasing values (from the left on the real number line). This is indicated by

$$\lim_{x \to x_0^-} f(x) = A$$

Only when the left-hand limit and the right-hand limit exist and *are equal to* each other are we able to state that *a* (single) limit of a function exists. That is, a single limit of a function $f(x)$ exists if and only if the following holds:

$$\lim_{x \to x_0^-} f(x) = \lim_{x \to x_0^+} f(x) = \lim_{x \to x_0} f(x) = A \qquad \text{where } A \text{ is a finite value}$$

A quick review of the function $y = f(x) = x^2$ and its limit in Table 3.1 reveals that as $x \to 3$ from both the right and the left, the value of the function $f(x) \to 9$. Both the left-hand limit and the right-hand limit are the finite value 9. Therefore we can state that both the right-hand and the left-hand limits exist such that $f(x) \to 9$ as $x \to 3$. A glance at Table 3.2 reveals that both the left-hand and the right-hand limits exist for the function

$$y = f(x) = \frac{x^2 - 1}{x - 1} \qquad \text{as } x \to 1$$

This limit is 2 despite the fact that (a) the value 1 is not in the domain of $f$, and (b) the value 2 is not in the range of $f$.

■ We must be careful to analyze and consider both the left-hand and right-hand limits of a function, if they exist. The existence of a left-hand limit does not guarantee the existence of a right-hand limit, and vice versa.

EXAMPLE Figure 3.4 illustrates the graph of a *step function*[4] such that $y = A_1$ for $0 \leq x < x_0$ and $y = A_2$ for $x_0 \leq x$. That is, for all values of variable $x$ that are less than $x_0$, the value of the function is $A_1$. For values of $x$ that are equal to or greater than $x_0$, the value of the function is $A_2$. The left-hand and right-hand limits are *not* the same; $\lim_{x \to x_0^-} f(x) = A_1$, but $\lim_{x \to x_0^+} f(x) = A_2$, and $A_1 \neq A_2$. Hence the function does not have *a* limit as $x \to x_0$.

### Infinite Limits

Our definition of a limit states that both $x$ and $f(x)$ approach finite numbers ($x_0$ and $A$, respectively) in the limit. It is possible, nonetheless, that either $x$ or $f(x)$, or both, will assume arbitrarily large positive or negative values in the limit. That is, it is possible for $x$ and/or $f(x)$ to increase or decrease indefinitely.

[4] We can intuitively define a *step function* as a combination of two or more constant functions defined for specified intervals, with a finite discontinuity separating each function. We shall discuss the concepts of step function, continuity, etc., later in this chapter.

Figure 3.4 Graph of a step function

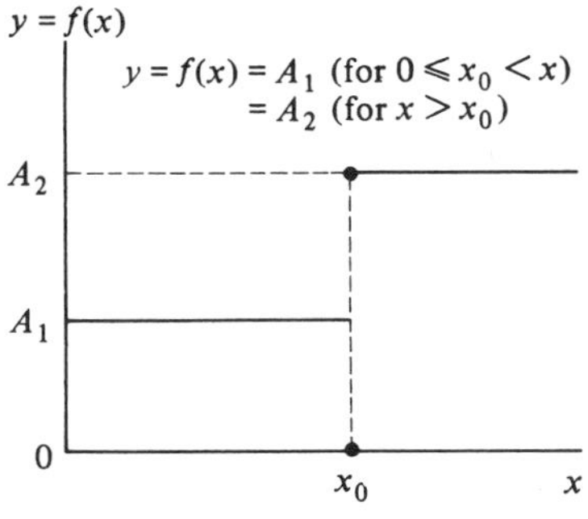

The mathematical symbol that we use when a variable increases without bound is $+\infty$, while the symbol we use to illustrate the case in which a variable decreases without bound is $-\infty$. These symbols are referred to as *plus infinity* and *minus infinity*.

We shall now consider five separate cases dealing with the function $f(x)$, in which: (1) $x$ approaches $+\infty$; (2) $x$ approaches $-\infty$; (3) $x$ approaches some finite value $x_0$ and the limit of the function is $+\infty$; (4) $x$ approaches some finite value $x_0$ and the limit of the function is $-\infty$; and (5) the value of variable $x$ and the value of the function $f(x)$ can tend to either plus infinity or minus infinity.

CASE 1 $f(x)$ approaches $A$ as $x$ approaches $+\infty$, usually written $\lim_{x\to\infty} f(x) = A$. This is read, "the limit of $f(x)$, as $x$ tends to plus infinity is $A$." In this case, we can make the value of $f(x)$ arbitrarily close to the finite number $A$ by considering positive values of variable $x$ that are sufficiently large. An example of such a situation is contained in Table 3.4, where $\lim_{x\to\infty} f(x) = \lim_{x\to\infty} 1/x = 0$. As the value of $x$ increases without bound in Table 3.4, we can see that in the limit the value of $1/x$ tends to 0.

CASE 2 $\lim_{x\to-\infty} f(x) = A$, which is read, "the limit of $f(x)$, as $x$ tends to minus infinity, is $A$." This situation reverses that of Case 1. Here we can make the value of function $f(x)$ arbitrarily close to the finite number $A$ by allowing variable $x$ to assume values that are ever-decreasing. Table 3.5 contains an example involving the function $y = f(x) = 1/x$, where $\lim_{x\to-\infty} 1/x = 0$. As the values of $x$ become increasingly small, the value of the function $1/x$ approaches 0.

CASE 3 $\lim_{x\to x_0} f(x) = \infty$. This is read, "the limit of $f(x)$, as $x$ tends to $x_0$, is infinity." In this situation, the function $f(x)$ takes on arbitrarily large values as $x$ approaches $x_0$. Consider the example illustrated in Table 3.6, where $y = f(x) = 1/x$ and $\lim_{x\to 0^+} 1/x = \infty$. We can see that as the values of variable $x$ approach 0, the values of $f(x)$ become increasingly large. Some mathemati-

Table 3.4 The limiting process: $\lim\limits_{x\to+\infty} \dfrac{1}{x} = 0$

| $x$ | $f(x) = \dfrac{1}{x}$ |
|---:|---|
| 1 | 1.0 |
| 5 | 0.2 |
| 10 | 0.1 |
| 100 | 0.01 |
| 1,000 | 0.001 |
| 10,000 | 0.0001 |

Table 3.5 The limiting process: $\lim_{x \to -\infty} \frac{1}{x} = 0$

| $x$ | $f(x) = \frac{1}{x}$ |
|---|---|
| −1 | −1.0 |
| −5 | −0.2 |
| −10 | −0.1 |
| −100 | −0.01 |
| −1,000 | −0.001 |
| −10,000 | −0.0001 |

cians are inclined to argue that there is no limit to the function $1/x$ as $x$ approaches 0. This is correct in the sense that there is no finite value that limits the value of $f(x)$. Nonetheless, following custom, we shall assume that the limit of $f(x)$ as $x$ approaches 0 is "positive infinity." That is, we assume that an "infinite limit" exists in this and similar cases.

CASE 4 $\lim_{x \to x_0} f(x) = -\infty$. This is read, "the limit of $f(x)$, as $x$ tends to $x_0$, is negative infinity." This means that as the value of $x$ approaches a finite value $x_0$, the function $f(x)$ takes on ever-decreasing values. Table 3.7 illustrates the case in which the limit of a function is negative infinity. As the value of variable $x$ becomes larger and approaches 0, the value of the function $1/x$ becomes progressively smaller and diverges from zero (to the left along the real number line).

CASE 5 It is possible that both the value of variable $x$ and the value of function $f(x)$ tends to either plus infinity or minus infinity. The four possibilites that result are as follows.

(a) $\lim_{x \to +\infty} f(x) = +\infty$ (b) $\lim_{x \to +\infty} f(x) = -\infty$

Table 3.6 The limiting process: $\lim_{x \to 0^+} \frac{1}{x} = \infty$

| $x$ | $f(x) = \frac{1}{x}$ |
|---|---|
| 10.0 | 0.1 |
| 5.0 | 0.2 |
| 1.0 | 1.0 |
| 0.5 | 2.0 |
| 0.1 | 10.0 |
| 0.01 | 100.0 |
| 0.001 | 1,000.0 |
| 0.0001 | 10,000.0 |

Table 3.7 The limiting process: $\lim_{x \to 0^-} \frac{1}{x} = -\infty$

| $x$ | $f(x) = \frac{1}{x}$ |
|---|---|
| −5.0 | −0.2 |
| −1.0 | −1.0 |
| −0.1 | −10.0 |
| −0.01 | −100.0 |
| −0.001 | −1,000.0 |
| −0.0001 | −10,000.0 |

(c) $\lim_{x \to -\infty} f(x) = +\infty$ (d) $\lim_{x \to -\infty} f(x) = -\infty$

EXAMPLES

1. Given $f(x) = e^x$, find $\lim_{x \to +\infty} f(x)$.

$$\lim_{x \to +\infty} e^x = e^{+\infty} = +\infty$$

2. Given $f(x) = e^x$, find $\lim_{x \to -\infty} f(x)$.

$$\lim_{x \to -\infty} e^x = e^{-\infty} = \frac{1}{e^{\infty}} = 0$$

3. Given $f(x) = \frac{x}{x-1}$ find $\lim_{x \to 1} f(x)$.

$$\lim_{x \to 1} \frac{x}{x-1} = \frac{1}{0} = \infty$$

*Cases 1 through 5: A summary*

In Cases 1 and 2, we observed that the limit of the function $f(x) = 1/x$ approaches plus infinity when the value of $x$ approaches 0 from the right-hand side, and that it approaches minus infinity when the value of $x$ approaches 0 from the left-hand side. Similarly, we found that the limit of the function $f(x) = 1/x$ approaches 0 when the value of $x$ approaches positive infinity, and also approaches 0 when the value of $x$ approaches minus infinity. Figure 3.5 demonstrates these relationships graphically. The graph of the function $y = f(x) = 1/x$, which is illustrated in Figure 3.5, confirms these summary observations.

**Limits That Imply Division by Zero**

In an earlier example of the limit of a function, we found that the limit of the function $y = f(x) = (x^2 - 1)/(x - 1)$ was 2 as $x$ approached 1 from either direction. However, you can see a potential problem here, for when $x = 1$, the

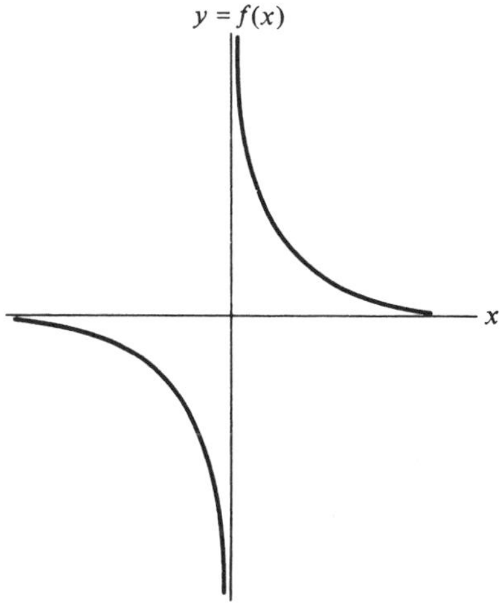


Figure 3.5 Graph of $y = f(x) = 1/x$

value of $(x^2 - 1)/(x - 1)$ is 0/0. Division by zero is undefined. Hence it would appear that the limit in this case is indeterminate.

Fortunately, there is a method by which we can often circumvent the "division by zero" problem. In the example above, where $y = f(x) = (x^2 - 1)/(x - 1)$, it is the denominator $x - 1$ that is the source of the problem as $x$ approaches 1. We therefore factor the numerator such that $x^2 - 1 = (x - 1)(x + 1)$. This gives us

$$\lim_{x \to 1} \frac{x^2 - 1}{x - 1} = \lim_{x \to 1} \frac{(x - 1)(x + 1)}{(x - 1)} = \lim_{x \to 1} (x + 1) = 2 \tag{3.9}$$

This trick in reality consists of factoring the numerator and the denominator whenever possible. The expression to be factored out and eliminated is the one that is making the denominator approach 0 in the limit. This enables us to transform the function into one that has a limit.

EXAMPLES

1. Given $f(x) = \dfrac{x + 3}{x^2 - x - 12}$, find $\lim\limits_{x \to -3} f(x)$.

$$\lim_{x \to -3} \frac{x + 3}{(x + 3)(x - 4)} = \lim_{x \to -3} \frac{1}{x - 4} = -\frac{1}{7}$$

2. Given $f(x) = \dfrac{x^2 + x - 2}{x^2 - 1}$, find $\lim\limits_{x \to 1} f(x)$.

$$\lim_{x + 1} \frac{(x + 2)(x - 1)}{(x - 1)(x + 1)} = \lim_{x \to 1} \frac{x + 2}{x + 1} = \frac{3}{2}$$

3. Given $f(x) = \dfrac{x^3 - 27}{x^2 - 9}$, find $\lim_{x \to 3} f(x)$.

$$\lim_{x \to 3} \frac{(x - 3)(x^2 + 3x + 9)}{(x - 3)(x + 3)} = \lim_{x \to 3} \frac{x^2 + 3x + 9}{x + 3} = \frac{9}{2}$$

**Limits That Are $\infty/\infty$**

Another type of indeterminate form involving limits occurs when the limit of a function is $\infty/\infty$. We shall discuss this problem in greater detail in a later chapter. However, once again, there is a method that often enables us to find a determinate limit in this case. Simply stated, the method suggests that we divide *both* the numerator and the denominator of the function whose limit we wish to find by the highest power of the independent variable that appears in either the numerator or the denominator of the function.

For example, consider the function

$$f(x) = \frac{4x^2 + 2x - 3}{x^3 - 6x + 2}$$

It is clear that as $x \to \infty$, both the numerator and denominator become infinitely large. That is,

$$\lim_{x \to \infty} \frac{4x^2 + 2x - 3}{x^3 - 6x + 2} = \frac{\infty}{\infty}$$

However, we are able to find a finite limit for this function by first dividing both the numerator and the denominator by the highest power of $x$ that appears in either the numerator or denominator of the function. In this particular problem, $x^3$ is the highest-powered $x$ term. Therefore the limit problem becomes

$$\lim_{x \to \infty} \frac{\dfrac{4}{x} + \dfrac{2}{x^2} - \dfrac{3}{x^3}}{1 - \dfrac{6}{x^2} + \dfrac{2}{x^3}} = \frac{0 + 0 - 0}{1 - 0 + 0} = \frac{0}{1} = 0$$

EXAMPLES

1. Given $f(x) = \dfrac{9x - 2}{3x + 7}$, find $\lim_{x \to \infty} f(x)$.

$$\lim_{x \to \infty} \frac{9 - \dfrac{2}{x}}{3 + \dfrac{7}{x}} = \frac{9 - 0}{3 + 0} = 3$$

2. Given $f(x) = \dfrac{6x^2 + 9x - 10}{4x^3 - x}$, find $\lim_{x \to \infty} f(x)$.

$$\lim_{x \to \infty} \frac{\dfrac{6}{x} + \dfrac{9}{x^2} - \dfrac{10}{x^3}}{4 - \dfrac{1}{x^2}} = \frac{0 + 0 - 0}{4 - 0} = \frac{0}{4} = 0$$

3. Given $f(x) = \dfrac{2x^3 + 8x - 1}{6x^2 + 5x + 10}$, find $\lim_{x \to \infty} f(x)$.

$$\lim_{x \to \infty} \frac{2 + \dfrac{8}{x^2} - \dfrac{1}{x^3}}{\dfrac{6}{x} + \dfrac{5}{x^2} + \dfrac{10}{x^3}} = \frac{2 + 0 + 0}{0 + 0 + 0} = \frac{2}{0} = \infty$$

**EXERCISE 3.2**

Evaluate the following limits.

1. $\lim_{x \to -1} \dfrac{x^2 - 1}{x + 1}$
2. $\lim_{x \to 2} \dfrac{x^2 - 5x + 6}{x - 2}$
3. $\lim_{x \to \infty} \dfrac{x + 10}{x^2 - 5}$
4. $\lim_{x \to 4} \dfrac{x^2 - x - 12}{x - 4}$
5. $\lim_{x \to \infty} \dfrac{3x^2 + 2x + 1}{3x^2 - 4x - 5}$
6. $\lim_{x \to \infty} \dfrac{4x^3 - 3}{x^2 + x - 1}$
7. $\lim_{x \to \infty} \dfrac{x^2 + 4}{3x^3}$
8. $\lim_{x \to 2} \dfrac{x - 2}{x^2 - 4}$
9. $\lim_{x \to -1} \dfrac{x^2 + 3x + 2}{x^2 + 4x + 3}$
10. $\lim_{x \to \infty} \dfrac{1}{1 + 2^{1/x}}$
11. $\lim_{x \to -\infty} \dfrac{1}{1 + 2^{1/x}}$
12. $\lim_{x \to \infty} \dfrac{2x^2 + 1}{8 + 3x - x^2}$
13. $\lim_{x \to \infty} \dfrac{x^2 - 5x + 6}{x - 3}$
14. $\lim_{x \to \infty} \dfrac{x + 3}{x^2 + 5x + 6}$
15. $\lim_{x \to \infty} \dfrac{1}{x + (1/x)}$
16. $\lim_{x \to \infty} \left(x + \dfrac{1}{x}\right)$
17. $\lim_{x \to 3} \dfrac{x + 3}{x^2 - 9}$
18. $\lim_{x \to 2} \dfrac{(x - 2)^2}{x^2 - 3x + 2}$
19. $\lim_{x \to 0} \dfrac{(a + x)^2 - a^2}{x}$
20. $\lim_{x \to 2} \dfrac{x^2 - 5x + 6}{x^2 - 6x + 8}$

## CONTINUITY

The first major step in defining the derivative of a function is to have a clear understanding of the concept of a limit. The second step involves using the limit concept to define the concept of *continuity* of a function. We shall begin with an intuitive approach to the idea of continuity, and later proceed to a formal definition.

Our definition of a limit made no assertion whatsoever about what happens to the value of the function at the point $x_0$. Hence, given that $\lim_{x \to x_0} f(x) = A$, we made no statement about what was true when the value of variable $x$ was actually equal to $x_0$. This meant that we excluded the point $(x_0, A)$ from our consideration and actually considered only the intervals around $x_0$ and $A$. In fact, it was not necessary for the function to be defined at $x_0$ in order for our definition of a limit to hold true.[5]

We now must consider the case in which the function $y = f(x)$ has the value $f(x_0)$ at a certain point $x = x_0$. The function $y = f(x)$ is said to be *continuous* at $x_0$ when $f(x)$ is defined at $x_0$ and, at the same time, $f(x_0) = A$. That is, the function $y = f(x)$ is continuous if and only if the point $(x_0, A)$ at which $A = \lim_{x \to 0} f(x)$ lies on the graph of the function.

A function that is continuous at every point in (or on) an interval $a \leq x \leq b$ (or $a < x < b$) is said to be *continuous* on that interval. When a function is said to be continuous without any further specification (this is often the case in functions used in business and economics problems), then the function is assumed to be continuous at *every* point in its domain.

Very roughly speaking, the classical example of a continuous function on a particular interval is one whose graph can be drawn without lifting one's pencil or pen from the paper in that interval. We need, however, to be more rigorous than this in our notion of continuity, and we shall therefore develop a formal definition.

DEFINITION A function $y = f(x)$ is said to be continuous at $x = x_0$ if the following three requirements are fulfilled: (1) $f(x_0)$ exists such that point $x_0$ is in the domain of the function, (2) $\lim_{x \to x_0} f(x)$ exists, and (3) $\lim_{x \to x_0} f(x) = f(x_0) = A$.

EXAMPLES

1. In an earlier example, in Table 3.1, we found $\lim_{x \to 3} x^2 = 9$. We shall now apply the three requirements for the continuity of a function in order to determine whether this function $y = x^2$ is continuous at the point (3, 9). First, we note that $f(3)$ does exist and that $x = 3$ is in the domain of the function. The first test is therefore passed. Second, the limit of the function, which we found previously, does exist and is 9. The second test is passed. Third, $f(x_0) = A$, because $f(3) = 3^2 = 9$. The third test is passed, and we can therefore assert that the function $y = x^2$ is continuous at the point (3, 9).

[5] Even if the function were defined at $x_0$, the value of the function might not be equal to $A$.

2. We have used the function $y = f(x) = (x^2 - 1)/(x - 1)$ several times in this chapter, initially in Table 3.2. We found that

$$\lim_{x \to 1} \frac{x^2 - 1}{x - 1} = 2$$

Is this function continuous when $x = 1$? First, we observe that $f(1)$ does *not* exist and that $x = 1$ is *not* in the domain of the function. This is sufficient to establish that the function is *not* continuous where $x = 1$, that is, where $x = x_0$. This type of discontinuity, at $x = 1 = x_0$, is referred to as a *missing-point discontinuity*. We'll discuss it later in this chapter.

***The Concept of Continuity: A More Rigorous Approach**

We utilized the notions of $\varepsilon$ and $\delta$ in developing our definition of a limit. Applying these concepts to the above definition of a continuous function results in an alternative, more rigorous definition.

DEFINITION A function $y = f(x)$ is continuous at $x_0$ if, for any $\varepsilon > 0$, however small, there is a $\delta > 0$ such that $|f(x) - f(x_0)| < \varepsilon$, or $|f(x) - A| < \varepsilon$ whenever $|x - x_0| < \delta$.

We shall attempt to clarify the meaning of a continuous function by referring to Figure 3.6. Those of you with a sharp memory will realize that this is

* The material in this section may be omitted without loss of continuity [no pun intended!]. If you are interested in a more formal and rigorous mathematical approach however, you should master the material in this section.

Figure 3.6 Geometric interpretation of continuity

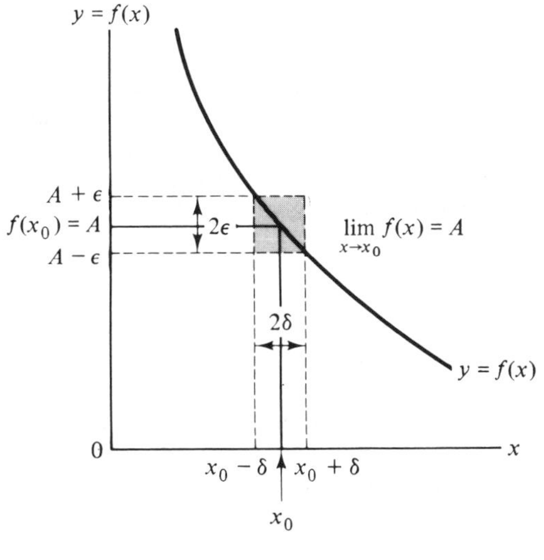

precisely the same function that we graphed in Figure 3.2, except that Figure 3.6 demonstrates what occurs when the limiting value $A$ equals $f(x_0)$. In Figure 3.2, the graph of the function $y = f(x)$ was not defined for $A = f(x_0)$. Consequently the graph of the function $y = f(x)$ was discontinuous at $A = f(x_0)$ in Figure 3.2. The gap in the function $y = f(x)$ is readily observable. Such is not the case in the function $y = f(x)$ in Figure 3.6, however. The function is continuous at $A = f(x_0)$, and no gap exists. The limiting value is $A = f(x_0)$ in Figure 3.6.

### A Helpful Theorem Dealing with Continuity

In the preceding examples concerning continuity, we examined each of the three requirements for continuity to see whether any was violated. Such a process can be laborious. The following theorem can help us avert some of this labor in many cases.

THEOREM 3.11 Let $f(x)$ and $g(x)$ be two continuous functions at the point $x_0$. The sum $f(x) + g(x)$, the difference $f(x) - g(x)$, the product $f(x) \cdot g(x)$, and the quotient $f(x)/g(x)$, given that $g(x) \neq 0$ in the denominator, are also continuous functions at point $x_0$.

*Proof* Given that $f(x)$ and $g(x)$ are continuous, the requirements for continuity must hold. Hence

$$\lim_{x \to x_0} f(x) = f(x_0) = A \qquad \text{and} \qquad \lim_{x \to x_0} g(x) = g(x_0) = B$$

Therefore, by applying the basic limit theorems found in Table 3.3, we can deduce the above theorem.

We can extend the result of the preceding theorem to more than two continuous functions and say that the sum, difference, product, or quotient of any finite number of continuous functions is another function that is continuous.

EXAMPLES

1. We shall now apply Theorem 3.11, on continuity, to polynomial functions. Let $f(x)$ and $g(x)$ be continuous functions that are both equal to $x$. The product of two continuous functions is also continuous. Hence we know that the function $x^2$ is continuous. Extending this, we can assert that the function $cx^n$, where $c$ is a real constant and $n$ is a positive integer, is also continuous (for all values of $x$). Given a polynomial of the general form

   $$y = f(x) = a_0 + a_1 x + a_2 x^2 + \cdots + a_n x^n$$

   As $x \to x_0$,

   $$\lim_{x \to x_0} (a_0 + a_1 x + a_2 x^2 + \cdots + a_n x^n) = a_0 + a_1 x_0 + a_2 x_0^2 + \cdots + a_n x_0^n$$

   Since $x_0$ is a point in the domain of the function, the limit does exist, and the limit equals the value of the function at point $x_0$. So the three conditions for continuity are satisfied. This means that *any* polynomial function is continuous.

2. A rational function is the quotient of two polynomial functions. Our theorem dealing with continuous functions tells us that the quotient of continuous functions is another function that is also continuous. Therefore any rational function is continuous in its domain. Consider $y = f(x) = (x^2 - 1)/(x - 1)$ as an example in support of this assertion. We have already shown that this function is *not* continuous at the point $x = 1$. However, the function could be continuous for any other point in the domain. Applying the three conditions for continuity, we find that: (a) $f(x_0)$ exists, except for $x = 1$; (b) $\lim_{x \to x_0} f(x)$ does exist; and (c) $\lim_{x \to x_0} f(x) = f(x_0)$ for all values except $x_0 = 1$. Thus, for any $x = x_0$ *except* $x_0 = 1$, the three requirements for continuity are met. The function $y = (x^2 - 1)/(x - 1)$ is therefore continuous at all points in the domain of the function except $x = 1 = x_0$.

**Classifying Discontinuities**

Whenever any one of the three conditions required for continuity is not satisfied, the function in question is said to be *discontinuous.* In a previous example, we briefly mentioned one particular type of discontinuity, the missing-point discontinuity. This is one of three different types of discontinuities that can be present: infinite, finite, and missing-point.

1. *Infinite discontinuity*
   An infinite discontinuity occurs at $x_0$ if either

$$\lim_{x \to x_0^-} f(x) = \pm\infty \qquad \text{or} \qquad \lim_{x \to x_0^+} f(x) = \pm\infty$$

EXAMPLE The function $y = f(x) = 1/x$, whose limit we found in Table 3.5, is infinitely discontinuous at the point $x = 0$. This follows because $f(0)$ is undefined and

$$\lim_{x \to 0^+} 1/x = +\infty \neq \lim_{x \to 0^-} 1/x = -\infty$$

Figure 3.5 illustrated the graph of the function $y = f(x) = 1/x$ and Figure 3.7 reproduces it. Note that the graph of the function is clearly discontinuous at $x = 0$. Further, given that $x = 0$, the function is discontinuous regardless of the value assumed by $y$. At the same time, the function $y = 1/x$ is continuous for all other values of $x$.

2. *Finite or "jump" discontinuity*
   A finite or jump discontinuity occurs when the first condition for continuity is satisfied, but the second condition is violated. That is, $f(x_0)$ is defined, but $\lim_{x \to x_0} f(x)$ does not exist. This situation arises when $f(x_0)$ is a finite number, but $f(x)$ changes value abruptly at $x = x_0$.

EXAMPLE A step function, such as that illustrated in Figure 3.4 and reproduced in Figure 3.8, is characterized by a finite discontinuity. Assume that $y = A_1$ for $0 \leq x < x_0$ and that $y = A_2$ for $x_0 \leq x$. This function, as Figure 3.8 demonstrates, is discontinuous at $x = x_0$ because the limit does not exist. Even

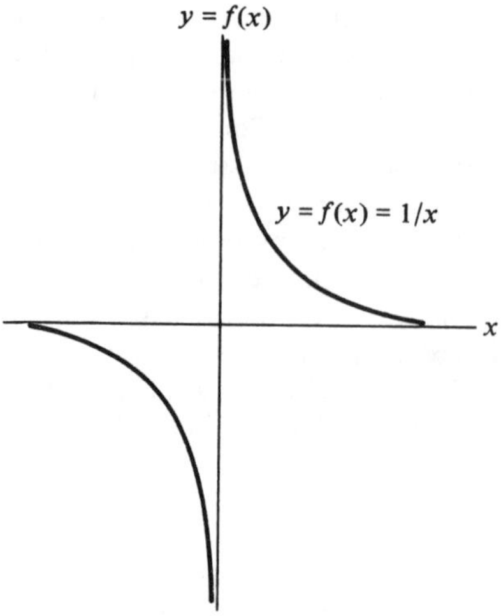


Figure 3.7 Infinite discontinuity at $x = 0$

though the step function is defined at $x = x_0$ such that $f(x_0) = A_2$, and the left-hand and right-hand limits both exist, it is also true that

$$\lim_{x \to x_0^-} f(x) = A_1 \neq \lim_{x \to x_0^+} f(x) = A_2$$

In general, a function has a finite or jump discontinuity at $x = x_0$ if both the left-hand and the right-hand limits exist, but are *not* equal.

3. *Missing-point or "removable" discontinuity*
   A function that exhibits a missing-point discontinuity satisfies all three conditions for continuity except at the single point $x = x_0$, which is missing or undefined.

Figure 3.8 Finite or "jump" discontinuity at $x = x_0$

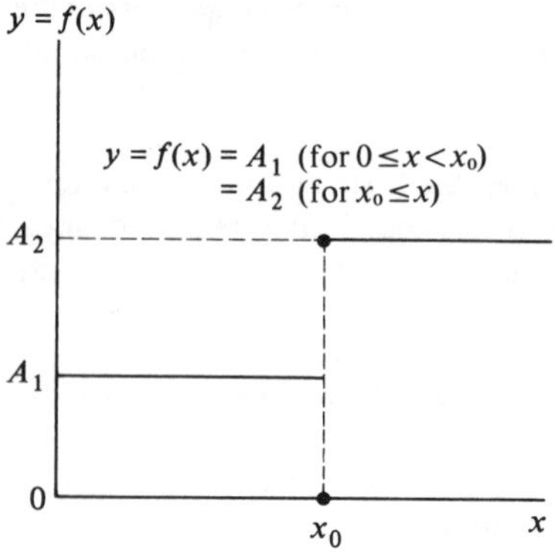

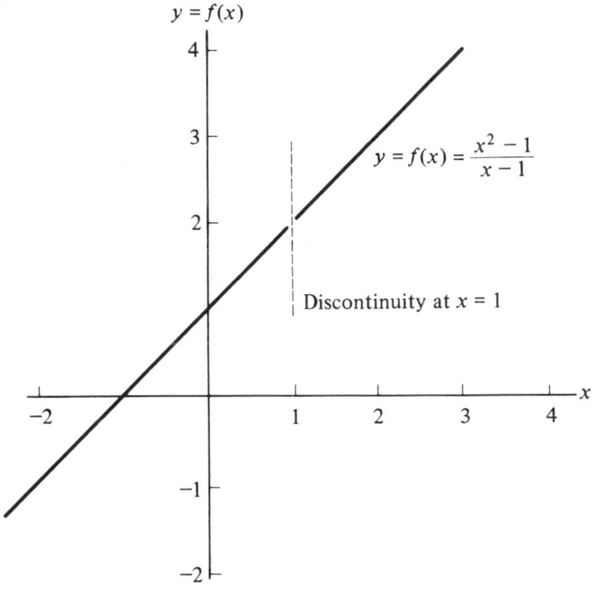


Figure 3.9 Missing-point discontinuity

EXAMPLE We have used the function $y = f(x) = (x^2 - 1)/(x - 1)$ several times for illustrative purposes in this chapter. This function has a missing-point discontinuity at $x = 1$. This follows because $f(1)$ is undefined, since it results in a 0/0 quotient, and $\lim_{x \to 1} f(x)$ does exist. The graph of the function $y = (x^2 - 1)/(x - 1)$ is illustrated in Figure 3.9. We can see that the graph is continuous everywhere except where $x = 1$.

Of the three different types of discontinuities, only the missing-point type is amenable to algebraic manipulations (for example, factoring) that enable us to find the limit of the function despite the discontinuity. That is, only with the missing-point discontinuity are we able to satisfy all three conditions for a continuous function after our manipulation. We are able to do this for the missing-point discontinuity because the limit does exist if only we can remove the discontinuity. One way to do so is to redefine the function at $x_0$ such that $f(x_0) = A$. In the cases of infinite and finite discontinuities, the limit itself does not exist. Hence changing the value of the function at one point does not solve our problem.

EXAMPLES

1. We can make the function $y = (x^2 - 1)/(x - 1)$ continuous at the point $x = 1$ by defining $f(1) = 2$. This recognizes that

$$y = \frac{x^2 - 1}{x - 1} = \frac{(x - 1)(x + 1)}{(x - 1)} = x + 1 \qquad \text{when } x \neq 1$$

Hence we define $f(1) = 1 + 1 = 2$. The three conditions for continuity are now met: (a) $f(1)$ is defined; (b) $\lim_{x \to 1} f(x)$ does exist; and (c) $\lim_{x \to 1} f(x) = f(1)$.

2. The function

$$y = f(x) = \frac{2x^2 - 3x + 1}{x^2 + x - 2}$$

has discontinuities at $x = 1$ and $x = -2$. The point $x = 1$ is a missing-point or removable discontinuity, whereas the point $x = -2$ is an infinite discontinuity. That is, when $x = 1, f(1)$ is not defined because $f(1) = 0/0$, even though

$$\lim_{x \to 1} \frac{2x^2 - 3x + 1}{x^2 + x - 2} = \frac{1}{3}$$

We can remove this discontinuity by defining $f(1) = \frac{1}{3}$. This recognizes that

$$y = \frac{2x^2 - 3x + 1}{x^2 + x - 2} = \frac{(2x - 1)(x - 1)}{(x - 1)(x + 2)} = \frac{2x - 1}{x + 2} \qquad \text{when } x \neq 1$$

and the limit of this quotient is $\frac{1}{3}$. Hence, by factoring and defining $f(1) = \frac{1}{3}$, we meet all three conditions for continuity. When $x = -2$, however, we have the following: $f(-2)$ is not defined, for $f(-2) = \frac{3}{0}$; and

$$\lim_{x \to -2^-} f(x) = +\infty \qquad \text{and} \qquad \lim_{x \to -2^+} f(x) = -\infty$$

Therefore, at the point $x = -2$, there is an infinite, nonremovable discontinuity about which we can do nothing.

**EXERCISE 3.3**

For what values of $x$ are the following functions continuous? If a discontinuity exists, identify the type of discontinuity and correct any removable discontinuities.

1. $f(x) = 3x^3 + 2x^2 + x + 1$
2. $f(x) = \dfrac{x}{x + 1}$
3. $f(x) = \dfrac{x^2 - 3x + 2}{x - 2}$
4. $f(x) = \dfrac{x^3 - 27}{x^2 - 9}$
5. $f(x) = \dfrac{x^2 + x - 2}{(x - 1)^2}$
6. $f(x) = \dfrac{x^2 - 4x - 21}{x - 7}$
7. $f(x) = \sqrt{4 - x^2}$
8. $f(x) = |x|$
9. $f(x) = \dfrac{8}{x - 4}$
10. $f(x) = \dfrac{x^2 + 5x + 6}{x^2 + 4x + 4}$
11. $f(x) = \dfrac{5}{1 - 2^x}$
12. $f(x) = e^x$

13. $f(x) = \dfrac{1}{x(x-4)}$ 14. $f(x) = \dfrac{(x-6)}{6}$

15. $f(x) = \dfrac{x+4}{x^2+2x-8}$ 16. $f(x) = \dfrac{1}{x^2+1}$

17. $f(x) = \dfrac{1}{3x^2-27}$ 18. $f(x) = \dfrac{x^2-16}{x+4}$

19. $f(x) = \sqrt{x}$ 20. $f(x) = \dfrac{1}{2e^x-2}$

## THE DERIVATIVE OF A FUNCTION

The concepts of a limit and of a continuous function constitute the foundation for our study of the derivative of a function. Consider the function $y = f(x)$. We now wish to focus on the effect that an incremental change in $x$—which we denote $\Delta x$—has on $y = f(x)$. The magnitude of any $\Delta y$ that does occur depends not only on the magnitude of $\Delta x$, but also on the specific form of the functional relationship that exists between $y$ and $x$.

In Chapter 2, a linear function $y = f(x)$ was graphed as a straight line with a constant slope. We found that the slope of a straight line that passed through any two points $(x_1, y_1)$ and $(x_2, y_2)$, or in functional notation $[x_1, f(x_1)]$ and $[x_2, f(x_2)]$, was given by the quotient

$$m = \frac{\Delta y}{\Delta x} = \frac{y_2 - y_1}{x_2 - x_1} = \frac{f(x_2) - f(x_1)}{x_2 - x_1} \tag{3.10}$$

Since $x_2$ differs from $x_1$ by some increment only, we can write $x_2$ as $x_1 + \Delta x$. Similarly, we can write $y_2$ as $y_1 + \Delta y = f(x_1 + \Delta x)$. We can rewrite Equation (3.10) as

$$m = \frac{\Delta y}{\Delta x} = \frac{f(x_1 + \Delta x) - f(x_1)}{(x_1 + \Delta x) - x_1} = \frac{f(x_1 + \Delta x) - f(x_1)}{\Delta x} \tag{3.11}$$

The definition of the slope $m$ provided in Equation (3.11) is hereafter referred to as the *difference quotient*.

EXAMPLE Using the concept of a difference quotient as defined in Equation (3.11), we shall verify that the slope of a specific linear function, $y = 10 + 2x$, is a constant. One particular point on the graph of this function is (5, 20), while another is (7, 24). For our purposes, $x_1 = 5$, $x_2 = 7$, $y_1 = 20$, and $y_2 = 24$. We now progressively reduce the difference between $x_1$ and $x_2$.

Table 3.8 records what happens as the value of $x_2$ falls from 7 and gradually approaches 5. Note that the value of $y_2$ also changes and progressively falls from 24 to arbitrarily close to 20. Most important, note that the slope of the function is given by $\Delta y/\Delta x$ and that this remains constant at a value of 2. For example, when the value of $x_2$ falls from 7 to 6, $\Delta x = 1$. This causes the value of $y_2$ to fall from 24 to 22 $[y = 10 + 2x = 10 + 2(6) = 22]$. The value of $\Delta y/\Delta x$ is therefore $2/1 = 2$. Similarly, when the value of $x_2$ falls from 6 to 5.5, the value of $y_2$ falls from 22 to 21. Once again $\Delta y/\Delta x = 2$. In general, the application of the concept of a difference quotient confirms that the slope of a linear function is a constant.

Unfortunately, life is not so simple in the real world. We cannot always use linear functions in decision and choice problems. The assumption of a constant slope is not fulfilled when the underlying function is nonlinear in character. We must determine the slope of a nonlinear function at each particular point of interest, since it is possible (indeed, likely) that the slope of the function differs at different points on that function.

EXAMPLE Consider the nonlinear function $y = f(x) = x^2$. We commence by selecting a particular point on the graph of that function, namely $(3, 9) = (x_1, y_1)$. Then, as in the preceding example, we select values of a variable $x_2$ that become progressively closer to $x_1$. Each of the incremental changes in variable $x_2$ becomes smaller and smaller. We can see that the slope of the function $y = x^2$ is different for every different value of $x_2$ we select.

The difference quotient method helps us find the slope of a line between two points. It measures an *average rate of change* rather than the slope of the function at a specific point. Given two points $(x_1, y_1)$ and $(x_2, y_2)$, $\Delta y/\Delta x$ measures the average rate of change in $y$ that occurs over the interval between the two points due to the change in the value of $x$.

Both Tables 3.8 and 3.9 illustrate that as the change in variable $x$, $\Delta x$, becomes infinitesimally small, and approaches 0 in the limit, the difference quotient approaches some finite value as a limit. In the case of $y = x^2$, as $x \to 3$, $\Delta y/\Delta x \to 6$. This is true whether we approach $x = 3$ from above or from below. When this is the case, this limit is called *the derivative of $y = f(x)$ with respect to $x$.*

DEFINITION Given the function $y = f(x)$, the derivative of $y$ with respect to $x$ is given by

$$\frac{dy}{dx} = \lim_{\Delta x \to 0} \frac{\Delta y}{\Delta x} = \lim_{\Delta x \to 0} \frac{f(x + \Delta x) - f(x)}{\Delta x}$$

provided that the limit exists.

Table 3.8 Difference quotients and the slope of a linear function

*Given $y = f(x) = 10 + 2x$. Commence at $(5, 20) = (x_1, y_1)$ and $(7, 24) = (x_2, y_2)$.*

| $x_1$ | $x_2$ | $\Delta x$ | $y = f(x_2)$ | $\Delta y$ | $\frac{\Delta y}{\Delta x}$ |
|---|---|---|---|---|---|
| 5 | 7.00 | 2.00 | 24.00 | 4.00 | 2 |
| 5 | 6.00 | 1.00 | 22.00 | 2.00 | 2 |
| 5 | 5.50 | 0.50 | 21.00 | 1.00 | 2 |
| 5 | 5.30 | 0.30 | 20.60 | 0.60 | 2 |
| 5 | 5.10 | 0.10 | 20.20 | 0.20 | 2 |
| 5 | 5.01 | 0.01 | 20.02 | 0.02 | 2 |

This definition of a derivative still measures a rate of change. A derivative is not an average rate of change between two points. For that reason, a derivative may be thought of intuitively as being taken at a particular point on a curve.



EXAMPLES

1. Find the derivative of the function $y = 10 + 2x$ when $x = 5$. Using the definition of a derivative, we have

$$\lim_{\Delta x \to 0} \frac{\Delta y}{\Delta x} = \lim_{\Delta x \to 0} \frac{f(x+\Delta x) - f(x)}{\Delta x} = \lim_{\Delta x \to 0} \frac{10 + 2(x + \Delta x) - (10 + 2x)}{\Delta x}$$

$$= \lim_{\Delta x \to 0} \frac{10 + 2x + 2\Delta x - 10 - 2x}{\Delta x} = \lim_{\Delta x \to 0} = \frac{2\,\Delta x}{\Delta x} = 2$$

2. Find the derivative of the function $y = x^2$ when $x$ is arbitrary. Using the definition of a derivative, we have

$$\lim_{\Delta x \to 0} \frac{\Delta y}{\Delta x} = \lim_{\Delta x \to 0} \frac{f(x+\Delta x) - f(x)}{\Delta x} = \lim_{\Delta x \to 0} \frac{(x + \Delta x)^2 - x^2}{\Delta x}$$

$$= \lim_{\Delta x \to 0} \frac{x^2 + 2x\Delta x + (\Delta x)^2 - x^2}{\Delta x}$$

$$= \lim_{\Delta x \to 0} (2x + \Delta x) = \lim_{\Delta x \to 0} 2x + \lim_{\Delta x \to 0} \Delta x = 2x$$

Therefore, when $x = 3$, the derivative of $y = x^2$ with respect to $x$ is $2 \cdot 3 = 6$.

Table 3.9 Difference quotients and the slope of a nonlinear function

*Given* $y = f(x) = x^2$. *Commence at* $(3, 9) = (x_1, y_1)$.

| $x_2$ | $\Delta x$ | $y_2$ | $\Delta y$ | $\frac{\Delta y}{\Delta x}$ | |
|---|---|---|---|---|---|
| 1.000 | 2.000 | 1.000 | 8.000 | 4.000 | |
| 2.000 | 1.000 | 4.000 | 5.000 | 5.000 | |
| 2.500 | 0.500 | 6.250 | 2.750 | 5.500 | |
| 2.700 | 0.300 | 7.290 | 1.710 | 5.700 | (From below) |
| 2.900 | 0.100 | 8.410 | 0.590 | 5.900 | |
| 2.990 | 0.010 | 8.940 | 0.060 | 5.990 | |
| 2.999 | 0.001 | 9.994 | 0.006 | 5.999 | |
| 5.000 | 2.000 | 25.000 | 16.000 | 8.000 | |
| 4.000 | 1.000 | 16.000 | 7.000 | 7.000 | |
| 3.500 | 0.500 | 12.250 | 3.250 | 6.500 | |
| 3.300 | 0.300 | 10.090 | 1.890 | 6.300 | (From above) |
| 3.100 | 0.100 | 9.610 | 0.610 | 6.100 | |
| 3.010 | 0.010 | 9.060 | 0.060 | 6.010 | |
| 3.001 | 0.001 | 9.006 | 0.006 | 6.001 | |

As the second example indicates, the derivative of a function is, in general, a new function derived from the original or "primitive" function. If the original function was a function of variable $x$, then the derivative may also be a function of $x$ (but of no other variable), as was the case in Example 2.

The process of finding the derivative of a function such as $y = f(x) = x^2$ is called *differentiation*. We found that the derivative of $y = x^2$ with respect to $x$ was $2x$. This is the *first derivative* of the function $y = x^2$ with respect to $x$. "First derivative" signifies that we have carried out the process of differentiation one time, as opposed to more than one time. A function such as $y = x^2$ is said to be *differentiable* when we can find the derivative of the function.

## EXERCISE 3.4

For the following functions, find $dy/dx$, using the limit difference quotient.

1. $f(x) = x^3$
2. $f(x) = x^2 + 3x + 4$
3. $f(x) = 4x - 1$
4. $f(x) = \dfrac{1}{x + 1}$
5. $f(x) = \sqrt{x}$
6. $f(x) = 4 - 3x$
7. $f(x) = a + bx$
8. $f(x) = bx^2$
9. $f(x) = 144 - 32x$

## GEOMETRIC INTERPRETATION OF THE DERIVATIVE

The formal definition of a derivative can be illustrated geometrically. The geometric interpretation of a derivative also leads us directly to the idea of a derivative as the slope of a tangent line at a point on a curve. We begin with the geometric interpretation of a difference quotient. Consider the function $y = f(x) = x^2$, whose graph is illustrated in Figure 3.10. Assume that $A$ and $B$

Figure 3.10 Geometric interpretation of a difference quotient

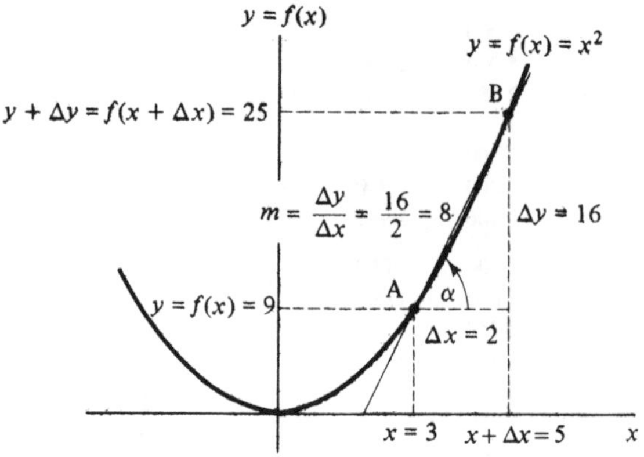

are any two points on the graph $y = x^2$ with coordinates $[x, f(x)] = (3, 9)$ and $[x + \Delta x, f(x + \Delta x)] = (5, 25)$, respectively. The slope of the line connecting points $A$ and $B$, that is, the difference quotient here, is

$$m = \frac{\Delta y}{\Delta x} = \frac{f(x + \Delta x) - f(x)}{\Delta x} = \frac{25 - 9}{2} = 8 \tag{3.12}$$

The value $m = 8$ is here interpreted as the average rate of change of $y = f(x) = x^2$ with respect to $x$ between points $A$ and $B$.

In trigonometric terms, the difference quotient illustrated in Figure 3.10 is the tangent of angle $\alpha$, where angle $\alpha$ is formed by the right triangle with the hypotenuse $AB$. The value of $\tan \alpha$ measures the slope of line $AB$.

Figure 3.11 illustrates various values that the slope $m$ might assume. When a line represented in Figure 3.11 is horizontal, then the slope $m$ of that line is 0. If the value of $m$ is $0 < m < \infty$, then the slope is positive, that is, the graph of the line rises as we move from left to right. A value of $m$ such that $m < 0$ indicates a line that falls as we move from left to right. Hence the slope is negative. For $m = \infty$, the line is vertical and the slope of the line is undefined.

A derivative is an infinitesimally small rate of change rather than an average rate of change. What would happen if we wanted to measure the infinitesimally small rate of change in $y$ with respect to $x$, that is, find the derivative of $y$ with respect to $x$ when $x = 3$? Geometrically, we ask the question, what value does the difference quotient in Equation (3.12) tend toward in the limit as $\Delta x$ approaches 0? As point $B$ moves along the curve $y = x^2$ toward point $A$, the line segment $AB$ continually changes its slope.

As indicated in Figure 3.12, the slope of the line connecting points $A$ and $B$ becomes more and more flat as point $B$ approaches point $A$. In the limit, as the changes in point $B$ are reduced in size and become arbitrarily small, line

Figure 3.11 Values of tangent $\alpha$ and their relationship to slope

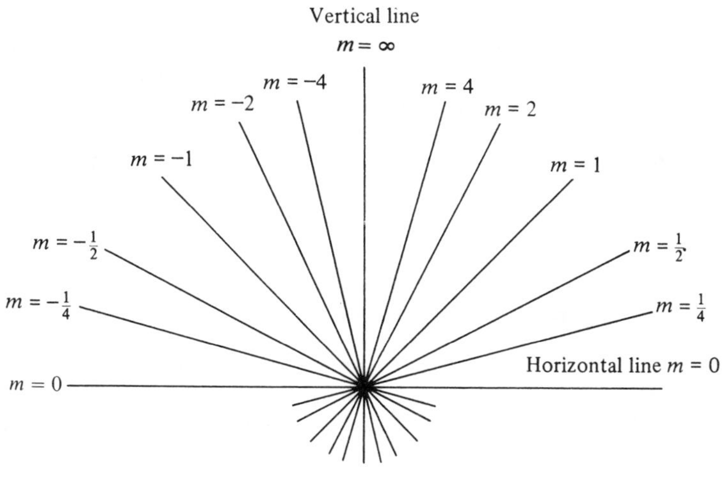

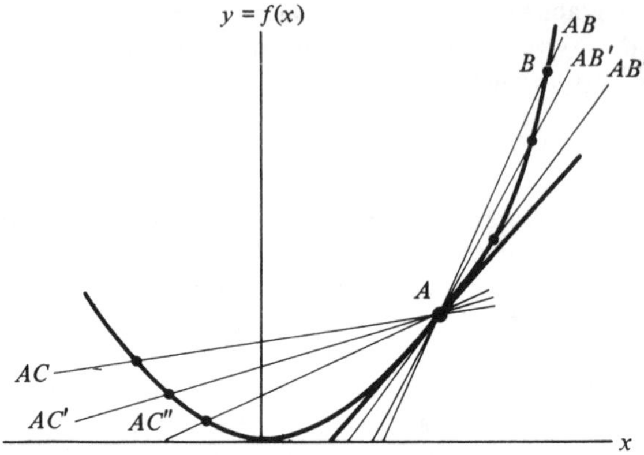


Figure 3.12 Geometric interpretation of a derivative. Limiting position or tangency at point $A$ is the derivative of $y$ with respect to $x$

segment $AB$ reaches a limiting position or tangency at point $A$. The heavier line in Figure 3.12 is that limiting position and is tangent to point $A$. Thus the slope of line segment $AB$ does approach a constant or finite limiting value. This limiting value at point $A$ is the derivative of the function $y = x^2$ at point $A$, and is variously indicated $dy/dx$, $y'$, or $f'(x)$.

The geometric limiting process in Figure 3.12, which resulted in the heavier line segment tangent to the curve at point $A$, is strictly analogous to the limiting value of the function $y = x^2$ that was demonstrated arithmetically in Table 3.9. It was demonstrated in Table 3.9 that, as $x \to 3$, $\Delta y/\Delta x \to 6.00$. At $x = 3$, the derivative of $y$ with respect to $x$ is 6.00. Table 3.9 demonstrates this arithmetically, while the visual interpretation of this limiting process is demonstrated in Figure 3.12, where at point $A$, the derivative is $f'(A)$. Since we have already seen that the derivative of $y$ with respect to $x^2$ is $2x$, when $x = A = 3, f'(3) = 2 \cdot 3 = 6.00$, as expected.

As Figure 3.11 illustrates, and the definition of a derivative demands, we must undertake the limiting process that results in a derivative independent of the direction from which we approach a point $x = A$. This means that should we choose two points, perhaps $A$ and $C$, and then move point $C$ progressively closer to fixed point $A$, we must obtain the same limit that we would obtain if we approached point $A$ from the other direction. The direction in which we approach the fixed point on the curve does *not* influence either the sign or the magnitude of the derivative.

## CONTINUITY AND DIFFERENTIABILITY

Not all functions can be differentiated. A function $y = f(x)$ is differentiable at a point $x$ *only if* it is also continuous at that same point $x$. A necessary, but not a sufficient, condition for a derivative to exist at a point is that the function be continuous at that point.

*Proof* Given $y = f(x)$. Assume that $f'(x)$ does exist. We start with an identity:

$$\frac{f(x+\Delta x)-f(x)}{\Delta x}=\frac{f(x+\Delta x)-f(x)}{\Delta x} \tag{3.13}$$

This can be written as

$$f(x+\Delta x)=f(x)+\Delta x\left[\frac{f(x+\Delta x)-f(x)}{\Delta x}\right] \tag{3.14}$$

As $\Delta x \to 0$, we have

$$\lim_{\Delta x\to 0} f(x+\Delta x)=\lim_{\Delta x\to 0}\left[f(x)+\Delta x\,\frac{f(x+\Delta x)-f(x)}{\Delta x}\right]$$

$$=\lim_{\Delta x\to 0} f(x)+\lim_{\Delta x\to 0}\left[\Delta x\,\frac{f(x+\Delta x)-f(x)}{\Delta x}\right]$$

$$=\lim_{\Delta x\to 0} f(x)+0\cdot f'(x) \tag{3.15}$$

$$\lim_{\Delta x\to 0} f(x+\Delta x)=f(x) \tag{3.16}$$

This is another way of saying that, given that the derivative exists at point $x$, then the function is also continuous at that point.

The above proof asserts that the fact that a function is differentiable at a point also means that it is continuous at that point. The converse is not true, however. The fact that a function is continuous does not necessarily mean that it is differentiable. A case in point is the function $y = |x|$. This function is continuous everywhere but is not differentiable at $x = 0$. The graph of this function is portrayed in Figure 3.13. When $x = 0$, the function satisfies all three conditions for continuity: (a) $f(0)$ exists; (b) $\lim_{x\to 0} f(x)$ exists; and, (c) $\lim_{x\to 0} f(x) = 0$. However, even though there is continuity at $x=0$, there is no derivative at $x=0$. The difference quotient in this case is

$$\frac{f(x+\Delta x)-f(x)}{\Delta x}=\frac{f(0+\Delta x)-f(0)}{\Delta x} \tag{3.17}$$

$$=\frac{|\Delta x|}{\Delta x} \tag{3.18}$$

As $\Delta x$ approaches 0 from the left, $|\Delta x|/\Delta x$ approaches negative 1. However, when $\Delta x$ approaches 0 from the right, $|\Delta x|/\Delta x$ approaches positive 1. Thus the limiting process does not produce a unique value when we approach 0 from the left and from the right. This implies that there is *more than one tangent line* at $x = 0$ for this function. Hence there is no derivative, because in order for there to be one, one unique value must result from the limiting process. When more than one value results from the limiting process (from the right and from the left), there is no derivative at that point.

In sum, differentiability implies continuity. Continuity is necessary if we are to find a derivative. Continuity, however, does not guarantee that a derivative exists or that the continuous function is differentiable. In logical notation, we can state that differentiability $\Rightarrow$ continuity.

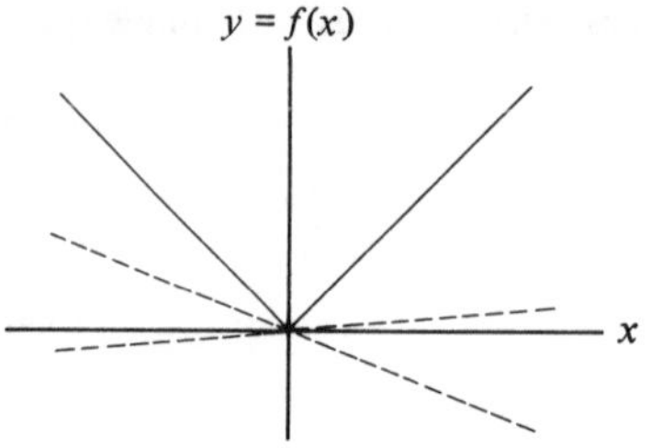


Figure 3.13 Graph of $y = f(x) = |x|$. Note that the dashed lines are tangent to the graph of $y = f(x)$ at the origin. There are an infinite number of such tangent lines at the origin. Hence a unique limit does not exist at the origin (where $x = 0$), and therefore there is no derivative at that point

## APPLICATIONS INVOLVING LIMITS, CONTINUITY, AND DERIVATIVES

Decision problems in business and economics rely very heavily on marginal analysis, in which concepts such as marginal sales, marginal revenue, and marginal cost are used repeatedly. Marginal analysis requires that one be able to determine and measure the changes that occur in a dependent variable when very small changes are made in an independent variable. A problem sometimes arises when one or more of the variables being examined is discrete in nature, so that the smallest possible change allowable is one whole unit. Fractional unit changes are not allowed. It is usually possible, however, to approximate any discrete function by a continuous function so that we can make infinitesimally small changes in a variable. In such a case, marginal analysis is viewed in a limiting sense. That is, the variations in the independent variable conceptually approach 0.

An example of the continuous–discrete problem is contained in a typical demand function. A *demand function* tells us the quantity of a good that a consumer would be willing and able to purchase at any possible price during a specified period of time and at a specified place. Table 3.10 presents data relating to the demand function of a hypothetical consumer for pizza during a given year.

Table 3.10 Demand function for pizza for a hypothetical consumer

| *Price per pizza* | *Quantity of pizzas demanded per unit of time* |
|---|---|
| \$5.00 | 0 |
| \$4.00 | 20 |
| \$3.00 | 40 |
| \$2.00 | 60 |
| \$1.00 | 80 |
| \$0.00 | 100 |

The price–quantity combinations in Figure 3.14(a) are nothing more than the data of Table 3.10 plotted graphically. Note that there are six discrete points. We can also represent the locus of the plotted points by the demand curve illustrated in Figure 3.14(b). The demand curve in part (b) is generated by the continuous demand function $q = f(p) = 100 - 20p$. This continuous demand curve includes all six discrete points found in part (a). However, it has the advantage of including all other permissible price–quantity combinations. Finally, in its continuous form, the demand function that we see in part (b) is easier to analyze in terms of its basic properties. For these reasons, we customarily work with continuous functions, although we must remember that these continuous functions are sometimes approximations of discrete data.

**Price Elasticity of Demand**

An inverse relationship between price and quantity demanded is evident in the demand function depicted in Table 3.10 and Figure 3.14. The negative slope of the demand curve reflects this inverse relationship. However, it does not tell us how sensitive quantity demanded is to changes in price. The coefficient of price

Figure 3.14 (a) Discrete demand curve. (b) Continuous demand curve. (It is customary in mathematics to place the dependent variable on the vertical axis of a graph and the independent variable on the horizontal one.)

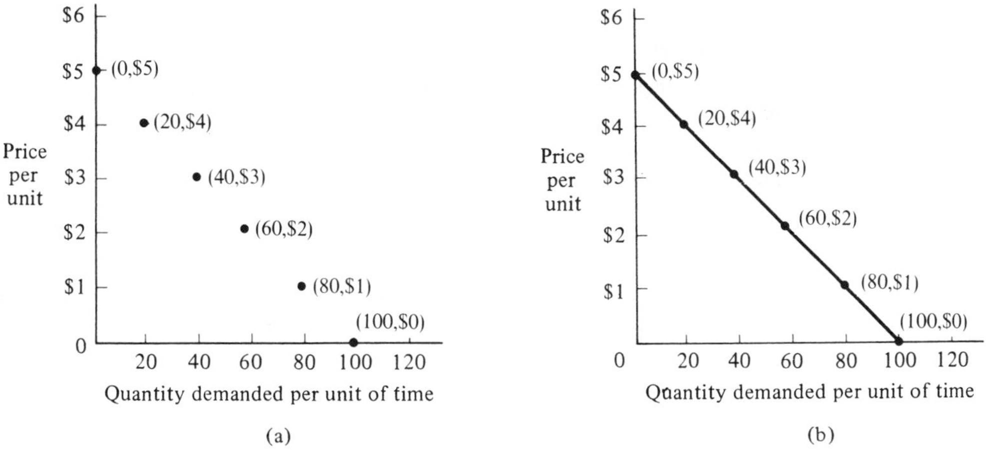


■ *Note*: It is customary in mathematics to place the dependent variable on the vertical axis of a graph, and the independent variable on the horizontal axis of the same graph. This is the usual convention also in economics, except where graphs of demand curves are concerned. Even though $q = f(p)$, it has long been customary in economic analysis to place the variable $q$ on the horizontal axis, even though it is the dependent variable. Similarly, in economics, $p$ is placed on the vertical axis, even though it is the independent variable. This is a historical curiosum that dates back to the nineteenth-century work of Alfred Marshall.

elasticity of demand, which is frequently represented by the Greek letter $\eta$, is used to measure the sensitivity or responsiveness of quantity demanded to changes in price.

DEFINITION The coefficient of price elasticity of demand $\eta$ is the percentage change in quantity demanded of a good divided by the percentage change in the price of that good.

Applying the verbal definition, we see that

$$\eta = \frac{\%\text{ change in quantity demanded}}{\%\text{ change in price}}$$

Hence

$$\eta = \frac{\Delta Q/Q}{\Delta P/P} = \frac{\Delta Q}{\Delta P} \cdot \frac{P}{Q}$$

In terms of the differential calculus, $\eta$ is defined at a particular point on the demand curve:

$$\eta = \lim_{\Delta P \to 0} \frac{\Delta Q}{\Delta P} \cdot \frac{P}{Q} = \frac{P}{Q} \lim_{\Delta P \to 0} \frac{\Delta Q}{\Delta P} = \frac{P}{Q} \cdot \frac{dQ}{dP} \tag{3.19}$$

We shall deal with the concept of price elasticity of demand in great detail in the next two chapters. For the present, it suffices to show that we can express the coefficient of price elasticity of demand in terms of a derivative.

### Marginal Cost

Assume that the total cost TC of producing pizzas is a function of the number of pizzas $Q$ produced by the pizza palace. That is, $\text{TC} = f(Q)$. One piece of information that any profit-making pizza parlor must be interested in is the incremental cost of producing an additional pizza.

DEFINITION Marginal cost MC is the change in total cost that occurs when an additional unit of output is produced.

Marginal cost is therefore the incremental cost of producing an additional pizza, and is equal to $\text{MC} = \Delta\text{TC}/\Delta Q$. In terms of the differential calculus, we can express MC as

$$\text{MC} = \lim_{\Delta Q \to 0} \frac{\Delta \text{TC}}{\Delta Q} = \frac{d\text{TC}}{dQ} \tag{3.20}$$

Once again, we shall use the concept of MC many times in subsequent chapters.

### Marginal Product

Another piece of information that a well-run pizza parlor would like to have is how many additional pizzas could be produced if, for example, an additional worker were hired. Assume that $Q = f(L)$, where $Q$ is the output of pizzas, and $L$ is the number of workers.

DEFINITION The marginal product of an input MP is the change in total output that occurs when an additional unit of the input is employed.

Marginal product expressed the additional number of pizzas that are forthcoming when the pizza parlor hires an additional worker. That is, $\text{MP} = \Delta Q/\Delta L$. Using the differential calculus, marginal product can be expressed as

$$\text{MP} = \lim_{\Delta L \to 0} \frac{\Delta Q}{\Delta L} = \frac{dQ}{dL} \tag{3.21}$$

We shall utilize the concept of marginal product in a wide range of different contexts in the next few chapters.

**Marginal Revenue**

The well-run pizza parlor is also interested in the incremental sales revenue that it actually realizes when it sells an extra pizza. Assume that the price $P$ that the pizza parlor charges for its pizzas is a function of the quantity of pizzas $Q$ that it sells. That is, $P = f(Q)$. The total sales revenue that the pizza parlor realizes is the product of $P$ times $Q$, or $PQ$.

DEFINITION Marginal revenue MR is the change in total revenue that occurs when the firm sells an additional unit.

Marginal revenue can therefore be expressed as $\text{MR} = \Delta\text{TR}/\Delta Q$. In terms of the differential calculus, this becomes

$$\text{MR} = \lim_{\Delta Q \to 0} \frac{\Delta \text{TR}}{\Delta Q} = \frac{d\text{TR}}{dQ} \tag{3.22}$$

The entire body of demand theory that economists teach relies heavily on the concept of marginal revenue. We shall therefore have frequent opportunity to use this concept in the future.

**Marginal Depreciation**

The pizza parlor presumably owns some capital equipment, such as an oven. As this oven grows older, it is worth less in terms of resale value, and may be less efficient in baking pizzas as well. Whatever the case, the Internal Revenue Service (IRS) typically allows pizza parlors and firms of all types to *depreciate* the value of their capital equipment. Depreciation is sometimes referred to as a *capital consumption allowance*. This label reflects the fact that the productivity of an oven, a house, or an open-hearth furnace typically declines as it ages. The depreciation that the firm realizes can, if the firm wishes, be accumulated and used to replace the worn-out piece of capital when the appropriate moment arrives.

Assume that depreciation $D$ is a function of the age of the equipment in years $A$. Hence $D = f(A)$. The depreciation that the firm can claim in a specific year is therefore dependent on the age of the piece of equipment that is being depreciated.

DEFINITION Marginal depreciation is the additional depreciation that a firm can claim when a piece of equipment is one year older.

That is, marginal depreciation MD is given by MD $= \Delta D/\Delta A$. In terms of the differential calculus, this becomes

$$\text{MD} = \lim_{\Delta A \to 0} \frac{\Delta D}{\Delta A} = \frac{dD}{dA} \tag{3.23}$$

**MPS, MPC, and the National Income Multiplier**

Most beginning economics courses spend a substantial portion of time dealing with national income determination models. The differential calculus is implicitly being used in these models also.

Let $Y$ = disposable income and $Y = C + S$, where $C$ is the consumption of private individuals and $S$ is the saving of private individuals. The consumption function of any individual indicates how much consumption that individual will undertake at any level of disposable income. We can write $C = f(Y)$, which indicates that consumption depends on disposable income.

DEFINITION The marginal propensity to consume MPC measures the change in consumption that results from a change in disposable income.

MPC is therefore MPC $= \Delta C/\Delta Y$. In terms of the differential calculus,

$$\text{MPC} = \lim_{\Delta Y \to 0} \frac{\Delta C}{\Delta Y} = \frac{dC}{dY} \tag{3.24}$$

Since all disposable income must be either consumed or saved, it follows that the marginal propensity to save MPS is equal to 1 minus the marginal propensity to consume.

DEFINITION The marginal propensity to save MPS measures the change in saving that results from a change in disposable income.

That is, MPS $= \Delta S/\Delta Y$, and it can be expressed in terms of the differential calculus as

$$\text{MPS} = \lim_{\Delta Y \to 0} \frac{\Delta S}{\Delta Y} = \frac{dS}{dY} = 1 - \text{MPC} = 1 - \frac{dC}{dY} \tag{3.25}$$

Equation (3.25) follows directly from the fact that MPC + MPS = 1.00. If you thrive on the usual Keynesian macroeconomic models that are introduced in beginning economics courses, you will also be able to add that the national income multiplier is equal to

$$\text{Multiplier} = \frac{1}{1 - \text{MPC}} = \frac{1}{\text{MPS}}$$

**The Kinked Demand Curve**

A recurring explanation of the pricing behavior of large "oligopolistic" firms such as those that characterize the American automobile industry is the kinked oligopoly demand curve. Although the empirical validity of the kinked-demand-curve hypothesis is a matter of some dispute, the mathematics associated with it is not. Of particular interest to us are two facts related to the kinked demand curve: (1) The kinked demand curve is a combination of two functions, and (2) the marginal revenue curve associated with the kinked demand curve is a discontinuous step function.

Figure 3.15 illustrates a kinked demand curve as it is usually assumed to be shaped. Assume that the oligopolistic firm whose demand curve is represented in Figure 3.15 feels that at all prices above $P_1$, it faces the demand curve given by linear segment *AB*, whereas at all prices below $P_1$, it faces the demand curve given by linear segment *BC*. *ABC* is the overall demand curve that the firm believes it faces. The marginal revenue curve that corresponds to this demand curve is given by the discontinuous function *ADEF*.

A first derivative does not exist at point *B* in Figure 3.15, even though the demand function *ABC* is continuous at that point. That is, when $Q = 3.33$, the

Figure 3.15 Finite discontinuous demand equation that results in a kinked demand curve and a discontinuous marginal revenue function

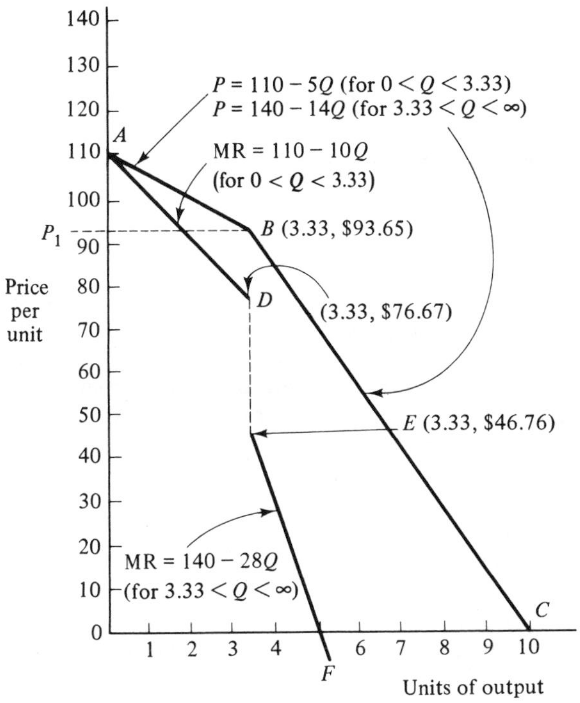

demand function satisfies all three conditions for continuity: (a) $f(3.33)$ exists; (b) $\lim_{Q\to 3.33} f(Q)$ exists; and (c) $\lim_{Q\to 3.33} f(Q) = 93.65$ exists. However, even though there is continuity at $Q = 3.33$, no derivative exists there. The difference quotient in this case for the function $P = 110 - 5Q$ is

$$\lim_{\Delta Q \to 0} \frac{110-(5Q+5\Delta Q)-(110-5Q)}{\Delta Q} = \lim_{\Delta Q \to 0} \frac{-5\Delta Q}{\Delta Q} = -5 \tag{3.26}$$

For the function $P = 140 - 140$, the difference quotient is

$$\lim_{\Delta Q \to 0} \frac{140 - (14Q + 14\,\Delta Q) - (110 - 5Q)}{\Delta Q} = \lim_{\Delta Q \to 0} \frac{-14\Delta Q}{\Delta Q} = -14 \tag{3.27}$$

Thus the limiting process does not produce a unique value when $\Delta Q \to 0$ is approached from left and right. This implies that *there is more than one tangent line* at $Q = 3.33$. Hence there is no derivative at that point.

The marginal revenue curve *ADEF* is a function that is characterized by a finite discontinuity. That is,

$$\text{MR} = 110 - 10Q \qquad \text{when } 0 < Q < 3.33$$

and

$$\text{MR} = 140 - 28Q \qquad \text{when } 3.33 < Q < \infty$$

The MR function is discontinuous at $Q = 3.33$ because the limit does not exist at $Q = 3.33$ for the MR function. Even though the function that is MR in Figure 3.15 is defined at $Q = 3.33$, and the left- and right-hand limits both exist, these two limits are not identical:

$$\lim_{Q \to 3.33^-} (110 - 10Q) = 76.67 \neq \lim_{Q \to 3.33^+} (140 - 28Q) = 46.76 \tag{3.28}$$

Hence the MR function is discontinuous at $Q = 3.33$.

## PROBLEMS

1. The amount of postage that one must pay (at the moment) in order to mail a first-class letter is 15 cents per ounce, or any fraction of an ounce. Thus $P = f(W)$, where $P$ = postage in cents, and $W$ = weight of the letter expressed in integer ounces such that any fraction is always rounded up to the next integer. (a) Write the precise algebraic equation that reflects the functional relationship between postage paid and letter weight. (b) Is this functional relationship continuous or discontinuous? If discontinuous, what type of discontinuity is it?
2. The relationship between the sales of automobile batteries by the Last-Ever Battery Company and the number of Last-Ever salespersons is given by the equation $S = (N^2 - 1)/(N - 2)$, where $S$ = sales in hundreds of thousands of dollars, and $N$ = number of salespersons. (a) How many sales are generated by five salespeople? (b) This sales function is discontinuous. Where? (c) What kind of discontinuity exists?

3. Samuel Academicus is a grade-school student who will start a four-year high school next year. Sam intends to work in order to make deposits of \$2000 in his savings account at the beginning of each year of high school. He will use the proceeds to finance his college education at Albuquerque Tech. Sam can earn a 7% rate of interest on his savings deposits. (a) At the end of four years of high school, how much money will Sam have available? (b) Write a general formula that expresses the relationship between Sam's saving, the rate of interest he can earn, and time. (c) As $r$, the rate of interest that Sam can earn, becomes very large, what value does Sam's savings approach?
4. An automobile tire factory in Akron emits pollution in direct relationship to the number of tires it produces. The total cost of this pollution is symbolized by TC, and is given by the equation $\text{TC} = 100 + 200Q$, where $Q$ is the number of tires produced, in thousands. (a) Find the average cost of pollution after 20,000 tires have been produced. (b) Find the marginal cost of pollution for the 20,000th tire produced.
5. The population in Timbuktoo is given by the equation $P(t) = t^2 + t$, where $t =$ years. (a) What will the population of Timbuktoo be at the end of five years if the population at $t = 0$ is 0? (b) What is the rate of increase per unit of time in Timbuktoo's population?
6. The cost $C$ of refining $N$ gallons of fuel oil (where $N$ is expressed in thousands) is given by the equation $C(N) = 10 + 10\sqrt{N}$. (a) Find the average cost of refining 50 gallons of fuel oil. (b) Find the marginal cost of refining the fiftieth gallon of fuel oil. (c) If the refining cost equation changes so that $C(N) = 10 + 0.5N^2$, then what are the average and marginal costs of refining the fiftieth gallon of fuel oil?
7. Suppose that $y = f(x) = x^2 + 3x + 3$. (a) Find the derivative of $y$ with respect to $x$ for *any* $x$. (b) Evaluate this difference quotient for $x_0 = 2, 1, \frac{1}{2}$, and 0.
8. The number of people $n$ who can be seated in a room is given by the function $n = f(s) = (2s + 5)/4s$, where $s$ is an index of factors such as space, available chairs, and so forth. (a) As $s$ becomes very large, how many people can be seated in the room? (b) Can your answer to (a) be interpreted as a limit? Why or why not?
9. An economist in the Department of Commerce has examined the history of the business cycle and has concluded that the contraction and recovery phases of the business cycle can be represented by the equation $y = f(t) = t^2 - t - 2$, where $y$ is an index of national income and is assumed to have a value of 0 when the business cycle was at its previous peak, and $t$ is time in years. When the index $y$ assumes increasingly negative values, then the economy is contracting. (a) If a particular business cycle contraction began one year ago (so that $t = -1$ then and $t = 0$ now), how many years will it take the economy to recover completely so that $y$ is once again equal to zero? (b) What is the rate of change in the index $y$ per year? (c) Using the rate of change found in (b), find the change in the index that occurs when $t$ changes from 1 to 2. (d) As $t \to \infty$, what value does the index $y$ approach? (e) Keeping in mind the limit

found in (d), critically evaluate the economist's use of the function $y = f(t)$ as a means to represent and predict the business cycle. What faults, if any, can you find with the economist's use of this particular functional form?

10. The marginal revenue curve for Germania Beer is $MR = 10 - 0.5Q$ for $0 \leq Q \leq 5$, and $MR = 7.50 - 0.7Q$ for $5 \leq Q \leq \infty$. (a) Graph this marginal revenue function. (b) Is the marginal revenue function discontinuous, and if so, at what value(s) of $Q$? (c) What kind of discontinuity is this, if a discontinuity exists?

# DIFFERENTIATION: FUNCTIONS OF ONE VARIABLE

# 4

Marginal analysis is the backbone of much of modern economic theory and analysis. Marginal analysis examines the effects on other variables of small changes in a particular parameter or exogenous variable. For example, what will happen to the number of riders on Chicago Transit Authority (CTA) subways and buses if the fare per person is raised by 5 cents?

A host of business and economics problems are susceptible to marginal analysis, where the rate of change of one variable (such as the number of passengers on the CTA) in response to a small change in another variable (CTA fares) is the heart of the matter. We can express the rate of change in one variable in response to small changes in another variable as the first derivative of the function involved. In the case at hand, the first and second derivatives of the demand function for CTA travel with respect to CTA fares supply much needed information.

In Chapter 3 we introduced the concept of a derivative and its geometric interpretation. In this chapter, we derive and utilize rules that will assist us in differentiating functions of one variable in everyday situations. Mastery of the technique of differentiation will not only enable us to speak to concrete problems such as that facing the CTA, but also will enhance our understanding of a wide range of concepts such as marginal cost, marginal revenue, marginal utility, elasticities, and population growth.

The initial objective of this chapter is therefore to study the specific rules that assist us in finding the derivative of a wide variety of functional expressions. Subsequently we shall highlight numerous business and economics problems where differentiation is of use.

## RULES OF DIFFERENTIATION

Finding the derivative of a function with respect to a particular variable can be tedious when we have to compute the derivative as the limit of a difference quotient, as defined in the previous chapter. Fortunately there is a set of time-saving rules that enables us to find the derivative of a function without going through the formal process of computing it as a limit of a difference quotient. The rules for differentiation are actually nothing more than general formulas that emerge when we take the limit of a difference quotient. The rules amount to a time-saving method of computing the derivative of a function. However, we shall prove the existence of each rule in order to quash the feeling that the rules might result from some type of sleight-of-hand maneuver.

The notation that we use to indicate the derivative of a function with respect to a certain variable is sometimes a greater source of problems than is the determination of the derivative itself. Given that $y = f(x)$, then the derivative of $y$ with respect to $x$ is equivalently symbolized by $dy/dx$, $y'$, and $f'(x)$. We shall ordinarily use the symbols $y'$ and $f'(x)$, and shall reserve the use of $dy/dx$ to situations in which we wish to make absolutely clear the function and variables involved in the differentiation.

### Derivatives of Polynomial Functions

RULE I (DERIVATIVE OF A CONSTANT) Given that $y = f(x) = k$, where $k$ is a constant, then

$$\frac{d(k)}{dx} = y' = f'(x) = 0$$

That is, the derivative of a constant is 0. Regardless of the value of $x$, the value of the function $y = f(x)$ is still equal to some constant $k$. Therefore any change in variable $x$ has no effect on $y$. Hence the derivative of function $y$ with respect to $x$, which measures the change in $y$ with respect to a change in $x$, must be 0.

*Proof* Given that $y = f(x) = k$, the difference quotient is

$$f'(x) = \lim_{\Delta x \to 0} \frac{\Delta y}{\Delta x} = \lim_{\Delta x \to 0} \frac{f(x + \Delta x) - f(x)}{\Delta x}$$

$$= \lim_{\Delta x \to 0} \frac{k - k}{\Delta x} = 0$$

As $\Delta x \to 0$, given that $y = f(x) = k$, then $f'(x) = 0$.

EXAMPLES

1. Given that $y = 6$, then $f'(x) = 0$.
2. Given that $y = \sqrt{6}$, then $f'(x) = 0$.
3. Given that $y = 6^6$, then $f'(x) = 0$.
4. Given that total cost TC is a function of fixed cost FC only, and FC is a constant amount of \$100, then the derivative of TC with respect to output $Q$ is $d\text{TC}/dQ = 0$.

RULE 2 (DERIVATIVE OF A POWER)[1] Given that $y = f(x) = x^n$, where $n$ is a positive integer, then

$$\frac{d(x^n)}{dx} = y' = f'(x) = nx^{n-1}$$

*Proof* Given that $y = f(x) = x^n$, then the difference quotient is

$$f'(x) = \lim_{\Delta x \to 0} \frac{f(x + \Delta x) - f(x)}{\Delta x} = \lim_{\Delta x \to 0} \frac{(x + \Delta x)^n - x^n}{\Delta x}$$

Using the binomial expansion, we get

$$\lim_{\Delta x \to 0} \frac{x^n + \binom{n}{1}x^{n-1}(\Delta x) + \binom{n}{2}x^{n-2}(\Delta x)^2 + \cdots + \binom{n}{n-1}x(\Delta x)^{n-1} + (\Delta x)^n - x^n}{\Delta x}$$

$$= \lim_{\Delta x \to 0} \left[\binom{n}{1}x^{n-1} + \binom{n}{2}x^{n-2}(\Delta x) + \cdots + \binom{n}{n-1}x(\Delta x)^{n-2} + (\Delta x)^{n-1}\right]$$

In the limit, this expansion reduces to

$$f'(x) = \lim_{\Delta x \to 0} \frac{\Delta y}{\Delta x} = \binom{n}{1}x^{n-1} = nx^{n-1}$$

EXAMPLES

1. Given that $y = f(x) = x$, then $f'(x) = 1$.
2. Given that $y = f(x) = x^2$, then $f'(x) = 2x$.
3. Given that $y = f(x) = x^{1/2}$, then $f'(x) = \frac{1}{2}x^{-1/2}$.
4. Given that $y = f(x) = x^{100}$, then $f'(x) = 100x^{99}$.

RULE 3 (DERIVATIVE OF A CONSTANT TIMES A FUNCTION) Given that $y = kf(x)$, then

$$\frac{d[kf(x)]}{dx} = y' = k \cdot f'(x)$$

where $d[kf(x)]/dx = dy/dx$, the derivative of $y$ with respect to $x$, and $f'(x) = d[f(x)]/dx$, the derivative of $f(x)$ with respect to $x$. Stated in words, the derivative of a constant times a function is the constant times the derivative of the function.

[1] We prove Rule 2 for the case in which $n$ is a positive integer. For cases in which $n$ is a negative integer or in which $n$ is a rational number, a very lengthy proof is required. See Louis Leithold, *The Calculus with Analytic Geometry*, third edition, Harper and Row, Publishers, Inc., New York, 1977, pp. 136–144.

*Proof* Given that $y = kf(x)$, then the difference quotient is

$$y^{1} = \lim_{\Delta x \to 0} \frac{f(x + \Delta x) - f(x)}{\Delta x} = \lim_{\Delta x \to 0} \frac{kf(x + \Delta x) - kf(x)}{\Delta x}$$

$$= \lim_{\Delta x \to 0} \left\{ k \left[ \frac{f(x + \Delta x) - f(x)}{\Delta x} \right] \right\} = k \left[ \lim_{\Delta x \to 0} \frac{f(x + \Delta x) - f(x)}{\Delta x} \right]$$

$$= kf'(x)$$

EXAMPLES

1. Given that $y = 6x$, then $f'(x) = 6$.
2. Given that $y = 6x^2$, then $f'(x) = 12x$.
3. Given that $y = 2x^{1/2}$, then $f'(x) = x^{-1/2}$.
4. Given that $y = 3x^4$, then $f'(x) = 12x^3$

EXERCISE 4.1

Find $dy/dx$ for the following.

1. $y = \frac{1}{2}$
2. $y = 1{,}000{,}000$
3. $y = e^2$
4. $y = \pi$
5. $y = x^{n+1}$
6. $y = x^2$
7. $y = x^{3/2}$
8. $y = -x^2$
9. $y = ax^b$, where $a$, $b$ are constants
10. $y = -x^{0.5}$

**Derivatives of Algebraic Functions**

Before we develop rules for the differentiation of algebraic functions, we must take note of a fundamental theorem that provides us with the basis for rules for differentiation of algebraic functions that are either sums or differences, products, or quotients.

THEOREM 4.1 Let $f(x)$ and $g(x)$ be two functions defined on a common interval. At every point on this common interval at which the functions $f(x)$ and $g(x)$ have a derivative, so also will the functions that are the sum or difference of the two functions $[f(x) \pm g(x)]$, the product of the two functions $[f(x) \cdot g(x)]$, and the quotient of the two functions $[f(x)/g(x)]$, where $g(x) \neq 0$ when $g(x)$ is the denominator of the quotient.

In nonrigorous language, this means that if two functions [call them $f(x)$ and $g(x)$] are differentiable, then other functions that take the form $f(x) + g(x)$, $f(x) - g(x)$, $f(x) \cdot g(x)$, or $f(x)/g(x)$ are also differentiable.

The derivatives of these functions and their proofs are given in differentiation rules 4 to 6.

RULE 4 (DERIVATIVE OF A SUM OR DIFFERENCE) Given that $y = f(x) \pm g(x)$, where $f(x)$ and $g(x)$ have derivatives, then

$$\frac{d[f(x) \pm g(x)]}{dx} = y' = f'(x) \pm g'(x)$$

That is, the derivative of a sum (difference) of two functions is the sum (difference) of the derivatives of the two functions.

*Proof* We shall prove that the derivative of the sum of two functions is the sum of the derivatives of the two functions, and leave the corresponding proof that the derivative of a difference between two functions is the difference between the derivatives of the two functions to you.

Given that $y = f(x) + g(x)$, then the difference quotient is

$$y' = \lim_{\Delta x \to 0} \frac{f(x + \Delta x) + g(x + \Delta x) - f(x) - g(x)}{\Delta x}$$

$$= \lim_{\Delta x \to 0} \frac{f(x + \Delta x) - f(x) + g(x + \Delta x) - g(x)}{\Delta x}$$

$$= \lim_{\Delta x \to 0} \frac{f(x + \Delta x) - f(x)}{\Delta x} + \lim_{\Delta x \to 0} \frac{g(x + \Delta x) - g(x)}{\Delta x}$$

$$= f'(x) + g'(x).$$

We can now combine Rules 3 and 4 and obtain a useful result. Given two constants $k_1$ and $k_2$, if $y = k_1 f(x) + k_2 g(x)$, then $y' = k_1 f'(x) + k_2 g'(x)$. This result is referred to as the *linearity property* of the derivatives. In general, given that

$$y = \sum_{i=1}^{n} k_i f_i(x) \qquad \text{for all } i = 1, 2, \ldots, n$$

where each $f_i(x)$ has a derivative, then

$$y' = \sum_{i=1}^{n} k_i f_i'(x) \qquad \text{where } k_1, k_2, \ldots, k_n \text{ are constants}$$

▣ When a constant is included in a function as a separate term, that is, when the constant is *not* multiplied by a function of $x$, then the values of the constant (whatever they might be) have no effect on the derivative with respect to $x$, because the derivative of a constant term is 0. However, if the constant term is a multiplicative function of $x$—that is, if it is a constant times a function—then it does affect the derivative with respect to $x$.

For example, assume that a firm has a total-cost function given by $TC = FC + VC = 100 + 2Q^2$, where TC = total cost, FC = fixed cost = 100, VC = variable cost = $2Q^2$, and $Q$ = output. Then

$$\frac{dTC}{dQ} = 0 + 4Q = 4Q$$

The size of the fixed-cost term has no effect on the derivative of TC with respect to $Q$. (Incidentally, $dTC/dQ$ is marginal cost.) On the other hand, note that the constant 2 in the multiplicative term $2Q^2$ is retained in the process of differentiation.

EXAMPLES

1. Given that $y = 100 - 2x + 8x^2$, then $y' = -2 + 16x$.
2. Given that $y = a + bx$, then $y' = b$.
3. Given that $y = 1 + 2x - 3x^2 + 4x^3$, then $y' = 2 - 6x + 12x^2$.

RULE 5 (DERIVATIVE OF A PRODUCT) Given that $y = f(x) \cdot g(x)$, where $f(x)$ and $g(x)$ have derivatives, then

$$\frac{d[f(x)g(x)]}{dx} = y' = f'(x) \cdot g(x) + f(x) \cdot g'(x)$$

That is, the derivative of the product of two functions is the derivative of the first function times the second function plus the first function times the derivative of the second function.

*Proof* Given that $y = f(x)g(x)$, then the difference quotient is

$$y' = \lim_{\Delta x \to 0} \frac{f(x+\Delta x)g(x+\Delta x) - f(x)g(x)}{\Delta x}$$

$$= \lim_{\Delta x \to 0} \frac{f(x+\Delta x)g(x+\Delta x) - f(x)g(x) + [f(x)g(x+\Delta x) - f(x)g(x+\Delta x)]}{\Delta x}$$

$$= \lim_{\Delta x \to 0} \frac{f(x+\Delta x)g(x+\Delta x) - f(x)g(x+\Delta x) - f(x)g(x) + f(x)g(x+\Delta x)}{\Delta x}$$

$$= \lim_{\Delta x \to 0} \frac{[f(x+\Delta x) - f(x)]g(x+\Delta x) + f(x)[g(x+\Delta x) - g(x)]}{\Delta x}$$

$$= \lim_{\Delta x \to 0} \frac{[f(x+\Delta x) - f(x)]g(x+\Delta x)}{\Delta x} + \lim_{\Delta x \to 0} \frac{f(x)[g(x+\Delta x) - g(x)]}{\Delta x}$$

$$= \lim_{\Delta x \to 0} \frac{f(x+\Delta x) - f(x)}{\Delta x} \cdot \lim_{\Delta x \to 0} g(x+\Delta x) + \lim_{\Delta x \to 0} f(x) \times \lim_{\Delta x \to 0} \frac{g(x+\Delta x) - g(x)}{\Delta x}$$

$$= f'(x)g(x) + f(x)g'(x)$$

In general, given that

$$y = \prod_{i=1}^{n} f_i(x) \qquad \text{for all } i = 1, 2, \ldots, n$$

then

$$y' = \frac{d}{dx}\left[\prod_{i=1}^{n} f_i(x)\right] = \sum_{i=1}^{n}\left[f_i'(x)\prod_{\substack{j=1\\(j\neq i)}}^{n} \mu_j\right]$$

where $\mu_j = f_j(x)$ are differentiable functions of $x$ for $j = 1, 2, \ldots, n$.

For example, given that $y = f(x)g(x)h(x)$, then $y' = f'(x)g(x)h(x) + f(x)g'(x)h(x) + f(x)g(x)h'(x)$.

■ Note that if $y = f(x) \cdot g(x)$, then $y' = f'(x) \cdot g(x) + f(x) \cdot g'(x)$, and also that $y' = g'(x) \cdot f(x) + f'(x) \cdot g(x)$. The order in which we take the derivative for each of the functions of $x$ is not important. However, note that *it is incorrect to state* that the derivative of a product is the product of the derivatives, that is, $y' \neq f'(x)g'(x)$.

EXAMPLES

1. Given that $y = x^2(8x + 5)$, then

$$y' = 2x(8x + 5) + x^2(8) = 16x^2 + 10x + 8x^2$$
$$= 24x^2 + 10x = 2x(12x + 5)$$

2. Given that $y = (x + 1)(x^3 - 2)$, then

$$y' = (1)(x^3 - 2) + (x + 1)(3x^2) = x^3 - 2 + 3x^3 + 3x^2 = 4x^3 + 3x^2 - 2$$

3. Given that $y = (x^3 - 3x^2)(4x + 6)$, then

$$y' = (3x^2 - 6x)(4x + 6) + (x^3 - 3x^2)(4)$$
$$= 12x^3 + 18x^2 - 24x^2 - 36x + 4x^3 - 12x^2$$
$$= 16x^3 - 18x^2 - 36x = 2x(8x^2 - 9x - 18)$$

RULE 6 (DERIVATIVE OF A QUOTIENT) Given that $y = f(x)/g(x)$, where $f(x)$ and $g(x)$ have derivatives, then

$$\frac{d[f(x)/g(x)]}{dx} = y' = \frac{f'(x) \cdot g(x) - f(x) \cdot g'(x)}{[g(x)]^2}$$

That is, the derivative of the quotient of two functions of $x$ is the derivative of the numerator times the denominator minus the numerator times the derivative of the denominator, all divided by the denominator squared. You are forewarned that there is no substitute for memorizing this rule, perhaps as one might memorize a jingle.

*Proof* Given that $y = f(x)/g(x)$, then the difference quotient is

$$y' = \lim_{\Delta x \to 0} \frac{\dfrac{f(x+\Delta x)}{g(x+\Delta x)} - \dfrac{f(x)}{g(x)}}{\Delta x}$$

$$= \lim_{\Delta x \to 0} \frac{f(x+\Delta x)g(x) - f(x)g(x+\Delta x)}{(\Delta x)g(x)g(x+\Delta x)}$$

$$= \lim_{\Delta x \to 0} \frac{f(x+\Delta x)g(x) - f(x)g(x+\Delta x) + [f(x)g(x) - f(x)g(x)]}{(\Delta x)g(x)g(x+\Delta x)}$$

$$= \lim_{\Delta x \to 0} \frac{[f(x+\Delta x)g(x) - f(x)g(x)] - [f(x)g(x+\Delta x) - f(x)g(x)]}{(\Delta x)g(x)g(x+\Delta x)}$$

$$= \lim_{\Delta x \to 0} \frac{[f(x+\Delta x) - f(x)]g(x) - f(x)[g(x+\Delta x) - g(x)]}{(\Delta x)g(x)g(x+\Delta x)}$$

$$= \lim_{\Delta x \to 0} \frac{[f(x+\Delta x) - f(x)]g(x)}{(\Delta x)g(x)g(x+\Delta x)} - \lim_{\Delta x \to 0} \frac{f(x)[g(x+\Delta x) - g(x)]}{(\Delta x)g(x)g(x+\Delta x)}$$

$$= \lim_{\Delta x \to 0} \frac{\dfrac{[f(x+\Delta x) - f(x)]g(x)}{\Delta x}}{g(x)g(x+\Delta x)} - \lim_{\Delta x \to 0} \frac{\dfrac{f(x)[g(x+\Delta x) - g(x)]}{\Delta x}}{g(x)g(x+\Delta x)}$$

$$= \frac{f'(x)g(x)}{g(x)g(x)} - \frac{f(x)g'(x)}{g(x)g(x)}$$

$$= \frac{f'(x)g(x) - f(x)g'(x)}{[g(x)]^2}$$

■ It is important to note that the order in which each function [$f(x)$ and $g(x)$] are differentiated is of crucial importance. If $y = f(x)/g(x)$, then $y' = [f'(x)g(x) - f(x)g'(x)]/[g(x)]^2$, and *this is not equivalent to* $[g'(x)f(x) - f'(x)g(x)]/[g(x)]^2$. The function $f(x)$, which is in the numerator of the original quotient that we seek to differentiate, is differentiated first and appears in the term with the positive sign in the numerator of the derivative. The function $g(x)$, which is in the denominator of the original quotient that we seek to differentiate, is differentiated second, and appears in the term with the negative sign in the numerator of the derivative. You can verify the importance of this point by differentiating the function $y = (x^2 + 2x - 1)/x^2$ with respect to $x$.

$$y' = \frac{(2x+2)x^3 - (x^2 + 2x - 1)2x}{(x^2)^2} \quad \text{or} \quad \frac{2(1-x^2)}{x^3}$$

If the order of differentiation is reversed, then the derivative obtained (*which is incorrect*) is $2(x-1)/x^3$.

1. Given that $y = (x^4 + x^2 - 3)/x^3$, then

$$y' = \frac{(4x^3 + 2x)(x^3) - (x^4 + x^2 - 3)(3x^2)}{(x^3)^2}$$

$$= \frac{4x^6 + 2x^4 - 3x^6 - 3x^4 + 9x^2}{x^6} = \frac{x^6 - x^4 + 9x^2}{x^6}$$

$$= \frac{x^4 - x^2 + 9}{x^4}$$

2. Given that $y = 1/x^3$, then

$$y' = \frac{(0)x^3 - (1)3x^2}{(x^3)^2} = \frac{-3x^2}{x^6} = \frac{-3}{x^4}$$

3. Given that $y = 1/x^n$ where $n > 0$, then

$$y' = \frac{(0)x^n - (1)nx^{n-1}}{(x^n)^2} = -\frac{nx^{n-1}}{x^{2n}} = -\frac{n}{x^{n+1}}$$

4. Given that $y = (3 - 4x)/(3 + 4x)$, then

$$y' = \frac{-4(3 + 4x) - (3 - 4x)(4)}{(3 + 4x)^2} = \frac{-12 - 16x - 12 + 16x}{(3 + 4x)^2}$$

$$= \frac{-24}{(3 + 4x)^2}$$

**EXERCISE 4.2**

Find $dy/dx$ for the following.

1. $y = \frac{x^3}{3} + \frac{x^2}{2} - x + \frac{3}{2}$
2. $y = 2 - 6x + 12x^2 - 20x^3$
3. $y = 8x^3(6x + 4)$
4. $y = (x^3 - x^2 + 5)(3x^2 + 5)$
5. $y = (x^2 + 3)(2x^3 - 5)$
6. $y = (2x^2 + 4x)(8 + 2x)$
7. $y = (x^3 + 4x^2 - 4)(5x)$
8. $y = (x - 1)(x - 2)(x - 3)$
9. $y = (1 - x)(2 - x^2)(3 - x^3)$
10. $y = \frac{3x^2 - 2}{x}$
11. $y = \frac{4x^2 + 2x + 1}{4x^2 + 2x}$
12. $y = \frac{1}{x} + \frac{2}{x^2} - \frac{3}{x^3}$
13. $y = \frac{x^2 + 2}{2 - x^2}$
14. $y = \frac{x^4 + x - 5}{x^3}$
15. $y = \frac{5 - 2x}{x^2(x - 2)}$

Rules 1 through 6 each dealt with the derivative of a function of the form $y = f(x)$. Rule 7 deals with a composite function, that is, two or more functions, each of which has a *different* independent variable. Mastery of this rule substantially increases the number of functions that we can differentiate.

RULE 7 (DERIVATIVE OF A FUNCTION OF A FUNCTION) Given that $y = f(u)$ and $u = g(x)$ such that $y = f[g(x)]$, then

$$\frac{d\{f[g(x)]\}}{dx} = y' = \frac{dy}{dx} = \frac{dy}{du} \cdot \frac{du}{dx} = f'(u) \cdot g'(x)$$

That is, the derivative of $f[g(x)]$ at point $x$ is the derivative of $y$ at point $u$, where $u = g(x)$, times the derivative $g'(x)$. In words, $y'$ is the derivative of $y$ with respect to $u$ times the derivative of $u$ with respect to $x$.

*Proof* Using the limit definition of a derivative that we developed in Chapter 3, we have

$$\frac{dy}{dx} = \lim_{\Delta x \to 0} \frac{\Delta y}{\Delta x} = \lim_{\Delta x \to 0} \left[\frac{\Delta y}{\Delta u} \cdot \frac{\Delta u}{\Delta x}\right]$$

However, as $\Delta x \to 0$, then $\Delta u \to 0$ also. And as $\Delta u \to 0$, so also $\Delta y \to 0$. Since, as we have seen, the limit of a product is the product of the limits, it follows that

$$\lim_{\Delta x \to 0} \frac{\Delta y}{\Delta x} = \lim_{\Delta u \to 0} \frac{f(u + \Delta u) - f(u)}{\Delta u} \cdot \lim_{\Delta x \to 0} \frac{g(x + \Delta x) - g(x)}{\Delta x}$$

Applying our definitions, we have

$$\frac{dy}{dx} = y' = \frac{dy}{du}\frac{du}{dx} = f'(u) \cdot g'(x)$$

We can easily extend the previous rule, which is often labeled the *chain rule*, to cover the case in which more than two functions are involved. Assume that $y = f(u)$, $u = g(v)$, and $v = h(x)$. Then

$$\frac{dy}{dx} = y' = \frac{dy}{du} \cdot \frac{du}{dv} \cdot \frac{dv}{dx} = f'(u) \cdot g'(v) \cdot h'(x)$$

EXAMPLES

1. Given that $y = 2u$ and $u = 8x$, then

$$\frac{dy}{dx} = \frac{dy}{du}\frac{du}{dx} = 2 \cdot 8 = 16$$

We can verify this by noting that

$$y = 2(8x) = 16x \qquad \text{and} \qquad \frac{d}{dx}[16x] = 16$$

2. Given that $y = u^5$ and $u = 2x^3 - 5x + 10$, then

$$\frac{dy}{dx} = \frac{dy}{du}\frac{du}{dx} = 5u^4(6x^2 - 5) = 5(2x^3 - 5x + 10)^4(6x^2 - 5)$$

3. Given that $y = u^2 + 18$ and $u = x^2 + 1$, then

$$\frac{dy}{dx} = \frac{dy}{du}\frac{du}{dx} = 2u(2x) = 2(x^2 + 1)(2x) = 4x(x^2 + 1)$$

RULE 8 (DERIVATIVE OF A CHAIN WITH AN EXPONENT) Given that $y = [u(x)]^n$, where $n$ is any integer, then (by the chain rule)

$$\frac{d\{[u(x)]^n\}}{dx} = y' = n[u(x)]^{n-1} \cdot \frac{du}{dx} = n[u(x)]^{n-1} \cdot u'(x)$$

*Proof* The definition of the chain rule is

$$\frac{dy}{dx} = \frac{dy}{du}\frac{du}{dx}$$

By Rule 2, we also know that

$$\frac{dy}{du} = \frac{d(u^n)}{du} = nu^{n-1}$$

in the case at hand. Therefore we have

$$\frac{dy}{dx} = nu^{n-1} \cdot \frac{du}{dx} = nu^{n-1} \cdot u'(x)$$

An interesting special case of Rule 8 occurs when $u = f(x) = x$. In such a case, $u^n = x^n$. Therefore the derivative becomes

$$\frac{dy}{dx} = \frac{dy}{du}\frac{du}{dx} = nx^{n-1}(1) = nx^{n-1}$$

You will recognize that this is a restatement of Rule 2, and that Rule 2 is a special case of Rule 8 where $u = f(x) = x$.

EXAMPLES

1. Given that $y = (x^2 + 5)^{1/2}$, then

   $y' = \frac{1}{2}(x^2 + 5)^{-1/2}(2x)$

2. Given that $y = (x^2 - x)^{-2}$, then

   $y' = -2(x^2 - x)^{-3}(2x - 1)$

3. Given that $y = (2x^3 - 5x + 10)^5$, then

   $y' = 5(2x^3 - 5x + 10)^4(6x^2 - 5)$

**Logarithmic Functions**

We reviewed the definition and use of logarithms in Chapter 2. Now we shall consider two general classes of logarithmic functions for purposes of differentiation.

RULE 9 (DERIVATIVE OF A LOGARITHMIC FUNCTION OF BASE $b$) Given that $y = \log_b u$, where $u = f(x)$, then (by the chain rule)

$$\frac{d(\log_b u)}{dx} = y' = \frac{dy}{du} \cdot \frac{du}{dx} = \frac{\log_b e}{u} \cdot \frac{du}{dx} = \frac{\log_b e}{u} \cdot u'(x)$$

*Proof* Given that $y = \log_b u$, then the difference quotient is

$$y' = \frac{d(\log_b u)}{du} = \lim_{\Delta x \to 0} \frac{\Delta y}{\Delta x} = \lim_{\Delta x \to 0} \frac{\log_b (u + \Delta x) - \log_b (u)}{\Delta x}$$

$$= \lim_{\Delta x \to 0} \frac{\log_b [(u + \Delta x)/u]}{\Delta x} = \lim_{\Delta x \to 0} \left[\frac{1}{\Delta x} \cdot \log_b \left(1 + \frac{\Delta x}{u}\right)\right]$$

$$= \lim_{\Delta x \to 0} \left[\frac{1}{u} \cdot \frac{u}{\Delta x} \cdot \log_b \left(1 + \frac{\Delta x}{u}\right)\right] = \lim_{\Delta x \to 0} \left[\frac{1}{u} \cdot \log_b \left(1 + \frac{\Delta x}{u}\right)^{u/\Delta x}\right]$$

$$= \frac{1}{u} \lim_{\Delta x \to 0} \left[\log_b \left(1 + \frac{\Delta x}{u}\right)^{u/\Delta x}\right]$$

If we set $\Delta x/u = n$, then $u/\Delta x = 1/n$, and, as $\Delta x \to 0$, $n \to 0$. Substituting, we have

$$y' = \lim_{\Delta x \to 0} \frac{\Delta y}{\Delta x} = \frac{1}{u} \cdot \lim_{\Delta n \to 0} \log_b (1 + n)^{1/n}$$

From Chapter 2, we know that $\lim_{\Delta n \to 0} (1 + n)^{1/n} = e$. Therefore

$$\frac{d}{du}(\log_b u) = \frac{1}{u} \cdot \log_b e$$

Substituting, we have

$$y' = \frac{dy}{dx} = \frac{\log_b e}{u} \cdot \frac{du}{dx}$$

EXAMPLES

1. Given that $y = \log_b x^2$, then

$$y' = \frac{\log_b e}{x^2}(2x) = \frac{2 \log_b e}{x}$$

2. Given that $y = \log_b x$, then

$$y' = \frac{\log_b e}{x}$$

3. Given that $y = \log_b (4x^2 + x)$, then

$$y' = \frac{\log_b e}{4x^2 + x}(8x + 1) = \frac{(8x + 1)\log_b e}{4x^2 + x}$$

RULE 10 (DERIVATIVE OF A LOGARITHMIC FUNCTION OF BASE $e$) Given that $y = \log_b u$, where $b = e$ and $u = f(x)$, then $y = \ln u$, and

$$\frac{f(\ln u)}{dx} = y' = \frac{1}{u} \cdot \frac{du}{dx} = \frac{1}{u} \cdot u'(x)$$

This rule is a special case of Rule 9.

*Proof* The proof of Rule 10 is analogous to that of Rule 9, and is left to you.

EXAMPLES

1. Given that $y = \ln x$, then

$$y' = \frac{1}{x}$$

2. Given that $y = \ln x^2$, then

$$y' = \left(\frac{1}{x^2}\right)(2x) = \frac{2}{x}$$

3. Given that $y = \ln (x^2 - 2x)$, then

$$y' = \frac{1}{x^2 - 2x} \cdot \frac{2x - 2}{1} = \frac{2(x - 1)}{x(x - 2)}$$

4. Given that $y = \ln [x(x^2 + 1)] = \ln x + \ln (x^2 + 1)$, then

$$y' = \frac{1}{x} + \frac{2x}{x^2 + 1}$$

5. Given that $y = \ln (x^2 + 1)^{1/2} = \frac{1}{2} \ln (x^2 + 1)$, then

$$y' = \frac{1}{2}\frac{1}{x^2 + 1} \cdot 2x = \frac{x}{x^2 + 1}$$

RULE 11 (DERIVATIVE OF A GENERAL EXPONENTIAL FUNCTION) Given that $y = a^u$, where $a > 0$, $a \neq 1$, and $u = f(x)$, then by the chain rule we have

$$\frac{d(a^u)}{dx} = y' = \frac{dy}{du} \cdot \frac{du}{dx} = a^u \ln a \frac{du}{dx}$$

*Proof* Given that $y = a^u$, then $\ln y = \ln a^u = u \ln a$ when both sides of the equation are stated in natural logarithms. Differentiating both sides, we have

$$\frac{d(\ln y)}{dx} = \left(\frac{du}{dx}\right) \ln a + u\left[\frac{d(\ln a)}{dx}\right]$$

$$\frac{1}{y}\frac{dy}{dx} = \frac{du}{dx} \cdot \ln a + 0 = \frac{du}{dx} \cdot \ln a$$

Therefore

$$\frac{dy}{dx} = y\frac{du}{dx} \ln a = a^u \cdot \ln a \cdot \frac{du}{dx}$$

■ You should be aware that you must take care in writing the derivatives of exponential chain functions. For example, assume that $y = a^{x^2}$; then $y' = a^{x^2}(\ln a)(2x)$; $y' \neq a^{x^2}(\ln 2xa)$. That is, the natural logarithm of some constant $a$ times $2x$ *is not equal to* the natural logarithm of the quantity $2xa$.

EXAMPLES

1. Given that $y = a^x$, then $y' = a^x \ln a$.
2. Given that $y = a^{x^2}$, then $y' = a^{x^2}(\ln a)(2x) = a^{x^2}(2x)(\ln a)$
3. Given that $y = 8^{-2x^3}$, then $y' = 8^{-2x^3}(\ln 8)(-6x^2)$.

RULE 12 (DERIVATIVE OF AN EXPONENTIAL FUNCTION OF BASE $e$) Given that $y = a^u$, where $a = e$ and $u = f(x)$, then

$$\frac{d(e^u)}{dx} = y' = e^u \cdot \ln e \cdot \frac{du}{dx} = e^u \cdot \frac{du}{dx}$$

This is a special case of Rule 11 where $a = e$ in the function $y = a^u$.

*Proof* The proof of Rule 12 is analogous to that of Rule 11, and is left to you.

EXAMPLES

1. Given that $y = e^x$, then $y' = e^x$.
2. Given that $y = e^{x^2}$, then $y' = e^{x^2}(2x)$.
3. Given that $y = e^{-2x^3}$, then $y' = e^{-2x^3}(-6x^2)$.

RULE 13 (DERIVATIVE OF AN EXPONENTIAL CHAIN FUNCTION) Given that $y = u^v$, where $u = f(x)$ and $v = g(x)$. Then by the chain rule we have

$$\frac{d(u^v)}{dx} = y' = u^v \cdot \ln u \cdot \frac{dv}{dx} + vu^{v-1} \cdot \frac{du}{dx}$$

*Proof* Given that $y = u^v$, then $\ln y = v \cdot \ln u$ and

$$\frac{d}{dx}(\ln y) = \left(\frac{dv}{dx}\right)\ln u + v\left[\frac{d(\ln u)}{dx}\right]$$

$$\frac{1}{y} \cdot \frac{dy}{dx} = \frac{dv}{dx} \cdot \ln u + v\left(\frac{1}{u}\right)\left(\frac{du}{dx}\right)$$

$$\frac{dy}{dx} = y\left(\frac{dv}{dx} \cdot \ln u + \frac{v}{u}\frac{du}{dx}\right) = u^v\left(\frac{dv}{dx} \cdot \ln u + vu^{-1}\frac{du}{dx}\right)$$

$$\frac{dy}{dx} = u^v \cdot \ln u \cdot \frac{dv}{dx} + vu^{v-1}\frac{du}{dx}$$

EXAMPLES

1. Given that $y = x^x$, then

   $y' = xx^{x-1} + x^x \cdot \ln x = x^x(1 + \ln x)$

   An alternative method of solving this problem involves stating both sides of the original equation in natural logarithms and then differentiating both sides.

   $$\ln y = x \ln x$$

   $$\frac{1}{y} \cdot \frac{dy}{dx} = \ln x + x\left(\frac{1}{x}\right) = \ln x + 1$$

   Therefore

   $$\frac{dy}{dx} = y(\ln x + 1) = x^x(\ln x + 1)$$

2. Given that $y = x^{x^5+5}$, then

   $y' = (x^5 + 5)x^{(x^5+5)-1} + x^{x^5+5}(\ln x)(5x^4)$

   Again, one may solve this problem by initially stating all terms in natural logarithms such that $\ln y = (x^5 + 5)\ln x$. Differentiating both sides, we have

   $$\frac{1}{y} \cdot \frac{dy}{dx} = 5x^4 \cdot \ln x + (x^5 + 5)\left(\frac{1}{x}\right)$$

   Therefore

   $$\frac{dy}{dx} = y\left(5x^4 \ln x + x^4 + \frac{5}{x}\right)$$

   $$\frac{dy}{dx} = \left[(5 \cdot \ln x + 1)x^4 + \frac{5}{x}\right]x^{x^5+5}$$

## Trigonometric Functions

Business and economic problems involving trigonometric functions are not as frequent as problems that involve the functions used in Rules 1 through 13. Therefore you may omit this section without loss of continuity with the remainder of the text. We present the rules for differentiating trigonometric functions primarily as a bow to completeness and also because you may need to resort to such rules in work elsewhere. We present the rules without proof.

RULE 14 (DERIVATIVES OF TRIGONOMETRIC FUNCTIONS) Assume that $u = f(x)$.

(a) Given that $y = \sin u$, then $$\frac{dy}{dx} = \cos u \frac{du}{dx}$$

(b) Given that $y = \cos u$, then $$\frac{dy}{dx} = -\sin u \frac{du}{dx}$$

(c) Given that $y = \tan u$, then $$\frac{dy}{dx} = \sec^2 u \frac{du}{dx}$$

(d) Given that $y = \cot u$, then $$\frac{dy}{dx} = -\csc^2 u \frac{du}{dx}$$

(e) Given that $y = \sec u$, then $$\frac{dy}{dx} = \sec u \tan u \frac{du}{dx}$$

(f) Given that $y = \csc u$, then $$\frac{dy}{dx} = -\csc u \cot u \frac{du}{dx}$$

EXAMPLES

1. Given that $y = \sin 8x$, then $y' = 8 \cos 8x$.
2. Given that $y = \tan (x^2/2)$, then

$$y' = \sec^2 \left(\frac{x^2}{2}\right)(x)$$

3. Given that $y = \sin x/\cos x$, then

$$y' = \frac{(\cos x)(\cos x) - (\sin x)(-\sin x)}{\cos^2 x}$$

$$= \frac{\cos^2 x + \sin^2 x}{\cos^2 x} = \frac{1}{\cos^2 x}$$

RULE 15 (DERIVATIVE OF AN INVERSE FUNCTION) Assume that the function $y = f(x)$ is strictly increasing and continuous on an interval $(a, b)$. If the function $y = f(x)$ is such that permissible values of $x$ always uniquely determine specific values of $y$, then the function $y = f(x)$ has an inverse function of the form $x = f^{-1}(y) = g(y)$. That is, the function $y = f(x)$ serves to define a new function $g$ whose value at each point $y$ is the number $x$ such that $y = f(x)$. This means that not only does a given value of $x$ yield a unique value of $y$ because $y = f(x)$, but also that a given value of $y$ yields a unique value of $x$ because $x = g(y)$. There is a one-to-one correspondence between $y$ and $x$.

THEOREM 4.2 Assume that $y = f(x)$ and $x = g(y)$ are inverse functions of each other. If the derivative $f'(x)$ exists and is nonzero at a point $x$ in the interval $[a, b]$, then the derivative $g'(y)$ also exists and is nonzero at the corresponding point $y$, where $y = f(x)$. Also the two derivatives are reciprocals of each other such that

$$g'(y) = \frac{1}{f'(x)} \qquad \text{and} \qquad \frac{dx}{dy} = \frac{1}{dy/dx}$$

*Proof of Theorem* Assume that point $x$ lies in the interval $[a, b]$ where $f'(x)$ exists and is nonzero, and further assume that $y = f(x)$. We want to show that the difference quotient $[g(y + \Delta y) - g(y)]/\Delta y$ approaches $1/f'(x)$ in the limit as $\Delta y \to 0$. Let $\Delta x = g(y + \Delta y) - g(y)$. Given that $x = g(y)$, we can write

$$\Delta x = g(y + \Delta y) - x \qquad \text{or} \qquad x + \Delta x = g(y + \Delta y)$$

Therefore

$$y + \Delta y = f(x + \Delta x) \qquad \text{and hence} \qquad \Delta y = f(x + \Delta x) - f(x)$$

Note that $\Delta x \neq 0$ if $\Delta y \neq 0$ because $g$ is strictly increasing (monotonically). Therefore, if $\Delta y \neq 0$, then the difference quotient is

$$\frac{g(y + \Delta y) - g(y)}{\Delta y} = \frac{\Delta x}{f(x + \Delta x) - f(x)} = \frac{1}{\dfrac{f(x + \Delta x) - f(x)}{\Delta x}}$$

As $\Delta y \to 0$, the difference $[g(y + \Delta y) - g(y)] \to 0$ because of the continuity of $g$ at $y$. This means that $\Delta x \to 0$ as $\Delta y \to 0$. But, as $\Delta x \to 0$, the difference quotient in the denominator of the expression

$$\frac{1}{\dfrac{f(x + \Delta x) - f(x)}{\Delta x}}$$

approaches $f'(x)$. Therefore, when $\Delta x \to 0$, the quotient

$$\frac{g(y + \Delta y) - g(y)}{\Delta y}$$

approaches the limit $1/f'(x)$.

■ Note that $x = f^{-1}(y)$ *is not equal to* $1/f(y)$.

■ If $f$ is not increasing (monotonic) in the interval $[a, b]$, then an inverse function *is not* uniquely determined.

EXAMPLES

1. Given that $y = 50 + x + x^2$ for $x > 0$, then

$$\frac{dy}{dx} = 1 + 2x \qquad \text{and} \qquad \frac{dx}{dy} = \frac{1}{dy/dx} = \frac{1}{1 + 2x}$$

2. Given that $y = x^3 + x + 3$, then

$$\frac{dy}{dx} = 3x^2 + 1 \qquad \text{and} \qquad \frac{dx}{dy} = \frac{1}{3x^2 + 1}$$

3. Given that $x = y + y^3 + y^5$, then

$$\frac{dx}{dy} = 1 + 3y^2 + 5y^4 \qquad \text{and} \qquad \frac{dy}{dx} = \frac{1}{1 + 3y^2 + 5y^4}$$

**EXERCISE 4.3**

Find $dy/dx$ for the following.

1. $y = u^2 + 3u + 7$ and $u = x^2 - 7$
2. $y = u^3 + 4,\ u = x^2 + 2x$
3. $y = u^2,\ u = \dfrac{1}{x^2}$
4. $y = u^{1/2},\ u = \dfrac{x^2 - 3}{x^2 + 4}$
5. $y = u^3 + 4,\ u = v^2 + 2v,\ v = x^2$
6. $y = (x^2 + 4)^2$
7. $y = (2x^3 + 1)^3$
8. $y = \sqrt{3x}$
9. $y = (4x^2 + x^4 - 1)^5$
10. $y = \left(\dfrac{x^2 - 1}{2x^2 + 1}\right)^3$
11. $y = \left(\dfrac{x}{1 + x}\right)^5$
12. $y = (x^2 + 3)^4(2x^3 - 5)^3$
13. $y = \log_a (x^2 + 1)$
14. $y = \log_b (x^2 + 1)^2$
15. $y = \log_b (2x^3 + 3x)$
16. $y = \ln x^2$
17. $y = \ln x$
18. $y = \ln (x^2 + 1)$
19. $y = \ln 3x^2$
20. $y = \ln (x^2 + x - 1)^3$
21. $y = \ln \left(\dfrac{1 + x^2}{x^2 - 1}\right)^2$
22. $y = \dfrac{\ln x}{x}$
23. $y = x \ln x$
24. $y = [\ln(x^2 + 4)]^2$
25. $y = \ln \left(\dfrac{1}{x}\right)$
26. $y = x^2 \ln x^2$
27. $y = [\ln (x^2 + 2)](x^3 + 3)$
28. $y = a^x x^a$
29. $y = a^{x2 + 1}$
30. $y = 3^{x-2}$
31. $y = e^x$
32. $y = a^x e^x$

33. $y = e^{\ln x^2}$

34. $y = e^{ex}$

35. $y = e^x \ln x$

36. $y = \dfrac{e^x + e^{-x}}{e^x - e^{-x}}$

37. $y = x^2 e^{x^2 + 4x + 2}$

38. $y = e^{-x^2/2}$

39. $y = \dfrac{1}{\sigma\sqrt{2\pi}} e^{-(1/2)x^2}$

40. $y = x^{ex}$

41. $y = x^{2x^4 + x}$

42. $y = x^{x^5}$

43. $y = \sin kx$, where $k$ is a constant

44. $y = \dfrac{\sin x^2}{x}$

45. $y = -12 \cos 3x^2$

46. $y = \tan 6x$

47. $y = 8 \cot \dfrac{x}{4}$

48. $y = \frac{1}{3} \sec 9x$

49. $y = \frac{1}{4} \csc 2x$

50. $y = \tan 4x^2$

51. $y = x^2 \sec x$

52. $y = \tan x \sin x$

53. $y = e^x \cos x$

54. $y = \dfrac{\csc x^2}{x^2}$

55. $y = x^2 = \cot x$

56. Find $\dfrac{dy}{dx}$, when $x = (1 + 2y)^3$

57. Find $\dfrac{dy}{dx}$, when $x = \dfrac{\ln 4}{y}$

58. Find $\dfrac{dy}{dx}$, when $x = y^3$

59. Find $\dfrac{dy}{dx}$, when $x = 12y^2 + 8y + 1$

60. Find $\dfrac{dx}{dy}$, when $y = \frac{1}{3}x^3 + 6x$

## SUMMARY OF RULES OF DIFFERENTIATION

RULE 1 (DERIVATIVE OF A CONSTANT) Given that $y = f(x) = k$, where $k$ is a constant, then

$$\frac{d[f(x)]}{dx} = y' = f'(x) = 0$$

RULE 2 (DERIVATIVE OF A POWER) Given that $y = f(x) = x^n$, where $n$ is any real number, then

$$\frac{d[f(x)]}{dx} = y' = f'(x) = nx^{n-1}$$

RULE 3 (DERIVATIVE OF A CONSTANT TIMES A FUNCTION) Given that $y = kf(x)$, then

$$\frac{d[kf(x)]}{dx} = y' = k \cdot f'(x)$$

RULE 4 (DERIVATIVE OF A SUM OR DIFFERENCE) Given that $y = f(x) \pm g(x)$, then

$$\frac{d[f(x) \pm g(x)]}{dx} = y' = f'(x) \pm g'(x)$$

RULE 5 (DERIVATIVE OF A PRODUCT) Given that $y = f(x) \cdot g(x)$, then

$$\frac{d[f(x) \cdot g(x)]}{dx} = y' = f'(x) \cdot g(x) + f(x) \cdot g'(x)$$

RULE 6 (DERIVATIVE OF A QUOTIENT) Given that $y = f(x)/g(x)$, then

$$\frac{d[f(x)/g(x)]}{dx} = y' = \frac{f'(x) \cdot g(x) - f(x) \cdot g'(x)}{[g(x)]^2}$$

RULE 7 (DERIVATIVE OF A FUNCTION OF A FUNCTION) Given that $y = f(u)$ and $u = g(x)$ such that $y = f[g(x)]$, then

$$\frac{d[f(g(x))]}{dx} = y' = \frac{dy}{du} \cdot \frac{du}{dx} = f'(u)g'(x)$$

RULE 8 (DERIVATIVE OF A CHAIN WITH AN EXPONENT) Given that $y = [u(x)]^n$, where $n$ is any real number, then

$$\frac{d[u(x)^n]}{dx} = y' = nu^{n-1}\frac{du}{dx} = nu^{n-1}u'(x)$$

RULE 9 (DERIVATIVE OF A LOGARITHMIC FUNCTION OF BASE $b$) Given that $y = \log_b u$, where $u = f(x)$, then

$$\frac{d(\log_b u)}{dx} = y' = \frac{\log_b e}{u}\frac{du}{dx} = \frac{\log_b e}{u}u'(x)$$

RULE 10 (DERIVATIVE OF A LOGARITHMIC FUNCTION OF BASE $e$) Given that $y = \log_b u$, where $b = e$ and $u = f(x)$, then $y = \ln u$ and

$$\frac{d(\ln u)}{dx} = y' = \frac{1}{u} \cdot \frac{du}{dx} = \frac{1}{u} \cdot u'(x)$$

RULE 11 (DERIVATIVE OF A GENERAL EXPONENTIAL FUNCTION) Given that $y = a^u$, where $a > 0$, $a \neq 1$, and $u = f(x)$, then

$$\frac{d(a^u)}{dx} = y' = \frac{dy}{du} \cdot \frac{du}{dx} = a^u \cdot \ln a \cdot u'(x)$$

RULE 12 (DERIVATIVE OF AN EXPONENTIAL FUNCTION OF BASE $e$) Given that $y = e^u$, where $u = f(x)$, then

$$\frac{d(e^u)}{dx} = y' = \frac{dy}{du} \cdot \frac{du}{dx} = e^u \cdot \ln e \cdot u'(x) = e^u \cdot u'(x)$$

RULE 13 (DERIVATIVE OF AN EXPONENTIAL CHAIN FUNCTION) Given that $y = u^v$, where $u = f(x)$ and $v = g(x)$, then

$$\frac{d(u^v)}{dx} = y' = u^v \cdot \ln u \cdot \frac{dv}{dx} + vu^{v-1} \cdot \frac{du}{dx}$$

$$= u^v \cdot \ln u \cdot v'(x) + vu^{v-1} \cdot u'(x)$$

RULE 14 (DERIVATIVES OF TRIGONOMETRIC FUNCTIONS) Given that $u = f(x)$.

(a) Given that $y = \sin u$, then

$$\frac{d(\sin u)}{dx} = y' = \cos u \cdot \frac{du}{dx} = \cos u \cdot u'(x)$$

(b) Given that $y = \cos u$, then

$$\frac{d(\cos u)}{dx} = y' = -\sin u \cdot \frac{du}{dx} = -\sin u \cdot u'(x)$$

(c) Given that $y = \tan u$, then

$$\frac{d(\tan u)}{dx} = y' = \sec^2 u \cdot \frac{du}{dx} = \sec^2 u \cdot u'(x)$$

(d) Given that $y = \cot u$, then

$$\frac{d(\cot u)}{dx} = y' = -\csc^2 u \cdot \frac{du}{dx} = -\csc^2 u \cdot u'(x)$$

(e) Given that $y = \sec u$, then

$$\frac{d(\sec u)}{dx} = y' = \sec u \cdot \tan u \cdot \frac{du}{dx} = \sec u \cdot \tan u \cdot u'(x)$$

(f) Given that $y = \csc u$, then

$$\frac{d(\csc u)}{dx} = y' = -\csc u \cdot \cot u \cdot \frac{du}{dx} = -\csc u \cdot \cot u \cdot u'(x)$$

RULE 15 (DERIVATIVE OF AN INVERSE FUNCTION) Given that $y = f(x)$ and

$x = g(y)$ are inverse functions of each other, then the derivatives $f'(x)$ and $g'(y)$ exist and are reciprocals of each other, such that

$$g'(y) = \frac{1}{f'(x)} \qquad \text{and} \qquad f'(x) = \frac{dy}{dx} \qquad \text{where } \frac{1}{dy/dx} = \frac{dx}{dy}$$

## HIGHER-ORDER DERIVATIVES

Not all functions have derivatives. However, we have seen that many functions of the form $y = f(x)$ have derivatives, which we symbolized by $f'(x)$. It is frequently the case that $f'(x)$, which we can also regard as a function, has its own derivative. This "derivative of a derivative" is referred to as a *second derivative* and is symbolized by $f''(x)$, $y''$, $d^2y/dx^2$, or $D_x^2(y)$.

DEFINITION The second derivative of $y = f(x)$ with respect to $x$ is given by

$$\lim_{\Delta x \to 0} \frac{f'(x + \Delta x) - f'(x)}{\Delta x}$$

provided that $f'(x)$ is smooth and continuous.

The derivative of the function that constitutes the second derivative is referred to as the *third derivative*, and so forth. Often, however, the value of a higher derivative is 0. Assume that $y = f(x) = 3x^2$. Then $y' = 6x$; $y'' = 6$; and $y''' = 0$.

▣ The fact that a higher-order derivative of a function assumes the value of 0 does not mean that the higher-order derivative "does not exist." It merely means that the value of the higher-order derivative is 0.

EXAMPLES

1. Given that $y = x^2 + x^3$, then $y' = 2x + 3x^2$, $y'' = 2 + 6x$, $y''' = 6$, and $y'''' = 0$.
2. Given that $y = e^x$, then $y' = e^x$, $y'' = e^x$, and so forth.
3. Given that $y = (x^3 + 2x^2)^3$, then

$$y' = 3(x^3 + 2x^2)^2(3x^2 + 4x)$$

$$y'' = 6(x^3 + 2x^2)(3x^2 + 4x)(3x^2 + 4x) + 3(x^3 + 2x^2)^2(6x + 4)$$

$$= 6(x^3 + 2x^2)(3x^2 + 4x)^2 + 3(x^3 + 2x^2)^2(6x + 4)$$

▣ You should be aware that the $n$th derivative of $y$ with respect to $x$ does not equal the first derivative of $y$ with respect to $x$ taken to the $n$th power. That is,

$$D_x^n(y) \neq [D_x(y)]^n$$

## INTUITIVE MEANING OF THE SECOND DERIVATIVE

The second derivative $y''$ measures the rate of change of the first derivative with respect to small changes in $x$. That is, the second derivative measures the "rate of change of the rate of change" of the primary function $y = f(x)$. An example of the "rate of change of the rate of change" is acceleration. The acceleration of an automobile, the acceleration of population growth, and the deceleration of the rate of business failures are all phenomena that we can represent by a second derivative. Second derivatives are also useful in describing the convexity and concavity of functions in graphical analysis, as we shall see in Chapter 6.

## IMPLICIT DIFFERENTIATION

Functions of the form $y = f(x)$, which express $y$ explicitly in terms of $x$, can be differentiated according to the rules stated earlier in this chapter. However, there are other types of functions, known as *implicit functions*, where $f(x, y) = 0$. Such an equation is said to define variable $y$ implicitly as a function of variable $x$ instead of the explicit formulation $y = f(x)$. The process of obtaining the derivative $dy/dx$ from the equation $f(x, y) = 0$ is referred to as *implicit differentiation*. We find the derivative $dy/dx$ in such a case by treating $y$ as an unknown but nonetheless differentiable function of $x$, then differentiating each term of the equation using the rules developed earlier in this chapter.

For example, assume that $f(x, y) = r^2 = x^2 + y^2$. We shall treat the variable $y$ as a differentiable function of variable $x$. Therefore $x^2 + [f(x)]^2 = r^2$. We now differentiate each term in the previous expression with respect to $x$.

$$\frac{d(x^2)}{dx} + \frac{d[f(x)]^2}{dx} = \frac{d(r^2)}{dx}$$

Since $y = f(x)$ by assumption, the term $y^2$ in the original equation is of the form $u^n$. This implies that

$$\frac{d(y^2)}{dx} = 2y\frac{d(y)}{dx} = 2yy'$$

Hence we can write

$$\frac{d(x^2)}{dx} + \frac{d(y^2)}{dx} = 2x + 2yy' = 0$$

Solving for $y'$, which is our final goal, we get

$$y' = -\left(\frac{x}{y}\right)$$

EXAMPLES

1. $xy = 8, \qquad xy - 8 = 0$

   Taking the first derivative with respect to $x$, we have

   $$y + xy' = 0, \qquad xy' = -y, \qquad y' = -\left(\frac{y}{x}\right)$$

2. $x^2 + y^2 = 16, \qquad 2x + 2yy' = 0,$

$$2yy' = -2x, \qquad y' = -\left(\frac{x}{y}\right)$$

3. $xy - y + 4x = 0, \qquad y + xy' - y' + 4 = 0$

$$(x-1)y' = -(y+4), \qquad y' = -\left(\frac{y+4}{x-1}\right)$$

A more lengthy example of the use of implicit functions in economic theory is contained in a typical utility function of the form $U = U(x, y)$, where $U$ is utility and $x$ and $y$ are goods. An *indifference curve* (an isoutility curve) is given by $U(x, y) = k$, where $k$ is a constant. Differentiating $U(x, y)$ with respect to $x$, we obtain

$$\frac{dU}{dx} + \frac{dU}{dy}\frac{dy}{dx} = \frac{dk}{dx}$$

Hence,

$$U_x + U_y\frac{dy}{dx} = 0 \qquad \text{where } U_x = \frac{dU}{dx} \qquad \text{and} \qquad U_y = \frac{dU}{dy}$$

It follows that

$$-\frac{dy}{dx} = \frac{U_x}{U_y}$$

The negative of the derivative $dy/dx$ is the marginal rate of substitution (MRS) of good $x$ for good $y$.

$$\text{MRS}_{x\text{ for }y} = -\frac{dy}{dx} = \frac{U_x}{U_y}$$

where we can interpret $U_x$ and $U_y$ as the marginal utility of $x$ and $y$, respectively.

The *theory of consumer choice* in economic theory deals with the attempts of individual consumers to maximize their utility, given the incomes that they have to spend and the prices that they face. The combination of goods and services that is utility-maximizing is given by the condition that requires the slope of the consumer's indifference curve to be the same as the slope of the consumer's budget line. In a two-good world, we can write the equation of the consumer's budget line as

$$M = x(P_x) + y(P_y)$$

where $M$ is the consumer's income, $x$ and $y$ are goods, and $P_x$ and $P_y$ are the parametric prices of the goods. This budget equation can be written with good $y$ as the dependent variable:

$$y = \frac{M}{P_y} - \frac{P_x}{P_y}(x)$$

The slope of the budget line is therefore $-P_x/P_y$.

Since the utility-maximizing condition for the consumer requires that the slope of the budget line $-P_x/P_y$ be equal to the slope of the most desirable indifference curve the consumer can attain, we can write the utility-maximizing condition as

$$\frac{dy}{dx} = -\frac{P_x}{P_y}$$

Finally, because

$$\frac{dy}{dx} = -\frac{U_x}{U_y}$$

we can express the equilibrium position of the consumer in terms of maximizing utility as

$$\text{MRS}_{x \text{ for } y} = -\frac{dy}{dx} = \frac{P_x}{P_y} = \frac{U_x}{U_y} \text{ or } \frac{U_y}{P_y} = \frac{U_x}{P_x}$$

**EXERCISE 4.4**

1. $y = 8x^3$; find $y'''$
2. $y = x^{1/2}$; find $y''$
3. $y = x^4 + x^2 + 1$; find $y^5$
4. $y = e^x$; find $y^n$
5. $y = \ln x$; find $y^n$
6. $xy - x + 2y = 1$; find $dy/dx$
7. $x^2 + y^2 - 49 = 0$; find $dy/dx$
8. $x^2 - xy + y^2 = 1000$; find $dy/dx$
9. $x^2y = 6$; find $dy/dx$
10. $e^x + e^y + e^{xy} = 10$; find $dy/dx$
11. $\ln xy + xy = 4$; find $dy/dx$

## APPLICATIONS OF THE DERIVATIVE IN BUSINESS AND ECONOMICS

The concept of a derivative is useful in a wide range of business and economic problems. The following examples are designed to give you facility in using the derivative in concrete situations.

### The Costs of Production

*Total cost* is defined as the sum of fixed cost plus variable cost at a given level of output. Let the total cost function $\text{TC} = k + g(Q)$, where $k$ is *total fixed cost* (TFC) and $g(Q)$ represents the *total variable cost* (TVC) associated with each level of output $Q$. We have the equation[2]

$$\text{TFC} + \text{TVC} = \text{TC}$$

[2] The derivatives of total cost and variable cost with respect to quantity are identical, since fixed cost vanishes upon differentiation. That is,

$$\frac{d\text{TC}}{dQ} = \frac{d\text{TFC}}{dQ} + \frac{d\text{TVC}}{dQ} = g'(Q)$$

*Average fixed cost* (AFC) is defined as

$$\frac{\text{TFC}}{Q} = \frac{k}{Q}$$

and the slope of the AFC function is given by

$$\frac{d(k/Q)}{dQ} = -\frac{k}{Q^2}$$

*Average variable cost* (AVC) is defined as

$$\frac{\text{TVC}}{Q} = \frac{g(Q)}{Q}$$

and the slope of the AVC function is given by

$$\frac{d[g(Q)/Q]}{dQ} = \frac{g'(Q)(Q) - g(Q)}{Q^2} = \frac{1}{Q}\left[g'(Q) - \frac{g(Q)}{Q}\right]$$

*Average total cost* (ATC) is the sum of AFC + AVC and is equal to TC/$Q$. The slope of the ATC function is given by

$$\frac{d\dfrac{k + g(Q)}{Q}}{dQ} = \frac{Q[g'(Q)] - [k + g(Q)](1)}{Q^2} = \frac{-k}{Q^2} + \frac{1}{Q}\left[g'(Q) - \frac{g(Q)}{Q}\right]$$

For infinitesimally small changes in output, *marginal cost* (MC) is defined as the addition to TC that results from the production of additional units of output $Q$.

$$\text{MC} = \frac{d(\text{TC})}{dQ} = \frac{d[k + g(Q)]}{dQ} = g'(Q)$$

The slope of the MC function is given by

$$\frac{d(\text{MC})}{dQ} = \frac{d^2(\text{TC})}{dQ^2} = g''(Q)$$

Referring back to AVC, we see that the slope of the AVC curve was given by

$$\frac{1}{Q}\left[g'(Q) - \frac{g(Q)}{Q}\right]$$

We can now restate this as

$$\frac{1}{Q}[\text{MC} - \text{AVC}]$$

We shall give more attention to the relationship among TC, AVC, AFC, and MC (and their slopes) in Chapter 6 when we discuss the extreme points of functions.

EXAMPLE Figure 4.1 depicts a set of cost curves for a representative firm. The equations of these cost curves are as follows: $TC = 100 + 25Q - 5Q^2 + Q^3$. Hence $TVC = 25Q - 5Q^2 + Q^3$ and TFC = the additive constant 100. AVC is

$$\frac{TVC}{Q} = \frac{25Q - 5Q^2 + Q^3}{Q} = 25 - 5Q + Q^2$$

Figure 4.1 Equations and slopes of the cost curves of the representative firm. (a) Total cost, total variable cost, and total fixed cost. (b) Average cost, average variable cost, and marginal cost

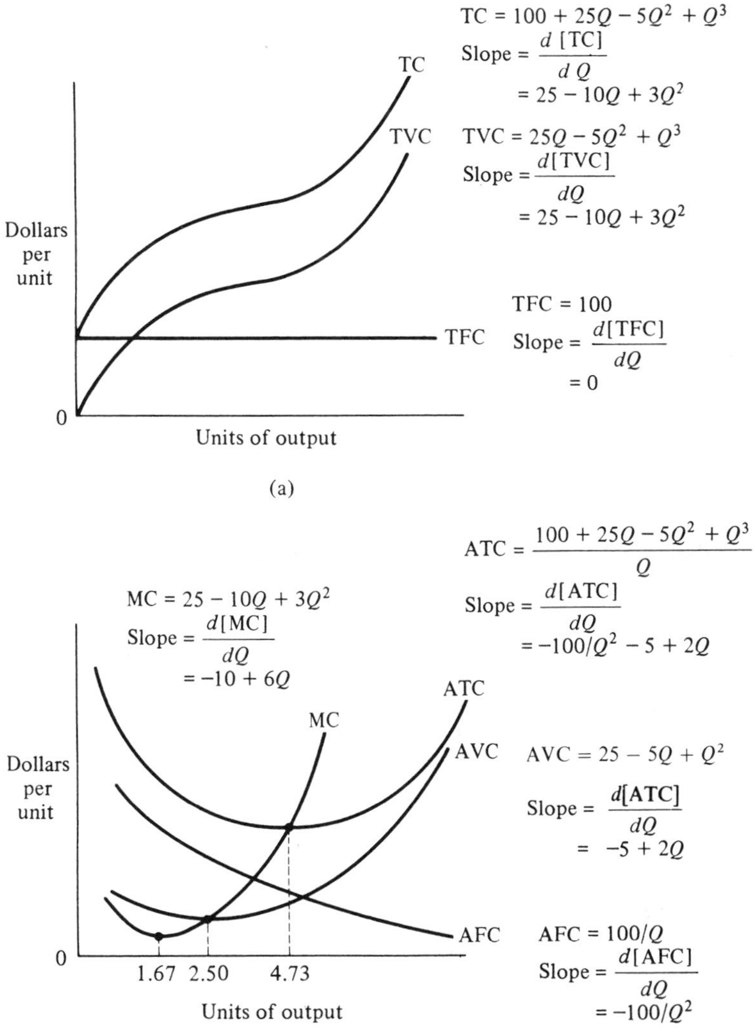

The slope of the AVC function is given by

$$\frac{d(\text{AVC})}{dQ} = \frac{d(25 - 5Q + Q^2)}{dQ} = -5 + 2Q$$

AFC is

$$\frac{\text{TFC}}{Q} = \frac{100}{Q}$$

and the slope of the AFC function is given by

$$\frac{d(100/Q)}{dQ} = -\frac{100}{Q^2}$$

ATC is

$$\frac{\text{TC}}{Q} = \frac{100 + 25Q - 5Q^2 + Q^3}{Q} = \frac{100}{Q} + 25 - 5Q + Q^2$$

and the slope of the ATC function is

$$\frac{d(\text{ATC})}{dQ} = \frac{-100}{Q^2} - 5 + 2Q$$

MC is

$$\frac{d(\text{TC})}{dQ} = 25 - 10Q + 3Q^2$$

and the slope of the MC function is given by

$$\frac{d(\text{MC})}{dQ} = \frac{d^2(\text{TC})}{dQ^2} = -10 + 6Q$$

Each of these functions is graphed in Figure 4.1, which also notes the slopes of the functions.

**Demand and Revenue**

Let $P$ be price per unit and $Q$ be quantity demanded such that the demand function (in inverse form) $P = f(Q)$ exists for a representative consumer. *Total sales revenue* (TR) realized by the firm that sells to this consumer is equal to $P \cdot Q = f(Q) \cdot Q$. The average revenue the firm realizes on sales to the consumer is

$$\frac{\text{TR}}{Q} = \frac{f(Q) \cdot Q}{Q} = f(Q) = P$$

We can see that average revenue and price are synonymous.

The *marginal revenue* (MR) the firm realizes on the sale of an extra unit to the consumer is

$$\frac{d(\text{TR})}{dQ} = \frac{d[f(Q) \cdot Q]}{dQ} = f(Q) + Q \cdot f'(Q)$$

If the demand curve of the consumer is downward-sloping, then

$$\frac{dP}{dQ} = f'(Q) < 0$$

EXAMPLE Assume that $P = f(Q) = a - bQ$, where $a$ and $b$ are constants and $a, b > 0$. The total revenue function is $\text{TR} = P \cdot Q = aQ - bQ^2$. Hence

$$\text{AR} = \frac{\text{TR}}{Q} = \frac{aQ - bQ^2}{Q} = a - bQ = P,$$

$$\text{MR} = \frac{d[\text{TR}]}{dQ} = \frac{d[aQ - bQ^2]}{dQ} = a - 2bQ$$

The slope of the MR function is therefore $-2b$, which is twice the slope of the demand function.

Figure 4.2 illustrates demand and MR functions for the case in which $P = a - bQ$. Note that both the demand (AR) function and the MR function have the same intercept on the ordinate, namely, the constant $a$. The slope of the AR function, however, is $-b$, while the slope of the MR function is $-2b$. Hence the MR function falls twice as fast as the AR function. Since both the AR function and the MR function are linear and they both have the same ordinate intercept, it follows that the MR function bisects the distance between the origin and the abscissa intercept of the demand function. That is, the MR function bisects the distance $OX$ in Figure 4.2.

EXAMPLE In this example, we assume a demand function of the form $P = a - bQ$ as in the previous example. Assume that $P = 25 - Q$.

$$\text{TR} = P \cdot Q = (25 - Q)(Q) = 25Q - Q^2$$

Figure 4.2 Demand and marginal revenue curves: linear case

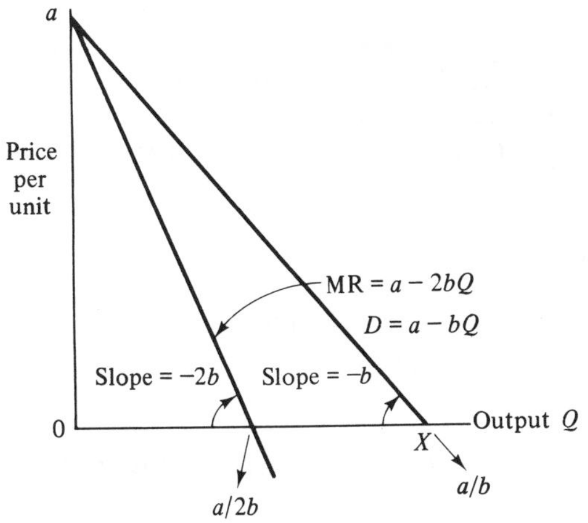

Hence

$$\text{AR} = \frac{25Q - Q^2}{Q} = 25 - Q = \text{P},$$

$$\text{MR} = \frac{d(\text{TR})}{dQ} = \frac{d(25Q - Q^2)}{dQ} = 25 - 2Q$$

The slope of the MR function is

$$\frac{d(25 - 2Q)}{dQ} = -2$$

Both the demand function and the MR function are linear and both have ordinate intercepts of 25. However, the MR function has a slope of $-2$, while the demand function has a slope of $-1$. Hence the MR function bisects the distance between the origin and the abcissa intercept of the demand function.

▣ The MR function does not in general bisect the distance between the origin and the $x$ intercept of the demand curve unless the demand function is linear. For example, assume that $P = 50 - 10Q - Q^2$, a quadratic. Then

$$\text{TR} = (50 - 10Q - Q^2)(Q) = 50Q - 10Q^2 - Q^3,$$

$$\text{MR} = \frac{d(\text{TR})}{dQ} = 50 - 20Q - 3Q^2$$

Note that both the demand function and the MR function are nonlinear in this case, and that they both have the same ordinate intercepts. However, the slope of the demand (average revenue) function is $d(\text{AR})/dQ = -10 - 2Q$, whereas the slope of the MR function is $d(\text{MR})/dQ = -20 - 6Q$. Not only are the slopes not the same, but the absolute value of the slope of the MR function is *not* twice the absolute value of the slope of the AR function, as in the linear case.

### Population

Assume that the population of an area in time $t$ is growing at an exponential rate such that $P(t) = P(o)e^{rt}$, where $P(t)$ = population in time $t$, $P(o)$ = population in time $o$, $r$ = the instantaneous rate of growth, and $t$ = time. Thus $P(t)$ is given for each point of time $t$, and the rate of change of $P(t)$ with respect to time is given by

$$\frac{dP(t)}{dt} = rP(o)e^{rt} = rP(t)$$

The *rate of growth* of $P(t)$ per time period is given by

$$\frac{dP(t)/dt}{P(t)} = rP(t)/P(t) = r$$

$r$ is interpreted as the rate of change of $P(t)$ expressed in percentage or relative terms.

Consider the following empirical example. In 1960, the population of the United States was 179.3 million people. The rate of growth of the population was $P(t) = 179.3e^{1.71t}$, where $t$ denotes time in years. The rate of change of $P(t)$ with respect to $t$ is

$$\frac{dP(t)}{dt} = 1.71(179.3e^{1.71}) = 1.71P(t)$$

The rate of growth of population $P(t)$ was

$$\frac{dP(t)/dt}{P(t)} = \frac{1.71P(t)}{P(t)} = 1.71$$

**Elasticities**

DEFINITION Given the function $y = f(x)$, the elasticity of $y$ with respect to $x$ for a given value of $x$ is defined as the percentage change in $y$ brought about by a percentage change in $x$. That is, $\eta_{yx}$, the elasticity of $y$ with respect to $x$, is equal to

$$\frac{dy}{dx} \cdot \frac{x}{y}$$

We can compute elasticities by using natural logarithms. Rule 10 concerning differentiation tells us that if $y = f(x)$, then

$$\frac{1}{y} \cdot \frac{dy}{dx} = f'(x)$$

when both sides of the original equation are stated in terms of natural logarithms and differentiated. That is,

$$\frac{d(\ln y)}{dx} = \frac{1}{y} \cdot \frac{dy}{dx}$$

Hence we can write

$$\frac{d(\ln y)/dx}{d(\ln x)/dx} = \frac{(1/y) \cdot (dy/dx)}{(1/x) \cdot (dx/dx)} = \frac{dy}{dx} \cdot \frac{x}{y} = \eta_{yx}$$

Assume a demand function of the form $Q = 50 - 10P - P^2$. When $P = \$2$ per unit, then $Q = 50 - 20 - 4 = 26$ units, and $dQ/dP = -10 - 2P = -10 - 2(2) = -14$. Therefore $\eta_{QP}$ at $P = \$2$ per unit is

$$\frac{dQ}{dP} \cdot \frac{P}{Q} = (-14)\left(\frac{2}{26}\right) = -1.076$$

That is, price elasticity of demand when price is \$2 per unit is $-1.076$.

Not all demand functions are quadratic in form as the previous one was. Given the demand function $Q = 50/P^k$, where $k$ is a constant,

$$\frac{dQ}{dP} = \frac{-(k)50}{P^{k+1}} \qquad \eta_{QP} = \frac{dQ}{dP} \cdot \frac{P}{Q} = \frac{-50(k)}{P^{k+1}} \cdot \frac{P}{Q} = \frac{-50(k)}{p^k(Q)}$$

The demand function itself tells us that $Q = 50/P^k$. Substituting this value into the right-hand side of the equation

$$\eta_{QP} = -k50p^{-k-1} \cdot \frac{P}{Q}, \qquad \text{we have} \qquad \eta_{QP} = \frac{-Q(k)}{Q} = -k$$

That is, price elasticity of demand is equal to $-k$. For example, if $Q = 50/P^1$, then price elasticity of demand $= -1.00$. The expression $Q = C/P^k$, where $C$ and $k$ are constants and $C > 0$, is a general form for a "constant price elasticity of demand" demand function. Price elasticity of demand $= -k$ at every point on the demand curve.

▣ The price elasticity of demand of every downward-sloping demand curve is negative in sign. You should be aware that the absolute value of price elasticity of demand (a positive number) is sometimes used in economic analysis. The use of an absolute-value measure of price elasticity of demand does *not* imply that the demand curve is upward-sloping.

**Demand, Revenue, and Price Elasticity**

Given a demand function of the form $P = f(Q)$, where $dP/dQ < 0$. Therefore the demand curve is downward-sloping. Total revenue is given by $\text{TR} = P \cdot Q = f(Q) \cdot Q$. Marginal revenue

$$\text{MR} = \frac{d(\text{TR})}{dQ} = \frac{d[f(Q) \cdot Q]}{dQ} = f(Q) + Qf'(Q) = f(Q) + Q\left(\frac{dP}{dQ}\right)$$

Since $P = f(Q)$, we can write

$$\text{MR} = P + Q\left(\frac{dP}{dQ}\right) = P\left[1 + \frac{Q}{P}\left(\frac{dP}{dQ}\right)\right]$$

Since

$$\eta_{QP} = \frac{dQ}{dP} \cdot \frac{P}{Q} \qquad \text{then} \qquad \frac{1}{\eta_{QP}} = \frac{dP}{dQ} \cdot \frac{Q}{P}$$

Substituting this latter value into the previous equation, we have

$$\text{MR} = P\left(1 + \frac{1}{\eta}\right) \qquad \text{where } \eta = \eta_{QP}$$

The equation $\text{MR} = P(1 + 1/\eta)$ is extremely useful. You can use it in studies as diverse as the measurement of monopoly power of firms, the measurement of sexual and racial discrimination, and the measurement of price flexibility. There are three unknowns (MR, $P$, and $\eta$) in the equation. Given values for any two of these unknowns, we can compute a value for the third.

Lerner[3] and others have suggested the $\text{MR} = P(1 + 1/\eta)$ equation as a

[3] Abba P. Lerner, "The Concept of Monopoly and the Measurement of Monopoly Power," *Review of Economic Studies*, 1 (June 1934), 157–175.

measure of the monopoly power of firms.[4] The *Lerner index of monopoly power* $I$ is equal to $(P - \text{MC})/P$ and is derived as follows:

1. $\text{MR} = P\left(1 + \frac{1}{\eta}\right)$
2. $\text{MC} = P\left(1 + \frac{1}{\eta}\right)$ Assume profit maximization.
3. $\text{MC} = P + \frac{P}{\eta}$ Clear parentheses on right side.
4. $\text{MC} - P = \frac{P}{\eta}$ Subtract $P$ from both sides.
5. $\frac{\text{MC} - P}{P} = \frac{1}{\eta}$ Divide both sides by $P$.
6. $\frac{P - \text{MC}}{P} = -\frac{1}{\eta}$ Multiply both sides by $-1$.

It is interesting to note that the Lerner index is equal to the negative of the reciprocal of price elasticity of demand. Several studies have estimated the Lerner index empirically in a wide range of industries.[5] The index is generally highest in industries in which there are barriers to entry that prevent new firms from entering the industry to compete with existing firms.

The notion of price elasticity of demand is intimately related to MR and TR. Assume a demand function of the form $P = 50 - 0.7Q$. Total revenue $\text{TR} = P \cdot Q = 50Q - 0.7Q^2$. [Figure 4.3 illustrates both the demand function $P = 50 - 0.7(Q)$ and the total revenue function $\text{TR} = 50Q - 0.7Q^2$.] Marginal revenue $\text{MR} = d(\text{TR})/dQ = 50 - 1.4Q$. Setting $\text{MR} = 0$, we have $50 - 1.4Q = 0$, and $Q$ is therefore equal to 35.7 when $\text{MR} = 0$. Figure 4.3(a) demonstrates this fact. Note also that the TR function in Figure 4.3(b) is at its maximum at \$892 when $Q = 35.7$.

Generalizing the relationship between MR and TR illustrated in Figure 4.3, we see that TR is rising whenever $\text{MR} > 0$. Total revenue is neither rising nor falling when $\text{MR} = 0$. Total revenue is falling whenever $\text{MR} < 0$. This information is intuitively sensible, since the slope of the TR function is $d(\text{TR})/dQ = \text{MR}$.

The connection between MR, TR, and $\eta$ (the coefficient of price elasticity of demand) is the following: When price is decreasing and $\text{MR} > 0$, TR is rising, and demand is elastic with respect to price changes. For example, price elasticity of demand at point $X$ on the demand curve in Figure 4.3(b) is

$$\eta = \frac{dQ}{dP} \cdot \frac{P}{Q} = \left(\frac{1}{dP/dQ}\right)\frac{P}{Q} = -1.42\left(\frac{P}{Q}\right)$$

[4] The term *monopoly power* here means the power of the firm to price its product above the marginal cost of producing that product.

[5] See, among many, David R. Kamerschen, "An Estimation of the Welfare Losses in the American Economy," *Western Economic Journal*, 4 (Summer 1966), 221–236.

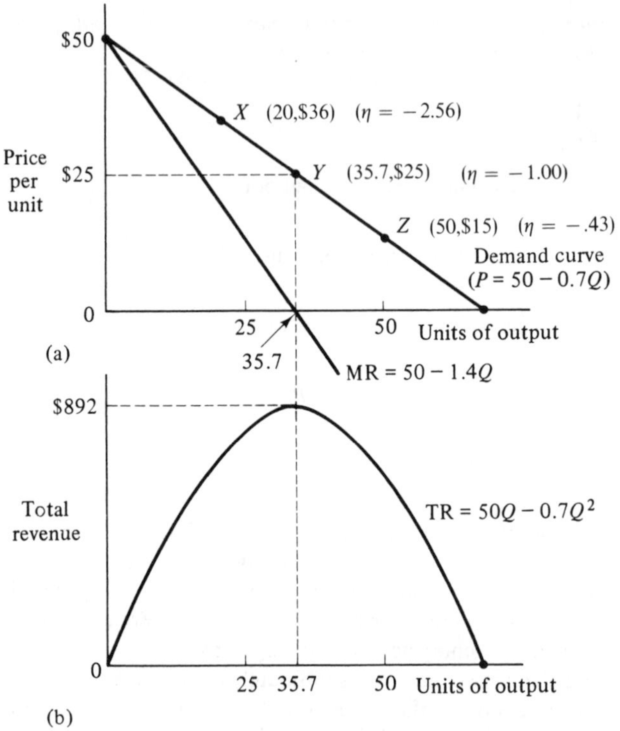


Figure 4.3 Total revenue, marginal revenue, and price elasticity of demand: the case of price reductions. (a) Demand curve, marginal revenue curve. (b) Total revenue curve

Since point $X$ is given by $P = \$36$ and $Q = 20$,

$$\eta = -1.42(\tfrac{36}{20}) = -2.56$$

Definitionally, demand is price elastic in nature when $\eta < -1.00$, since this indicates that a given percentage change in $P$ evokes a greater percentage change in $Q$ of the opposite sign. In the case at hand, a decrease in price of 10% would cause an increase in quantity demanded of 25.6%.

Similarly, demand at point $Z$ on the demand curve in Figure 4.3(a) is price inelastic.

$$\eta = -1.42(\tfrac{15}{50}) = -0.43$$

Demand is said to be price inelastic when $-1 < \eta < 0$; MR $< 0$ when demand is price inelastic and price is decreased.

Finally, demand is unit elastic ($\eta = -1.00$) at point $Y$, where MR $= 0$.

$$\eta = -1.42\left(\frac{25.0}{35.7}\right) = -1.00$$

Figure 4.3 and Table 4.1 summarize our findings with respect to MR, TR, and $\eta$. When price is decreased and demand is price elastic, MR > 0, and this means that TR is rising. When price is decreased and demand is price inelastic, MR < 0, and therefore TR must be falling. Finally, when price is decreased and demand is unit elastic, then MR = 0, and TR is neither rising nor falling. Hence any change in price elicits changes in quantity demanded that exactly counteract the price change, so that TR is not altered.

An actual example of the relevance of price elasticity of demand to decision-making can drive home the importance of the concept. The authors have estimated a simple demand function for student enrollment at almost 1700 colleges and universities in the United States.[6] Student enrollment at college $i$ ($Q_i$) was made a function of the price of attending institution $i$ in terms of tuition and fees ($P_i$). That is,

$$Q_i = f(P_i) \qquad \text{as } i = 1, 2, \ldots, 1700$$

The equation estimated was of the form $Q = a + b_i(P_i)$. The coefficient $b_i$ indicates the effects of a 1-dollar increase in tuition and fees at college $i$ on student enrollment at college $i$. That is,

$$b_i = \frac{d(Q_i)}{dP_i}$$

The elasticity of $Q$ with respect to $P$ is

$$\frac{d(Q_i)}{dP_i} \cdot \frac{P_i}{Q_i} = b_i \cdot \frac{P_i}{Q_i}$$

The actual value of $b_i$ estimated was $-2.17$. The mean values of $P$ and $Q$ for the 1700 colleges were \$2867 and 3638, respectively. Hence the price elasticity of demand "about the mean" for student enrollment was

$$\eta = -2.17\left(\tfrac{2867}{3638}\right) = -1.71$$

[6] Portions of this work were reported in James V. Koch, "Student Choice of Undergraduate Major Field of Study and Private Internal Rates of Return," *Industrial and Labor Relations Review*, 26 (October 1972), 680–685.

Table 4.1 The behavior of total revenue in response to price changes under varying price elasticities of demand

| *Price elasticity of demand* | *Price increase* | *Price decrease* |
|---|---|---|
| Elastic ($\eta < -1.00$) | TR ↓ | TR ↑ |
| Inelastic ($-1.00 < \eta < 0$) | TR ↑ | TR ↓ |
| Unit elastic ($\eta = -1.00$) | TR ↔ | TR ↔ |

This means that an increase in tuition and fees undertaken by one college actually *decreases* that college's total revenues from tuition and fees, because the demand for enrollment at a *particular* college is price elastic.[7]

**Operating Rates and Employment Decisions**

The Curtis Engine Company has a research department that has discovered the following relationship between the profit $\pi$ of the company and its output $Q$ of customized engines:

$$\pi = -100 + 116Q - 0.01Q^2 \tag{4.1}$$

The researchers have also discovered that there is a strict relationship between the company's output of customized engines and the size of the company's labor force $L$. That relationship is given by

$$Q = 3L + 0.02L^2 \tag{4.2}$$

Curtis Engine Company currently employs 50 workers. This means that the company's output of customized engines in this time period is

$$\begin{aligned} Q &= 3(50) + 0.02(50)^2 \\ &= 150 + 50 = 200 \text{ customized engines} \end{aligned} \tag{4.3}$$

When 50 workers are employed, the total profit of the company is

$$\begin{aligned} \pi &= -100 + 116(3L + 0.02L^2) - 0.01(3L + 0.02L^2)^2 \\ &= -100 + 348(50) + 2.32(50)^2 - 0.09(50)^2 - 0.0012(50)^3 - .000004(50)^4 \\ &= -100 + 17{,}400 + 5800 - 225 - 150 - 25 = 22{,}700 \end{aligned} \tag{4.4}$$

The operating rate when 50 workers are employed is a profitable one. However, the research team is interested in determining whether the company could profitably hire more workers. To do so, they compute the derivative of total profit with respect to the size of the labor force, or $d\pi/dL$:

$$\frac{d\pi}{dL} = 348 + 4.64L - 18L - 0.0036L^2 - 0.000016L^3 \tag{4.5}$$

When $L = 50$, then

$$\begin{aligned} \frac{d\pi}{dL} &= 348 + 4.64(50) - 0.18(50) - 0.0036(50)^2 - 0.000016(50)^3 \\ &= 348 + 232 - 9 - 9 - 200 = 362 \end{aligned} \tag{4.6}$$

Since $d\pi/dL > 0$, it would be profitable for the Curtis Engine Company to hire an additional worker. The company should continue to hire additional workers (and to increase its operating rate) as long as $d\pi/dL > 0$. When $d\pi/dL$

[7] The most appropriate demand function for college enrollment is multivariate in nature. However, the computation of an elasticity in such a case involves a partial derivative, and that topic will not be introduced until Chapter 5.

finally falls to 0 (and it must, since $d^2\pi/dL^2 < 0$), it will no longer be profitable for the Curtis Engine Company to hire additional workers. As we shall see in Chapter 6, satisfying $d\pi/dL = 0$ is a necessary condition for the maximization of profit.



**Logistic Curves**

The growth pattern of a wide range of phenomena can be usefully approximated by a *logistic curve.* A logistic curve exhibits a very rapid initial rate of growth, followed by a decline in that rate of growth and an eventual asymptotic approach to some limit. Figure 4.4 illustrates a typical logistic curve. In this case, the logistic curve represents the growth of the sales of a popular textbook. Logistic curves can also be used successfully to represent phenomena as diverse as the adoption of new products and production processes, for example, the basic oxygen steel refining process; the growth of animal, insect, and human populations; the growth of particular industries, such as electronic computers and television; and the mastery by students of particular modules of knowledge.

The general form of a logistic curve is given by[8]

$$y = \frac{k}{1 + e^{f(t)}}. \tag{4.7}$$

where $y$ = the dependent variable whose growth is being approximated, $k$ = a constant that reflects the limit to potential growth, and $f(t)$ = a polynomial function in which $t$ represents time periods.

The slope and the shape of a logistic curve are determined by (1) the sign and the form of the function $f(t)$, and (2) the sign and the magnitude of the constant $k$.

The most commonly used situation is that illustrated in Figure 4.5, where

[8] The number 10 is occasionally substituted for $e$, which is equal to 2.71828 … .

Figure 4.4 Logistic curve

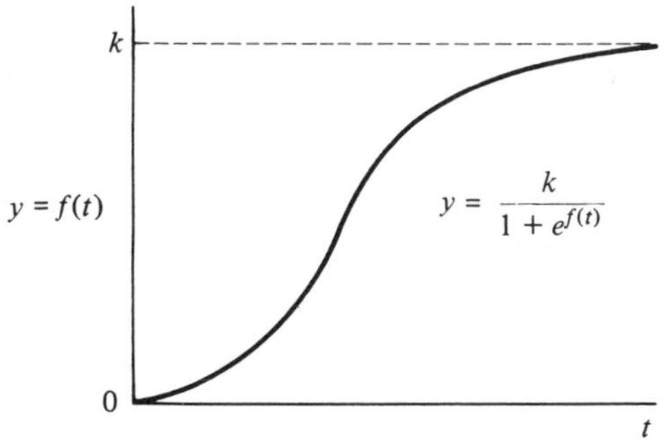

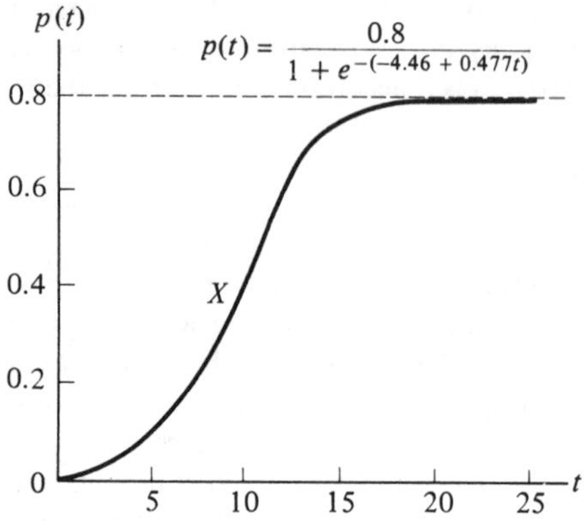


| $t$ | 1 | 2 | 3 | 4 | 5 | 6 | 7 | 8 | 9 | 10 | 11 | 12 | 13 | 14 | 15 | 16 | 17 | 18 | 19 | 20 |
|---|---|---|---|---|---|---|---|---|---|---|---|---|---|---|---|---|---|---|---|---|
| $p(t)$ | .01 | .02 | .04 | .06 | .09 | .13 | .20 | .28 | .37 | .46 | .55 | .63 | .68 | .72 | .75 | .77 | .78 | .78 | .79 | .79 |

Figure 4.5 Logistic curve describing the adoption of numerical control

$k > 0$ and $f(t) < 0$. Given that $k > 0$, the value of $f(t)$ must be decreasing as $t$ grows larger in order for the logistic curve to have a positive slope. The value of the constant $k$ determines the limit that the logistic function asymptotically approaches. For example, assume that

$$y = \frac{10{,}000}{1 + e^{-0.3t}}$$

The logistic curve that is the graph of this equation has a positive slope and asymptotically approaches 10,000. If, on the other hand,

$$y = \frac{10{,}000}{1 + e^{0.3t}}$$

then the logistic curve begins at 10,000, and asymptotically approaches 0. A negative sign on the constant $k$ implies that the logistic curve asymptotically approaches $-k$ when the value of $f(t)$ is increasing as $t$ becomes larger, and begins at $-k$ and asymptotically approaches 0 when the value of $f(t)$ is decreasing as $t$ becomes larger.

We can determine the slope of any logistic curve of the form $y = k/(1 + e^{f(t)})$ by finding $dy/dt$. Given that $k > 0$ and that the value of $f(t)$ is decreasing as $t$ becomes larger, the logistic curve initially rises, increasingly rapidly (and $dy/dt$ initially is increasingly large) as the value of $f(t)$ becomes increasingly small. Thus, when $f(t) = -0.3t$, the logistic curve initially rises less rapidly than when $f(t) = -0.6t$. This means that the logistic curve approaches $k$ more slowly in the first case than in the second case.

EXAMPLE Edwin Mansfield has examined the rapidity with which newly available productive processes are diffused throughout an industry and adopted by firms.[9] In one such case, he analyzed the diffusion of numerical control of machine tools. Numerical control is a system by which numerical instructions are prepared in code on tapes or cards. The instructions control the operation of the machine; for example, its speed. The instructions are placed in a control unit attached to the machine that directs (automatically) the operation of the machine. Numerical control results in machine tool operation that is simultaneously less expensive and more flexible.

Mansfield used the following logistic function to analyze the diffusion of numerical control:

$$p(t) = \frac{0.80}{1 + e^{-(a+bt)}} \tag{4.8}$$

where $p(t)$ = percentage of firms using numeric control in year $t$.

In this case, the assumption is that the percentage of firms using numerical control would increase until it was arbitrarily close to 0.80.[10] Mansfield found that $a = -4.46$, while $b = 0.477$. Hence, when $t = 1$, $-(a + bt) = -[-4.46 + 0.477(1)] = 3.983$. Therefore

$$p(1) = \frac{0.8}{1 + e^{3.983}} = \frac{0.8}{54.677} = 0.01$$

Similarly $p(3) = 0.04$, $p(10) = 0.46$, $p(15) = 0.75$, and $p(20) = 0.79$. Hence, after 20 years, the percentage of firms using numerical control would be estimated to be arbitrarily close to 80. Figure 4.5 illustrates the estimated relationship. The first derivative of $p(t)$ with respect to $t$ $[dp(t)/dt]$ is positive and increasing until point $X$ and decreasing thereafter. It is apparent that the limit of $dp(t)/dt$ as $t \to \infty$ is zero. This can be demonstrated in this case as follows: Given

$$p(t) = \frac{k}{1 + e^{-(a+bt)}}$$

then

$$\frac{dp(t)}{dt} = \frac{kbe^{-(a+bt)}}{1 + 2e^{-(a+bt)} + e^{-2(a+bt)}} \tag{4.9}$$

[9] Edwin Mansfield, "The Diffusion of a Major Manufacturing Innovation," in *Research and Innovation in the Modern Corporation* W. W. Norton and Company, Inc., New York, 1971, pp. 186–205.

[10] We can defend this assumption as follows: Let

$$p(t) = \frac{k}{1 + e^{-(a+bt)}}$$

where $a > 0$ and $b < 0$. Then

$$p(t) = \frac{k}{1 + (e^a/e^{bt})}$$

which has a limit of $k$ as $t$ becomes large. That is, $\lim_{t \to \infty} p(t) = k$.

Evaluating this derivative at $t = 5$, we find that

$$p'(5) = \frac{0.8(0.477)(2.716)^{2.07}}{1 + 2(2.716)^{2.07} + (2.716)^{4.15}} = 0.04 \tag{4.10}$$

Using similar methods, we find that $dp(t)/dt = 0.05$ when $t = 6$. Hence we conclude that the function $p(t)$ is upward-sloping in this region and that it is increasing at an increasing rate.[11] It can also be shown that $dp(t)/dt = 0.08$ when $t = 11$, but $dp(t)/dt = 0.07$ when $t = 12$. This establishes that the function $p(t)$ is upward-sloping in this region, and also that it is increasing at a decreasing rate.[12]

Hence the function $p(t)$ increases at an increasing rate until point $X$.[13] Thereafter it increases at a decreasing rate. As $t \to \infty$, the value of $dp(t)/dt$ approaches zero.

### Production

Consider a simple production function of the form $Q = f(L)$, where $Q$ is output and $L$ is the input labor. The average product AP of the variable input $L$ is $Q/L = f(L)/L$, and the marginal product MP of $L$ is $dQ/dL = d[f(L)]/dL = f'(L)$.

The so-called *law of diminishing returns* states that the application of an increasing number of units of a variable input such as $L$ to a fixed input (perhaps land) eventually results in a decline in the MP of $L$. That is, $dQ/dL$ eventually declines absolutely. We shall see in Chapter 5 that we can use the second derivative of $Q$ with respect to $L$ to describe the operation of the law of diminishing returns with greater precision.

The Cobb-Douglas production function is a widely used production function in economic analysis.[14] In the Cobb-Douglas function, $Q = f(L, K)$ and both $L$ and $K$ (which is units of capital) are considered to be inputs that can be varied in amount. The usual specification of the Cobb-Douglas production function is $Q = AL^\alpha K^{1-\alpha}$, where $A$ and $\alpha$ are constants and $0 < \alpha < 1$. Assume that we are in the short run in terms of production, so that one of the inputs ($K$) is fixed in amount. Then

$$AP_L = \frac{Q}{L} = \frac{AL^\alpha K^{1-\alpha}}{L} = A\left(\frac{K}{L}\right)^{1-\alpha}$$

and $$\text{MP}_L = \frac{dQ}{dL} = \frac{d(AL^\alpha K^{1-\alpha})}{dL} = \alpha A\left(\frac{K}{L}\right)^{1-\alpha} = \frac{\alpha Q}{L}$$

One of the early applications of the Cobb-Douglas production function in-

[11] We can verify this by determining that $d^2p(t)/dt^2 > 0$ in the same region.

[12] This can also be verified by finding $d^2p(t)/dt^2$. In this case, $d^2p(t)/dt^2 < 0$ in this region, and hence the function $p(t)$ must be increasing at a decreasing rate.

[13] In Chapter 6 we shall acquire the means to locate point $X$ precisely.

[14] The Cobb-Douglas production function was originally developed by Paul Douglas, a University of Chicago economist who later became a United States senator, and Charles Cobb, an Amherst College mathematician. See a general discussion of this in Paul Douglas, "Are There Laws of Production?" *American Economic Review*, 38 (March 1948), 1–41.

volved an empirical estimation of production in the manufacturing sector of the American economy. Cobb and Douglas estimated that $A = 1.01$ and $\alpha = 0.75$. Hence, if 1000 units of capital and 250 units of labor exist in such a case, the Cobb-Douglas production function predicts total output of 357.08:

$$Q = 1.01(250)^{0.75}(1000)^{0.25} = 1.01(62.87)(5.62) = 357.08$$

Similarly, the marginal product of an incremental unit of labor in this situation is 1.06:

$$\text{MP}_L = \frac{d(AL^{\alpha}K^{1-\alpha})}{dL} = \alpha A\left(\frac{K}{L}\right)^{1-\alpha} = 0.75(1.01)(\tfrac{1000}{250})^{0.25} = 1.06$$

**Consumption, Saving, and the National Income Multiplier**

Let $Y =$ disposable income and $Y \equiv C + S$, where $C =$ the consumption of private individuals and $S$ is the saving of private individuals. The individual's consumption function is given by $C = f(Y)$, and indicates the consumption that the individual would undertake at various levels of disposable income. The individual's *average propensity to consume* (APC) is given by $\text{APC} = C/Y$, and the individual's *marginal propensity to consume* (MPC) is given by $\text{MPC} = dC/dY$. Since all disposable income must be either consumed or saved, it follows that MPS, the *marginal propensity to save*, is given by $\text{MPS} = dS/dY = 1 - dC/dY$. Definitionally,

$$\text{MPC} + \text{MPS} = \frac{dC}{dY} + \frac{dS}{dY} = 1.00$$

The national income multiplier $k$ is defined as

$$k = \frac{1}{1 - \text{MPC}} = \frac{1}{\text{MPS}} = \frac{1}{1 - dC/dY} = \frac{1}{dS/dY}$$

The greater (smaller) the value of MPC, the larger (smaller) the value of $k$, the multiplier.

**The Chicago Transit Authority**

At the beginning of this chapter, we indicated that the concept of the derivative was useful in a wide variety of situations. One situation that was suggested involved the fare-making policy of the Chicago Transit Authority (CTA). Like many urban rapid transit systems, the CTA has been afflicted with falling ridership and rising costs. Hence there has been continual pressure on the CTA to raise its fares in order to increase the revenues that it realizes from customer fares.

Whether or not the CTA can actually increase the total revenue it realizes from customer fares by increasing customer fares depends on the value of price elasticity of demand. Unfortunately, while the price elasticity of demand for CTA travel is inelastic with respect to fares in the short run (30 days or less), price elasticity of demand is elastic with respect to fares as time passes. That is,

CTA passengers react substantially to higher fares as time passes, and many switch to private automobiles or commuter railroads when CTA fares rise. Table 4.1 confirms the fact that a price increase under conditions of price-elastic demand decreases total sales revenues. Hence a fare increase is actually counterproductive.

Assume a demand function for CTA travel of the form $Q = f(P)$, where $Q$ = the number of CTA passengers who pay fares in a given year, and $P$ = the average CTA fare.[15] Given that

$$\dot{Q} = 300{,}000{,}000 - 6{,}920{,}000P = 3 \times 10^8 - (6.92 \times 10^6)P$$

then

$$\text{TR} = (3 \times 10^8)P - (6.92 \times 10^6)P^2$$

$$\text{MR} = \frac{d(\text{TR})}{dQ} = 3 \times 10^8 - (13.84 \times 10^6)P$$

The slope of the demand function is given by $dQ/dP = -(6.92 \times 10^6)$.

The coefficient of price elasticity of demand $\eta$ is defined as

$$\frac{dQ}{dP} \cdot \frac{P}{Q}$$

If 127,000,000 passengers ride the CTA annually when the average fare is \$0.25, then the price elasticity of demand for CTA travel is

$$\eta = -(6.92 \times 10^6)\left(\frac{0.25}{127{,}000{,}000}\right) = -1.36$$

Hence a 1% increase in CTA fares will cause a 1.36% decrease in CTA ridership over the space of a year and a *decline* in total revenues realized by the CTA. (See Table 4.1 to confirm this statement.)

We can see the inadvisability of a fare increase by the CTA when it faces a price-elastic demand if we experimentally raise the average fare to \$0.30 per passenger. When the average fare was \$0.25 per passenger, the CTA's annual revenues were 127,000,000 × \$0.25 = \$31,750,000. However, a rise in the average fare to \$0.30 produces only 92,400,000 × \$0.30 = \$27,720,000 in revenue. Over the time space of a year, therefore, a policy of increasing fares is counterproductive in terms of revenue received. The CTA seems to be continually deceived by the fact that the demand for CTA travel is inelastic with respect to fares in the short run, but elastic with respect to fares in the long run.

## PROBLEMS

1. Find $dy/dx$ and $d^2y/dx^2$, if they exist.
   (a) $y = 3x^6$ (b) $y = 3x(4x^3)(\sin x)$
   (c) $y = \frac{3}{7}x$ (d) $y = 9x/0.25x^4$

[15] The work presented here is based on work performed by one of the authors. The numbers used in the example, while fictitious, are realistic in terms of their implications.

(e) $y = 10u$, where $u = 4x^3 + 5x$ (f) $y = 6x^4$
(g) $y = 10^{x/3x^3+8}$ (h) $y = \log_e 2x$
(i) $y = \log_5 2x^{x^2}$
(j) $y = g(x)$, where $g(x) = \sin\,(x^2/5)^2$

2. The growth of the electronic calculator industry can perhaps be approximated by a logistic curve of the form $N = f(t)$, where $N =$ the number of calculators in use and $t =$ time in years. In the context of electronic calculators, this implies that the number of calculators in use will initially grow very rapidly, subsequently taper off in growth, and ultimately asymptotically approach a saturation point.

   Assume that the logistic curve representing the growth of the electronic calculator industry is given by

$$N = \frac{12{,}000{,}000}{1 + 0.5e^{-0.2t}}$$

   Find $dN/dt$ and $d^2N/dt^2$. When $t = 15$, is the number of calculators in use growing at an increasing or a decreasing rate? When $t = 50$? Continue to make $t$ larger. Can you make an educated guess concerning the number of electronic calculators that will be in use when the market is saturated? (The tools that we shall acquire in Chapter 6 will make the solution of this last question much easier.)

3. Henry Schultz became famous for his estimates of demand functions for a wide range of agricultural commodities. For the period 1915–1929, Schultz found the demand function for corn to be $P = 6{,}570{,}000/Q^{1.3}$, where $P =$ price per bushel of corn, and $Q =$ bushels of corn.[16] If 300,000 bushels of corn are produced, what is the price per bushel? What is price elasticity of demand at that point on the demand curve? Could farmers increase their total revenues from the sale of corn by increasing the price of corn per bushel? Why?

4. The decision as to whether the Alaskan oil pipeline should be built was an important decision that confronted the United States in the early 1970s. One of the alternatives to building the pipeline was to transport the oil via large oil tankers. The presumption was that economies of scale existed such that the average cost of transporting oil per barrel would decline as the size of the oil tankers increased. In order to test this assumption, an average cost curve was estimated such that

$$\text{AC} = 0.03 + \frac{10}{S} - \frac{200}{S^2}$$

   where AC = average cost of transporting a barrel of oil 1000 nautical miles, and $S =$ size of the oil tanker in terms of deadweight tons.[17] Use the first derivative of AC with respect to $S$ (and selected values of $S$) to judge whether any potential economies of scale did exist with respect to

[16] Henry Schultz, *The Theory and Measurement of Demand.*
[17] See "Use of Satellite Data on the Alaskan Oil Marine Link," *Practical Applications of Space Systems: Cost and Benefits,* National Academy of Sciences, (Washington, D.C., 1975), p. B-23.

the use of large oil tankers. Use the second derivative, $d^2AC/dS^2$, to judge whether any economies of scale that do exist disappear when exceptionally large oil tanker sizes are introduced.

5. A ball is thrown vertically into the air. After $t$ seconds, the ball's height above the ground is $H$ feet. In general, $H = 96t - 16t^2$. What is the velocity of the ball at time $t = 2$? (Velocity is given by $dH/dt$ evaluated at a particular $t$.) What is the height of the ball when $t = 2$?
6. A real estate firm pays its salespeople a fixed salary per month plus a commission, which is a percentage of the total sales of real estate engineered by the salesperson. The monthly wage $W$ of a salesperson is given by $W = 100 + 0.01S + 0.0000001S^2$, where $S$ = dollars of sales for which the salesperson is responsible. A particular salesperson sells \$100,000 worth of real estate in a given month. What is that person's total wage that month? What meaning can be attached to the first derivative, $dW/dS$? Use the second derivative, $d^2W/dS^2$, to determine whether the wage structure provides decreasing or increasing incentive to salespeople selling real estate. Why?
7. The most common method of depreciating an asset is the straight-line method. Under such a system, the depreciated value of an asset in year $t$ ($V_t$) is given by $V(t) = \text{PP} - bt$ (as $t = 1, 2, \ldots, n$), where PP = the purchase price of the asset, $b = \text{PP}/n$, and $n$ = number of depreciable years of life of the asset. Assume that a new house, with an estimated depreciable life of 25 years, is purchased for a price of \$50,000. What is the depreciated value of the house after 5 years? What meaning can be attached to the derivative $dV/dt$? Observe that the second derivative, $d^2V/dt^2$, is equal to 0. Relate this to the concept of straight-line (even) depreciation.
8. The Morton Lumber Company faces a demand curve given in inverse form by $P = 10 - 0.1Q$. The marginal cost curve of the company is given by $\text{MC} = 2 + 0.05Q$. Find the profit-maximizing price and output for Morton. What is price elasticity of demand for Morton's product at the profit-maximizing price and output?
9. Several empirical studies have revealed that the relationship between the number of police officers employed by a city and the total number of arrests can be represented by a quadratic function of the form $\text{NA} = a + b(\text{NP}) + c(\text{NP})^2$, where NA = the number of arrests and NP = the number of police officers. The empirical studies suggest that $d\text{NA}/d\text{NP} > 0$ and that $d^2\text{NA}/d\text{NP}^2 < 0$.[18] What is the practical meaning of these derivatives?
10. Both marketing and economics textbooks suggest that it is possible for a firm to increase its profit by engaging in price discrimination. We can nonrigorously define price discrimination as selling identical units of output to different customers at different prices. Profit maximization requires that one of the conditions that the firm must satisfy in such a situation in order to increase its profit is to equate the marginal revenue MR it receives from each customer with the marginal cost MC of the

[18] See A. Gus Rogers III, *The Economics of Crime*, Dryden Press, Hinsdale, Ill., 1973.

firm's output. That is, if there are two customers A and B, then one condition the firm must satisfy is $MR_A = MR_B = MC$. Assume that customer A's demand curve is given in inverse form by $P = 10 - 0.2Q$, whereas customer B's analogous demand curve is given by $P = 8 - 0.5Q$. Let MC be constant at \$2 per unit. What prices should be charged customers A and B in order to maximize profit? Is this price discriminatory?

# DIFFERENTIATION: FUNCTIONS OF SEVERAL VARIABLES

# 5

In Chapter 4 we examined the effect of a change in subway and bus fares on the number of riders of subways and buses. Our analysis presumed a simple demand function for Chicago Transit Authority (CTA) travel of the form $Q = f(P)$, where $Q$ = number of CTA riders and $P$ = fare per rider. We were aware that many other factors, in addition to fares, influence ridership. Nonetheless, we were unable to consider these other factors jointly with the influence of fares because our ability to differentiate was restricted to functions of one variable.

The tools that we shall acquire in this chapter will enable us to differentiate many functions of several variables. We can enhance the realism of our CTA example by considering a demand function for CTA travel of the form $Q = f(P, Y, N, A)$, where $Y$ = the income of potential riders, $N$ = number of potential riders, and $A$ = cost of operating an automobile. We shall be able to consider the rate of change of $Q$ with respect to small changes in $P$, while at the same time holding $Y$, $N$, and $A$ constant at their mean values. Similarly, we can look at the rate of change of $Q$ with respect to small changes in $Y$, or $N$, or $A$, while holding the other variables constant.

A multivariate function approach to the CTA ridership problem is intuitively and theoretically much more attractive. We can now consider the effects of changes in $P$ on $Q$, having already controlled for $Y$, $N$, and $A$. Specifically, we can investigate the effects of $P$ on $Q$ under the assumption that variables $Y$, $N$, and $A$ are at specific values. This is a major step forward, since we have strong reason to believe that income, population, and the cost of operating an automobile do affect ridership on public transit. We shall return to the CTA ridership problem after we have acquired the mathematical tools necessary to analyze it in greater detail.

## PARTIAL DIFFERENTIATION

This chapter is concerned with functions of two or more independent variables. Consider $z = f(x, y)$, where $z$ is the dependent variable and $x$ and $y$ are independent variables. Given any permissible values of $x$ and $y$, we can determine a value for $z$. For example, if $z = x \cdot y$, and $x = 2$ and $y = 4$, then $z = 8$.

The multivariate functions that we deal with in this chapter are all characterized by *independence* among the independent variables. That is, the occurrence or nonoccurrence of one independent variable is completely unrelated to the occurrence or nonoccurrence of any other independent variable.

In general, we shall deal with functions of the form

$$y = f(x_1, x_2, \ldots, x_n) \tag{5.1}$$

The $x_i$ are independent variables that are also independent of one another.

In Equation (5.1), if $x_1$ varies while $x_2, \ldots, x_n$ are held constant, then $y$ is a function of $x_1$ and the limiting difference quotient becomes

$$\lim_{\Delta x_1 \to 0} \frac{\Delta y}{\Delta x_1} = \lim_{\Delta x_1 \to 0} \frac{f(x_1 + \Delta x_1, x_2, \ldots, x_n) - f(x_1, x_2, \ldots, x_n)}{\Delta x_1} \tag{5.2}$$

The derivative taken in Equation (5.2) measures the rate of change of $y$ with respect to $x_1$ and is referred to as the *partial derivative* of $y$ with respect to $x_1$. The partial derivative indicates the effect of a change in a single independent variable on the dependent variable, with all other independent variables in the function held constant while this particular derivative is taken. If all independent variables were allowed to change their values simultaneously, then it would be impossible to isolate the effect of a change in one independent variable on the dependent variable.

The process of partial differentiation is denoted by the variant form of the lower-case Greek delta: $\partial$. Suppose that we have a function of the form $y = f(x_1, x_2)$. We represent the partial derivative of $y$ with respect to $x_1$ by

$$\frac{\partial y}{\partial x_1}$$

Equivalently, we could state this as

$$\left.\frac{\partial y}{\partial x_1}\right| x_2 = \text{constant}$$

This indicates that we are finding the partial derivative of $y$ with respect to $x_1$ and that $x_2$ is being held constant. Other notations for a partial derivative include

$$\frac{\partial f}{\partial x_1} \qquad \frac{\partial}{\partial x_1} f(x_1, \ldots, x_n) \qquad f_{x_1} \qquad f_1 \qquad y_{x_1} \qquad \text{and} \qquad f_{x_1}(x_1, \ldots, x_n)$$

### Rules of Differentiation

Fortunately the rules of differentiation that we derived in Chapter 4 can also be put to use to find partial derivatives when we deal with functions of several independent variables. The major alteration in our differentiation procedure is that all independent variables not explicitly involved in the differentiation are treated as constants and are differentiated accordingly.

Given $y = f(x_1, x_2, \ldots, x_n)$. The computation of $\partial y/\partial x_n$ requires that the remaining $n - 1$ independent variables be regarded as constants and differentiated accordingly.

EXAMPLES

1. Let $z = f(x, y) = x^2 + 4xy + y^2$

$$\frac{\partial z}{\partial x} = z_x = f_x = \frac{\partial(x^2)}{\partial x} + \frac{\partial(4xy)}{\partial x} + \frac{\partial(y^2)}{\partial x}$$

$$= 2x + 4y + 0 = 2x + 4y$$

$$\frac{\partial z}{\partial y} = z_y = f_y = \frac{\partial(x^2)}{\partial y} + \frac{\partial(4xy)}{\partial y} + \frac{\partial(y^2)}{\partial y}$$

$$= 0 + 4x + 2y = 4x + 2y$$

2. Let

$$z = f(x, y) = \frac{4x}{y} + \frac{2y}{x}$$

$$\frac{\partial z}{\partial x} = z_x = f_x = \frac{4}{y} - \frac{2y}{x^2}, \qquad \frac{\partial z}{\partial y} = z_y = f_y = -\frac{4x}{y^2} + \frac{2}{x}$$

In both these examples, the partial derivative $\partial z/\partial x$ is itself a function of $x$ and $y$. Similarly, $\partial z/\partial y$ is a function of $x$ and $y$. This is often the case. This means that we can evaluate the partial derivatives for any values of $x$ and $y$.

We can generalize the results of the previous examples. Given $y = f(x_1, x_2, \ldots, x_n)$, where the $x_i$ are independent variables that are independent of one another. It is in principle possible to compute a partial derivative of $y$ with respect to each of the $x_i$. There are a total of $n$ such partial derivatives in this situation.

EXAMPLE Let $z = f(x, y, r, s, t, u) = 3x^2r + 4y^2 - 10rstu$

$$\frac{\partial z}{\partial x} = 6xr, \qquad \frac{\partial z}{\partial y} = 8y, \qquad \frac{\partial z}{\partial r} = 3x^2 - 10stu,$$

$$\frac{\partial z}{\partial s} = -10rtu, \qquad \frac{\partial z}{\partial t} = -10rsu, \qquad \frac{\partial z}{\partial u} = -10rst$$

EXERCISE 5.1

In each case compute all first-order partial derivatives.

1. $f(x, y) = x^4 + y^4 - 4x^2y^2$
2. $f(x, y) = xy + \dfrac{x}{y} \quad (y \neq 0)$
3. $f(x, y) = \sqrt{x^2 + y^2}$
4. $f(x, y) = \dfrac{x + y}{x - y} \quad (x \neq y)$
5. $f(x, y) = e^{x^2 + xy}$
6. $f(x, y, z) = xyz$

7. $f(x, y) = \frac{x}{y^2} + \frac{y}{x^2}$

8. $f(x, y) = \ln(xy + y^2)$

9. $f(x, y) = x \cos y - y \cos x$

10. $f(x, y) = x \sin(x + y)$

11. $f(x, y) = \sqrt{xy}$

12. $f(x, y, z) = \frac{x^2/2 + 3y^3}{xy + yz}$

13. $f(x, y) = \log \sqrt{x + 5y^2}$

**Geometric Interpretation of the Partial Derivative**

We learned in Chapter 4 that when $y = f(x)$, the derivative of $y$ with respect to $x$ can be given a geometric interpretation. $dy/dx$ is the slope of the curve of that function in a plane. Similarly, a partial derivative has a geometric interpretation that we shall now demonstrate.

Consider a typical two-factor input production function used in economics, such as $Q = f(L, K)$, where $Q$ = output, $L$ = labor, and $K$ = capital. This production function is assumed to be continuous. We can find two partial derivatives. $\partial Q/\partial L$ is the partial derivative of output with respect to labor and is more commonly known as the marginal product of labor. $\partial Q/\partial K$ is the partial derivative of output with respect to capital and is the marginal product of capital. Therefore $\partial Q/\partial L$ holds the number of units of capital constant, while $\partial Q/\partial K$ holds the number of units of labor constant.

Figure 5.1 is a three-dimensional production surface based on the production function $Q = f(L, K)$. Two of the dimensions of the production surface in

Figure 5.1 Production surface

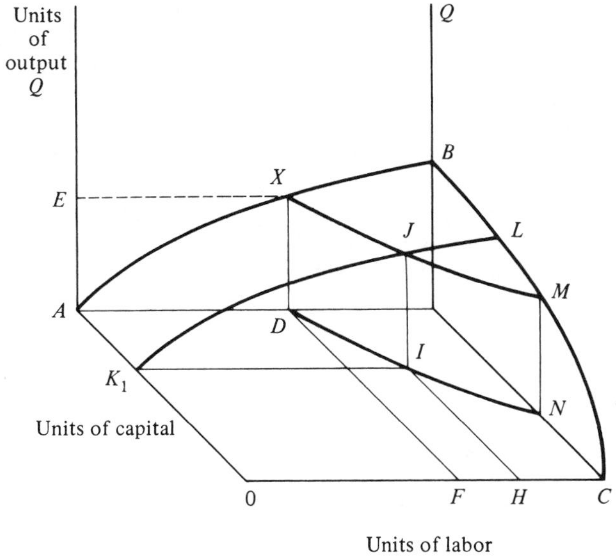

Figure 5.1 are given by the inputs $L$ and $K$, while the third dimension is given by $Q$. The overall production surface is given by $OABC$. We can evaluate any given point on the production surface (for example, point $X$) in each of the three dimensions. Point $X$ represents the use of $OF$ units of labor, the use of $OA$ units of capital, and total output of $DX = AE$.

Let us now consider the effect on output of changes in the labor input that occur when capital is held constant at amount $K_1$ in Figure 5.1. The curve $K_1JL$ is the total product curve of labor, given $K_1$ units of capital. The slope of curve $K_1JL$ at a given point measures the rate of change of output with respect to changes in labor, with capital held constant at level $K_1$. That is, this slope represents the partial derivative of output with respect to labor, given $K_1$ units of capital, and is symbolized by

$$\left.\frac{\partial Q}{\partial L}\right| K = K_1$$

We can follow a similar process in order to generate a geometric interpretation of $\partial Q/\partial L$ given levels of capital other than $K_1$. Or we can hold the number of units of labor constant and depict $\partial Q/\partial K$.

## DIFFERENTIALS

In Chapter 4 we defined the derivative as

$$\lim_{\Delta x \to 0} \frac{\Delta y}{\Delta x} = \lim_{\Delta x \to 0} \frac{f(x + \Delta x) - f(x)}{\Delta x} = \frac{dy}{dx} \tag{5.3}$$

The symbol $dy/dx$ expressed the result of a limiting process, and we did not regard it as the quotient of the quantities $dy$ and $dx$. That is, we did not address ourselves to the issue of whether or not $dy/dx$ was the division of $dy$ by $dx$. We can see, however, that in Equation (5.3) we found $dy/dx$ by taking the limit of a quotient. The symbol $dy/dx$ can, therefore, also be interpreted as the quotient of $dy$ divided by $dx$. This piece of information, which we shall now discuss, will be quite useful in later sections of this chapter.

Figure 5.2 presents the graph of a differentiable function $y = f(x)$. The slope of the tangent to the curve at point $A$ is the derivative of $y$ with respect to $x$. This derivative measures the slope of the curve at point $A$ because $\Delta x$ is very small at point $A$. Consider point $B$, however. The error in the linear approximation to the curve at $A$ is equal to the vertical distance $CB$ in Figure 5.2. That is, $CD$ represents the linear approximation to the change in $y$ where $CD = f'(x) \cdot \Delta x$, but

$$\Delta y = \left(\frac{\Delta y}{\Delta x}\right)\Delta x = \left(\frac{BD}{AD}\right)AD$$

$$= BD \qquad \text{represents the actual change in } y$$

Hence the difference in the true value of $\Delta y$ and the linear approximation to $\Delta y$ is $BD - CD = CB$.

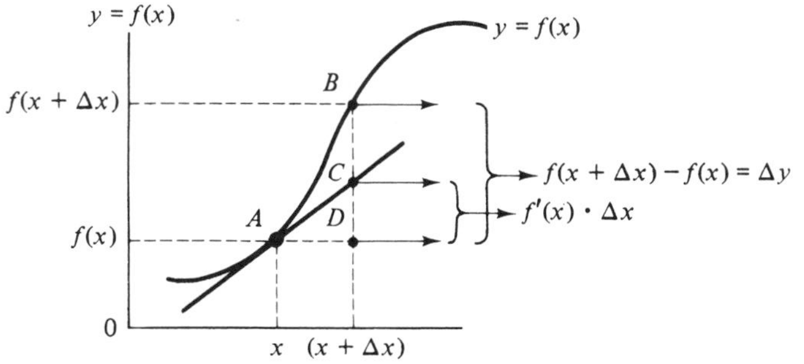


Figure 5.2 The derivative and the differential

that it is proper to regard the derivative $dy/dx$ as the quotient of two quantities, $dy$ and $dx$.[1] Thus, when $dx$ is small, $dy$ is a good approximation to $\Delta y$, as shown in the following example.

EXAMPLE If $dx = \Delta x$ is infinitesimally small, then $dy$ is a good approximation for $\Delta y$.

Let $y = x^3$, and allow $x$ to change from $x_1 = 2$ to $x_2 = 2.01$. The actual change in $y$ is

$$\Delta y = f(x_2) - f(x_1) = (2.01)^3 - 2^3 = 0.1206$$

Using differential $dy$, obtained by taking $x = 2$ and $dx = 0.01$, to measure the approximate change of $\Delta y$, one obtains

$$dy = f'(x)dx = 3x^2dx = 3(2)^2(0.01) = 0.12$$

Therefore the error involved using the approximate $dy$ is 0.0006.

## TOTAL DIFFERENTIALS

In this section we extend the concept of a differential to include functions of two or more independent variables. We begin by noting that a partial derivative measures the rate of change of the dependent variable with respect to an infinitesimal change in one of the independent variables, all other independent variables held constant. A *total differential* of a function, however, is a linear approximation of the rate of change of the dependent variable when *all* the

[1] Observe that we must have two separate pieces of information, $x$ and $\Delta x$, before we can compute the differential $dy$. The value of $x$, moreover, must be one for which $f'(x)$ exists.

independent variables change by an infinitesimal amount. The total differential is the sum of the changes in the dependent variable caused by simultaneous infinitesimal changes in all the dependent variables.

Given the differentiable function $z = f(x, y)$. The total differential of this function is defined as

$$dz = \frac{\partial f}{\partial x}\, dx + \frac{\partial f}{\partial y}\, dy \tag{5.5}$$

Using abbreviated notation, Equation (5.5) becomes

$$dz = f_x\, dx + f_y\, dy \tag{5.6}$$

The total differential of the function of only one independent variable, such as $z = f(x)$, is

$$dz = \frac{\partial f}{\partial x}\, dx \tag{5.7}$$

Equation (5.7) is equivalent to Equation (5.4), where we found the differential of a function of only one independent variable. When we add an additional independent variable, and the function becomes $z = f(x, y)$, then the total differential is the sum of the differentials with respect to each independent variable, as our definition in Equation (5.5) indicates.

In general, the total differential of a function of $n$ independent variables, such as $z = f(x_1, x_2, \ldots, x_n)$, is defined as

$$dz = \frac{\partial f}{\partial x_1}\, dx_1 + \frac{\partial f}{\partial x_2}\, dx_2 + \cdots + \frac{\partial f}{\partial x_n}\, dx_n \tag{5.8}$$

EXAMPLES

1. Given the utility function $U = f(Q_1, Q_2)$, where $U$ = utility and $Q_1$ and $Q_2$ are commodities. The total differential of this utility function is

$$dU = \frac{\partial f}{\partial Q_1}\, dQ_1 + \frac{\partial f}{\partial Q_2}\, dQ_2$$

2. Given the production function $Q = f(L, K) = AL^{\alpha}K^{1-\alpha}$, where $Q$ = output, $L$ = labor, and $K$ = capital. The total differential of this production function (which is known as the Cobb–Douglas) is

$$dQ = f_L d_L + f_K d_K = A\alpha\left(\frac{K}{L}\right)^{1-\alpha} dL + A(1-\alpha)\left(\frac{L}{K}\right)^{\alpha} dK$$

EXERCISE 5.2

Find the total differential, given:

1. $y = \frac{1}{2}x^2 + \frac{1}{3}x^3$
2. $z = x^2 + xy + y^2$
3. $z = \ln(x^2 + 8y^3)$
4. $w = xyz$
5. $w = e^{x^2} + y^2 + z^2$
6. $w = z^2(2x + 3y)$
7. $z = x \sin y + y \sin x$

## TOTAL DERIVATIVES OF COMPOSITE FUNCTIONS

In the previous section, we developed the concept of a total *differential*. In this section, we develop the concept of a total *derivative*. The slight difference in terminology represents a substantial difference in the type of function with which we are dealing.

Our discussion of partial derivatives and total differentials relied on the assumption that the independent variables were independent of one another. There are many examples in which such an assumption cannot be fulfilled, however. Let us now direct our attention to such situations.

### Case 1: Interrelated Independent Variables

Given the function $z = f(x, y)$, where it also is true that $y = g(x)$. Hence $z = f[x, g(x)]$, which is a composite function in which $x$ is the only independent variable. An important underlying assumption of a partial derivative is no longer fulfilled when we encounter a function such as $z = f[x, g(x)]$. Variable $y = g(x)$ does not remain constant when variable $x$ varies. That is, $x$ and $y$ are not independent of each other.

When $z = f(x, y)$ and $y = g(x)$, the total differential of the function is

$$dz = \frac{\partial f}{\partial x}\,dx + \frac{\partial f}{\partial y}\,dy \tag{5.9}$$

We divide Equation (5.9) by $dx$ and obtain

$$\frac{dz}{dx} = \frac{\partial f}{\partial x}\frac{dx}{dx} + \frac{\partial f}{\partial y}\frac{dy}{dx} = \frac{\partial f}{\partial x} + \frac{\partial f}{\partial y}\frac{dy}{dx} \tag{5.10}$$

The term $dz/dx$ is referred to as the *total derivative* of $z$ with respect to $x$. This total derivative has two parts. The first part, $\partial f/\partial x$, measures the change in $z$ brought about by changes in $x$, all other variables held constant.[2] The second part, $(\partial f/\partial y) \cdot (dy/dx)$, measures the change in $z$ brought about by changes in variable $x$ that work through intermediate variable $y$. The first part of Equation (5.10) is often called the *direct effect*, while the second part is often called the *indirect effect*. The indirect effect takes account of the fact that changes in variable $x$ affect variable $y$, which in turn affects variable $z$.

▣ Rule 7 in Chapter 4 dealt with the derivative of a function of a function. It stated that when $z = f(u)$, where $u = f(x)$,

$$\frac{dz}{dx} = \frac{dz}{du} \cdot \frac{du}{dx}$$

This is similar to, *but not the same as*, the indirect effect of the total derivative noted in Equation (5.10). When $z = f(x, y)$ and $y = g(x)$, the total derivative is

$$\frac{dz}{dx} = \frac{\partial z}{\partial x} + \frac{\partial z}{\partial y} \cdot \frac{dy}{dx}$$

[2] The partial derivative designation, $\partial f/\partial x$, is needed because of the two independent variables, $x$ and $y$, in the function $z = f(x, y)$. Technically, however, it is impossible in some situations for $x$ to change unless $y$ also changes.

The derivative of a function of a function $[(dz/du) \cdot (du/dx)]$ and the indirect effect of a total derivative $[(\partial z/\partial y) \cdot (dy/dx)]$ are not the same. There is only one independent variable in the function of a function case; that is why we use the ordinary derivative sign. There are two independent variables when a total derivative is taken; therefore we must use the partial derivative sign.

In general, if $z = f(x, y_1, y_2, \ldots, y_n)$, and $y_1 = g(x)$, $y_2 = h(x)$, $\ldots$, $y_n = k(x)$, then the total derivative of $z$ with respect to $x$ is

$$\frac{dz}{dx} = \frac{\partial f}{\partial x} + \frac{\partial f}{\partial y_1}\frac{dy_1}{dx} + \frac{\partial f}{\partial y_2} \cdot \frac{dy_2}{dx} + \cdots + \frac{\partial f}{\partial y_n} \cdot \frac{dy_n}{dx} \tag{5.11}$$

EXAMPLES

1. $z = x^2 + 2xy + y^2, \qquad y = e^x$

$$\frac{dz}{dx} = f_x + f_y\frac{dy}{dx} = (2x + 2y) + (2x + 2y)e^x$$

$$= 2(x + y)(1 + e^x)$$

2. $z = e^{x2 - y2}, \qquad x = 2y^3$

$$\frac{dz}{dy} = f_x\frac{dx}{dy} + f_y = e^{x2 - y2}(2x)(6y^2) + e^{x2 - y2}(-2y)$$

$$= 12xy^2e^{x2 - y2} - 2ye^{x2 - y2}$$

3. $w = 2x^2 + 3y^3 + 4z^4 \qquad y = e^x \qquad z = \ln x$

$$\frac{dw}{dx} = f_x + f_y\frac{dy}{dx} + f_z\frac{dz}{dx}$$

$$= 4x + 9y^2e^x + 16z^3\left(\frac{1}{x}\right)$$

**Case 2: Both Independent Variables a Function of Another Variable**

Given the function $z = f(x, y)$, where $x = g(t)$ and $y = h(t)$. That is, both independent variables are themselves dependent on another variable, $t$. Once again we have a variety of composite function, since $z = f[g(t), h(t)]$. Function $z$ can change directly as $x$ and/or $y$ vary, or indirectly through intermediate variables $x$ and $y$ when variable $t$ changes.

The total differential of the function $z = f[g(t), h(t)]$ is

$$dz = \frac{\partial f}{\partial x}\,dx + \frac{\partial f}{\partial y}\,dy \tag{5.12}$$

Dividing by $dt$, we obtain the total derivative, given in Equation (5.13):

$$\frac{dz}{dt} = \frac{\partial f}{\partial x}\frac{dx}{dt} + \frac{\partial f}{\partial y}\frac{dy}{dt} \tag{5.13}$$

The change in $z$ with respect to a small change in $t$ is transmitted through $x$ and $y$ via functions $g$ and $h$. Note once again the use of both the partial derivative sign ($\partial$) and the regular derivative sign ($d$) in Equation (5.13). We did this in order to indicate functions involving more than one independent variable ($\partial$) or only one independent variable ($d$).

In some cases, it may be true that $x = g(t)$, but $y \neq h(t)$. If so, then $dy/dt = 0$, and $dz/dt$ reduces to the indirect effect analyzed in Case 1, where

$$\frac{dz}{dt} = f_x \frac{dx}{dt}$$

In general, if $z = f(x_1, x_2, \ldots, x_n)$ and $x_1 = g(t), x_2 = h(t), \ldots, x_n = k(t)$, then the total derivative of $z$ with respect to $t$ is

$$\frac{dz}{dt} = f_1 \frac{dx_1}{dt} + f_2 \frac{dx_2}{dt} + \cdots + f_n \frac{dx_n}{dt} \tag{5.14}$$

EXAMPLES

1. $z = x^2 y^3 \qquad x = \frac{1}{2}t^2 \qquad y = 3t^3$

$$\frac{dz}{dt} = f_x \frac{dx}{dt} + f_y \frac{dy}{dt} = 2xy^3 t + 3x^2y^2 \cdot 9t^2$$
$$= 2xy^3 t + 27x^2y^2t^2$$

2. $Q = AL^\alpha K^{1-\alpha}, \qquad K = 2M^2, \qquad L = 4M$

$$\frac{dQ}{dM} = f_L \frac{dL}{dM} + f_K \frac{dK}{dM} = \alpha AL^{\alpha-1}K^{1-\alpha}(4) + (1-\alpha)AL^\alpha K^{-\alpha}(4M)$$
$$= 4A\alpha\left(\frac{K}{L}\right)^{1-\alpha} + 4AM(1-\alpha)\left(\frac{L}{K}\right)^\alpha$$

3. $w = e^{xyz}, \qquad x = e^t, \qquad y = \ln t, \qquad z = t^2$

$$\frac{dw}{dt} = f_x \frac{dx}{dt} + f_y \frac{dy}{dt} + f_z \frac{dz}{dt} = yze^{xyz}e^t + xze^{xyz}\frac{1}{t} + 2txye^{xyz}$$

### Case 3: Independent Variables Dependent on Two Other Variables

Given the function $z = f(x, y)$, where $x = g(t_1, t_2)$ and $y = h(t_1, t_2)$. The composite function here is written $z = f[g(t_1, t_2), h(t_1, t_2)]$. Function $z$ can change directly as $x$ and/or $y$ vary, or indirectly through intermediate variables $x$ and $y$ when variables $t_1$ and $t_2$ change. The total differential of function $z$ is given by

$$dz = \frac{\partial f}{\partial x}\,dx + \frac{\partial f}{\partial y}\,dy \tag{5.15}$$

Dividing by $dt_1$, we obtain the total derivative, given in Equation (5.16):

$$\frac{\partial z}{\partial t_1} = f_x \frac{\partial x}{\partial t_1} + f_y \frac{\partial y}{\partial t_1} \tag{5.16}$$

■ Note that the total derivative in this case is actually a partial derivative. $\partial z/\partial t_1$ is sometimes referred to as the total "partial" derivative. The partial derivative sign is necessary because variables $x$ and $y$ are functions of two variables, $t_1$ and $t_2$.

We can also find the total derivative $\partial z/\partial t_2$ by following the now familiar procedure. We find the total differential of $z$, divide by $dt_2$, and obtain

$$\frac{\partial z}{\partial t_2} = f_x \frac{\partial x}{\partial t_2} + f_y \frac{\partial y}{\partial t_2} \tag{5.17}$$

In general, if $z = f(x_1, x_2, \ldots, x_n)$ and $x_1 = g(t_1, t_2)$, $x_2 = h(t_1, t_2)$, ..., $x_n = k(t_1, t_2)$, then the total derivatives of $z$ with respect to $t_1$ and $t_2$, respectively, are

$$\frac{\partial z}{\partial t_1} = f_1 \frac{\partial x_1}{\partial t_1} + f_2 \frac{\partial x_2}{\partial t_1} + \cdots + f_n \frac{\partial x_n}{\partial t_1}$$

$$\frac{\partial z}{\partial t_2} = f_1 \frac{\partial x_1}{\partial t_2} + f_2 \frac{\partial x_2}{\partial t_2} + \cdots + f_n \frac{\partial x_n}{\partial t_2}$$

The occasion may arise in which one of the independent variables such as $y$ is a function only of $t_2$, but not of $t_1$. In such a case, we find that

$$\frac{\partial y}{\partial t_1} = 0 \qquad \text{and} \qquad \frac{\partial z}{\partial t_1} = f_x \frac{\partial x}{\partial t_1}$$

We can find this total derivative by extending Rule 7 in Chapter 4 (function-of-a-function rule).

EXAMPLES

1. $z = 2x^2 + y^3, \qquad x = 3s^2 + 2t^3, \qquad y = 2s^3 - 3t^2$

$$\frac{\partial z}{\partial s} = f_x \frac{\partial x}{\partial s} + f_y \frac{\partial y}{\partial s} = 4x(6s) + 3y^2(6s^2) = 24xs + 18y^2s^2$$

$$\frac{\partial z}{\partial t} = f_x \frac{\partial x}{\partial t} + f_y \frac{\partial y}{\partial t} = 4x(6t^2) + 3y^2(-6t) = 24xt^2 - 18y^2t$$

2. $w = e^{xyz}, \qquad x = s^2 + t^2, \qquad y = s^2 - t^2, \qquad z = s^2t^2$

$$\frac{\partial w}{\partial s} = f_x \frac{\partial x}{\partial s} + f_y \frac{\partial y}{\partial s} + f_z \frac{\partial z}{\partial s}$$

$$= yze^{xyz}(2s) + xze^{xyz}(2s) + xye^{xyz}(2st^2)$$

$$= 2syze^{xyz} + 2sxze^{xyz} + 2st^2xye^{xyz}$$

$$\frac{\partial w}{\partial t} = f_x \frac{\partial x}{\partial t} + f_y \frac{\partial y}{\partial t} + f_z \frac{\partial z}{\partial t}$$

$$= yze^{xyz}(2t) + xze^{xyz}(-2t) + xye^{xyz}(2ts^2)$$

$$= 2tyze^{xyz} - 2txze^{xyz} + 2ts^2xye^{xyz}$$

Given the following:

1. $z = x^2y + xy^2$, $y = 2x^3$; find $dz/dx$
2. $z = e^{x^2y}$, $y = \sqrt{x}$; find $dz/dx$
3. $z = \ln xy^2$, $y = 8x + 8$; find $dz/dx$
4. $z = x/y + xy$, $x = 2t$, $y = t^2$; find $dz/dt$
5. $z = \sqrt{x + 8y}$, $x = t^2 + 2t + 4$, $y = t^3 + t$; find $dz/dt$
6. $w = x^2z^2 + xyz + y^2t^2$, $x = 2t$, $y = 2t + 2$, $z = t^2$; find $dw/dt$
7. $z = \sqrt{x^2 - y^2}$, $x = s - t$, $y = s + t$; find $\partial z/\partial s$, $\partial z/\partial t$
8. $z = (x^2 + xy^2)^3$, $x = s + t$, $y = 25 - 2t$; find $\partial z/\partial s$, $\partial z/\partial t$
9. $w = \ln xyz$, $x = s^2t^2$, $y = st^2$, $z = st$; find $\partial z/\partial s$, $\partial z/\partial t$

## IMPLICIT DIFFERENTIATION

Many of the functions one encounters in the study of business and economics are *implicit functions* of the form $F(x, y) = 0$. For example, the isoquants and indifference curves of economic analysis are based on functions of this type. It is sometimes possible to solve such an equation for one of the variables explicitly in terms of the other variable. Thus it may be possible to reduce the equation $F(x, y) = 0$ to an explicit function of the form $y = f(x)$ or $x = f(y)$.[3]

Given an implicit function $F(x, y) = 0$, where it is possible to solve for $y$ in terms of $x$ such that $y = g(x)$. We wish to find $dy/dx$. The implicit function can be rewritten as

$$F[x, g(x)] = 0 \tag{5.18}$$

We now introduce a new variable, $z$.

$$z = h(x, y) = F[x, g(x)] \tag{5.19}$$

Differentiating $z$ with respect to $x$ by means of the procedure developed in Case 1 yields

$$\frac{dz}{dx} = \frac{\partial h}{\partial x} + \frac{\partial h}{\partial y} \cdot \frac{dy}{dx} \tag{5.20}$$

Equation (5.18) requires that $F[x, g(x)] = 0$, while Equation (5.19) states that $z = h(x, y) = F[x, g(x)]$. Hence $z = h(x, y) = 0$. This means that $dz/dx$ must also equal 0. Therefore Equation (5.20) may also be set equal to 0

$$\frac{dz}{dx} = \frac{\partial h}{\partial x} + \frac{\partial h}{\partial y} \cdot \frac{dy}{dx} = 0$$

$$= \frac{\partial F}{\partial x} + \frac{\partial F}{\partial y} \cdot \frac{dy}{dx} = 0 \tag{5.21}$$

[3] Notice the difference between the functional notation used in the above paragraph. An implicit function such as $F(x, y)$ is indicated by the capital $F$ notation, whereas an explicit function such as $y = f(x)$ is indicated by the lower-case $f$ notation.

Solving Equation (5.21) for $dy/dx$, we obtain

$$\frac{dy}{dx} = -\frac{F_x}{F_y} \quad \text{where } F_y \neq 0 \tag{5.22}$$

Equations (5.18) through (5.22) demonstrate that it is possible to find $dy/dx$ given an implicit function of the form $F(x, y) = 0$, provided that we can solve for $y$ in terms of $x$ such that $y = g(x)$. It is also possible to find $dx/dy$ by the same type of process. Assume that $F(x, y) = 0$ and $x = g(y)$, so that $F[g(y), y] = 0$. Differentiating this new function with respect to $y$, we obtain

$$\frac{\partial F}{\partial x} \cdot \frac{dx}{dy} + \frac{dF}{dy} = 0 \tag{5.23}$$

Solving Equation (5.23) for $dx/dy$, we obtain

$$\frac{dx}{dy} = -\frac{F_y}{F_x} \quad \text{where } F_x \neq 0 \tag{5.24}$$

EXAMPLES

1. $x^2 + y^2 = 10$ $\qquad \dfrac{dy}{dx} = -\dfrac{F_x}{F_y} = -\dfrac{2x}{2y} = -\dfrac{x}{y}$

2. $e^x + e^y = 20$ $\qquad \dfrac{dy}{dx} = -\dfrac{F_x}{F_y} = -\dfrac{e^x}{e^y}$

3. $y^3 + xy - 12 = 0$ $\qquad \dfrac{dy}{dx} = -\dfrac{F_x}{F_y} = -\dfrac{y}{3y^2 + x}$

We can extend the concept of implicit differentiation to a function of $n$ variables. Given the implicit function $F(x_1, x_2, \ldots, x_n) = 0$. Let one of the $x$'s, $x_n$, be a function of the remaining $n - 1$ variables. That is, $x_n = f(x_1, x_2, \ldots, x_{n-1})$. We can now compute the partial derivative of $x_n$ with respect to any $x_j$ by means of the implicit differentiation formula used in Equations (5.22) and (5.24):

$$\frac{\partial x_n}{\partial x_j} = -\frac{F_{x_j}}{F_{x_n}} \quad \text{where } F_{x_n} \neq 0 \tag{5.25}$$

▣ When an implicit function contains more than two variables, for example, $F(x_1, x_2, \ldots, x_n)$, it is necessary to use a partial derivative to measure the rate of change of one of the $x$'s with respect to another of the $x$'s. This emphasizes the fact that at least one other variable is being held constant. By way of contrast, one needs only the ordinary derivative sign when one is dealing with the implicit function $F(x, y)$. No other variable is being held constant when $dy/dx$ or $dx/dy$ are computed. Observe that the partial derivative $\partial x_n/\partial x_j$ is equal to the negative of the ratio of the partial derivatives of the function with respect to $x_j$ and $x_n$. There is a reciprocal relationship in the positioning of variables $x_n$ and $x_j$ on each side of Equation (5.25).

EXAMPLES

1. $F(x, y, z) = x^2 + 3xy + y^2 - 3xz + z^2 = 0$

$$\frac{\partial y}{\partial x} = -\frac{F_x}{F_y} = -\frac{2x + 3y - 3z}{3x + 2y}$$

$$\frac{\partial z}{\partial x} = -\frac{F_x}{F_z} = -\frac{2x + 3y - 3z}{2z - 3x}$$

2. $e^{xyz} + \ln xyz = 0$

$$\frac{\partial z}{\partial x} = -\frac{F_x}{F_z} = -\frac{yze^{xyz} + [1/(xyz)](yz)}{xye^{xyz} + [1/(xyz)](xy)} = -\frac{yze^{xyz} + 1/x}{xye^{xyz} + 1/z}$$

## HIGHER-ORDER PARTIAL DERIVATIVES

Given the differentiable function $z = f(x, y)$. We have shown that the process of partial differentiation produces two new functions, namely

$$\frac{\partial z}{\partial x} = \frac{\partial f(x, y)}{\partial x} \quad \text{and} \quad \frac{\partial z}{\partial y} = \frac{\partial f(x, y)}{\partial y} \tag{5.26}$$

When these new functions are themselves functions of variables $x$ and $y$, we can differentiate them once again in order to obtain the rate of change of the partial derivative with respect to either $x$ or $y$. The partial derivative of a partial derivative is referred to as a *higher-order partial derivative*. Standard notation for the case in which we take a "second-order partial derivative" (the partial derivative of a partial derivative) is as follows:

$$\begin{aligned} z_{xx} &= \frac{\partial}{\partial x}\left(\frac{\partial z}{\partial x}\right) = \frac{\partial^2 z}{\partial x^2} = \frac{\partial^2 f}{\partial x^2} = f_{xx} \\ z_{yy} &= \frac{\partial}{\partial y}\left(\frac{\partial z}{\partial y}\right) = \frac{\partial^2 z}{\partial y^2} = \frac{\partial^2 f}{\partial y^2} = f_{yy} \\ z_{xy} &= \frac{\partial}{\partial y}\left(\frac{\partial z}{\partial x}\right) = \frac{\partial^2 z}{\partial y\, \partial x} = \frac{\partial^2 f}{\partial y\, \partial x} = f_{xy} \\ z_{yx} &= \frac{\partial}{\partial x}\left(\frac{\partial z}{\partial y}\right) = \frac{\partial^2 z}{\partial x\, \partial y} = \frac{\partial^2 f}{\partial x\, \partial y} = f_{yx} \end{aligned} \tag{5.27}$$

We refer to $z_{xy}$ and $z_{yx}$ as *cross (or mixed) partial derivatives*. They result when one differentiates function $z$ first with respect to one variable and then with respect to the other variable. For example, let $z = 5x^2y$. Then we find $z_{xy}$ in two steps. First we differentiate $z$ with respect to $x$, and obtain $10xy$. Then we differentiate $10xy$ with respect to $y$, and obtain $10x$, which is $z_{xy}$.

In many cases, $z_{xy} = z_{yx}$. When this is the case, it makes no difference whether we first differentiate function $z$ with respect to $x$, then with respect to $y$, or vice versa. We obtain the same result. For example, $z_{xy} = z_{yx}$ when $z = 5x^2y$. In general, $z_{xy} = z_{yx}$ when the following theorem holds.

THEOREM 5.1 (YOUNG'S THEOREM) Given the function $f(x, y)$. If the function $f(x, y)$, its two first-order partial derivatives, and both cross partial derivatives are continuous, then $f_{xy} = f_{yx}$.

This theorem may be generalized to functions of $n$ variables. It enables us to disregard the ordering of our differentiation when we find cross partial derivatives, provided that the continuity property holds as outlined. The proof of this theorem is lengthy. You are referred to footnote 4 for a reference to a rigorous proof.[4]

EXAMPLES

1. $z = x^2 + 2xy + y^2$

$z_x = 2x + 2y = 2(x + y) \qquad z_y = 2x + 2y = 2(x + y)$

$z_{xx} = 2 \qquad z_{yy} = 2$

$z_{xy} = 2 = z_{yx} \qquad z_{yx} = 2$

2. $z = x^2y + x^2y^2 + xy^2$

$z_x = 2xy + 2xy^2 + y^2 \qquad z_y = x^2 + 2x^2y + 2xy$

$z_{xx} = 2y + 2y^2 \qquad z_{yy} = 2x^2 + 2x$

$z_{xy} = 2x + 4xy + 2y = z_{yx} = 2x + 4xy + 2y$

EXERCISE 5.4

Using implicit differentiation, find $\partial z/\partial x$ and $\partial z/\partial y$, given

1. $2x^2 + 3y^2 + 4z^2 = 24$
2. $x^3 + y^3 + z^3 + xy + 2yz + 3xz = 0$
3. $-x^2 - 4y^2 + 2z^3 = 60$
4. $3x^2 - 4y - z^2 + x^2yz^2 = 20$
5. $e^x + e^y + e^z = 1000$
6. $\ln xyz = 10$
7. $\ln x + \ln y + \ln z = e^y$
8. $\sin(x + y) + \sin(y + z) + \sin(z + x) = 0$
9. $xy - e^x \sin y = 1$
10. $x + y - \ln z = 0$
11. $ax + by + cz = e$
12. $(x^2 + 8yz)(x^3 + 5) = 8$

Determine the following higher-order partial derivatives.

13. Given that $z = x^2 + 2xy + y^2$, find $z_{xx}$, $z_{yy}$
14. Given that $z = 4x^2y^2$, find $z_{xx}$, $z_{yy}$
15. Given that $z = e^{x^2+y^2} + 4x^3y^2$, find $z_{xx}$, $z_{yy}$
16. Given that $z = \frac{x}{y} - \frac{y}{x}$, find $z_{xx}$, $z_{yy}$
17. Given that $z = \cos y + y \sin x$, find $z_{xx}$, $z_{yy}$
18. Given that $z = zx^2 + 2y^2 - 4x - 8xy^2$, show that $z_{xy} = z_{yx}$
19. Given that $z = \frac{x - y}{x + y}$, show that $z_{xy} = z_{yx}$
20. Given that $z = \ln(x^2 + y^2)$, show that $z_{xx} + z_{yy} = 0$
21. Given that $z = x^2y^2 + 4x^3y$, show that $z_{xyy} = z_{yxy} = z_{yyx}$

[4] See David Widder, *Advanced Calculus*, Prentice-Hall, Englewood Cliffs, N.J., 1961, p. 52.

We shall devote the remainder of this chapter to applications of the partial derivative that you may encounter in business and economics.

### Partial Elasticities

Assume that a certain consumer has a demand function for a particular good $i$ of the form $Q_i = f(P_i, P_j, Y)$, where $Q_i$ = quantity demanded of good $i$, $P_i$ = price of good $i$, $P_j$ = price of some other good $j$, and $Y$ = the consumer's income. The *direct price elasticity of demand*, initially defined in Chapter 4 for a demand function with only one independent variable, may now be defined as

$$\eta_{Q_i, P_i} = \frac{\partial Q_i}{\partial P_i} \cdot \frac{P_i}{Q_i} \tag{5.28}$$

When the demand curve the consumer faces is downward-sloping, then $\partial Q_i / \partial P_i < 0$. The signs of $Q_i$ and $P_i$ are always positive in the first quadrant. Hence $\eta_{Q_i, P_i}$ always assumes a negative sign under such conditions.

We can also define $\eta_{Q_i, Y}$, a partial elasticity with respect to the final argument in the demand function. *Income elasticity of demand* ($\eta_{Q_i, Y}$) relates percentage changes in quantity demanded to percentage changes in the consumer's income.

$$\eta_{Q_i, Y} = \frac{\partial Q_i}{\partial Y} \cdot \frac{Y}{Q_i} \tag{5.29}$$

When $\eta_{Q_i, Y} > 0$, we label the good in question *income superior* ("normal"), whereas when $\eta_{Q_i, Y} < 0$, we label the good *income inferior*. A knowledgeable forecaster can make considerable use of information about income elasticity of demand. For example, Chow found that the income elasticity of demand for new automobiles was +3.0, and concluded that rising incomes would greatly stimulate automobile sales.[5] This is important information for economic policy making. On the other hand, Wold found the income elasticity of demand for margarine to be −0.20.[6] Rising incomes would cause consumers to decrease their expenditures for margarine.

Our ability to differentiate functions of more than one independent variable also means that we can define the *cross price elasticity of demand*. Cross price elasticity of demand relates the percentage change in the quantity demanded of one good to percentage changes in the price of some other good. In the case at hand, we relate $Q_i$ to $P_j$.

$$\eta_{Q_i, P_j} = \frac{\partial Q_i}{\partial P_j} \cdot \frac{P_j}{Q_i} \tag{5.30}$$

The sign of $\eta_{Q_i, P_j}$ is used to define the goods in question (goods $i$ and $j$) as

[5] Gregory C. Chow, *Demand for Automobiles in the United States*, North-Holland Publishing Company, Amsterdam, 1957.

[6] Herman Wold, *Demand Analysis*, John Wiley and Sons, New York, 1953, p. 265.

having either a *substitute relationship* or a *complementary relationship.* When $\eta_{Q_i, P_j} > 0$, the goods in question have a substitute relationship. For example, Wold found the cross price elasticity of demand between the quantity of margarine sold and the price of butter to be +0.81.[7] When $\eta_{Q_i, P_j} < 0$, the goods in question have a complementary relationship. An example is the relationship between the quantity of cameras sold and the price of camera film.

EXAMPLE The CTA. Given the demand function for CTA travel specified at the beginning of the chapter, in which $Q = f(P, Y, N, A)$, where $Q$ = number of riders, $Y$ = income of potential riders, $N$ = number of potential riders, and $A$ = cost of operating an automobile. Let our best estimate of this demand function be

$$Q = 200{,}000{,}000 - 400{,}000{,}000P - 0.001Y + 5.1N + 300{,}000{,}000A$$

(a) When $P = \$0.25$, $Y = \$20$ billion, $N = 2$ million, and $A = \$0.10$, then

$$\text{Estimated } Q = 200{,}000{,}000 - 400{,}000{,}000(0.25) - 0.001(20{,}000{,}000{,}000) + 5.1(2{,}000{,}000) + 300{,}000{,}000(0.10) = 120{,}200{,}000$$

(b) Price elasticity of demand when $P = \$0.25$ and $Q = 120{,}200{,}000$ is

$$\frac{\partial Q}{\partial P} \cdot \frac{P}{Q} = (-400{,}000{,}000)\left(\frac{0.25}{120{,}200{,}000}\right) = -0.832$$

Hence attempts by the CTA to increase total sales revenues by increasing prices would be successful in this general price range.

(c) Income elasticity of demand is

$$\frac{\partial Q}{\partial Y} \cdot \frac{Y}{Q} = (-0.001)\left(\frac{20{,}000{,}000{,}000}{120{,}200{,}000}\right) = -0.167$$

Rising incomes will lead to less usage of the CTA, presumably because increased incomes enable consumers to afford other types of transportation, such as automobiles. CTA travel is an income-inferior good here.

(d) The elasticity of CTA travel with respect to the potential number of riders is

$$\frac{\partial Q}{\partial N} \cdot \frac{N}{Q} = (5.1)\left(\frac{2{,}000{,}000}{120{,}200{,}000}\right) = 0.085$$

An increase in the number of potential riders will increase the total number of rides actually taken. However, CTA ridership expands much less rapidly than the number of potential riders.

(e) Cross price elasticity of demand is

$$\frac{\partial Q}{\partial A} \cdot \frac{A}{Q} = (300{,}000{,}000)\left(\frac{0.10}{120{,}200{,}000}\right) = 0.250$$

[7] Wold, p. 285. Note that there is a distinct cross price elasticity of demand between the quantity of butter sold and the price of margarine. Wold found this to be +0.67.

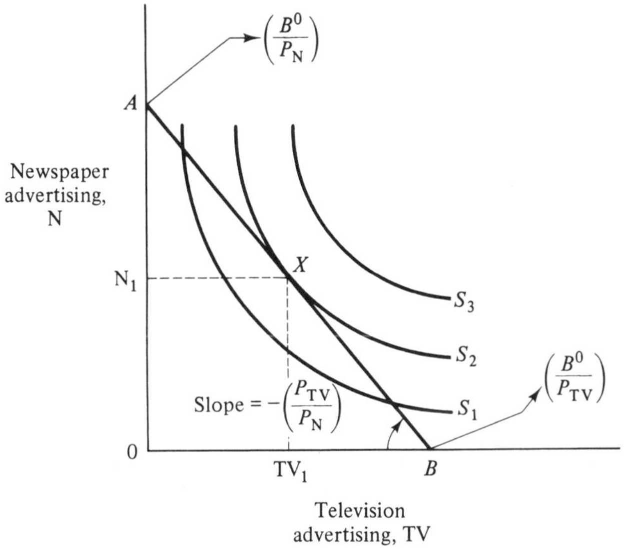


Figure 5.3 Media selection in advertising

An increase in the cost of operating an automobile ($0.10 a mile in the example here) will increase CTA ridership. CTA ridership and automobile travel are substitute goods.[8]

#### Selection of Media in Advertising

Consider a firm with a fixed budget of $B^0$ dollars that it is willing to spend on advertising in either of two media, television (TV) or newspapers (N). The price of television advertising and the price of newspaper advertising are $P_{TV}$ and $P_N$, respectively. The firm can make any expenditures on advertising that do not violate the budget constraint, given by

$$B^0 \geq P_{TV}(\mathrm{TV}) + P_N(\mathrm{N}) \tag{5.31}$$

Assume that the firm chooses to spend all the $B^0$ dollars at its disposal. Then $B^0 = P_{TV}(\mathrm{TV}) + P_N(\mathrm{N})$. Advertising budget line $AB$ in Figure 5.3 depicts this equation. We can find the slope $-P_{TV}/P_N$ and ordinate intercept $B^0/P_N$ of this budget equation by solving it for variable N.

$$\begin{aligned} B^0 &= P_{TV}(\mathrm{TV}) + P_N(\mathrm{N}) \\ P_N(\mathrm{N}) &= B^0 - P_{TV}(\mathrm{TV}) \\ \mathrm{N} &= \frac{B^0}{P_N} - \frac{P_{TV}}{P_N}(\mathrm{TV}) \end{aligned} \tag{5.32}$$

[8] Once again, the numbers used in this example are fictitious, though realistic, and are based on work performed by one of the authors.

The firm realizes additional sales $S$ when it advertises in either medium. That is,

$$S = f(\text{TV}, \text{N}) \qquad \text{where } \frac{\partial S}{\partial(\text{TV})} > 0 \text{ and } \frac{\partial S}{\partial \text{N}} > 0$$

However, the firm experiences diminishing returns at the margin when it increases advertising in one medium and holds advertising in the other medium constant. This means that

$$\frac{\partial^2 S}{\partial(\text{TV})^2} < 0 \qquad \text{and} \qquad \frac{\partial^2 S}{\partial \text{N}^2} < 0$$

The total differential of the advertising sales function is given by

$$dS = \frac{\partial S}{\partial(\text{TV})} d(\text{TV}) + \frac{\partial S}{\partial \text{N}} d\text{N} \tag{5.33}$$

Define an "isosales curve" as the locus of all combinations of television and newspaper advertising that yield a given, constant level of sales. That is, an isosales curve is given by the equation $S^0 = f(\text{TV}, \text{N})$. Along any isosales curve, the change in sales is 0, and we can therefore rewrite Equation (5.33) as

$$\begin{aligned} 0 &= \frac{\partial S}{\partial(\text{TV})} d(\text{TV}) + \frac{\partial S}{\partial \text{N}} d\text{N} \\ -\frac{d\text{N}}{d(\text{TV})} &= \frac{\partial S/\partial(\text{TV})}{\partial S/\partial \text{N}} = \frac{f_{\text{TV}}}{f_{\text{N}}} \end{aligned} \tag{5.34}$$

The term $-d\text{N}/d(\text{TV})$ is the marginal rate of substitution between television advertising and newspaper advertising.[9] This rate of substitution is also the slope of any isosales curve at any point on that isosales curve. Note that the rate of substitution between media (holding sales constant along a given isosales curve) depends on the marginal sales produced by additional expenditures on each medium. Figure 5.3 presents several among an infinite number of different possible isosales curves. These isosales curves are labeled $S_1$, $S_2$, and $S_3$.

The firm wishes to manipulate its expenditures on advertising in each medium so that it maximizes the total sales that it receives when it spends $B^0$ dollars on advertising. The particular combination of advertising on television and advertising in newspapers that will maximize sales (given $B^0$ dollars spent) is indicated by $\text{TV}_1$ and $\text{N}_1$ in Figure 5.3. This particular selection of media enables the firm to realize the level of sales given by isosales curve $S_2$. The firm cannot achieve a place on a superior isosales curve if it restricts itself to spending $B^0$ dollars on advertising. Likewise, the firm cannot rearrange its selection of media so that sales are increased. Any alternative selection of media other than $\text{TV}_1$, $\text{N}_1$ reduces sales when the firm spends $B^0$ dollars.

Media selection $\text{TV}_1$, $\text{N}_1$ in Figure 5.3 is given by the tangency of advertising

[9] We can also find $-d\text{N}/d(\text{TV})$ by using the implicit function rule.

budget line $AB$ with isosales curve $S_2$ at point $X$. We know that the following condition must hold at point $X$:

$$-\frac{dN}{d(TV)} = \frac{f_{TV}}{f_N} = \frac{P_{TV}}{P_N} \tag{5.35}$$

This follows because the two left-hand terms define the slope of isosales curve $S_2$ at point $X$, while the right-hand term defines the slope of the advertising budget line at point $X$.

EXAMPLE Acme Construction Company (ACC) is willing to spend \$10,000 on advertising during this time period. The price of television advertising is \$1000 per minute, while the price of newspaper advertising is \$10 per line. ACC's advertising budget constraint is given by

$$\$10{,}000 = \$1000\text{TV} + \$10\text{N} \tag{5.36}$$

The sales function that ACC faces is given by

$$S = f(\text{TV}, \text{N}) = K(\text{TV})^3\text{N} \qquad \text{where } K = \text{a positive number}$$

The total differential of this sales function is

$$dS = \frac{\partial S}{\partial(\text{TV})}\,d\text{TV} + \frac{\partial S}{\partial \text{N}}\,d\text{N} \tag{5.37}$$

Along any isosales curve, $dS = 0$. Hence we can see that the marginal rate of substitution between newspaper advertising and television advertising $[-d\text{N}/d(\text{TV})]$ is equal to 3N/TV.

$$\begin{aligned} 0 &= \frac{\partial S}{\partial(\text{TV})}\,d\text{TV} + \frac{\partial S}{\partial \text{N}}\,d\text{N} \\ -\frac{d\text{N}}{d(\text{TV})} &= \frac{\partial S/\partial(\text{TV})}{\partial S/\partial \text{N}} = \frac{f_{TV}}{f_N} = \frac{3K(\text{TV})^2\text{N}}{K(\text{TV})^3} = \frac{3\text{N}}{\text{TV}} \end{aligned} \tag{5.38}$$

Sales are maximized when expenditures on media are distributed such that

$$\begin{aligned} -\frac{d\text{N}}{d(\text{TV})} &= \frac{f_{TV}}{f_N} = \frac{P_{TV}}{P_N} \\ \frac{3\text{N}}{\text{TV}} &= \frac{1000}{10} \\ \text{N} &= \frac{100}{3}\text{TV} \end{aligned} \tag{5.39}$$

Substituting the value of N found in Equation (5.39) into the advertising budget equation given by Equation (5.36), we obtain

$$\begin{aligned} 10{,}000 &= 1000\text{TV} + \frac{1000}{3}\text{TV} \\ 10{,}000 &= 1333\text{TV} \\ \text{TV} &= 7.5 \end{aligned} \tag{5.40}$$

When TV = 7.5, then N = 250:

$$\begin{aligned} 10{,}000 &= 1000(7.5) + 10\text{N} \\ 2500 &= 10\text{N} \\ \text{N} &= 250 \end{aligned} \tag{5.41}$$

Hence the sales-maximizing choice of advertising media for ACC is to purchase 7.5 minutes of television advertising and 250 lines of newspaper advertising. Any alternative choice of media results in a lower level of sales, the maximum of which, in this case, is equal to

$$S = (\text{TV})^3\text{N} = (7.5)^3(250) = \$105{,}469 \tag{5.42}$$

**Production Theory**

A production function indicates the maximum output that a firm can obtain from any given set of inputs that it uses. Assume a production function of the form $Q = f(L, K)$, where $Q$ = output, $L$ = units of labor, and $K$ = units of capital. The marginal product of labor ($\text{MP}_L$) measures the change in output that results when a very small change is made in the amount of labor being used, the amount of capital being held constant.

$$\text{MP}_L = \frac{\partial Q}{\partial L} = f_L$$

Similarly, we can define the marginal product of capital as

$$\text{MP}_K = \frac{\partial Q}{\partial K} = f_K$$

The law of diminishing returns, mentioned in Chapter 4, can also hold with respect to some or all of the inputs in multiple-input production functions. Diminishing returns with respect to labor (capital held constant) implies that, at some point, successive increments in the number of units of labor used eventually cause $\partial Q/\partial L$ to decline and possibly even become negative. We shall be able to describe the law of diminishing returns with much greater precision when we have mastered the concept of concavity and have learned to find maximum and minimum points (Chapter 6).

*Output-maximizing, cost-minimizing firm*

Assume that a firm possesses a production function of the form $Q = f(L, K)$. The firm is willing to spend $C^0$ dollars on inputs $L$ and $K$. $P_L$ and $P_K$, the prices of $L$ and $K$, respectively, are given to the firm and cannot be altered by the firm's activities. Therefore the firm faces a cost constraint given by

$$C^0 = P_L(L) + P_K(K) \tag{5.43}$$

The graph of Equation (5.43) is isocost line $AB$ in Figure 5.4. We can find the slope of isocost line $AB$ by solving Equation (5.43) for $K$:

$$K = \frac{C^0}{P_K} - \frac{P_L}{P_K}L \tag{5.44}$$

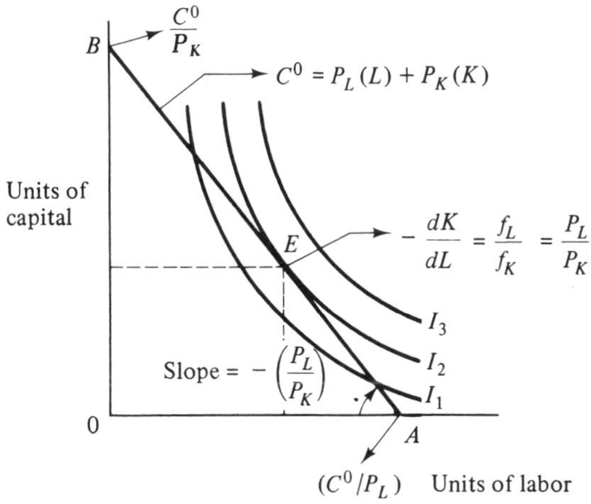


Figure 5.4 Output-maximizing, cost-minimizing firm

The slope is therefore $-P_L/P_K$, while the intercept of the isocost line on the ordinate is given by $C^0/P_K$.

We may represent the firm's production function by means of the isoquants ($I_1$, $I_2$, $I_3$) found in Figure 5.4. An *isoquant* is an isoproduct curve describing all the combinations of $L$ and $K$ that will produce a given $Q$. The equation of an isoquant is $Q^0 = f(L, K)$, where $Q^0$ is a specific level of output.

Taking the total differential of the production function, we find that

$$dQ = f_L\, dL + f_K\, dK \tag{5.45}$$

Since $dQ = 0$ along any isoquant, we know that

$$0 = f_L\, dL + f_K\, dK \tag{5.46}$$

Rearranging Equation (5.46), we obtain

$$-\frac{dK}{dL} = \frac{f_L}{f_K} \tag{5.47}$$

The expression $-dK/dL$ is referred to as the *marginal rate of technical substitution* between $K$ and $L$ and is the slope of any isoquant at any point. Note that the marginal rate of technical substitution of $K$ for $L$ is equal to $MP_L/MP_K$.

The firm wishes to produce the maximum output possible given cost expenditure $C^0$. This means that the firm wishes to produce at a point on the highest possible isoquant consistent with isocost line $AB$. Figure 5.4 demonstrates that this occurs when isocost line $AB$ is tangent to isoquant $I_2$ at point $E$. At point $E$, the slope of cost constraint $AB$ is the same as the slope of isoquant $I_2$. Hence we know that

$$-\frac{dK}{dL} = \frac{f_L}{f_K} = \frac{P_L}{P_K} \tag{5.48}$$

Equation (5.48) describes a necessary or equilibrium condition that the firm must satisfy if it is to maximize output given cost expenditure $C^0$. Equation (5.48) is also the condition the firm must satisfy if it wishes to minimize the cost of producing a given level of output.

*Homogeneous production functions*

Many production functions are *linear homogeneous.* This means that they realize constant returns to scale such that when all inputs are changed by a given proportion, output changes by the same proportion. Linear homogeneous functions also have a number of other interesting properties that are outlined in the footnote below.[10]

DEFINITION A production function is homogeneous of degree $n$ if output changes by the proportion $\lambda^n$ when all inputs are changed by proportion $\lambda$.

Assume a production function of the form $Q = f(L, K)$. Multiply all inputs by the constant $\lambda$. If output expands by the factor $\lambda^n$, then the production function is said to be homogeneous of degree $n$ in all inputs. For example, let the quantity of all inputs double, so that $\lambda = 2$. Then, if output also doubles, $n = 1$, and the production function exhibits *constant returns to scale.* When $n < 1$ and output less than doubles, the production function exhibits *decreasing returns to scale.* When $n > 1$ and output more than doubles, the production function exhibits *increasing returns to scale.*

EXAMPLES

1. Let $Q = AL^\alpha K^{1-\alpha}$, the Cobb-Douglas production function. Multiply all inputs by $\lambda$, a constant.

$$Q = A(\lambda L)^\alpha(\lambda K)^{1-\alpha} = A\lambda^\alpha L^\alpha \lambda^{1-\alpha}K^{1-\alpha}$$
$$= \lambda(AL^\alpha K^{1-\alpha})$$

[10] Given a linear homogeneous production function of the form $Q = f(L, K)$, where $Q$ is output and $L$ and $K$ are inputs. In addition to the definitional characteristic of a linear homogeneous production function, the following characteristics also hold:

1. Euler's theorem holds, such that

$$nQ = \frac{\partial Q}{\partial L}L + \frac{\partial Q}{\partial K}K$$

2. The average and marginal products of each input depend only on the capital-to-labor ratio and are independent of the absolute magnitudes of the inputs used.
3. The average and marginal products of either input attain their maximum at a certain constant amount, regardless of the amounts of each input used.
4. The marginal products of the inputs are homogeneous of degree zero in all inputs.
5. We can construct the isoquants by drawing rays from the origin so that a production level to $tQ$ will be exactly $t$ times farther from the origin than a production level of $Q$.
6. Every isoquant on a ray from the origin has the same slope and $MRTS$ where the ray cuts those isoquants.
7. The expansion path is linear.
8. The ridge lines are linear.

Output expands by $\lambda$, the constant. The Cobb-Douglas production function is therefore linear homogeneous and realizes constant returns to scale. $n = 1$.

2. Let $Q = L^{0.5} + K^{0.5}$. Multiply all inputs by $\lambda$, a constant.

$$Q = (\lambda L)^{0.5} + (\lambda K)^{0.5} = \lambda^{0.5}L^{0.5} + \lambda^{0.5}K^{0.5}$$
$$= \lambda^{0.5}(L^{0.5} + K^{0.5})$$

Output expands by $\lambda^{0.5}$, which is less than $\lambda$. That is, this production function realizes decreasing returns to scale. $n = 0.5$.

3. Let $Q = L^2 + K^2$. Multiply all inputs by $\lambda$, where $\lambda > 1$.

$$Q = (\lambda L)^2 + (\lambda K)^2 = \lambda^2L^2 + \lambda^2K^2$$
$$= \lambda^2(L^2 + K^2)$$

Output expands by $\lambda^2$, which is greater than $\lambda$. The production function realizes increasing returns to scale. $n = 2$.

▣ A linear homogeneous production function implies constant returns to scale. It does not mean that the underlying production function itself is linear. For example, the Cobb-Douglas production function is linear homogeneous. However, it is not linear in its form. That is, $Q = AL^{\alpha}K^{1-\alpha}$ is not of the form $y = mx + b$, and therefore it is not linear. Total output $Q$ in the Cobb-Douglas production function cannot be described by a straight line.

*Euler's theorem and distribution*

Euler's theorem plays a central role in the theory of marginal productivity in economics. Suppose that the question arises as to whether or not the value of the output produced by the factors of production are sufficient to pay each factor of production the value of its marginal product. Let $PQ$ = total value of the output produced, while $(P_i)(MP_i) = VMP_i$ = the value of the marginal product produced by factor input $i$. Will

$$PQ \lesseqgtr \sum_{i=1}^{n} VMP_i?$$

Can each factor of production be paid the value of its marginal product without bankrupting the firm? Euler's theorem bears directly on this issue.

Given a production function of the form $Q = f(L, K)$, which is homogeneous of degree $n$. The following condition holds:

$$L\left(\frac{\partial Q}{\partial L}\right) + K\left(\frac{\partial Q}{\partial K}\right) = nQ = nf(L, K)$$
$$L(f_L) + K(f_K) = nQ = nf(L, K) \qquad (5.49)$$

Equation (5.49) is known as *Euler's theorem.* It states that the sum of the number of units of each input used times the marginal product of that input is equal to $n$, the degree of homogeneity, times output.

Euler's theorem is derived as follows.

*Given*: $f(\lambda L, \lambda K) = \lambda^n f(L, K)$ (5.50)

Using the chain rule and taking the partial derivative with respect to $\lambda$ on both sides, we obtain

$$\frac{\partial f(\lambda L, \lambda K)}{\partial \lambda L} \cdot \frac{\partial \lambda L}{\partial \lambda} + \frac{\partial f(\lambda L, \lambda K)}{\partial \lambda K} \cdot \frac{\partial \lambda K}{\partial \lambda} = \frac{\partial[\lambda^n f(L, K)]}{\partial \lambda} \tag{5.51}$$

$$L(f_{\lambda L}) + K(f_{\lambda K}) = n\lambda^{n-1} f(L,K) \tag{5.52}$$

Since $\lambda$ is any positive, real constant, we may (for example) set $\lambda = 1$. In this case, Equation (5.52) reduces to

$$\begin{aligned} L(f_L) + K(f_K) &= nf(L, K) \\ L(f_L) + K(f_K) &= nQ \end{aligned} \tag{5.53}$$

We can recognize Equation (5.53) as being identical to Equation (5.49).

Let us now "monetize" Equation (5.53) by multiplying both sides by $P$, the price of the output produced by the inputs. This results in

$$\begin{aligned} L \cdot P \cdot f_L + K \cdot P \cdot f_K &= n(PQ) \\ L(\text{VMP}_L) + K(\text{VMP}_K) &= n(PQ) \end{aligned} \tag{5.54}$$

Equation (5.54) tells us that when each factor of production is paid the value of its marginal product, the sum of those factor payments is equal to $n(PQ)$, where $PQ$ is the total value of the output produced by those factor inputs. Three possible situations may hold.

1. $n = 1$ (constant returns). In this case, $L(\text{VMP}_L) + K(\text{VMP}_K) = PQ$, and the payments to the factors of production exactly exhaust the value of the output these factors produce.
2. $n < 1$ (decreasing returns). In this case, $L(\text{VMP}_L) + K(\text{VMP}_K) < PQ$, and the payments to the factors of production are less than the value of the output these factors produce.
3. $n > 1$ (increasing returns). In this case, $L(\text{VMP}_L) + K(\text{VMP}_K) > PQ$, and the payments to the factors of production are greater than the value of the output these factors produce.

EXAMPLE Let $Q = AL^\alpha K^{1-\alpha}$, the Cobb-Douglas production function. Euler's theorem says that

$$\begin{aligned} AL^\alpha K^{1-\alpha} &= L \cdot f_L + K \cdot f_K \\ &= L\left[A\alpha\left(\frac{L}{K}\right)^{\alpha-1}\right] + K\left[A(1-\alpha)\left(\frac{K}{L}\right)^{-\alpha}\right] \\ &= A\alpha L^\alpha K^{1-\alpha} + A(1-\alpha)K^{1-\alpha}L^\alpha = \alpha(Q) + (1-\alpha)Q \\ &= Q[\alpha + (1-\alpha)] = Q \end{aligned} \tag{5.55}$$

Hence we see that in the Cobb-Douglas function, $L(f_L) + K(f_K) = nQ$, where $n = 1$. The Cobb-Douglas production function is linear homogeneous and exhibits constant returns to scale.

*Elasticity of substitution*

An increase in the wage paid to human dishwashers is likely (*ceteris paribus*) to lead to a reduction in the employment of human dishwashers and an increase in the employment of dishwashing machines. The point is that changes in the prices of factor inputs stimulate changes in the levels of employment of those factor inputs. The *elasticity of substitution* $\sigma$ (lower-case sigma) measures the way that the firm alters its factor input ratio when changes in factor prices occur. We can also use $\sigma$ to make some important statements about the distribution of income among the factors of production.

Given the production function $Q = f(L, K)$. The elasticity of substitution of $K$ for $L$ is defined as

$$\sigma = \frac{dk}{dp} \cdot \frac{p}{k} \tag{5.56}$$

where $k = K/L$, $p = w/r$, $w$ = wage of labor, and $r$ = price of capital.

EXAMPLE Let $Q = L^2K$. Then $\partial Q/\partial L = 2LK$ and $\partial Q/\partial K = L^2$. Since $\sigma = (dk/dp) \cdot (p/k)$ and $p = w/r = f_L/f_K$,

$$\frac{dp}{dk} = \frac{d(2LK/L^2)}{dk} = \frac{d(2K/L)}{dk}$$

$$= \frac{d[2(k)]}{dk} = 2.00$$

Then

$$\frac{dk}{dp} = \frac{1}{2} = 0.5$$

Therefore

$$\sigma = \frac{dk}{dp} \cdot \frac{p}{k} = (0.5)\frac{2(k)}{(k)} = 1.00$$

In the above example, $\sigma = 1$. This means that a proportionate increase in the ratio $w/r$ would bring about an equiproportionate increase in $K/L$. When $\sigma > 1$, a given proportionate change in $w/r$ elicits a greater-than-proportionate change in $K/L$. When $\sigma < 1$, a given proportionate change in $w/r$ elicits a less-than-proportionate change in $K/L$. Each of these three situations ($\sigma = 1$, $\sigma > 1$, $\sigma < 1$) has implications for the distribution of income between labor and capital.

Consider the case in which $w/r$ increases more rapidly than $K/L$. This causes the share of labor to increase while the share of capital decreases. This is because an increase in labor's wage (relative to the price of capital) causes firms to substitute relatively cheap capital for relatively expensive labor. However, because factor input proportions are not as flexible as factor input price ratios, firms cannot substitute capital for labor in the same proportion as the factor price ratio has risen. Hence the employment of labor does not fall sufficiently, nor does the employment of capital rise sufficiently, to offset the rise in labor's wage. This means that labor's share of the value of total output ($wL/PQ$) rises, while capital's share ($rK/PQ$) falls.

Table 5.1 summarizes the relationship between the elasticity of substitution and the relative distribution of income between labor and capital.

*Output elasticities*

Output elasticities measure the proportionate response in total output that is elicited by proportionate changes in the quantity of one input, all other inputs being held constant. Given the production function $Q = f(X_1, X_2, \ldots, X_n)$, where $X_i$ = factor input. The output elasticity with respect to input $X_i$ is defined as

$$\varepsilon_{Q,X_i} = \frac{\partial Q}{\partial X_i} \cdot \frac{X_i}{Q} \tag{5.57}$$

The elasticity of output with respect to input $X_i$ is equal to the marginal product of input $X_i$ divided by the average product of input $X_i$. This follows from the definition of $\varepsilon_{Q,X_i}$.

$$\varepsilon_{Q,X_i} = \frac{\partial Q}{\partial X_i} \cdot \frac{X_i}{Q} = \frac{\partial Q/\partial X_i}{Q/X_i} = \frac{\mathrm{MP}_i}{\mathrm{AP}_i} \tag{5.58}$$

EXAMPLE Given the Cobb-Douglas production function, where $Q = AL^{\alpha}K^{1-\alpha}$. The elasticity of output with respect to $L$ is equal to $\alpha$.

$$\begin{aligned}\varepsilon_{Q,L} &= \frac{\partial Q}{\partial L} \cdot \frac{L}{Q} = \left[\alpha A\left(\frac{L}{K}\right)^{\alpha-1}\right]\left(\frac{L}{Q}\right) \\ &= \frac{\alpha AL^{\alpha}K^{1-\alpha}}{AL^{\alpha}K^{1-\alpha}} = \alpha\end{aligned} \tag{5.59}$$

The elasticity of output with respect to $K$ is equal to $1 - \alpha$.

$$\begin{aligned}\varepsilon_{Q,K} &= \frac{\partial Q}{\partial K} \cdot \frac{K}{Q} = \left[A(1-\alpha)\left(\frac{L}{K}\right)^{\alpha}\right]\left(\frac{K}{Q}\right) \\ &= \frac{A(1-\alpha)L^{\alpha}K^{1-\alpha}}{AL^{\alpha}K^{1-\alpha}} = 1 - \alpha\end{aligned} \tag{5.60}$$

Table 5.1 Elasticity of substitution and factor shares

| *Change in factor input price ratio* | *Value of $\sigma$* | | |
|---|---|---|---|
| | $\sigma < 1$ | $\sigma = 1$ | $\sigma > 1$ |
| $w/r$ decreases | Labor's share decreases | Labor's share constant | Labor's share increases |
| | Capital's share increases | Capital's share constant | Capital's share decreases |
| $w/r$ increases | Labor's share increases | Labor's share constant | Labor's share decreases |
| | Capital's share decreases | Capital's share constant | Capital's share increases |

The sum of the output elasticities is also equal to the degree of homogeneity of the production function. For example, the Cobb-Douglas production function is homogeneous of degree 1, and the sum of $\alpha$ plus $(1-\alpha)=1$. We shall prove this assertion by means of a generalized production function in which $Q=f(L, K)$. Euler's theorem requires that

$$L(f_L)+K(f_K)=nf(L, K) \tag{5.61}$$

Dividing both sides of Equation (5.61) by $Q=f(L, K)$, we obtain

$$\frac{L(f_L)}{Q}+\frac{K(f_K)}{Q}=n \tag{5.62}$$

Inverting $L/Q$ and $K/Q$ in Equation (5.62), and applying our finding of Equation (5.58) that the elasticity of output with respect to an input is equal to the marginal product of that input divided by the average product of that input, we can write

$$\frac{\partial Q/\partial L}{Q/L}+\frac{\partial Q/\partial K}{Q/K}=n, \qquad \varepsilon_{Q,L}+\varepsilon_{Q,K}=n \tag{5.63}$$

*The Cobb-Douglas production function*
The Cobb-Douglas production function,[11] which we have referred to throughout the last two chapters, takes the form $Q=AL^{\alpha}K^{1-\alpha}$, where $A$ and $\alpha$ are constants, $A>0$, and $0<\alpha<1$.

$$\text{MP}_L=\frac{\partial Q}{\partial L}=A\alpha\left(\frac{L}{K}\right)^{\alpha-1} \qquad \text{and} \qquad \text{MP}_K=\frac{\partial Q}{\partial K}=A(1-\alpha)\left(\frac{L}{K}\right)^{\alpha}$$

We have already demonstrated that the Cobb-Douglas production function is linear homogeneous and realizes constant returns to scale. The marginal rate of technical substitution is given by

$$-\frac{dK}{dL}=\frac{f_L}{f_K}=\frac{\alpha A(L/K)^{\alpha-1}}{(1-\alpha)A(K/L)^{-\alpha}}=\frac{\alpha}{1-\alpha}\left(\frac{K}{L}\right) \tag{5.64}$$

The elasticity of substitution $\sigma$ in the Cobb-Douglas is equal to 1.

$$\sigma=\frac{dk}{dp}\cdot\frac{p}{k} \qquad \text{where } k=\frac{K}{L} \text{ and } p=\frac{w}{r}$$

$$p=\frac{w}{r}=\frac{f_L}{f_K} \qquad \text{Therefore} \qquad \frac{dp}{dk}=\frac{d[(\alpha/1-\alpha)(k)]}{dk}=\frac{\alpha}{1-\alpha} \tag{5.65}$$

Hence

$$\frac{dk}{dp}=\frac{1-\alpha}{\alpha}$$

[11] One of the initial expositions of the Cobb-Douglas production function is found in Paul Douglas and Martin Bronfenbrenner, "Cross-Section Studies in the Cobb-Douglas Function," *Journal of Political Economy*, 47 (December 1939), 761–785.

Therefore

$$\sigma = \left(\frac{1-\alpha}{\alpha}\right)\left[\frac{[\alpha/(1-\alpha)](k)}{k}\right] = 1.00$$

The elasticity of output with respect to labor $\varepsilon_{Q,L}$ is equal to $\alpha$ in the Cobb-Douglas production function, whereas the elasticity of output with respect to capital $\varepsilon_{Q,K}$ is equal to $1-\alpha$.

$$\varepsilon_{Q,L} = \frac{\mathrm{MP}_L}{\mathrm{AP}_L} = \frac{\alpha A(L/K)^{\alpha-1}}{AL^{\alpha}K^{1-\alpha}/L} = \frac{\alpha AL^{\alpha-1}K^{1-\alpha}}{AL^{\alpha-1}K^{1-\alpha}} = \alpha \tag{5.66}$$

$$\varepsilon_{Q,K} = \frac{\mathrm{MP}_K}{\mathrm{AP}_K} = \frac{(1-\alpha)A(K/L)^{-\alpha}}{AL^{\alpha}K^{1-\alpha}/K} = \frac{(1-\alpha)AK^{-\alpha}L^{\alpha}}{AL^{\alpha}K^{-\alpha}} = 1-\alpha \tag{5.67}$$

The Cobb-Douglas production function was the first attempt by economists to estimate a production function from actual input and output data. It has proved to be remarkably durable as a functional form, however, because of two factors.

First, it is a linear homogeneous production function and realizes constant returns to scale. This means that the Cobb-Douglas production function exhibits several characteristics that are both theoretically attractive and empirically realistic in many cases.

Second, when the Cobb-Douglas production function is subjected to a logarithmic transformation, the inputs $L$ and $K$ are linear in the logarithms. That is, $\log Q = \log A + \alpha \log L + (1-\alpha)\log K$. This means that the Cobb-Douglas function can be estimated as the linear form with which so many economists are familiar. Also, the log-linear transformation means that we can interpret $\alpha$ and $(1-\alpha)$ as output elasticities.

*The CES production function*

The CES (constant elasticity of substitution) production function[12] is a popular recent form that is more general than the Cobb-Douglas. The Cobb-Douglas production function can be shown to be a special case of the CES. As its name implies, the elasticity of substitution in the CES production function is equal to a constant, specifically $1/(1+\rho)$.

The functional form of the CES is

$$Q = \gamma[\delta K^{-\rho} + (1-\delta)L^{-\rho}]^{-1/\rho}$$

where $A$, $\delta$, and $\rho$ are three parameters, $A > 0$, $0 < \delta < 1$, $\rho > 1$, and $L$ and $K$ represent labor and capital, respectively. The marginal product of labor $\mathrm{MP}_L$ is given by

$$\mathrm{MP}_L = \frac{\partial Q}{\partial L} = \left(-\frac{1}{\rho}\right)\gamma[\delta K^{-\rho} + (1-\delta)L^{-\rho}]^{-(1/\rho)-1}[(1-\delta)(-\rho)L^{-\rho-1}]$$

[12] See K. Arrow, H. Chenery, B. Minhas, and R. Solow, "Capital-Labor Substitution and Economic Efficiency," *Review of Economics and Statistics*, 43 (August 1961), 228–232.

Since

$$\left(-\frac{1}{\rho}\right)\cdot(-\rho)=1 \qquad \text{and} \qquad -\left(\frac{1}{\rho}\right)-1=-\left(\frac{1}{\rho}\right)(1+\rho)$$

we can say that

$$\frac{\partial Q}{\partial L}=(1-\delta)\gamma[\delta K^{-\rho}+(1-\delta)L^{-\rho}]^{-(1/\rho)(1+\rho)}L^{-\rho-1}$$

Since $\gamma^{\rho+1}/\gamma^{\rho}=\gamma$, we can say that

$$\frac{\partial Q}{\partial L}=(1-\delta)\left(\frac{\gamma^{\rho+1}}{\gamma^{\rho}}\right)[\delta K^{-\rho}+(1-\delta)L^{-\rho}]^{-(1/\rho)(1+\rho)}L^{-\rho-1}$$

Define

$$Q^{1+\rho}=\{\gamma[\delta K^{-\rho}+(1+\delta)L^{-\rho}]^{-1/\rho}\}^{1+\rho}$$

Then

$$\frac{\partial Q}{\partial L}=\frac{1-\delta}{\gamma^{\rho}}\left(\frac{Q}{L}\right)^{1+\rho} \tag{5.68}$$

The marginal product of capital ($\mathrm{MP}_K$) is given by

$$\mathrm{MP}_K=\frac{\partial Q}{\partial K}=\left(-\frac{1}{\rho}\right)\gamma[\delta K^{-\rho}+(1-\delta)L^{-\rho}]^{-(1/\rho)-1}(-p)\delta K^{-p-l}$$

$$=(\gamma)(\delta)[\delta K^{-\rho}+(1-\delta)L^{-\rho}]^{-(1/\rho)(1+\rho)}\cdot\frac{1}{K^{1+\rho}}$$

Since $\gamma^{\rho+1}/\gamma^{\rho}=\gamma$, we can say that

$$\frac{\partial Q}{\partial K}=\frac{\gamma^{\rho+1}}{\gamma^{\rho}}(\delta)[\delta K^{-\rho}+(1-\delta)L^{-\rho}]^{-(1/\rho)(1+\rho)}\cdot\frac{1}{K^{1+\rho}}$$

Define

$$Q^{1+\rho}=\{\gamma[\delta K^{-\rho}+(1-\delta)L^{-\rho}]^{1/\rho}\}^{1+\rho}$$

Then

$$\frac{\partial Q}{\partial K}=\frac{\delta}{\gamma^{\rho}}\left(\frac{Q}{K}\right)^{1+\rho} \tag{5.69}$$

The marginal rate of technical substitution of $K$ for $L$ in the CES production function is given by

$$-\frac{dK}{dL}=\frac{f_L}{f_K}=\frac{(1-\delta)\gamma^{-\rho}(Q/L)^{1+\rho}}{(\delta)\gamma^{-\rho}(Q/K)^{1+\rho}}=\left(\frac{1-\delta}{\delta}\right)\left(\frac{K}{L}\right)^{1+\rho} \tag{5.70}$$

The elasticity of substitution in the CES production function is equal to $1/(1+\rho)$. This is demonstrated as follows:

$$\sigma = \frac{dk}{dp} \cdot \frac{p}{k} \qquad \text{where } k = \frac{K}{L} \text{ and } p = \frac{w}{r}$$

$$p = \frac{w}{r} = \frac{f_L}{f_K}$$

$$\frac{dp}{dk} = \frac{d[(1-\delta)/\delta]k^{1+\rho}}{dk} = (1+\rho)\left(\frac{1-\delta}{\delta}\right)k^{\rho}$$

Hence

$$\frac{dk}{dp} = \frac{1}{(1+\rho)[(1-\delta)/\delta]k^{\rho}} = \frac{\delta}{(1+\rho)(1-\delta)k^{\rho}}$$

$$\sigma = \frac{dk}{dp} \cdot \frac{p}{k} = \frac{\delta}{(1+\rho)(1-\delta)k^{\rho}} \cdot \frac{(1-\delta)k^{1+\rho}}{(\delta)(k)} = \frac{1}{1+\rho} \tag{5.71}$$

The elasticity of output with respect to $L$ in the CES production function is equal to

$$\frac{\text{MP}_L}{\text{AP}_L} = \frac{dQ}{dL} \cdot \frac{L}{Q} = \frac{1-\delta}{\gamma^{\rho}}\left(\frac{Q}{L}\right)^{1+\rho} \cdot \frac{L}{Q} = \frac{1-\delta}{\gamma^{\rho}}\left(\frac{Q}{L}\right)^{\rho} \tag{5.72}$$

The elasticity of output with respect to $K$ in the CES production function is equal to

$$\frac{\text{MP}_K}{\text{AP}_K} = \frac{dQ}{dK} \cdot \frac{K}{Q} = \frac{\delta}{\gamma^{\rho}}\left(\frac{Q}{K}\right)^{1+\rho} \cdot \frac{K}{Q} = \frac{\delta}{\gamma^{\rho}}\left(\frac{Q}{K}\right)^{\rho} \tag{5.73}$$

**PROBLEMS**

1. Find $\partial z/\partial x$, $\partial^2 z/\partial x^2$, $\partial z/\partial y$, $\partial^2 z/\partial y^2$, and $\partial^2 z/\partial x\,\partial y$, if they exist.

   (a) $z = 6x^2y$ (b) $z = \dfrac{0.3x^4}{y^2}$

   (c) $z = \dfrac{0.3x^{\alpha}}{y^{\alpha}}$ (d) $z = xy^2 + y$

   (e) $z = e^{x+1}y^2$ (f) $z = \ln 5x^4y$

   (g) $z = \log_7 x^3y^2$ (h) $z = \log_e x^y$

   (i) $z = Ax^{\alpha}y^{1-\alpha}$

2. Let $u = t^3 + 2$, $u = 1 + t^2$, and $w = u^2 - u$. Find $\partial w/\partial t$.
3. Stone estimated a demand function for beer in pre-World War II Great Britain such that $Q = 177.6Y^{-0.023}P^{-1.040}R^{0.939}$, where $Q$ = quantity of beer demanded, $Y$ = aggregate real income, $P$ = mean retail price of beer, and $R$ = mean retail price of all other commodities.[13] Find own price elasticity of demand; income elasticity of demand; cross price elasticity of demand.

[13] Richard Stone, "The Analysis of Market Demand," *Journal of the Royal Statistical Society*, 108 (1945), 286–382.

4. In February 1966, Pope Paul VI issued an apostolic decree that gave local Roman Catholic bishops the authority to decide whether or not Catholics would continue to be required to eat fish on Fridays and during the Lenten season. Catholic bishops in the United States duly terminated meatless Fridays, except during Lent. Bell has demonstrated that this decision shifted downward the demand curve for fish in New England such that there was a 12.5% fall in the landing price of fish.[14] Using monthly data encompassing months both prior to the decree and after the decree, Bell estimated a demand function of the form $P = KX_i^{\alpha}D^{\beta}$, where $P$ = landing price of fish per pound, $K$ = a constant, $X_i$ = explanatory variables such as income, prices of other goods, and so forth, and $D$ = a dummy variable that assumed a value of 1 for months prior to the decree and a value of 10 for all months in which the decree was in effect. Bell performed a log-linear transformation such that

$$\log P = K + \alpha \log X_i + \beta \log D$$

What meaning can we attach to $\beta$? What is the meaning of $(d \log P)/(d \log D)$? Bell concluded that prices fell by 12.5%. Which parameter in the log-linear transformation reflects that fact?

5. The Apex Calculator Company sells its Model 50 calculator in college bookstores at a price of $25 each. The cost per calculator of manufacturing the Model 50 (in production runs of up to 10,000 calculators) is an increasing function of the number of calculators produced.

$$\text{TC} = \$5000 + 10Q + .00005Q^2$$

Demonstrate that it is profitable to produce additional calculators, and indicate how many additional calculators should be produced.

6. The Rockford Detergent Company has allocated an advertising budget of $2,000,000 to spread the word about its new deodorant, "Cool 'n' Fresh." The cost of a 1-minute advertisement during prime television time is $100,000. The cost of a one-page advertisement in *Newstime* magazine is $40,000. Based on past sales experience with these advertising media, Rockford estimates that sales react to these types of advertising in the following fashion: $S = 5(\text{TV})^4P$, where $S$ = sales of Cool 'n' Fresh, TV = minutes of television advertising time, and $P$ = pages of advertising in *Newstime*. How many pages of advertising and how many minutes of television advertising should Rockford purchase?

7. The cost $C$ of building a house is given by $C = f(L_1, L_2)$, where $L_1$ = the daily number of carpenters used and $L_2$ = the daily number of electricians used. Specifically, $C = 15{,}000 + 50L_1^2 + 60L_2^2$. What is the marginal cost of adding (a) a carpenter, and (b) an electrician, when 10 of each are already employed?

8. The First National Bank of Paranoia has determined that the two major factors that influence whether or not an individual will pay back a loan

[14] Frederick W. Bell, "The Pope and the Price of Fish," *American Economic Review*, 58 (December 1968), 1346–1350.

are (a) the borrower's income and (b) the rate of unemployment. Payback (PB) is a function of income $I$ and the rate of unemployment $U$. That is, $PB = f(I, U)$, where $\partial PB/\partial I > 0$ and $\partial PB/\partial U < 0$. Payback is represented by a variable that assumes a value of 1 when the loan is paid back and 0 otherwise. Specifically, First National has found that $PB = 0.0001I - 12U$. Find $\partial PB/\partial I$ and $\partial PB/\partial U$. If my income is \$15,000 and the rate of unemployment is 6% (0.06), am I likely to pay back the loan? What would be the effect on the probability of payback of an increase in income to \$70,000 (rate of unemployment held constant)?

9. The First National Bank of Paranoia has also attempted to determine the size of a mortgage that it can safely give to a Paranoid who wished to buy a house. First National determines ability to pay ATP on the basis of $ATP = 0.00005I^2 + 3DP$, where $I$ = the applicant's income and DP = the size of the down payment on the mortgage. Find $\partial ATP/\partial I$ and $\partial ATP/\partial DP$. What meaning can you attach to these derivatives? What size of mortgage could a Paranoid support who has an income of \$20,000 and who is able to make a down payment of \$10,000?
10. The present value PV of 1 dollar that is to be received $t$ years from now is given by

$$PV = \frac{1}{(1 + r)^t}$$

Find $\partial PV/\partial r$ and $\partial PV/\partial t$.
11. The production function for widgets is given by $Q = f(L, K) = 2L^{0.5}K^{0.25}$, where $Q$ = output in units, $L$ = labor in units, and $K$ = capital in units. The firm is currently employing 100 workers and 81 units of capital. Find the marginal products of $L$ and $K$. Does the law of diminishing returns apply to either or both inputs? Why?
12. The production function relating to performance on accounting examinations is given by $G = 10HI - 0.2H^2 - 0.1I^2$, where $G$ = grade on the accounting examination, $H$ = hours of study for the examination, and $I$ = the student's IQ. Find $\partial G/\partial H$, $\partial^2G/\partial H^2$, $\partial G/\partial I$, and $\partial^2G/\partial I^2$. Under what circumstances are the marginal productivities of $H$ and $I$ positive? (For example, what value of $H$ is necessary for $\partial G/\partial I$ to be positive?)

# MAXIMA AND MINIMA

# 6

The objective of an accountant, business person, or economist is usually to maximize or minimize some function. Thus attention is given to minimizing the cost of achieving a certain objective. Or the decision-maker wants to maximize some magnitude, such as sales or output. It is also true, however, that the actions of the decision-maker are nearly always constrained by limitations such as the amount of money available for expenditure on this activity, or the minimum acceptable level of performance or output.

This chapter initially demonstrates how one may find the maxima or minima of a differentiable function. This finding is then generalized to the case in which one wishes to find the maxima or minima of a differentiable function subject to some constraint. This adds considerable realism to our work and enables you to deal with a wide range of problems in practical and theoretical situations. While it is an exaggeration to say that we can describe all activities as the maximization or minimization of some function subject to some constraint, it is not an overstatement to say that we can describe an extremely large number of activities by constrained optimization models. The goal of this chapter is to provide you with the tools you need to deal with many such situations.

## INCREASING OR DECREASING FUNCTIONS

It is often useful to be able to specify under what circumstances a function is increasing or decreasing. That is, for what values of the independent variable does the function increase, decrease, or remain stationary? For what values of the independent variable, if any, does the function increase (decrease) at an increasing (decreasing) rate?

The concept of an increasing or decreasing function is found in many places in business and economic problems. For example, in the law of diminishing returns, the "point of diminishing returns" occurs where the production function changes from increasing at an increasing rate to increasing at a decreasing rate.

DEFINITION A function $f(x)$ is said to be an increasing function for an interval if and only if $f(x_1) < f(x_2)$ when $x_1 < x_2$, for all $x_1$ and $x_2$ on the interval. Similarly, $f(x)$ is a decreasing function if and only if $f(x_1) > f(x_2)$ when $x_1 < x_2$, for all $x_1$ and $x_2$.

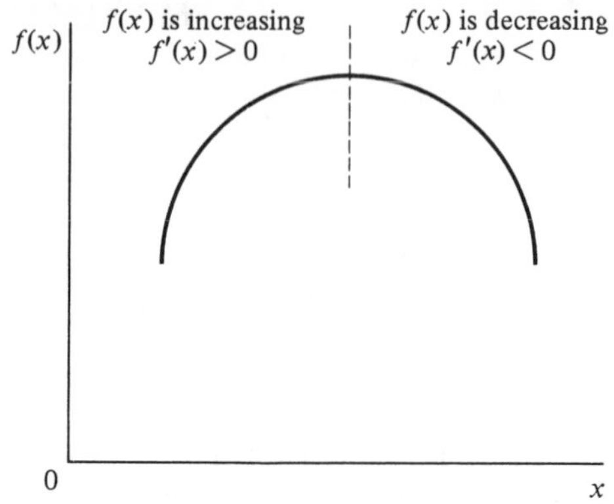


Figure 6.1 Increasing and decreasing functions

Figure 6.1 illustrates the graph of a function $f(x)$ that increases for an interval, becomes stationary, and then decreases. We already know that the first derivative of the function $f(x)$ represents the slope of that function at a given point $x$. When $f'(x)$ has a positive value, $f(x)$ is increasing. That is, when $f'(x) > 0$ for all values of $x$ on the interval, then $f(x)$ is increasing on that interval. Similarly, we can define $f'(x) < 0$ to be a decreasing function for all values of $x$ on that interval. When $f'(x) < 0$, $f(x)$ is decreasing.

EXAMPLES

1. Given $y = f(x) = 2 + 4x$. $f'(x) = 4$. Since $f'(x) > 0$, $f(x)$ is an increasing function for all values of $x$.

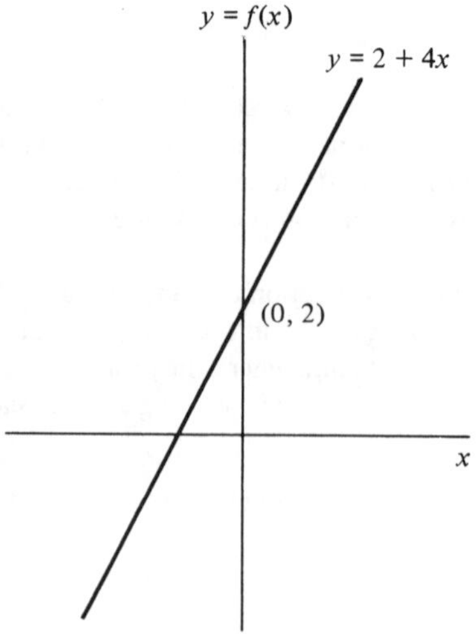

2. Given $y = f(x) = x^2$. $f'(x) = 2x$. Since $f'(x) > 0$ for $x > 0$ and $f'(x) < 0$ for $x < 0$, $f(x)$ is an increasing function of $x$ for all positive values of $x$ and a decreasing function of $x$ for all negative values of $x$.

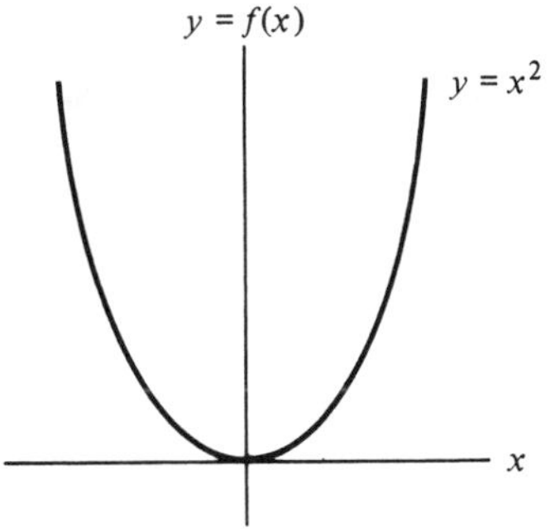


3. Given $y = f(x) = 2x^3 + 3x^2 - 12x$. $f'(x) = 6x^2 + 6x - 12$. Since $f'(x) > 0$ for $x > 1$ or $x < -2$, and $f'(x) < 0$ for $-2 < x < 1$, $f(x)$ is an increasing function of $x$ for those values of $x > 1$ or $x < -2$, and $f(x)$ is a decreasing function of $x$ for $-2 < x < 1$.

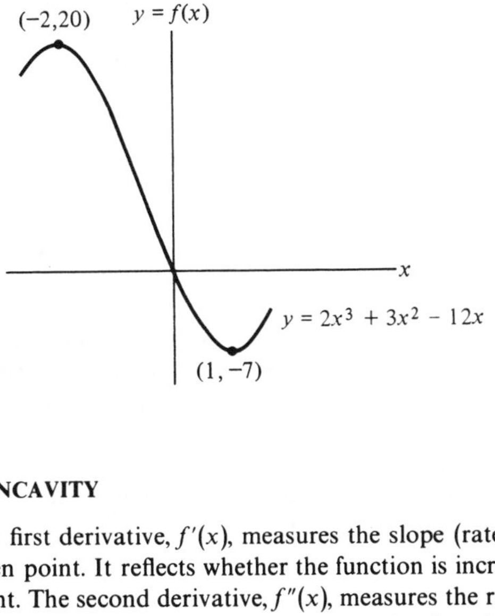


## CONCAVITY

The first derivative, $f'(x)$, measures the slope (rate of change) of a curve at a given point. It reflects whether the function is increasing or decreasing at that point. The second derivative, $f''(x)$, measures the rate of change of the slope of the function $f(x)$. It reflects whether the function $f(x)$ is increasing at an increasing (decreasing) rate or decreasing at an increasing (decreasing) rate.[1]

[1] A commonly used physical interpretation of the first and second derivatives relates to a moving automobile. The first derivative of distance with respect to time measures velocity ("speed"), while the second derivative of distance with respect to time measures acceleration.

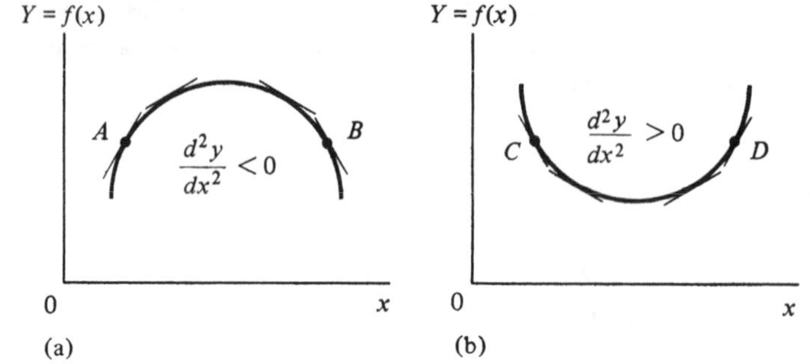


Figure 6.2 Concave functions. (a) Concave downward. (b) Concave upward

DEFINITION Given that $f'(x)$ and $f''(x)$ exist for all $x$ in some interval. Then, if $f''(x) > 0$, the curve $f(x)$ is said to be *concave upward* at $x$. If $f''(x) < 0$, then the curve $f(x)$ is said to be *concave downward* at $x$.

Figure 6.2(a) illustrates the case in which the curve of the function is *concave downward*. At point $A$, the first derivative, $f'(x)$, is positive and the second derivative, $f''(x)$, is negative. This means that the function is increasing, but at a decreasing rate. At point $B$, $f'(x) < 0$ and $f''(x) < 0$, indicating that the function is decreasing at an increasing rate, that is, that the slope of the function is becoming increasingly negative.

Figure 6.2(b) depicts the case where the curve of the function is *concave upward*. At point $C$, $f'(x) < 0$, but $f''(x) > 0$. This implies that the function is decreasing at a decreasing rate, that is, that the slope of the function is becoming less negative. At point $D$, $f'(x) > 0$ and $f''(x) > 0$. This means that the function is increasing at an increasing rate, that is, that the slope of the function is becoming increasingly positive.

■ One must be careful in assessing the implications of $f''(x)$ for $f'(x)$. For example, assume that a function $f(x)$ is decreasing at a increasing rate. That is, $f'(x) < 0$ and $f''(x) < 0$. This does *not* mean that the rate of change (slope) of the function is changing from (for example) $-5$ to $-4$. Instead, it implies that the rate of change (slope) is changing from $-5$ to $-6$. That is, $f'(x)$ is becoming increasingly negative. When the rate of change (slope) of the function is changing from $-5$ to $-4$, $f'(x)$ is becoming less negative.

## POINTS OF INFLECTION

DEFINITION A function $f(x)$ is said to have a *point of inflection* at point $x_0$ when the concavity of the function changes from downward to upward or from upward to downward at point $x_0$.

Figure 6.3 illustrates the two different types of points of inflection. In the upper portion of part (a), the point of inflection occurs where the concavity of

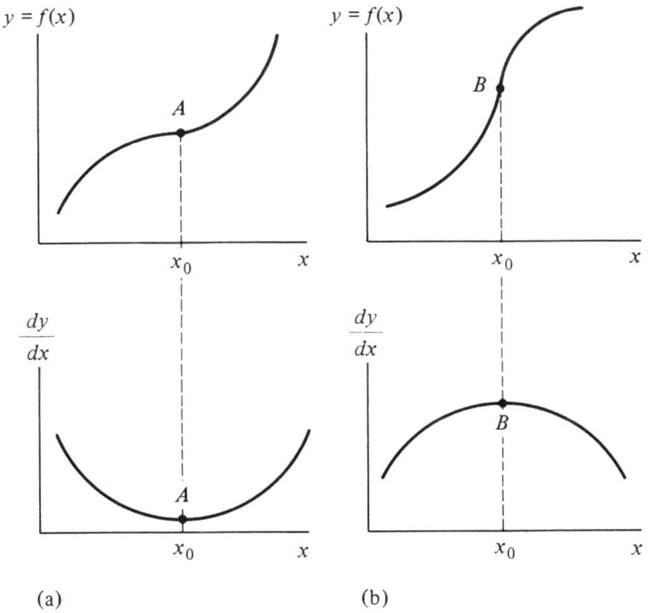


Figure 6.3 Points of inflection. (a) Concavity changes from downward to upward. (b) Concavity changes from upward to downward

the function changes from downward to upward and is indicated by point $A$. The point of inflection in the upper portion of part (b) occurs where the concavity of the function changes from upward to downward and is indicated by point $B$.

Points of inflection have definite implications for the first and second derivatives. We can see in the lower portion of part (a) that the point of inflection is the *minimum* value of $f'(x)$ when concavity is changing from downward to upward. Analogously, the point of inflection in the lower portion of part (b) is the *maximum* value of $f'(x)$ in the case in which the concavity of the function is changing from upward to downward.[2]

Whether the concavity of the function is changing from downward to upward [part (a)] or upward to downward [part (b)], it is true that $f''(x) = 0$. Hence $f''(x) = 0$ at both points $A$ and $B$ in Figure 6.3. This reflects the fact that the function $f(x)$ in part (a) is changing from increasing at a decreasing rate to increasing at an increasing rate. The function $f(x)$ in part (b) is changing from increasing at an increasing rate to increasing at a decreasing rate.

[2] The minimum and maximum referred to in this paragraph are "neighborhood" minima and maxima. It is possible that somewhere else $f'(x)$ assumes a value that is less than (greater than) the local "neighborhood" minimum and maximum points indicated here. We shall discuss local "neighborhood" minimum and maximum points further in the next section.

We can make a more general statement about points where the concavity of a function is changing. Given a differentiable function $f(x)$. If $f'(x)$ and $f''(x)$ are also continuous, and the value of the function $f''(x)$ is changing from a negative value to a positive value as in Figure 6.3(a), then there *must* be one point at which the value of the function $f''(x)$ is equal to 0. That is, if a function such as $f(x)$ in part (a) is changing from increasing at a decreasing rate to increasing at an increasing rate, then $f''(x)$ must be equal to 0 at one point on that interval.

▣ Given the function $f(x)$. If $f(x)$ has a point of inflection at point $x_0$, then it must be true that $f''(x) = 0$ at point $x_0$. The converse is not true. The fact that $f''(x) = 0$ at point $x_0$ is not sufficient to guarantee the existence of a point of inflection at point $x_0$. Therefore $f''(x)$ is a necessary rather than a sufficient condition for a point of inflection.

For example, suppose that $y = 4x$. Then $f'(x) = 4$ and $f''(x) = 0$. The graph of $y = 4x$ is a straight line, however, and there is no point of inflection anywhere along it.

Or consider $y = x^4$. Then $f'(x) = 4x^3$ and $f''(x) = 12x^2$. Setting $12x^2 = 0$, we find that $x = 0$. This does not mean that there is a point of inflection at $x = 0$. A point of inflection exists only if the concavity of the function changes from downward to upward or from upward to downward. We can ascertain whether this is the case by evaluating $f''(x)$ for $x < 0$ and $x > 0$. When $x < 0$, then $12x^2 > 0$. When $x > 0$, then $12x^2 > 0$. Hence $f''(x)$ is positive both for values of $x$ that are less than zero and for values of $x$ that are greater than zero. This implies that the concavity of the function is not changing. For a point of inflection to exist in this case, the sign of $f''(x)$ must change when we go from values of $x$ less than 0 to values of $x$ greater than 0. Hence there is no point of inflection at $x = 0$.

## MAXIMA AND MINIMA: FUNCTIONS OF ONE INDEPENDENT VARIABLE

Given the function $y = f(x)$. The value(s) of $x$ for which $f(x)$ attains a maximum or a minimum are referred to as *extreme points*. It is necessary, however, to distinguish between *absolute* and *relative* extreme points.

DEFINITION Let $y = f(x)$ be a real-valued function defined on a set $S$ of real numbers. Then the function $f(x)$ has an *absolute maximum* at $x = x_0$ if $f(x_0) \geq f(x)$ for all $x$ in $S$.

DEFINITION Given $y = f(x)$ as above. Then the function $f(x)$ has an *absolute minimum* at $x = x_0$ if $f(x_0) \leq f(x)$ for all $x$ in $S$.

DEFINITION Given $y = f(x)$ as above. Then the function $f(x)$ has a *relative (local) maximum* at $x = x_0$ if $f(x_0) \geq f(x)$ for all values of $x$ in a neighborhood of $x_0$ in $S$.

DEFINITION Given $y = f(x)$ as above. Then the function $f(x)$ has a *relative*

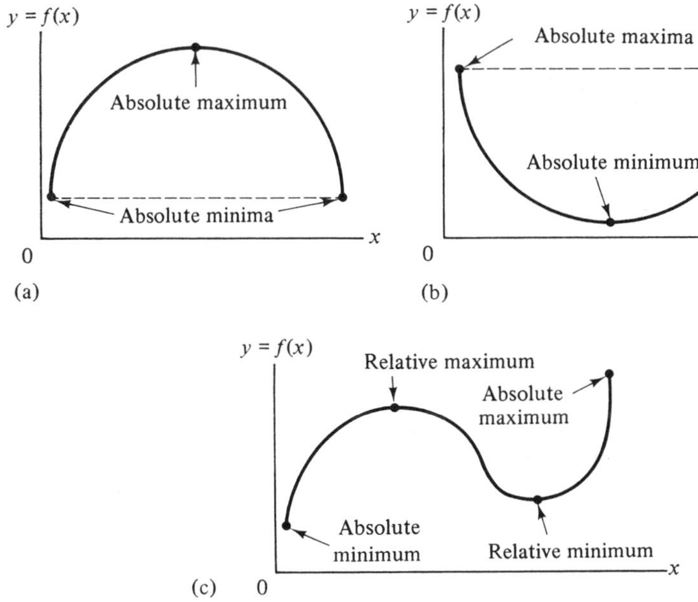


Figure 6.4 Relative and absolute maxima and minima. (a) Absolute maxima and minima (concave downward). (b) Absolute maxima and minima (concave upward). (c) Relative versus absolute maxima and minima

(*local*) *minimum* at $x = x_0$ if $f(x_0) \leq f(x)$ for all values of $x$ in a neighborhood of $x_0$ in $S$[3].

Figure 6.4(a), (b), and (c) illustrates examples of absolute and relative maximum and minimum points. Note that an absolute maximum (minimum) is also a relative maximum (minimum). The converse, however, is not true. A relative maximum (minimum) is not always an absolute maximum (minimum). For example, in part (c), the point labeled "absolute minimum" is also a relative minimum in the neighborhood of the point. The point labeled "relative minimum" is only that, however, and is not an absolute minimum.

There are two tests that enable us to identify extreme points. One, the first derivative test, is only a necessary condition for an extreme point; when satisfied, it does not guarantee that an extreme point exists. The other, the second derivative test, is a sufficient condition for an extreme point; when satisfied, it guarantees that an extreme point exists.

**First Derivative Test**

1. Given that the first derivative of a function $f(x)$ is $f'(x_0) = 0$ when $x = x_0$. Solve the equation $f'(x_0) = 0$ for its critical roots.

[3] A neighborhood of $x_0$ is an interval containing $x_0$. Formally, a $\delta$ neighborhood of $x_0$ is the interval $(x_0 - \delta, x_0 + \delta)$.

2. Examine each critical root separately. If, within a given interval, $f'(x)$ changes sign, then an extreme point exists at $x = x_0$.
3. One of the following three conditions must hold:
   (a) If $f'(x) > 0$ for $x < x_0$ and $f'(x) < 0$ for $x > x_0$, then a *relative* (*local*) *maximum* exists at $x = x_0$.
   (b) If $f'(x) < 0$ for $x < x_0$ and $f'(x) > 0$ for $x > x_0$, then a *relative* (*local*) *minimum* exists at $x = x_0$.
   (c) If $f'(x) > 0$ for $x \lesseqgtr x_0$ or if $f'(x) < 0$ for $x \lesseqgtr x_0$, then *no relative extreme point exists* at $x = x_0$.

The first derivative test is illustrated graphically in Figure 6.5(a), (b), and (c). Point $A$ in part (a) is a *relative maximum* for the function $y = f(x)$, because $f'(x) = 0$ and the sign of $f'(x)$ changes from positive to negative as $x$ assumes values that are initially less than $x_0$ and subsequently greater than $x_0$. There is a relative minimum at point $B$ in part (b), because $f'(x) = 0$ and the sign of $f'(x)$ changes from negative to positive as $x$ assumes values that are initially less than $x_0$ and subsequently greater than $x_0$. There is no relative maximum or minimum point at point $C$ in Figure 6.5(c). This is because $f'(x) > 0$ for $x < x_0$ as well as for $x > x_0$. Alternatively, no relative maximum or minimum point would exist at point C if $f'(x) < 0$ for $x < x_0$ as well as for $x > x_0$. Hence point C is not a relative extreme point. It is, however, a point of inflection according to our previous discussion.

EXAMPLES

1. Find the relative maxima and minima (if any) of the function $y = f(x) = x^2$ (see Example 2, page 179 for graph).

   $$f'(x) = 2x = 0$$

   This function has one extreme point, $x = 0$. If $x < 0$, $f'(x) < 0$, and if $x > 0$, $f'(x) > 0$, we can conclude that when $x = 0$, the function has a relative minimum.
2. Find the relative maxima and minima (if any) of the function $y = f(x) = 2x^3 + 3x^2 - 12x$ (see Example 3, page 179 for graph).

   $$\begin{aligned} f'(x) &= 6x^2 + 6x - 12 = 0 \\ &= 6(x^2 + x - 2) = 0 \\ &= 6(x + 2)(x - 1) = 0 \end{aligned}$$

   This function has two critical roots, $x = -2$ and $x = 1$. Since $f'(x) > 0$ for $x < -2$ and $f'(x) < 0$ for $x > -2$, then $x = -2$ is a relative maximum. Since $f'(x) < 0$ for $x < 1$ and $f'(x) > 0$ for $x > 1$, then $x = 1$ is a relative minimum.

▣ You must clearly understand that the first derivative test is only a necessary condition for the existence of a relative maximum or minimum. That is, if the function $y = f(x)$ has a relative maximum or minimum at $x = x_0$, then

$f'(x_0) = 0$. However, it does not follow that because we find $f'(x_0) = 0$, we must have a relative maximum or minimum point at $x_0$. Instead, we may have a point of inflection at $x_0$.

**EXERCISE 6.1**

For each of the following functions, find any extreme points that exist and determine whether each such point is a relative maximum, a relative minimum, or a point of inflection.

1. $y = x^2 - 4x + 16$
2. $y = x^3 - 6x^2 + 9x + 24$
3. $y = (x - 1)^3 + 8$
4. $y = x(x - 1)^2$
5. $y = xe^x$
6. $y = x + \dfrac{1}{x}$
7. $y = x^3$
8. $y = e^{2x} - 2x$
9. $y = \frac{1}{3}x^3 - x^2 + x + 1$

For each of the following functions, find the absolute maximum and/or minimum values in the designated intervals.

10. $y = x^2$ where $-8 \le x \le 16$
11. $y = (25 - 3x)^{0.5}$ where $0 \le x \le 3$
12. $y = (x - 8)^2$ where $-2 \le x \le 4$
13. $y = 150 + 0.8x$ where $0 \le x \le 10$

Solve the following problems.

14. When an automobile is traveling at $s$ miles per hour, the cost per hour (in dollars) of operating it is given by $C = 0.1 + 1.1s - 0.01s^2$, where $0 < s \le 55$. At what speed $s$ is the cost per hour of operating an automobile at a minimum?
15. An entrepreneur faces the following demand equation for a product

    $$q = 8 - p$$

    where $q$ is output and $p$ is price per unit. What price should the producer set for the product in order to maximize total sales revenues ($pq$)?

**Second Derivative Test**

Earlier in this chapter, we used the second derivative to indicate whether a given function was concave upward or concave downward. We shall now use the second derivative to determine whether the critical roots found by the first derivative test are actually relative maxima or minima.

1. Given that the first derivative of a function $f(x)$ exists. Solve the equation $f'(x) = 0$ for its critical roots. (This step is identical to the first step of the first derivative test.)
2. If the second derivative $f''(x)$ also exists, then one of the following three conditions must hold:

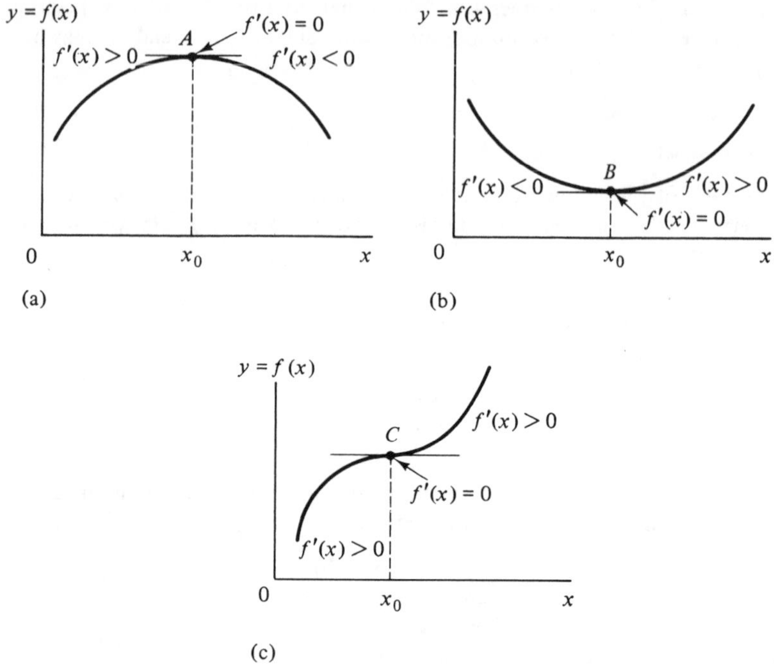


Figure 6.5 Graphical illustration of first derivative test. (a) Relative maximum. (b) Relative minimum. (c) No relative extreme point

(a) If $f''(x_0) < 0$, then the function $f(x)$ has a *relative maximum* at $x = x_0$.
(b) If $f''(x_0) > 0$, then the function $f(x)$ has a *relative minimum* at $x = x_0$.
(c) If $f''(x_0) = 0$, then the second derivative test *fails*. We must return to the first derivative test to ascertain whether a relative maximum or minimum exists.[4]

Figure 6.6(a), (b), and (c) illustrates the second derivative test graphically. In part (a) a *relative maximum* exists because $f'(x_0) = 0$ and $f''(x) < 0$. In part (b) a *relative minimum* exists because $f'(x_0) = 0$ and $f''(x) > 0$. The second derivative test is incapable of detecting whether or not a relative maximum or minimum exists at $x = x_0$ in part (c), for $f''(x_0) = 0$ at point $C$ in Figure 6.6 (c). Hence we cannot be certain what we have.

In order to clarify this matter, we must either retreat back to the first derivative test or invoke the higher-order test. (We shall consider the higher-order test shortly.) One portion of the first derivative test states that if $f'(x) > 0$ for $x \lessgtr x_0$, or if $f'(x) < 0$ for $x \lessgtr x_0$, then no relative extreme point exists at $x = x_0$. That is, if (1) $f'(x) > 0$ both when $x < x_0$ and when $x > x_0$; *or* (2) $f'(x) < 0$ both when $x < x_0$ and when $x > x_0$, then no relative extreme point

[4] Alternatively, we may be able to use the higher derivative test, which is discussed in the next section.

exists. We can see in Figure 6.5(c) that $f'(x) > 0$ for $x < x_0$ and also for $x > x_0$. This means that no relative extreme point exists at point $C$. Consistent with our previous work, however, we can classify point $C$ as a point of inflection.



**Summarizing the First and Second Derivative Tests**

| | *Maximum* | *Minimum* |
|---|---|---|
| Necessary or first-order condition | $\frac{dy}{dx} = 0$ | $\frac{dy}{dx} = 0$ |
| Sufficient or second-order condition | $\frac{d^2y}{dx^2} < 0$ | $\frac{d^2y}{dx^2} > 0$ |

■ There are two situations that do not conform to the above arrangement and that can therefore cause students substantial grief. First, consider Figure 6.7, in which there is an absolute minimum point at point $A$ and an absolute maximum point at point $B$. At both points, $f'(x) \neq 0$. Hence the first derivative test leads to the conclusion that there is no extreme point. This is because an extreme point *does not exist* when one is dealing with a linear function and no

Figure 6.6 Graphical illustration of second derivative test. (a) Relative maximum. (b) Relative minimum. (c) Second derivative test fails

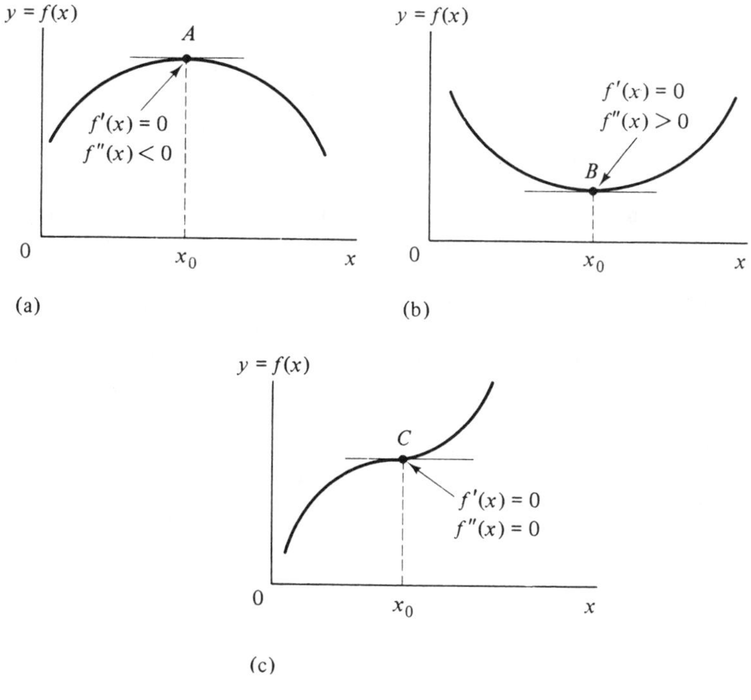

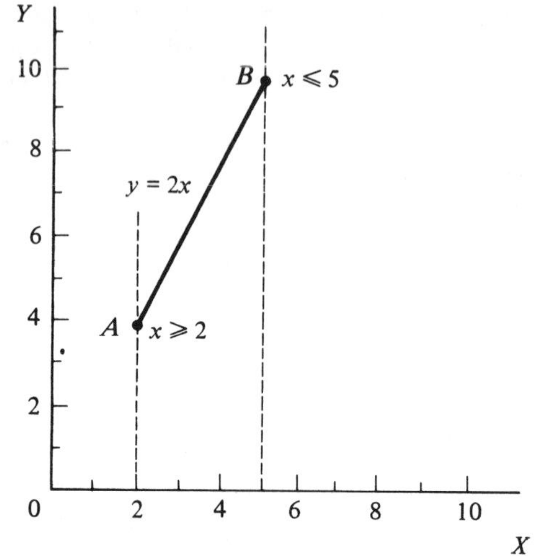


Figure 6.7 Linear functions and the first derivative test

further conditions are imposed. For example, the graph of the equation $y = 2x$ ordinarily extends infinitely far out into the first quadrant. Hence there is no extreme point to be found. If, however, a further condition that $2 \leq x \leq 5$ is imposed, then absolute maximum and minimum points exist. That is the case in Figure 6.7.

The functions that we encounter in business and economic problems are not often constrained in this fashion. Hence we can usually apply the first derivative test and get a relative extreme point. This relative extreme point is also an absolute extreme point when the second derivative test is satisfied. [Note: You should assume throughout that we are interested in relative maxima and minima when no constraints on the domain are given. On the other hand, we are interested in both relative and absolute maxima and minima if there are constraints on the domain.]

The second circumstance in which the first and second derivative tests sometimes cause confusion is the case in which $f''(x) = 0$. In this case, a maximum or minimum point may or may not exist. Also, a point of inflection may exist. In order to determine the truth in this situation, we can apply the first derivative test, as we did in the previous section. This amounts to analyzing the slope of the function for values of $x$ that are less than—and those that are greater than—the value of $x$ at the possible extreme point. Alternatively, we may apply the higher-order test, which we shall now develop.

**Higher-Order Test**

Let $f^{(n)}(x_0)$ signify the $n$th derivative of the function $y = f(x)$ at $x = x_0$. Assume that

$$f'(x_0) = f''(x_0) = \cdots = f^{(n-1)}(x_0) = 0$$

but $f^{(n)}(x_0) \neq 0$. That is, assume that the first $n - 1$ derivatives of the function $y = f(x)$ are equal to zero when $x = x_0$. The $n$th derivative, however, is not equal to zero. Then one of the following two situations must hold: (a) When $n$ is even, $f(x)$ has a relative minimum at $x = x_0$ if $f^{(n)}(x_0) > 0$, and has a relative maximum at $x_0$ if $f^{(n)}(x_0) < 0$; *or* (b) when $n$ is odd, then there is neither a relative maximum nor a relative minimum at $x_0$.[5]

We can apply the higher-order test when $f''(x) = 0$ and there is doubt whether any extreme point exists. This test tells us to successively compute higher-order derivatives until we find one that is not equal to zero. If the first higher derivative that is nonzero is the $n$th derivative, then we reach our conclusion concerning the existence or nonexistence of an extreme point by determining whether $n$ is an even or an odd number. When $n$ is odd, no extreme point exists.

EXAMPLES

1. Find the extreme values of the function $y = x^2$.

   $y' = 2x = 0$ The critical point is $x = 0$

   $y'' = 2 > 0$ Hence $y$ has a minimum value of 0 at $x = 0$

2. Examine $y = x^3 - 27x + 12$ for maxima and minima.

   $y' = 3x^2 - 27 = 0$

   $3(x^2 - 9) = 0$ The critical values are $x = \pm 3$

   $y'' = 6x$ For $x = 3$, $y'' > 0$.

   Hence $y$ has a minimum value of $-42$ at $x = 3$.

   For $x = -3$, $y'' < 0$.

   Hency $y$ has a maximum value of 66 at $x = -3$.

3. Using the higher-order test, determine whether $y = x^5$ has a maximum or minimum point.

   $y^{\text{I}} = 5x^4 = 0;$ $x = 0$

   $y^{\text{II}} = 20x^3 = 0;$ $x = 0$

   $y^{\text{III}} = 60x^2 = 0;$ $x = 0$

   $y^{\text{IV}} = 120x = 0;$ $x = 0$

   $y^{\text{V}} = 120 \neq 0$

   Since $n = 5$ is an odd number, we conclude that the point (0, 0) represents an inflection point. We can verify this by checking the concavity of the function. When $x < 0$, $y^{\text{II}} < 0$, and when $x > 0$, $y^{\text{II}} > 0$; thus the concavity changes.

[5] The relative extreme point is also an absolute extreme point when the domain of $x$ is not subject to additional restrictions such as $x \leq 5$, $x \geq 10$, or whatever.

## EXERCISE 6.2

Find the extreme values of the following functions, and determine by use of the second derivative test whether they are maxima or minima.

1. $y = x^2 - 8x + 10$
2. $y = x(6 - x)^2$
3. $y = x^2 + 8$
4. $y = x^4 - 2x^2 + 6$
5. $y = x^3 - 3x^2 + 12$
6. $y = xe^{-x}$
7. $y = \frac{x^3}{3} + \frac{x^2}{2} - 12x$
8. $y = \frac{x}{x + 1}$
9. $y = \frac{1}{x + 4}$
10. $y = x + \frac{1}{x}$

Determine by the higher-order test whether the following functions have maxima, minima, or inflection points.

11. $y = x^4$
12. $y = -x^6$
13. $y = x^3$
14. $y = (2 - x)^4$
15. $y = (x - 5)^5$

## MAXIMA AND MINIMA: FUNCTIONS OF TWO INDEPENDENT VARIABLES

The previous section dealt with the finding of extreme points for functions of only one independent variable. Let us now extend this discussion to include functions of two independent variables. We shall defer a discussion of how to identify extreme points in functions of more than two independent variables until our work with matrix algebra in Chapter 8.

In the following discussion, we use the term *absolute extreme point* synonymously with *global extreme point*. This underlines the fact that an absolute extreme point is global in nature with respect to the function in question. We shall also occasionally refer to a relative extreme point as a local extreme point. This emphasizes the fact that a given function may have several extreme points, one for each locality or neighborhood of the function. Only one of these local extreme points can be a global extreme point, however.

DEFINITION Let $z = f(x, y)$ be a real-valued function defined on a set $S$ of ordered pairs of real numbers. When $x = x_0$ and $y = y_0$, the function $f(x, y)$ has an *absolute* (*global*) *maximum* if $f(x_0, y_0) \geq f(x, y)$ for all $(x, y)$ in $S$.

DEFINITION Let $z = f(x, y)$ be a real-valued function defined on a set $S$ of ordered pairs of real numbers. When $x = x_0$ and $y = y_0$, the function $f(x, y)$ has an *absolute* (*global*) *minimum* if $f(x_0, y_0) \leq (x, y)$ for all $(x, y)$ in $S$.

DEFINITION Let $z = f(x, y)$ be a real-valued function defined on a set $S$ of ordered pairs of real numbers. When $x = x_0$ and $y = y_0$, the function $f(x, y)$

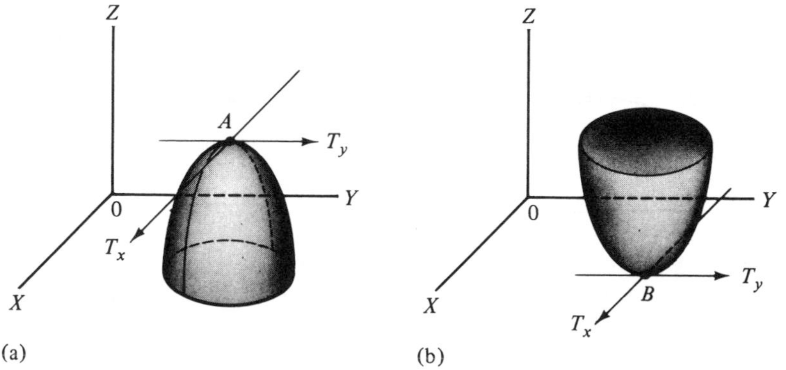


Figure 6.8 Relative maxima and minima in the case of two independent variables. (a) Relative maximum. (b) Relative minimum

has a *relative* (*local*) *maximum* if $f(x_0, y_0) \geq f(x, y)$ for all $(x, y)$ in the immediate vicinity or neighborhood[6] of $(x_0, y_0)$ in $S$.

DEFINITION Let $z = f(x, y)$ be a real-valued function defined on a set $S$ of ordered pairs of real numbers. When $x = x_0$ and $y = y_0$, the function $f(x, y)$ has a *relative* (*local*) *minimum* if $f(x_0, y_0) \leq f(x, y)$ for all $(x, y)$ in the immediate vicinity or neighborhood of $(x_0, y_0)$ in $S$.

Figure 6.8(a) and (b) illustrates two different functions, each with two independent variables. The function in part (a) has a relative maximum at point $A$, and the function in part (b) has a relative minimum at point $B$. Point $A$ in part (a) is a relative maximum because the value of function $z$ at this point is greater than it would be for any other values of $x$ and $y$ in the neighborhood. Similarly, point $B$ in part (b) illustrates a relative minimum because the value of function $z$ at this point is less than it would be for any other values of $x$ and $y$ in the neighborhood.

Assume that the two functions of the form $z = f(x, y)$ illustrated in Figure 6.8(a) and (b) have relative extreme points at points $A$ and $B$, respectively. When the first partial derivatives of either of these functions are continuous, then $\partial z/\partial x = 0 = \partial z/\partial y$. That is, tangent lines $T_x$ and $T_y$, which are parallel to the $XZ$ plane and the $YZ$ plane, respectively, both have zero slopes.

Extreme points $A$ and $B$ in Figure 6.8(a) and (b) are represented in three dimensions. You should bear in mind, however, that our usual two-dimensional diagram can depict the same thing in the context of a single plane.

For example, Figure 6.9(a) demonstrates that when we consider only the $XZ$ plane of Figure 6.8(a), a two-dimensional diagram is sufficient to represent an extreme point. In this case, we ignore the fact that in the context of plane $YZ$, there is also an extreme point at point $A$. Note that tangent lines $T_x$

[6] A neighborhood of $(x_0, y_0)$ is a circular area around the $(x_0, y_0)$. Formally, a $\delta$ neighborhood of $(x_0, y_0)$ is the disk $(x - x_0)^2 + (y - y_0)^2 < \delta^2$.

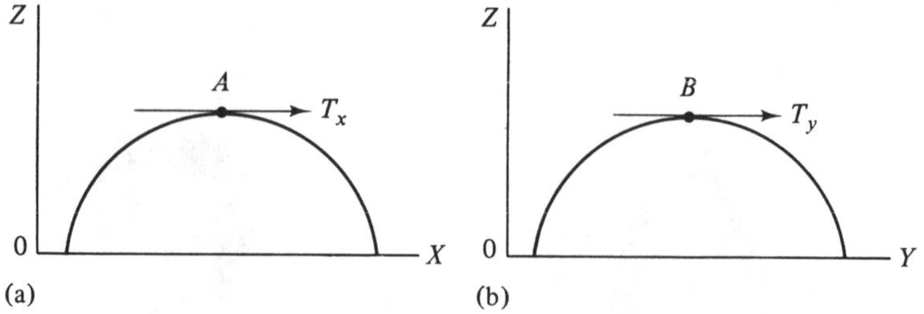


Figure 6.9 Two-dimensional view of three-dimensional extreme points portrayed in Figure 6.8

and $T_y$ are parallel to the abcissa in Figure 6.8(a) and (b), respectively. This means that $\partial z/\partial x = 0$ and that $\partial z/\partial y = 0$ at point $A$. The lesson is that when we deal with functions of two independent variables, we can illustrate extreme points in two different planes. Our maximization (minimization) process, then, concentrates on one plane at a time.

**First-Order (Necessary) Condition**

1. Given that the first partial derivatives of a function $z = f(x, y)$ exist and are set equal to zero,

$$\frac{\partial z}{\partial x} = \frac{\partial z}{\partial y} = 0$$

   solve these two equations for their critical roots.
2. For every critical root of $f(x, y)$, one of the following must hold:
   (a) If $f(x_0, y_0) \geq f(x, y)$ for all values $x = x_0$ and $y = y_0$, then we have a *relative maximum.*
   (b) If $f(x_0, y_0) \leq f(x, y)$ for all values in the interval of $x = x_0$ and $y = y_0$, then we have a *relative minimum.*
   (c) *No relative extreme point exists.* Instead, we have either a point of inflection or a "saddle point" (see below). This is an instance in which we must observe special caution. We'll talk about the reasons for this in the next paragraph.

We are already aware from our work with functions of one independent variable that a first-order condition (such as $dy/dx = 0$) is a necessary condition for an extreme point to exist. It is not, however, a sufficient condition. The analogous situation holds in the case of functions of two independent variables. Given $z = f(x, y)$. If $\partial z/\partial x = \partial z/\partial y = 0$ at $x = x_0$ and $y = y_0$, this does not guarantee that an extreme point exists at $x = x_0$, $y = y_0$. Instead, either a point of inflection or a saddle point may exist at $x = x_0$, $y = y_0$. We shall consider each of these possibilities in turn.

Figure 6.10(a) illustrates the possibility that a point of inflection may exist when $\partial z/\partial x = \partial z/\partial y = 0$. Consider point $A$, at which $x = x_0$ and $y = y_0$. It is

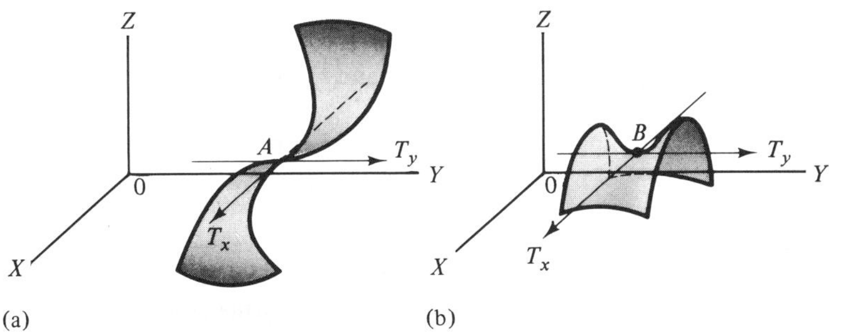


Figure 6.10 First-order condition yields (a) point of inflection or (b) saddle point

evident that $\frac{\partial z}{\partial x} > 0$ and $\frac{\partial z}{\partial y} > 0$ when $x > x_0$ and $y > y_0$, as well as when $x < x_0$ and $y < y_0$. Hence there is a point of inflection at point $A$, despite the fact that the first-order condition for an extreme point has been satisfied.

Figure 6.10(b) illustrates the possibility that a saddle point may exist when $\partial z/\partial x = \partial z/\partial y = 0$. The term *saddle point* is taken from the appearance of the graph in such a case. A saddle point exists at point $B$, at which $x = x_0$ and $y = y_0$. When $x < x_0$ and $y < y_0$, $\partial z/\partial x > 0$ and $\partial z/\partial y < 0$. And when $x > x_0$ and $y > y_0$, $\partial z/\partial x < 0$ and $\partial z/\partial y > 0$. Hence there is no extreme point at point $A$.

#### Second-Order (Sufficient) Condition

In the case of functions of one independent variable of the form $y = f(x)$, $f'(x) = 0$ was a necessary condition for an extreme point. Also $f''(x) < 0$ and $f''(x) > 0$ were sufficient conditions for the existence of a maximum or minimum point, respectively. The second-order (sufficient) condition for the existence of an extreme point in the case of a function of two independent variables is analogous, though more extensive. A second partial derivative such as $f_{xx}$ considers the shape of a surface only in reference to the plane $XZ$. Similarly, $f_{yy}$ considers the shape of a surface only in reference to the plane $YZ$.

Neither second partial derivative considers the shape of any cross section of the surface. For example, $f_{xx}$ ignores the $YZ$ plane as well as the $XY$ plane. This means that we cannot rely on the sign of the second partial derivative to identify extreme points, as we did in the case of functions of only one independent variable. For example, $f_y = 0$ and $f_{yy} < 0$ is not a guarantee of a maximum point because we have not also considered $f_{xx}$ and $f_{xy}$.

The second-order test consists of the following.[7]

1. Given that the first partial derivatives of $z = f(x, y)$ exist and have been set equal to zero such that $\partial z/\partial x = \partial z/\partial y = 0$. Solve these two equations for their critical roots, for example, $(x_0, y_0)$.

[7] The second-order test is stated without proof. The interested reader is directed to Richard Courant, *Differential and Integral Calculus*, Vol. 1, E. J. McShane translation, Interscience Publishers, New York, 1936, pp. 183–209, for a rigorous proof.

2. If $f_{xx}$, $f_{yy}$, and $f_{xy}$ exist at $x = x_0$, $y = y_0$, then one of the following conditions must hold:
   (a) When $f_{xx} f_{yy} - (f_{xy})^2 > 0$ and $f_{xx}$ and $f_{yy} < 0$, we have a *relative maximum* at $x = x_0$, $y = y_0$.
   (b) When $f_{xx} f_{yy} - (f_{xy})^2 > 0$ and $f_{xx}$ and $f_{yy} > 0$, we have a *relative minimum* at $x = x_0$, $y = y_0$.
   (c) When $f_{xx} f_{yy} - (f_{xy})^2 < 0$, we have a *saddle point* at $x = x_0$, $y = y_0$.
   (d) When $f_{xx} f_{yy} - (f_{xy})^2 = 0$, the second-order test *fails*. A relative extreme point may exist; however, the second-order test is incapable of indicating whether or not that is the case. Further, the first-order test or higher-derivative test, applied in the case of one independent variable, are not appropriate in the case of two independent variables. One must examine the original function $z = f(x, y)$ in the neighborhood of $x = x_0$, $y = y_0$ in order to determine whether an extreme point may exist.

**Summary of Conditions for Unconstrained Extremum:** $z = f(x, y)$

*First-order condition*:

$$f_x, f_y = 0$$

*Second-order condition*

| | | |
|---|---|---|
| 1. *Maximum:* | $f_{xx} f_{yy} - (f_{xy})^2 > 0$ | and $f_{xx}, f_{yy} < 0$ |
| 2. *Minimum:* | $f_{xx} f_{yy} - (f_{xy})^2 > 0$ | and $f_{xx}, f_{yy} > 0$ |
| 3. *Saddle point:* | $f_{xx} f_{yy} - (f_{xy})^2 < 0$ | |
| 4. *Test fails:* | $f_{xx} f_{yy} - (f_{xy})^2 = 0$ | |

EXAMPLES

1. Find the extreme value of $z = f(x, y) = 8 - x^2 - y^2$.

   $z_x = -2x = 0 \qquad x = 0$

   $z_y = -2y = 0 \qquad y = 0$

   The function may have an extreme value at (0, 0).

   $z_{xx} = -2 < 0 \qquad z_{yy} = -2 < 0 \qquad \text{and} \qquad z_{xy} = 0$

   Hence the second-order condition is

   $z_{xx} z_{yy} - (z_{xy})^2 = 4 - 0 = 4 > 0 \qquad$ and $z_{xx}$ and $z_{yy} < 0$

   There is a relative maximum at (0, 0).
2. Find the extreme values of $z = f(x, y) = x^3 + y^3 - 3xy$.

   $z_x = 3x^2 - 3y = 0 \qquad x^2 - y = 0$

   $z_y = 3y^2 - 3x = 0 \qquad y^2 - x = 0$

Therefore the possible extreme points are (0, 0) and (1, 1).

$z_{xx} = 6x \qquad z_{yy} = 6y \qquad z_{xy} = -3$

Hence

$z_{xx}z_{yy} - (z_{xy})^2 = (6x)(6y) - (-3)^2$

*(0, 0) Case*

$z_{xx} = 6x = 0$

$z_{yy} = 6y = 0$

$z_{xx}z_{yy} - (z_{xy})^2 = 0 - 9 < 0$

Thus $z$ has a saddle point at (0, 0).

*(1, 1) Case*

$z_{xx} = 6x = 6 > 0$

$z_{yy} = 6y = 6 > 0$

$z_{xx}z_{yy} -. z_{xy} = 36 - 9 = 27 > 0$

Thus $z$ is a minimum at (1, 1).

3. Determine whether the function $z = x^2 + y^2$ has an extreme value.

$z_x = 2x = 0 \qquad x = 0$

$z_y = 2y = 0 \qquad y = 0$

The second-order condition ascertains whether (0, 0) is an extreme point.

$z_{xx} = 2 > 0$

$z_{yy} = 2 > 0$

$z_{xy} = 0$

Thus $z_{xx}z_{yy} - (z_{xy})^2 = 4 - 0 = 4 > 0$. Hence there is a minimum at (0, 0).

**EXERCISE 6.3**

Examine the following functions for extreme values, and determine whether these values are maxima, minima, or saddle points.

1. $z = x^2 + (y - 4)^2$
2. $z = x^2 - xy + y^2 - 2x + y$
3. $z = x^2 - 2xy + y^2$
4. $z = x^2 + y^2 - 2x - 2y - xy + 4$
5. $z = x^3 - 3x + y^3 - 12y + 6$
6. $z = x^2 + y^2 + xy + 5x + 4y$
7. $z = x^2 + 2y^2 - 4x + 8y$

## MAXIMA AND MINIMA SUBJECT TO CONSTRAINTS

Rare is the decision-maker who is able to make decisions in a vacuum without reference to any constraints on choices. Business people and consumers alike have limited budgets, resources, and time. As a consequence, many of the most realistic maximization and minimization problems in business and economics involve finding an extreme point subject to one or more constraints.

For example, the task of a salesperson may be to maximize the sales in a territory subject to a budget that limits the salesperson's ability to travel and service that territory. An academic administrator may wish to construct a schedule of courses that maximizes the usage of classrooms during certain key time periods during the day. However, the administrator must do so without violating constraints on how many classes can be offered, how many classes can be offered in a single time slot, and so forth. The number of decision-making problems that involve constrained maximization or minimization is as large and diverse as the world itself.

A constraint acts as a prohibiting, limiting agent in an optimization problem. That is, the constraint reduces the feasible or workable area of the objective function. Figure 6.11 illustrates the effect of a constraint on a function $z = f(x, y)$. The shaded area indicates the feasible area of the objective function. Point $A$ is the maximum point for the entire surface $z = f(x, y)$. However, when the constraint labeled $CC'$ is imposed, the constrained maximum is indicated by point $B$. That is, point $B$ is the maximum when constraint $CC'$ is imposed and the range of the objective function is limited to the shaded area in Figure 6.11.

In general, a constraint must result in an extreme point whose value is less than or equal to the extreme value obtained when the same objective function is maximized in the absence of the constraint. Similarly, imposing a constraint on a minimization problem must result in an extreme point whose value is greater than or equal to the value obtained when the same objective function is minimized in the absence of the constraint.

We generally try to solve a constrained optimization problem by one of two methods. The first involves substituting the constraint into the objective function, then proceeding as if one were maximizing or minimizing an uncon-

Figure 6.11 Graphical representation of constrained maximization

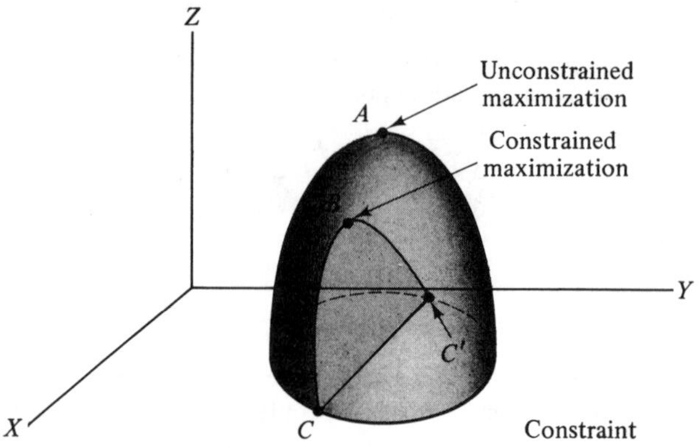

strained function. This method seems straightforward. Unfortunately, it often becomes complicated and quite troublesome when the objective function and constraint are something other than very simple functions. Hence the most popular method of maximizing or minimizing in the face of a constraint is by the use of *Lagrange multipliers.*

### Lagrange Multipliers

Assume an objective function of the form $z = f(x, y)$ that is to be maximized or minimized subject to the constraint given by $g(x, y) = 0$. We now form a new objective function that contains both the original objective function and the constraint:

$$L = L(x, y, \lambda) = f(x, y) - \lambda g(x, y) \tag{6.1}$$

New objective function — Original objective function — Constraint

The Greek letter $\lambda$ (lambda) in Equation (6.1) is a newly created unknown variable that has the property of being able to apply to the constrained objective function precisely the same first-order condition applied when an extremum is found in the absence of a constraint. We often refer to $\lambda$ as an *undetermined multiplier* or Lagrange multiplier. However, $\lambda$ does represent the change in the objective function per unit change in the constraint.

*First-order (necessary) condition*

Differentiating the new objective function in Equation (6.1) with respect to $x$, $y$, and $\lambda$, and setting these partial derivatives equal to 0, we obtain Equations (6.2) through (6.4):

$$L_x = f_x - \lambda g_x = 0 \tag{6.2}$$

$$L_y = f_y - \lambda g_y = 0 \tag{6.3}$$

$$L_\lambda = g(x, y) = 0 \tag{6.4}$$

We can solve Equations (6.2) through (6.4) for the critical roots of the function $L(x, y, \lambda)$. Note that Equation (6.4) is actually nothing more than the constraint that must be satisfied when the extreme point is found.

EXAMPLE Maximize the utility function $U = x_1 \cdot x_2$ subject to the budget constraint given by $y = p_1 x_1 + p_2 x_2$, where $y = \$100$, $p_1 = \$2$, and $p_2 = \$5$. Construct the Lagrangian function:

$$L = L(x_1, x_2, \lambda) = x_1 \cdot x_2 - \lambda(2x_1 + 5x_2 - 100)$$

Differentiating, we obtain

$$\frac{\partial L}{\partial x_1} = x_2 - 2\lambda = 0 \tag{6.5}$$

$$\frac{\partial L}{\partial x_2} = x_1 - 5\lambda = 0 \tag{6.6}$$

$$\frac{\partial L}{\partial \lambda} = 100 - 2x_1 - 5x_2 = 0 \tag{6.7}$$

Working with Equations (6.5) and (6.6), we have

$$\frac{x_2}{2} = \lambda \quad \text{and} \quad \frac{x_1}{5} = \lambda \tag{6.8}$$

Therefore

$$\frac{x_2}{2} = \frac{x_1}{5} \quad \text{and} \quad x_1 = 2.5x_2 \tag{6.9}$$

Equation (6.9) represents the relative values of $x_1$ and $x_2$. We must substitute these into the constraint Equation (6.7) in order to obtain values of $x_1$ and $x_2$ that satisfy the equilibrium, or first-order, condition.

$$100 - 2x_1 - 5x_2 = 0$$

$$100 - 2(2.5x_2) - 5x_2 = 0 \tag{6.10}$$

$$100 = 10x_2, \qquad x_2 = 10$$

Therefore

$$100 - 2x_1 - 5(10) = 0$$

$$50 = 2x_1, \qquad x_1 = 25 \tag{6.11}$$

By inspection, we can see that $x_1 = 25$ and $x_2 = 10$ does not violate the constraint given by Equation (6.7). These values satisfy the first-order condition for utility maximization.

▣ You will occasionally see a plus sign (+) used in front of the constraint in a Lagrangian expression, such as that in Equation (6.1). We can do this without changing the critical roots of the independent variables in the original objective function. For example, in the previous problem, the Lagrangian function would become

$$L = x_1 \cdot x_2 + \lambda(100 - 2x_1 - 5x_2) \tag{6.12}$$

You may confirm for yourself that the constrained maximization process once again results in $x_1 = 25$, $x_2 = 10$. There is an intuitive explanation of why the sign of the constraint term in Equations (6.1) and (6.12) is of no consequence. The value of the constraint term, when the objective function is being maximized or minimized, as appropriate, is equal to zero. For example, in Equation (6.12), $100 - 2x_1 - 5x_2 = 0$ when utility is being maximized. The addition or subtraction of zero is of no concern.

*Second-order (sufficient) test*

The method of Lagrange identifies only those values of the independent variables that satisfy first-order or necessary conditions for an extreme point. These values may or may not actually represent an extreme point. A second-order test is necessary to provide further information on this matter. The second-order test is as follows.[8]

1. Given $L_x = L_y = 0$ at $x = x_0$, $y = y_0$. Given also that $L_{xx}$, $L_{yy}$, $L_{xy}$ exist at $x = x_0$, $y = y_0$.
2. Then, one of the following conditions must hold:
   (a) If $L_{xx} L_{yy} - (L_{xy})^2 > 0$, and $L_{xx}$ and $L_{xy} < 0$, then we have a *relative maximum* at $x = x_0$, $y = y_0$.
   (b) If $L_{xx} L_{yy} - (L_{xy})^2 > 0$, and $L_{xx}$ and $L_{xy} > 0$, then we have a *relative minimum* at $x = x_0$, $y = y_0$.
   (c) If $L_{xx} L_{yy} - (L_{xy})^2 \leq 0$, then the second-order test *fails* and is incapable of indicating whether or not a relative extreme point exists. A relative extreme point may exist. Once again, there is no first-order test or higher-order test to retreat to in this case. Instead, one must analyze the function $z = f(x, y)$ in the neighborhood of $x = x_0$, $y = y_0$ in order to ascertain whether an extreme point exists at $x = x_0$, $y = y_0$.

▣ The second-order test outlined above is quite similar to the second-order test described for the case when an unconstrainted extreme point is being sought. There is, however, an important difference. Assume that $L_{xx} L_{yy} - (L_{xy})^2 \leq 0$. In the unconstrained case, a saddle point exists when $f_{xx} f_{yy} - (f_{xy})^2 < 0$, and an extreme point may exist when $f_{xx} f_{yy} - (f_{xy})^2 = 0$. In the constrained case, however, we can say nothing about the existence of a saddle point when $L_{xx} L_{yy} - (L_{xy})^2 < 0$. An extreme point may exist when $L_{xx} L_{yy} - (L_{xy})^2 = 0$ as well as when $L_{xx} L_{yy} - (L_{xy})^2 < 0$ in the constrained case.

**Summary of Conditions for Constrained Extremum:** $z = f(x, y)$ subject to $g(x, y) = 0$.

*First-order condition*

$$L_x = L_y = L_\lambda = 0$$

*Second-order condition*

| | | | |
|---|---|---|---|
| 1. *Maximum:* | $L_{xx} L_{yy} - (L_{xy})^2 > 0$ | and | $L_{xx}, L_{yy} < 0$ |
| 2. *Minimum:* | $L_{xx} L_{yy} - (L_{xy})^2 > 0$ | and | $L_{xx}, L_{yy} > 0$ |
| 3. *Test fails:* | $L_{xx} L_{yy} - (L_{xy})^2 \leq 0$ | | |

[8] This condition is asserted without proof. The interested reader may find a proof of the second-order condition in the case of constrained optimization of a function of two or more independent variables in Courant, pp. 194–202.

EXAMPLES

1. Find the extremum of $z = x^2 + y^2 + 2x + 2y + 4$ subject to $x + y = 4$. Form the Lagrangian function

   $$L = x^2 + y^2 + 2x + 2y + 4 + \lambda(x + y - 4)$$

   Thus

   $$L_x = 2x + 2 + \lambda = 0$$

   $$L_y = 2y + 2 + \lambda = 0$$

   $$L_\lambda = x + y - 4 = 0$$

   Solving these three equations, we find

   $$x = 2 \qquad y = 2 \qquad \text{and} \qquad \lambda = -6$$

   The second-order condition is

   $$L_{xx} = 2 \qquad L_{yy} = 2 \qquad L_{xy} = 0$$

   Thus

   $$L_{xx}L_{yy} - (L_{xy})^2 = 4 - 0 = 4 > 0 \qquad \text{and} \qquad L_{xx} \text{ and } L_{yy} > 0$$

   Hence there is a minimum when $x = 2$ and $y = 2$ and $z = 20$.
2. Find the extremum of $z = x^2 + y^2$ subject to $x + y = 1$. Form the Lagrangian function

   $$L = x^2 + y^2 + \lambda(x + y - 1)$$

   Thus

   $$L_x = 2x + \lambda = 0$$

   $$L_y = 2y + \lambda = 0$$

   $$L_\lambda = x + y - 1 = 0$$

   Solving these three equations, we find $x = \frac{1}{2}$, $y = \frac{1}{2}$, and $\lambda = -1$. The second-order condition is

   $$L_{xx} = 2 \qquad L_{yy} = 2 \qquad L_{xy} = 0$$

   Thus

   $$L_{xx}L_{yy} - (L_{xy})^2 = 4 - 0 = 4 > 0 \qquad \text{and} \qquad L_{xx} \text{ and } L_{yy} > 0.$$

   Hence there is a minimum when $x = \frac{1}{2}$, $y = \frac{1}{2}$ and $z = \frac{1}{2}$.

**EXERCISE 6.4**

Solve the following constrained optimization problems by the method of Lagrange multipliers.

1. $z = 2x^2 + y^2$ subject to $x + y = 1$
2. $z = x^2 - 2xy + y^2$ subject to $x + y = 2$

3. $z = x^2 + 4y^2 + 24$ subject to $x - 4y = 10$
4. $z = 4x^2 - xy + 3y^2$ subject to $x + 2y = 21$
5. $z = 6x^2 - xy + 5y^2$ subject to $2x + y = 24$
6. $z = 3x^2 + y^2 - 2xy - 8$ subject to $x + y = 1$

## APPLICATIONS OF MAXIMA AND MINIMA

Let us now apply the tools that we have acquired in this chapter to specific problems in business and economics.

### Profit Maximization: Perfect Competition

A fundamental problem in business and economics is that of the firm maximizing profit. We shall assume that the representative firm that we are examining in this section purchases its inputs and sells its output in perfectly competitive markets. That is, the firm's purchases of inputs, and its sales of the output it produces, are sufficiently small and insignificant that its actions do not perceptibly influence the prices of either inputs or outputs.

Let $p = f(q)$ be the firm's inverse demand function. Assume that $p$, the price of the firm's output, is a constant and is unaffected by $q$, the firm's output. The total sales revenue $R$ of the firm is given by $pq$, or $qf(q)$, and it can be seen that $R = R(q)$.

The firm's total cost $C$ function is given by $C(q) = k + g(q)$, and we can see that $C = C(q)$. Note also that total cost is the sum of fixed cost $k$ plus variable cost $g(q)$.

The profit of the firm, $\pi$, is defined as total revenue minus total cost, and is given by

$$\pi = qf(q) - k - g(q) \tag{6.13}$$

We can find the profit-maximizing level of output by satisfying the first- and second-order conditions for an unconstrained maximum, namely, $d\pi/dq = 0$ and $d^2\pi/dq^2 < 0$. Differentiating Equation (6.13) with respect to $q$ and setting this derivative equal to zero, we obtain Equation (6.14), which describes the equilibrium or first-order condition for profit maximization. Note that $f'(q) = 0$ because $f(q) = p$, a constant.

$$\begin{aligned} \frac{d\pi}{dq} &= f(q) + qf'(q) - g'(q) = 0 \\ f(q) &= g'(q) \end{aligned} \tag{6.14}$$

Equation (6.14) requires that the firm equate the price of its output $p$ and the marginal cost of its output $g'(q)$. This is a slightly differentiated version of the usual "marginal revenue equals marginal cost" rule for profit maximization. When the firm operates in perfect competition, price is equal to marginal revenue.

Profit maximization by the firm in perfect competition is shown graphically in Figure 6.12(a), (b), and (c). The total cost and total revenue func-

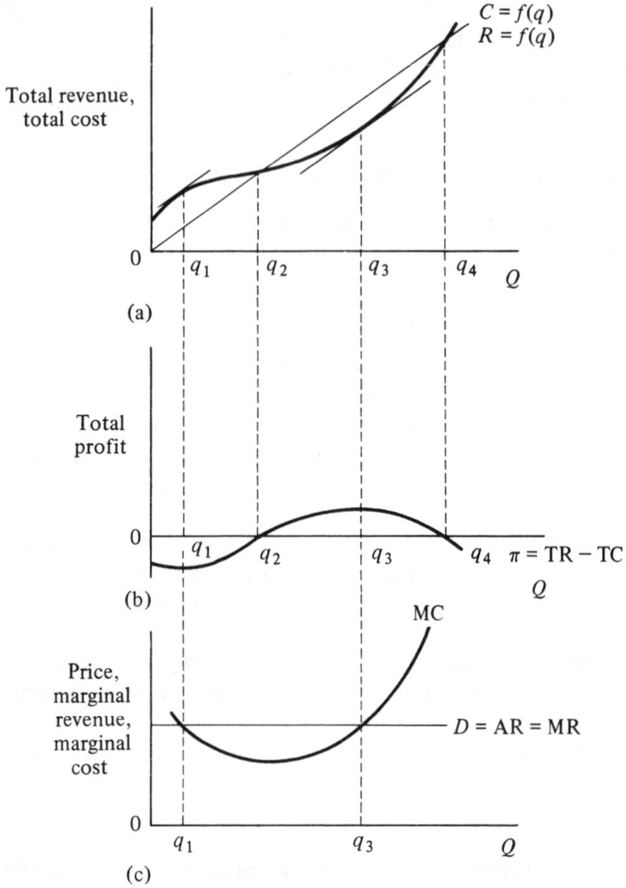


Figure 6.12 Profit maximization: Perfect competition

tions shown in part (a) intersect twice, initially at output level $Oq_2$, and subsequently at output level $Oq_4$. At these two levels of output, total profit is equal to zero. Intervals $(0, q_2)$ and $(q_4, \infty)$ represent negative profit, whereas the open interval $(q_2, q_4)$ represents positive profit. The total profit curve illustrated in part (b) reflects these considerations.

The first-order condition for profit maximization, $d\pi/dq = 0$, implies that the slope of the total revenue curve must be equal to the slope of a tangent to the total cost curve. In Figure 6.12(a), two different levels of output ($Oq_1$ and $Oq_3$) satisfy this first-order condition. We can see in part (c) that the first-order condition $d\pi/dq = 0$ also implies that marginal revenue is equal to marginal cost.

It is apparent in Figure 6.11(a) that even though output level $Oq_1$ satisfies the first-order condition $d\pi/dq = 0$, it nonetheless involves a negative profit (a loss) for the firm. In the absence of a graph such as part (a), we must use the second-order condition for profit maximization to determine that output level $Oq_3$ is preferable to output level $Oq_1$. The second-order condition for profit maximization is that $d^2\pi/dq^2 < 0$. In the case at hand, $d^2\pi/dq^2 = -g''(q) < 0$. This means that $g''(q) > 0$. Since $g(q)$ is total cost, $g'(q)$ is marginal cost. Hence, for the second-order condition $g''(q) > 0$, marginal cost must be *rising* at the profit-maximizing output. This requirement eliminates output level $Oq_1$ and identifies output level $Oq_3$ as profit-maximizing.

**Profit Maximization: Imperfect Competition**

Let the imperfectly competitive firm's demand function (in inverse form) be $p = f(q)$, where $f'(q) < 0$. The firm's total cost function is once again given by $C(q) = k + g(q)$. Hence the firm's profit function is given by

$$\pi = qf(q) - k - g(q) \tag{6.15}$$

The first-order condition for profit maximization requires that $d\pi/dq = 0$.

$$\frac{d\pi}{dq} = f(q) + qf'(q) - g'(q) = 0 \tag{6.16}$$

The term $[f(q) + qf'(q)]$ is the derivative of $qf(q)$ with respect to $q$, and is marginal revenue. The term $g'(q)$ represents marginal cost. Therefore we can restate the first-order condition as

$$\begin{aligned} f(q) + qf'(q) &= g'(q) \\ \text{MR} &= \text{MC} \end{aligned} \tag{6.17}$$

The second-order condition for profit maximization requires that $d^2\pi/dq^2 < 0$. Performing this differentiation, we find that

$$\frac{d^2\pi}{dq^2} = f'(q) + f'(q) + qf''(q) - g''(q) < 0 \tag{6.18}$$

or

$$2f'(q) + qf''(q) < g''(q)$$

Equation (6.18) indicates that the second-order condition for profit maximization requires that the slope of the marginal revenue curve be less than the slope of the marginal cost curve. That is, the marginal cost curve must cut the marginal revenue curve from below.

Figure 6.13(a), (b), and (c) illustrates profit maximization for the imperfectly competitive firm. Output levels $Oq_1$ and $Oq_3$ both satisfy the first-order necessary condition that $d\pi/dq = 0$. Only output level $Oq_3$, however, also satisfies the second-order condition that requires the slope of the marginal revenue curve to be less than the slope of the marginal cost curve. Hence output level $Oq_3$ is profit-maximizing.

EXAMPLE The Co-op Bookstore is anxious to maximize profit on its sales of Adam Smith's *The Wealth of Nations*. The demand for the book is given by

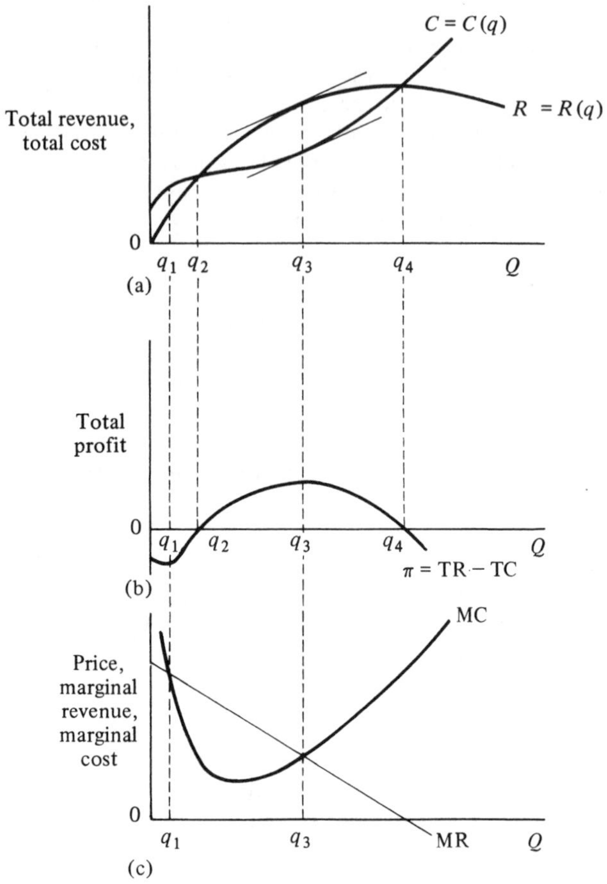


Figure 6.13 Profit maximization: imperfect competition

$p = 10 - 0.01(q)$, while the total cost function with respect to sales of the book is given by $\text{TC} = 5q + 0.025q^2 + 0.0333q^3$. The Co-op's total profit function on the sales of *The Wealth of Nations* is given by

$$\pi = 10q - 0.01q^2 - 5q - 0.025q^2 - 0.0333q^3 \tag{6.19}$$

The first-order condition for profit maximization requires that $\partial\pi/\partial q$ be set equal to zero.

$$\frac{\partial\pi}{\partial q} = 10 - 0.02q - 5 - 0.05q - 0.1q^2 = 0 \tag{6.20}$$

Therefore $-0.1q^2 - 0.07q + 5 = 0$. This is a quadratic equation, and we can solve it using the quadratic formula, $(-b \pm \sqrt{b^2 - 4ac})/2a$, where $a = -0.1$, $b = -0.07$, and $c = +5$.

$$\textit{Solution 1} = \frac{+0.07 + \sqrt{(-0.07)^2 - 4(-0.1)(+5)}}{2(-0.1)} = -7.43$$

$$\textit{Solution 2} = \frac{+0.07 - \sqrt{(-0.07)^2 - 4(-0.1)(+5)}}{2(-0.1)} = 6.73$$

Solution 1 involves negative sales and is thus nonsensical. Hence the solution is $q = 6.73$. Given $q = 6.73$, $p = 10 - 0.01(6.73) = \$9.93$. Therefore, the profit-maximizing strategy for the Co-op Bookstore is to sell 6.73 books at a price of \$9.93 per book. If an integer solution is required (and, after all, what bookstore has ever sold 6.73 books?), then the Co-op must choose between selling 6.00 books and 7.00 books. When $q = 6.00$, $p = 10 - 0.01(6.00) = \$9.94$, and

$$\pi = 10(6) - 0.01(6)^2 - 5(6) - 0.025(6)^2 - 0.0333(6)^3 = \$21.55$$

When $q = 7.00$, $p = 10 - 0.01(7) = \$9.93$, and

$$\pi = 10(7) - 0.01(7)^2 - 5(7) - 0.025(7)^2 - 0.0333(7)^3 = \$21.87$$

Note, however, that this is less than the profit that the Co-op Bookstore would make if it were not restricted to integer sales. The noninteger solution yielded a profit of

$$\pi = 10(6.73) - 0.01(6.73)^2 - 5(6.73) - 0.025(6.73)^2 - 0.0333(6.73)^3 = \$21.92$$

**Production: Marginal and Average Products**

Consider a production function of the form $Q = f(L, K)$, where $Q$ = output, and $L$ and $K$ are the labor and capital inputs, respectively. Assume a short-run situation such that the amount of capital is fixed at $K = K_0$. Thus $Q = f(L)$, given $K = K_0$.

The average product of labor $\text{AP}_L$ is given by

$$\text{AP}_L = \frac{Q}{L} = \frac{f(K_0, L)}{L} = \frac{f(L)}{L} \tag{6.21}$$

The marginal product of labor $\text{MP}_L$ is given by

$$\text{MP}_L = \frac{d[f(L)]}{dL} = f'(L) \tag{6.22}$$

As Figure 6.14 illustrates, the $\text{MP}_L$ curve cuts the $\text{AP}_L$ curve at the $\text{AP}_L$ curve's highest point. That is, $\text{MP}_L = \text{AP}_L$ at point $B'$, when $\text{AP}_L$ is at a maximum. We can demonstrate this mathematically by showing the conditions under which $\text{AP}_L$ is at a maximum. We differentiate $\text{AP}_L = Q/L$ with respect to $L$, and set this derivative equal to zero in order to find a maximum.

$$\frac{d(Q/L)}{dL} = \frac{d[f(L)/L]}{dL} = \frac{f'(L)L - f(L)}{L^2} = \frac{1}{L}\left[f'(L) - \frac{f(L)}{L}\right] = 0 \tag{6.23}$$

Since $L > 0$, Equation (6.23) can be equal to 0 only if $f'(L) - f(L)/L = 0$. This implies that $f'(L) = f(L)/L$, that is, that $\text{MP}_L = \text{AP}_L$. Hence the $\text{AP}_L$ curve is

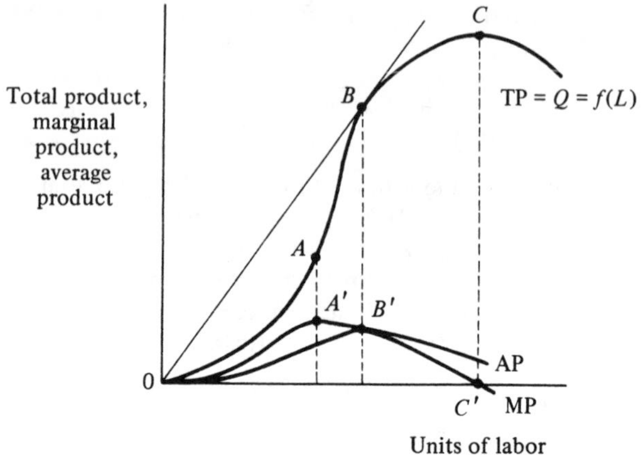


Figure 6.14 Total, marginal, and average products

at a maximum when the $MP_L$ curve cuts it from above, and $MP_L = AP_L$ at that point.

In Chapter 4, we designated the point of diminishing returns as that place at which the marginal product of the variable input is at its maximum. In Figure 6.14, this occurs at point $A$ on the total product curve, which is equivalently represented by point $A'$ on the marginal product curve, where $dQ/dL$ is at a maximum. Note also that the concavity of the total product curve in Figure 6.14 changes from upward to downward. This means that $d^2Q/dL^2 > 0$ from the origin to point $A$, that $d^2Q/dL^2 = 0$ at point $A$, and that $d^2Q/dL^2 < 0$ to the right of point $A$, where the total product curve is concave downward.

### The Costs of Production

In Chapter 4, we analyzed the costs of production. Since that time, we have acquired the ability to analyze the concavity of a function, and we have also gained the ability to find extreme points (if they exist) on a given function. We can now use this added knowledge to extend our understanding of cost curves substantially beyond where we left it in Chapter 4.

Consider Figure 6.15, which is identical to Figure 4.1, which we used previously. The total cost function in part (a) is given by $TC = 100 + 25Q - 5Q^2 + Q^3$. Hence marginal cost $MC = d(TC)/dQ = 25 - 10Q + 3Q^2$. This MC curve is shown in part (b). The slope of the MC curve is given by $d^2(TC)/dQ^2 = -10 + 6Q$. Marginal cost MC attains a minimum when $d^2(TC)/dQ^2 = 0$ and $d^3(TC)/dQ^3 > 0$. Solving $-10 + 6Q = 0$ for $Q$, we find $Q = 1.67$. Further, $d^3(TC)/dQ^3 = 6$. Hence the MC curve in part (b) has a minimum at $Q = 1.67$.

The average variable cost AVC curve in Figure 6.15(b) is given by $\text{AVC} = 25 - 5Q + Q^2$. The slope of the AVC curve is $d(\text{AVC})/dQ = -5 + 2Q$. The AVC curve attains a minimum when $d(\text{AVC})/dQ = 0$. Solving the equation $-5 + 2Q = 0$ for $Q$, we find that $Q = 2.5$. We confirm that this is a minimum point by determining that $d^2(\text{AVC})/dQ^2 = 2 > 0$. We can see from part (b) that the MC curve cuts the AVC curve at the minimum point ($Q = 2.5$)

Figure 6.15 Equations and slopes of the cost curves of the representative firm. (a) Total cost, total variable cost, and total fixed cost. (b) Average cost, average variable cost, and marginal cost

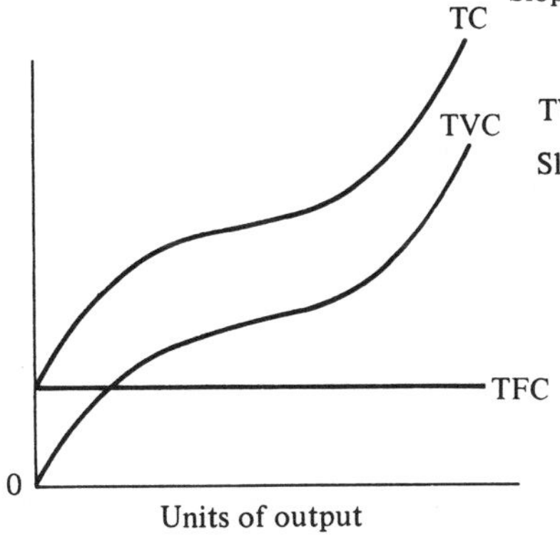

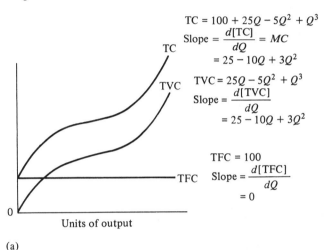

$$\text{TC} = 100 + 25Q - 5Q^2 + Q^3$$
$$\text{Slope} = \frac{d[\text{TC}]}{dQ} = MC$$
$$= 25 - 10Q + 3Q^2$$

$$\text{TVC} = 25Q - 5Q^2 + Q^3$$
$$\text{Slope} = \frac{d[\text{TVC}]}{dQ}$$
$$= 25 - 10Q + 3Q^2$$

$$\text{TFC} = 100$$
$$\text{Slope} = \frac{d[\text{TFC}]}{dQ}$$
$$= 0$$

(a)

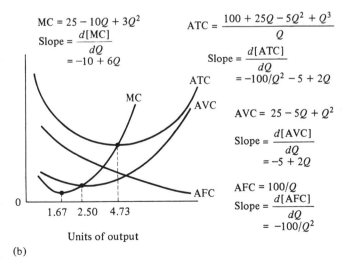

$$\text{MC} = 25 - 10Q + 3Q^2$$
$$\text{Slope} = \frac{d[\text{MC}]}{dQ}$$
$$= -10 + 6Q$$

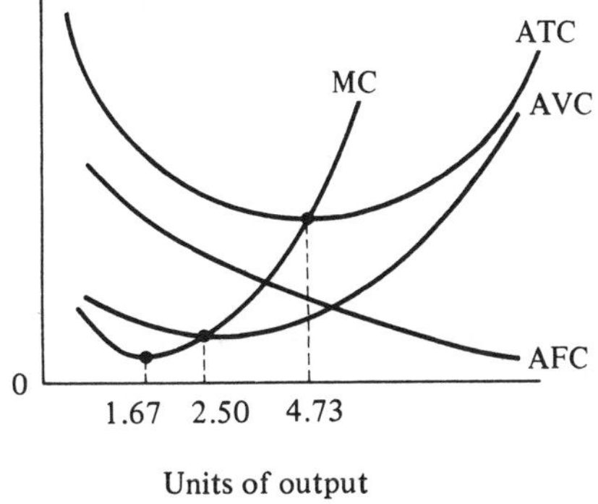


$$\text{ATC} = \frac{100 + 25Q - 5Q^2 + Q^3}{Q}$$
$$\text{Slope} = \frac{d[\text{ATC}]}{dQ}$$
$$= -100/Q^2 - 5 + 2Q$$

$$\text{AVC} = 25 - 5Q + Q^2$$
$$\text{Slope} = \frac{d[\text{AVC}]}{dQ}$$
$$= -5 + 2Q$$

$$\text{AFC} = 100/Q$$
$$\text{Slope} = \frac{d[\text{AFC}]}{dQ}$$
$$= -100/Q^2$$

(b)

on the AVC curve.[9] The average total cost ATC curve in Figure 6.15(b) attains a minimum when $d(\text{ATC})/dQ = 0$ and $d^2(\text{ATC})/Q^2 > 0$. Setting $d(\text{ATC})/dQ = -100/Q^2 + 2Q - 5 = 0$, we find $Q = 4.73$ as the value that minimizes ATC. We confirm this minimum point by finding that $d^2(\text{ATC})/Q^2 = 200/Q^3 + 2Q > 0$. It is also apparent in part (b) that the MC curve cuts the ATC curve at the minimum point ($Q = 4.73$) on the ATC curve.[10]

### Taxation and Imperfectly Competitive Output

Assume an imperfectly competitive firm whose total revenue and total cost functions are as follows:

$$\begin{aligned} \text{Total revenue} &= R(q) = qf(q) \\ \text{Total cost} &= C(q) = k + g(q) \end{aligned} \tag{6.24}$$

[9] This can be demonstrated as follows: Given a total cost function $\text{TC} = k + g(q)$ such that variable cost is $g(q)$ and $\text{AVC} = g(q)/q$. The AVC attains a minimum when

$$\frac{d[g(q)]/q}{dq} = 0$$

Then

$$\frac{1}{q}\left[g'(q) - \frac{g(q)}{q}\right] = 0$$

Since $q > 0$, then $1/q > 0$. Hence, in order for the entire derivative to be equal to 0, it follows that

$$g'(q) - \frac{g(q)}{q} = 0$$

This means that

$$g'(q) = \frac{g(q)}{q}$$

Hence AVC attains a minimum when MC = AVC.

[10] This can be demonstrated as follows. Given

$$\text{TC} = k + g(q) \qquad \text{and} \qquad \text{ATC} = \frac{\text{TC}}{q} = \frac{k + g(q)}{q}$$

Then ATC attains a minimum when

$$\frac{d(\text{ATC})}{dq} = \frac{q[g'(q)] - k - g(q)}{q^2} = 0$$

Since the quantity $q^2 > 0$, it is apparent that $q[g'(q)] - k - g(q)$ must be equal to 0 if the entire derivative is equal to 0. Hence

$$g'(q) = \frac{k + g(q)}{q}$$

and ATC attains a minimum when MC = ATC.

The government is planning to levy a tax of $t$ dollars per unit on the firm's output in order to raise revenues to pay for governmental services. The government wants to maximize $T$, the total revenue it realizes from the tax. However, the government does not know what tax rate $t$ will accomplish that end.

The tax revenue function facing the government is $T = t\bar{q}$, where $\bar{q}$ is the output the imperfectly competitive firm produces *after* the tax $t$ has been imposed. The firm wants to maximize profit; however, the imposition of the tax alters the firm's total cost function. Let $C(q)^*$ be the firm's total cost function after the imposition of the tax. Then

$$\text{Total cost after tax} = C(q)^* + tq$$

$$= k + g(q) + tq \tag{6.25}$$

The profit-maximizing firm produces where marginal cost after tax MC* is equal to marginal revenue.

$$\text{MC}^* = \frac{dC(q)^*}{dq} = \text{MR} = \frac{dR(q)}{dq} \tag{6.26}$$

or

$$g'(q) + t = f(q) + qf'(q)$$

Solving Equation (6.26) for $q$, we obtain $\bar{q}$, the output of the firm when the tax $t$ is taken into consideration. However, this optimal $\bar{q}$ is a function of $t$ such that $\bar{q} = \bar{q}(t)$. Substituting this value into the government's tax revenue function, we find that

$$T = t\bar{q} = t\bar{q}(t) \tag{6.27}$$

The first-order condition for maximizing $T$ requires taking the first derivative of $T$ with respect to $t$ and setting that derivative equal to 0.

$$\frac{dT}{dt} = \bar{q}(t) + t\bar{q}'(t) = 0 \tag{6.28}$$

Solving Equation (6.28) for $t$, and subject to $d^2T/dt^2 < 0$, we have found the tax rate $t$ that maximizes total tax revenue $T$ for the government.

EXAMPLE Assume that an imperfectly competitive firm's total revenue and total cost functions are

$$\text{Total revenue} = \text{TR} = 12Q - 2Q^2$$

$$\text{Total cost} = \text{TC} = 4Q$$

The government is going to impose a tax of $t$ dollars per unit quantity on a commodity $Q$ produced by the firm. The object of the taxation is to maximize total revenue $T$ from the tax. Thus the objective function to be maximized is $T = t\bar{Q}$, where $\bar{Q}$ is the equilibrium quantity for which the firm's profit is maximized after taxation. Then

$$\text{Total cost after tax} = \text{TC}^* = \text{TC} + tQ = 4Q + tQ$$

Profit after taxation is

$$\text{MR} = \text{MC}^* = \frac{d\text{TC}^*}{dQ}$$

or

$$12 - 4Q = 4 + t$$

Thus

$$\bar{Q} = \frac{8 - t}{4}$$

Substituting this value into the tax revenue function, Equation (6.29), we find that

$$T = t\bar{Q} = \frac{t(8 - t)}{4} = \frac{8t - t^2}{4}$$

To maximize $T$, we have

$$\frac{dT}{dt} = \frac{8 - 2t}{4} = 0 \qquad \text{or} \qquad t = 4$$

and $d^2T/dt^2 = -\tfrac{1}{2} < 0$. Hence the maximum tax $t$ equals 4, equilibrium output is $\bar{Q} = (8 - t)/4 = 1$, and total tax revenue is $T = t\bar{Q} = 4$.

#### Inventories and Reordering

Most business firms live in a world where their production is not perfectly synchronized with their sales. Any particular firm therefore typically maintains some sort of inventory of unsold units of its output. There is a direct relationship between the number of units of inventory and the cost of keeping that inventory. Hence the firm wants to maintain as small an inventory as possible and still be able to meet anticipated customer orders. At the same time, however, there are costs associated with starting up production and reordering when the firm's inventory is depleted. As a result, the firm must balance these two types of costs when it makes a decision about how large an inventory to keep and how often to reorder. A large inventory increases inventory storage costs but reduces reorder costs. A small inventory decreases inventory storage costs but increases reorder costs. The optimal inventory (that inventory that minimizes the storage and reorder costs of the firm) must take both types of costs into account.

Let $Q$ be the expected sales of the firm in units in a particular time period, which we will designate a year. Suppose that $Q = 50{,}000$; this implies that the firm expects to sell 50,000 units over the space of the next year. Let us further assume that these sales will be spaced evenly throughout the year, so that $50{,}000/12 = 4166$ units will be sold each month.

*Storage cost*
Let $U$ represent the number of units that the firm receives when it reorders. This means that the average number of units the firm has in its inventory (assuming that the sales of the units are spaced evenly throughout time) is $U/2$. There are costs associated with maintaining a unit of inventory in terms of protection, storage, and so forth. Let $c$ represent the cost of maintaining a unit of inventory for one year. Hence $c(U/2)$ is the total cost of maintaining an average inventory of $U/2$ units.

Total yearly cost of maintaining an average inventory of

$$\frac{U}{2} \text{ units} = c\left(\frac{U}{2}\right) \tag{6.29}$$

*Reordering cost*
Assume that there are two separate types of costs associated with reordering to replenish the inventory. The first type of cost is fixed in nature and does not vary with the size of the order. The cost of recording an order (which presumably does not depend on the size of the order) is an example of this type of cost. We shall represent this fixed cost by the letter $f$. The second type of cost varies directly with the size of the order and covers the incremental cost of shipping and packaging each unit in the order. Let $b$ refer to the incremental cost associated with reordering $U$ units. The total cost of reordering in a specific instance is therefore equal to the sum of $f + bU$. Since a total of $Q$ units is eventually needed for sale, and $U$ units are reordered each time, a total of $Q/U$ reorders are made. This means that the total cost of reordering during the entire year is given by

$$\text{Total yearly cost of reordering} = (f + bU)\left(\frac{Q}{U}\right) \tag{6.30}$$

*Total cost (storage and reordering)*
The total cost associated with storing and reordering is given by Equation (6.31):

$$\text{TC} = c\left(\frac{U}{2}\right) + (f + bU)\left(\frac{Q}{U}\right) \tag{6.31}$$

This can be rewritten as

$$\text{TC} = \frac{cU}{2} + \frac{fQ}{U} + bQ \tag{6.32}$$

Equation (6.32) is in principle rather easy to solve for the optimal size of order $U$ that the firm should undertake. The parameters $b$, $c$, and $f$ are assumed to be known to the firm. Only the size of the firm's order $U$ is unknown. Differentiating Equation (6.33) with respect to the unknown $U$, we obtain

$$\frac{d\text{TC}}{dU} = \frac{c}{2} - \frac{fQ}{U^2} \tag{6.33}$$

Setting $d\text{TC}/dU$ equal to zero, we have

$$\frac{c}{2} - \frac{fQ}{U^2} = 0 \tag{6.34}$$

and

$$\frac{c}{2} = \frac{fQ}{U^2} \tag{6.35}$$

and

$$U^2 = \frac{2fQ}{c} \tag{6.36}$$

The optimal size of order (in the sense of minimizing total storage and reorder costs) is therefore given by

$$U = \sqrt{\frac{2fQ}{c}} \tag{6.37}$$

We know that Equation (6.37) describes a minimum rather than a maximum because $d\text{TC}^2/d^2U > 0$. Specifically, $d\text{TC}^2/d^2U = 2fQ/U^3$, which is always positive because $f$, $Q$, and $U$ are all positive.

Let $Q = 50{,}000$, as above, while $f = \$500.00$ and $c = \$20.00$ per unit per year. Then the optimal size of order is given by

$$U = \sqrt{\frac{2fQ}{c}} = \sqrt{\frac{2(500)(50{,}000)}{20}} = 1581.14 \tag{6.38}$$

This implies that the firm should reorder a total of $Q/U$ times, or $50{,}000/1581.14 = 31.62$ times, and that each reorder should be of size $U = 1581.14$ units.

The "square-root rule" of Equation (6.38) is one particular form of a common and very powerful inventory rule. Whether the subject of the inventory is Ford Motors (and we are talking about Pintos) or the subject is a bank (and we are talking about cash balances), some form of the square-root rule ordinarily applies if we are interested in the optimal size of inventory holdings, the optimal size of orders, or the number of orders that must be placed. If you are interested, you should do additional reading in the area of operations research to augment your knowledge in this area.[11]

### Method of Least Squares: Linear Regression

Business and economic decision-makers are frequently concerned with the relationship between two variables—for example, the relationship between depreciation and new investment, or the relationship between the number of sales representatives in a territory and total sales in that territory. It is seldom

[11] One example of an operations research textbook in which inventory theory is covered in detail is Frederick S. Hillier and Gerald J. Lieberman, *Operations Research*, Second Edition, Holden-Day, San Francisco, 1974, Chapter 11.

possible to predict the exact value of one variable merely on the basis of knowing the value of the other variable. Hence it is seldom possible to predict the precise total dollar value of sales in a territory even if one knows how many sales people are operating in that territory.

Let \$ be the total dollar value of sales in a given territory, and $N$ be the number of sales people operating in that territory. Then $\$ = f(N)$, and assuming the relationship to be linear, we can write

$$\$ = \alpha + \beta N \tag{6.39}$$

where $\alpha$, $\beta$ are unknown parameters to be estimated.

Suppose that we have available paired observations of \$ and $N$ from the territories of the Acme Manufacturing Corporation. Table 6.1 summarizes those paired observations, while Figure 6.16 plots them graphically.

Equation (6.39) is capable of representing any linear relationship. While it appears that the paired observations in Figure 6.16 can be roughly represented by some type of linear line segment, it is also apparent that not all the paired observations in Figure 6.16 lie on a single straight line. The dashed line labeled $AA$ in Figure 6.16 is one such straight line; the dashed line labeled $BB$ is another possibility. Neither straight line ($AA$ or $BB$) perfectly represents the paired observations. It is clear, however, that straight line $AA$ is a "better fit" of the paired observations than $BB$. On that basis we prefer $AA$ to $BB$ as a representation of the relationship between sales and number of sales people.

What we want is that straight line that "best" represents the relationship between sales and the number of sales people. This straight line is expressed in the form $\$ = \alpha + \beta N$. Casual eyeballing indicates that straight line $AA$ is a good representation of the relationship between sales and the number of sales people. It fits the paired observations "better" than straight line $BB$ and "looks" good. Is straight line $AA$, however, the best possible fit of the paired observations?

The usual procedure used to determine the best straight line to fit paired observations is called the *method of least squares*. The method of least squares is the foundation of most *linear regression analysis*. Linear regression analysis

Table 6.1 Relationship between monthly total sales revenues and number of sales people in the Acme Manufacturing Corporation

| *Territory* | *Monthly total dollar value of sales (000s)* | *Number of sales people* |
|---|---|---|
| 1 | 9 | 1 |
| 2 | 12 | 2 |
| 3 | 8 | 1 |
| 4 | 6 | 1 |
| 5 | 15 | 3 |
| 6 | 13 | 3 |
| 7 | 11 | 2 |

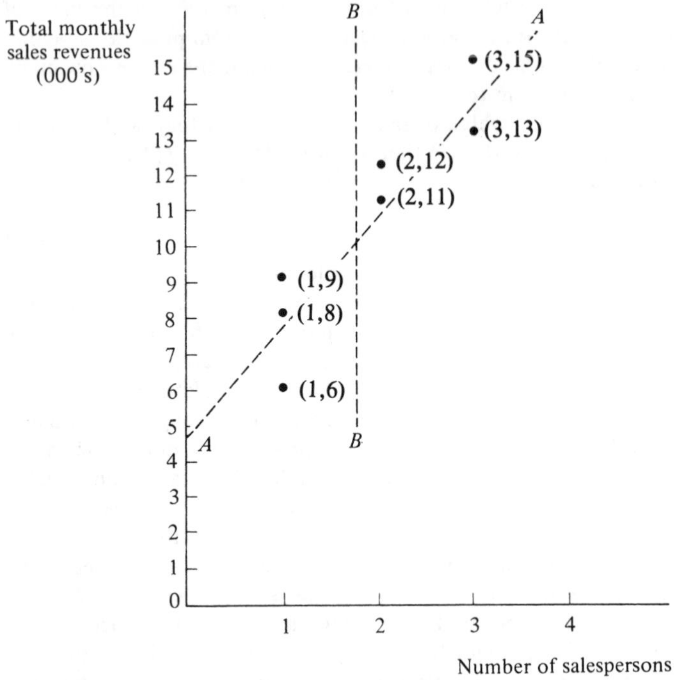


Figure 6.16 Monthly sales and number of salespersons

is a general label applied to attempts to estimate the best-fit straight line for paired observations. The method of least squares is the most common means of obtaining that best-fit estimate.

DEFINITION *Linear regression analysis* is a technique whereby one estimates the relationship between a dependent variable and one or more independent variables by means of a linear equation.

The method of least squares determines the equation of a straight line that minimizes the sum of squares of the vertical distances from each paired observation to the line. Figure 6.17 plots the paired observations of Table 6.1, these vertical distances are represented by dashed lines in the figure. The best-fit line, according to the method of least squares, is that line which minimizes the sum of the squares of the dashed distances in Figure 6.17.

As it happens, the straight line labeled $MM$ in Figure 6.17 does minimize the sum of the squares as desired. We need to develop a technique by which we can demonstrate that such is the case here, and that we can use in other situations in which we confront a similar problem.

Consider the paired observation (6, 1) in Figure 6.17. It is not on the best-fit straight line $MM$. We shall refer to the vertical distance between the paired observation (6, 1) and line $MM$ as an *error*. In general, if we are analyzing the

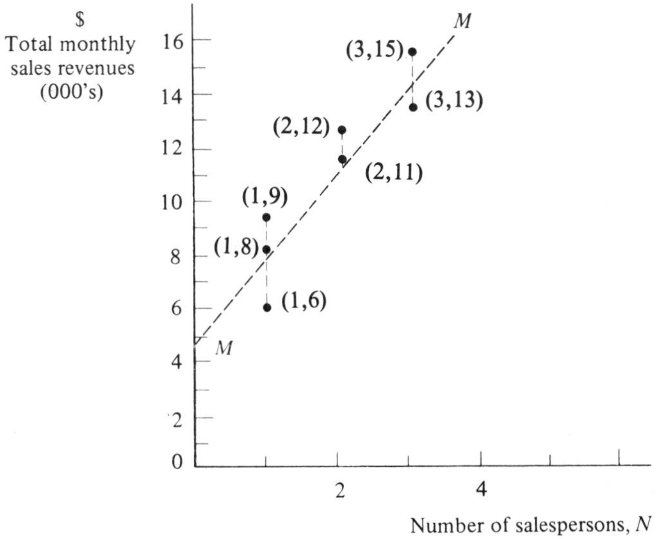


Figure 6.17 Method of least squares and best-fit line. Least-squares estimate of equation that is "best" fit is: $\$ = 4.62 + 3.21N$. This is the equation of line $MM$

$i$th paired observations $(N_i, \$_i)$, the error $e_i$ associated with that paired observation is given by

$$\$_i = \alpha + \beta N + e_i \tag{6.40}$$

Equation (6.40) is a form of Equation (6.39) rewritten to take into account the fact that the straight line that is the best fit is usually not a perfect fit, and that therefore estimation errors $e_i$ will exist.

The method of least squares is concerned with minimizing the sum of the squared errors. Let SS be that sum. SS is equal to

$$\text{SS} = e_1^2 + e_2^2 + e_3^2 + \cdots + e_n^2 \tag{6.41}$$

where 1, 2, 3, ..., $n$ are paired observations.

From Equation (6.40) we know that $e_i = \$_i - \alpha - \beta N_i$. Substituting this into Equation (6.41), we obtain

$$\text{SS} = (\$_1 - \alpha - \beta N_1)^2 + (\$_2 - \alpha - \beta N_2)^2 + \cdots + (\$_n - \alpha - \beta N_n)^2 \tag{6.42}$$

The method of least squares requires that we minimize the value of Equation (6.42). Differentiating Equation (6.42) first with respect to $\alpha$ and then with respect to $\beta$, and solving, we obtain

$$\frac{\partial \text{SS}}{\partial \alpha} = -2(\$_1 - \alpha - \beta N_1) - 2(\$_2 - \alpha - \beta N_2) - \cdots - 2(\$_n - \alpha - \beta N_n)$$

$$= -2\sum_{i=1}^{n} \$_i + 2\alpha n + 2\beta \sum_{i=1}^{n} N_i = 0 \tag{6.43}$$

$$\Sigma\$_i = \alpha n + \beta\Sigma N_i \tag{6.44}$$

$$\frac{\partial SS}{\partial \beta} = -2N_1(\$_1 - \alpha - \beta N_1) - 2N_2(\$_2 - \alpha - \beta N_2) - \cdots$$

$$- 2N_n(\$_n - \alpha - \beta N_n)$$

$$= -2\sum_{i=1}^{n} N_i\$_i + 2\alpha\sum_{i=1}^{n} N_i + 2\beta\sum_{i=1}^{n} N_i^2 = 0 \tag{6.45}$$

$$\Sigma N_i\$_i = \alpha\Sigma N_i + \beta\Sigma N_i^2 \tag{6.46}$$

Solving Equations (6.44) and (6.46) simultaneously for $\alpha$ and $\beta$ yields

$$\hat{\alpha} = \frac{\Sigma N_i^2\Sigma\$_i - \Sigma N_i\Sigma N_i\$_i}{n\Sigma N_i^2 - (\Sigma N_i)^2}, \qquad \hat{\beta} = \frac{n\Sigma N_i\$_i - \Sigma N_i\Sigma\$_i}{n\Sigma N_i^2 - (\Sigma N_i)^2} \tag{6.47}$$

Thus $\hat{\alpha}$ and $\hat{\beta}$ are estimates of the true values $\alpha$ and $\beta$ found in Equation (6.47). The solution values of $\alpha$ and $\beta$ in light of the seven paired observations provided in Table 6.1 are as follows.

| $\$_i$ | $N_i$ | $N_iS_i$ | $N_i^2$ |
|---|---|---|---|
| 9 | 1 | 9 | 1 |
| 12 | 2 | 24 | 4 |
| 8 | 1 | 8 | 1 |
| 6 | 1 | 6 | 1 |
| 15 | 3 | 45 | 9 |
| 13 | 3 | 39 | 9 |
| 11 | 2 | 22 | 4 |
| $\Sigma$ = 74 | 13 | 153 | 29 |

$$\alpha = \frac{29(74) - 13(153)}{7(29) - 13(13)} = 4.62, \qquad \beta = \frac{7(153) - 13(74)}{7(29) - 13(13)} = 3.21 \tag{6.48}$$

Hence the best-fit estimate of the relationship between the total monthly dollar value of sales in a territory and the number of sales people in that territory is $\$ = 4.62 + 3.21N$. Since the dollar value of sales is stated in thousands, the addition of one salesperson in a typical territory would add an estimated \$3210 of sales on a monthly basis. Two sales people would yield $4.62 + 3.21(2) = 4.62 + 6.42 = 11.04$ or \$11,040 of sales.

We can generalize the least-squares estimating equation given in Equation (6.40) to handle any linear functional relationship of the form $y = f(x)$ such that $y = \alpha + \beta x$. We can find $\hat{\alpha}$ and $\hat{\beta}$ as follows.

$$\hat{\alpha} = \frac{\Sigma x_i^2\Sigma y_i - \Sigma x_i\Sigma x_i y_i}{n\Sigma x_i^2 - (\Sigma x_i)^2}, \qquad \hat{\beta} = \frac{n\Sigma x_i y_i - \Sigma x_i\Sigma y_i}{\Sigma x_i^2 - (\Sigma x_i)^2} \tag{6.49}$$

EXAMPLE Assume that the data in Table 6.2 represent the performance of individual students on an accounting examination. The scores of the students on the test are paired with the hours of study that each student reported having undertaken for the examination.

We wish to know the relationship between examination scores and hours of study. We can use the method of least squares to estimate a best-fit regression line for the above paired observations. The assumption is that $y = \alpha + \beta x$, where $y$ = score on examination and $x$ = hours of study. We assemble the needed intermediate data and find that

$$\hat{\alpha} = \frac{1440(1911) - 182(15{,}313)}{26(1440) - (182)^2} = -8.14$$

$$\hat{\beta} = \frac{26(15{,}313) - 182(1911)}{26(1440) - (182)^2} = 11.66$$

This means that the best-fit straight line describing the previous paired observations is given by the equation $y = -8.14 + 11.66x$. This implies that,

Table 6.2 Hypothetical student examination and study data

| (1) *Student* | (2) *Score on examination* $(y)$ | (3) *Hours studied* $(x)$ | (4) $(x)\cdot(y)$ | (5) $(x)^2$ |
|---|---|---|---|---|
| A | 76 | 7 | 532 | 49 |
| B | 83 | 8 | 664 | 64 |
| C | 55 | 4 | 220 | 16 |
| D | 100 | 9 | 900 | 81 |
| E | 89 | 8 | 712 | 64 |
| F | 63 | 5 | 315 | 25 |
| G | 94 | 11 | 1,034 | 121 |
| H | 85 | 9 | 765 | 81 |
| I | 77 | 3 | 231 | 9 |
| J | 20 | 2 | 40 | 4 |
| K | 79 | 6 | 474 | 36 |
| L | 96 | 10 | 960 | 100 |
| M | 71 | 6 | 426 | 36 |
| N | 91 | 5 | 455 | 25 |
| O | 97 | 10 | 970 | 100 |
| P | 72 | 4 | 288 | 16 |
| Q | 86 | 7 | 602 | 49 |
| R | 98 | 11 | 1,078 | 121 |
| S | 91 | 7 | 637 | 49 |
| T | 47 | 3 | 141 | 9 |
| U | 79 | 7 | 553 | 49 |
| V | 84 | 8 | 672 | 64 |
| W | 67 | 6 | 402 | 36 |
| X | 88 | 10 | 880 | 100 |
| Y | 72 | 6 | 432 | 36 |
| Z | 93 | 10 | 930 | 100 |
|  | $\Sigma$ = 1911 | 182 | 15,313 | 1440 |

*at the margin*, an additional hour's study raises the typical student's examination score by 11.66 points.

Note that the inference that an additional hour's study raises the typical student's examination score by 11.66 points is valid only at the margin. One could not validly infer that if a particular student studied 10 additional hours, then his or her examination score would rise by $11.66 \cdot 10 = 111.66$ points. One obvious objection is that the highest possible examination score is 100 points. Therefore an examination score of 111.66 is impossible. The general lesson, however, is that the estimated regression coefficient $\beta$ relates only to what happens to $y$ when small changes are made in $x$. The regression coefficient does not imply that this marginal relationship holds true forever and in all circumstances.

***Point of Inflection: Normal Distribution**

A random variable $y$ is said to be normally distributed if its density function is

$$y = f(x) = \frac{1}{\sqrt{2\Pi}(\sigma)} e^{-(x-\mu)^2/2\sigma^2} \tag{6.50}$$

Here $\mu$ and $\sigma^2$ are the parameters of this particular distribution function. If the variable $x$ is distributed $N(0, 1)$, then we say that $y$ has a standard normal distribution with zero mean and unit variance. This implies that we can write Equation (6.50) as

$$y = f(x) = \frac{1}{\sqrt{2\Pi}} e^{-0.5x2} \tag{6.51}$$

A point of inflection on the curve representing a standard normal distribution indicates a point at which the concavity of the curve representing that density function is changing. As we shall see, the points of concavity for a curve representing a standard normal distribution have interesting properties. These points of inflection are given by $f''(x) = 0$. Differentiating Equation (6.51) with respect to $x$, we obtain

$$f'(x) = \frac{1}{\sqrt{2\Pi}} e^{-0.5x^2}(-x) = -\frac{x}{\sqrt{2\Pi}} e^{-0.5x2} \tag{6.52}$$

and

$$\begin{aligned} f''(x) &= -\frac{1}{\sqrt{2\Pi}} e^{-0.5x2} - \frac{x}{\sqrt{2\Pi}} e^{-0.5x^2}(-x) \\ &= -\frac{1}{\sqrt{2\Pi}} e^{-0.5x2} + \frac{x^2}{\sqrt{2\Pi}} e^{-0.5x2} \\ &= (x^2 - 1)\frac{1}{\sqrt{2\Pi}} e^{-0.5x2} \end{aligned} \tag{6.53}$$

* This section contains more difficult material and may be omitted without loss of continuity.

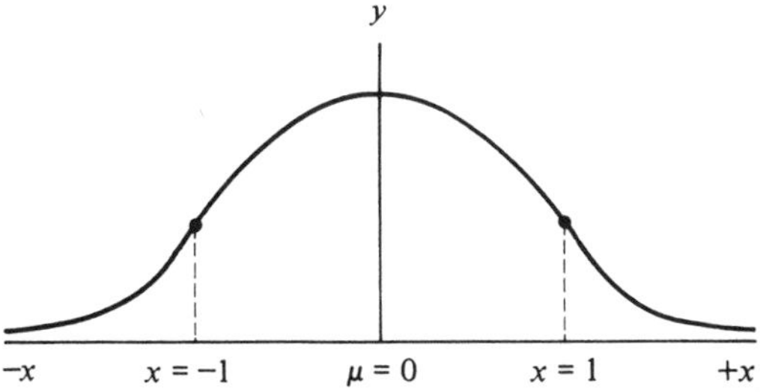


Figure 6.18 Standard normal curve $N(0, 1)$

The only circumstance under which $f''(x)$ can equal zero in Equation (6.53) is if $x^2 - 1 = 0$. This implies that $x^2 = \pm 1$, and that there are points of inflection at $x = -1$ and $x = +1$. We can confirm that $x = -1$ is a point of inflection by observing that when $x = -2, f''(x) > 0$, and that when $x = 0, f''(x) < 0$. Hence concavity changes at $x = -1$. Similarly, we can determine that $x = +1$ is a point of inflection by observing that when $x = 0$, $f''(x) < 0$ and that when $x = +2, f''(x) > 0$. Hence concavity changes when $x = +1$.

Figure 6.18 illustrates the graph of a standard normal curve $N(0, 1)$. There are points of inflection at $x = -1$ and $x = +1$.

## *Portfolio Choice[12]

An important area of finance deals with the question of what is the appropriate portfolio that an investor should seek and maintain. There are many different assets that an investor can purchase. Each asset, however, has distinctive characteristics in terms of rate of return, risk, liquidity,[13] and so forth. Modern theories of portfolio choice generally concentrate on two characteristics: rate of return and risk. The individual investor is assumed to want the highest possible rate of return consistent with whatever level of risk he or she is willing to bear. That is, the investor is assumed to like higher returns and dislike higher risk.

The rate of return on an asset is often represented by $\mu$, the mean rate of return. The riskiness of the asset is typically represented by the standard deviation of the rate of return ($\sigma$) or the variance of the rate of return ($\sigma^2$). For our purposes, assume a representative investor who possesses a utility function of the form $U = U(\mu, \sigma^2)$, where $\partial U/\partial\mu > 0$ and $\partial U/\partial\sigma^2 < 0$. The specific form of this utility function is given by Equation (6.54):

$$U = a\mu + c\omega \qquad \text{where } \omega = \sigma^2 \text{ and } a > 0, c < 0 \qquad (6.54)$$

Such a utility function generates linear indifference curves of the type illustrated in Figure 6.19.

*This section contains more difficult material. It can be omitted without loss of continuity.

[12]William Perry, "A Mathematical Analysis of Efficient Portfolio Theory," Master's Thesis, Illinois State University, May 1976.

[13]Liquidity is often measured by the ease with which a particular asset can be converted into cash.

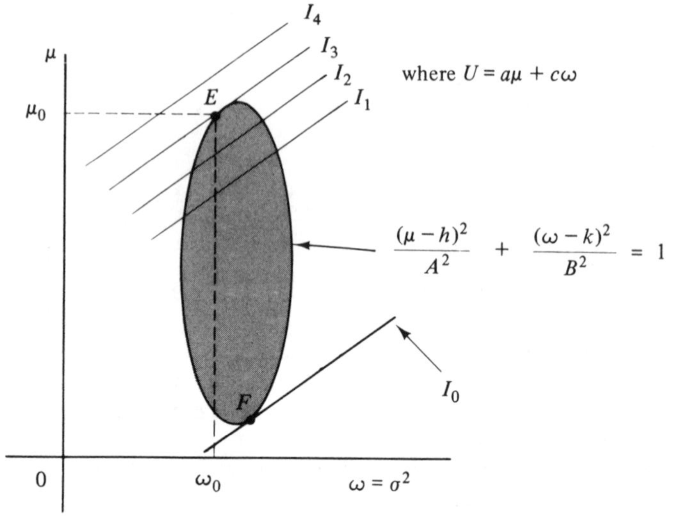


Figure 6.19 Portfolio choice

The constraint that the investor faces is the available set of asset returns and risks. Certain combinations of return and risk are ordinarily not available; for example, a 30% rate of return accompanied by no risk. Hence it is necessary to specify precisely what return–risk combinations the investor may consider. We shall assume that the set of return–risk combinations is enclosed by the ellipse in Figure 6.19. This ellipse is generated by an equation of the form

$$\frac{(\mu - h)^2}{A^2} + \frac{(\omega - k)^2}{B^2} = 1 \tag{6.55}$$

We require that $h > A$ and $k > B$, so that the ellipse is located in the first quadrant. This means that all values of $\mu$ and $\omega$ are positive. The ellipse in Figure 6.19 also has the ordinate as its major axis. This means intuitively that the ellipse is elongated along the vertical axis (ordinate); this is always the case when $B < A$.

It is apparent from Figure 6.19 that the utility-maximizing combination of return and risk is given by point $E$, where indifference curve $I_3$ is tangent to the ellipse that encloses the possible return–risk combinations. At point $E$, the investor realizes the rate of return given by $\mu_0$ and assumes the level of risk represented by $\omega_0$. We shall now demonstrate this choice process by means of the calculus.

We wish to maximize Equation (6.54) subject to the constraint given by Equation (6.55). The Lagrangian function becomes

$$L = a\mu + c\omega + \lambda\left[\frac{(\mu - h)^2}{A^2} + \frac{(\omega - k)^2}{B^2} - 1\right] \tag{6.56}$$

First-order conditions are

$$\frac{\partial L}{\partial \mu} = L_\mu = a + \frac{2\lambda(\mu - h)}{A^2} = 0 \tag{6.57}$$

$$\frac{\partial L}{\partial \omega} = L_\omega = c + \frac{2\lambda(\omega - k)}{B^2} = 0 \tag{6.58}$$

$$\frac{\partial L}{\partial \lambda} = L_\lambda = \frac{(\mu - h)^2}{A^2} + \frac{(\omega - k)^2}{B^2} - 1 = 0 \tag{6.59}$$

We eliminate $\lambda$ from Equations (6.57) and (6.58) and obtain

$$\frac{\mu - h}{aA^2} = \frac{\omega - k}{cB^2} \tag{6.60}$$

This gives us two equations [(6.60) and (6.59)] in two unknowns ($\mu$ and $\omega$). Solving these two equations for $\omega$, we obtain

$$\omega = k \pm \frac{cB^2}{\sqrt{a^2A^2 + c^2B^2}} \tag{6.61}$$

Using the value of $\omega$ obtained in Equation (6.61), we solve for $\mu$, which is equal to

$$\mu = h \pm \frac{aA^2}{\sqrt{a^2A^2 + c^2B^2}} \tag{6.62}$$

Solving in turn for $\lambda$, we obtain

$$\lambda = \pm \frac{\sqrt{a^2A^2 + c^2B^2}}{2} \tag{6.63}$$

Two critical points exist:

(1) $(h + s_1, k + s_2)$ and (2) $(h - s_1, k - s_2)$

where

$$s_1 = \frac{aA^2}{\sqrt{a^2A^2 + c^2B^2}} \quad \text{and} \quad s_2 = \frac{cB^2}{a^2A^2 + c^2B^2}.$$

Note that when $\lambda$ is negative in sign,

$\omega = k + s_2$ and $\mu = h + s_1$

whereas when $\lambda$ is positive in sign,

$\omega = k - s_2$ and $\mu = h - s_1$

The second-order condition for utility maximization requires that

$$L_{\mu\mu} = \frac{2\lambda}{A^2} = \pm \frac{\sqrt{a^2A^2 + c^2B^2}}{A^2} \tag{6.64}$$

$$L_{\omega\omega} = \frac{2\lambda}{B^2} = \pm \frac{\sqrt{a^2A^2 + c^2B^2}}{B^2} \tag{6.65}$$

$$L_{\mu\omega} = 0 \tag{6.66}$$

Equivalently, the second-order conditions are that

$$L_{\mu\mu}L_{\omega\omega} - (L_{\mu\omega})^2 > 0 \qquad \text{and} \qquad L_{\mu\mu},\ L_{\omega\omega} < 0 \tag{6.67}$$

The second-order conditions stated in Equations (6.64) through (6.67) can be satisfied only when $\mu = h + s_1$ and $\omega = k + s_2$. That is, only the first critical point above satisfies the second-order conditions. This places us on the extreme northwest frontier of the ellipse in Figure 6.19. This is point $E$. It ensures that we shall not obtain some point that satisfies the first-order condition (but not the second-order condition), such as point $F$ in Figure 6.19.

Let us now illustrate this procedure by means of an empirical example. Let $a = 2$, $A = 3$, $B = 8$, $c = -1$, $h = 6$, and $k = 12$. Such values are consistent with the linear indifference curves and the ellipse depicted in Figure 6.19. Then

$$\omega = \sigma^2 = k + \frac{cB^2}{a^2A^2 + c^2B^2} \qquad\qquad \mu = h + \frac{aA^2}{a^2A^2 + c^2B^2}$$

$$= 12 + \frac{(-1)(8)^2}{(2)^2(3)^3 + (-1)^2(8)^2} \qquad\qquad = 6 + \frac{(2)(3)^2}{(2)^2(3)^2 + (-1)^2(8)^2}$$

$$= 12 - 6.4 \qquad\qquad = 6 + 1.8$$

$$= 5.6 \qquad\qquad = 7.8$$

Hence the utility-maximizing investor would arrange a portfolio such that he or she would realize the risk represented by a variance of 5.6, and also such that he or she would realize a rate of return of 7.8%.

## THE OUTPUT-MAXIMIZING, COST-MINIMIZING FIRM

In the applications section of Chapter 5, we developed an example of the output-maximizing, cost-minimizing firm in detail. We shall now demonstrate how we can use the more sophisticated tools of this chapter to solve the same problems we introduced in Chapter 5.

### Maximizing Output Subject to a Cost Constraint

Given a production function for a representative firm that takes the form

$$Q = f(L, K) \tag{6.68}$$

where $Q$ = output, $L$ = labor, $K$ = capital. The representative firm has $C^0$ dollars to spend on inputs and faces a cost constraint given by

$$C^0 = P_L L + P_K K \tag{6.69}$$

The task of the firm is tọ maximize Equation (6.68) subject to the constraint given by Equation (6.69). We construct a Lagrangian function reflecting these facts.

$$\Omega(L, K, \lambda) = f(L, K) + \lambda(C^0 - P_L L - P_K K) \tag{6.70}$$

Setting the first partial derivatives of $\Omega$ with respect to $L$, $K$, and $\lambda$ equal to zero, we obtain

$$\Omega_L = f_L - \lambda P_L = 0 \qquad \text{where } f_L = \frac{\partial Q}{\partial L} \tag{6.71}$$

$$\Omega_K = f_K - \lambda P_K = 0 \qquad \text{where } f_K = \frac{\partial Q}{\partial K} \tag{6.72}$$

$$\Omega_\lambda = C^0 - P_L L - P_K K = 0 \tag{6.73}$$

Solving Equations (6.71) and (6.72) for $\lambda$, we obtain

$$\frac{f_L}{P_L} = \lambda \qquad \text{and} \qquad \frac{f_K}{P_K} = \lambda \tag{6.74}$$

Hence

$$\frac{f_L}{P_L} = \frac{f_K}{P_K} \qquad \text{and} \qquad \frac{f_L}{f_K} = \frac{P_L}{P_K} \tag{6.75}$$

Since $f_L$ is the marginal product of labor and $f_K$ is the marginal product of capital, we can write

$$\frac{f_L}{f_K} = \frac{\text{MP}_L}{\text{MP}_K} = \frac{P_L}{P_K} \tag{6.76}$$

Definitionally, any of the three ratios in Equation (6.76) is the "marginal rate of technical substitution of capital for labor." Geometrically, the equilibrium condition set out in Equation (6.76) is satisfied by a point of tangency between the firm's cost constraint and one of its isoquants. Figure 5.4 in Chapter 5 illustrated this first-order condition for constrained output maximization. The second-order condition does not vary from that introduced in Chapter 5.

#### Cost Minimization Given a Level of Output

Assume that the representative firm wishes to minimize the cost of producing a certain level of output $Q^0$. That is, the firm wishes to minimize its cost function $C = P_L L + P_K K$ subject to the constraint that it must produce $Q^0$ of output, where $Q^0 = f(L, K)$. The Lagrangian function to be minimized is

$$\phi(L, K, \psi) = P_L L + P_K K - \psi[Q^0 - f(L, K)] \tag{6.77}$$

Setting the first partial derivatives of $\phi$ with respect to $L$, $K$, and $\psi$ equal to zero, we obtain

$$\phi_L = P_L + \psi f_L = 0 \qquad \text{where } f_L = \frac{\partial Q}{\partial L} \tag{6.78}$$

$$\phi_K = P_K + \psi f_K = 0 \qquad \text{where } f_K = \frac{\partial Q}{\partial K} \tag{6.79}$$

$$\phi_\psi = -[Q^0 - f(L, K)] = 0 \tag{6.80}$$

Solving the first two equations for $\psi$, we obtain

$$\frac{P_L}{f_L} = \psi \quad \text{and} \quad \frac{P_K}{f_K} = \psi$$

Hence

$$\frac{P_L}{f_L} = \frac{P_K}{f_K} \quad \text{and} \quad \frac{f_L}{f_K} = \frac{\text{MP}_L}{\text{MP}_K} = \frac{P_L}{P_K} \tag{6.81}$$

Equation (6.76), which describes the behavior of an output-maximizing firm, and Equation (6.81), which describes the behavior of a cost-minimizing firm, are identical. Hence the equilibrium point labeled $E$ in Figure 5.4 describes the position that both an output-maximizer and a cost-minimizer would attain. It is the first-order condition. The second-order condition does not vary from that introduced in Chapter 5.

**Profit Maximization**

The representative firm that we deal with in this example is a perfect competitor in both the product and the factor markets. This means that it takes as given the price $p$ of its output $Q$ and the price $w$ of the single factor input, labor $L$, that it purchases. The firm's production function is given by $Q = f(L)$, and the firm's cost function is given by $C = wL + k$, where $k$ is fixed cost that is incurred independent of the level of output chosen by the firm.

The firm wishes to maximize profit. This means that it seeks to maximize Equation (6.82):

$$\begin{aligned} \pi &= \text{TR} - \text{TC} = pQ - (wL + k) \\ &= pf(L) - (wL + k) \end{aligned} \tag{6.82}$$

Setting the first derivative of $\pi$ with respect to $L$ equal to zero, we obtain

$$\frac{d\pi}{dL} = pf'(L) - w = 0 \tag{6.83}$$

Hence

$$pf'(L) = w \tag{6.84}$$

Equation (6.84) expresses the first-order condition for profit maximization when the firm has a production function with only one variable input. The left-hand member of Equation (6.84) is $pf'(L)$, which is defined as the "value of the marginal product of labor" ($\text{VMP}_L$). That is, it is the cash value of the marginal product produced by labor. Equation (6.84) requires that the value of the marginal product of labor be equated to the wage paid labor, $w$. The rational, profit-maximizing firm will hire an additional unit of labor whenever $\text{VMP}_L > w$. The firm should hire fewer units of labor when $\text{VMP}_L < w$. It is in equilibrium in the sense of Equation (6.84) when $\text{VMP}_L = w$. This is the first-order condition. The second-order condition does not vary from that introduced in Chapter 5.

## UTILITY MAXIMIZATION

In Chapter 4, we illustrated utility maximization subject to a budget constraint by means of an implicit function. We shall now illustrate utility maximization by means of a Lagrangian function.

Given the utility function $U = U(x, y)$, where $U$ is utility and $x$ and $y$ are goods. The representative consumer who has this utility function also faces a budget constraint of the form $M = P_x x + P_y y$, where $M$ is money income and $P_x$ and $P_y$ are the prices of goods $x$ and $y$, respectively. The task is to maximize the utility function subject to the budget constraint.

We form the Lagrangian expression given by Equation (6.85):

$$L(x, y, \lambda) = U(x, y) + \lambda(M - P_x x - P_y y) \tag{6.85}$$

First-order conditions require that we set all first partial derivatives equal to zero:

$$\frac{\partial L}{\partial x} = L_x = \frac{\partial U}{\partial x} - \lambda P_x = 0 \tag{6.86}$$

$$\frac{\partial L}{\partial y} = L_y = \frac{\partial U}{\partial y} - \lambda P_y = 0 \tag{6.87}$$

$$\frac{\partial L}{\partial \lambda} = L_\lambda = M - P_x x - P_y y = 0 \tag{6.88}$$

We solve for $\lambda$ in the first two equations [(6.86) and (6.87)], and set these equations equal to each other.

$$\frac{\partial U/\partial x}{P_x} = \lambda \quad \text{and} \quad \frac{\partial U/\partial y}{P_y} = \lambda \tag{6.89}$$

$$\frac{\partial U/\partial x}{P_x} = \frac{\partial U/\partial y}{P_y} \tag{6.90}$$

We can rewrite Equation (6.70) as:

$$\frac{\partial U/\partial x}{\partial U/\partial y} = \frac{P_x}{P_y} \tag{6.91}$$

Since we can interpret the partial derivative of the utility function with respect to a variable such as $x$ as the "marginal utility of $x$," we can write

$$\frac{\mathrm{MU}_x}{\mathrm{MU}_y} = \frac{P_x}{P_y} \tag{6.92}$$

The ratio of the marginal utility of $x$ to the marginal utility of $y$ (which is equal to the ratio of the price of $x$ to the price of $y$) defines the "marginal rate of substitution of good $x$ for good $y$" and is strictly analogous to the result we found in Chapter 4.

The second-order condition requires that

$$L_{xx}L_{yy} - (L_{xy})^2 > 0$$
$$= U_{xx}U_{yy} - (U_{xy})^2 > 0$$
$$\text{and } U_{xx}, U_{yy} < 0 \tag{6.93}$$

The second-order condition is satisfied when the representative consumer's indifference curves are concave upward, that is, bowed in toward the origin.

**PROBLEMS**

1. Find the extrema, if such exist, and determine whether they are maxima or minima.
   (a) $z = f(x, y) = 2x^3 + y^2$
   (b) $z = f(x, y) = x^2 + x^2y + y^2$
   (c) $z = f(x, y) = x^3 - xy^2$
   (d) $z = f(r, s) = r + 2r^2 + s - s^3$
   (e) $z = f(P, Y) = 12PY - PY^2$
   (f) $z = f(L, K) = 1.01L^{0.75}K^{0.25}$
2. Heinz Westphal, Vertrater, imports Rhein and Mosel wines. The value of the wine V increases as time passes according to the following formula: $V = 6(2.5)^{t^{0.5}}$, where $t$ = time in years. The present value of the wine PV, given a discount rate $r$ and continuous appreciation, is $PV = 6(2.5)^{t^{0.5}}e^{-rt}$. How long should Westphal hold the wine before selling it in order to maximize the present value of the wine? That is, what $t$ maximizes PV? If $r = 0.08$, what is the corresponding $t$ that maximizes PV?
3. The Des Moines Packing Company has a total cost (TC) function of the form $TC = f(M, L)$, where $M$ = meat in pounds and $L$ = hours of labor. Specifically, $TC = 3M + 7L$. The production function for finished, butchered meat ($Q$) in pounds is $Q = 2M^{0.5}L^{0.5}$. The Des Moines Packing Company wishes to produce 10,000 pounds of finished, butchered meat in this time period. Find the quantities of $M$ and $L$ that minimize the cost of doing so. With respect to the production function, do diminishing returns exist with respect to $M$, $L$, or both? Does the production function exhibit increasing, decreasing, or constant returns to scale? Does Euler's theorem apply?
4. The following data represent the results of a study that sought to determine the relationship between worker productivity per worker hour and the experience per worker in years.

   Use the method of least squares to estimate a best-fit linear function that considers productivity per worker hour $y$ to be a function of experience $x$. The following computations will help you: $\sum y^2 = 5830$; $\sum x^2 = 488$; $\sum xy = 1535$. What is the estimated effect of an additional year of worker experience on productivity per worker hour?

| Employee | *Productivity per worker hour* | *Years experience* |
|---|---|---|
| 1 | 20 | 2 |
| 2 | 31 | 14 |
| 3 | 17 | 1 |
| 4 | 25 | 6 |
| 5 | 22 | 4 |
| 6 | 27 | 9 |
| 7 | 24 | 5 |
| 8 | 27 | 8 |
| 9 | 19 | 1 |
| 10 | 26 | 8 |

5. Determine (if possible) whether the following functions are increasing or decreasing, whether points of inflection exist and where, whether extreme points exist and where, and whether the extreme points, if any, are maxima or minima.
   (a) $y = f(x) = 2x^2$
   (b) $y = f(x) = 6 + 0.15x$
   (c) $y = f(x) = 6x^2 + 2x + 1$
   (d) $y = f(x) = a + bx + cx^2 + dx^3$
   (e) $y = f(x) = 10 + 5x + 2x^2 - x^3$
   (f) $y = f(x) = \sin x$
   (g) $y = f(x) = \sin x^2$
   (h) $y = f(x) = 15 - x + 2x^2 + x^3$
   (i) $y = f(x) = \dfrac{100}{x^2}$

6. An electric power company has two generator plants, which we label A and B. The total cost functions in each plant are given by

$$\mathrm{TC_A} = 8 + 5Q - Q^2 + 0.5Q^3, \qquad \mathrm{TC_B} = 2 + 2Q + Q^2$$

where TC = total cost and $Q$ = kilowatt hours generated (in thousands). The company wishes to minimize the cost of generating any given amount of electricity. How should it allocate production among the two generating plants if it must produce 10,000 kilowatt hours?

7. Harold Hedonist has a utility function of the form $U = Q_1 Q_2$, where $U$ = utility, and $Q_1$ and $Q_2$ are quantities of two different goods and services. Mr. Hedonist has \$100 to spend in this time period. He faces parametric prices such that $P_1 = \$1$ and $P_2 = \$2$. Using the Lagrange multiplier technique, determine the utility-maximizing quantities of $Q_1$ and $Q_2$.

8. Assume that $f(x)$ is a monotonic transformation of $x$ given that $f(x_1) > f(x_0)$ whenever $x_1$ was previously greater than $x_0$. Monotonic transformations are order-preserving. With respect to ordinal utility

maximization, the maximization of a monotonic transformation of a utility function yields exactly the same results as the maximization of the original utility function. Demonstrate that maximizing $U = Q_1^2 Q_2^2$ subject to $100 = Q_1 + 2Q_2$ yields the same results as those found in Problem 7 above.

9. The West Mifflin Ford Company expects to sell 1000 new Fords during the next year. These sales will be evenly spaced throughout the year. The cost of storing an unsold Ford for 1 year is \$150. The cost of placing a new order for Fords from Detroit is \$100 plus \$25 per new automobile ordered. What is the optimal size of order that West Mifflin should place when it orders new Fords? How many such orders should West Mifflin place during this year?
10. The state of Taxonia wishes to maximize the total tax revenue $T$ that it receives from a per-unit tax of amount $t$ per unit that it is going to place on the output of Monopoly, Inc. The total revenue TR function of Monopoly, Inc., is given by $\text{TR} = 6Q - Q^2$, while its total cost (TC) function is given by $\text{TC} = 2Q$, where $Q$ is units of output. What tax per unit $t$ will maximize total tax receipts for the state of Taxonia? How much tax revenue ($T$) will this tax raise? What are the equilibrium price and output in this situation?

# INTEGRAL CALCULUS

# 7

In the previous four chapters, we have studied the differential calculus. We considered a function such as $y = f(x)$, and learned how to find a new function, $dy/dx$, which we termed the derivative of the function $y$ with respect to $x$. We found that the first derivative of a function is the slope of the graph of that function at a particular point.

In this chapter we introduce the second main branch of the calculus: the *integral calculus.* The integral calculus is notable in two specific ways. First, it enables us to define and measure the concept of area; for example, the area under a curve. As with the differential calculus, we apply the limit notion when we work with an integral. A few of the very many applications of the integral calculus to business and economics include: measuring consumer's surplus, determining the total amount of depreciation that a firm will realize in a specific time span, measuring the deadweight loss due to monopoly, and finding total product when one knows only marginal product.

The second way in which the integral calculus is notable is that the technique of integration is operationally the inverse of differentiation. Whereas in the differential calculus a function is given and one must find the corresponding derivative, in the integral calculus the derivative of the function is given and we must work backward to find the original function. This relationship is useful, for example, when we know marginal sales revenue, but wish to find total sales revenue. The backward direction of this process of *integration* is the reason that an integral of a function is often called the *antiderivative* of that function.

## THE INDEFINITE INTEGRAL

DEFINITION If $F(x)$ is a function such that $dF(x)/dx = F'(x) = f(x)$ is its derivative for a given interval on the $x$ axis, then $F(x)$ is defined to be the antiderivative or integral of $f(x)$.

The process of integration is symbolized as follows:

$$\int f(x)\,dx = F(x) + C \tag{7.1}$$

The left-hand side of Equation (7.1) is read, "the integral $f$ of $x$ with respect to $x$." The elongated $\int$ symbol is an *integral sign* (which, as we shall soon see, implies the summation of continuous values). We call $f(x)$ the *integrand*, that is, the function that is being integrated. The delta $x$ (or dee $x$) symbol, $dx$, indicates that we are integrating with respect to a variable $x$. On the right-hand side of Equation (7.1), $F(x) + C$ is the *indefinite integral*, while $C$ itself is any arbitrary *constant of integration*.

The inclusion of the $dx$ symbol on the left-hand side of Equation (7.1) may seem superfluous. However, we cannot omit it, since it indicates the variable with respect to which we are integrating. If $dx$ were absent in Equation (7.1), the equation would be just as incomplete as a derivative that was written $df(x)/d$. One might presume that the differentiation is taking place with respect to $x$. However, that cannot be assumed and may not be true.

In the process of finding the antiderivative or integral of a given function $f(x)$, we produce another function of $x$, $F(x) + C$. This, too, is analogous to the process of differentiation, where we differentiated a function of $x$ and thereby generated another function that was, in general, also a function of $x$.

When we find the antiderivative or integral of a function, it will in general not be unique. That is, there are many alternative functions that could have the same derivative. For example, when $y = F(x) = 2x$, $dy/dx = 2$; however, when $y = F(x) = 2x + 1000$, $dy/dx = 2$ also. "$2x$" is an antiderivative of 2; however, "$2x + 1000$" is also an antiderivative of 2. So also are "$2x + 1500$" and "$2x + 4224$."

Hence there can be an infinite number of antiderivatives (integrals) associated with a particular derivative. By way of contrast, in the past four chapters, when we found the derivative of a function, that derivative was unique. For example, if $y = F(x) = 2x^2$, then $dy/dx = 4x$, which is unique. There is no other value or function that is the first derivative of the function $y = 2x^2$.

We need to stress the nonuniqueness of an antiderivative (integral), since it is important to the understanding of the process of integration. In general, the indefinite integral of $f(x) = 2x$ would be

$$F(x) = x^2 + C, \qquad \text{for} \qquad \frac{dF(x)}{dx} = \frac{d(x^2 + C)}{dx} = 2x = f(x)$$

Geometrically, $y = x^2 + C$ represents a family of curves that are parallel to one another, but have a vertical displacement from one another of $C$ units.

Figure 7.1 illustrates such a family of curves for the function $F(x) = x^2 + C$. Unless we know the value of the arbitrary constant $C$, we are unable to determine the unique antiderivative of a given function. When additional information is supplied concerning the value of the constant $C$, we state that the *initial conditions* or *boundary conditions* have been specified. In the example depicted in Figure 7.1, if we are given the initial condition that $x = 0$, and the value $F(x) = F(0) = 3$, then the value of the constant $C$ is determined. $F(0)$ now is equal to $F(x) + C = F(0) + C = 3$; hence $(0)^2 + C = 3$, and $C = 3$. Thus $F(x) = x^2 + C$ becomes $x^2 + 3$.

The $F(x)$ term of the indefinite integral $F(x) + C$ is entirely a function of $x$ and has no definite numerical value. That is why $F(x) + C$ is referred to as the

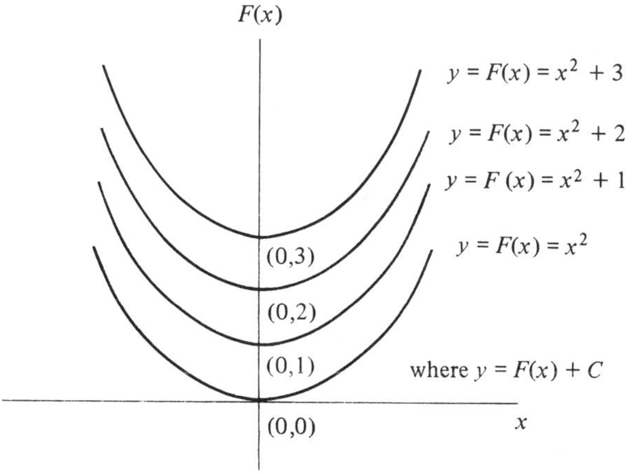


Figure 7.1 A graphical interpretation of the constant of integration

*indefinite integral.* In the absence of additional information, the value of $F(x) + C$ is unknown and indefinite.

You must pay careful attention to the notation you use when you are finding an antiderivative or integral. Whereas $f'(x)$ denoted a derivative of a function in the differential calculus, $F(x)$ is the antiderivative or original function in the integral calculus, and $f(x)$ now refers to the derivative.

In describing the process of integration in Equation (7.1), we used a function of the form $y = f(x)$. Functions involving the letter $x$ are customarily used to illustrate the process of integration, just as we used functions involving the letter $x$ to illustrate the process of differentiation. There is nothing magical about the symbol $x$. We could use any other letter, such as, $s$, $t$, $u$, $v$, or $w$, to illustrate integration with equal validity.

## RULES AND PROPERTIES RELATING TO THE INTEGRAL

In Chapter 4 we developed a series of rules that greatly simplified the task of finding the derivative of a function. We shall now state a series of rules that will help you integrate a wide variety of functions.

Since differentiation and integration have an inverse relationship to each other, it should come as no surprise that many of the rules relating to integration are closely related to the rules that we have already developed for differentiation. Specifically, it is often the case that one need only reverse a specific rule for differentiation to get the needed rule for integration. Nevertheless, this is *not* always the case. Some integrals are not easy to evaluate. It is customary to use published tables, such as the one found in Appendix A at the end of this book, to assist one in evaluating integrals because of the multitude of mathematical forms that are involved. In the next few pages, therefore, we shall consider only a few of the rules that you can use to find integrals. You can find the remainder of these rules, many of which are quite complicated, in Appendix A.

### The Power Rule

$$\int x^n \, dx = \frac{1}{n+1} x^{n+1} + C \qquad (n \neq -1)$$

*Proof* Remembering that the differential of any variable $x$ is $f_x \, dx$, the differential of the right-hand side of the power-rule equation above is

$$\frac{d\left(\dfrac{1}{n+1} x^{n+1} + C\right)}{dx} \cdot dx = \frac{n+1}{n+1} x^n \, dx \tag{7.2}$$

or

$$f_x \, dx = x^n \, dx \tag{7.3}$$

Equation (7.3) is actually the integrand that we started with on the left-hand side of the power-rule equation. Hence the power rule is proved.

The proof above correctly suggests that the derivative of an integral must always be equal to the integrand. That is, if the correct integration has been performed, $d[F(x) + C]/dx$ must be equal to $f(x)$.

EXAMPLES

1. $\int x^5 \, dx = \frac{1}{6}x^6 + C$ *Check:* $\dfrac{d(\frac{1}{6}x^6 + C)}{dx} = x^5$

2. $\int x \, dx = \frac{1}{2}x^2 + C$ *Check:* $\dfrac{d(\frac{1}{2}x^2 + C)}{dx} = x$

3. $\int dx = \int 1 \, dx = \int x^0 \, dx = x + C$ *Check:* $\dfrac{d(x + C)}{dx} = 1$

4. $\int \sqrt{x} \, dx = \int x^{1/2} \, dx = \frac{2}{3}x^{3/2} + C$ *Check:* $\dfrac{d(\frac{2}{3}x^{3/2} + C)}{dx} = x^{1/2} = \sqrt{x}$

5. $\int \left(\frac{1}{x^2}\right) dx = \int x^{-2} \, dx = -\left(\frac{1}{x}\right) + C$

   *Check:* $\dfrac{d[-(1/x) + C]}{dx} = \dfrac{d[-x^{-1} + C]}{dx} = x^{-2} = \dfrac{1}{x^2}$

The power rule of integration explicitly requires that $n \neq -1$. The following example demonstrates why this restriction is necessary. Let us try to find the integral of $f(x) = 1/x$. $\int (1/x) \, dx = \int x^{-1} \, dx = (1/0)x^0$. Hence, when $n = -1$, the power rule is no longer applicable because the integral is undefined due to division by 0. The following rule deals with this type of situation, however.

**The General Logarithmic Rule**

$$\int \frac{1}{x}\,dx = \int x^{-1}\,dx = \ln|x| + C \qquad (x \neq 0)$$

*Proof* The differential of the right-hand side of the equation describing the general logarithmic rule is $d(\ln|x| + C)$, which is equal to $(1/x)\,dx$. Since we started our integration with $(1/x)\,dx$ on the left-hand side, the general logarithmic rule is proved.

The antiderivative in the general logarithmic rule has an absolute-value sign contained within it. This is used because logarithms do not exist for negative values of any variable $x$. When we are working with a problem in which we are certain that the domain of a variable consists only of positive values, we may omit the absolute-value sign.

■ We use the general logarithmic rule *only* when we have the specific integrand $f(x) = 1/x$. We cannot apply the rule to any integrand containing a multiplicative constant. For example,

$$\int \left(\tfrac{1}{2}x\right) dx \neq \ln|2x| + C \qquad \text{because} \qquad \frac{d(\ln|2x| + C)}{dx} = \frac{1}{2x}(2) = \frac{1}{x} \neq \tfrac{1}{2}x$$

**The General Exponential Rule**

$$\int a^x\,dx = \frac{a^x}{\ln a} + C$$

*Proof* The differential of the right-hand side of the equation expressing the general exponential rule is

$$\frac{d\left(\dfrac{a^x}{\ln a} + C\right)}{dx} \cdot dx = \left[\frac{a^x}{\ln a}\ln a(1)\right] dx = a^x\,dx$$

which is the integrand with which we started on the left-hand side of the expression of the general exponential rule.

**The Exponential Rule: Base *e***

$$\int e^x\,dx = e^x + C$$

*Proof* The differential of the right-hand side of the equation expressing the exponential rule of base $e$ is $d(e^x + C) = e^x\,dx$.

■ Rules 3 and 4 above apply *only* to the cases in which the integrands are $a^x$ and $e^x$, respectively. Any multiplicative constant applied to the function $x$, or the raising of variable $x$ to a power other than 1, invalidates the use of the rules.

EXAMPLES

1. $\int e^{2x}\,dx \neq e^{2x} + C$ Check: $\dfrac{d(e^{2x} + C)}{dx} = 2e^{2x} \neq e^{2x}$

2. $\int e^{x^2}\,dx \neq e^{x^2} + C$ Check: $\dfrac{d(e^{x^2} + C)}{dx} = 2xe^{x^2} \neq e^{x^2}$

3. $\int a^{2x^2}\,dx \neq a^{2x^2} + C$ Check: $\dfrac{d(a^{2x^2} + C)}{dx} = a^{2x^2} \ln a(4x) \neq a^{2x^2}$

■ Before we develop additional rules that will enable us to deal with exponential functions that are not of the precise form $y = a^x$ or $y = e^x$, we must confront a problem that often confuses people who are learning about integration. We have already mentioned that in order to get rid of the arbitrary constant of integration, *initial conditions* (*boundary conditions*) must be specified. In general, the initial condition is the value of the arbitrary constant itself. For example, $\int 2x\,dx = x^2 + C$. If the initial condition is $x = 0$ and $F(0) = 3$, then the constant of integration would also be 3: $F(0) = 0^2 + C = 3$, or $C = 3$.

However, *it is possible* for the initial condition to have a value different from that of the constant of integration. Exponential functions sometimes furnish examples of this phenomenon. Consider the integral $\int e^x\,dx$ with the initial condition $F(0) = 3$. Thus $F(x) = \int e^x\,dx = e^x + C$. Hence $F(0) = e^0 + C = 3$, and $1 + C = 3$, and $C = 2$. That is, $F(0) = 3 \neq C = 2$, and we should not always assume that the constant of integration and the initial condition of the function are identical.

### Four Fundamental Theorems of Integration

In order to progress in our evaluation of integrals, we must state four important theorems that enable us to develop further useful techniques and rules for integration.

THEOREM 7.1 (THE ADDITIVE PROPERTY) If both $f(x)$ and $g(x)$ are integrable, then the integral of a sum of a finite number of functions is equal to the sum of the integrals. That is,

$$\int [f(x) + g(x)]\,dx = \int f(x)\,dx + \int g(x)\,dx$$
$$= F(x) + C_1 + G(x) + C_2 = F(x) + G(x) + C$$

where $C_1 + C_2 = C$ is a single arbitrary constant of integration.

THEOREM 7.2 (HOMOGENEOUS PROPERTY) The integral of $K$, a constant, times an integral is equal to $K$ times the integral of the integrand. That is,

$$\int Kf(x)\,dx = K \int f(x)\,dx = KF(x) + C$$

Theorem 7.2 states that if we multiply a function of $x$ by some constant $K$, then the resulting integral is also multiplied by that same constant $K$. This rule is analogous to the rule in the differential calculus that tells us that $d(2x)/dx = 2$, but $d[5(2x)]/dx = 5 \cdot 2 = 10$.

THEOREM 7.3 (LINEARITY PROPERTY) If both $f(x)$ and $g(x)$ are integrable, so is $K_1 f(x) + K_2 g(x)$ for every pair of constants $K_1$ and $K_2$. That is,

$$\begin{aligned} \int [K_1 f(x) + K_2 g(x)]\, dx &= K_1 \int f(x)\, dx + K_2 \int g(x)\, dx \\ &= K_1 F(x) + C_1 + K_2 G(x) + C_2 \\ &= K_1 F(x) + K_2 G(x) + C \end{aligned}$$

Theorem 7.3 may be generalized to $n$ functions of $x$.

THEOREM 7.4 (GENERALIZED LINEARITY) If $f_1(x), \ldots, f_n(x)$ are integrable, then so is $K_1 f_1(x) + \cdots + K_n f_n(x)$ for all real $K_1, \ldots, K_n$. That is,

$$\int \sum_{i=1}^{n} K_i f_i(x)\, dx = \sum_{i=1}^{n} K_i \int f_i(x)\, dx = \sum_{i=1}^{n} [K_i F_i(x) + C_i] = \sum_{i=1}^{n} K_i F_i(x) + C$$

where $F_i(x)$ is the antiderivative of $f_i(x)$, for all $i = 1, 2, \ldots, n$ and

$$\sum_{i=1}^{n} C_i = C$$

the sum of the arbitrary constants of integration.

EXAMPLES

1. $\int -4x^2\, dx = -4 \int x^2\, dx = -\frac{4}{3}x^3 + C$

   *Check*: $\dfrac{d(-\frac{4}{3}x^3 + C)}{dx} = -4x^2$

2. $$\begin{aligned} \int (3x^2 - 5x + 1)\, dx &= 3 \int x^2 - 5 \int x\, dx + \int dx \\ &= 3(\tfrac{1}{3})x^3 + C_1 - 5(\tfrac{1}{2})x^2 + C_2 + x + C_3 \\ &= x^3 - (\tfrac{5}{2})x^2 + x + C \end{aligned}$$

3. $\int \frac{8}{x}\, dx = 8 \int \frac{dx}{x} = 8 \ln |x| + C$

4. $$\begin{aligned} \int (2e^x + x^{-2})\, dx &= 2 \int e^x + \int x^{-2}\, dx \\ &= (2e^x + C_1) + (-x^{-1} + C_2) = 2e^x - \frac{1}{x} + C \end{aligned}$$

**Integration by Substitution**

Our rules of integration, and the theorems stated above, deal with relatively uncomplicated integrands. As we have seen, however, more complicated integrands do exist and cannot be handled by the rules and theorems. We need a process by which we can transform a complicated integrand into the simple integrands utilized in the rules and theorems. One such process is known as the *substitution method* of integration, which "substitutes" a new variable of integration for the original variable. The object of the substitution is to transform the complicated integrand into one of the simple integrands that our rules and theorems can deal with.

The technique of integration by substitution is applicable whenever we can transform the original integral $\int f(x)\,dx$ as follows:

$$\int f(x)\,dx = \int f[g(x)]g'(x)\,dx = \int f(u)\frac{du}{dx}\,dx = \int f(u)\,du \tag{7.4}$$

The substitution involved concerns the replacement of $g(x)$ by $u$ and $g'(x)\,dx$ by $du$. This substitution transforms the operation $\int dx$ into the operation $\int du$. When we integrate with respect to the variable $u$, we obtain an indefinite integral that is a function of $u$, such as $F(u) + C$. We can then transform this indefinite integral back into a function of the original variable, $x$, by making the opposite substitution, that is, replacing $u$ with $g(x)$ and replacing $du$ with $g'(x)\,dx$. This accomplishes the needed integration by means of substitution.

We can now rewrite our four integration rules for the cases in which substitution is carried out:

1′. *The power rule*: $\int u^n\,du = \dfrac{u^{n+1}}{n+1} + C \qquad n \neq -1$

2′. *The general logarithmic rule*: $\int \dfrac{1}{u}\,du = \ln |u| + C$

3′. *The general exponential rule*: $\int a^u\,du = \dfrac{a^u}{\ln a} + C$

4′. *The exponential rule: Base e*: $\int e^u\,du = e^u + C$

If you are alert, you may already have seen the connection between integration by substitution and the use of the chain rule in differentiation. Integration is, as we have pointed out, the reverse of differentiation. This means that when we introduce a new function $u = g(x)$ in the process of integration, the usual checking process (by which we ascertain whether our integral is correct) must utilize the chain rule of differentiation. That is, since integration by substitution involves the introduction of a new function $u$, which is a function of $x$, the checking process must use the function-of-a-function rule (the chain rule) in order to return us to the original function.

*Proof* Given a function of a function, $y = F[g(x)]$. The derivative of this function with respect to $x$ is, by the chain rule,

$$\frac{dy}{dx} = F'[g(x)]g'(x) \tag{7.5}$$

Assume that the function $F[g(x)]$ is the integral of another function, $f(x)$. That is,

$$F'[g(x)] = f(x) \tag{7.6}$$

or

$$F'[g(x)] = f[g(x)] \tag{7.7}$$

Now we substitute Equation (7.7) into Equation (7.5):

$$\frac{dy}{dx} = F[g(x)]g'(x) \tag{7.8}$$

Integrating, we obtain

$$\int F'[g(x)]\,dx = \int f(x)\,dx = F(x) + C \tag{7.9}$$

Therefore

$$\int f[g(x)]g'(x)\,dx = F[g(x)] + C \tag{7.10}$$

We now substitute $u = g(x)$ and $du = g'(x)\,dx$ into Equation (7.10):

$$\int f(u)\,du = F(u) + C \tag{7.11}$$

Equation (7.11) is the general formula for integration by substitution.

EXAMPLES

1. Evaluate $\int \frac{1}{2}(e^{2x} + 1)^2 e^{2x}\,dx$. Let

   $$u = e^{2x} + 1, \qquad du = 2e^{2x}dx \qquad \text{or} \qquad dx = \tfrac{1}{2}e^{-2x}du$$

   Thus

   $$\int \tfrac{1}{2}(e^{2x} + 1)^2 e^{2x}\,dx = \int \tfrac{1}{2}u^2 e^{2x}(2e^{-2x})\,dx = \int u^2\,dx$$
   $$= \tfrac{1}{3}u^3 + C = \tfrac{1}{3}(e^{2x} + 1)^3 + C$$

2. Evaluate $\int 3x^2(x^3 - 4)^2\,dx$. Let $u = x^3 - 4$. Then

   $$du = 3x^2\,dx \qquad \text{or} \qquad dx = \frac{1}{3x^2}\,du$$

Thus

$$\int 3x^2(x^3 - 4)^2\,dx = \int 3x^2u^2\left(\frac{1}{3x^2}\,du\right) = \int u^2\,du$$

$$= \tfrac{1}{3}u^3 + C = \tfrac{1}{3}(x^3 - 4)^3 + C$$

3. Evaluate

$$\int \frac{dx}{x-2}$$

Let $u = x - 2$. Then $du = dx$. Thus

$$\int \frac{dx}{x-2} = \int \frac{du}{u} = \ln|u| + C = \ln|x-2| + C$$

The above examples indicate clearly that an appropriate substitution consists of two parts that are related to each other. One part of the substitution is the derivative of the other part of the substitution. It is also possible that integration by substitution may result in a constant multiple of $f(u)\,du$. However, as the examples below demonstrate, this does not present a problem. The homogeneous property allows us to factor this constant multiple and to place it in front of the integral sign.

EXAMPLES

1. Evaluate $\int 2e^{4x}\,dx$. Let $u = 4x$. Then $du = 4\,dx$ or $dx = \frac{1}{4}\,du$. Thus

$$\int 2e^{4x}\,dx = 2\int e^u(\tfrac{1}{4}\,du) = \tfrac{1}{2}\int e^u\,du$$

$$= \tfrac{1}{2}e^u + C = \tfrac{1}{2}e^{4x} + C$$

2. Evaluate

$$\int \frac{dx}{2x-5}$$

Let $u = 2x - 5$. Then $du = 2\,dx$ or $dx = \frac{1}{2}\,du$. Thus

$$\int \frac{dx}{2x-5} = \int \frac{1}{u}(\tfrac{1}{2}\,du) = \tfrac{1}{2}\int \frac{du}{u} = \tfrac{1}{2}\ln|u| + C$$

$$= \tfrac{1}{2}\ln|2x-5| + C$$

3. Evaluate $\int K^{4x}\,dx$, where $K$ is a constant. Let $u = 4x$; then $du = 4\,dx$ or $dx = \frac{1}{4}\,du$. Thus

$$\int K^{4x}\,dx = \int K^u[\tfrac{1}{4}\,du] = \tfrac{1}{4}\int K^u\,du = \tfrac{1}{4}K^u \cdot \frac{1}{\ln K} + C$$

$$= \frac{K^{4x}}{4\ln K} + C$$

■ In order for the technique of integration by substitution to work, we must always completely transform the original integrand from one that involves one variable, say $x$, to a completely different function involving another variable, say $u$. If substitution is impossible, or is carried out improperly so that a function or functions of two or more variables results, then we must try a new substitution, for there is no general way in which we can find the integral of this new quantity.

EXAMPLE Evaluate

$$\int \frac{2x-3}{x^2-3x}\,dx$$

Let $u = 2x - 3$. Then $du = 2dx$ or $dx = \tfrac{1}{2}du$. Thus

$$\int \frac{2x-3}{x^2-3x}\,dx = \int \frac{u}{x^2-3x}\,(\tfrac{1}{2})du$$

which is not integrable, since the substitution created a new function with two variables, $x$ and $u$. The proper substitution should have been $u = x^2 - 3x$. Then

$$du = (2x-3)\,dx \qquad \text{or} \qquad dx = \frac{1}{2x-3}\,du$$

Thus

$$\int \frac{2x-3}{x^2-3x}\,dx = \int \frac{2x-3}{u}\,\frac{1}{2x-3}\,du = \int \frac{1}{u}\,du$$

$$= \ln|u| + C = \ln|x^2-3x| + C$$

It is often possible to decide on the appropriate substitution by simple observation of the original integrand. That ability, however, usually means that you have acquired the knowledge and foresight that seem to come only with experience, some trial and error, and hard work. Integration is generally considered to be a more difficult process to master than differentiation. The correct way to integrate a function is not always readily apparent. Also, if the substitution is carried out improperly so that a function or functions of two or more variables results, then you must try a new substitution. There is no completely general way to find the needed integral by means of substitution. All these difficulties are reasons why tables of integrals typically accompany any book that purports to teach the integral calculus.

**EXERCISE 7.1**

Evaluate the following integrals.

1. $\int (4x^3 - 3x^2 + 2x - 6)\,dx$
2. $\int \frac{2-3x+x^3}{x^2}\,dx$

3. $\int (4x - 3)^2\, dx$

4. $\int 4x\sqrt{1 + 2x^2}\, dx$

5. $\int \frac{x}{x^2 - 6}\, dx$

6. $\int \sqrt{1 + 2x}\, dx$

7. $\int \frac{x\, dx}{\sqrt{1 - x^2}}$

8. $\int \frac{x + 1}{x^2 + 2x + 3}\, dx$

9. $\int (2x - 5)^3\, dx$

10. $\int (1 - x)\, dx$

11. $\int \frac{x^5}{\sqrt{1 - x^6}}\, dx$

12. $\int (1 - x^3)^2 x^2\, dx$

13. $\int e^{-x}\, dx$

14. $\int \frac{e^{1/x}}{x^2}\, dx$

15. $\int e^{x2+4}x\, dx$

16. $\int x^2 e^{x^3}\, dx$

17. $\int \frac{e^{3x}}{e^{3x} + 3}\, dx$

18. $\int a^{8x}\, dx$

**Integration by Parts**

Another popular method used to transform complex, seemingly unworkable integrands into more workable forms is known as *integration by parts.* Just as integration by substitution was seen to be the inverse of the chain rule for differentiation, the technique of integration by parts may be viewed as the inverse of the product rule for differentiation.

Integration by parts is applicable whenever the original integral $\int h(x)\, dx$ can be transformed as follows:

$$\int f(x)g'(x)\, dx = f(x)g(x) - \int f'(x)g(x)\, dx + C \tag{7.12}$$

We can rewrite Equation (7.12) in more abbreviated form by making the following substitutions:

$$u = f(x), \qquad v = g(x), \qquad du = f'(x)\, dx, \qquad dv = g'(x)\, dx$$

Then Equation (7.12) becomes

$$\int u\, dv = uv - \int v\, du + C \tag{7.13}$$

A proof of Equation (7.12), which is the heart of the integration-by-parts technique, follows. We shall prove Equation (7.12) by working in the opposite direction. That is, we shall begin with the rule for the derivative of a product and then demonstrate how it can be transformed into the formula for integration by parts.

*Proof* If $h(x) = f(x) \cdot g(x)$, then

$$h'(x) = f'(x)g(x) + f(x)g'(x) \tag{7.14}$$

This is the definition of the derivative of a product. Translating this into the process of integration, we have

$$\int f'(x)g(x)\,dx + \int f(x)g'(x)\,dx = f(x) \cdot g(x) + C \tag{7.15}$$

We can find the integration-by-parts formula, which we stated above in Equation (7.12), by rewriting Equation (7.15) as

$$\int f(x)g'(x)\,dx = f(x)g(x) - \int f'(x)g(x)\,dx + C \tag{7.16}$$

In review, the procedure that we must follow when attempting to evaluate an integral by parts is to transform any original integral of the form $\int f(x)g(x)\,dx$ into an integral in which the only term to evaluate is $\int f'(x)g(x)\,dx$. If we have made appropriate choices when we substituted for $f(x)$ and $g(x)$, then the transformed integral will be easier to evaluate than the original.

EXAMPLES

1. Evaluate $\int xe^x\,dx$. Let $u = x$ and $dv = e^x\,dx$. Then $du = dx$ and $v = e^x$. Thus

$$\int xe^x\,dx = xe^x - \int e^x\,dx = xe^x - e^x + C$$

2. Evaluate $\int \ln x\,dx$. Let $u = \ln x$ and $dv = dx$. Then $du = 1/x\,dx$ and $v = x$. Thus

$$\int \ln x\,dx = x \ln x - \int x \frac{1}{x}\,dx = x \ln x - x + C$$
$$= x(\ln x - 1) + C$$

Occasionally we need to use the integration procedure several times before we obtain an integral that we can solve using the general rules stated earlier in this chapter, by substitution, or by means of tables such as the one in Appendix A at the back of this book.

EXAMPLES

1. Evaluate $\int x\sqrt{1 + x}\,dx$. Let $u = x$ and $dv = \sqrt{1 + x}\,dx$. Then $du = dx$ and $v = \frac{2}{3}(1 + x)^{3/2}$. Thus

$$\int x\sqrt{1 + x}\,dx = \tfrac{2}{3}x(1 + x)^{3/2} - \tfrac{2}{3}\int (1 + x)^{3/2}\,dx$$

To evaluate $\int (1 + x)^{3/2}$ we must substitute $u = (1 + x)$ and $du = dx$. Thus

$$\int x\sqrt{1 + x}\,dx = \tfrac{2}{3}x(1 + x)^{3/2} - \tfrac{2}{3}\left(\int u^{3/2}\,du\right)$$
$$= \tfrac{2}{3}x(1 + x)^{3/2} - \tfrac{2}{3}(\tfrac{2}{5}u^{5/2}) + C$$
$$= \tfrac{2}{3}x(1 + x)^{3/2} - \tfrac{4}{15}(1 + x)^{5/2} + C$$

2. Evaluate $\int x^3e^{2x}\,dx$. Let $u = x^3$ and $dv = e^{2x}\,dx$. Then $du = 3x^2\,dx$ and $v = \frac{1}{2}e^{2x}$. Thus

$$\int x^3e^{2x}\,dx = \tfrac{1}{2}x^3e^{2x} - \tfrac{3}{2}\int x^2e^{2x}\,dx$$

To evaluate $\int x^2e^{2x}\,dx$, let $u = x^2$ and $dv = e^{2x}\,dx$. Then $du = 2x\,dx$ and $v = \frac{1}{2}e^{2x}$, and

$$\int x^3e^{2x}\,dx = \tfrac{1}{2}x^3e^{2x} - \tfrac{3}{2}\left(\tfrac{1}{2}x^2e^{2x} - \int xe^{2x}\,dx\right)$$

To evaluate $\int xe^{2x}\,dx$, let $u = x$ and $dv = e^{2x}\,dx$. Then $du = dx$ and $v = \frac{1}{2}e^{2x}$, and

$$\int x^3e^{2x}\,dx = \tfrac{1}{2}x^3e^{2x} - \tfrac{3}{4}x^2e^{2x} + \tfrac{3}{2}\left(\tfrac{1}{2}xe^{2x} - \tfrac{1}{2}\int e^{2x}\,dx\right)$$
$$= \tfrac{1}{2}x^3e^{2x} - \tfrac{3}{4}x^2e^{2x} + \tfrac{3}{4}xe^{2x} - \tfrac{3}{8}e^{2x} + C$$

It should by now be clear that there is unfortunately no general rule that dictates the best way to transform a complex integral into a more pliable one. There are, however, a few helpful hints that can reduce the difficulty of what is otherwise often a frustrating procedure.

First, when we make a substitution, we know that $f(x)$ and $g'(x)\,dx$ are the two terms that make up the left-hand side of the equation. $g'(x)\,dx$ is the differential of $g(x)$. This means that we should choose the differential of $g(x)$ for substitution purposes. However, that differential must be integrable so that we can find $g(x)$, which is part of the right-hand side of the equation.

Second, the object of transforming the integral is to produce an integral that is more amenable to ordinary rules of integration. Hence we should choose the most complicated substitution that is possible, yet integrable, for $g'(x)\,dx$. That is, a more complex substitution that is integrable is preferred to a simple substitution that is also integrable. The more complete the substitution, the easier $\int f'(x)g(x)\,dx$, the transformed function, will be to integrate. In everyday terms, you should accomplish as much as possible with the substitution.

**EXERCISE 7.2**

Evaluate the following integrals.

1. $\int x \ln x\,dx$
2. $\int \ln 2x\,dx$
3. $\int x^2e^{2x+3}\,dx$
4. $\int xe^{2x}\,dx$
5. $\int x^2e^{-3x}\,dx$
6. $\int (x + 4)\ln x\,dx$
7. $\int xe^{-x}\,dx$
8. $\int \frac{\ln x}{\sqrt{x}}\,dx$

## APPLICATIONS OF THE INDEFINITE INTEGRAL IN BUSINESS AND ECONOMICS

We shall now look at several examples in which a marginal function, represented by a first derivative, is known. For example, we know marginal cost, which is $d\text{TC}/dQ$. What we do not know is the total cost function itself, which is $\text{TC} = f(Q)$. In brief, we shall now examine situations in which we know the derivative of a function, and can use that knowledge to construct the function itself.

### Marginal Cost and Total Cost

Marginal cost MC, which is the addition to total cost TC that occurs when an incremental unit of output is produced, is given by

$$\text{MC} = \frac{d\text{TC}}{dQ} \tag{7.17}$$

We can find the total cost function, where $\text{TC} = C(Q)$, by integrating the marginal cost function with respect to output:

$$\text{TC} = \int \text{MC}\, dQ = C(Q) + K \tag{7.18}$$

That is, the total cost function is the sum of $C(Q)$, which represents total variable cost, plus the constant of integration $K$, which represents total fixed cost. When $Q = 0$, then $C(Q) = 0$, and only $K$ remains in terms of total cost. That is, when $Q = 0$, there are no variable costs, only fixed costs.

EXAMPLE Let $\text{MC} = 25 - 10Q + 3Q^2$ and fixed cost = 100. Then total cost can be written as

$$\int \text{MC}\, dQ = \int (25 - 10Q + 3Q^2)\, dQ = C(Q) + K \tag{7.19}$$

$$\text{TC} = 25Q - 5Q^2 + Q^3 + K \tag{7.20}$$

When $Q = 0$, then

$$\text{TC} = 25(0) - 5(0)^2 + (0)^3 + 100 = 100$$

Hence the total cost function is

$$\text{TC} = 100 + 25Q - 5Q^2 + Q^3$$

We can check this by observing that

$$\text{MC} = \frac{d\text{TC}}{dQ} = 25 - 10Q + 3Q^2$$

### Marginal Revenue and Total Revenue

Marginal revenue MR is the additional sales revenue a firm obtains when it sells an additional unit of output. $\text{MR} = d\text{TR}/dQ$, where TR = total sales revenue in dollars. If we know the form of the marginal revenue function, then we can find the total revenue function by integrating the marginal revenue function with respect to output.

$$\text{TR} = \int \text{MR}\, dQ = R(Q) + C \tag{7.21}$$

The arbitrary constant of integration $C$ has a value of 0 in a total revenue function. This recognizes the fact that usually the firm will realize no revenue if it does not sell any of its output. We can therefore state the total revenue function as $\text{TR} = R(Q)$.

EXAMPLE Given the marginal revenue function $\text{MR} = 25 - 2Q$. Then it follows that total revenue is given by

$$\text{TR} = \int (25 - 2Q)\, dQ = 25Q - Q^2 + C \tag{7.22}$$

$$\text{TR} = 25Q - Q^2 \qquad \text{since } C = 0 \tag{7.23}$$

We can check this result by observing that $d\text{TR}/dQ = 25 - 2Q$, which is our original MR function.

**Consumption, Saving, and Investment**

Let $Y =$ disposable income and $Y = C + S$, where $C$ is the consumption of private individuals and $S$ is the saving of private individuals. The *marginal propensity to consume* MPC is given by $\text{MPC} = dC/dY$. All disposable income must be either consumed or saved. Hence it follows that MPS, the *marginal propensity to save*, is given by $\text{MPS} = dS/dY$. By definition,

$$\text{MPC} + \text{MPS} = \frac{dC}{dY} + \frac{dS}{dY} = 1.00$$

We can find disposable income either by integrating MPC + MPS with respect to income $Y$ or by finding the consumption and savings functions by integrating MPC and MPS, respectively, with respect to income. This latter process yields $C(Y)$ and $S(Y)$, which when summed give us $Y$.

$$Y = \int (\text{MPC} + \text{MPS})\, dY = C(Y) + K_1 + S(Y) + K_2 = C(Y) + S(Y) + K \tag{7.24}$$

Alternatively,

$$C = \int \text{MPC}\, dY = C(Y) + K_1 \tag{7.25}$$

$$S = \int \text{MPS}\, dY = S(Y) + K_2 \tag{7.26}$$

Since $Y = C + S$, we sum Equations (7.25) and (7.26) to yield

$$Y = C + S = C(Y) + K_1 + S(Y) + K_2 = C(Y) + S(Y) + K \tag{7.27}$$

Equations (7.24) and (7.27) are identical, demonstrating that we may find disposable income $Y$ by means of either integration.

EXAMPLE Given the marginal propensity to consume MPC as MPC = $dC/dY = 0.75$, it follows that MPS, the marginal propensity to save, is given by

$$\text{MPS} = \frac{dS}{dY} = 0.25$$

Thus disposable income is given by

$$Y = \int (\text{MPC} + \text{MPS})\, dY = 0.75Y + 0.25Y = Y$$

That is, total disposable income must be either consumed or saved.

**Demand Functions, Total Revenue, and Price Elasticity of Demand**

An interesting application of indefinite integrals involves the determination of a demand function when we know that the point price elasticity of demand $\eta$ of that demand function is equal to some constant $-K$. That is, we know that

$$\eta_{Q,P} = \frac{dQ}{dP} \cdot \frac{P}{Q} = \frac{dQ}{Q} \cdot \frac{P}{dP} = -K \tag{7.28}$$

Rearranging Equation (7.28), we obtain

$$\frac{dQ}{Q} = -K \cdot \frac{dP}{P} \tag{7.29}$$

We now integrate both sides of Equation (7.29):

$$\int \frac{dQ}{Q} = -K \int \frac{dP}{P} \tag{7.30}$$

Utilizing the general logarithmic rule, we have

$$\ln |Q| + C_1 = -K \ln |P| + C_2 \tag{7.31}$$

We combine the constants of integration such that $C_1 + C_2 = C_3$. Recognizing that $P$ and $Q$ are both positive-valued variables, we can remove the absolute-value signs. This gives us

$$\ln Q = -K \cdot \ln P + C_3 \tag{7.32}$$

If $C_3 = \ln C$, where $C > 0$, then Equation (7.32) becomes

$$\ln Q = \ln C - K \cdot \ln P \tag{7.33}$$

Since the quantity $(-K \cdot \ln P)$ is equal to the quantity $(-\ln P^K)$, we can again restate our finding as

$$\ln Q = \ln C - \ln P^K = \ln \frac{C}{P^K} \tag{7.34}$$

Equation (7.34) tells us that $\ln Q = \ln (C/P^K)$. Taking the exponential of both sides yields

$$Q = \frac{C}{P^K} \tag{7.35}$$

Equation (7.35), which states that $Q = C/P^K$, is a general form of a *constant price elasticity of demand* demand function.

## THE DEFINITE INTEGRAL

The integral calculus was introduced in order to measure the area under a curve. Archimedes (287–212 B.C.) successfully utilized the "method of exhaustion" in order to find the approximate area contained in a region by placing inside that region a polygonal region that more or less approximated the original region of interest. Successive polygonal regions were then introduced, each with an additional side, in order to give a closer approximation of the original region of interest. Eventually, if the process were carried out long enough, the method of exhaustion would lead to a close approximation of the area of a particular region.

We shall use the method of exhaustion to give you an intuitive and visual idea of how the integral calculus is used to find the area under a curve. The major difference between the ancient methods of Archimedes and modern methods of finding the area under a curve is that instead of using a many-sided polygon, the modern approach uses a rectangle (which is actually a four-sided polygon).

Figure 7.2 illustrates the continuous function $y = f(x)$, where the domain of the function is the closed interval $[a, b]$. The problem confronting us is to calculate the shaded area labeled with a capital $A$, which is the area enclosed by the curve and the abscissa between points $a$ and $b$. As a first approximation to the area $A$, we divide the interval $[a, b]$ into $n$ (where $n = 5$ in our example) subintervals as shown in Figure 7.3(a) and (b). Part (a) approximates the area under the curve by inscribing five rectangles below the curve between points $a$

Figure 7.2 The closed interval $[a, b]$

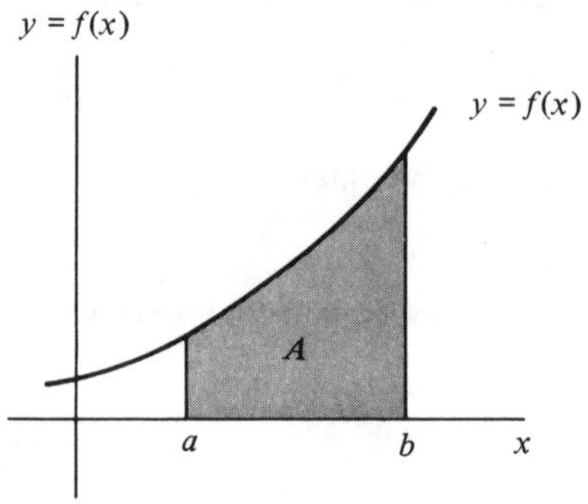

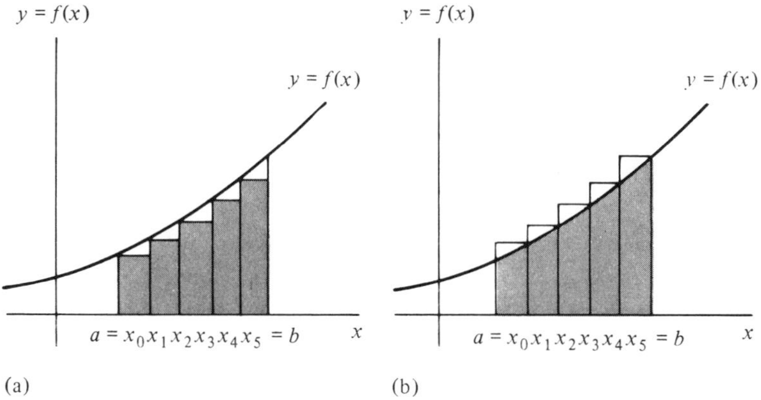


Figure 7.3 Approximating the area underneath a curve by means of rectangles. (a) Approximation from below. (b) Approximation from above

and $b$. Part (b) approximates the area under the curve between points $a$ and $b$ by inscribing five rectangles from above the curve. The left-hand boundary of each rectangle in part (a) has a minimum height of $y = f(x)$, whereas the right-hand boundary of each rectangle in part (b) has a height that represents the maximum value that $y = f(x)$ assumes in that subinterval.

The area of a rectangle is given by the product of the height and the width of that rectangle. The first rectangle in Figure 7.3(a) has a height of $f(x_0)$ and a width of $\Delta x_0 = x_1 - x_0$. To generalize, the $i$th rectangle in part (a) has a height of $f(x_i)$ and a width of $\Delta x_i$. The area of the $i$th rectangle is given by: $\text{Area}_i = f(x_i)\,\Delta x_i$. The total area in the five rectangles between points $a$ and $b$ in part (a) is given by

$$A_n^- = \sum_{i=0}^{4} f(x_i)\,\Delta x_i$$

We can see that this is an *under*estimate of the total area under the curve between points $a$ and $b$.

In similar fashion, we can measure the area of each rectangle in Figure 7.3(b). This yields an *over*estimate of the area under the curve between points $a$ and $b$ that is equal to

$$A_n^+ = \sum_{i=1}^{5} f(x_i)\,\Delta x_i$$

In this case, each rectangle has a height of $f(x_i)$ and a width of $\Delta x_i = x_i - x_{i-1}$.

The two approximations to the area under the curve between points $a$ and $b$ are labeled $A_n^-$ (underestimate) and $A_n^+$ (overestimate). It is apparent that $A_n^- < A < A_n^+$. The unshaded portions of the rectangles under the curve in part (a) and above the curve in part (b) are responsible for the difference between $A_n^-$, $A$, and $A_n^+$.

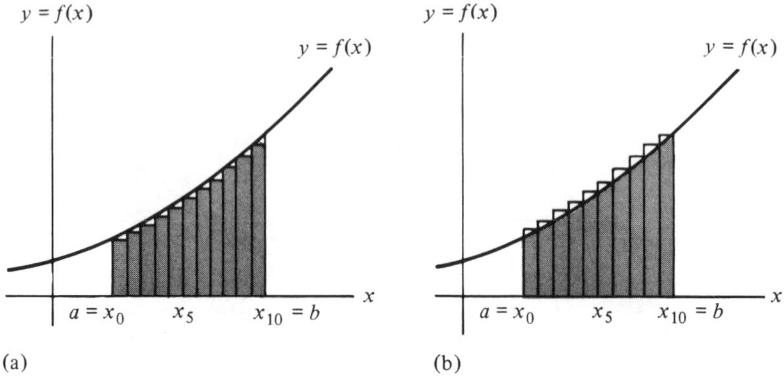


Figure 7.4 Approximating the area underneath a curve by means of successively smaller rectangles. (a) Approximation from below. (b) Approximation from above

It is possible to achieve an even better approximation of the area under the curve in the closed interval $[a, b]$ by further subdividing that interval. Figure 7.4(a) and (b) illustrate the effects of increasing the number of subdivisions from 5 to 10. We can see that as $n$ increases from 5 to 10, and $\Delta x_i$ becomes smaller, areas $A^-$ and $A^+$ differ less from each other, and also become closer approximations of the true area $A$.

In the limit, as $\Delta x_i \to 0$, areas $A^-$ and $A^+$ approach the true area $A$. That is, when the area of the inscribed rectangles in part (a) is equal to the area in the circumscribed rectangles in part (b), we have found the area under curve $A$. This area is known as the *Riemann* or *definite integral.*

DEFINITION Let $A_n^+$ be the upper estimate and $A_n^-$ the lower estimate of the area under the graph of $y = f(x)$ when the interval $[a, b]$ is divided into $n$ subintervals. If

$$\lim_{n\to\infty} A_n^- = \lim_{n\to\infty} A_n^+ = \int_a^b f(x)dx = A$$

the function $f(x)$ is said to be *Riemann integrable*, and $A$ is said to be the Riemann or definite integral of $f(x)$ on $[a, b]$.

The expression $\int_a^b f(x)\,dx = A$ is read, "the integral of $f(x)$ from $a$ to $b$ is $A$." The letters $a$ and $b$ signify the limits of integration. That is, the lower limit or bound of the variable $x$ is equal to $a$, while the upper limit or bound of variable $x$ is equal to $b$. For example, the definite integral $\int_2^4 f(x)\,dx$ indicates that we shall integrate the function $y = f(x)$ between the values of 2 and 4 for variable $x$.

There are four matters relating to our definition of the definite integral that are worthy of additional discussion. First, the integral sign ($\int$) functions in place of the summation sign ($\sum$), which we have used so often previously in a wide range of different contexts. The integral sign indicates that the number of terms (or rectangles) to be summed is infinite, that is, that $n \to \infty$. The integral sign is actually a special case of a $\sum$-type summation.

Second, the symbol representing change, $\Delta x_i$, has now been replaced by the integration notation $dx$ and represents an infinitesimal change.

Third, the indefinite integral with which we previously worked resulted in a function of variable $x$, whereas the definite integral results in a numeric answer that represents a specific area.

Fourth, when we evaluate $\int_a^b f(x)\,dx$, the constant of integration that we used with the indefinite integral now disappears. The second fundamental theorem of the calculus, which we will shortly introduce, gives us the following result:

$$\int_a^b f(x)\,dx = F(x)\Big|_a^b = F(b) + C - [F(a) + C] = F(b) - F(a) \tag{7.36}$$

That is, when we integrate $f(x)$ over the interval from $a$ to $b$, the constant of integration disappears.

### First Fundamental Theorem of the Calculus

There are two important theorems dealing with integral calculus that are called—not so originally—the first and second fundamental theorems of the calculus. Let us consider each of these in turn.

THEOREM 7.5 Given an integrable function $f(t)$ on a closed interval $[a, b]$, that is, given $\int_a^x f(t)\,dt = F(t)$ if $a \le x \le b$, then the derivative of $F(t)$ exists at each point $x$ and is equal to $f(t)$. That is, $F'(t) = f(t)$.

*Proof* A geometric proof of this theorem is less demanding and more easily understood. Figure 7.5 depicts the graph of a positive function

Figure 7.5 Utilizing the first fundamental theorem of the calculus

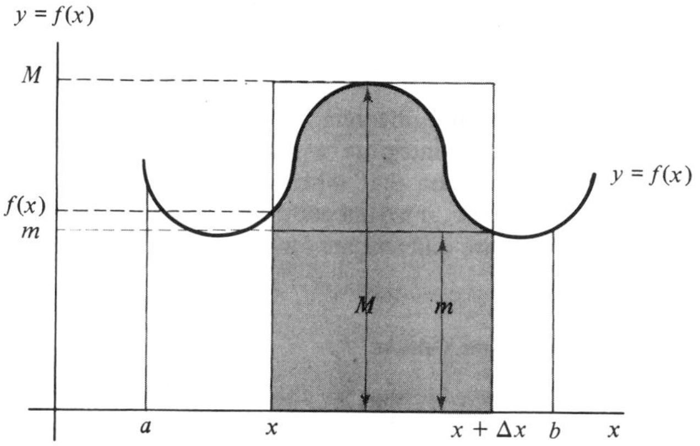

$y = f(x)$ over an interval $[a, b]$. We construct an interval given by $[x, x + \Delta x]$. Corresponding to this interval on the $x$ axis is an interval given by $[m, M]$ on the $y$ axis, where $m$ is the minimum value of $f(x)$ on $[x, x + \Delta x]$ and $M$ is the corresponding maximum value. Using the definition of the definite integral, we can measure the shaded area in Figure 7.5.

$$\int_a^x f(t)\,dt = F(x) \tag{7.37}$$

and

$$\int_a^{x+\Delta x} f(t)\,dt = F(x + \Delta x) \tag{7.38}$$

Equation (7.38) implies that

$$\begin{aligned}\int_x^{x+\Delta x} f(t)\,dt &= \int_a^{x+\Delta x} f(t)\,dt - \int_a^x f(t)\,dt \\ &= F(x + \Delta x) - F(x)\end{aligned} \tag{7.39}$$

That is, Equation (7.38) implies that the shaded area of Figure 7.5 is given by Equation (7.39).

$M$ is the upper bound or largest value of $f(x)$ in the interval $[x, x + \Delta x]$, while $m$ is the lowest bound or smallest value of $f(x)$ in that interval. A comparison of the area under the curve in this interval with the shaded area indicates that

$$m < F(x + \Delta x) - F(x) < M \tag{7.40}$$

We can rewrite this as

$$m < \frac{F(x + \Delta x) - F(x)}{\Delta x} < M \tag{7.41}$$

We know that as $\Delta x \to 0$, the lower limit $m$ and the upper limit $M$ approach $f(x)$, provided that $f(x)$ is continuous. Therefore the difference quotient $[F(x + \Delta x) - F(x)]/\Delta x$ approaches $F'(x)$ in the limit. Hence, if we let $\Delta x \to 0$, $m$ and $M$ approach a common limit and $F'(x) = f(x)$.

What does the first fundamental theorem of the calculus say to us intuitively? It states that when we integrate a continuous function, perhaps $y = f(x)$, we obtain a new function that, when differentiated, results in the original function $y = f(x)$. That is, if we integrate some function $A$ and obtain some function $B$, then when we differentiate function $B$, we shall once again obtain function $A$.

### Second Fundamental Theorem of the Calculus

There are two pieces of knowledge that we shall use in order to prove the second fundamental theorem of the calculus. First, we shall use the first fundamental theorem, which we just proved. Second, we shall use the fact that two antiderivatives of the same function differ only by a constant. That is,

$$G(x) = F(x) + C \text{ for } G'(x) = F'(x) = f(x)$$

THEOREM 7.6 Let $f(x)$ be continuous on $[a, b]$ and $F'(x) = f(x)$ for each $x$ in $[a, b]$. Then

$$\int_a^b f(x)\, dx = F(b) - F(a)$$

*Proof* If $F(x)$ is an antiderivative of $f(x)$ on $[a, b]$, then $F(x) = \int_a^x f(t)\, dt + C$ for some constant $C$.

When $x = a$, we get

$$F(a) = \int_a^a f(t)\, dt + C = C$$

When $x = b$, we get

$$F(b) = \int_a^b f(t)\, dt + C = \int_a^b f(t)\, dt + F(a)$$

It follows that

$$F(b) - F(a) = \int_a^b f(t)\, dt$$

which can be written with $x$ as the variable of integration as

$$\int_a^b f(x)\, dx = F(b) - F(a) \tag{7.42}$$

Note that we often write $F(x)\big|_a^b$ to denote $F(b) - F(a)$, the value of the integral.

EXAMPLES

1. $\displaystyle\int_0^3 x\, dx = \frac{x^2}{2}\bigg|_0^3 = \frac{3^2}{2} - \frac{0^2}{2} = \frac{9}{2}$

2. $\displaystyle\int_{-1}^2 (x^3 - 3x^2)\, dx = \frac{x^4}{4} - x^3\bigg|_{-1}^2 = \left(\frac{16}{4} - 8\right) - \left(\frac{1}{4} + 1\right) = -\frac{21}{4}$

3. $\displaystyle\int_3^9 \frac{dx}{x} = \ln|x|\bigg|_3^9 = \ln 9 - \ln 3 = \ln 3$

The following examples show that when we use the change-of-variable technique in order to integrate a function, that is, when we integrate by substitution, we must always use *new* limits of integration.

EXAMPLES

1. Evaluate $\int_4^{10} dx/(2x - 5)$. Let $u = 2x - 5$. Then $du = 2\,dx$ or $dx = \frac{1}{2}\,du$. Note that when we integrate with respect to $u$, the new limits of integration are: When $x = 4$, $u = 3$ and when $x = 10$, $u = 15$. Thus

$$\int_3^{15} \frac{1}{2}\frac{du}{u} = \frac{1}{2} \ln |u| \Big|_3^{15} = \frac{1}{2}(\ln 15 - \ln 3) = \frac{1}{2} \ln 5$$

Alternatively, before we evaluate the integral, we can convert the antiderivative back from $u$ to $x$ and then use the original limits of 4 and 10. That is,

$$\int \frac{1}{2}\frac{du}{u} = \frac{1}{2} \ln |u| = \frac{1}{2} \ln |2x - 5| \Big|_4^{10} = \frac{1}{2}(\ln 15 - \ln 3) = \frac{1}{2} \ln 5$$

2. Evaluate $\int_0^2 3x^2(x^3 - 1)^2\,dx$. Let $u = x^3 - 1$. Then $du = 3x^2\,dx$ or $dx = 1/3x^2\,du$. Thus, when integrating with respect to $u$, the limits of integration become $u = -1$ when $x = 0$ and $u = 7$ when $x = 2$. Thus

$$\int_{-1}^{7} u^2\,du = \frac{1}{3}u^3 \Big|_{-1}^{7} = \frac{1}{3}(343 + 1) = \frac{344}{3} = 114\frac{2}{3}$$

Once again we can convert $u$ back to $x$ and then use the original limits of 0 and 2 to get the same answer:

$$\int u^2\,du = \frac{1}{3}u^3 = \frac{1}{3}(x^3 - 1)^3 \Big|_0^2 = \frac{1}{3}(343 + 1) = 114\frac{2}{3}$$

**Dealing with Negative Areas**

Consider the continuous function $y = f(x)$, which was depicted in Figure 7.2. We wish to find the area that lies under the curve, but above the $x$ axis, between points $a$ and $b$. That area is shaded in Figure 7.2 and is labeled $A$.

It is possible, however, that a function may assume both positive and negative values. This means that the graph of such a function lies *below* the abscissa for some values of $x$, and *above* the $x$ axis for other values of $x$. Figure 7.6(a) illustrates such a possibility. The area between the curve and the $x$ axis for the interval $[c, d]$, which is indicated by $\int_c^d f(x)\,dx$, is negative in sign. It is negative because the height of the rectangles that are circumscribed or inscribed in that region is negative.

DEFINITION Negative area is the area measured by the definite integral that lies below the $x$ axis and above the curve representing the function being integrated.

When we measure the area for the interval $[a, b]$, that is, when we find $\int_a^b f(x)\,dx$ in Figure 7.6(a), the positive and negative areas counteract each other. Specifically, the area for the interval $[c, d]$ is subtracted from the sum of the areas for the intervals $[a, c]$ and $[d, b]$. However, if you are interested in the numeric or absolute value of these three areas, then you must sum the areas of the regions above the $x$ axis, *minus* any areas of regions below the $x$ axis.

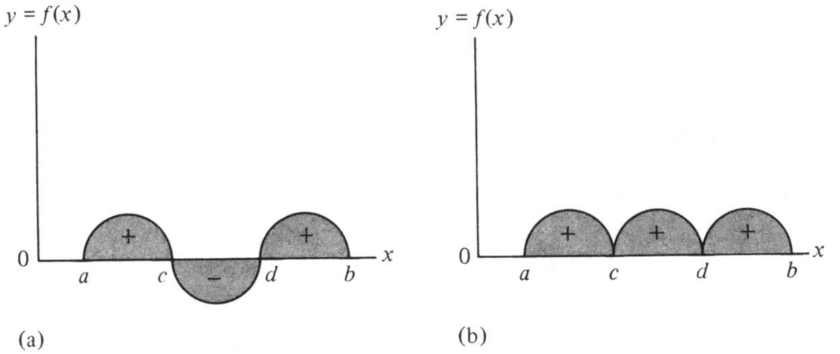


Figure 7.6 Integrating negative areas. (a) Algebraic sum of the area. (b) Absolute value of the area

[Remember, $-(-A) = +A$.] That is, the total or absolute area between the curve illustrated in Figure 7.6(a) and the $x$ axis is, in the interval $[a, b]$, given by

$$\int_a^b |f(x)|\, dx \tag{7.43}$$

The absolute-value sign in Equation (7.43) implies that the graph of $|f(x)|$, which is illustrated in Figure 7.6(b), coincides with the graph of $f(x)$ when $f(x) \geq 0$. When $f(x) < 0$ in some intervals, as is the case in part (a), we can obtain $f(x)$ by finding its mirror image with respect to the $x$ axis. The area between the curve and the $x$ axis in the interval $[c, d]$ is equivalent in absolute size in both parts (a) and (b). The area between the curve and the $x$ axis in the interval $[c, d]$ in part (b) is the mirror image of the area between the curve and the $x$ axis in the same interval in part (a).

As we shall shortly be able to demonstrate, the function $|f(x)|$ is integrable on the interval $[a, b]$ whenever $f(x)$ is integrable on the same interval. That is, we can show that Equation (7.43) is the sum of the positive areas *minus* the sum of the negative areas. Hence

$$\int_a^b |f(x)|\, dx = \int_a^c f(x)\, dx - \int_c^d f(x)\, dx + \int_d^b f(x)\, dx \tag{7.44}$$

EXAMPLES

1. Find the area bounded by the curve $y = x^3 - 6x^2 + 8x$, the $x$ axis, and the lines $x = 0$ and $x = 4$. (See the shaded area of Figure 7.7.)

$$\text{Area} = \int_0^2 (x^3 - 6x^2 + 8x)\, dx - \int_2^4 (x^3 - 6x^2 + 8x)\, dx$$

$$= \left(\frac{x^4}{4} - 2x^3 + 4x^2\right)\Bigg|_0^2 - \left(\frac{x^4}{4} - 2x^3 + 4x^2\right)\Bigg|_2^4$$

$$\text{Area} = 4 + 4 = 8$$

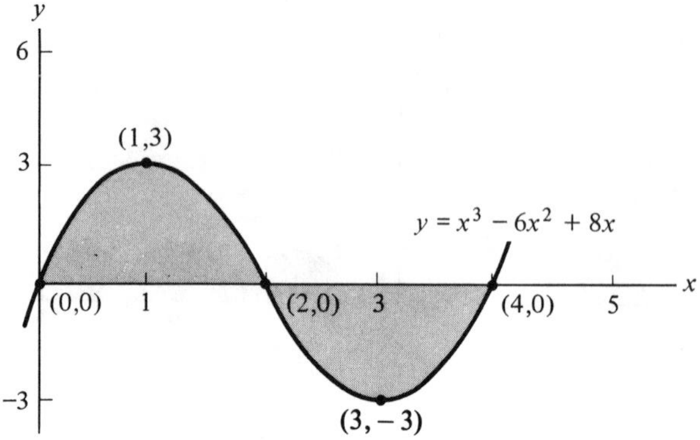


Figure 7.7 Graph of $y = x^3 - 6x^2 + 8x$

2. Find the area bounded by the curve $y = x^2 - 4x$ and the $x$ axis such that only positive values of $x$ are permitted.

$$\text{Area} = \int_0^4 -(x^2 - 4x)\,dx = -\left(\frac{x^3}{3} - 2x^2\right)\Big|_0^4$$

$$= -\left(\tfrac{64}{3} - 32\right) - 0 = 10\tfrac{2}{3}$$

(See the shaded area of Figure 7.8.)

**Some Additional Properties of Integrals**

We can now state some additional properties of integrals that are useful in practical situations.

Figure 7.8 Graph of $y = x^2 - 4x$

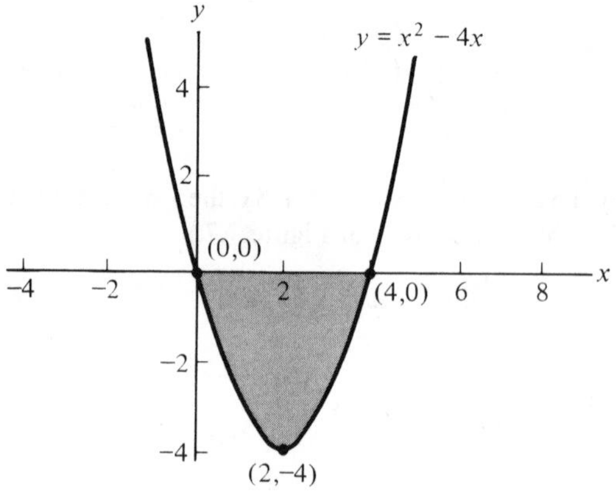

PROPERTY 1

$$\int_a^b f(x)\,dx = -\int_b^a f(x)\,dx \tag{7.45}$$

Equation (7.45) tells us that if we interchange the limits of integration, the sign of the definite integral also changes.

*Proof* We know that $\int_a^b f(x)\,dx = F(b) - F(a)$. This, in turn, can be restated as

$$F(b) - F(a) = -[F(a) - F(b)] = -\int_b^a f(x)\,dx$$

EXAMPLES

1. $\displaystyle\int_0^3 x^2\,dx = \tfrac{1}{3}x^3\Big|_0^3 = 9$ However $\displaystyle\int_3^0 x^2\,dx = \tfrac{1}{3}x^3\Big|_3^0 = -9$

2. $\displaystyle\int_{-1}^2 (2 + x)\,dx = \left(2x + \frac{x^2}{2}\right)\Bigg|_{-1}^2 = (4 + 2) - (-2 + \tfrac{1}{2}) = 7\tfrac{1}{2}$

   However,

$$\int_2^{-1} (2 + x)\,dx = \left(2x + \frac{x^2}{2}\right)\Bigg|_2^{-1} = (-2 + \tfrac{1}{2}) - (4 + 2)$$

$$= -7\tfrac{1}{2}$$

PROPERTY 2

$$\int_a^a f(x)\,dx = 0 \tag{7.46}$$

Property 2 tells us that the area of a single point is zero.

*Proof*

$$\int_a^a f(x)\,dx = F(a) - F(a) = 0$$

EXAMPLE

$$\int_3^3 x\,dx = \frac{x^2}{2}\Bigg|_3^3 = \frac{9}{2} - \frac{9}{2} = 0$$

PROPERTY 3

$$\int_a^b f(x)\,dx + \int_b^c f(x)\,dx + \cdots + \int_{n-1}^n f(x)\,dx = \int_a^n f(x)\,dx \tag{7.47}$$

Equation (7.47) tells us that we can successfully divide a definite integral into a sum of $n$ finite subintegrals.

EXAMPLE The definite integral $\int_a^b f(x)\,dx$ is, in the case of Figure 7.6(b), given by

$$\int_a^c f(x)\,dx + \int_c^d f(x)\,dx + \int_d^b f(x)\,dx = \int_a^b f(x)\,dx \tag{7.48}$$

Property 3 is quite robust and has several interesting implications. First, the limits of integration usually seem to suggest that one is counting some points or areas twice. For example,

$$\int_a^c f(x)\,dx = \int_a^b f(x)\,dx + \int_b^c f(x)\,dx$$

We can see that point $b$ is both the upper limit for one integral and the lower limit for another. Is this a double counting of point $b$? The answer is no, because Property 2 has already demonstrated that the integral of a single point is zero. Therefore it is entirely appropriate to use a point such as $b$ as both an upper and a lower limit in the process of integration.

Property 3 also enables us to find the area under the graph of a function that is discontinuous. The definition of a definite integral explicitly states that the function being integrated must be continuous over the interval $[a, b]$, if it is $\int_a^b f(x)\,dx$ that we wish to find. This would seem to pose a problem if the function is discontinuous at one or more points within that interval $[a, b]$. However, Property 3 enables us to break the original integral into several subintegrals in order to avoid the problem of a discontinuous function.

Consider Figure 7.9(a) and (b). Both parts depict functions that are discontinuous at point $c$. Hence it is impossible to integrate either of these functions over the entire interval $[a, b]$. The solution[1] is to break the overall integral for the interval $[a, b]$ into two subintegrals, as follows:

$$\int_a^b f(x)\,dx = \int_a^c f(x)\,dx + \int_c^b f(x)\,dx \tag{7.49}$$

[1] This discontinuity must be of either a jump or point variety in order to apply the method described here. It cannot be an infinite discontinuity.

Figure 7.9 The use of subintegrals with discontinuous functions

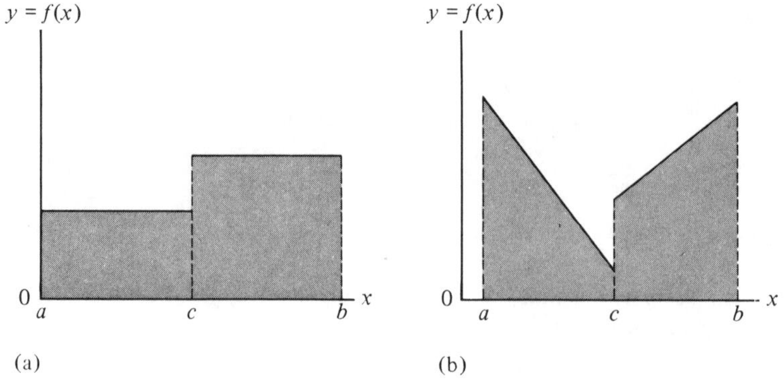

Since integration over an interval requires continuity within that integral, we integrate over the interval $[a, c]$ and then separately integrate over the interval $[c, b]$, and sum the results. The functions illustrated in parts (a) and (b) are both continuous within these subintervals, and therefore the integration can be carried out.

EXAMPLE

$$\int_0^4 (2 + x)\, dx = \int_0^1 (2 + x)\, dx + \int_1^4 (2 + x)\, dx$$

$$= \left(2x + \frac{x^2}{2}\right)\Bigg|_0^1 + \left(2x + \frac{x^2}{2}\right)\Bigg|_1^4$$

$$= \left(2 + \frac{1}{2}\right) - 0 + (8 + 8) - \left(2 + \frac{1}{2}\right) = 16$$

*Check*: $\int_0^4 (2 + x)\, dx = \left(2x + \frac{x^2}{2}\right)\Bigg|_0^4 = (8 + 8) - 0 = 16$

**EXERCISE 7.3**

Evaluate the following integrals:

1. $\int_0^3 x^2\, dx$
2. $\int_{-1}^2 (2x + 3x^2)\, dx$
3. $\int_1^3 (x^2 - 3x + 8)\, dx$
4. $\int_0^2 (8x^3 + 6x^2 - 2x + 5)\, dx$
5. $\int_{-2}^4 (x - 1)(x - 2)\, dx$
6. $\int_{-1}^0 (x + 1)^2\, dx$
7. $\int_{-2}^2 (x - 5)^4\, dx$
8. $\int_2^4 \frac{4x^3\, dx}{x^4 + 1}$
9. $\int_1^e \ln x\, dx$
10. $\int_4^9 \frac{dx}{\sqrt{x}}$
11. $\int_{-1}^1 x^2(x^3 + 1)\, dx$
12. $\int_0^3 e^{-2x}\, dx$
13. $\int_0^1 xe^x\, dx$
14. $\int_{-1}^1 3x^2(x^3 - 4)^2\, dx$
15. $\int_4^{10} \frac{2x - 3}{x^2 - 3x}\, dx$

**Integrating the Area between Curves**

An interesting and occasionally difficult problem arises when we wish to find the area of a region that is formed and enclosed by several curves. For example, consider Figure 7.10(a) and (b). How do we proceed when we wish to find

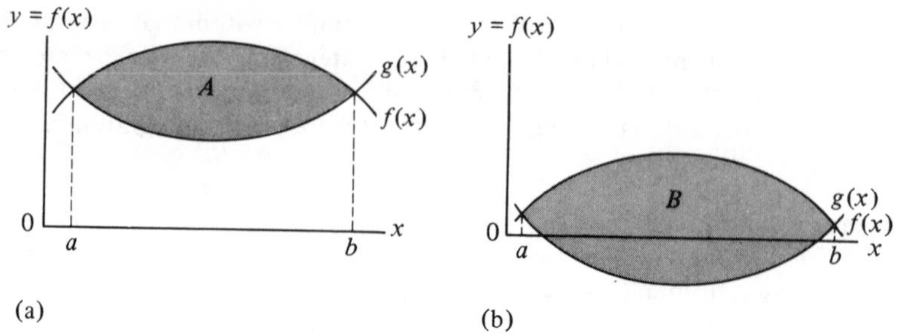


Figure 7.10 Finding the area between curves: I

the shaded area labeled $A$ in part (a), or the shaded area labeled $B$ in part (b)? We need only to reformulate slightly our basic approach to finding an integral in order to accommodate this situation.

DEFINITION Given two functions $f(x)$ and $g(x)$, both of which are integrable on the interval $[a, b]$. $f(x) \geq g(x)$ in the interval $[a, b]$. Then $\int_a^b [f(x) - g(x)]\, dx$ is the area between the curves of these two functions.

Hence, when we wish to find an area such as $A$ in Figure 7.10(a), we find the integral $\int_a^b [f(x) - g(x)]\, dx$. It is possible, however, that the condition $f(x) \geq g(x)$ does not always hold. Figure 7.11(a) illustrates such a case for the interval $[a, b]$, where the value of $f(x)$ is initially greater than the value of $g(x)$, but subsequently $f(x) \leq g(x)$, and finally $f(x) \geq g(x)$. In such a case, we are interested in the total *absolute* area between the two curves, and we must reformulate our definition of the area between two curves, as follows.

DEFINITION Given two functions $f(x)$ and $g(x)$, both of which are integrable on the interval $[a, b]$. The total absolute area between the curves of these two functions is given by

$$\int_a^b |f(x) - g(x)|\, dx$$

Figure 7.11 Finding the area between curves: II. (a) Graphs of $y = f(x)$ and $y = g(x)$. (b) Graph of $y = f(x) - g(x)$. (c) Graph of $y = |f(x) - g(x)|$

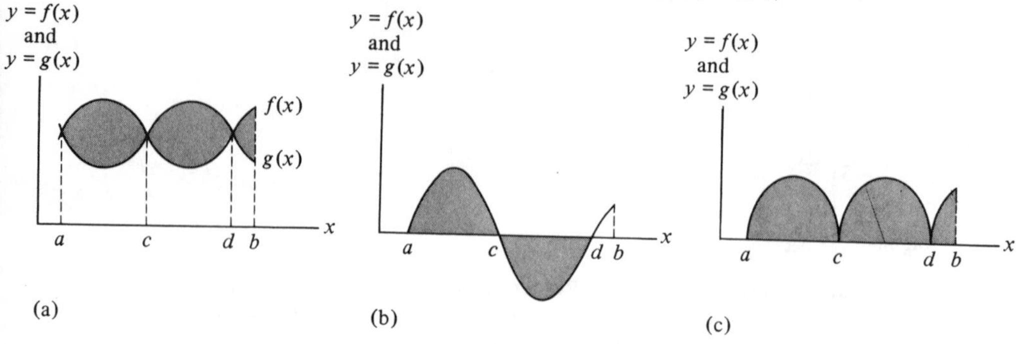

The absolute area definition can be explained visually. Figure 7.11(b) is the graph of $f(x) - g(x)$, and is derived from part (a). We can see that the area of $f(x) - g(x)$ is negative in the interval $[c, d]$. When we take the absolute value $|f(x) - g(x)|$, we make this area positive. This transforms the problem into one of integrating the area under the curve, but above the $x$ axis, in Figure 7.11(c). The area in the interval $[c, d]$ in part (b) is the same size as the area in the interval $[c, d]$ in part (c).

Occasions sometimes arise when it is easier to find the area between two curves if one conceptually interchanges the roles of the $x$ and $y$ axes. Consider the two curves illustrated in Figure 7.12. We wish to find the shaded area in the interval $[c, d]$ between the two curves. We write the relationship between variables $x$ and $y$ as $x = g(y)$ for the curve farthest to the left, and the relationship between variables for the curve farthest to the right as $x = f(y)$. The two functions $g(y)$ and $f(y)$ are integrable over the interval $[c, d]$, as follows:

$$\int_c^d [f(y) - g(y)]\, dy \tag{7.50}$$

In the previous example, we integrated the area between two curves with respect to the $y$ variable. The choice between integrating with respect to the $x$ variable or the $y$ variable is largely immaterial, since we obtain identical results.

■ We must be careful in applying this knowledge, however. When integrating, we *must* assign the limits of integration in light of the variable of integration that we are using. You can verify that integrating with respect to the $x$ variable will *not* yield the same answer as integrating with respect to the $y$ variable when integration is carried out with respect to the interval $[c, d]$ in Figure 7.12. That is,

$$\int_c^d [f(y) - g(y)]\, dy \neq \int_c^d [f(x) - g(x)]\, dx \tag{7.51}$$

Figure 7.12 Integrating with respect to the variable $y$

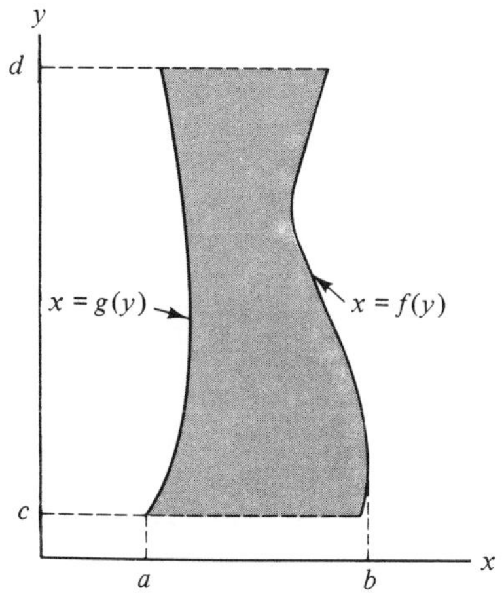

On the other hand, if the two curves illustrated in Figure 7.12 are truncated at points $c$ and $d$, then it is true that

$$\int_c^d [f(y) - g(y)]\, dy = \int_a^b [f(x) - g(x)]\, dx \tag{7.52}$$

EXAMPLES

1. Find the area bounded by the curves $y^2 = 2x$ and $y = 2x - 2$. (See Figure 7.13.) The two curves intersect at (2, 2) and $(\frac{1}{2}, -1)$, which are found by solving the two equations simultaneously. Thus

$$\text{Area} = \int_0^{1/2} [\sqrt{2x} - (-\sqrt{2}\,x)]\, dx + \int_{1/2}^2 [\sqrt{2x} - (2x - 2)]\, dx$$

$$= \int_0^{1/2} 2\sqrt{2x}\, dx + \int_{1/2}^2 (\sqrt{2x} - 2x + 2)\, dx$$

$$= \frac{2}{3}(2x)^{3/2}\Big|_0^{1/2} + \left[\frac{1}{3}(2x)^{3/2} - x^2 + 2x\right]\Big|_{1/2}^2 = \frac{27}{12}$$

Alternatively, we could have found the area by integrating with respect to $y$. Thus

$$\int_{-1}^2 \left(\frac{y+2}{2} - \frac{y^2}{2}\right) dy = \frac{1}{2}\left(\frac{1}{2}y^2 + 2y - \frac{1}{3}y^3\right)\Big|_{-1}^2 = \frac{27}{12}.$$

2. Find the area bounded by the curves $y = x^2$ and $y = 2x$. (See Figure 7.14.) Solving the two equations simultaneously, we find that the points of intersection are (0, 0) and (2, 4). Thus

$$\text{Area} = \int_0^2 (2x - x^2)\, dx = \left(x^2 - \frac{1}{3}x^3\right)\Big|_0^2 = \frac{4}{3}$$

Figure 7.13 Graphs of $y^2 = 2x$ and $y = 2x - 2$

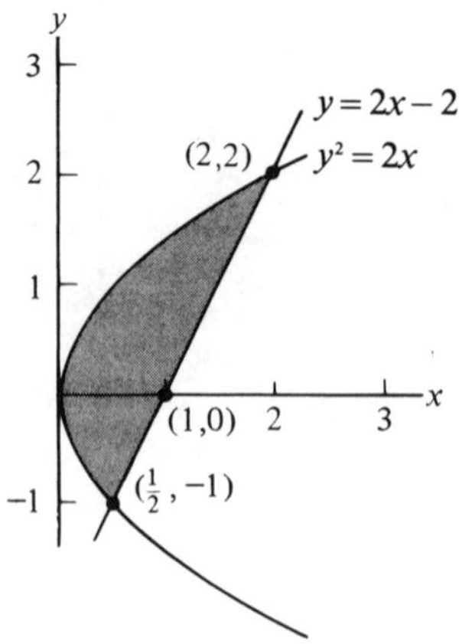

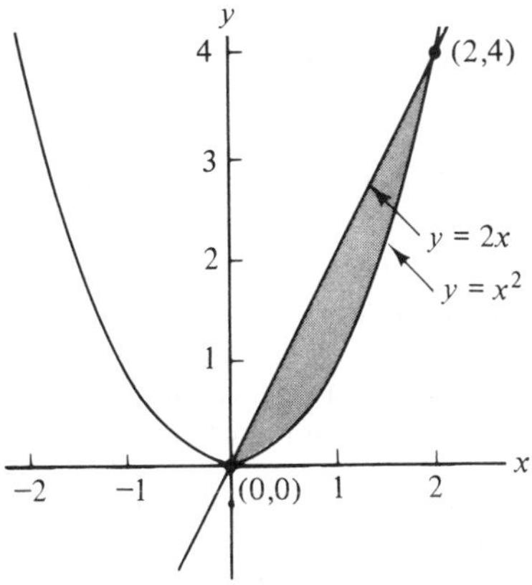


Figure 7.14 Graphs of $y = x^2$ and $y = 2x$

or

$$\text{Area} = \int_0^4 \left(\sqrt{y} - \frac{y}{2}\right) dy = \left(\frac{2}{3}y^{3/2} - \frac{1}{4}y^2\right)\Bigg|_0^4 = \frac{4}{3}$$

**EXERCISE 7.4**

Draw a sketch and find the area bounded by the following curves.

1. $y = x^3$, $y = 0$, $x = 0$, $x = 2$
2. $y = 9 - x^2$, $y = x + 3$
3. $y = 3 - x^2$, $y = -2x$
4. $y = 6 - x$, $y = x + 2$, $y = 0$
5. $y = 6x - x^2$, $y = x^2 - 2x$
6. $y^2 = x$, $y = \frac{1}{2}x - \frac{3}{2}$
7. $y = x^3$, $y = 2x + 4$, $x = 0$
8. $y = x$, $y = 10 - 4x$, $y = 0$, $x = 0$

**Improper Integrals**

Our examination of integration has thus far assumed a continuous function of the form $y = f(x)$, which is defined for the closed finite interval $[a, b]$. When an integral satisfies these restrictions, it is said to to be a *proper* integral. This section discusses integrals that are said to be *improper*. Specifically, we shall give our attention to situations in which the restrictions for a definite integral are relaxed.

We shall consider two general types of improper integrals. The first, which we shall consider shortly, occurs in cases in which there are infinite limits of integration. The second case involves a situation in which there is an infinite integrand.

*Case 1: Improper integral due to an infinite limit of integration*
When the limits of integration are no longer finite, for example, when we wish to study the definite integral $\int_a^b f(x)\,dx$ as $a \to -\infty$, and/or $b \to \infty$, we have an

improper integral. In such a case, it is not possible to find a finite value for the integral. This is because $F(\infty) - F(a)$ is meaningless, as are $F(b) - F(-\infty)$ and $F(\infty) - F(-\infty)$.

DEFINITION An improper integral with an infinite limit of integration is formally symbolized by

$$\int_a^\infty f(x)\,dx = \lim_{b\to\infty} \int_a^b f(x)\,dx \qquad \text{or} \qquad \lim_{b\to\infty} \left[ F(x)\Big|_a^b \right]$$

Such an integral is said to be *convergent* when the limit exists and is finite, whereas it is said to be *divergent* when the limit does not exist.

We can use the definition in any particular case by initially finding $\int_a^b f(x)\,dx$, that is, by finding the indefinite integral $F(x)$. Second, we evaluate $F(x)$ for $a$ and $b$, then find the limit as $b \to \infty$. If the limit is finite, then the integral exists and is convergent. If the limit is infinite, then the integral is diverging and has no finite value.

It is not uncommon to see an improper integral written without the limit notation in front of the integral. That is, instead of

$$\lim_{b\to\infty} \int_a^b f(x)\,dx$$

one often sees in many books the shorthand expression

$$\int_a^\infty f(x)\,dx = F(x)\Big|_a^\infty$$

This shorthand notation nevertheless *must* be evaluated with the limit concept held firmly in mind. This implicit step must be carried out, since the limit may be divergent, and if it is, the integral has no finite value.

The existence of an improper integral with an infinite limit for its upper bound does not change the fact that we are measuring the area under a curve. Figure 7.15 illustrates the graph of a function $y = f(x)$ where the upper limit of integration $b$ is infinite. That is,

$$\int_a^b f(x)\,dx = \int_a^\infty f(x)\,dx$$

If the improper integral is convergent, that is, if the limit exists, then the shaded region under the curve is considered to be a finite area. However, if the improper integral is divergent, then a limit does not exist and the shaded area under the curve is infinite in size.

It is possible, of course, for the lower bound of integration to be infinite as well. In this case, the lower bound $a$ tends to $-\infty$. We can define the improper integral $\int_{-\infty}^b f(x)\,dx$ as

$$\int_{-\infty}^b f(x)\,dx = \lim_{a\to-\infty} \int_a^b f(x)\,dx \qquad (7.53)$$

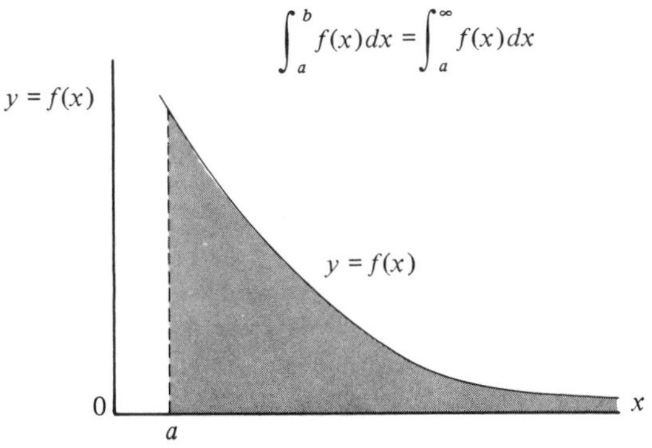


Figure 7.15 Improper integral: the case of an infinite limit

We then use the usual procedure to determine whether the improper integral is convergent or divergent.

A more complicated case is the situation in which both limits of integration are infinite; that is, we wish to find $\int_{-\infty}^{\infty} f(x)\,dx$.

DEFINITION An improper integral with both limits of integration infinite exists when, for any real number $C$,

$$\int_{-\infty}^{\infty} f(x)\,dx = \int_{-\infty}^{C} f(x)\,dx + \int_{C}^{\infty} f(x)\,dx = \lim_{\substack{a \to -\infty \\ b \to \infty}} \int_a^b f(x)\,dx \tag{7.54}$$

Both integrals, $\int_{-\infty}^{C} f(x)\,dx$ and $\int_C^\infty f(x)\,dx$, must be convergent in order for the improper integral $\int_{-\infty}^{\infty} f(x)\,dx$ to be convergent. If either of the two integrals in the middle of Equation (7.54) is divergent, then the improper integral $\int_{-\infty}^{\infty} f(x)\,dx$ is divergent.

EXAMPLES

1. $\displaystyle\int_{-\infty}^{0} e^{3x}\,dx = \lim_{a \to -\infty} \int_a^0 e^{3x}\,dx = \lim_{a \to -\infty} \tfrac{1}{3}e^{3x}\Big|_a^0 = \tfrac{1}{3} - 0 = \tfrac{1}{3}$

2. $\displaystyle\int_1^\infty \frac{dx}{\sqrt{x}} = \lim_{b \to \infty} \int_1^b \frac{dx}{\sqrt{x}} = \lim_{b \to \infty} 2\sqrt{x}\Big|_1^b = \lim_{b \to \infty} (2\sqrt{b} - 2)$

   The integral is said to diverge, for the limit does not exist.

3. $\displaystyle\int_{-\infty}^{\infty} e^x\,dx = \lim_{\substack{a \to -\infty \\ b \to \infty}} \int_a^b e^x\,dx = \lim_{\substack{a \to -\infty \\ b \to \infty}} e^x\Big|_a^b = \lim_{\substack{a \to -\infty \\ b \to \infty}} (e^b - e^a)$

   The integral is also divergent, for the limit does not exist.

*Case 2: Improper integral due to an infinite integrand*

The second type of improper integral occurs whenever the integrand becomes infinite (due to an infinite discontinuity). It does not matter here that the limits of integration are finite. There are three instances involving improper integrands that we need to examine.

*Infinite integrand at lower limit*

DEFINITION Given an integral $\int_x^b f(t)\,dt$ that exists for the interval $a < t \leq b$. Define a new function $F(x)$ such that:

$$F(x) = \int_x^b f(t)\,dt \qquad \text{for } a < t \leq b \tag{7.55}$$

The function $F(x)$ is said to be an improper integral at the point $x = a$ and is denoted by the symbol

$$\lim_{x \to a} \int_x^b f(t)\,dt = \lim_{x \to a} F(t)\,\Big|_x^b \tag{7.56}$$

*Infinite integrand at upper limit*
The above definition considers the circumstance in which the integrand becomes infinite at the lower limit of integration. It is also possible for the integrand to become infinite at the upper limit of integration:

$$\lim_{x \to b} \int_a^x f(t)\,dt = \lim_{x \to b} F(t)\,\Big|_a^x \qquad \text{for } a \leq t < b \tag{7.57}$$

Either of the improper integrals noted in Equations (7.56) and (7.57) can be evaluated in the limit to determine whether the improper integral is convergent or divergent. This analysis duplicates that in which we were concerned with infinite limits to integration, but the integrand was finite.

EXAMPLES

1. Given $\int_0^3 dx/(x-3)$. The integrand is discontinuous at $x = 3$. Thus

$$\int_0^3 \frac{dx}{x-3} = \lim_{b \to 3} \int_0^b \frac{dx}{x-3} = \lim_{b \to 3} \ln|x-3|\,\Big|_0^b$$
$$= \lim_{b \to 3} (\ln|b-3| - \ln|-3|)$$

The limit does not exist, and the integral is divergent.

2. Given $\int_0^1 dx/x$. The integrand is discontinuous at $x = 0$. Thus

$$\int_0^1 \frac{dx}{x} = \lim_{a \to 0} \int_a^1 \frac{dx}{x} = \lim_{a \to 0} \ln|x|\,\Big|_a^1 = \lim_{a \to 0} (\ln|1| - \ln|a|)$$

The limit does not exist, and the integral is divergent.

3. $\int_0^1 dx/\sqrt{x}$ has a discontinuity at $x = 0$. Thus

$$\int_0^1 \frac{dx}{\sqrt{x}} = \lim_{a \to 0} \int_a^1 \frac{dx}{\sqrt{x}} = \lim_{a \to 0} 2\sqrt{x}\,\Big|_a^1 = \lim_{a \to 0} (2 - 2\sqrt{a}) = 2$$

*Infinite integrand due to an infinite discontinuity*

The case sometimes arises in which a function $y = f(x)$ is discontinuous at some point $c$. Then the integral $\int_a^b f(x)\,dx$ is defined for the interval $[a, b]$, except at point $c$, when $a < c < b$. The additivity theorem relating to integrals tells us that we can write

$$\int_a^b f(x)\,dx = \int_a^c f(x)\,dx + \int_c^b f(x)\,dx \tag{7.58}$$

Only when the two integrals on the right-hand side of Equation (7.58) converge can we be certain that the improper integral $\int_a^b f(x)\,dx$ also converges. It is not sufficient for only one of the integrals on the right-hand side of Equation (7.58) to be convergent.

The analysis in Equation (7.58) relates to a situation in which one finite discontinuity exists. We can extend Equation (7.58) to deal with the situation in which a finite number of such infinite discontinuities exist. For example, assume that $y = f(x)$ is infinitely discontinuous at points $c$ and $d$, where $a < c$, $d < b$. Then we have

$$\int_a^b f(x)\,dx = \int_a^c f(x)\,dx + \int_c^d f(x)\,dx + \int_d^b f(x)\,dx \tag{7.59}$$

All three of the integrals on the right-hand side of Equation (7.59) must be convergent in order for us to assert that the improper integral $\int_a^b f(x)\,dx$ is convergent.

EXAMPLES

1. Evaluate $\int_1^5 dx/(x-2)^2$. The integrand is discontinuous at $x = 2$. Thus

$$\int_1^5 \frac{dx}{(x-2)^2} = \int_1^2 \frac{dx}{(x-2)^2} + \int_2^5 \frac{dx}{(x-2)^2}$$

However,

$$\int_1^2 \frac{dx}{(x-2)^2} = \lim_{b\to 2} \int_1^b \frac{dx}{(x-2)^2} = \lim_{b\to 2} \frac{-1}{x-2}\bigg|_1^b = \lim_{x\to 2}\left(\frac{-1}{b-2} - 1\right) = \infty$$

which is divergent.

2. Evaluate $\int_{-1}^2 dx/x^3$. The integrand has a discontinuity when $x = 0$. Thus

$$\int_{-1}^2 \frac{dx}{x^3} = \int_{-1}^0 \frac{dx}{x^3} + \int_0^2 \frac{dx}{x^3}$$

However,

$$\int_{-1}^0 \frac{dx}{x^3} = \lim_{b\to 0} \int_{-1}^b \frac{dx}{x^3} = \lim_{b\to 0}\left(-\frac{1}{2x^{-2}}\right)\bigg|_{-1}^b$$

$$= \lim_{b\to 0} -\frac{1}{2}\left(\frac{1}{b^2} - 1\right) = \infty$$

Thus the integral diverges.

**EXERCISE 7.5**

Evaluate the following integrals.

1. $\int_0^\infty \frac{x^2}{\sqrt{x^3+1}}\,dx$
2. $\int_{-1}^1 \frac{dx}{x}$
3. $\int_0^3 \frac{dx}{3-x}$
4. $\int_1^\infty \frac{dx}{x^2}$
5. $\int_{-\infty}^0 xe^x\,dx$
6. $\int_{-\infty}^\infty xe^{-x^2}\,dx$
7. $\int_0^\infty e^{-x}\,dx$
8. $\int_0^1 \ln x\,dx$
9. $\int_{-1}^1 \frac{dx}{x^4}$
10. $\int_{-1}^8 \frac{dx}{1/x^3}$
11. $\int_{-1}^0 \frac{x}{x^2-1}\,dx$
12. $\int_1^\infty x\ln x\,dx$
13. $\int_0^2 \frac{x}{\sqrt{4-x^2}}\,dx$

## APPLICATIONS OF THE DEFINITE INTEGRAL IN BUSINESS AND ECONOMICS

The concept of the definite integral is useful in a wide range of business and economics problems. The following examples are illustrative and do not exhaust the list of possible applications.

### Consumer's Surplus

The concept of *consumer's surplus* is often used in applied welfare economics to help decision-makers make judgments about the desirability of particular actions. For example, one can use the idea of consumer's surplus to measure the loss that consumers realize as a result of the exercise of business and labor monopoly power. One can also use consumer's surplus to help make a decision about the desirability of building a new highway, a new lock and dam, or a new nuclear accelerator.

Figure 7.16 illustrates a demand curve for pizza of the form $P = f(Q)$, where the equilibrium price and quantity are $P_E$, $Q_E$ when there is competition in the marketplace. At price $P_1$, consumers of this good would be willing and able to purchase $Q_1$ units of pizza. At price $P_2$, they would be willing and able to purchase $Q_2$ units of pizza, and so forth. Now let $P_1 \cdot Q_1$ represent the marginal (additional) utility that consumers receive from the purchase of a first pizza. This is a rough but appropriate measure of the marginal utility that consumers attach to that first pizza, because it is the most money that they are willing to pay for it. Similarly, let $P_2 \cdot Q_2$ represent the marginal utility associated with the purchase of a second pizza. Then the total utility that consumers receive from the purchase of $Q_E$ units of pizza is given by $\int_0^Q Ef(Q)\,dQ$. This definite integral, $\int_0^Q Ef(Q)\,dQ$, is closely approximated by the area inside $ODEQ_E$ when the units of pizza are very, very small.

The "surplus" context of consumer's surplus relates to the fact that consumers would have been willing to pay price $P_1$ for a first pizza, but did not

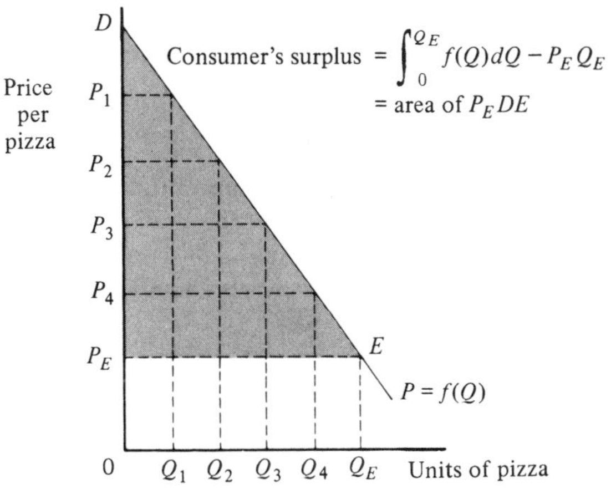


Figure 7.16 The definite integral and consumer's surplus

have to do so. Instead, they paid only $P_E$ for that pizza. Hence the difference between $P_1$ and $P_E$ is (for the first pizza) consumer's surplus—marginal utility that the consumer receives that he or she would have been willing to pay for, but did not have to.

DEFINITION Consumer's surplus is the difference between the maximum the consumer would have been willing to pay for the units that he or she purchased, and what he or she actually had to pay for those same units.

The definition implies that the total consumer's surplus derived by consumers of pizza closely approximates the area of the triangle $P_E DE$ when the units of pizza are very, very small. In terms of a definite integral, we can express consumer's surplus as[2]

$$\text{Consumer's surplus} = \int_0^{Q_E} [f(Q) - P_E]\, dQ = \int_0^{Q_E} f(Q)\, dQ - \int_0^{Q_E} P_E\, dQ$$

$$= \int_0^{Q_E} f(Q)\, dQ - P_E Q_E \qquad (7.60)$$

We can also find the area that comprises consumer's surplus by integrating with respect to the price variable. That is, given the demand function $Q = g(P)$, consumer's surplus becomes[3]

$$\text{Consumer's surplus} = \int_{P_E}^{P_D} g(P)\, dP \qquad (7.61)$$

[2] We assume a demand function of the form $P = f(Q)$ and an equilibrium price–quantity combination of $P_E$, $Q_E$.

[3] The demand function is of the form $Q = g(P)$, $P_E$, $Q_E$ is once again the equilibrium price–quantity combination, and $P_D$ is the intercept of the demand function on the ordinate (price) axis.

EXAMPLES

1. Find the consumer's surplus given that the demand and supply functions, under perfect competition, for a particular commodity are

   Demand: $P = 30 - 2Q^2$, Supply: $P = 3 + Q^2$

   We find equilibrium by setting demand equal to supply. Thus

   $$30 - 2Q^2 = 3 + Q^2, \qquad 3Q^2 = 27, \qquad Q = \pm 3$$

   Therefore the equilibrium quantity $Q_E = 3$ and the equilibrium price $P_E = 12$.

   $$\text{Consumer's surplus} = \int_0^3 (30 - 2Q^2)\, dQ - (12)(3)$$

   $$= \left(30Q - \tfrac{2}{3}Q^3\right)\Big|_0^3 - 36 = 36$$

2. The demand function for a particular commodity is $P = 28 - 5Q$, and the marginal cost to the monopolist of producing and marketing the commodity is $\text{MC} = 2Q + 4$. Determine the consumer's surplus.

   We find maximum profit by setting marginal revenue equal to marginal cost and finding equilibrium output. That is,

   $$\text{MR} = \text{MC} \qquad \text{or} \qquad 28 - 10Q = 2Q + 4$$

   Thus

   $$Q = 2 \qquad \text{and} \qquad P = 18$$

   $$\text{Consumer's surplus} = \int_0^2 (28 - 5Q)\, dQ - (18)(2)$$

   $$= \left(28Q - \tfrac{5}{2}Q^2\right)\Big|_0^2 - 36 = 10$$

   Alternatively,

   $$\text{Consumer's surplus} = \int_{18}^{28} \left(\frac{28 - P}{5}\right) dP = \left(\frac{28}{5}P - \frac{1}{10}P^2\right)\Bigg|_{18}^{28} = 10$$

**Producer's Surplus**

The analogous concept of producer's surplus is also susceptible to analysis by means of a definite integral. Figure 7.17 illustrates a supply curve for a firm. This supply curve takes the form $P = f(Q)$. Once again, $P_E$ and $Q_E$ represent the equilibrium price–quantity combination in this market. The firm is willing to supply $Q_1$ units at a price of $P_1$ per unit. However, it will receive price $P_E$ per unit when it supplies $Q_1$ units. The difference between $P_E$ and $P_1$ is the producer's surplus associated with $Q_1$ units. We can approximate total producer's surplus by the area of $P_S P_E E$ when the units of $Q_1$ are very small.

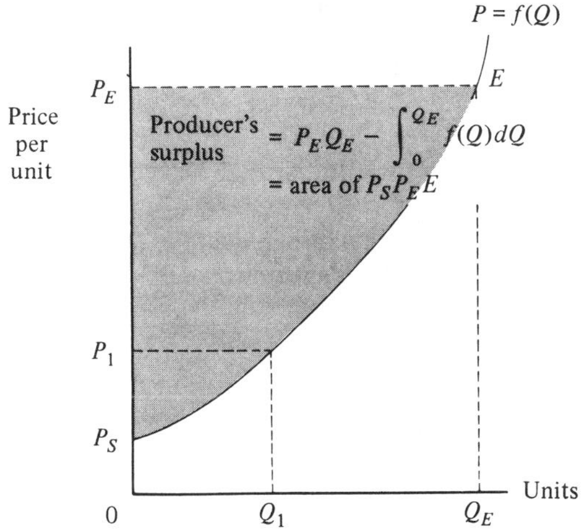


Figure 7.17 The definite integral and producer's surplus

DEFINITION Producer's surplus is the difference between the equilibrium price per unit and the price per unit for which the firm would have been willing to supply each unit.

In terms of the integral calculus, producer's surplus can be expressed as[4]

$$\text{Producer's surplus} = \int_0^{Q_E} [P_E - f(Q)]\, dQ = \int_0^{Q_E} P_E\, dQ - \int_0^{Q_E} f(Q)\, dQ$$

$$= P_E Q_E - \int_0^{Q_E} f(Q)\, dQ \tag{7.62}$$

Equation (7.62) expresses producer's surplus when we integrate with respect to quantity $Q$. We can also find producer's surplus by integrating with respect to price $P$:[5]

$$\text{Producer's surplus} = \int_{P_S}^{P_E} g(P)\, dP \tag{7.63}$$

EXAMPLES

1. Given the demand function $P = 30 - 2Q^2$ and the supply function $P = 3 + Q^2$ for a particular commodity under perfect competition, find the producer's surplus.

   $D = S, \qquad 30 - 2Q^2 = 3 + Q^2, \qquad Q = \pm 3$

[4] A supply function of the form $P = f(Q)$ is assumed.

[5] A supply function of the form $Q = g(P)$ is assumed, and $P_S$ is the price intercept of the supply function.

Thus equilibrium quantity $Q_E = 3$ and equilibrium price $P_E = 12$.

$$\text{Producer's surplus} = (12)(3) - \int_0^3 (3 + Q^2)\, dQ$$

$$= 36 - (3Q + \tfrac{1}{3}Q^3)\Big|_0^3 = 18$$

2. Given the supply function $P = 8Q + 2$, equilibrium quantity $Q_E = 3$, and equilibrium price $P_E = 26$, find the producer's surplus.

$$\text{Producer's surplus} = (26)(3) - \int_0^3 (8Q + 2)\, dQ$$

$$= 78 - (4Q^2 + 2Q)\Big|_0^3 = 36$$

**Choice of Manufacturing Technique**

Firms must often make decisions concerning the manner in which they produce their products. Assume that a new technique of production promises to generate cost $C$ reductions $R$ over $t$ years, such that $R = f(t)$. The cost of installing this new technique is also spread over time such that $C = g(t)$. The company wishes to install this new technique in one additional assembly line per year until the cost of a new installation exceeds the cost reductions that the new technique will achieve. That is, the firm wishes to continue new installations until $R = C$. How long should the firm make new installations, and how much money will it save by making new installations until $R = C$?

Figure 7.18 The net cost savings due to the adoption of a new technique

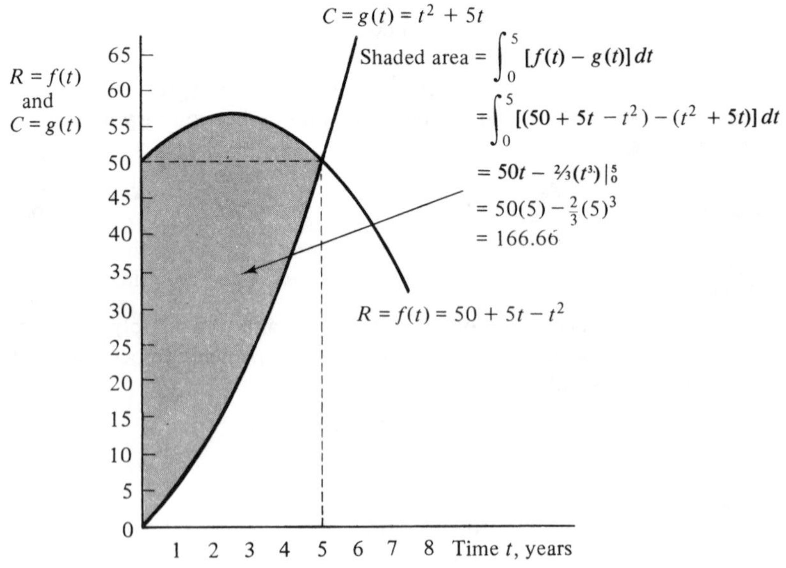

Suppose that $R = f(t) = 50 + 5t - t^2$, while $C = g(t) = t^2 + 5t$, where both $R$ and $C$ are expressed in thousands. Then the optimal number of years of installation is given by

$$R = C \tag{7.64}$$

$$50 + 5t - t^2 = t^2 + 5t \tag{7.65}$$

$$2t^2 - 50 = 0 \tag{7.66}$$

$$t^2 = 25 \tag{7.67}$$

$$t = 5 \tag{7.68}$$

The number of years that the firm should install the new technique is therefore 5. Figure 7.18 demonstrates this visually. The net total cost savings that the firm will realize is the shaded area in Figure 7.18. It is given by the definite integral

$$\int_0^5 [f(t) - g(t)]\,dt = \int_0^5 [(50 + 5t - t^2) - (t^2 + 5t)]\,dt \tag{7.69}$$

$$= \int_0^5 (50 - 2t^2)\,dt \tag{7.70}$$

$$= 50t - \tfrac{2}{3}(t^3)\Big|_0^5 \tag{7.71}$$

$$= 50(5) - \tfrac{2}{3}(5)^3 \tag{7.72}$$

$$= 250 - 83.34 \tag{7.73}$$

$$= 166.66 \tag{7.74}$$

Hence the shaded area in Figure 7.18, which is equivalent to the *net* saving that the firm will realize, is \$166,660, spread over five years.

### Profit Maximization

In Chapter 6 we demonstrated that the first-order or necessary condition for profit maximization on the part of the firm was that the firm must equate marginal revenue MR with marginal cost MC. We shall now use integration to measure the area between the MR and MC curves. The result is the maximum total profit of the firm, that is,

$$\text{Total maximum profit } (\pi) = \int_0^{Q_m} (\text{MR} - \text{MC})\,dQ \tag{7.75}$$

where $Q_m$ = output in units that maximizes $\pi$.

■ When we integrate a marginal revenue function, we obtain a total revenue function plus an arbitrary constant of integration. In the case of total revenue, this constant is equal to zero. Similarly, when we integrate a marginal cost function, we obtain a total cost function plus a constant of integration. In this case, the constant of integration is interpreted as the fixed costs of production. Since all costs are variable in the long run because we can make any adjustments necessary, this constant disappears in the long run. There is no reason, however, that the constant of integration obtained when we integrate marginal revenue must be equal to the constant of integration that we obtain when we integrate the marginal cost function. The two constants do not, in general, cancel each other in magnitude. Therefore we must subtract fixed costs (the constant of integration in the short run) from total profit when we are in a short-run situation.

EXAMPLE Given a total revenue function TR and a total cost function TC,

$$\mathrm{TR} = 26Q - 3Q^3 \tag{7.76}$$

$$\mathrm{TC} = 3Q^2 + 2Q + 14 \tag{7.77}$$

Then

$$\mathrm{MR} = \frac{d(\mathrm{TR})}{dQ} = 26 - 9Q^2 \tag{7.78}$$

$$\mathrm{MC} = \frac{d(\mathrm{TC})}{dQ} = 6Q + 2 \tag{7.79}$$

Total profit $\pi$ is given by:

$$\pi = \mathrm{TR} - \mathrm{TC} = 24Q - 3Q^2 - 3Q^3 - 14 \tag{7.80}$$

Maximum profit is found by setting the first derivative of profit with respect to output equal to 0:

$$\frac{d\pi}{dQ} = 24 - 6Q - 9Q^2 = 0 \tag{7.81}$$

$$(Q + 2)(-3Q + 4) = 0 \tag{7.82}$$

$$Q = -2 \quad \text{or} \quad \tfrac{4}{3} \tag{7.83}$$

The $Q = -2$ solution is extraneous, since it involves negative production. Hence $Q = \frac{4}{3}$ when profit is maximized. Substituting $Q = \frac{4}{3}$ into the profit Equation (7.80), we obtain $\pi = \frac{50}{9}$.

Now we shall work with the MR and MC functions and construct a solution by means of the integral calculus.

$$\pi \text{ maximization} = \int_0^{Q_m} (\mathrm{MR} - \mathrm{MC})\, dQ \tag{7.84}$$

$$= \int_0^{4/3} (24 - 6Q - 9Q^2)\, dQ \tag{7.85}$$

$$= (24Q - 3Q^2 - 3Q^3)\Big|_0^{4/3} \tag{7.86}$$

$$= \tfrac{176}{9} \tag{7.87}$$

Why is the answer that we have just obtained in Equation (7.87) using the integral calculus not the same as the answer we obtained using Equation (7.80)? That is, why does profit maximization on the part of the firm lead to $\pi = \frac{176}{9}$ when we use the integral calculus, but only $\frac{50}{9}$ when we rely on the differential calculus? The reason is that the TC function included a fixed cost component equal to 14.



$$\frac{176}{9} - 14 = \frac{50}{9}$$

Total profit, when found by means of integration, must have the fixed-cost component subtracted from it before it is consistent with the "true" magnitude of total profit found using the differential calculus. The 14 disappears in the long run when fixed costs are 0. Hence, in the long run, the differential and the integral calculus yield the same answer.

### The Normal Distribution

One of the cornerstones of modern statistics at all levels of sophistication is the normal distribution. An astonishingly broad range of physical and human phenomena can be accurately represented by a normal distribution. Examples include the performance of athletes, students, and workers.

DEFINITION A random variable $x$ is said to have a normal distribution if its density function is given by the equation

$$N(x) = \frac{1}{\sqrt{2\pi}\,\sigma} \cdot e^{-(x-\mu)^2/2\sigma^2} \tag{7.88}$$

where $\sigma$ is the standard deviation, $\mu$ is the mean of random variable $x$, and $-\infty < x < \infty$.

The characteristic bell-shaped curve that identifies the normal distribution is illustrated in Figure 7.19. The area under the normal curve is given by the improper integral $\int_{-\infty}^{\infty} N(x)\,dx$ and is equal to 1.00.[6]

[6] A formal proof of this assertion may be found in John E. Freund, *Mathematical Statistics*, Prentice-Hall, Englewood Cliffs, N.J., 1962, pp. 129–30.

Figure 7.19 Integrating the area under the normal curve

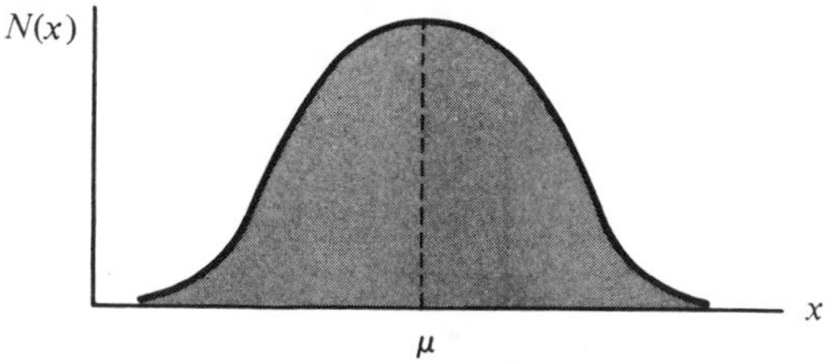

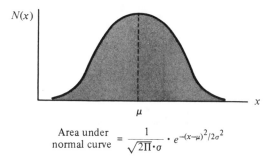

Area under normal curve $= \frac{1}{\sqrt{2\Pi}\cdot\sigma} \cdot e^{-(x-\mu)^2/2\sigma^2}$

## The Lorenz Curve and the Gini Coefficient

A Lorenz curve is a graphical device used to illustrate the inequality of the distribution of some variable, such as income, intelligence, or wealth. We can construct (conceptually) a Lorenz curve reflecting the distribution of incomes. The first step is to rank-order all individuals according to their incomes, from lowest to highest. Then we observe the cumulative percentage of total income held by various percentages of individuals. For example, the lowest 20% of individuals might hold only 10% of all income.

Perfect equality of incomes (a state in which all individuals have the same income) means that the lowest 20% of individuals have 20% of the income, the lowest 75% of individuals have 75% of the income, and so forth. The Lorenz curve that corresponds to this particular distribution of income is depicted in Figure 7.20. It is a straight line that is characterized by a 45° angle from left to right. We can see that the cumulative percentage of individuals (measured along the horizontal axis) is everywhere the same as the cumulative percentage of income (measured along the vertical axis). For example, the lowest 50% of individuals have 50% of the income.

When the distribution of income is unequal, then the Lorenz curve that depicts it is bowed out toward the southeast corner of the diagram. The Lorenz curve in Figure 7.21 is one such example. It is based on the income-distribution data compiled in Table 7.1.

Both the graph and the table inform us that the lowest 10% of individuals have only 2% of the income. The highest 10% of individuals, however, have 16% of the income. Notice that a Lorenz curve need not be symmetric in its tails, or about a point such as 50%, or any other point.

The more unequal the distribution of income, the more deviation we observe

Figure 7.20 A Lorenz curve representing precise equality of incomes. The cumulation is from lowest to highest. Hence the first 50% of individuals, taken from left to right, are those with the lowest incomes, in rank order from lowest to highest

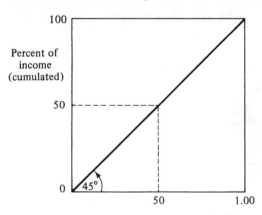

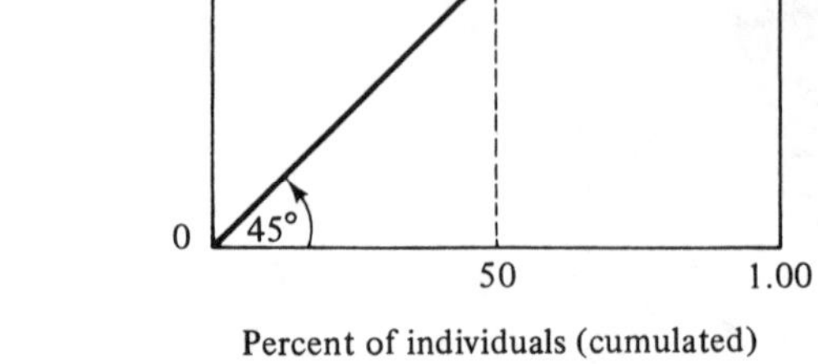

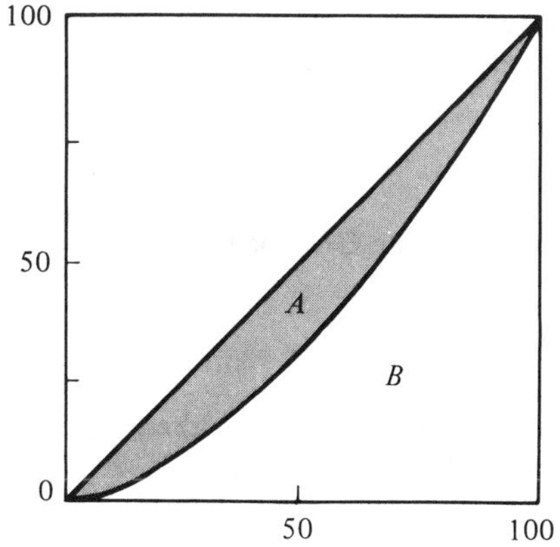


Figure 7.21 A Lorenz curve depicting inequality of incomes

in the Lorenz curve relative to the 45° line that would represent a precisely equal distribution of income. We can measure the precise degree of inequality of the income distribution by means of a Gini coefficient. In Figure 7.21, the Gini coefficient is the shaded area labeled $A$, divided by the sum of areas $A$ and $B$. That is,

$$\text{Gini coefficient} = \frac{A}{A + B} \tag{7.89a}$$

We know that the sum of areas $A$ and $B$ in Figure 7.21 is equal to one-half

Table 7.1 A cumulative and percentage ranking of the distribution of income

| *Percentage of families, ranked by income* | *Cumulative percentage of families* | *Percentage of income received by a particular group* | *Cumulative percentage of income* |
|---|---|---|---|
| Lowest 10% | 10% | 2% | 2% |
| 10–20 | 20 | 4 | 6 |
| 20–30 | 30 | 7 | 13 |
| 30–40 | 40 | 9 | 22 |
| 40–50 | 50 | 11 | 33 |
| 50–60 | 60 | 12 | 45 |
| 60–70 | 70 | 12 | 57 |
| 70–80 | 80 | 13 | 70 |
| 80–90 | 90 | 14 | 84 |
| Highest 10% | 100 | 16 | 100 |

*Note*: Although the data above are hypothetical, they nonetheless give a substantially accurate picture of the distribution of family incomes in the United States.

the area of the square that comprises the entire Lorenz curve diagram. Therefore we can reformulate the Gini coefficient as follows:

$$\text{Gini coefficient} = \frac{\frac{1}{2} - B}{\frac{1}{2}} = 1 - 2B \tag{7.89b}$$

In terms of a definite integral, we can write the Gini coefficient

$$1 - 2B = 1 - 2\int_0^{100} (\text{Lorenz curve function})\, dx \tag{7.90}$$

The $dx$ in Equation (7.90) tells us that we must integrate with respect to the variable on the horizontal axis, which, in the case of Figure 7.21, is the cumulated percentage of individuals.

EXAMPLE The Olympia Savings and Loan Association occasionally has liquidity problems such that it has difficulty meeting depositors' demands for funds. Existing research on the subject has suggested to Olympia that the instability of its deposits and withdrawals tends to be greater when there is greater inequality in the size distribution of deposits. The presence of several large depositors can sharply alter Olympia's liquidity picture if one or more of these large depositors chooses to make a major withdrawal of funds.

The Lorenz curve for Olympia's deposits is the following:

$$\text{PDD} = 0.5\text{PA} + 0.005\text{PA}^2 \tag{7.91}$$

where PDD = percentage of dollars deposited in Olympia, cumulated, and PA = percentage of savings accounts at Olympia, cumulated.

How many percent of Olympia's deposits do the highest cumulative 10% of depositors hold? We can answer this by evaluating PDD for PA = 90 and PA = 100.

$$\text{PDD} = 0.5(90) + 0.005(90)^2 = 85.5$$

while

$$\text{PDD} = 0.5(100) + 0.005(100)^2 = 100.$$

Therefore the 10% of the depositors with the largest savings deposits own 14.5% of the deposit dollars.

Suppose that research indicates that savings and loan associations that have a Gini coefficient that exceeds 0.6 are likely to have liquidity troubles due to instability of deposits. Is Olympia an example of such a savings and loan association? The answer is no. The entire area of the triangle that a Lorenz curve can enclose is the area that we labeled $A + B$ in Figure 7.21. Since the area of a triangle is given by $\frac{1}{2}bh$, where $b$ = the base and $h$ = height, the area of $A + B = (\frac{1}{2})(100)(100) = 5000$. The Gini coefficient itself is given by $A/(A + B)$. We can find area $A$ by finding the value of the following definite integral:

$$\text{Area } A = 5000 - \int_0^{100} (0.5\text{PA} + 0.005\text{PA}^2)\, d\text{PA} \tag{7.92}$$

$$= 5000 - \left(\frac{\text{PA}^2}{4} + \frac{\text{PA}^3}{600}\right)\Bigg|_0^{100} \tag{7.93}$$

$$= 5000 - 4166.67 = 833.33 \tag{7.94}$$

Therefore the Gini coefficient for Olympia's savings deposits is 833.33/5000 = 0.167, and Olympia's deposit structure is not a source of instability according to the rule.

We could also have found the Gini coefficient by using Equation (7.90) and regarding the total available area $(A + B)$ as 10,000. Then

$$\text{Gini coefficient} = 10{,}000 - 2B \tag{7.95}$$

$$= 10{,}000 - 2\int_0^{100} (0.5\text{PA} + 0.005\text{PA}^2)\, d\text{PA} \tag{7.96}$$

$$= 10{,}000 - 2(4166.67) \tag{7.97}$$

$$= 0.167 \tag{7.98}$$

**Capital Accumulation**

Capital accumulation is the process of adding to a given stock of capital by the process known as investment. The capital stock in time $t$ is designated by $K(t)$. The rate at which the stock of capital is being depleted or increased over time is given by the derivative,

$$\frac{dK}{dt} \equiv \dot{K} \tag{7.99}$$

The dot above the $K$ in Equation (7.99) denotes the derivative of that variable with respect to time. Hence $\dot{K} = dK/dt$. This notation is often used in dynamic economic analyses.

The rate at which capital accumulates at time $t$ is also the rate of net investment at time $t$, which we indicate by $I(t)$. The relationship between $K(t)$ and $I(t)$ is as follows:

$$\frac{dK}{dt} \equiv \dot{K} \equiv I(t) \tag{7.100}$$

and

$$K(t) = \int \frac{dK}{dt}\, dt = \int dK = \int I(t)\, dt \tag{7.101}$$

The capital stock $K(t)$ refers to the *stock* or total amount of capital that has been accumulated and is available at a given point in time. It is a stock in the same sense that we can meaningfully talk about the existing stock of automobiles owned by students. On the other hand, net investment $I(t)$ is a *flow* concept that indicates the rate of net investment per time period. We can talk meaningfully about the *change* in the stock of student automobiles, in which case we refer to a flow.

In order to find the precise amount of net investment or capital accumulation for a period of time, we must know the length of the particular period of time. That is, we must know the limits of integration. We can rewrite Equation (7.101) as

$$\int_a^b I(t)\,dt = K(t)\Big|_a^b = K(b) - K(a) \tag{7.102}$$

Equation (7.102) represents the *area* under the $I(t)$ curve illustrated in Figure 7.22. Total capital accumulation, which is the stock of capital, is given by $K(b) - K(a)$. Its size depends not only on the rate of net investment $I(t)$, but also on the length of the time interval $[a, b]$. In Figure 7.22, the size of the capital stock at time $b$ is the shaded area given by the definite integral $\int_a^b I(t)\,dt$.

EXAMPLE The Economic Planning Bureau of the kingdom of Middle Volta is making a strenuous attempt to increase Middle Volta's ability to produce electric power. Middle Volta already has \$30 million worth of generators producing electricity, and according to the five-year plan, the number of dollars invested in generators during the five years of the plan will be $\$(t) = 3t + 0.5t^2 - 0.001t^3$, where $t$ is the year of the plan and \$ are expressed in millions. What will the value of Middle Volta's generator capacity be at the end of the five-year plan? How much net investment in generators will Middle Volta undertake in the final year of the plan?

The total dollar value of the generator stock after 5 years is given by

$$30 + \int_0^5 (3t + 0.5t^2 - 0.001t^3)\,dt \tag{7.103}$$

$$= 30 + \frac{3}{2}t^2 + \frac{1}{6}t^3 - \frac{t^4}{4000}\Big|_0^5 \tag{7.104}$$

$$= 88.174 \tag{7.105}$$

Figure 7.22 The flow of net investment and the capital stock

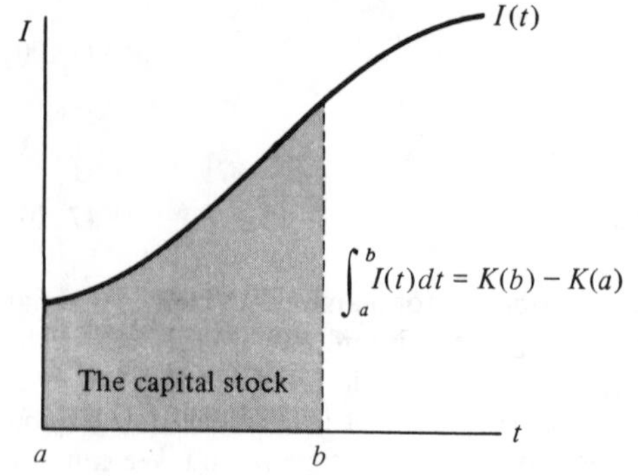

During the fifth year, the net investment in generators is given by

$$\$(5) - \$(4) = 58.174 - 34.603 = 23.571 \tag{7.106}$$

***Domar's Growth Model**

Assume that investment in capital $I(t)$ is the only type of expenditure that is capable of increasing or decreasing the flow of income. Any change in $I(t)$ affects both the productive capacity of the economy and aggregate demand. Evsei Domar has attempted to determine whether there is some rate of growth in $I(t)$ that is necessary in order to have a stable economy with full employment in which available productive capacity is precisely utilized to satisfy aggregate demand.

We define the following terms and symbols:

$I(t) = I$ = rate of investment per year (flow)

$Y(t) = Y$ = rate of income per year (flow)

$K(t) = K$ = stock of capital at time (stock)

$s$ = MPS = marginal propensity to save (constant)

$k = 1/s$ = multiplier (constant)

$\rho$ = potential productive capacity

$\sigma = \rho/K$ = potential social average productivity of investment

Any change in investment has two effects. First, the change in investment affects aggregate demand via the operation of the multiplier, so that

$$\frac{dY}{dt} = \frac{dI}{dt} \cdot \frac{1}{s} \tag{7.107}$$

Second, the capital stock is potentially capable of producing a national income of

$$\rho = \sigma K \qquad \text{dollars} \tag{7.108}$$

It follows from Equation (7.108) that a change in the potential ability to generate income from a particular capital stock is defined by

$$d\rho = \sigma\, dK \tag{7.109}$$

Hence

$$\frac{d\rho}{dt} = \sigma \frac{dK}{dt} = \rho I \tag{7.110}$$

* This section contains more difficult material that may be omitted without loss of continuity. Further details concerning the Domar growth model may be found in Evsei D. Domar, "Capital Expansion, Rate of Growth, and Employment," *Econometrica*, 14 (April 1946), pp. 137–147; reprinted in Domar, *Essays in the Theory of Economic Growth*, Oxford University Press, Fair Lawn, N.J., 1957, pp. 70–82.

Equilibrium in the system is attained when supply equals demand, that is, when productive capacity equals aggregate demand, or $\rho = Y$. The system remains in equilibrium when $d\rho/dt = dY/dt$. Let us now substitute Equations (7.107) and (7.110) into the stability condition $d\rho/dt = dY/dt$. This yields

$$\rho I = \frac{dI}{dt} \cdot \frac{1}{s} \tag{7.111}$$

or

$$s\rho\, dt = \frac{dI}{I} = \frac{dI(t)}{I(t)} \tag{7.112}$$

Since investment occurs over time, we integrate Equation (7.112) from 0 to $t$ in order to ascertain the conditions that investment must satisfy in order to have equilibrium in the system:

$$\int_0^t s\rho\, dt = \int_0^t \frac{1}{I(t)}\, dI(t) \tag{7.113}$$

$$s\rho t \Big|_0^t = \ln I(t) \Big|_0^t \tag{7.114}$$

$$s\rho t = \ln I(t) - \ln I(0) = \ln \frac{I(t)}{I(0)} \tag{7.115}$$

$$e^{s\rho t} = \frac{I(t)}{I(0)} \tag{7.116}$$

Therefore we can rewrite Equation (7.112) to include the result of Equation (7.116), as follows:

$$I(t) = I(0)e^{s\rho t} \tag{7.117}$$

That is, in order to maintain an equilibrium (at whatever level of national income), investment must grow at the rate of $s\rho$.

EXAMPLE Domar illustrated his equilibrium condition by collecting data on United States savings and capacity–capital ratio from 1899 to 1941 and found that $s = 12\%$ and $\rho = 30\%$. Thus the equilibrium rate in the Domar model would be 3.6% per year.

## PROBLEMS

1. The Wenatchee Electric Company has a marginal cost MC function given by $\text{MC} = C'(x) = 0.0001 + 3.0 \cdot 10^{-8}x$, where MC is stated in terms of cost per kilowatthour, and $x$ is tons of coal burned. Additionally, there is a fixed cost of \$500 associated with electricity generation in a given time period. (a) Find the total cost function $C(x)$ for the generation of electricity. (b) What is the total cost associated with the generation of 1,000,000 kilowatthours of electricity? (c) What is the marginal cost of

generating an additional kilowatthour of electricity when 100,000 kilowatthours have already been generated?

2. The department of economics at Ivy League University has bought a new duplicating machine. The savings in labor per hour associated with the use of this machine ($S$) are given by the function $S(t) = 2.00 + 0.50t$, where $t$ is the number of hours the new machine is used. Suppose that the new machine costs \$200. Disregarding present values, will the machine pay for itself if it is used for 1000 hours in a given time period? What is the breakeven point (in hours) for the machine?

3. Rent-a-Car, Inc., knows that the cost of maintaining a newly purchased fleet car is given by $C(t) = 60(1 + t^2)$, where $t$ is the number of years that the car is used. (a) Suppose that a car is leased for 3 years. What will be the total maintenance cost to the firm? (b) What monthly charge would meet the expected maintenance costs of two automobiles?

4. The Widget Manufacturing Corporation has installed a new production control device that promises savings $S$ that will decline with respect to the time $t$ that the control device is used. The cost $C$ of operating the control device will rise with respect to time. The savings function is given by $S(t) = 90 - t^2$, while the cost function is given by $C(t) = t^2 + 4t$. (a) For how many years will the firm realize net savings by using the control device? (b) What will be the total amount of net savings realized by the firm during this period? (c) Suppose that there is a fixed charge of \$50 associated with the purchase of the control device. How will this change your answers to (a) and (b)?

5. The demand function for tennis shoes at Tennis Everyone is given by $Q_d = f(P)$, where $Q_d$ = quantity demanded and $P$ = price per unit. Tennis Everyone's supply function for shoes is given by $Q_s = f(P)$, where $Q_s$ = quantity supplied. The precise demand and supply functions are given by $Q_d = 850 - 20P - P^2$ and $Q_s = P^2 + 15P$. (a) Find the equilibrium price and quantity for tennis shoes. (b) At the equilibrium price, some consumer's surplus is realized by those who purchase the tennis shoes. How much is it? (c) Similarly, a producer's surplus is realized. How much is it?

6. The Stutz Bearcat Auto Company has been forced by the Environmental Protection Agency to install a new pollution-control device on the automobiles that it produces. The marginal cost MC of this per auto produced ($Q$) is given by $\text{MC} = 20 + 0.01Q - 0.003Q^2$. The marginal savings from pollution reduction, realized by society, are given by $\text{MS} = 15 - 0.05Q + 0.005Q^2$, where MS = marginal savings per auto. (a) At what point in terms of auto production will it no longer pay society to force Stutz to install the pollution-control device? (b) What will the total savings realized by society from pollution control be at that point?

7. The derivative of a certain exponential function is $xe^{x^2}$. What is the original exponential function?

8. Fertilizer is being used in McLean County according to the following exponential growth curve: $Q(t) = Q_0 e^{rt}$, where $Q(t)$ = usage of fertilizer in year $t$, and $r$ is the annual rate of increase in the use of fertilizer.

Suppose that $Q_0 = 10{,}000$ tons in 1977, and $r = 0.06$. (a) What will be the usage of fertilizer in McLean County in 1990? (b) How much fertilizer will have been used in the time period 1976–1990?

9. Professor McCarney has invested \$1000 in a savings account that pays 6% per year. (a) What will the value of that savings account be after 10 years? (b) Assume that Professor McCarney also has an opportunity to buy an asset that will pay \$100 per year for 10 years. Assume that Professor McCarney's rate of discount is 7%. What is the present value of that asset? (c) Should Professor McCarney accept the current owner of the asset's offer to sell it for \$900? [*Hint*: Remember that present value PV is given by

$$\text{PV} = \int_0^n \$(t)e^{-rt}\,dt$$

where $t$ is the time period in years, $\$(t)$ is the dollars received in time period $t$, $r$ is the rate of discount, and $n$ is the number of years the money is received.]

10. The oil well in my back yard yields 100 barrels of oil per month, and will run dry in 5 years at that rate. The price of oil today is \$14 per barrel, and it has been estimated to be $14 + 0.5 \ln t$ dollars in year $t$. (a) What will be the price of oil per barrel in the fifth year? (b) What is the total revenue that I will realize from my oil well over the 5-year period?

11. The total sales $S$ of a new soap are a function of the days of a month $d$ such that $S(d) = 100 + 0.9e^{0.01t}$ as $t = 1, 2, \ldots, 30$ each month. (a) What will the sales of soap be in units on the twenty-fifth day? (b) What will total soap sales be in a 30-day month? (c) Suppose that the supermarket that sells the soap receives shipments of 5000 bars of soap whenever it requests a shipment. How often should the supermarket reorder soap in order to replenish its inventory?

12. The manager of a frozen pizza company expects daily sales to grow at such a rate that she will be able to sell $200 + 3d$ pizzas per day, where $d$ = number of days from today. (a) When will the pizza company sell 5000 pizzas? (b) Suppose that each pizza sells for \$4. How much revenue will the firm realize after 100 days?

13. The marginal cost MC of producing widgets $W$ is given by $\text{MC} = 2 + 0.10W$. The marginal revenue MR realized from the sale of widgets is given by $\text{MR} = 15 - 0.5W$. (a) Find the profit-maximizing price and output of widgets. (b) How much profit will the firm earn when it follows the profit-maximizing solution?

14. A study of new employees at Game Designers Workshop indicates that a new employee there will take $10 + 10e^{-0.02n}$ minutes to package and mail the $n$th game to a customer. What is the total time the new worker will take to package and mail 100 games?

# MATRIX ALGEBRA

# 8

In Chapter 1 we used Stigler's diet problem to demonstrate the power of mathematics in formulating and solving an important problem. The crux of the diet problem is to find the least expensive combination of 80 foods available to a consumer that will nevertheless satisfy nine recommended daily dietary allowances. The dietary allowances were established by the Food and Nutrition Board of the National Academy of Sciences.

Formally, we can write the diet problem as follows:

*Minimize*:

$$C = P_1X_1 + P_2X_2 + \cdots + P_{80}X_{80} \tag{8.1}$$

*Subject to*:

$$\begin{aligned} a_{11}X_1 + a_{12}X_2 + \cdots + a_{1,80}X_{80} &= R_1 \\ a_{21}X_1 + a_{22}X_2 + \cdots + a_{2,80}X_{80} &= R_2 \\ \vdots \qquad \vdots \qquad\qquad \vdots \qquad & \quad \vdots \\ a_{91}X_1 + a_{92}X_2 + \cdots + a_{9,80}X_{80} &= R_9 \end{aligned} \tag{8.2}$$

where $X_j$ = quantity of food $j$ in ounces, $P_j$ = price of food $j$ per ounce, $R_i$ = minimum recommended daily dietary allowance of requirement $i$ in units, $a_{ij}$ = units of requirement $i$ obtained from 1 ounce of food $j$, and

$$C = \sum_{i=1}^{80} P_jX_j = \text{total expenditure by consumer on all 80 foods}$$

Equations (8.1) and (8.2) represent a shorthand way of expressing a detailed series of 10 equations (the objective function that we are trying to minimize plus the nine constraint equations) in which there are 80 unknowns (the 80 different foods that can be consumed). Equations (8.1) and (8.2) express all this in a compact, linear form. They are an example of applied *linear algebra*.

DEFINITION Linear algebra is the study of systems of linear equations and the attempt to find a simultaneous solution for the unknowns of those equations, if such a solution exists.

It is important to note that linear algebra deals with linear equations. You have probably already observed that linear equations are generally easier to deal with than are nonlinear equations. Nonlinear equations and nonlinear models often cannot be solved without the help of a computer. It is also true, however, that we can usefully approximate many business and economics relationships by linear functional forms. Hence we are not severely disadvantaged by the fact that matrix algebra is restricted to the study, manipulation, and solution of *linear* equations.

## MATRICES AND VECTORS: DEFINITIONAL MATTERS

We begin with a very general case involving a system of $m$ linear equations in $n$ variables:

$$\begin{aligned} a_{11}x_1 + a_{12}x_2 + \cdots + a_{1n}x_n &= c_1 \\ a_{21}x_1 + a_{22}x_2 + \cdots + a_{2n}x_n &= c_2 \\ \vdots \qquad \vdots \qquad\qquad \vdots \quad &\quad \vdots \\ a_{m1}x_1 + a_{m2}x_2 + \cdots + a_{mn}x_n &= c_n \end{aligned} \tag{8.3}$$

The $n$ variables, $x_1, x_2, \ldots, x_n$ above, are carefully and specifically aligned in a particular fashion. The variable denoted $x_1$ is the first variable and must appear in the first column. The variable $x_2$ is the second variable and must appear in the second column. Any variable $x_j$ must appear in the $j$th column. Similarly, the subscript $a_{ij}$ is definitive with respect to location in the system of equations. For example, $a_{24}$ represents the coefficient of the variable that appears in the second row and the fourth column of the system of equations. In general, $a_{ij}$ refers to the coefficient of the variable located in the $i$th row and the $j$th column. Finally, the parameters $c_1$, $c_2, \ldots, c_m$ are $m$ in number and are unattached to any of the variables $x_j$. The constant $c_3$ belongs in the third row such that

$$\sum_{j=1}^{n} a_{3j}x_j = c_3$$

For any particular row $i$,

$$\sum_{j=1}^{n} a_{ij}x_j = c_i$$

DEFINITION A matrix is a rectangular, ordered array of elements or entries consisting of numbers, parameters, or variables.

The existence of a matrix is signaled by the use of brackets [ ] or parentheses ( ), or by the use of double vertical lines ‖ ‖. We are using the bracket notation [ ] in this text.

Even though it is written in standard notation, the system of equations found in Equation (8.3) is cumbersome and unwieldy. Fortunately, this system of equations can be simply rewritten using a shorthand notation. Let $AX = C$ represent the system of equations found in Equation (8.3), where

$$A = \begin{bmatrix} a_{11} & a_{12} & \cdots & a_{1n} \\ a_{21} & a_{22} & \cdots & a_{2n} \\ \vdots & \vdots & & \vdots \\ a_{m1} & a_{m2} & \cdots & a_{mn} \end{bmatrix} \qquad X = \begin{bmatrix} x_1 \\ x_2 \\ \vdots \\ x_n \end{bmatrix} \qquad \text{and} \qquad C = \begin{bmatrix} c_1 \\ c_2 \\ \vdots \\ c_m \end{bmatrix} \tag{8.4}$$

$A$, $X$, and $C$ are each matrices, and $AX = C$.[1] The elements in a particular matrix are not separated by commas, but by blank spaces. It is customary to symbolize a matrix by an upper-case (capital) letter, such as $A$, $X$, or $C$, whereas the elements in a particular matrix are customarily denoted by lower-case (small) letters, such as $a$, $a_{ij}$, and $b$. It is possible for the elements of the matrix to be numeric values, such as 5, 7, or 11.24. In this case, the numeric values are used in preference to lower-case letters.

The matrix labeled $A$ above represents the coefficients of the variables in the system of equations. The $A$ matrix has $m$ rows and $n$ columns. This can be contrasted with the variable matrix, labeled $X$, which consists of $n$ rows and only one column. In general, there is no relationship between the number of rows and the number of columns in a matrix. The number of rows is not necessarily related to the number of columns, and vice versa. What is the case, however, is that the number of rows and the number of columns define the *dimension* (or *order*) of a matrix. For example, matrix $A$ has $m$ rows and $n$ columns and is therefore said to be an $m \times n$ matrix (which is read, "$m$ by $n$ matrix"). The dimension of a matrix is always read rows first, columns second. A $5 \times 7$ matrix has five rows and seven columns, *not* vice versa. In the special case in which $m = n$, for example, a $5 \times 5$ matrix, one is dealing with a *square matrix*.

■ You will occasionally encounter the notation $A = [a_{ij}]$, which represents a matrix composed of the elements that take the form $a_{ij}$. The number of rows and columns is unspecified. Note well that $[a_{ij}]$, which represents a matrix, is not equivalent to $a_{ij}$, which represents a specific element in a matrix. That is, $[a_{ij}] \neq a_{ij}$ unless the dimensions of the matrix are $1 \times 1$.

It is instructive to rewrite Stigler's diet problem, which we formally stated in Equations (8.1) and (8.2), in matrix notation. We can denote the objective function that we seek to minimize by $PX = C$, and we can represent the constraint equations by $AX = R$, where

$$P = [P_1 P_2 \cdots P_{80}] \qquad \text{a } 1 \times 80 \text{ matrix}$$

$$X = \begin{bmatrix} X_1 \\ X_2 \\ \vdots \\ X_{80} \end{bmatrix} \qquad \text{an } 80 \times 1 \text{ matrix}$$

[1] The matrix notation $AX = C$ can also be written as $XA = C$, where $X = [x_1, x_2, \ldots, x_n]$ and $C = [c_1, c_2, \ldots, c_m]$. Matrix $A$ must have $n$ rows and $m$ columns for this relationship to hold.

$C = [C]$  a $1 \times 1$ matrix

$$A = \begin{bmatrix} a_{11} & a_{12} & \cdots & a_{1,80} \\ a_{21} & a_{22} & \cdots & a_{2,80} \\ \vdots & \vdots & & \vdots \\ a_{91} & a_{92} & & a_{9,80} \end{bmatrix} \quad \text{a } 9 \times 80 \text{ matrix}$$

$$R = \begin{bmatrix} R_1 \\ R_2 \\ \vdots \\ R_9 \end{bmatrix} \quad \text{a } 9 \times 1 \text{ matrix}$$

EXAMPLES

1. $\begin{bmatrix} 1 & 2 & -4 \\ 3 & 0 & 8 \end{bmatrix}$ is a $2 \times 3$ matrix

2. $\begin{bmatrix} -3 \\ 4 \\ 2 \end{bmatrix}$ is a $3 \times 1$ matrix

3. $[6 \quad 9 \quad -2 \quad 0]$ is a $1 \times 4$ matrix

4. $\begin{bmatrix} 2 & -4 & 6 & 18 \\ 7 & 1 & -3 & 2 \\ 1 & 2 & 3 & 4 \end{bmatrix}$ is a $3 \times 4$ matrix

Matrices $X$ and $C$ in Equation (8.4) have the dimensions $n \times 1$ and $m \times 1$, respectively. Both matrices have only one column and are referred to as *column vectors.* Had we defined matrices $X$ and $C$ as horizontal rather than vertical arrays—that is, had we said that

$$X = [x_1 x_2 \cdots x_n] \qquad \text{and} \qquad C = [c_1 c_2 \cdots c_m]$$

then each of these matrices would have only one row, and they would be referred to as *row vectors* with the dimensions $1 \times n$ and $1 \times m$, respectively.

We can use the concept of a vector to view a matrix as a series of related row and/or column vectors. Consider the matrix

$$A = \begin{bmatrix} a_{11} & a_{12} & \cdots & a_{1n} \\ a_{21} & a_{22} & \cdots & a_{2n} \\ \vdots & \vdots & & \vdots \\ a_{m1} & a_{m2} & \cdots & a_{mn} \end{bmatrix} \tag{8.5}$$

We can consider this matrix to be an ordered set of $m$ row vectors,[2] namely,

$$\begin{aligned} A_1 &= [a_{11} \quad a_{12} \quad \cdots \quad a_{1n}] \\ A_2 &= [a_{21} \quad a_{22} \quad \cdots \quad a_{2n}] \\ \vdots \quad & \quad \vdots \qquad \vdots \qquad\quad \vdots \\ A_m &= [a_{m1} \quad a_{m2} \quad \cdots \quad a_{mn}] \end{aligned} \tag{8.6}$$

[2] We could also view the matrix given by Equation (8.5) as an ordered set of $n$ column vectors.

We can therefore represent matrix $A$ of Equation (8.5) as

$$A = \begin{bmatrix} A_1 \\ A_2 \\ \vdots \\ A_m \end{bmatrix} = \begin{bmatrix} a_{11} & a_{12} & \cdots & a_{1n} \\ a_{21} & a_{22} & \cdots & a_{2n} \\ \vdots & \vdots & & \vdots \\ a_{m1} & a_{m2} & \cdots & a_{mn} \end{bmatrix} \tag{8.7}$$

■ It is absolutely essential that an $m \times n$ matrix be read as $m$ rows by $n$ columns. An $m \times n$ matrix is not equivalent to an $n \times m$ matrix except in the special circumstances in which $m = n$ and we have a square matrix. For example, we define matrices $J$ and $K$ as follows:

$$J = \begin{bmatrix} 1 & 2 & 3 \\ 4 & 5 & 6 \end{bmatrix} \quad \text{and} \quad K = \begin{bmatrix} 1 & 4 \\ 2 & 5 \\ 3 & 6 \end{bmatrix} \tag{8.8}$$

Matrices $J$ and $K$ do not have identical dimensions. $J$ is a $2 \times 3$ matrix, whereas $K$ is a $3 \times 2$ matrix.

A matrix is an *ordered array* of elements, according to our definition. Each element of the matrix has an assigned location in the matrix. Any alteration of that assigned location will, in general, alter the matrix and the system of equations it represents. Consider the following system of equations:

$$\begin{aligned} 8x_1 + 10x_2 + 12x_3 &= 1 \\ 3x_1 \qquad\quad + 2x_3 &= 0 \\ x_1 - 2x_2 - 5x_3 &= 8 \end{aligned} \tag{8.9}$$

The coefficient matrix of this system of equations is given by

$$A = \begin{bmatrix} 8 & 10 & 12 \\ 3 & 0 & 2 \\ 1 & -2 & -5 \end{bmatrix} \tag{8.10}$$

The element in the second row and second column ($a_{22}$) of the coefficient matrix is 0 and must be included. Further, should we interchange the elements in the first and second columns of the first row, that is, should we interchange $a_{11}$ and $a_{12}$, then the matrix would become

$$A^* = \begin{bmatrix} 10 & 8 & 12 \\ 3 & 0 & 2 \\ 1 & -2 & -5 \end{bmatrix} \tag{8.11}$$

Matrix $A^*$ now represents the coefficients in the following system of equations:

$$\begin{aligned} 10x_1 + 8x_2 + 12x_3 &= 1 \\ 3x_1 \qquad\quad + 2x_3 &= 0 \\ x_1 - 2x_2 - 5x_3 &= 8 \end{aligned} \tag{8.12}$$

Matrices $A$ and $A^*$ are not the same; they represent different sets of coefficients.

We must finally observe that a matrix has no numeric value *per se*. One cannot state that a matrix has a value of 5, 7, 14, or any other number. A matrix is simply a shorthand, efficient method of writing an array of elements.

EXAMPLES

1. Given the system of linear equations

$$\begin{aligned} x_1 + 5x_2 + 6x_3 &= 8 \\ 8x_1 - 3x_2 - x_3 &= 7 \\ 2x_1 + 8x_2 - 7x_3 &= 3 \end{aligned}$$

the coefficient matrix $A$ is

$$A = \begin{bmatrix} 1 & 5 & 6 \\ 8 & -3 & -1 \\ 2 & 8 & -7 \end{bmatrix}$$

2. Given the system of linear equations

$$\begin{aligned} x_1 + x_2 + x_3 &= 3 \\ 3x_1 \qquad + 2x_3 &= 7 \\ x_2 + x_3 &= 10 \end{aligned}$$

the coefficient matrix $A$ is

$$A = \begin{bmatrix} 1 & 1 & 1 \\ 3 & 0 & 2 \\ 0 & 1 & 1 \end{bmatrix}$$

## MATRIX OPERATIONS

We have already seen that a matrix is a compact and logical way to write an array of elements. We represented a system of $m$ linear equations in $n$ variables as $AX = C$. We have yet to indicate how one matrix is related to another. We have not touched on such interesting questions as: Why did we choose to write $X$ and $C$ as column vectors rather than as row vectors? How do we multiply matrices? When are two matrices equal? Do the laws governing the addition and subtraction of real numbers also hold for matrices? We shall discuss these and other matters in this section. We shall consider the following matrix algebra concepts: (1) equality, (2) addition, (3) subtraction, (4) the commutative and associative laws of addition and subtraction, (5) scalar multiplication, (6) matrix multiplication, and (7) the commutative and associative laws of multiplication.

### Matrix Equality

DEFINITION Two matrices $A = [a_{ij}]$ and $B = [b_{ij}]$ are said to be equal, such that $A = B$, if and only if $A$ and $B$ have the same dimensions and all corresponding elements in their arrays are identical. That is, $A = B$ if and only if $a_{ij} = b_{ij}$ for all $i$ and $j$.

EXAMPLES

1. $A = \begin{bmatrix} 1 & 0 \\ 0 & 1 \end{bmatrix} \qquad B = \begin{bmatrix} 1 & 0 \\ 1 & 1 \end{bmatrix} \qquad A \neq B$, since $a_{21} \neq b_{21}$

2. $A = \begin{bmatrix} 1 & 2 \\ 3 & 4 \\ 5 & 6 \end{bmatrix} \qquad B = \begin{bmatrix} 1 & 2 \\ 3 & 4 \\ 5 & 6 \end{bmatrix}$ Therefore $A = B$

3. $A = \begin{bmatrix} 1 & 4 \\ 2 & 5 \\ 3 & 6 \end{bmatrix} \qquad B = \begin{bmatrix} 1 & 2 & 3 \\ 4 & 5 & 6 \end{bmatrix}$

   $A \neq B$ because $A$ is a $3 \times 2$ matrix, whereas $B$ is a $2 \times 3$ matrix

4. $A = \begin{bmatrix} x_1 \\ x_2 \\ x_3 \end{bmatrix} \qquad B = \begin{bmatrix} 1 \\ 0 \\ 8 \end{bmatrix}$

   *If* $A = B$, then $x_1 = 1$, $x_2 = 0$, and $x_3 = 8$

### Addition of Matrices

DEFINITION We can add two matrices, $A = [a_{ij}]$ and $B = [b_{ij}]$, if and only if $A$ and $B$ have the same dimensions. $A + B = C$ such that $[a_{ij}] + [b_{ij}] = [c_{ij}]$, where $c_{ij} = a_{ij} + b_{ij}$ for all $i$ and $j$. Matrix $C$ has the same dimensions as $A$ and $B$.

The definition tells us that we can add two matrices of the same dimension; we cannot add two matrices of dissimilar dimensions. For example, we can add a $2 \times 3$ matrix to another $2 \times 3$ matrix. We cannot, however, add a $2 \times 3$ matrix to a $3 \times 2$ matrix. The definition also tells us that addition involves adding *corresponding* elements in each matrix. That is, given that the two matrices are of the same dimension, we may add them by summing the corresponding elements of each matrix. This means that we add the element that is in the first row, first column of matrix $A$ to the element that is in the first row, first column of matrix $B$. The result is the element that appears in the first row, first column of the summed matrix $C$.

Similarly, we pair and add the elements in the first row, second column of each matrix, and so forth. Formally, we can write this process as follows:

$$\begin{bmatrix} a_{11} & a_{12} & \cdots & a_{1n} \\ a_{21} & a_{22} & \cdots & a_{2n} \\ \vdots & \vdots & & \vdots \\ a_{m1} & a_{m2} & \cdots & a_{mn} \end{bmatrix} + \begin{bmatrix} b_{11} & b_{12} & \cdots & b_{1n} \\ b_{21} & b_{22} & \cdots & b_{2n} \\ \vdots & \vdots & & \vdots \\ b_{m1} & b_{m2} & \cdots & b_{mn} \end{bmatrix}$$

$$= \begin{bmatrix} a_{11} + b_{11} & a_{12} + b_{12} & \cdots & a_{1n} + b_{1n} \\ a_{21} + b_{21} & a_{22} + b_{22} & \cdots & a_{2n} + b_{2n} \\ \vdots & \vdots & & \vdots \\ a_{m1} + b_{m1} & a_{m2} + b_{m2} & \cdots & a_{mn} + b_{mn} \end{bmatrix} \tag{8.13}$$

EXAMPLES

1. $A = \begin{bmatrix} 1 & 2 \\ 3 & 4 \end{bmatrix} \qquad B = \begin{bmatrix} 5 & 6 \\ 7 & 8 \end{bmatrix} \qquad A + B = \begin{bmatrix} 6 & 8 \\ 10 & 12 \end{bmatrix}$

2. $A = \begin{bmatrix} 1 & 2 & 3 \\ 4 & 5 & 6 \end{bmatrix}$ $B = \begin{bmatrix} 4 & 5 & 6 \\ 1 & 2 & 3 \end{bmatrix}$ $A + B = \begin{bmatrix} 5 & 7 & 9 \\ 5 & 7 & 9 \end{bmatrix}$

3. $A = \begin{bmatrix} 1 & 2 & 3 \\ 4 & 5 & 6 \end{bmatrix}$ $B = \begin{bmatrix} 1 & 4 \\ 2 & 5 \\ 3 & 6 \end{bmatrix}$

We cannot find $A + B$ because matrices $A$ and $B$ have differing dimensions. $A$ is a $2 \times 3$ matrix, while $B$ is a $3 \times 2$ matrix.

**Subtraction of Matrices**

DEFINITION We can subtract two matrices $A = [a_{ij}]$ and $B = [b_{ij}]$ if and only if $A$ and $B$ have the same dimensions. $A - B = D$ such that $[a_{ij}] - [b_{ij}] = [d_{ij}]$, where $d_{ij} = a_{ij} - b_{ij}$ for all $i$ and $j$. Matrix $D$ has the same dimensions as $A$ and $B$.

Subtraction of matrices is analogous to addition of matrices. The matrices being subtracted must have the same dimension. The new matrix formed by the subtraction is composed of elements found by subtracting the corresponding elements of the original two matrices. Formally, we have

$$\begin{bmatrix} a_{11} & a_{12} & \cdots & a_{1n} \\ a_{21} & a_{22} & \cdots & a_{2n} \\ \vdots & \vdots & & \vdots \\ a_{m1} & a_{m2} & \cdots & a_{mn} \end{bmatrix} - \begin{bmatrix} b_{11} & b_{12} & \cdots & b_{1n} \\ b_{21} & b_{22} & \cdots & b_{2n} \\ \vdots & \vdots & & \vdots \\ b_{m1} & b_{m2} & \cdots & b_{mn} \end{bmatrix}$$

$$= \begin{bmatrix} a_{11} - b_{11} & a_{12} - b_{12} & \cdots & a_{1n} - b_{1n} \\ a_{21} - b_{21} & a_{22} - b_{22} & \cdots & a_{2n} - b_{2n} \\ \vdots & \vdots & & \vdots \\ a_{m1} - b_{m1} & a_{m2} - b_{m2} & \cdots & a_{mn} - b_{mn} \end{bmatrix} \tag{8.14}$$

EXAMPLES

1. $A = \begin{bmatrix} 4 & 8 \\ 10 & 12 \end{bmatrix}$ $B = \begin{bmatrix} 1 & 2 \\ 3 & 4 \end{bmatrix}$ $A - B = \begin{bmatrix} 3 & 6 \\ 7 & 8 \end{bmatrix}$

2. $A = \begin{bmatrix} 1 & 0 & 1 \\ 0 & 1 & 0 \end{bmatrix}$ $B = \begin{bmatrix} 1 & 2 & 3 \\ 4 & 5 & 6 \end{bmatrix}$ $A - B = \begin{bmatrix} 0 & -2 & -2 \\ -4 & -4 & -6 \end{bmatrix}$

3. $A = \begin{bmatrix} 2 & 5 \\ 4 & 6 \end{bmatrix}$ $B = \begin{bmatrix} 2 & 1 \\ 4 & 3 \\ 6 & 5 \end{bmatrix}$

$A - B$ cannot be found because the two matrices do not have the same dimensions.

**Commutative and Associative Laws for Matrix Addition and Subtraction**

*The Commutative Law*

The order in which we add or subtract matrices is irrelevant. The commutative law demonstrates this fact. You should observe that we treat subtraction as the addition of a negative number.

COMMUTATIVE LAW (ADDITION) Given two matrices $A$ and $B$,

$$A + B = B + A$$

*Proof*

$$A + B = [a_{ij}] + [b_{ij}] = [a_{ij} + b_{ij}] = [b_{ij} + a_{ij}] = [b_{ij}] + [a_{ij}] = B + A$$

EXAMPLE

$$A = \begin{bmatrix} 1 & 2 \\ 3 & 4 \end{bmatrix} \quad B = \begin{bmatrix} 5 & 6 \\ 7 & 8 \end{bmatrix} \quad A + B = \begin{bmatrix} 6 & 8 \\ 10 & 12 \end{bmatrix} = B + A$$

*The Associative Law*

The associative law deals with situations in which three or more matrices are being added. We can apply the associative law to subtraction by considering subtraction to be the addition of a negative number.

DEFINITION Given matrices $A$, $B$, and $C$,

$$A + (B + C) = (A + B) + C = A + B + C$$

*Proof*

$$\begin{aligned} A + (B + C) &= [a_{ij}] + [b_{ij} + c_{ij}] \\ &= [a_{ij} + b_{ij}] + [c_{ij}] = (A + B) + C \\ &= [a_{ij} + b_{ij} + c_{ij}] = A + B + C \end{aligned}$$

EXAMPLE

$$A = \begin{bmatrix} 1 & 0 \\ 0 & 1 \end{bmatrix} \quad B = \begin{bmatrix} 1 & 0 \\ 1 & 0 \end{bmatrix} \quad C = \begin{bmatrix} 0 & 1 \\ 0 & 1 \end{bmatrix}$$

$$A + (B + C) = \begin{bmatrix} 1 & 0 \\ 0 & 1 \end{bmatrix} + \begin{bmatrix} 1 & 1 \\ 1 & 1 \end{bmatrix} = \begin{bmatrix} 2 & 1 \\ 1 & 2 \end{bmatrix} = A + B + C$$

Also

$$(A + B) + C = \begin{bmatrix} 2 & 0 \\ 1 & 1 \end{bmatrix} + \begin{bmatrix} 0 & 1 \\ 0 & 1 \end{bmatrix} = \begin{bmatrix} 2 & 1 \\ 1 & 2 \end{bmatrix} = A + B + C$$

### Scalar Multiplication

The process of multiplying a matrix by a number (called a *scalar* in matrix terminology) is referred to as scalar multiplication.

DEFINITION Given a matrix $A = [a_{ij}]$ and a scalar $k$. The *scalar multiplication* of $k$ and $A$, written $kA$, is defined to be

$$kA = [ka_{ij}] = \begin{bmatrix} ka_{11} & ka_{12} & \cdots & ka_{1n} \\ ka_{21} & ka_{22} & \cdots & ka_{2n} \\ \vdots & \vdots & & \vdots \\ ka_{mn} & ka_{m2} & \cdots & ka_{mn} \end{bmatrix} = [a_{ij}k] = Ak$$

EXAMPLES

1. Let $k = 5$, and

$$A = \begin{bmatrix} 1 & 2 \\ 3 & 4 \end{bmatrix} \qquad \text{Then} \qquad kA = 5A = \begin{bmatrix} 5 & 10 \\ 15 & 20 \end{bmatrix}$$

2. Let $k = -3$, and

$$A = \begin{bmatrix} 1 & -2 & 3 \\ 4 & 5 & -6 \end{bmatrix} \qquad \text{Then} \qquad kA = -3A = \begin{bmatrix} -3 & 6 & -9 \\ -12 & -15 & 18 \end{bmatrix}$$

**Matrix Multiplication**

Matrix multiplication also has dimensional requirements associated with it. However, these requirements differ from those imposed in matrix addition and subtraction. Two matrices $A$ and $B$ can be multiplied together to form the product $AB$ if and only if the *column* dimension of $A$ is equal to the *row* dimension of $B$. That is, we may multiply an $m \times n$ matrix by an $n \times p$ matrix. An $m \times n$ matrix $A$ is said to be *postmultiplied* by an $n \times p$ matrix $B$ in order to form a new $m \times p$ matrix $C$. Or we could equivalently state that $n \times p$ matrix $B$ is *premultiplied* by $m \times n$ matrix $A$, once again yielding an $m \times p$ matrix $C$.

DEFINITION Given $A = [a_{ik}]$, an $m \times n$ matrix, and $B = [b_{kj}]$, an $n \times p$ matrix, where $a_{ik}$ is any element of $A$ and $b_{kj}$ is any element of $B$. Then $AB = C$, an $m \times p$ matrix whose elements are

$$c_{ij} = \sum_{k=1}^{n} a_{ik} b_{kj} \qquad \text{for all } i = 1, 2, \ldots, m \quad \text{and} \quad j = 1, 2, \ldots, p$$

Consider a $2 \times 2$ matrix

$$A = \begin{bmatrix} a_{11} & a_{12} \\ a_{21} & a_{22} \end{bmatrix} \qquad \text{which is postmultiplied by matrix} \qquad B = \begin{bmatrix} b_{11} \\ b_{21} \end{bmatrix}$$

a $2 \times 1$ matrix. The result is matrix

$$C = \begin{bmatrix} c_{11} \\ c_{12} \end{bmatrix}$$

a $2 \times 1$ matrix. $C$ is defined to be matrix $B$ premultiplied by matrix $A$. The reverse product, $BA$, is *not* defined because the dimensional requirements are not met. That is, $B$ is a $2 \times 1$ matrix, whereas $A$ is a $2 \times 2$ matrix. The number of columns in $B$ (which is 1) is not equal to the number of rows in $A$ (which is 2).

■ You must clearly understand the following concepts.

1. The product of matrices $A$ and $B$ is read, "$B$ is premultiplied by $A$" or "$A$ is postmultiplied by $B$."
2. In order to form the matrix product $AB$, the column dimension of $A$ must be equal to the row dimension of $B$.
3. If $AB$ is defined, then the result is a new matrix $C$ that exhibits the row dimension of $A$ and column dimension of $B$.

4. The happenstance that the product $AB$ is defined does not imply that the product $BA$ must also be defined.

EXAMPLES

1. $A = 2 \times 3$ matrix, while $B = 3 \times 3$ matrix. $AB = C = 2 \times 3$ matrix; however, $BA$ is not defined.
2. $A = 1 \times 3$ matrix, while $B = 3 \times 1$ matrix. $AB = C = 1 \times 1$ matrix and $BA = 3 \times 3$ square matrix. Even though both $AB$ and $BA$ are defined, they do not have the same dimensions.
3. $A = 5 \times 3$ matrix, while $B = 3 \times 2$ matrix. $AB = C = 5 \times 2$ matrix.
4. $A = \begin{bmatrix} 2 & 5 \\ 7 & 1 \\ 8 & 3 \end{bmatrix} \qquad B = \begin{bmatrix} 4 & 6 \\ 9 & 10 \end{bmatrix}$

$$AB = C = \begin{bmatrix} 2 & 5 \\ 7 & 1 \\ 8 & 3 \end{bmatrix} \cdot \begin{bmatrix} 4 & 6 \\ 9 & 10 \end{bmatrix}$$

$$= \begin{bmatrix} (2)(4) + (5)(9) & (2)(6) + (5)(10) \\ (7)(4) + (1)(9) & (7)(6) + (1)(10) \\ (8)(4) + (3)(9) & (8)(6) + (3)(10) \end{bmatrix}$$

$$= \begin{bmatrix} 53 & 62 \\ 37 & 52 \\ 59 & 78 \end{bmatrix}$$

Note that

$$c_{31} = 59 = \sum_{k=1}^{2} a_{3k} b_{k2} = (8)(4) + (3)(9)$$

The preceding examples indicate the dimensions of the matrix that results from matrix multiplication. Our approach to matrix multiplication has so far been mechanical. We shall now develop an intuitive understanding of matrix multiplication as well.

We have already dealt with linear equation systems of the form

$$\begin{aligned} a_{11}x_1 + a_{12}x_2 + \cdots + a_{1n}x_n &= c_1 \\ a_{21}x_1 + a_{22}x_2 + \cdots + a_{2n}x_n &= c_2 \\ \vdots \qquad \vdots \qquad\qquad \vdots \quad &\quad \vdots \\ a_{m1}x_1 + a_{m2}x_2 + \cdots + a_{mn}x_n &= c_m \end{aligned} \tag{8.15}$$

We previously learned how to abbreviate the system of linear equations given in Equation (8.15) as $AX = C$. Our definition of matrix equality enables us to state that matrix $C$ equals the product $AX$ if and only if element $c_i$ is given by

$$c_i = \sum_{k=1}^{n} a_{ik} x_k \qquad \text{for } i = 1, 2, \ldots, m \tag{8.16}$$

The subscripts of the terms in Equation (8.16) lead intuitively to the definition of matrix multiplication. Specifically, we observe that the subscript $k$ is used in both the $a_{ik}$ and the $x_k$ terms. This ensures that the number of columns in matrix $A$ is the same as the number of rows in matrix $X$. In more detailed form, the matrix multiplication $AX = C$ involves the following:

$$\begin{matrix} a_{11}x_1 + a_{12}x_2 + \cdots + a_{1n}x_n \\ a_{21}x_1 + a_{22}x_2 + \cdots + a_{2n}x_n \\ \vdots \qquad \vdots \qquad \vdots \\ a_{m1}x_1 + a_{m2}x_2 + \cdots + a_{mn}x_n \end{matrix} = \begin{bmatrix} \sum_{k=1}^{n} a_{1k}x_k \\ \sum_{k=1}^{n} a_{2k}x_k \\ \vdots \\ \sum_{k=1}^{n} a_{mk}x_k \end{bmatrix} = \begin{matrix} c_1 \\ c_2 \\ \vdots \\ c_m \end{matrix} \tag{8.17}$$

We now need to go from the somewhat familiar case above to the general case in which $A$ is once again an $m \times n$ matrix and $X$ is an $n \times p$ matrix. Any element $c_{ij}$ of the new matrix $AX = C$ is given by

$$c_{ij} = \sum_{k=1}^{n} a_{ik}x_{kj} \qquad \text{as } i = 1, 2, \ldots, m \text{ and } j = 1, 2, \ldots, p \tag{8.18}$$

In detail, the product $AX = C$ is given by

$$[a_{ik}][x_{kj}] = \begin{bmatrix} \sum_{k=1}^{n} a_{1k}x_{k1} & \cdots & \sum_{k=1}^{n} a_{1k}x_{kp} \\ \sum_{k=1}^{n} a_{2k}x_{k1} & \cdots & \sum_{k=1}^{n} a_{2k}x_{kp} \\ \vdots & & \vdots \\ \sum_{k=1}^{n} a_{mk}x_{k1} & \cdots & \sum_{k=1}^{n} a_{mk}x_{kp} \end{bmatrix} = [c_{ij}] \text{ as } i = 1, 2, \ldots, m \text{ and } j = 1, 2, \ldots, p \tag{8.19}$$

EXAMPLE The system of linear equations

$$\begin{aligned} 3x_1 + 4x_2 - x_3 &= 8 \\ 2x_1 - 5x_2 + 4x_3 &= 10 \\ 9x_1 + 11x_2 - 3x_3 &= 4 \end{aligned}$$

can be written in matrix notation as

$$\begin{bmatrix} 3 & 4 & -1 \\ 2 & -5 & 4 \\ 9 & 11 & -3 \end{bmatrix} \cdot \begin{bmatrix} x_1 \\ x_2 \\ x_3 \end{bmatrix} = \begin{bmatrix} 8 \\ 10 \\ 4 \end{bmatrix}$$

The coefficient matrix $A$ is $\begin{bmatrix} 3 & 4 & -1 \\ 2 & -5 & 4 \\ 9 & 11 & -3 \end{bmatrix}$

The column vector of variables $x$ is $\begin{bmatrix} x_1 \\ x_2 \\ x_3 \end{bmatrix}$

The column vector of constants $c$ is $\begin{bmatrix} 8 \\ 10 \\ 4 \end{bmatrix}$

Following the definition of matrix multiplication that we have developed,

$$c_2 = \sum_{k=1}^{3} a_{2k} x_k$$

that is,

$$10 = (2)(x_1) + (-5)(x_2) + (4)(x_3)$$

which is simply the second equation in the system.

Equation (8.19) above may appear a bit frightening. There is, however, a relatively simple way to remember what is supposed to be multiplied and what is supposed to be added. Note that the number of columns in matrix $A = [a_{ik}]$ is $n$, while the number of rows in matrix $X = [x_{kj}]$ is also $n$. Hence the multiplication is defined. The result of the multiplication $C = [c_{ij}]$ is a matrix of $m$ rows and $p$ columns. Matrix $A$ must have $i$ rows; matrix $X$ must have $j$ columns. The individual elements in matrix $C$ are given by

$$c_{ij} = \sum_{k=1}^{n} a_{ik} x_{kj} \qquad \text{as } i = 1, 2, \ldots, m \quad \text{and} \quad j = 1, 2, \ldots, p \tag{8.20}$$

That is, each element $c_{ij}$ depends on the elements in row $i$ of matrix $A$ and the elements in column $j$ of matrix $X$. Figure 8.1 demonstrates this relationship visually. The $i$th row of matrix $A$ times the $j$th column of matrix $X$ results in element $c_{ij}$ ($i$th row, $j$th column) in matrix $C$. The $i$th row in matrix $A$, the $j$th column in matrix $X$, and element $c_{ij}$ in matrix $C$ are each enclosed in a shaded box in Figure 8.1.

A specific example should drive home what Equation (8.19) and Figure 8.1 have tried to demonstrate. Consider a $2 \times 2$ matrix $A$ and a $2 \times 3$ matrix $B$. $A \cdot B =$ another matrix $C$, which must have the dimension $2 \times 3$.

Figure 8.1 Matrix multiplication $AX = C$

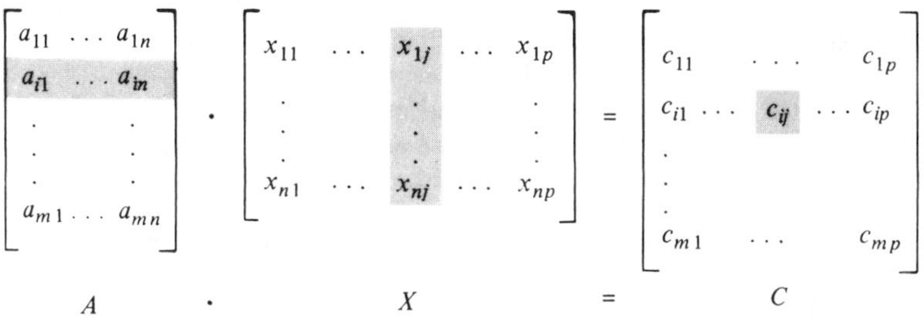

$$\underset{A}{\begin{bmatrix} a_{11} & a_{12} \\ a_{21} & a_{22} \end{bmatrix}} \quad \underset{B}{\begin{bmatrix} b_{11} & b_{12} & b_{13} \\ b_{21} & b_{22} & b_{23} \end{bmatrix}} = \underset{C}{\begin{bmatrix} c_{11} & c_{12} & c_{13} \\ c_{21} & c_{22} & c_{23} \end{bmatrix}} \tag{8.21}$$

where

$c_{11} = a_{11}b_{11} + a_{12}b_{21}$ (row 1 entries in $A$; column 1 entries in $B$)
$c_{21} = a_{21}b_{11} + a_{22}b_{21}$ (row 2 entries in $A$; column 1 entries in $B$)
$c_{12} = a_{11}b_{12} + a_{12}b_{22}$ (row 1 entries in $A$; column 2 entries in $B$)
$c_{22} = a_{21}b_{12} + a_{22}b_{22}$ (row 2 entries in $A$; column 2 entries in $B$)
$c_{13} = a_{11}b_{13} + a_{12}b_{23}$ (row 1 entries in $A$; column 3 entries in $B$)
$c_{23} = a_{21}b_{13} + a_{22}b_{23}$ (row 2 entries in $A$; column 3 entries in $B$)

Any element $c_{ij}$ is the result of an operation performed on the $i$th row of matrix $A$ and the $j$th column of matrix $B$. For example, $c_{13}$ involves the first row of matrix $A$ and the third column of matrix $B$.

EXAMPLES

1. Let $A = \begin{bmatrix} 1 & 2 \\ 3 & 4 \end{bmatrix}$ $\quad B = \begin{bmatrix} 1 & 0 & 2 \\ 5 & 6 & 3 \end{bmatrix}$

$$AB = \begin{bmatrix} (1 \times 1) + (2 \times 5) & (1 \times 0) + (2 \times 6) & (1 \times 2) + (2 \times 3) \\ (3 \times 1) + (4 \times 5) & (3 \times 0) + (4 \times 6) & (3 \times 2) + (4 \times 3) \end{bmatrix}$$

$$= \begin{bmatrix} 11 & 12 & 8 \\ 23 & 24 & 18 \end{bmatrix}$$

2. Let $A = [1 \quad 2 \quad 3]$ $\quad B = \begin{bmatrix} 3 & 1 \\ 2 & 0 \\ 1 & 2 \end{bmatrix}$ $\quad AB = [10 \quad 7]$

3. Let $A = [1 \quad 2 \quad 3]$ $\quad B = \begin{bmatrix} 3 \\ 2 \\ 1 \end{bmatrix}$ $\quad AB = 10 = \text{scalar}$

$$BA = \begin{bmatrix} 3 & 6 & 9 \\ 2 & 4 & 6 \\ 1 & 2 & 3 \end{bmatrix} = \text{square matrix}$$

*Commutative, Associative, and Distributive Laws of Matrix Multiplication*

1. *Commutative law*
Matrix multiplication requires that the column dimension of the premultiplier be equal to the row dimension of the postmultiplier in order for multiplication to be defined. This requirement virtually *eliminates* the property of commutability! In general, even if the products $AB$ and $BA$ are both defined, $AB \neq BA$. Hence they do not "commute," and the commutative law does not hold.[3] Example 3 above illustrates this circumstance.

[3] If you are observant, you will note that there actually are exceptions to this rule. When scalar $k$ and matrix $A$ are multiplied, then $kA = Ak$. The case of an identity matrix (to be defined shortly) is another exception.

2. *Associative law*
The associative law of matrix multiplication tells us that $A(BC) = (AB)C = ABC$, *provided* that the dimensional requirements for multiplication are satisfied. The following dimensional requirements must hold:

*Dimension*

$$\underset{m\times n}{A}\cdot(\underset{n\times p}{B}\cdot\underset{p\times q}{C}) = (\underset{m\times n}{A}\cdot\underset{n\times p}{B})\cdot\underset{p\times q}{C} = \underset{m\times n}{A}\cdot\underset{n\times p}{B}\cdot\underset{p\times q}{C}$$

$$\text{where } B\cdot C \text{ is } n\times q, \quad A\cdot B \text{ is } m\times p, \quad A\cdot B\cdot C \text{ is } m\times q$$

EXAMPLE Let

$$A = \begin{bmatrix} 1 & 2 \\ 3 & 4 \end{bmatrix} \quad B = \begin{bmatrix} 1 & 0 & 2 \\ 5 & 6 & 3 \end{bmatrix} \quad C = \begin{bmatrix} 1 & 0 \\ 0 & 2 \\ 3 & 1 \end{bmatrix}$$

$$(AB)C = \begin{bmatrix} 11 & 12 & 8 \\ 23 & 24 & 18 \end{bmatrix} \cdot \begin{bmatrix} 1 & 0 \\ 0 & 2 \\ 3 & 1 \end{bmatrix} = \begin{bmatrix} 35 & 32 \\ 77 & 66 \end{bmatrix} = ABC$$

$$A(BC) = \begin{bmatrix} 1 & 2 \\ 3 & 4 \end{bmatrix} \cdot \begin{bmatrix} 7 & 2 \\ 14 & 15 \end{bmatrix} = \begin{bmatrix} 35 & 32 \\ 77 & 66 \end{bmatrix} = ABC$$

3. *Distributive law*
With respect to matrix multiplication, the distributive law tells us that $A(B + C) = AB + AC$ and that $(B + C)A = BA + CA$, *provided* once again that the dimensional requirements for addition and multiplication are satisfied. That is, the following dimensional requirements must be met:

$$\underset{m\times n}{A}\cdot(\underset{n\times p}{B}+\underset{n\times p}{C}) = (\underset{m\times n}{A}\cdot\underset{n\times p}{B}+\underset{m\times n}{A}\cdot\underset{n\times p}{C}) = \underset{m\times p}{D}$$

$$m\times n \quad n\times p \quad n\times p = m\times n \quad n\times p \quad m\times n \quad n\times p = m\times p$$

*Proof*

$$\sum_j a_{ij}(b_{jk} + c_{jk}) = \sum_j a_{ij}b_{jk} + \sum_j a_{ij}c_{jk}$$

EXAMPLE Let

$$A = \begin{bmatrix} 1 & 2 \\ 3 & 4 \end{bmatrix} \quad B = \begin{bmatrix} 1 & 0 & 2 \\ 5 & 6 & 3 \end{bmatrix} \quad C = \begin{bmatrix} 1 & 0 & 3 \\ 0 & 2 & 1 \end{bmatrix}$$

$$A(B + C) = \begin{bmatrix} 1 & 2 \\ 3 & 4 \end{bmatrix} \cdot \begin{bmatrix} 2 & 0 & 5 \\ 5 & 8 & 4 \end{bmatrix} = \begin{bmatrix} 12 & 16 & 13 \\ 26 & 32 & 31 \end{bmatrix}$$

$$AB + AC = \begin{bmatrix} 11 & 12 & 8 \\ 23 & 24 & 18 \end{bmatrix} + \begin{bmatrix} 1 & 4 & 5 \\ 3 & 8 & 13 \end{bmatrix} = \begin{bmatrix} 12 & 16 & 13 \\ 26 & 32 & 31 \end{bmatrix}$$

**EXERCISE 8.1**

1. Find the coefficient matrix for each of the following linear equation systems.

(a)
$$\begin{aligned} 3x_1 + 2x_2 + 4x_3 &= 17 \\ x_1 + 2x_2 + x_3 &= 4 \\ 5x_1 + x_2 + 3x_3 &= -2 \end{aligned}$$

(b)
$$\begin{aligned} x_1 + x_2 &= 4 \\ 3x_1 + 2x_2 &= 0 \end{aligned}$$

(c)
$$\begin{aligned} 3x_1 + 4x_2 - x_3 &= 4 \\ 0.5x_1 - x_2 + 3x_3 &= 8 \\ x_1 + 0.25x_2 - 8x_3 &= 0 \end{aligned}$$

(d)
$$\begin{aligned} x + y - z &= 10 \\ -5y + 3z &= 4 \\ -3x + 2y &= -3 \end{aligned}$$

(e)
$$\begin{aligned} x + 2y + 4z - w &= -6 \\ -4x + 2w &= 7 \\ 3y + z - 4w &= 0 \\ -x - y + z &= 6 \end{aligned}$$

2. State the dimension of the following matrices.

(a) $A = \begin{bmatrix} 1 & 2 & 1 \\ 3 & 4 & 0 \\ 0 & 0 & 2 \end{bmatrix}$ (b) $B = \begin{bmatrix} 1 & 2 & 3 \\ 4 & 5 & 6 \end{bmatrix}$

(c) $C = \begin{bmatrix} 1 \\ 2 \end{bmatrix}$ (d) $D = \begin{bmatrix} 0 & 19 & 9 \\ 0 & 26 & 12 \\ 0 & 33 & 15 \\ 2 & 7 & 4 \end{bmatrix}$

(e) $E = \begin{bmatrix} 9 & 12 & 15 \\ 19 & 26 & 33 \end{bmatrix}$ (f) $F = \begin{bmatrix} 2 & 3 \\ 4 & 5 \end{bmatrix}$

(g) $G = [-9 \quad 5 \quad 1]$ (h) $H = \begin{bmatrix} 1 & 2 & -1 & 2 & 1 \\ 3 & 0 & -6 & 0 & 1 \\ 0 & 0 & 8 & 0 & 1 \\ 2 & -11 & 10 & 15 & 5 \end{bmatrix}$

Perform the indicated matrix operations whenever the matrices meet the required dimensional constraints.

3. Given that

$$A = \begin{bmatrix} -5 & -6 & 2 \\ 3 & 5 & 4 \end{bmatrix} \quad \text{and} \quad B = \begin{bmatrix} 3 & 0 & 8 \\ 3 & 2 & -4 \end{bmatrix}$$

find (a) $A + B$, (b) $A - B$, (c) $AB$, (d) $BA$, (e) $3A$.

4. Given that

$$A = \begin{bmatrix} 3 & 1 & 4 \\ 2 & 5 & 6 \end{bmatrix} \quad \text{and} \quad B = \begin{bmatrix} 1 & 3 \\ 2 & 1 \\ 4 & 0 \end{bmatrix}$$

find (a) $A + B$, (b) $AB$, (c) $BA$.

5. Given that $A = [1 \quad 2 \quad 3]$, $B = [4 \quad 5 \quad 6]$, and $C = [7 \quad 8 \quad 9]$, find (a) $A + B + C$, (b) $A - (B + C)$, (c) $2A + 3B - 4C$.
6. Given that

$$A = \begin{bmatrix} -2 \\ 0 \\ 4 \end{bmatrix} \qquad B = [1 \quad 1 \quad 2] \qquad \text{and} \qquad C = [2 \quad 6 \quad 0]$$

find (a) $AB$, (b) $BA$, (c) $A(B + C) = AB + AC$.
7. Given that

$$A = \begin{bmatrix} 2 & 3 \\ 4 & 5 \end{bmatrix} \qquad B = \begin{bmatrix} 3 & 5 \\ 2 & 0 \end{bmatrix} \qquad C = \begin{bmatrix} 5 & 4 \\ 0 & -4 \end{bmatrix}$$

find (a) $A + B$, (b) $A(B + C)$, (c) $ABC$, (d) $CBA$.
8. Given that

$$A = \begin{bmatrix} 5 & 6 & 1 & 3 \\ 1 & 2 & 0 & -1 \end{bmatrix} \qquad \text{and} \qquad B = \begin{bmatrix} 2 & 1 & 4 \\ 1 & 3 & 1 \\ 1 & 0 & -2 \\ 0 & 2 & -1 \end{bmatrix} \qquad \text{find } AB$$

## SPECIAL TYPES OF MATRICES

Certain types of matrices occur with such frequency that they are easily worth additional study. Other matrices have elements or dimensions that sometimes present problems. In this section we consider the following specific situations: the identity matrix, the diagonal matrix, the scalar matrix, the null matrix, and the transpose of a matrix.

### Identity Matrix

In the real number system, the number one (1) has the unique property that for any number $a$, we have $1 \cdot a = a \cdot 1 = a$, and $1 \cdot 1 = 1$. In matrix algebra, the identity or unit matrix plays the same role as does the number 1 in ordinary algebra.

DEFINITION The identity matrix of order $n$, denoted by the symbol $I$ or $I_n$, is a square matrix whose main, or principal, diagonal contains no other elements except the number 1. All other elements in the identity matrix are zeros.

$I_n$ is the identity matrix if

$$I_n = \begin{bmatrix} 1 & 0 & 0 & \cdots & 0 \\ 0 & 1 & 0 & \cdots & 0 \\ 0 & 0 & 1 & \cdots & 0 \\ \vdots & \vdots & \vdots & & \vdots \\ 0 & 0 & 0 & \cdots & 1 \end{bmatrix} \qquad (8.22)$$

The subscript $n$ on the identity matrix $I_n$ indicates the dimension of the matrix. We can see that the main diagonal of the identity matrix in Equation (8.22) consists of the elements beginning with the element in the upper left-hand corner of the matrix and proceeding diagonally to the lower right-hand corner of the matrix. The main diagonal therefore contains the elements $a_{11}$, $a_{22}$, $a_{33}, \ldots, a_{nn}$. In the case at hand, every element of the main diagonal is the number 1.

The identity matrix is sometimes written in shorthand as

$$I = [\delta_{ij}]. \qquad \delta_{ij}, \text{ known as } \textit{Kronecker's delta,} \qquad = \begin{cases} 1, & i = j \\ 0, & i \neq j \end{cases}$$

EXAMPLES

1. $I = I_2 = \begin{bmatrix} 1 & 0 \\ 0 & 1 \end{bmatrix}$  2. $I = I_3 = \begin{bmatrix} 1 & 0 & 0 \\ 0 & 1 & 0 \\ 0 & 0 & 1 \end{bmatrix}$

If $A$ is a square matrix of order $n$, and $I_n$ is the identity matrix, then

$$IA = AI = A \tag{8.23}$$

■ There is a peculiarity associated with the dimensional requirements for matrix multiplication about which you should be aware. When $A$ is a non-square matrix, say $m \times n$, then Equation (8.23) above still holds, but in a very particular and limited way.

$$\underset{m \times m}{I} \cdot \underset{m \times n}{A} = \underset{m \times n}{A} \quad \text{and} \quad \underset{m \times n}{A} \cdot \underset{n \times n}{I} = \underset{m \times n}{A} \quad \text{but } I_m \neq I_n$$

That is, the identity matrix in the term $IA$ is not the same identity matrix found in the term $AI$. The dimensional requirements for an identity matrix are different, depending on whether we premultiply ($IA$) or postmultiply ($AI$).

Another circumstance of interest occurs when $A = I$. Then

$$AI = I \cdot I = I^2 = I \tag{8.24}$$

In general, Equation (8.24) implies that

$$(I)^k = I \qquad \text{where } k = 1, 2, \ldots, n \tag{8.25}$$

Equation (8.25) tells us that an identity matrix raised to any power is in fact equal to itself. Such a matrix is an *idempotent matrix.*

DEFINITION An *idempotent matrix* is one that, when raised to any power, does not change in value. $A$ is an idempotent matrix if $A \cdot A = A$.

### Diagonal Matrix

The concept of a diagonal matrix is directly related to the idea of the principal diagonal of a matrix.

DEFINITION A *diagonal matrix* is a square matrix in which all elements both above and below the main diagonal are zero.

Equation (8.26) shows an $n \times n$ diagonal matrix.

$$D = \begin{bmatrix} a_{11} & 0 & \cdots & 0 \\ 0 & a_{22} & \cdots & 0 \\ 0 & 0 & \cdots & 0 \\ \vdots & \vdots & \vdots & \vdots \\ 0 & 0 & 0 & a_{nn} \end{bmatrix} \tag{8.26}$$

EXAMPLES

1. $\begin{bmatrix} 1 & 0 \\ 0 & 2 \end{bmatrix}$ is a diagonal matrix.
2. $\begin{bmatrix} 1 & 0 & 0 \\ 0 & 0 & 0 \\ 0 & 0 & 2 \end{bmatrix}$ is a diagonal matrix. Note that only one nonzero value is required on the main diagonal.
3. $\begin{bmatrix} 1 & 0 & 0 \\ 0 & 1 & 0 \\ -1 & -1 & 0 \end{bmatrix}$ is an idempotent matrix.
4. The identity matrix is an example of a diagonal matrix: $\begin{bmatrix} 1 & 0 \\ 0 & 1 \end{bmatrix}$

### Scalar Matrix

DEFINITION A scalar matrix is any square matrix $S$ such that

$S = \lambda I = [\lambda s_{ij}]$, where $\lambda$ is any scalar.

EXAMPLE

$$\begin{bmatrix} 3 & 0 & 0 \\ 0 & 3 & 0 \\ 0 & 0 & 3 \end{bmatrix} = 3 \begin{bmatrix} 1 & 0 & 0 \\ 0 & 1 & 0 \\ 0 & 0 & 1 \end{bmatrix} = 3I \qquad \text{a scalar matrix}$$

### Null Matrix

In the real number system, zero has the unique property that for any number $a$, we have $0 \cdot a = a \cdot 0 = 0$. Also, $a + 0 = 0 + a = a$. In matrix algebra, the *null* or *zero* matrix plays a role similar to that of zero in the real number system.

DEFINITION A null or zero matrix consists of elements that are all equal to zero.

EXAMPLE

$$0 = \begin{bmatrix} 0 & 0 \\ 0 & 0 \end{bmatrix} \qquad 0 = \begin{bmatrix} 0 \\ 0 \\ 0 \end{bmatrix} \qquad 0 = [0 \quad 0 \quad 0]$$

The null matrix is not restricted to being a square matrix, as are the identity, diagonal, and scalar matrices. A square null matrix is idempotent, although a nonsquare null matrix is not.

The null matrix, like the number 0 in the real number system, has several unique qualities. For instance, the commutative law for addition of matrices holds when the null matrix and another matrix $A$ are added if both the null matrix and the $A$ matrix satisfy the usual dimensional requirements. That is,

$$\underset{m \times n}{A} + \underset{m \times n}{0} = \underset{m \times n}{0} + \underset{m \times n}{A} = \underset{m \times n}{A} \tag{8.27}$$

■ The commutative law with respect to the multiplication of matrices presents a more difficult problem when a null matrix is involved. The two products $A \cdot 0 = 0$ and $0 \cdot A = 0$ both result in a null matrix. However, if matrix $A$ is nonsquare in nature, then the products ($A \cdot 0$ and $0 \cdot A$) *will not commute.* That is,

$$\underset{m \times n}{A} \cdot \underset{n \times p}{0} = \underset{m \times p}{0} \neq \underset{q \times m}{0} \cdot \underset{m \times n}{A} = \underset{q \times n}{0} \tag{8.28}$$

On the other hand, if both matrix $A$ and the null matrix are square, then the two products will commute.

$$\underset{m \times m}{A} \cdot \underset{m \times m}{0} = \underset{m \times m}{0} \cdot \underset{m \times m}{A} = \underset{m \times m}{0} \tag{8.29}$$

### A Digression on Matrix Algebra

There are three instances in which the intuition we have developed with reference to the algebra of numbers interferes with the proper application of matrix algebra.

CASE 1 We have already discussed the situation in which the product $AB$ does commute in the algebra of numbers, but does not commute in matrix algebra. For example, $5 \cdot 6 = 6 \cdot 5 = 30$, while

$$\begin{bmatrix} 1 & 0 \\ 2 & 1 \end{bmatrix} \cdot \begin{bmatrix} 2 & 3 \\ 2 & 4 \end{bmatrix} = \begin{bmatrix} 2 & 3 \\ 6 & 10 \end{bmatrix} \neq \begin{bmatrix} 2 & 3 \\ 2 & 4 \end{bmatrix} \cdot \begin{bmatrix} 1 & 0 \\ 2 & 1 \end{bmatrix} = \begin{bmatrix} 8 & 3 \\ 10 & 4 \end{bmatrix}$$

CASE 2 Given two real numbers $a$ and $b$, we know from number algebra that if $ab = 0$, then $a = 0$ and/or $b = 0$. However, in matrix algebra, the product $AB = 0$ *does not imply* that $A = 0$ and/or that $B = 0$.

EXAMPLES

1. Let $A = \begin{bmatrix} 0 & 0 \\ -2 & 3 \end{bmatrix}$ $\quad B = \begin{bmatrix} 0 & 3 \\ 0 & 2 \end{bmatrix}$ $\quad AB = \begin{bmatrix} 0 & 0 \\ 0 & 0 \end{bmatrix}$

2. Let $A = \begin{bmatrix} 1 & 3 \\ 2 & 6 \end{bmatrix}$ $\quad B = \begin{bmatrix} -3 & 6 \\ 1 & -2 \end{bmatrix}$ $\quad AB = \begin{bmatrix} 0 & 0 \\ 0 & 0 \end{bmatrix}$

CASE 3 Given three real numbers $a$, $b$, and $c$, we know from number algebra that when $ab = ac$ (with $a \neq 0$), $b = c$. Once again, however, we find that this relationship does not hold in matrix algebra. For example, given matrices $A$, $B$, and $C$ such that $AB = AC$, it does not follow that $B$ and $C$ are identical matrices such that $B = C$.

EXAMPLE Let

$$A = \begin{bmatrix} 1 & 3 \\ 2 & 6 \end{bmatrix} \qquad B = \begin{bmatrix} 2 & 2 \\ 2 & 4 \end{bmatrix} \qquad C = \begin{bmatrix} -4 & 2 \\ 4 & 4 \end{bmatrix}$$

Then

$$AB = \begin{bmatrix} 8 & 14 \\ 16 & 28 \end{bmatrix} = AC.$$

However, $B \neq C$.

### The Transpose of a Matrix

We are now familiar with the meaning of the dimension of a matrix. The occasion sometimes arises, especially where matrix multiplication is concerned, when we need to form a new matrix whose rows and columns are interchanged in such a way that they reverse the dimension of the original matrix. Such a new matrix is referred to as the *transpose* of the original matrix.

DEFINITION Given an $m \times n$ matrix labeled $A$. The *transpose* of $A$, denoted by $A'$ or $A^T$, is a new matrix whose rows are the columns of $A$ and whose columns are the rows of $A$, so that the new matrix has the dimension $n \times m$. That is, if

$$A = \begin{bmatrix} a_{11} & a_{12} & \cdots & a_{1n} \\ a_{21} & a_{22} & \cdots & a_{2n} \\ \vdots & \vdots & & \vdots \\ a_{m1} & a_{m2} & \cdots & a_{mn} \end{bmatrix} = [a_{ij}]$$

then

$$A' = \begin{bmatrix} a_{11} & a_{21} & \cdots & a_{m1} \\ a_{12} & a_{22} & \cdots & a_{m2} \\ \vdots & \vdots & & \vdots \\ a_{1n} & a_{2n} & \cdots & a_{mn} \end{bmatrix} = [a_{ji}]$$

Note that the original matrix $A$ has the dimension $m \times n$, while the transpose of $A$, $A'$, has the dimension $n \times m$.

EXAMPLES

1. Let

$$A = \begin{bmatrix} 1 & 2 \\ 3 & 4 \\ 5 & 6 \end{bmatrix} \qquad \text{then} \qquad A' = \begin{bmatrix} 1 & 3 & 5 \\ 2 & 4 & 6 \end{bmatrix}$$

   $A$ is a $3 \times 2$ matrix, while $A'$ is a $2 \times 3$ matrix.

2. Let

$$B = [1 \quad 2 \quad 3] \qquad B' = \begin{bmatrix} 1 \\ 2 \\ 3 \end{bmatrix}$$

$B$ is a $1 \times 3$ matrix, while $B'$ is a $3 \times 1$ matrix. The transpose of an $n$-dimensional row vector is an $n$-dimensional column vector.

3. Given that

$$I = \begin{bmatrix} 1 & 0 & 0 \\ 0 & 1 & 0 \\ 0 & 0 & 1 \end{bmatrix} \qquad \text{then} \qquad I' = \begin{bmatrix} 1 & 0 & 0 \\ 0 & 1 & 0 \\ 0 & 0 & 1 \end{bmatrix}$$

That is, $I = I'$.

4. $$A = \begin{bmatrix} 2 & 0 & 0 \\ 0 & 4 & 0 \\ 0 & 0 & 6 \end{bmatrix} = A'$$

Examples 3 and 4 demonstrate that the transpose of a diagonal matrix is equal to itself.

*Properties of Transposed Matrices*

Transposed matrices exhibit four properties that are of immediate interest to us.

PROPERTY 1 $(A')' = A$. That is, the transposed matrix of an already transposed matrix is the original matrix.

*Proof* $A' = [a_{ij}]' = [a_{ji}]$ and $(A')' = [a_{ji}]' = [a_{ij}]$.

EXAMPLE Let

$$A = \begin{bmatrix} 1 & 5 \\ -3 & 6 \end{bmatrix} \qquad \text{then} \qquad A' = \begin{bmatrix} 1 & -3 \\ 5 & 6 \end{bmatrix} \qquad \text{and} \qquad (A')' = \begin{bmatrix} 1 & 5 \\ -3 & 6 \end{bmatrix} = A$$

PROPERTY 2 Given $A$, an $m \times n$ matrix, and $B$, an $m \times n$ matrix. $(A \pm B)' = A' \pm B'$, where $A'$ and $B'$ are both $n \times m$ matrices. In words, this property asserts that the transpose of a sum of two matrices is the sum of the transposes of those two matrices.

*Proof* Let $A = [a_{ij}]$ and $B = [b_{ij}]$ such that $C = [c_{ij}] = A \pm B$. Then

$$[c_{ij}]' = [c_{ji}] = [a_{ji}] \pm [b_{ji}] = [a_{ij}]' \pm [b_{ij}]'$$

We can extend this result to the addition or subtraction of a finite number of matrices such that

$$(A_1 \pm A_2 \pm \cdots \pm A_n)' = A_1' \pm A_2' \pm \cdots \pm A_n'$$

EXAMPLES

1. Let

$$A = \begin{bmatrix} 1 & 5 \\ 0 & 8 \\ 2 & 1 \end{bmatrix} \qquad B = \begin{bmatrix} 1 & 0 \\ 3 & 2 \\ -4 & 1 \end{bmatrix}$$

Then

$$A + B = \begin{bmatrix} 2 & 5 \\ 3 & 10 \\ -2 & 2 \end{bmatrix}$$

$$(A + B)' = \begin{bmatrix} 2 & 3 & -2 \\ 5 & 10 & 2 \end{bmatrix} \qquad A' = \begin{bmatrix} 1 & 0 & 2 \\ 5 & 8 & 1 \end{bmatrix}$$

$$B' = \begin{bmatrix} 1 & 3 & -4 \\ 0 & 2 & 1 \end{bmatrix} \quad \text{and} \quad A' + B' = \begin{bmatrix} 2 & 3 & -2 \\ 5 & 10 & 2 \end{bmatrix}$$

2. Let

$$C = \begin{bmatrix} 1 & 2 \\ 3 & 4 \end{bmatrix} \qquad D = \begin{bmatrix} 1 & 0 \\ 0 & 1 \end{bmatrix}$$

Then

$$(C + D) = \begin{bmatrix} 2 & 2 \\ 3 & 5 \end{bmatrix} \qquad (C + D)' = \begin{bmatrix} 2 & 3 \\ 2 & 5 \end{bmatrix} \qquad C' = \begin{bmatrix} 1 & 3 \\ 2 & 4 \end{bmatrix}$$

$$D' = \begin{bmatrix} 1 & 0 \\ 0 & 1 \end{bmatrix} \quad \text{and} \quad C' + D' = \begin{bmatrix} 2 & 3 \\ 2 & 5 \end{bmatrix}$$

PROPERTY 3 Given matrix $A$, which has the dimensions $m \times n$, and matrix $B$, which has the dimensions $n \times p$. Then $(AB)' = B'A'$. That is, the transpose of the product of these two matrices is the product of the individual transposes of these matrices in *reverse order*.

*Proof* Let $A = [a_{ik}]$; $B = [b_{kj}]$; $C = [c_{ij}] = AB$. Then

$$c_{ij} = \sum_k a_{ik} b_{kj} \qquad \text{and} \qquad c'_{ij} = c_{ji} = \sum_k a_{jk} b_{ki} = \sum_k a'_{kj} b'_{ik} = \sum_k b'_{ik} a'_{kj}$$

We can extend this result to include the product of a finite number of matrices, for example,

$$(A_1 \cdot A_2 \cdot \cdots \cdot A_n)' = A'_n \cdot \cdots \cdot A'_2 \cdot A'_1$$

EXAMPLES

1. Let

$$A = \begin{bmatrix} 3 & 2 \\ 0 & 5 \end{bmatrix} \qquad B = \begin{bmatrix} 2 & 0 \\ 1 & 3 \end{bmatrix}$$

Then

$$AB = \begin{bmatrix} 8 & 6 \\ 5 & 15 \end{bmatrix} \quad (AB)' = \begin{bmatrix} 8 & 5 \\ 6 & 15 \end{bmatrix} \quad A' = \begin{bmatrix} 3 & 0 \\ 2 & 5 \end{bmatrix} \quad B' = \begin{bmatrix} 2 & 1 \\ 0 & 3 \end{bmatrix}$$

and $B'A' = \begin{bmatrix} 8 & 5 \\ 6 & 15 \end{bmatrix}$ Thus $(AB)' = \begin{bmatrix} 8 & 5 \\ 6 & 15 \end{bmatrix} = B'A'$

2. Let

$$A = \begin{bmatrix} 1 & 3 & -1 \\ 2 & 0 & 0 \\ 0 & -1 & 6 \end{bmatrix} \quad B = \begin{bmatrix} 1 & 0 \\ -1 & 2 \\ 1 & 3 \end{bmatrix}$$

Then

$$AB = \begin{bmatrix} -3 & 3 \\ 2 & 0 \\ 7 & 16 \end{bmatrix} \quad (AB)' = \begin{bmatrix} -3 & 2 & 7 \\ 3 & 0 & 16 \end{bmatrix}$$

$$A' = \begin{bmatrix} 1 & 2 & 0 \\ 3 & 0 & -1 \\ -1 & 0 & 6 \end{bmatrix} \quad B' = \begin{bmatrix} 1 & -1 & 1 \\ 0 & 2 & 3 \end{bmatrix}$$

Then

$$B'A' = \begin{bmatrix} -3 & 2 & 7 \\ 3 & 0 & 16 \end{bmatrix}$$

Thus

$$(AB)' = \begin{bmatrix} -3 & 2 & 7 \\ 3 & 0 & 16 \end{bmatrix} = B'A'$$

3. Let

$$A = \begin{bmatrix} 2 & 1 \\ 3 & 4 \end{bmatrix} \quad B = \begin{bmatrix} 0 & 3 & -1 \\ 1 & 0 & 2 \end{bmatrix} \quad C = \begin{bmatrix} 3 & 2 & 1 \\ 2 & -1 & 0 \\ 1 & 0 & -1 \end{bmatrix}$$

Then

$$ABC = \begin{bmatrix} 15 & -4 & 1 \\ 35 & -1 & -1 \end{bmatrix} \quad \text{and} \quad (ABC)' = \begin{bmatrix} 15 & 35 \\ -4 & -1 \\ 1 & -1 \end{bmatrix}$$

$$A' = \begin{bmatrix} 2 & 3 \\ 1 & 4 \end{bmatrix} \quad B' = \begin{bmatrix} 0 & 1 \\ 3 & 0 \\ -1 & 2 \end{bmatrix}$$

$$C' = \begin{bmatrix} 3 & 2 & 1 \\ 2 & -1 & 0 \\ 1 & 0 & -1 \end{bmatrix} \quad \text{and} \quad C'B'A' = \begin{bmatrix} 15 & 35 \\ -4 & -1 \\ 1 & -1 \end{bmatrix}$$

PROPERTY 4 When the transpose of a square matrix results in the original matrix, the original matrix is said to be *symmetric about its main diagonal.* That is, if $A = A'$, then we have a symmetric matrix. The elements in matrix $A$ that are above the main diagonal are a mirror image of the elements of matrix $A$ that are below the main diagonal.

EXAMPLES

1. Let

$$A = \begin{bmatrix} 1 & 2 & 4 \\ 2 & 3 & 5 \\ 4 & 5 & 6 \end{bmatrix}$$

Then $A = A'$, so that $A$ is symmetric. Note that the elements above the main diagonal of $A$ are 2, 4, and 5, respectively. The elements below the main diagonal of $A$ are identical.

2. Let

$$I = \begin{bmatrix} 1 & 0 & 0 \\ 0 & 1 & 0 \\ 0 & 0 & 1 \end{bmatrix}$$

then $I = I'$, so that $I$ is symmetric. Matrix $I$ is both a diagonal matrix and an identity matrix. All diagonal matrices are symmetric.

EXERCISE 8.2

Find the transpose of each of the following matrices.

1. $\begin{bmatrix} 1 & 3 & 4 \\ 5 & -1 & -1 \end{bmatrix}$
2. $\begin{bmatrix} -12 & 5 \\ 0 & 8 \\ -5 & 4 \end{bmatrix}$
3. $\begin{bmatrix} 4 & -2 \\ -2 & 1 \end{bmatrix}$
4. $[1 \quad 2 \quad 5]$
5. $\begin{bmatrix} 4 \\ 0 \\ -3 \end{bmatrix}$
6. $\begin{bmatrix} 1 & -1 & 2 \\ 0 & 3 & 4 \end{bmatrix}$
7. $\begin{bmatrix} 1 & 2 & 4 \\ 2 & 3 & 4 \\ 4 & 4 & 4 \end{bmatrix}$
8. Given that

$$A = \begin{bmatrix} 2 & 4 \\ 1 & 2 \end{bmatrix}, \quad B = \begin{bmatrix} 1 & 3 \\ 0 & 5 \end{bmatrix}, \quad \text{and } C = \begin{bmatrix} 1 & 0 \\ -1 & 3 \end{bmatrix},$$

show that

(a) $(A + B)' = A' + B'$, (b) $(AB)' = B'A'$, (c) $(ABC)' = C'B'A'$, (d) $(A')' = A$

## DETERMINANTS

In the previous sections we have demonstrated how it is possible to write a linear equation system in shorthand by means of matrix algebra. For example, we developed the shorthand $AX = C$ to represent a typical system of linear equations. It's nice to be able to write a large system of equations in a concise, shorthand notation. However, the premium is on being able to *solve* that system of equations for the values of the unknown variables represented by the vector $X$.

There would be relatively little reason to study matrix algebra if we were always unable to solve sets of linear equations. However, we are able to find solutions in a large number of situations. For example, when we have two linear equations in two unknowns, we can find the solution values of the unknown variables by setting one unknown variable equal to the other, substituting, and solving. It is apparent, nonetheless, that the process of substitution becomes exceedingly complex when many equations and unknowns are involved. Therefore we must further develop our matrix-algebra tools so that we can find the solution values for a large set of simultaneous linear equations.

The first step we must take is to master the concept of the determinant of a matrix. Once we have found the value of the determinant, we ordinarily know whether or not we can solve the system of equations in question, and we often can find the precise solution values.

DEFINITION The *determinant* of a square matrix is a uniquely defined scalar (number) that is characteristic of that particular matrix.

Determinants are denoted by vertical straight lines, that is,

$$|A| = \begin{vmatrix} a_{11} & a_{12} & \cdots & a_{1n} \\ a_{21} & a_{22} & \cdots & a_{2n} \\ \vdots & \vdots & & \vdots \\ a_{n1} & a_{n2} & \cdots & a_{nn} \end{vmatrix} \tag{8.30}$$

The $n \times n$ matrix $A$ given in Equation (8.30) is said to be a determinant of the $n$th order, or, an $n \times n$ determinant.

Consider a second-order matrix that results in the second-order determinant

$$|A| = \begin{vmatrix} a_{11} & a_{12} \\ a_{21} & a_{22} \end{vmatrix} \tag{8.31}$$

This determinant may also be expressed as

$$|A| = \begin{vmatrix} a_{11} & a_{12} \\ a_{21} & a_{22} \end{vmatrix} = a_{11}a_{22} - a_{12}a_{21} \tag{8.32}$$

We obtained the expression $(a_{11}a_{22} - a_{12}a_{21})$ by cross-multiplying the elements of determinant $|A|$. That is, we obtained the scalar $(a_{11}a_{22} - a_{12}a_{21})$ by multiplying the two elements in the main diagonal and then subtracting from that the product of the two off-diagonal elements.

A third-order determinant is more complicated and is defined by

$$|A| = \begin{vmatrix} a_{11} & a_{12} & a_{13} \\ a_{21} & a_{22} & a_{23} \\ a_{31} & a_{32} & a_{33} \end{vmatrix}$$

$$= a_{11}a_{22}a_{33} + a_{12}a_{23}a_{31} + a_{13}a_{21}a_{32} - a_{31}a_{22}a_{13} - a_{32}a_{23}a_{11} - a_{33}a_{21}a_{12} \quad (8.33)$$

The third-order determinant is composed of six terms, three of which are added and three of which are subtracted in the process of cross-multiplication. Figure 8.2 illustrates how we find the various products when a third-order determinant is involved. The solid lines in Figure 8.2 form a cross product of three elements, beginning in each case with an element in the top row and including two other elements that are each from a different row and column. The dashed lines also form a cross product of three elements, beginning in each case with an element from the bottom row and including two other elements, each of which is from a different row and column. The six products together determine the value of the determinant, with the solid-line products to be added and the dashed-line products to be subtracted.

EXAMPLES

1. Given that

$$A = \begin{bmatrix} 4 & 2 \\ 1 & 5 \end{bmatrix} \qquad \text{then } |A| = 4 \cdot 5 - 1 \cdot 2 = 18$$

Figure 8.2 The value of a third-order determinant

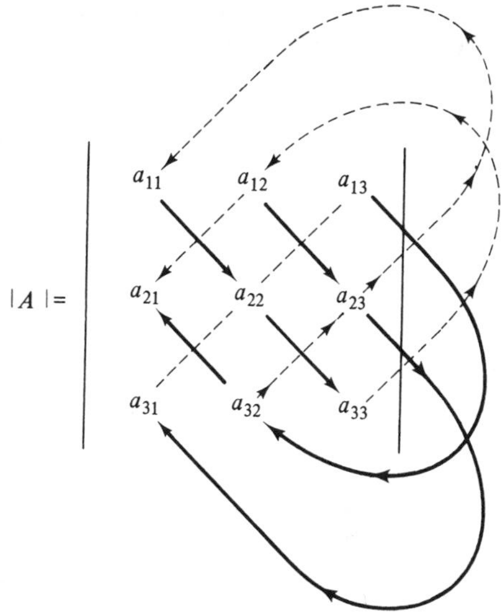


$$|A| = a_{11}a_{22}a_{33} + a_{12}a_{23}a_{31} + a_{13}a_{21}a_{32} - a_{31}a_{22}a_{13} - a_{32}a_{23}a_{11} - a_{33}a_{21}a_{12}$$

2. Given that

$$A = \begin{bmatrix} -3 & -4 \\ 1 & 5 \end{bmatrix} \qquad \text{then } |A| = (-3)(5) - (1)(-4) = -11$$

3. Given that

$$A = \begin{bmatrix} 2 & 0 & 1 \\ 3 & 2 & -3 \\ -1 & -3 & 5 \end{bmatrix}$$

then

$$|A| = (2)(2)(5) + (0)(-3)(-1) + (1)(3)(-3) - (-1)(2)(1) - (-3)(-3)(2) - (5)(3)(0) = -5$$

4. Given that

$$A = \begin{bmatrix} 1 & 0 & 0 \\ 3 & 2 & 4 \\ 4 & 1 & 3 \end{bmatrix}$$

then

$$|A| = 1 \cdot 2 \cdot 3 + 0 \cdot 4 \cdot 4 + 0 \cdot 3 \cdot 1 - 4 \cdot 2 \cdot 0 - 1 \cdot 4 \cdot 1 - 3 \cdot 3 \cdot 0 = 2$$

**Evaluating Determinants of Orders Higher than Three**

The cross-multiplication methods of evaluating determinants of orders two and three cannot be directly applied to determinants of orders higher than three. We must use another procedure to evaluate determinants of the fourth (and higher) orders. This new procedure is known as *expansion by cofactors*, and it operates on the principle of reducing a higher-order determinant to a series of second- or third-order determinants that we can evaluate by cross-multiplication.

Consider again a 3 × 3 determinant $|A|$:

$$|A| = \begin{vmatrix} a_{11} & a_{12} & a_{13} \\ a_{21} & a_{22} & a_{23} \\ a_{31} & a_{32} & a_{33} \end{vmatrix}$$

$$= a_{11}a_{22}a_{33} + a_{12}a_{23}a_{31} + a_{13}a_{21}a_{32} - a_{31}a_{22}a_{13} - a_{32}a_{23}a_{11} - a_{33}a_{21}a_{12} \tag{8.34}$$

$$= a_{11}(a_{22}a_{33} - a_{23}a_{32}) + a_{12}(a_{23}a_{31} - a_{21}a_{33}) + a_{13}(a_{21}a_{32} - a_{22}a_{31}) \tag{8.35}$$

$$= a_{11}\begin{vmatrix} a_{22} & a_{23} \\ a_{32} & a_{33} \end{vmatrix} - a_{12}\begin{vmatrix} a_{21} & a_{23} \\ a_{31} & a_{33} \end{vmatrix} + a_{13}\begin{vmatrix} a_{21} & a_{22} \\ a_{31} & a_{32} \end{vmatrix} \tag{8.36}$$

$$= a_{11}|A_{11}| - a_{12}|A_{12}| + a_{13}|A_{13}| \tag{8.37}$$

$$= \sum_{j=1}^{3} (-1)^{1+j} a_{1j} |A_{1j}| \tag{8.38}$$

Equation (8.36) transforms the $3 \times 3$ determinant in Equation (8.34) to a three-term expression. Each of the three terms in Equation (8.36) consists of an element from the first row of the original determinant multiplied by a second-order (actually $n - 1 = 3 - 1 =$ second order) determinant that we shall now call a *minor*. For example, the first term in Equation (8.36) is the element $a_{11}$ times $2 \times 2$ determinant (minor).

DEFINITION Given $A$, an $n \times n$ matrix. Then $|A_{ij}|$ is an $(n-1) \times (n-1)$ determinant of the submatrix formed from $A$ by deleting the $i$th row and the $j$th column of $A$. This determinant is known as a *minor* of $a_{ij}$ from matrix $A$.

$$\text{Let } A = \begin{bmatrix} a_{11} & \cdots & \boxed{a_{1j}} & \cdots & a_{1n} \\ \vdots & & \vdots & & \vdots \\ a_{i1} & \cdots & a_{ij} & \cdots & a_{in} \\ \vdots & & \vdots & & \vdots \\ a_{n1} & \cdots & a_{nj} & \cdots & a_{nn} \end{bmatrix} \tag{8.39}$$

We now delete the $i$th row and $j$th column from matrix $A$, giving us

$$|A_{ij}| = \begin{vmatrix} a_{11} & \cdots & a_{1,j-1} & a_{1,j+1} & \cdots & a_{1n} \\ \vdots & & \vdots & \vdots & & \vdots \\ a_{i-1,1} & \cdots & a_{i-1,j-1} & a_{i-1,j+1} & \cdots & a_{i-1,n} \\ a_{i+1,1} & \cdots & a_{i+1,j-1} & a_{i+1,j+1} & \cdots & a_{i+1,n} \\ \vdots & & \vdots & \vdots & & \vdots \\ a_{n1} & \cdots & a_{n,j-1} & a_{n,j+1} & \cdots & a_{nn} \end{vmatrix} \tag{8.40}$$

$|A_{ij}|$ is the minor of $a_{ij}$ from matrix $A$.

The concept of a minor may at this point seem to be obtuse and complicated. We can, however, use the $3 \times 3$ determinant of Equation (8.34) to demonstrate and clarify what we mean by the term minor. There are three minors that we can construct with reference to the top-row elements of this $3 \times 3$ determinant:

$$\text{Minor of } a_{11} = \begin{Vmatrix} a_{11} & a_{12} & a_{13} \\ a_{21} & a_{22} & a_{23} \\ a_{31} & a_{32} & a_{33} \end{Vmatrix} = \begin{vmatrix} a_{22} & a_{23} \\ a_{32} & a_{33} \end{vmatrix} = |A_{11}| \tag{8.41}$$

(The first row and first column are deleted.)

$$\text{Minor of } a_{12} = \begin{Vmatrix} a_{11} & a_{12} & a_{13} \\ a_{21} & a_{22} & a_{23} \\ a_{31} & a_{32} & a_{33} \end{Vmatrix} = \begin{vmatrix} a_{21} & a_{23} \\ a_{31} & a_{33} \end{vmatrix} = |A_{12}| \tag{8.42}$$

(The first row and second column are deleted.)

$$\text{Minor of } a_{13} = \left|\begin{array}{cc|c} a_{11} & a_{12} & a_{13} \\ \hline a_{21} & a_{22} & a_{23} \\ a_{31} & a_{32} & a_{33} \end{array}\right| = \begin{vmatrix} a_{21} & a_{22} \\ a_{31} & a_{32} \end{vmatrix} = |A_{13}| \qquad \text{(8.43}$$

(The first row and third column are deleted.)

Each minor, $|A_{11}|$, $|A_{12}|$, and $|A_{13}|$, is itself a determinant that has value. Further, Equation (8.37) has a sign (positive or negative) that must b affixed to it. That sign is positive when the sum of the rows and columns of th minor is an even number. The sign is negative when the sum of the rows an columns of the minor is an odd number. For example, the sign of minor $|A_{11}$ is positive because $1 + 1 = 2$, an even number. The sign of minor $|A_{12}|$ i negative because $1 + 2 = 3$, an odd number.

DEFINITION A *cofactor* or *signed minor* of the element $a_{ij}$ is a scalar given b $|C_{ij}| = (-1)^{i+j}|A_{ij}|$.

More formally, then, the cofactors (the signed minors) associated with th top-row elements $a_{11}$, $a_{12}$, and $a_{13}$ are

$$\text{Cofactor of } a_{11} = |C_{11}| = (-1)^{1+1}|A_{11}| = +|A_{11}| \qquad \text{(8.44}$$

$$\text{Cofactor of } a_{12} = |C_{12}| = (-1)^{1+2}|A_{12}| = -|A_{12}| \qquad \text{(8.45}$$

$$\text{Cofactor of } a_{13} = |C_{13}| = (-1)^{1+3}|A_{13}| = +|A_{13}| \qquad \text{(8.46}$$

We can expand any determinant by resorting to cofactors. Consider th $3 \times 3$ determinant originally given in Equation (8.34) and subsequently used i the cofactors expressed in Equations (8.44) through (8.46):

$$|A| = \begin{vmatrix} a_{11} & a_{12} & a_{13} \\ a_{21} & a_{22} & a_{23} \\ a_{31} & a_{32} & a_{33} \end{vmatrix} = a_{11}|A_{11}| - a_{12}|A_{12}| + a_{13}|A_{13}| \qquad \text{(8.47}$$

$$= a_{11}|C_{11}| + a_{12}|C_{12}| + a_{13}|C_{13}| \qquad \text{(8.48}$$

$$= \sum_{j=1}^{3} a_{1j}|C_{1j}| \qquad \text{(8.49}$$

It is important to remember that when the cofactor procedure is expresse in the form of Equation (8.49), the signs of each cofactor are found accordin to the "even-odd" rule cited above, with the sign of any cofactor given b $(-1)^{i+j}$, where $i$ is the index number of the deleted row and $j$ is the inde number of the deleted column. The sign of any particular cofactor is als shown in the $n \times n$ matrix of Figure 8.3. The sign of every cofactor on the mai diagonal of the $n \times n$ matrix is positive because the sum of the number of row and columns of any element on the diagonal is an even number.

We accomplished the expansion of the $3 \times 3$ determinant that was given i Equations (8.47) through (8.49) by means of three cofactors that related to th *first row* of that determinant. We could have accomplished a similar an

$$\begin{bmatrix} + & - & + & \cdots & & & \\ - & + & - & \cdots & & & \\ + & - & + & \cdots & & & \\ & & & \cdots & + & - & + \\ & & & \cdots & - & + & - \\ & & & \cdots & + & - & + \end{bmatrix}$$

Figure 8.3 The signs of the cofactors of an $n \times n$ matrix

equivalent expansion by finding the cofactors of *any row or column* in the determinant. Thus, in general,

$$|A| = \sum_{j=1}^{n} a_{ij}|C_{ij}| \qquad \text{for any row } i = 1, \ldots, n \tag{8.50}$$

*or*

$$|A| = \sum_{i=1}^{n} a_{ij}|C_{ij}| \qquad \text{for any column } j = 1, \ldots, n \tag{8.51}$$

EXAMPLES

1. Given a general $2 \times 2$ determinant $|A|$, we can find the value of that determinant by expanding and finding the cofactors of any row or column. Given

$$|A| = \begin{vmatrix} a_{11} & a_{12} \\ a_{21} & a_{22} \end{vmatrix} = a_{11}a_{22} - a_{12}a_{21}$$

This same result may be found as

$$|A| = a_{11}|C_{11}| + a_{12}|C_{12}| = a_{11}a_{22} - a_{12}a_{21} \qquad \text{(row 1)}$$

$$|A| = a_{21}|C_{21}| + a_{22}|C_{22}| = -a_{21}a_{12} + a_{22}a_{11} \qquad \text{(row 2)}$$

$$|A| = a_{11}|C_{11}| + a_{21}|C_{21}| = a_{11}a_{22} - a_{21}a_{12} \qquad \text{(column 1)}$$

$$|A| = a_{12}|C_{12}| + a_{22}|C_{22}| = -a_{12}a_{21} + a_{22}a_{11} \qquad \text{(column 2)}$$

2. Let

$$|A| = \begin{vmatrix} 2 & 1 \\ 3 & 8 \end{vmatrix} = 2 \cdot 8 - 1 \cdot 3 = 13$$

or by expanding by means of the first row of cofactors,

$$|A| = 2|8| - 1|3| = 13$$

3. Let

$$|A| = \begin{vmatrix} 3 & 0 & 1 \\ 2 & 4 & 5 \\ 1 & 3 & 6 \end{vmatrix}$$

$$= 3 \cdot 4 \cdot 6 + 0 \cdot 5 \cdot 1 + 1 \cdot 2 \cdot 3 - 1 \cdot 4 \cdot 1 - 3 \cdot 5 \cdot 3 - 6 \cdot 2 \cdot 0 = 29$$

or expanding by means of the first row of cofactors,

$$|A| = 3\begin{vmatrix} 4 & 5 \\ 3 & 6 \end{vmatrix} - 0\begin{vmatrix} 2 & 5 \\ 1 & 6 \end{vmatrix} + 1\begin{vmatrix} 2 & 4 \\ 1 & 3 \end{vmatrix} = 3(9) - 0(7) + 1(2) = 29$$

4. Let

$$|A| = \begin{vmatrix} 2 & 0 & 1 \\ 3 & 2 & -3 \\ -1 & -3 & 5 \end{vmatrix} = -5$$

as found in Example 3 on page 310, or expanding by means of the first row of cofactors,

$$|A| = 2\begin{vmatrix} 2 & -3 \\ -3 & 5 \end{vmatrix} - 0\begin{vmatrix} 3 & -3 \\ -1 & 5 \end{vmatrix} + 1\begin{vmatrix} 3 & 2 \\ -1 & -3 \end{vmatrix}$$

$$= 2(1) - 0(12) + 1(-7) = -5$$

In general, the problem of evaluating an $n \times n$ determinant reduces to one of evaluating $n$ determinants of order $(n-1)$. Applying the cofactor expansion method again reduces the task of evaluating $n$ determinants of order $(n-1)$ to one of evaluating $(n-1)$ determinants of order $(n-2)$, and so forth. Eventually, no matter how large the determinant, repeated application of the cofactor expansion method transforms the original large determinant into a series of more workable $2 \times 2$ or $3 \times 3$ determinants.

EXAMPLES

1. Let

$$|A| = \begin{vmatrix} 1 & 0 & 0 \\ 3 & 2 & 4 \\ 4 & 1 & 3 \end{vmatrix}$$

Expanding by means of the first row of cofactors,

$$|A| = 1\begin{vmatrix} 2 & 4 \\ 1 & 3 \end{vmatrix} = 1(2) = 2$$

2. Let

$$|A| = \begin{vmatrix} 3 & 4 & 1 & -5 \\ 1 & 0 & 0 & 0 \\ -2 & 0 & 3 & 3 \\ 2 & 1 & -1 & 2 \end{vmatrix}$$

Expanding by means of the second row of cofactors,

$$|A| = -1 \begin{vmatrix} 4 & 1 & -5 \\ 0 & 3 & 3 \\ 1 & -1 & 2 \end{vmatrix}$$

Expanding again by means of the first column of cofactors,

$$|A| = -\left[4\begin{vmatrix} 3 & 3 \\ -1 & 2 \end{vmatrix} + 1\begin{vmatrix} 1 & -5 \\ 3 & 3 \end{vmatrix}\right] = -[4(9) + 1(18)] = -54$$

3. Let

$$|A| = \begin{vmatrix} 1 & 1 & 0 & 5 \\ 1 & 2 & 1 & 0 \\ 0 & 2 & 1 & 1 \\ 3 & 0 & 0 & -4 \end{vmatrix}$$

Expanding by means of the last row of cofactors,

$$|A| = -3 \begin{vmatrix} 1 & 0 & 5 \\ 2 & 1 & 0 \\ 2 & 1 & 1 \end{vmatrix} + (-4) \begin{vmatrix} 1 & 1 & 0 \\ 1 & 2 & 1 \\ 0 & 2 & 1 \end{vmatrix}$$

Expanding each by the first row of cofactors,

$$|A| = -3\left[1\begin{vmatrix} 1 & 0 \\ 1 & 1 \end{vmatrix} + 5\begin{vmatrix} 2 & 1 \\ 2 & 1 \end{vmatrix}\right] - 4\left[1\begin{vmatrix} 2 & 1 \\ 2 & 1 \end{vmatrix} - 1\begin{vmatrix} 1 & 1 \\ 0 & 1 \end{vmatrix}\right]$$

$$= -3[1 \cdot 1 + 5 \cdot 0] - 4[1 \cdot 0 - 1 \cdot 1] = 1$$

The above example demonstrates that we can save considerable time and energy by selecting for expansion that row or column that contains the most zero elements.

### A Digression on the Differences between Matrices and Determinants

Matrices and determinants are not the same thing. A matrix, denoted by brackets or parentheses, has no numeric value. A matrix is a rectangular array of numbers, variables, and parameters. A determinant, on the other hand, does have a numeric value. A determinant is defined to be a scalar (number).

Matrices can be of any dimension and need not be square. Determinants must be square. A $2 \times 3$ determinant does *not* exist.

### The Properties of Determinants

We can usefully apply the following properties when we work with determinants. These properties apply to determinants of any dimension, although they are illustrated here only for a $2 \times 2$ determinant.

PROPERTY I $|A| = |A'|$. The determinant of a matrix $A$ has the same value as the determinant of its transpose $A'$.

EXAMPLES

1. Let

$$|A| = \begin{vmatrix} a & b \\ c & d \end{vmatrix} = ad - bc \qquad |A'| = \begin{vmatrix} a & c \\ b & d \end{vmatrix} = ad - cb$$

Hence $|A| = |A'|$

2. $|A| = \begin{vmatrix} 1 & 2 \\ 3 & 4 \end{vmatrix} = |A'| = \begin{vmatrix} 1 & 3 \\ 2 & 4 \end{vmatrix} = -2$

PROPERTY 2 Interchanging any two rows (or any two columns) of a determinant does not alter the value of that determinant. However, it alters the sign of the determinant.

EXAMPLES

1. $\begin{vmatrix} a & b \\ c & d \end{vmatrix} = ad - bc \qquad \begin{vmatrix} c & d \\ a & b \end{vmatrix} = cb - da$

Thus

$$\begin{vmatrix} a & b \\ c & d \end{vmatrix} = -\begin{vmatrix} c & d \\ a & b \end{vmatrix}$$

2. $\begin{vmatrix} 1 & 2 \\ 3 & 4 \end{vmatrix} = -2 = -\begin{vmatrix} 3 & 4 \\ 1 & 2 \end{vmatrix}$

3. $\begin{vmatrix} a & b & c \\ d & e & f \\ g & h & i \end{vmatrix} = -\begin{vmatrix} d & e & f \\ a & b & c \\ g & h & i \end{vmatrix} = \begin{vmatrix} d & e & f \\ g & h & i \\ a & b & c \end{vmatrix}$

PROPERTY 3 A determinant in which any two rows (or any two columns) are identical, or a determinant in which any two rows (or any two columns) are multiples of each other, has a value of zero.

EXAMPLES

1. $\begin{vmatrix} a & b \\ a & b \end{vmatrix} = 0$ and $\begin{vmatrix} ka & kb \\ a & b \end{vmatrix} = kab - kab = 0$

2. $\begin{vmatrix} 1 & 2 & 3 \\ 0 & 1 & 0 \\ 1 & 2 & 3 \end{vmatrix} = 1\begin{vmatrix} 1 & 3 \\ 1 & 3 \end{vmatrix} = 0$

3. $\begin{vmatrix} 1 & 2 & 3 \\ 0 & 1 & 0 \\ 2 & 4 & 6 \end{vmatrix} = 1\begin{vmatrix} 1 & 3 \\ 2 & 6 \end{vmatrix} = 0$

PROPERTY 4 A determinant in which any row or any column has all zero elements has a value of zero.

EXAMPLES

1. $\begin{vmatrix} a & b \\ 0 & 0 \end{vmatrix} = 0$ and $\begin{vmatrix} a & 0 \\ b & 0 \end{vmatrix} = 0$

2. $\begin{vmatrix} 1 & 2 & 3 \\ 0 & 1 & 0 \\ 0 & 0 & 0 \end{vmatrix} = 0$

PROPERTY 5 Adding (or subtracting) a multiple of one row of a determinant to (from) another row of that determinant, or adding (or subtracting) a multiple of one column of a determinant to (from) another column of that determinant does not change the value of the determinant.

EXAMPLES

1. $\begin{vmatrix} a & b \\ c & d \end{vmatrix} = \begin{vmatrix} a & b \\ c \pm ka & d \pm kb \end{vmatrix} = ad - bc$

2. $\begin{vmatrix} 1 & 2 & 3 \\ 0 & 1 & 0 \\ 4 & 2 & 1 \end{vmatrix} = \begin{vmatrix} 1 & 2 & 3 \\ 0 + 2 \cdot 1 & 1 + 2 \cdot 2 & 0 + 3 \cdot 2 \\ 4 & 2 & 1 \end{vmatrix}$

$$= \begin{vmatrix} 1 & 2 & 3 \\ 2 & 5 & 6 \\ 4 & 2 & 1 \end{vmatrix} = -11$$

PROPERTY 6 If every element in one row (or one column) is multiplied by a constant $k$, then the value of the determinant is also multiplied by $k$.

EXAMPLES

1. $\begin{vmatrix} a & b \\ c & d \end{vmatrix} = ad - bc$ Therefore $\begin{vmatrix} ka & kb \\ c & d \end{vmatrix} = k(ad - bc)$

2. Note, however, that if every *element* of a determinant of order $n$ is multiplied by a constant $k$, then the value of the determinant is multiplied by $k^n$. That is, $|kA| = k^n|A|$. Thus, if

   $\begin{vmatrix} a & b \\ c & d \end{vmatrix} = ad - bc,$ then $\begin{vmatrix} ka & kb \\ kc & kd \end{vmatrix} = k^2(ad - bc)$

**EXERCISE 8.3**

Evaluate each of the following determinants.

1. $\begin{vmatrix} 1 & 2 & 3 \\ 2 & 3 & 4 \\ 1 & 5 & 7 \end{vmatrix}$ 2. $\begin{vmatrix} 1 & 3 & 4 \\ 2 & 0 & 7 \\ 5 & 6 & 9 \end{vmatrix}$ 3. $\begin{vmatrix} 4 & 1 & 6 \\ 7 & 2 & 9 \\ 3 & 0 & 8 \end{vmatrix}$

4. $\begin{vmatrix} 2 & 1 \\ 3 & 4 \end{vmatrix}$

5. $\begin{vmatrix} 2 & 1 & -3 & 4 \\ 5 & -4 & 7 & -2 \\ 4 & 0 & 6 & -3 \\ 3 & -2 & 5 & 2 \end{vmatrix}$

6. $\begin{vmatrix} 1 & 1 \\ -3 & -3 \end{vmatrix}$

7. $\begin{vmatrix} 1 & 1 & 1 \\ 0 & 1 & 1 \\ 0 & 0 & 1 \end{vmatrix}$

8. $\begin{vmatrix} 2 & 1 & 1 \\ 0 & 5 & -2 \\ 1 & -3 & 4 \end{vmatrix}$

9. $\begin{vmatrix} 1 & 2 & -2 & 3 \\ 3 & -1 & 5 & 0 \\ 1 & 7 & 2 & -3 \\ 4 & 0 & 2 & 1 \end{vmatrix}$

## THE INVERSE OF A MATRIX

Much of our work in this chapter has dealt with a system of $n$ linear equations in $n$ unknowns, such as

$$\begin{aligned} a_{11}x_1 + a_{12}x_2 + \cdots + a_{1n}x_n &= c_1 \\ a_{21}x_2 + a_{22}x_2 + \cdots + a_{2n}x_n &= c_2 \\ \vdots \qquad \vdots \qquad\quad \vdots \quad &\quad \vdots \\ a_{n1}x_1 + a_{n2}x_2 + \cdots + a_{nn}x_n &= c_n \end{aligned} \tag{8.52}$$

We have already seen that we can write the system of equations given by Equation (8.52) shorthand as $AX = C$. We shall soon discuss the problem of solving such an equation system.

Solving a linear equation system of the form $AX = C$ seems to be easy at first glance. We are tempted to divide both sides of the equation system by $A$, giving us $X = C/A$. Unfortunately, we cannot do this. In matrix algebra, the division operator is not defined. That is, we cannot divide a matrix $C$ by another matrix $A$. Instead, we must use a technique that involves finding the *inverse* of a matrix. Symbolically, in ordinary algebra, $C/A = CA^{-1} = A^{-1}C$. In general, in matrix algebra, we must use the inverse of a matrix instead of dividing one matrix by another. However, we must be careful in doing so, for (as we have already seen) matrix multiplication does not commute. Given

$$\underset{n \times n}{A} \cdot \underset{n \times 1}{X} = \underset{n \times 1}{C}$$

if an inverse matrix does exist for $A$, then the solution for the $X$ matrix is

$$\underset{n \times 1}{X} = \underset{n \times n}{A^{-1}} \cdot \underset{n \times 1}{C}$$

This is in general *not* equivalent to $X = CA^{-1}$.

DEFINITION The *inverse* of a square matrix $A$ (if it exists) is another square matrix, denoted $A^{-1}$, that satisfies the relation $A^{-1}A = AA^{-1} = I$.

This definition of the inverse matrix is consistent with ordinary algebraic rules. For example, in ordinary algebra, $aa^{-1} = a^{-1}a = 1$. In the case of matrix algebra, it makes no difference whether $A$ is premultiplied or postmultiplied by $A^{-1}$. The product that results is always the identity matrix $I$.[4]

There are two important facts associated with our definition of the inverse of a matrix. First, if an inverse of a matrix does exist, then this inverse is unique. That is, $A^{-1}$ is the only matrix that, when multiplied by $A$, results in the identity matrix $I$.

*Proof* Assume that $A$ and $A^{-1}$ are matrices such that $A^{-1}A = AA^{-1} = I$. Assume also that another matrix $B$ exists such that $BA = AB = I$. Therefore $A^{-1}AB = IB = B$. Since $AB = I$, this implies that $A^{-1} = B$. Hence the inverse matrix $A^{-1}$ is unique in the sense that no matrix other than $A^{-1} = B$ is the inverse of matrix $A$.

The second major lesson to be drawn from our definition of an inverse matrix is that the commutative law of multiplication does hold when we multiply a square matrix by its inverse. That is, $AA^{-1} = A^{-1}A = I$.

*Proof* Assume two matrices $A$ and $B$ such that $B = A^{-1}$ and $AB = I$. Premultiplying $AB = I$ by $A^{-1}$, we obtain $B = A^{-1}$. Postmultiplying this result by $A$, we obtain $BA = I$. Therefore we obtain the result $BA = I$ when $AB = I$. This implies that either the premultiplication or the postmultiplication of a square matrix by its inverse results in the identity matrix.

### Finding the Inverse Matrix if It Exists

The following theorem yields both the necessary and the sufficient conditions for determining whether or not an inverse matrix exists, and how one can find it.

THEOREM 8.1 A square matrix $A$ has an inverse matrix $A^{-1}$ if and only if the determinant $|A| \neq 0$, in which case $A$ is said to be nonsingular. The inverse is given by $A^{-1} = (1/|A|) \cdot \text{adj } A$, where "adj $A$" implies the adjoint of matrix $A$.[5]

We must emphasize several points concerning this theorem. First, a square matrix is a necessary, but not a sufficient condition, for an inverse matrix to exist. Second, if matrix $A$ does have an inverse, $A$ is said to be nonsingular. If $A$ does not have an inverse, then $A$ is said to be singular. (We shall return to the concepts of singularity and nonsingularity when we solve systems of simultaneous equations.) Third, the condition $|A| \neq 0$ is a sufficient condition for an inverse to exist.

The theorem above uses the term *adjoint of matrix A*. We must now define this new concept.

DEFINITION The adjoint of matrix $A$, denoted by adj $A$, is the transpose of the cofactor matrix of $A$.

[4] This is yet another exception to the general dictum that matrix multiplication is not commutative.
[5] For a complete proof, see Sam Perlis, *Theory of Matrices*, Addison-Wesley, Reading, Mass., 1958.

Assume that the cofactor matrix of $A$ is given by

$$C = [|C_{ij}|] \tag{8.53}$$

Then the adjoint of $A$ is given by

$$C' = \begin{bmatrix} |C_{11}| & |C_{12}| & \cdots & |C_{1n}| \\ |C_{21}| & |C_{22}| & \cdots & |C_{2n}| \\ \vdots & \vdots & & \vdots \\ |C_{n1}| & |C_{n2}| & \cdots & |C_{nn}| \end{bmatrix}' = \text{adj } A$$

$$= \begin{bmatrix} |C_{11}| & |C_{21}| & \cdots & |C_{n1}| \\ |C_{12}| & |C_{22}| & \cdots & |C_{n2}| \\ \vdots & \vdots & & \vdots \\ |C_{1n}| & |C_{2n}| & \cdots & |C_{nn}| \end{bmatrix} \tag{8.54}$$

■ You should remember that a cofactor of an element is a signed minor given by $|C_{ij}| = (-1)^{i+j}|A_{ij}|$. The cofactor is *not* the element of a particular row and column multiplied by the signed minor. That is, $|C_{ij}| \neq a_{ij}(-1)^{i+j}|A_{ij}|$. Only when we expand by a particular row or column in order to find the determinant do we need to multiply the element and cofactor together.

EXAMPLES

1. Let

$$A = \begin{bmatrix} 2 & 1 \\ 3 & 4 \end{bmatrix} \qquad \text{Then} \qquad |A| = 5, \qquad [|C_{ij}|] = \begin{bmatrix} 4 & -3 \\ -1 & 2 \end{bmatrix}$$

and

$$\text{adj } A = \begin{bmatrix} 4 & -1 \\ -3 & 2 \end{bmatrix}$$

Thus

$$A^{-1} = \frac{1}{5}\begin{bmatrix} 4 & -1 \\ -3 & 2 \end{bmatrix}.$$

This is easily proved to be the inverse by computing

$$A^{-1}A = \begin{bmatrix} \frac{4}{5} & -\frac{1}{5} \\ -\frac{3}{5} & \frac{2}{5} \end{bmatrix}\begin{bmatrix} 2 & 1 \\ 3 & 4 \end{bmatrix} = \begin{bmatrix} 1 & 0 \\ 0 & 1 \end{bmatrix}$$

2. Let

$$A = \begin{bmatrix} 1 & 3 & 4 \\ 2 & 0 & 7 \\ 5 & 6 & 9 \end{bmatrix}$$

Then

$$|A| = 57, \qquad [|C_{ij}|] = \begin{bmatrix} -42 & 17 & 12 \\ -3 & -11 & 9 \\ 21 & 1 & -6 \end{bmatrix}$$

and

$$\text{adj } A = \begin{bmatrix} -42 & -3 & 21 \\ 17 & -11 & 1 \\ 12 & 9 & -6 \end{bmatrix}$$

Thus

$$A^{-1} = \frac{1}{57}\begin{bmatrix} -42 & -3 & 21 \\ 17 & -11 & 1 \\ 12 & 9 & -6 \end{bmatrix}$$

This is easily verified to be the inverse by computing

$$A^{-1}A = \begin{bmatrix} -\frac{42}{57} & -\frac{3}{57} & \frac{21}{57} \\ \frac{17}{57} & -\frac{11}{57} & \frac{1}{57} \\ \frac{12}{57} & \frac{9}{57} & -\frac{6}{57} \end{bmatrix}\begin{bmatrix} 1 & 3 & 4 \\ 2 & 0 & 7 \\ 5 & 6 & 9 \end{bmatrix} = \begin{bmatrix} 1 & 0 & 0 \\ 0 & 1 & 0 \\ 0 & 0 & 1 \end{bmatrix}$$

3. Let

$$A = \begin{bmatrix} 1 & 0 & 4 \\ 2 & -3 & 1 \\ 6 & -9 & 3 \end{bmatrix}$$

Then $|A| = 0$. This implies that the matrix is singular and does not have an inverse.

The above examples illustrate two very important points. First, the definition of an inverse matrix requires that $|A| \neq 0$. Not only does this mean that matrix $A$ is nonsingular, but also it recognizes that division by zero is undefined. Therefore $|A| \neq 0$ is a sufficient condition for an inverse matrix to exist. Second, it is always possible to check whether the theorem concerning inverse matrices has been applied correctly. One need only multiply the alleged inverse and the original matrix. If the theorem has been applied correctly, the result must be the identity matrix.

### Properties of Inverse Matrices

PROPERTY I If $A^{-1}$ exists, then $(A^{-1})^{-1} = A$. That is, the inverse of an inverse is the original matrix.

*Proof* Definitionally, $AA^{-1} = A^{-1}A = I$. We substitute $A^{-1}$ for matrix $A$, and the result of Property 1 follows.

EXAMPLE Let

$$A = \begin{bmatrix} 2 & 1 \\ 3 & 4 \end{bmatrix} \quad \text{and} \quad A^{-1} = \begin{bmatrix} \frac{4}{5} & -\frac{1}{5} \\ -\frac{3}{5} & \frac{2}{5} \end{bmatrix}$$

Then

$$[A^{-1}]^{-1} = \begin{bmatrix} \frac{4}{5} & -\frac{1}{5} \\ -\frac{3}{5} & \frac{2}{5} \end{bmatrix}^{-1} = \begin{bmatrix} 2 & 1 \\ 3 & 4 \end{bmatrix}$$

PROPERTY 2 If $A^{-1}$ and $B^{-1}$ exist, then $(AB)^{-1} = B^{-1} \cdot A^{-1}$. That is, the inverse of the product of two matrices is equal to the product of their inverses in reverse order.

*Proof* Given two matrices $A$ and $B$ such that $AB$ is defined. Premultiplying $AB$ by $B^{-1}A^{-1}$, we obtain

$$B^{-1}A^{-1}AB = B^{-1}IB = I$$

Similarly, if $BA$ is defined, then postmultiplying $BA$ by $A^{-1}B^{-1}$ yields

$$BAA^{-1}B^{-1} = BIB^{-1} = BB^{-1} = I$$

Hence $(AB)^{-1} = B^{-1}A^{-1}$. In general, the inverse of a product of a finite number of nonsingular matrices is equal to the product of the inverses in reversed order. That is,

$$(AB \cdots Z)^{-1} = Z^{-1} \cdots B^{-1}A^{-1}$$

EXAMPLE Let

$$A = \begin{bmatrix} 2 & 1 \\ 4 & 5 \end{bmatrix} \quad \text{and} \quad B = \begin{bmatrix} 0 & 1 \\ 3 & -2 \end{bmatrix}$$

Then

$$AB = \begin{bmatrix} 3 & 0 \\ 15 & -6 \end{bmatrix} \quad (AB)^{-1} = \begin{bmatrix} \frac{1}{3} & 0 \\ \frac{5}{6} & -\frac{1}{6} \end{bmatrix} \quad A^{-1} = \begin{bmatrix} \frac{5}{6} & -\frac{1}{6} \\ -\frac{2}{3} & \frac{1}{3} \end{bmatrix}$$

$$B^{-1} = \begin{bmatrix} \frac{2}{3} & \frac{1}{3} \\ 1 & 0 \end{bmatrix} \quad \text{and} \quad B^{-1}A^{-1} = \begin{bmatrix} \frac{1}{3} & 0 \\ \frac{5}{6} & -\frac{1}{6} \end{bmatrix}$$

Thus

$$AB^{-1} = \begin{bmatrix} \frac{1}{3} & 0 \\ \frac{5}{6} & -\frac{1}{6} \end{bmatrix} = B^{-1}A^{-1}$$

PROPERTY 3 If $A^{-1}$ exists, then $(A')^{-1} = (A^{-1})'$. That is, the inverse of the transpose is the transpose of the inverse.

*Proof* Using the definition of an inverse matrix, $AA^{-1} = A^{-1}A = I$. Taking the transpose of both sides, we obtain

$$(AA^{-1})' = (A^{-1}A)' = I' \quad \text{and} \quad (A^{-1})'A' = A'(A^{-1})' = I$$

Thus $(A^{-1})'$ is the inverse of $A'$.

EXAMPLE Let

$$A = \begin{bmatrix} 2 & 1 \\ 4 & 5 \end{bmatrix}$$

Then

$$A^{-1} = \begin{bmatrix} \frac{5}{6} & -\frac{1}{6} \\ -\frac{2}{3} & \frac{1}{3} \end{bmatrix} \quad (A^{-1})' = \begin{bmatrix} \frac{5}{6} & -\frac{2}{3} \\ -\frac{1}{6} & \frac{1}{3} \end{bmatrix} \quad A' = \begin{bmatrix} 2 & 4 \\ 1 & 5 \end{bmatrix}$$

and

$$(A')^{-1} = \begin{bmatrix} \frac{5}{6} & -\frac{2}{3} \\ -\frac{1}{6} & \frac{1}{3} \end{bmatrix}$$

Thus

$$(A')^{-1} = \begin{bmatrix} \frac{5}{6} & -\frac{2}{3} \\ -\frac{1}{6} & \frac{1}{3} \end{bmatrix} = (A^{-1})^{-1}$$

**Summary and Review: Finding the Inverse of a Matrix**

1. Determine whether or not the inverse matrix exists. That is, find $|A|$. If $|A| = 0$, then there is no inverse matrix.
2. Find the cofactor matrix. That is, find $C = [|C_{ij}|]$.
3. Find the adjoint of matrix $A$. That is, take the transpose of the cofactor matrix such that $C' = \text{adj } A$.
4. Divide adj $A$ by the determinant of $A$. That is,

$$A^{-1} = \frac{1}{|A|} \text{ adj } A$$

**EXERCISE 8.4**

For each of the following matrices, find the inverse, if it exists.

1. $\begin{bmatrix} 2 & 1 \\ 0 & 5 \end{bmatrix}$
2. $\begin{bmatrix} 1 & 1 & 1 \\ 0 & 1 & 1 \\ 0 & 0 & 1 \end{bmatrix}$
3. $\begin{bmatrix} 2 & 1 & 1 \\ 0 & 5 & -2 \\ 1 & -3 & 4 \end{bmatrix}$
4. $\begin{bmatrix} 7 & 6 & 5 \\ 1 & 2 & 1 \\ 3 & -2 & 1 \end{bmatrix}$
5. $\begin{bmatrix} -1 & 0 & 2 \\ 3 & 1 & -6 \\ -2 & -1 & 5 \end{bmatrix}$
6. $\begin{bmatrix} 1 & 0 & -2 \\ -3 & -1 & 6 \\ 2 & 1 & -5 \end{bmatrix}$
7. $\begin{bmatrix} 3 & -5 \\ -1 & 2 \end{bmatrix}$
8. $\begin{bmatrix} 0 & 5 \\ 6 & 4 \end{bmatrix}$
9. $\begin{bmatrix} 2 & 4 \\ -3 & -6 \end{bmatrix}$
10. $\begin{bmatrix} 2 & 1 & 3 \\ 3 & 0 & 1 \\ -1 & 1 & 4 \end{bmatrix}$

## SOLVING SIMULTANEOUS LINEAR EQUATIONS

By this juncture, we have become quite familiar with a simultaneous linear equation system of the form

$$\underset{n \times n}{A} \cdot \underset{n \times 1}{X} = \underset{n \times 1}{C}$$

If the inverse matrix $A^{-1}$ does exist, then premultiplying both sides of $AX = C$ by $A^{-1}$ yields

$$A^{-1}AX = A^{-1}C \tag{8.55}$$

$$\underset{n \times 1}{X} = \underset{n \times n}{A^{-1}} \cdot \underset{n \times 1}{C} = \underset{n \times 1}{D} \tag{8.56}$$

With respect to Equation (8.56), our definition of matrix equality tells us that the left side $n \times 1$ column vector of unknown variables represented by $X$ must be equal to the right side $n \times 1$ column vector of solution values represented by $D$ if the two sides are indeed equal.

We have also found that in order for us to be able to find an inverse matrix (such as $A^{-1}$), the matrix $A$ must be square. We stated this requirement by asserting that $A^{-1}A = AA^{-1} = I$, the identity matrix. This means that the number of equations is equal to the number of unknowns.

You must remember that when the value of the determinant of a matrix is zero, then you cannot find an inverse for that matrix. That is,

$$A^{-1} = \frac{1}{|A|} \text{ adj } A \qquad \text{and} \qquad |A| \neq 0$$

Thus, when $|A| \neq 0$, there is a unique solution for a linear equation system. Nonsingularity implies that an inverse can be found. When an inverse matrix can be found, then there is a unique solution. We may summarize the relationship between nonsingularity and the existence of a unique solution by stating that

$$\text{Nonsingularity} \Leftrightarrow \text{an inverse and a unique solution exist} \tag{8.57}$$

EXAMPLES

1. Solve the set of simultaneous linear equations using an inverse matrix. Given: $y - 4x = 12$ and $y + 3x = 5$. Then

$$|A| = \begin{vmatrix} 1 & -4 \\ 1 & 3 \end{vmatrix} = 7 \qquad [|C_{ij}|] = \begin{bmatrix} 3 & -1 \\ 4 & 1 \end{bmatrix}$$

and

$$\text{adj } A = \begin{bmatrix} 3 & 4 \\ -1 & 1 \end{bmatrix}$$

Thus

$$A^{-1} = \frac{1}{7}\begin{bmatrix} 3 & 4 \\ -1 & 1 \end{bmatrix}$$

and

$$\begin{bmatrix} y \\ x \end{bmatrix} = \frac{1}{7}\begin{bmatrix} 3 & 4 \\ -1 & 1 \end{bmatrix}\begin{bmatrix} 12 \\ 5 \end{bmatrix} \qquad \text{or} \qquad \begin{bmatrix} y \\ x \end{bmatrix} = \begin{bmatrix} 8 \\ -1 \end{bmatrix}$$

By definition of matrix equality, $y = 8$ and $x = -1$.

2. Solve the set of simultaneous linear equations using an inverse matrix. Given

$$\begin{aligned} 2x_1 - x_2 - x_3 &= 0 \\ -x_1 + 4x_2 - x_3 &= 0 \\ x_1 + x_2 \quad\quad &= 8 \end{aligned}$$

Then

$$|A| = \begin{vmatrix} 2 & -1 & -1 \\ -1 & 4 & -1 \\ 1 & 1 & 0 \end{vmatrix} = 8 \qquad [|C_{ij}|] = \begin{bmatrix} 1 & -1 & -5 \\ -1 & 1 & -3 \\ 5 & 3 & 7 \end{bmatrix}$$

and

$$\text{adj } A = \begin{bmatrix} 1 & -1 & 5 \\ -1 & 1 & 3 \\ -5 & -3 & 7 \end{bmatrix}$$

Thus

$$A^{-1} = \frac{1}{8}\begin{bmatrix} 1 & -1 & 5 \\ -1 & 1 & 3 \\ -5 & -3 & 7 \end{bmatrix}$$

and

$$\begin{bmatrix} x_1 \\ x_2 \\ x_3 \end{bmatrix} = \frac{1}{8}\begin{bmatrix} 1 & -1 & 5 \\ -1 & 1 & 3 \\ -5 & -3 & 7 \end{bmatrix}\begin{bmatrix} 0 \\ 0 \\ 8 \end{bmatrix} \quad \text{or} \quad \begin{bmatrix} x_1 \\ x_2 \\ x_3 \end{bmatrix} = \begin{bmatrix} 5 \\ 3 \\ 7 \end{bmatrix}$$

By definition of matrix equality, $x_1 = 5$, $x_2 = 3$, and $x_3 = 7$.

## CRAMER'S RULE

Although we can find the solution of a system of simultaneous linear equations by matrix inversion, there is another solution method that is also frequently used. This alternative method is *Cramer's rule*, which is derived from our theorem dealing with the procedure for finding the inverse of a matrix. Let us now derive Cramer's rule.

The inverse of a matrix $A$ is given by

$$A^{-1} = \left(\frac{1}{|A|}\right) \text{adj } A$$

The solution values of a system of $n$ equations in $n$ unknowns of the form $AX = D$ are given by

$$X = A^{-1}D = \left(\frac{1}{|A|}\right) \text{adj } A \cdot D \tag{8.58}$$

Equation (8.58) can be expressed in greater detail:

$$X = \begin{bmatrix} x_1 \\ x_2 \\ x_3 \\ \vdots \\ x_n \end{bmatrix} = \left(\frac{1}{|A|}\right) \begin{bmatrix} |c_{11}| & |c_{21}| & \cdots & |c_{n1}| \\ |c_{12}| & |c_{22}| & \cdots & |c_{n2}| \\ \vdots & \vdots & & \vdots \\ |c_{1n}| & |c_{2n}| & \cdots & |c_{nn}| \end{bmatrix} \begin{bmatrix} d_1 \\ d_2 \\ \vdots \\ d_n \end{bmatrix} \tag{8.59}$$

$$= \left(\frac{1}{|A|}\right) \begin{bmatrix} d_1|c_{11}| + d_2|c_{21}| + \cdots + d_n|c_{n1}| \\ d_1|c_{12}| + d_2|c_{22}| + \cdots + d_n|c_{n2}| \\ \vdots \\ d_1|c_{1n}| + d_2|c_{2n}| + \cdots + d_n|c_{nn}| \end{bmatrix} \tag{8.60}$$

$$= \left(\frac{1}{|A|}\right) \begin{bmatrix} \sum_{i=1}^{n} d_i|c_{i1}| \\ \sum_{i=1}^{n} d_i|c_{i2}| \\ \vdots \\ \sum_{i=1}^{n} d_i|c_{in}| \end{bmatrix} \tag{8.61}$$

Hence we can find any particular solution value $x_j$ as follows:

$$x_j = \left(\frac{1}{|A|}\right) \sum_{i=1}^{n} d_i|c_{ij}| \tag{8.62}$$

If you have a good memory, you will note that Equation (8.62) is very similar to Equation (8.51), which we used to find the determinant of matrix $A$ by means of expansion by cofactors for any column $j$. That is, in terms of column $j$, the determinant of matrix $A$ was given by

$$|A| = \sum_{i=1}^{n} a_{ij}|c_{ij}| \qquad \text{for any column } j = 1, \ldots, n \tag{8.63}$$

Equations (8.62) and (8.63) are identical, except that the $j$th column of $|A|$ has been replaced by the column vector $D$, with all other columns of the coefficient matrix intact.

In any case, we can use Equation (8.62) to find solution values. The solution value for variable $x_1$ in a system of $n$ linear equations in $n$ unknowns is given by

$$x_1 = \left(\frac{1}{|A|}\right) \sum_{i=1}^{n} d_1|c_{i1}| \tag{8.64}$$

$$= \left(\frac{1}{|A|}\right) \begin{vmatrix} d_1 & a_{12} & \cdots & a_{1n} \\ d_2 & a_{22} & \cdots & a_{2n} \\ \vdots & \vdots & & \vdots \\ d_n & a_{n2} & \cdots & a_{nn} \end{vmatrix} \tag{8.65}$$

$$= \frac{|A_1|}{|A|} \tag{8.66}$$

The first column of the coefficient matrix of Equation (8.65) is the $D$ column vector, because we wish to find the solution value of $x_1$. We can obtain the solution value for $x_2$ by replacing the second column in the coefficient matrix of Equation (8.62) with the $D$ column vector:

$$x_2 = \left(\frac{1}{|A|}\right) \sum_{i=1}^{n} d_2 |c_{i2}| \tag{8.67}$$

$$= \left(\frac{1}{|A|}\right) \begin{vmatrix} a_{11} & d_1 & \cdots & a_{1n} \\ a_{21} & d_2 & \cdots & a_{2n} \\ \vdots & \vdots & & \vdots \\ a_{n1} & d_n & \cdots & a_{nn} \end{vmatrix} \tag{8.68}$$

$$= \frac{|A_2|}{|A|} \tag{8.69}$$

Hence the solution value for any $x_j$ is given by

$$x_j = \left(\frac{1}{|A|}\right) \begin{vmatrix} a_{11} & a_{12} & \cdots & d_1 & \cdots & a_{1n} \\ a_{21} & a_{22} & \cdots & d_2 & \cdots & a_{2n} \\ \vdots & \vdots & & \vdots & & \vdots \\ a_{n1} & a_{n2} & \cdots & d_n & \cdots & a_{nn} \end{vmatrix} \tag{8.70}$$

$$= \frac{|A_j|}{|A|} \tag{8.71}$$

The subscript in the numerator of Equation (8.71) indicates which column has been replaced by the $D$ column vector in Equation (8.70). Equation (8.71) is the most general statement of Cramer's rule.

EXAMPLES

1. Solve the set of simultaneous linear equations by Cramer's rule. Given $y - 4x = 12$ and $y + 3x = 5$. Then solving,

$$y = \frac{|A_1|}{|A|} = \frac{\begin{vmatrix} 12 & -4 \\ 5 & 3 \end{vmatrix}}{\begin{vmatrix} 1 & -4 \\ 1 & 3 \end{vmatrix}} = \frac{56}{7} = 8$$

and

$$x = \frac{|A_2|}{|A|} = \frac{\begin{vmatrix} 1 & 12 \\ 1 & 5 \end{vmatrix}}{\begin{vmatrix} 1 & -4 \\ 1 & 3 \end{vmatrix}} = \frac{-7}{7} = -1$$

2. Solve the set of simultaneous linear equations by Cramer's rule. Given

$$2x_1 - x_2 - x_3 = 0$$

$$-x_1 + 4x_2 - x_3 = 0$$

$$x_1 + x_2 = 8$$

Then solving,

$$x_1 = \frac{|A_1|}{|A|} = \frac{\begin{vmatrix} 0 & -1 & -1 \\ 0 & 4 & -1 \\ 8 & 1 & 0 \end{vmatrix}}{\begin{vmatrix} 2 & -1 & -1 \\ -1 & 4 & -1 \\ 1 & 1 & 0 \end{vmatrix}} = \frac{40}{8} = 5$$

$$x_2 = \frac{|A_2|}{|A|} = \frac{\begin{vmatrix} 2 & 0 & -1 \\ -1 & 0 & -1 \\ 1 & 8 & 0 \end{vmatrix}}{\begin{vmatrix} 2 & -1 & -1 \\ -1 & 4 & -1 \\ 1 & 1 & 0 \end{vmatrix}} = \frac{24}{8} = 3$$

$$x_3 = \frac{|A_3|}{|A|} = \frac{\begin{vmatrix} 2 & -1 & 0 \\ -1 & 4 & 0 \\ 1 & 1 & 8 \end{vmatrix}}{\begin{vmatrix} 2 & -1 & -1 \\ -1 & 4 & -1 \\ 1 & 1 & 0 \end{vmatrix}} = \frac{56}{8} = 7$$

**EXERCISE 8.5**

Solve the following sets of simultaneous linear equations by Cramer's rule.

1. $\begin{aligned} x_1 + 3x_2 &= 15 \\ x_1 - 2x_2 &= -3 \end{aligned}$

2. $\begin{aligned} 2x_1 + 3x_2 &= 10 \\ -4x_1 + x_2 &= -6 \end{aligned}$

3. $\begin{aligned} 2x_1 - 3x_2 &= 7 \\ 3x_1 + 5x_2 &= 1 \end{aligned}$

4. $\begin{aligned} 10x_1 - x_2 - x_3 &= 0 \\ -x_1 + 12x_2 - 2x_3 &= 0 \\ x_1 + 2x_2 &= 24 \end{aligned}$

5. $\begin{aligned} 12x_1 - 2x_2 - x_3 &= 0 \\ 12x_1 - 6x_2 - x_3 &= 0 \\ x_1 + x_2 &= 16 \end{aligned}$

6. $\begin{aligned} x_1 + 2x_2 - 3x_3 &= -1 \\ 3x_1 - x_2 + 2x_3 &= 7 \\ 5x_1 + 3x_2 - 4x_3 &= 2 \end{aligned}$

7. $\begin{aligned} 2x_1 + x_2 - 2x_3 &= 10 \\ 3x_1 + 2x_2 - 2x_3 &= 1 \\ 5x_1 + 4x_2 + 3x_3 &= 4 \end{aligned}$

8. $\begin{aligned} x_1 + 2x_2 - 3x_3 &= 6 \\ 2x_1 - x_2 + 4x_3 &= 2 \\ 4x_1 + 3x_2 - 2x_3 &= 14 \end{aligned}$

9. $\begin{aligned} x_1 + 3x_2 - 2x_3 &= 0 \\ 2x_1 - 3x_2 + x_3 &= 0 \\ 3x_1 - 2x_2 + 2x_3 &= 0 \end{aligned}$

## MAXIMA AND MINIMA: FUNCTIONS OF $n$ INDEPENDENT VARIABLES

Chapter 6 dealt initially with the means of finding extreme points for functions of one independent variable, and subsequently with the same consideration for functions of two independent variables. The case(s) of three or more independent variables were said to flow directly from the one- and two-independent-variable cases. However, this was not formally demonstrated. With the help of matrix algebra, however, we shall discuss how to identify extreme points when we deal with functions that have $n$ independent variables.

### First-Order (Necessary) Condition

Consider a function of the form $z = f(x_1, x_2, \ldots, x_n)$, with the first partial derivatives of the function given by $f_1, f_2, \ldots, f_n$. In order for $z$ to have extreme points, whether maxima or minima, it is necessary for it to be in a "stationary" position. That is, it is necessary that $f_1 = f_2 = \cdots = f_n = 0$. This is the first-order condition for finding extreme points.

We demonstrated the first-order condition for extreme point(s) graphically in Figure 6.4 when we dealt with a function of one independent variable. This graphical representation had intuitive attractiveness, for it involved drawing a tangent to the curve of the function at all points at which the slope of that graph was equal to 0.

The analogous geometry for the case of two independent variables involves a three-dimensional diagram. A six-dimensional diagram is needed to illustrate extreme points when five independent variables are involved. In general, we need $n + 1$ dimensions to illustrate the case which involves $n$ independent variables. It is difficult to draw intelligible three-dimensional diagrams; four or more dimensions strain both graphical talents and understanding. For that reason, we cannot illustrate the geometry of maxima and minima where $n$ dimensions are involved.

### Second-Order (Sufficient) Condition

We shall state without proof the second-order condition for an extremum of a function. Given that the first partial derivatives of $z = f(x_1, x_2, \ldots, x_n)$ exist and have been set equal to 0 for solution purposes, we must find the *Hessian determinant* (or simply *Hessian*) relating to the function.

DEFINITION The *Hessian determinant* of a function $z = f(x_1, x_2, \ldots, x_n)$ is denoted by $|H|$, and is composed of elements that are second-order partial derivatives of the function such that

$$|H| = \begin{vmatrix} f_{11} & f_{12} & \cdots & f_{1n} \\ f_{21} & f_{22} & \cdots & f_{2n} \\ \vdots & \vdots & & \vdots \\ f_{n1} & f_{n2} & \cdots & f_{nn} \end{vmatrix} \tag{8.72}$$

Once we have found the Hessian determinant, one of the following conditions must hold:

(a) When $|H_1|, |H_2|, \ldots, |H_n| > 0$, we have a minimum at the critical point.
(b) When $|H_1| < 0$, $|H_2| > 0$, $|H_3| < 0, \ldots$, we have a maximum at the critical point.
(c) When neither (a) nor (b) is true, the test fails, and we must examine the function in the neighborhood of the critical point in order to determine whether an extreme point exists.

The Hessian determinant that is used in the second-order condition is a symmetric determinant. That is, the main diagonal of the Hessian consists of all second-order partial derivatives of the function with respect to the variables of the function; for example, $f_{11}, f_{22}, \ldots, f_{nn}$. The off-diagonal elements in the Hessian are composed of all mixed or cross-partial derivatives of the function, for example, $f_{12}$ or $f_{36}$, where, according to Young's theorem, $f_{ij} = f_{ji}$.

It is traditional to use the symbol $|H_i|$ to denote the $i$th *principal minor* of a Hessian determinant. Starting at the upper left-hand corner of the Hessian given in Equation (8.72), we have the following examples of principal minors:

$$|H_1| = |f_{11}| = f_{11} \qquad |H_2| = \begin{vmatrix} f_{11} & f_{12} \\ f_{21} & f_{22} \end{vmatrix} = \begin{vmatrix} f_{11} & f_{12} \\ f_{12} & f_{22} \end{vmatrix}$$

The principal minor $|H_3|$ is given by

$$|H_3| = \begin{vmatrix} f_{11} & f_{12} & f_{13} \\ f_{21} & f_{22} & f_{23} \\ f_{31} & f_{32} & f_{33} \end{vmatrix} = \begin{vmatrix} f_{11} & f_{12} & f_{13} \\ f_{12} & f_{22} & f_{23} \\ f_{13} & f_{23} & f_{33} \end{vmatrix} \tag{8.73}$$

We noted above that when one independent variable exists, and $|H_1| > 0$, then a minimum exists. However, when $|H_1| < 0$, a maximum exists. This is consistent with our work in Chapter 6, in which we stated that a function of one independent variable had a minimum at a critical point if $f''(x) > 0$, and a maximum if $f''(x) < 0$.

Analogously, a function of two independent variables satisfied the second-order condition for a minimum in Chapter 6 if

$$f_{xx} f_{yy} - (f_{xy})^2 > 0 \qquad \text{and} \qquad f_{xx}, f_{yy} > 0$$

at the critical point. A maximum existed if

$$f_{xx} f_{yy} - (f_{xy})^2 > 0 \qquad \text{and} \qquad f_{xx}, f_{yy} < 0$$

at the critical point. This is precisely what the second-order condition for the Hessian determinants requires.

$$|H_1| = |f_{xx}| = f_{xx} > 0$$

and

$$|H_2| = \begin{vmatrix} f_{xx} & f_{yy} \\ f_{yx} & f_{yy} \end{vmatrix} = f_{xx} f_{yy} - (f_{xy})^2 > 0$$

for a minimum. Similarly,



$$|H_1| = f_{xx} < 0$$

and

$$|H_2| = \begin{vmatrix} f_{xx} & f_{yy} \\ f_{yx} & f_{yy} \end{vmatrix} = f_{xx} f_{yy} - (f_{xy})^2 > 0$$

for a maximum.

A function with only one independent variable has only one principal minor. A function of two independent variables has only two principal minors. A function with $n$ independent variables has $n$ principal minors. We must examine each of those principal minors when we seek to determine whether an extreme point exists. If any one of those principal minors is found to have an incorrect sign, then we need go no further with the evaluation process.

It is wise to begin with $H_1$, proceed to $H_2$, and so forth. If, for example, we are testing for the existence of a maximum at a critical point, then the signs of the principal minors will alternate, beginning with a negative. If $H_1 < 0$ and $H_2 > 0$, but $H_3 > 0$, then a maximum point may not exist. In this case, the test fails, and we must examine the function in the neighborhood of the critical point in order to determine whether a maximum exists. In any case, we need not go beyond $|H_3|$ to determine that the test has failed. Finally, if there are $n$ independent variables, and $n$ is an even number, then the sign of the $n$th principal minor must be positive if a maximum exists. If $n$ is odd, then the sign of the $n$th principal minor must be negative for a maximum to exist.

## EXAMPLES

1. Find the extreme point(s) for the following function:

   $$z = x^2 + xy + y^2 - 3x + 2$$

   *First-order condition:*

   $$z_x = 2x + y - 3 = 0$$

   $$z_y = x + 2y = 0$$

   So the critical point $(2, -1)$ may be a maximum or a minimum.

   *Second-order condition:*

   $$|H_1| = |z_{xx}| = 2 > 0$$

   $$|H_2| = \begin{vmatrix} z_{xx} & z_{xy} \\ z_{yx} & z_{yy} \end{vmatrix} = \begin{vmatrix} 2 & 1 \\ 1 & 2 \end{vmatrix} = 3 > 0$$

   Thus $z$ has a minimum value at $(2, -1)$.

2. Find the extreme point(s) for the following function:

   $$z = -x_1^3 + 3x_1x_3 + 2x_2 - x_2^2 - 3x_3^2$$

*First-order condition:*

$$z_1 = -3x_1^2 + 3x_3 = 0$$

$$z_2 = 2 - 2x_2 = 0$$

$$z_3 = 3x_1 - 6x_3 = 0$$

The critical points (0, 1, 0) and $(\frac{1}{2}, 1, \frac{1}{4})$ may be maxima or minima.

*Second-order condition:*

(a) For the critical point $(\frac{1}{2}, 1, \frac{1}{4})$,

$$|H_1| = |z_{11}| = |-6x_1| = |-3| < 0$$

$$|H_2| = \begin{vmatrix} z_{11} & z_{12} \\ z_{21} & z_{22} \end{vmatrix} = \begin{vmatrix} -6x_1 & 0 \\ 0 & -2 \end{vmatrix} = \begin{vmatrix} -3 & 0 \\ 0 & -2 \end{vmatrix} = 12 > 0$$

$$|H_3| = \begin{vmatrix} z_{11} & z_{12} & z_{13} \\ z_{21} & z_{22} & z_{23} \\ z_{31} & z_{32} & z_{33} \end{vmatrix} = \begin{vmatrix} -6x_1 & 0 & 3 \\ 0 & -2 & 0 \\ 3 & 0 & -3 \end{vmatrix} = \begin{vmatrix} -3 & 0 & 3 \\ 0 & -2 & 0 \\ 3 & 0 & -3 \end{vmatrix} = -18 <$$

The critical point $(\frac{1}{2}, 1, \frac{1}{4})$ is a maximum.

(b) For the critical point (0, 1, 0),

$$|H_1| = |-6x_1| = 0$$

so the test fails, and we must therefore go back to the function and examine around the neighborhood of the critical point. The critical point is neither a maximum nor a minimum.

**EXERCISE 8.6**

Determine the critical point(s), if any, that maximize or minimize the following functions.

1. $z = 2x^2 + y^2 - 2xy + 5x - 3y + 1$
2. $z = 2x_1 + x_1x_2 + 4x_2 + x_1x_3 + x_3^2 + 8$
3. $z = 4x_1x_2 + 3x_3x_1^2 + x_2x_3$
4. $z = x_1^2 + x_2^2 + 8x_3^2 - x_1x_2 + 10$
5. $z = x_1^2 + x_2^2 + x_3^2 + x_1x_2 + x_2x_3 - 3x_1 - 8$
6. $w = x^3 + y^3 + z^3 - 3xyz$
7. $z = 5x^3 - 2xy + 3y^2$

## MAXIMA AND MINIMA SUBJECT TO CONSTRAINTS

We shall now extend the results of the previous section to deal with the situation in which we wish to identify extreme points in functions that have $n$ independent variables, and in which the functions are subject to one or more constraints.

### The Case of One Constraint

Consider a function of $n$ variables of the form $z = f(x_1, x_2, \ldots, x_n)$ subject to a constraint given by $g(x_1, x_2, \ldots, x_n) = 0$. We now form a new objective function of the form

$$L = L(x_1, x_2, \ldots, x_n, \lambda) = f(x_1, x_2, \ldots, x_n) - \lambda g(x_1, x_2, \ldots, x_n) \tag{8.74}$$

where $\lambda$ is a Lagrangian multiplier whose value is to be determined by the maximization (minimization) process.[6]

*First-order (necessary) condition*
We differentiate the new objective function given in Equation (8.74) with respect to the $n+1$ variables $x_1, x_2, \ldots, x_n, \lambda$, set these partial derivatives equal to 0, and solve for their critical roots. Only critical-root values can be extreme points. However, a critical-root value is not always an extreme point. We need a second-order (sufficient) condition in order to make a firm judgment.

*Second-order (sufficient) condition*
Given that the first partial derivatives of $L$ exist and have been set equal to 0 for solution purposes, we must find the bordered Hessian determinant relating to the function and its constraints.

DEFINITION The *bordered Hessian determinant* of a function $z = f(x_1, x_2, \ldots, x_n)$, subject to $g(x_1, x_2, \ldots, x_n) = 0$, is denoted by $|\bar{H}|$ such that

$$|\bar{H}| = \begin{vmatrix} 0 & g_1 & g_2 & \cdots & g_n \\ g_1 & L_{11} & L_{12} & \cdots & L_{1n} \\ g_2 & L_{21} & L_{22} & \cdots & L_{2n} \\ \vdots & \vdots & \vdots & & \vdots \\ g_n & L_{n1} & L_{n2} & \cdots & L_{nn} \end{vmatrix} \tag{8.75}$$

If all the first-order partial derivatives of the constraint and all the second-order partial derivatives of the function $L$ exist at the critical point(s), then one of the following conditions must hold.

(a) When $|\bar{H}_2|, |\bar{H}_3|, \ldots, |\bar{H}_n| < 0$, we have a minimum at the critical point.
(b) When $|\bar{H}_2| > 0$, $|\bar{H}_3| < 0$, $|\bar{H}_4| > 0, \ldots$, we have a maximum at the critical point.
(c) When neither (a) nor (b) is met, the test fails, and we must examine the function in the neighborhood around the critical point in order to determine whether a constrained extremum exists.

A bordered Hessian determinant is a symmetric determinant. It is simply a Hessian determinant that is bordered by the first partial derivatives of the constraint, and 0. The symmetry follows from the fact that a Hessian determinant, which is the major part of a bordered Hessian determinant, is also symmetric.

[6] The concept and use of the Lagrangian multiplier were initially introduced in Chapter 6.

It is customary to denote the $i$th bordered principal minor of a bordered Hessian determinant by the symbol $|\bar{H}_i|$. Among the bordered principal minors of the bordered Hessian found in Equation (8.75) are the following:

$$|\bar{H}_2| = \begin{vmatrix} 0 & g_1 & g_2 \\ g_1 & L_{11} & L_{12} \\ g_2 & L_{21} & L_{22} \end{vmatrix} \qquad |\bar{H}_3| = \begin{vmatrix} 0 & g_1 & g_2 & g_3 \\ g_1 & L_{11} & L_{12} & L_{13} \\ g_2 & L_{21} & L_{22} & L_{23} \\ g_3 & L_{31} & L_{32} & L_{33} \end{vmatrix} \tag{8.76}$$

■ The notation $|\bar{H}_2|$ means that we must take the Hessian determinant $|H_2|$ and place around it the appropriate border. $|\bar{H}_2|$ does *not* mean that we have a $2 \times 2$ determinant.

We should note carefully that the process of evaluating bordered Hessian determinants begins with $|\bar{H}_2|$, not with $|\bar{H}_1|$. We do not evaluate $|\bar{H}_1|$ when we maximize or minimize subject to a single constraint. We shall shortly state a general rule that deals with this situation.

EXAMPLES

1. Maximize or minimize the following function:

   $z = x_1^2 - 10x_2^2$

   subject to the constraint $x_1 - x_2 = 18$. Then

   $L(x_1, x_2, \lambda) = x_1^2 - 10x_2^2 - \lambda(x_1 - x_2 - 18)$

   *First-order condition:*

   $L_1 = 2x_1 - \lambda = 0$

   $L_2 = -20x_2 + \lambda = 0$

   $L_\lambda = -(x_1 - x_2 - 18) = 0$

   The critical point is therefore $x_1 = 20$, $x_2 = 2$, and $\lambda = 40$.

   *Second-order condition:*

   $$|\bar{H}_2| = \begin{vmatrix} 0 & 1 & -1 \\ 1 & 2 & 0 \\ -1 & 0 & -20 \end{vmatrix} = 18 > 0$$

   Thus there is a maximum at the critical point of (20, 2).
2. Maximize or minimize the following function:

   $z = 5x_1^2 + 10x_2^2 + x_3^2 - 4x_1x_2 - 2x_1x_3 - 36x_2$

   subject to the constraint $x_1 + 2x_2 + 4x_3 = 12$. Then

   $$L(x_1, x_2, x_3, \lambda) = 5x_1^2 + 10x_2^2 + x_3^2 - 4x_1x_2 - 2x_1x_3 - 36x_2 - \lambda(x_1 + 2x_2 + 4x_3 - 12)$$

   $L_1 = 10x_1 - 4x_2 - 2x_3 - \lambda = 0$

   $L_2 = 20x_2 - 4x_1 - 36 - 2\lambda = 0$

$L_3 = 2x_3 - 2x_1 - 4\lambda = 0$

$L_\lambda = -(x_1 + 2x_2 + 4x_3 - 12) = 0$

The critical point is therefore $x_1 = 1.23$, $x_2 = 2.14$, and $x_3 = 1.65$.

$$|\bar{H}_2| = \begin{vmatrix} 0 & 1 & 2 \\ 1 & 10 & -4 \\ 2 & -4 & 20 \end{vmatrix} = -76 < 0$$

and

$$|\bar{H}_3| = \begin{vmatrix} 0 & 1 & 2 & 4 \\ 1 & 10 & -4 & -2 \\ 2 & -4 & 20 & 0 \\ 4 & -2 & 0 & 2 \end{vmatrix} = -3528 < 0$$

Thus there is a minimum at the critical point $x_1 = 1.23$, $x_2 = 2.14$, $x_3 = 1.65$.

### The Case of Two or More Constraints

The problem of maximizing or minimizing a function of $n$ independent variables subject to two or more constraints is analogous to the situation in the preceding section, in which there was only one constraint. In terms of a bordered Hessian determinant, we simply add an additional border for each effective constraint.

Consider a function of the form $z = f(x_1, x_2, \ldots, x_n)$, which is subject to $m$ constraints ($m < n$) given by $g(x_1, x_2, \ldots, x_n) = 0$, $h(x_1, x_2, \ldots, x_n) = 0, \ldots,$ $k(x_1, x_2, \ldots, x_n)$. In order to find any extreme points that might exist, we form a new objective function of the form

$$\begin{aligned} L &= L(x_1, x_2, \ldots, x_n, \lambda_1, \lambda_2, \ldots, \lambda_m) \\ &= f(x_1, x_2, \ldots, x_n) - \lambda_1 g(x_1, x_2, \ldots, x_n) - \lambda_2 h(x_1, x_2, \ldots, x_n) \\ &\quad - \cdots - \lambda_m k(x_1, x_2, \ldots, x_n) \end{aligned} \tag{8.77}$$

where $\lambda_1, \ldots, \lambda_m$ are Lagrange multipliers.

*First-Order (Necessary) Condition*

The new objective function described in Equation (8.77) is differentiated with respect to each of the $n + m$ variables $(x_1, x_2, \ldots, x_n, \lambda_1, \lambda_2, \ldots, \lambda_m)$. The resulting partial derivatives are set equal to 0 and solved for critical points. These critical points may or may not identify actual extreme points. We must apply a second-order (sufficient) condition to identify those critical points that are extreme points.

*Second-Order (Sufficient) Condition*

Given that the first partial derivatives of $L$ exist and have been set equal to zero for solution purposes, we must find the appropriate bordered Hessian determinant. In this case, the bordered Hessian is given by

$$|\bar{H}| = \begin{vmatrix} 0 & \cdots & \cdots & 0 & k_1 & k_2 & \cdots & k_n \\ \vdots & & & \vdots & \vdots & \vdots & & \vdots \\ \cdot & \cdots & 0 & 0 & h_1 & h_2 & \cdots & h_n \\ 0 & \cdots & 0 & 0 & g_1 & g_2 & \cdots & g_n \\ k_1 & \cdots & h_1 & g_1 & L_{11} & L_{12} & \cdots & L_{1n} \\ k_2 & \cdots & h_2 & g_2 & L_{21} & L_{22} & \cdots & L_{2n} \\ \vdots & & \vdots & \vdots & \vdots & \vdots & & \vdots \\ k_n & \cdots & h_n & g_n & L_{n1} & L_{n2} & \cdots & L_{nn} \end{vmatrix} \tag{8.78}$$

If all the first-order partial derivatives of the constraints and all the second-order partial derivatives of the function $L$ exist at the critical point(s), then one of the following conditions must hold:

(a) When $|\bar{H}_{m+1}|, |\bar{H}_{m+2}|, \ldots, |\bar{H}_n|$ all have the same sign, namely $(-1)^m$, we have a constrained minimum at the critical point.
(b) When $|\bar{H}_{m+1}|, |\bar{H}_{m+2}|, \ldots, |\bar{H}_n|$ alternate in sign, where $|\bar{H}_{m+1}|$ has the sign $(-1)^{m+1}$, we have a constrained maximum at the critical point.
(c) When the requirements of neither (a) nor (b) are met, the test fails and we must examine the function in the neighborhood around the critical point in order to determine whether a constrained extremum exists.

The practice of beginning the evaluation of the bordered Hessians with something other than $|H_1|$ continues. The rule that guides this behavior requires that we begin with a bordered Hessian whose size is one bigger than the number of constraints. Hence, when $m$ constraints exist, we begin our analysis of the bordered Hessians with $|\bar{H}_{m+1}|$. We can now refer back to our previous work and explain our previous choices in this regard. When $m = 0$ and no constraint exists, we begin with $|H_1|$. When $m = 1$, we begin with $|\bar{H}_2|$; and so on.

The signs that are required for the successive bordered Hessian determinants follow a definite order. When we evaluate critical point(s) with respect to a maximum, the bordered Hessians must alternate in sign. In the case in which two constraints exist, the sign of $|\bar{H}_{m+1}| = |\bar{H}_3|$ must be negative, the sign of $|\bar{H}_4|$ must be positive, and so forth. The rule is that the sign is given by $(-1)^{m+1}$. Hence, if $m = 2$, the sign of $|\bar{H}_3|$ is $(-1)^3 = -1$, and $|\bar{H}_3|$ is negative.

The sign determination for the case of a constrained minimum differs from that of a constrained maximum. When $m = 0$, all bordered Hessians must be positive. When $m = 1$, all bordered Hessians must be negative. When $m = 2$, all bordered Hessians must once again be positive. In general, the sign of all bordered Hessians must be given by $(-1)^m$ if a minimum exists.

For example, when five constraints exist, then all bordered Hessian determinants must have a negative sign, for $(-1)^5 = -1$, which is negative. We can see that when the number of constraints is odd, the signs must all be negative, whereas when the number of constraints is even, the signs must all be positive.

**EXERCISE 8.7**

Maximize or minimize the following functions subject to the indicated constraints.

1. $z = 2x_1 + x_2 + 2x_1 x_2$, subject to the constraint $2x_1 + x_2 = 100$
2. $z = 25x_1 x_2 x_3$, subject to the constraint $x_1 + 2x_2 + 4x_3 = 180$
3. $w = \ln x + \ln y + \ln z$, subject to the constraint $5x + 2y + z = 120$
4. $z = x_1^2 + 4x_2^2 + x_3^2 - 4x_1 x_2 - 6x_3$, subject to the constraint $x_1 + x_2 + x_3 = 21$

## PROBLEMS

1. Write the following system of equations in matrix notation.

$$
\begin{array}{l}
a_{11}x_1 + a_{12}x_2 + a_{13}x_3 + \cdots + a_{1n}x_n = K_1 \\
a_{21}x_1 + a_{22}x_2 + a_{23}x_3 + \cdots + a_{2n}x_n = K_2 \\
\quad \vdots \qquad\quad \vdots \qquad\quad \vdots \qquad\qquad\quad \vdots \qquad \vdots \\
a_{n1}x_1 + a_{n2}x_2 + a_{n3}x_3 + \cdots + a_{nn}x_n = K_n
\end{array}
$$

2. Given the following national income equations:

   (1) $Y = C + I + G$, (2) $C = 200 + 0.7Y$,

   (3) $I = 75 + 0.1Y$, (4) $G = 100$

   (a) Find the equilibrium values of $C$, $I$, $G$, and $Y$.
   (b) What is the numeric value of the multiplier that we would use to determine the effects of autonomous changes in $I$ on $Y$?
   (c) Suppose that autonomous investment increases from 75 to 100. What is the reultant increase in $Y$? (Show this result algebraically and also by means of matrix algebra.)
   (d) Demonstrate that your numeric solutions to parts (a) and (c) are general equilibrium solutions in the sense that they are internally consistent with each other in magnitude.

3. A common utility function that is used in the theory of portfolio choice is one in which $U = U(\bar{R}, \sigma_{ij})$, where $\bar{R}$ is the expected rate of return realized on the portfolio and $\sigma_{ij}$ is the covariance of the rates of return on any two assets $i$ and $j$. Such a utility function is typically maximized subject to some type of constraint that requires that the investor's portfolio of assets ($A$'s), when summed, be equal to the investor's net wealth $W_n$. This means that the investor cannot allocate to the various investments more than the amount of net wealth without choosing to borrow. The typical Lagrangian expression that is maximized is a form of the following:

$$L = \sum_{i=1}^{n} \bar{r}_i A_i - C\left( \sum_{i=1}^{n} \sum_{j=1}^{n} A_i A_j \sigma_{ij} \right) + \lambda\left( W_n - \sum_{i=1}^{n} A_i \right)$$

   where $\bar{r}_i$ = expected rate of return on asset $i$, and $C$ = a constant.

(a) Differentiate the Lagrangian expression with respect to the $A_i$'s and $\lambda$, and set those partial derivatives equal to 0. The result should be a system of $N + 1$ equations in $N + 1$ unknowns.
(b) For the case of two assets, write the system of equations in matrix notation.
(c) Solve the system of equations in (b) by means of matrix algebra, and find the utility-maximizing combination of $A_1$, $A_2$.

4. Assume the following national income model:

$$Y = C + I + G, \qquad C = a + b(Y - T)$$

$$I = c + dY + ei \qquad c > 0,\ 0 < d < 1,\ e < 0$$

$$G = G_0, \qquad i = i_0$$

$$T = f + gY \qquad f, g > 0$$

where $Y$ is GNP; $C$ is consumption; $I$ is investment; $G$ is government spending; $T$ is taxation; $i$ is interest rate; and $a$, $b$, $c$, $d$, $e$, $f$, $g$ are parameters.
(a) List all the exogeneous and endogenous variables in the model.
(b) Solve for the equilibrium level of GNP, using Cramer's rule.

5. Find the equilibrium prices for $A$, $B$, and $C$ using inverse matrix algebra, then use Cramer's rule to check your answer.

$$Q_{D,A} = 8 - 2P_A + 3P_B - P_C$$

$$Q_{D,B} = 4 - 4P_B + P_A + 3P_C$$

$$Q_{D,C} = 6 - P_C + 3P_A + 3P_B$$

$$Q_{S,A} = 10$$

$$Q_{S,B} = 2P_B + 2$$

$$Q_{S,C} = 8 + P_C$$

6. Find the equilibrium position of a consumer, given the following utility function and budget information:

$$U = U(q_1, q_2, q_3) = \ln q_1 + \ln q_2 + \ln q_3$$

$$Y = 60 \qquad P_1 = 5 \qquad P_2 = 2 \qquad P_3 = 1$$

7. How much of goods $q_1$, $q_2$, and $q_3$ should a person consume so as to maximize utility if the utility function is given by

$$U = U(q_1, q_2, q_3) = 10q_1q_2q_3$$

The budget information is as follows: the price of $q_1$ is \$4, the price of $q_2$ is \$2, the price of $q_3$ is \$4, and the available budget is \$120.

# LINEAR PROGRAMMING AND INPUT-OUTPUT ANALYSIS

# 9

The knowledge of matrix algebra that we gained in Chapter 8 has several important uses beyond those already demonstrated. In particular, if we are familiar with the fundamentals of matrix algebra and its terminology, we can master two powerful quantitative techniques (linear programming and input-output analysis) with relative ease. We can appropriately regard these topics as a continuation of the matrix algebra application section of Chapter 8, and we devote a separate chapter to them only as a means of focusing attention on their importance to economists.

We shall initially consider linear programming in a matrix algebra framework, and subsequently examine input-output analysis in the same fashion.

## LINEAR PROGRAMMING

Linear programming is a mathematical technique that economists and others use to derive economically efficient solutions to problems that arise in a wide range of situations. Linear programming always involves the maximization or minimization of some function, subject to various constraints. For example, a school district may wish to minimize the cost of busing students from one location to another, with the students' initial locations considered as given. A firm might wish to maximize its output given that it faces certain input prices and has a finite limit on how much money it can spend on those inputs. Or a government agency, perhaps the Defense Department, may seek to minimize the cost of feeding, clothing, and equipping an infantry division, subject to constraints concerning the location of the resources used and how much of each resource is required.

DEFINITION *Linear programming* is a mathematical technique whereby one maximizes or minimizes a linear function subject to various *constraints*, or side conditions, stated in the form of linear inequalities.

### Stigler's Diet Problem Once Again

In Chapter 1 we considered a classic economic allocation exercise, Stigler's diet problem. We shall now recast the diet problem as a linear-programming problem that uses matrix algebra. The crux of the diet problem is to find the least expensive combination of foods available to consumers that will allow these same consumers to satisfy recommended daily dietary allowances established by the Food and Nutrition Board of the National Academy of Sciences. That is, Stigler's objective was to find the least expensive menu that would give the consumer required minimum levels of calories, vitamins, and so forth.

Stigler allowed the consumer to choose a menu from among 80 possible foods. Let $X_j$ refer to the quantity of food $j$ that an individual consumes. We can then represent the quantities of the 80 different foods consumed by the individual as $X_1, X_2, \ldots, X_{80}$. The $X_j$, with $j = 1, 2, \ldots, 80$, are *decision variables*, or unknowns, that are to be determined by solving the linear-programming problem.

Any attempt to determine the least expensive way to accomplish a given end must necessarily consider the prices of various alternatives. Let $P_j$ represent the dollar price of food $j$. Thus the prices of the 80 different foods that can be selected are represented by $P_1, P_2, \ldots, P_{80}$. For example, $P_1$ might be equal to $0.02 and represent the price of peanut butter per ounce. It follows that $P_1 X_1$, the price of peanut butter per ounce times the number of ounces of peanut butter purchased, is the consumer's total expenditure on peanut butter.

Equation (9.1) defines the total expenditure $C$ that the consumer makes on the 80 different foods. This equation is referred to as the *objective function*; it is this function that we seek to minimize as a part of Stigler's diet problem. Note that this objective function is *linear* in the $X_j$'s, the decision variables.[1]

$$C = P_1X_1 + P_2X_2 + \cdots + P_{80}X_{80} \tag{9.1}$$

The easiest way to minimize $C$ is to not spend any money on food, but this is not permissible, for such a menu plan would not satisfy the recommended daily dietary allowances, the *constraints*. Let $R$ symbolize a dietary requirement. Thus $R_1$ might represent the recommended intake of calories per individual per day. For example, in Stigler's 1945 version of the diet problem, the recommended intake of calories per individual per day was 3000. We can represent the nine different dietary requirements of Stigler's problem by the variables $R_1, R_2, \ldots, R_9$.

The diet problem is inherently challenging because two different foods seldom yield the same amount of nutrient per ounce of food. For example, in Stigler's 1945 exercise, 1 ounce of uncooked bacon yielded 186 calories, whereas 1 ounce of uncooked sirloin steak yielded only 88 calories. Let the symbol $a_{ij}$ represent the number of units of nutrient $i$ that are provided by 1 ounce of food $j$. Hence the $a_{ij}$ for uncooked bacon (in terms of calories) is 186, while the analogous $a_{ij}$ for uncooked sirloin steak is 88.

A consumer can satisfy a nutrient requirement by eating many different foods. The term $a_{ij}X_j$ represents the total number of units of nutrient $i$ that are obtained when one consumes a given number of ounces of food $j$. For example, if one consumes 6 ounces of uncooked bacon, then $X_j = 6$, and since $a_{ij} = 186$, $a_{ij}X_j = (186)(6) = 1116$ calories.

[1] Nonlinear objective functions are not permissible in a linear programming problem. If the researcher attempts to represent the underlying phenomenon by a linear equation when it is actually nonlinear, then the results obtained will be inaccurate and unreliable.

We have previously noted that Stigler assumed that the individual must obtain at least 3000 calories per day from the foods consumed. The consumer can choose among the 80 foods in order to satisfy this requirement. We can write this constraint as Equation (9.2), which states that the sum of all the calories the consumer derives from consuming various foods must be 3000 or greater:

$$a_{11}X_1 + a_{12}X_2 + a_{13}X_3 + \cdots + a_{1,80}X_{80} \geq 3000 \qquad (9.2)$$

The nine daily dietary requirements that Stigler imposed on his consumer in his diet problem were reported in Table 1.1 of Chapter 1. Each of these nine requirements constitutes a constraint on the consumer's activities that takes the form of a linear inequality similar to Equation (9.2). The nine constraints are

$$\begin{array}{cccc} a_{11}X_1 + & a_{12}X_2 + \cdots + & a_{1,80}X_{80} \geq & R_1 \\ a_{21}X_1 + & a_{22}X_2 + \cdots + & a_{2,80}X_{80} \geq & R_2 \\ \vdots & \vdots & \vdots & \vdots \\ a_{91}X_1 + & a_{92}X_2 + \cdots + & a_{9,80}X_{80} \geq & R_9 \end{array} \qquad (9.3)$$

The constraints or requirements given by Equations (9.3) are, like the objective function, linear in the decision variables $X_j$.

We must include one additional, seemingly obvious constraint, that $X_j \geq 0$ for all $j = 1, 2, \ldots, 80$. This restriction is known as a *nonnegativity constraint.* It explicitly restricts the solution values of the decision variables to be either zero or positive, thus eliminating the possibility of a nonsensical solution that might (for example) allow the individual to consume minus 5 ounces of uncooked bacon.

We can now state the diet problem directly as a linear-programming exercise. We wish to minimize the value of Equation (9.1), the objective function, subject to the nine nutrient requirements stated as constraints in Equation (9.3). In addition, we must satisfy the nonnegativity constraint.

*Minimize:*

$$C = P_1X_1 + P_2X_2 + \cdots + P_{80}X_{80}$$

*Subject to:*

$$\begin{array}{cccc} a_{11}X_1 + & a_{12}X_2 + \cdots + & a_{1,80}X_{80} \geq & R_1 \\ a_{21}X_1 + & a_{22}X_2 + \cdots + & a_{2,80}X_{80} \geq & R_2 \\ \vdots & \vdots & \vdots & \vdots \\ a_{91}X_1 + & a_{92}X_2 + \cdots + & a_{9,80}X_{80} \geq & R_9 \end{array} \qquad (9.4)$$

and $X_j \geq 0$, for all $j = 1, 2, \ldots, 80$

The solutions to Stigler's 1945-vintage diet problem and a more recent version may be found in Table 1.2.

**A Formal Definition of a Linear-Programming Model**

The previous example, which stated Stigler's diet problem as a linear-programming problem, exhibits the three fundamental properties of any linear-programming problem:

1. The object of the problem is to find optimal values for the decision variables or unknowns in the problem.
2. The optimal values of the decision variables are such that they either minimize or maximize an explicit linear objective function.
3. The minimization or maximization solution of the objective function must be feasible. That is, the values of the decision variables in the optimal solution must satisfy both the linear inequality constraints and the nonnegativity constraints.

Our general linear-programming model has the following structure:

*Maximize or Minimize:*

$$X_0 = C_1X_1 + C_2X_2 + \cdots + C_nX_n$$

*Subject to:*

$$\begin{aligned} &a_{11}X_1 + a_{12}X_2 + \cdots + a_{1n}X_n(\leq, =, \geq)b_1 \\ &a_{21}X_1 + a_{22}X_2 + \cdots + a_{2n}X_n(\leq, =, \geq)b_2 \\ &\ \vdots \qquad\quad \vdots \qquad\qquad\quad \vdots \qquad\qquad\qquad \vdots \\ &a_{m1}X_1 + a_{m2}X_2 + \cdots + a_{mn}X_n(\leq, =, \geq)b_m \\ &X_j \geq 0 \text{ for all } j = 1, 2, \ldots, n \end{aligned} \tag{9.5}$$

where $n$ = the number of decision variables, and $m$ = the number of constraints or side conditions.

Each of the decision variables ($X_j$'s) must appear in the objective function of a linear-programming problem. Only one sign ($\leq$, $=$, or $\geq$) can hold in any particular constraint. The $b_i$, $a_{ij}$, and $C_j$ are the parameters of the model. The $b_i$'s are the amounts of scarce resource $i$ available for allocation ($i = 1, 2, \ldots, m$). The parameter $a_{ij}$ represents the amount of resource $i$ that is consumed by, or allocated to, each unit of decision variable $j$ (for $i = 1, 2, \ldots, m$ and $j = 1, 2, \ldots, n$). The increase in $X_0$ that results from a unit increase in $X_j$ is represented by $C_j$. For example, if $C_j = -5$, then a one-unit increase in $X_j$ decreases $X_0$ by five units.

We can write the general linear-programming model more compactly using matrix notation. Equation (9.5) becomes

*Maximize or Minimize:*

$$X_0 = CX$$

*Subject to:*

$$AX(\leq, =, \geq)B$$

$$X \geq 0$$

where

$$X = \begin{bmatrix} X_1 \\ X_2 \\ \vdots \\ X_n \end{bmatrix} \qquad C = [C_1 C_2 \cdots C_n]$$

$$A = \begin{bmatrix} a_{11} & a_{12} & \cdots & a_{1n} \\ a_{21} & a_{22} & \cdots & a_{2n} \\ \vdots & \vdots & & \vdots \\ a_{m1} & a_{m2} & \cdots & a_{mn} \end{bmatrix} \qquad B = \begin{bmatrix} b_1 \\ b_2 \\ \vdots \\ b_m \end{bmatrix} \tag{9.6}$$

Although a graphical approach to solving linear programming problems is seldom very efficient in terms of either time or effort, the graphical approach does give you a clear understanding of what linear programming actually involves. We shall use the graphical approach in this section to solve a rather simple linear-programming problem. This should enable you to visualize exactly what is happening when you find a linear-programming solution (regardless of the formal methodology used).

We shall demonstrate the graphical approach to linear programming by a problem concerning a firm, Acme Manufacturing Company, that produces two products, $X_1$ and $X_2$. Acme charges a price of \$20 per unit for $X_1$ and \$15 per unit for $X_2$. Acme also believes that the demand for these two products is sufficiently strong that it can sell all that it wishes at these prices.

Acme's production is limited by three resource constraints. The production of $X_1$ and $X_2$ both require three inputs, which we shall label *a*, *b*, and *c*. Thus Acme really has two production functions: $X_1 = X_1(a, b, c)$ and $X_2 = X_2(a, b, c)$. Acme has only 60 units of input *a*, 24 units of input *b*, and 84 units of input *c* available. It is impossible for Acme to augment the quantities of these inputs during the current production period.

Each time a single unit of good $X_1$ is produced, Acme uses 5 units of input *a*, 3 units of input *b*, and 12 units of input *c*. The production of a single unit of good $X_2$ requires 15 units of input *a*, 4 units of input *b*, and 7 units of input *c*. Acme does not have the ability to alter these input-output relationships during the current production period. Table 9.1 summarizes the price, input, and output information that Acme has available.

Acme's objective is to maximize the revenue *R* that it receives from the sale of goods $X_1$ and $X_2$, while at the same time not violating any resource constraint that it faces. We can state this problem in linear-programming terms as follows:

*Maximize:*

$$R = P_1 X_1 + P_2 X_2 = 20X_1 + 15X_2$$

*Subject to:*

$$5X_1 + 15X_2 \leq 60 \quad \text{(input constraint } a\text{)}$$
$$3X_1 + 4X_2 \leq 24 \quad \text{(input constraint } b\text{)} \qquad (9.$$
$$12X_1 + 7X_2 \leq 84 \quad \text{(input constraint } c\text{)}$$
$$X_1, X_2 \geq 0 \quad \text{(nonnegativity constraint)}$$

Once we have formulated the linear programming problem, the next step i the graphical approach is to delineate the *solution space*. We do this by graph ing the constraints (as we shall do below). The constraints, when graphe enclose a set of feasible (possible) solutions that constitute the solution spac Linear programming selects the point within that solution space that maxi mizes (minimizes) the value of the objective function.

If we are willing to ignore, for the time being, the less-than sign in the linea constraints of Acme's linear programming problem, and therefore treat thes equations as if they had equals signs then we can begin to provide a visua representation of the linear-programming problem. From Chapter 2, we kno that we can graph a straight line without great difficulty if we are given tw points on that line. For example, if we know the horizontal intercept (abscissa and vertical intercept (ordinate) of a line, then we can connect these tw intercepts with a straight line and obtain the needed graph. We shall use thi technique to define the solution space for Acme. Figure 9.1 illustrates thi procedure.

The *a* constraint, made into an equality, is $5X_1 + 15X_2 = 60$. The intercep of this line with the $X_1$ axis is (12, 0), while the intercept with the $X_2$ axis i (0, 4). These two points, (12, 0) and (0, 4), are labeled *A* and *B*, respectively, i Figure 9.1. Straight line *AB* connects these points and is a visual representatio of the *a* constraint that Acme faces. The original *a* constraint was of a less than-or-equal-to variety. This means that we should interpret straight line *A* as telling us that the area to the *left* of straight line *AB* is a portion of th

Table 9.1 Price, input, and output data confronting Acme Manufacturing Company

1. Acme produces two goods, $X_1$ and $X_2$.
2. The price of good 1, $P_1$, is \$20. The price of good 2, $P_2$, is \$15. Acme can se whatever quantity it wishes during this production period without influencing thes prices.
3. Acme has available: 60 units of input *a*
   24 units of input *b*
   84 units of input *c*
4. The production of a single unit of $X_1$ requires: 5 units of input *a*
   3 units of input *b*
   12 units of input *c*
5. The production of a single unit of $X_2$ requires: 15 units of input *a*
   4 units of input *b*
   7 units of input *c*

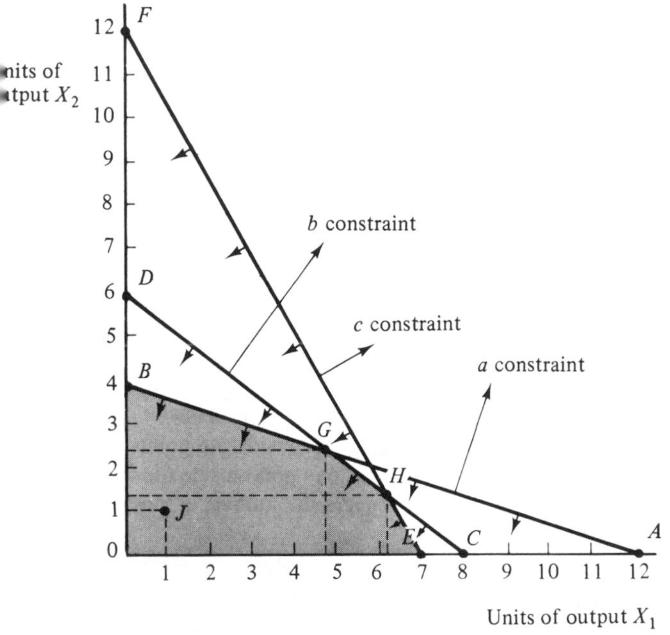


igure 9.1 The graphics of the Acme Manufacturing Company linear-programming roblem

asible solution area insofar as this constraint is concerned. The area to the *ght* of straight line *AB* is not in the feasible area and consists of points that re impossible for Acme to obtain. Similarly, the feasible area defined by the *b* onstraint is given by the area to the left of straight line *CD*, and the feasible rea defined by the *c* constraint is given by the area to the left of straight ne *EF*.

The nonnegativity constraint ($X_1, X_2 \geq 0$) specifies that the optimal soluon (the revenue-maximizing solution) for the objective function must lie in ıe first quadrant of Figure 9.1. Hence the shaded area *OBGHE*, which is ›rmed by the *a*, *b*, and *c* constraints, represents the area of feasible (possible) roduction combinations that Acme could undertake. The optimum solution › Acme's linear programming problem is a point that lies somewhere within ıis shaded solution space. Such a point maximizes Acme's sales revenues ithout violating any of the resource constraints that Acme faces.

An infinite number of points lie either within or on the boundary of shaded rea *OBGHE* in Figure 9.1. This means that an infinite number of possibilities onfront us when we attempt to identify the solution that is optimal.

To illustrate the search technique that linear programming performs, we ıall now consider a few specific points within the solution space. At the origin, $_1 = 0$ and $X_2 = 0$, so that total revenue is also 0. Since it is possible to produce positive quantities of goods $X_1$ and $X_2$ that will generate some sales revenue, we know that the solution at the origin is not optimal. We can do better.

One possible solution to the linear programming problem that we can easily see is permissible would have us produce one unit each of $X_1$ and $X_2$. This solution, represented by point $J$ in Figure 9.1, generates sales revenues equal to $\$20(1) + \$15(1) = \$35$. We also observe that increased production increases total sales revenues. For example, suppose that we produce two units of both $X_1$ and $X_2$; then total sales revenues would be $\$20(2) + \$15(2) = \$70$. Repeated experimentation of this type leads to the conclusion that we should increase both $X_1$ and $X_2$ as long as our constraints allow us to do so. Increased production of both goods always means increased total sales revenues.

Any point *inside* the solution space represents less production (and therefore less total sales revenue) than at least one point on the boundary of the solution space. The moral to this story is that *the optimal solution lies on the boundary of the solution space*, not inside it. When we are considering points as candidates for the optimal solution, we can discount any point inside the solution space. Knowledge of this fact *substantially reduces* the number of possible solutions with which we must contend.

We proceed therefore to consider only those solution points that are on the boundary of the shaded solution space in Figure 9.1. Corner point $E$ is the $X_1$ intercept. We can see that point $E$ represents a production of $X_1 = 7$ and $X_2 = 0$. Total sales revenues in this case are $\$20(7) + \$15(0) = \$140$. The $X_2$ intercept, corner point $B$, involves the production of $X_1 = 0$, $X_2 = 4$. Total sales revenues in this case are $\$20(0) + \$15(4) = \$60$.

We next consider corner point $G$ in Figure 9.1. Point $G$ is given by the intersection of the $a$ constraint and the $b$ constraint, and involves the production of both goods $X_1$ and $X_2$. We can determine the precise levels of output of $X_1$ and $X_2$ at point $G$ by solving (simultaneously) the equations of the $a$ and $b$ constraints.

$$\begin{aligned} 5X_1 + 15X_2 &= 60 \qquad (a \text{ constraint}) \\ 3X_1 + 4X_2 &= 24 \qquad (b \text{ constraint}) \end{aligned} \tag{9.8}$$

We can accomplish this either by eliminating a variable and substituting, by inverse matrix operation, or by using Cramer's rule. Using any of these solution techniques, we find that $X_1 = 4.8$ and $X_2 = 2.4$ at point $G$. This means that total sales revenue at point $G$ is $\$20(4.8) + \$15(2.4) = \$132$.

Similarly, we can find the solution values for $X_1$ and $X_2$ at point $H$. Point $H$ is formed by the intersection of the $b$ constraint and the $c$ constraint.

$$\begin{aligned} 3X_1 + 4X_2 &= 24 \qquad (b \text{ constraint}) \\ 12X_1 + 7X_2 &= 84 \qquad (c \text{ constraint}) \end{aligned} \tag{9.9}$$

We solve the equations of the $b$ constraint and the $c$ constraint for $X_1$ and $X_2$ and find that at point $H$, $X_1 = 6.22$ and $X_2 = 1.33$. Total sales revenue at point $H$ is therefore $\$20(6.22) + \$15(1.33) = \$144.35$.

Table 9.2 lists the four *corner solutions* that we have found thus far. It is apparent that the most attractive solution (the *optimal solution*) in terms of total sales revenues is given by point $H$, where Acme production is $X_1 = 6.22$, $X_2 = 1.33$, and total sales revenues are \$144.35. We shall now assert that one of the corner points of the solution space is always the optimal solution to a linear-programming problem. This assertion may not be intuitively obvious, however, and requires more explanation.

Consider Figure 9.2, which graphs the constraints of the Acme linear programming problem. Shaded area $OBGHE$ once again represents the solution space. However, superimposed on Figure 9.2 are various possible graphs of the objective function, $R = \$20X_1 + \$15X_2$. Each different graph of the objective function assumes a different value for $R$. For example, let $R = \$30$. Given the equation $30 = 20X_1 + 15X_2$, we find that the $X_1$ intercept is $(\frac{3}{2}, 0)$, while the $X_2$ intercept is (0, 2). The straight line connecting these two points (labeled $MN$) contains all those levels of production that generate total sales revenues of \$30. Similarly, straight line $BQ$ is the locus of points representing total sales revenues of \$60, and so forth. It is apparent in Figure 9.2 that the farther away from the origin a revenue line is, the higher the value of the objective function.

Since the object of the linear-programming problem is to maximize total sales revenue, we wish to attain a point on the highest revenue line that is consistent with the constraints that we face. The total revenue line labeled \$150 is highly attractive but is not possible, since it has no point in common with the solution space. The total revenue line labeled \$120 has many points inside the solution space (points $S$ and $T$ are two of these). However, we can see in Figure 9.2 that other total revenue lines farther from the origin are also possible. The highest possible total revenue line that contains at least one point in the solution space is the one that is tangent to the solution space. The total revenue line labeled \$144.35 is the one that we seek. It is tangent to the solution space at point $H$. There is no other feasible total revenue line that will generate

Table 9.2 Finding the optimal solution in the Acme linear-programming problem depicted in Figure 9.1

| *Solution point* | *Production at that point* | *Total sales revenue at that point* |
|---|---|---|
| Origin | $X_1 = 0$<br>$X_2 = 0$ | \$ 0.00 |
| Point $E$ | $X_1 = 7$<br>$X_2 = 0$ | \$140.00 |
| Point $B$ | $X_1 = 0$<br>$X_2 = 4$ | \$ 60.00 |
| Point $G$ | $X_1 = 4.8$<br>$X_2 = 2.4$ | \$132.00 |
| Point $H$ | $X_1 = 6.22$<br>$X_2 = 1.33$ | \$144.35 |

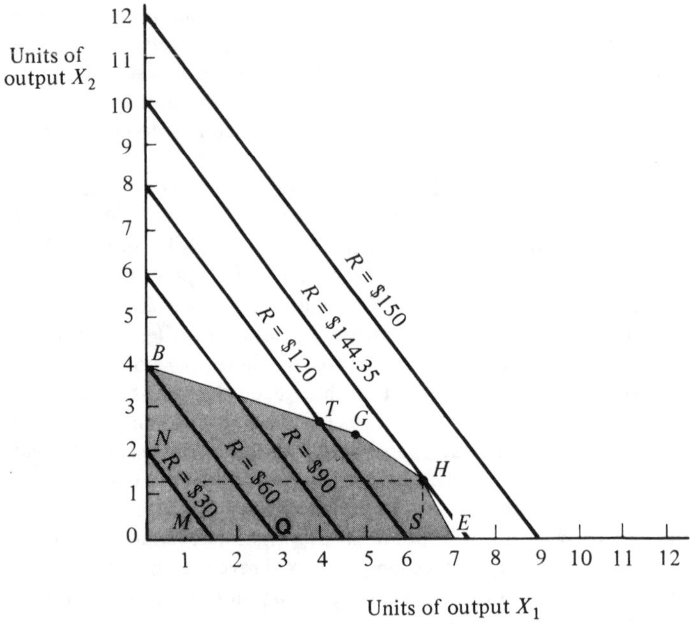


Figure 9.2 Finding the optimal solution by graphing the objective function

as much total sales revenue for Acme. Point $H$, therefore, defines the optimal solution.

In general, a corner of the solution space will always be the optimal solution to a linear programming problem. Only when the slope of the objective function is the same as the slope of a binding constraint will there be more than one optimal solution. For example, if the slope of the objective function in Figure 9.2 were the same as the slope of line segment $HG$, then all the points on line segment $HG$ (including the corner points $H$ and $G$) would be optimal.

We can now perform a conceptual experiment that demonstrates that point $H$ in Figures 9.1 and 9.2 is in fact the optimal solution. If a particular point is a unique optimal solution, then a movement away from that point but along the boundary of the solution space should result in lower total sales revenue. For example, as we move from point $H$ in the direction of point $G$, we move to progressively lower total revenue lines. Similarly, as we move from point $H$ in the direction of point $E$, we also find ourselves on progressively lower total revenue lines. We can visualize ourselves at the top of a total sales revenue hill when we are at point $H$. A movement in any direction from the top of the hill decreases altitude (total sales revenue).

We now see that we can depend on an optimal solution to occur at a corner point of the solution space. An efficient linear-programming solution technique is ordinarily to identify the corner points in a problem, evaluate them, and select the optimal solution from among those possibilities.

The *simplex algorithm* is one such technique that is frequently used. The simplex algorithm is a search technique that identifies and evaluates the corner points in a problem. It continually strives to find a better solution than the one at hand. When it reaches an optimal point, such as $H$ in Figures 9.1 and 9.2, it stops. A movement to any other corner (away from point $G$) would result in a worse solution.

### The Dual Problem

We can actually view every linear-programming problem as consisting of two separate problems. The original linear-programming problem is called the *primal problem*, while a second hybrid formulation of this original problem is known as the *dual problem*. The dual problem in linear programming often yields results that are quite useful to economists and other decision-makers. Also, the dual problem is sometimes easier to solve than the original (primal) problem. Therefore, when the primal problem is intractable and difficult to solve, we can sometimes solve the dual problem, then use the information from that dual to solve the primal problem.

Assume that the original (primal) linear-programming problem is

*Maximize:*

$$X_0 = C_1X_1 + C_2X_2 + \cdots + C_nX_n$$

*Subject to:*

$$\begin{aligned}
&a_{11}X_1 + a_{12}X_2 + \cdots + a_{1n}X_n \le b_1\\
&a_{21}X_1 + a_{22}X_2 + \cdots + a_{2n}X_n \le b_2\\
&\vdots \qquad \vdots \qquad \vdots \qquad \vdots\\
&a_{m1}X_1 + a_{m2}X_2 + \cdots + a_{mn}X_n \le b_m
\end{aligned} \tag{9.10}$$

$x_j \ge 0$ for all $j = 1, 2, \ldots, n$

The dual problem associated with this primal problem is

*Minimize:*

$$X_0 = b_1Y_1 + b_2Y_2 + \cdots + b_mY_m$$

*Subject to:*

$$\begin{aligned}
&a_{11}Y_1 + a_{21}Y_2 + \cdots + a_{m1}Y_m \ge C_1\\
&a_{12}Y_1 + a_{22}Y_2 + \cdots + a_{m2}Y_m \ge C_2\\
&\vdots \qquad \vdots \qquad \vdots \qquad \vdots\\
&a_{1n}Y_1 + a_{2n}Y_2 + \cdots + a_{mn}Y_m \ge C_n
\end{aligned} \tag{9.11}$$

$Y_i \ge 0$ for all $i = 1, 2, \ldots, m$

where $Y_1, Y_2, \ldots, Y_m$ are the dual variables.

A definite symmetry exists between a primal problem and its dual. When the primal problem involves the maximization of a function, then the dual involves the minimization of some function. When the constraints on the primal objective function require the firm to arrange its activities so that its input use and expenditures are less than or equal to certain constants, the constraints on the dual objective function require that certain of the firm's activities be equal to or exceed certain constant levels. For example, if the primal problem is to maximize output given a cost constraint of \$200, then the dual problem is to minimize the cost of producing a certain level of output, perhaps 10 units. We shall be more specific about the symmetry between the primal and dual linear-programming problems in a moment.

One of the most interesting results of many dual problems in linear programming is the idea of a *shadow price*. Decision-makers often wish to estimate the value of contributions that various inputs make to the optimal solution. On occasion, not all the available units of a particular input are used in the optimal solution. In such a circumstance, the decision-maker has little need for additional units of such inputs. Therefore the shadow price of such inputs is 0, because an additional unit of such an input would not alter the optimal solution. For example, the value of an extra seat in a classroom that already has many empty seats is 0. Similarly, the value of a second textbook to a student who already has one is 0 until the student loses the first textbook.

DEFINITION A *shadow price* indicates the value at the margin that an input has for the objective function's activities.

We can, in many situations, interpret the shadow price of an input as the value of the marginal product of that input. This is an interesting and quite useful result, particularly in decision situations in which the input in question is not purchased in the market, or in which the connection between that input and the ultimate output seems quite distant at best. The shadow price in this case indicates the price that the decision-maker would have to pay for this input in a competitive market, even when such a market does not formally exist!

Economic planners in nonmarket economies such as the Soviet Union have made considerable use of the shadow prices of linear programming. Since market prices often do not exist in the Soviet Union, it is difficult for planners to cost, price, and value things efficiently. Shadow prices enable them to do so. Similarly, large organizations (the military services are a prime example) that do not vend their wares in a conventional fashion can use shadow-pricing techniques to increase the efficiency of many activities, such as purchasing, routing, intrabranch transfers, and even determining the optimal antisubmarine defense.

### The Symmetry between the Primal and the Dual Problems

1. If the primal problem involves maximization, then the dual problem involves minimization, and vice versa.
2. If the primal problem involves $\leq$ constraints, then the dual problem involves $\geq$ constraints.

3. The coefficients of the variables in the primal objective function are the right-hand constants of the constraint equations in the dual problem.
4. The coefficients of the variables in the dual objective function are the right-hand constants of the constraint equations in the primal problem.
5. A new set of variables $Y_i$ appears in the dual objective function and constraint equations. These $Y_i$ are the shadow prices of the inputs.
6. If there are $n$ decision variables and $m$ constraint equations in the primal problem, then there will be $m$ variables and $n$ constraints in the dual problem.
7. The coefficients of the constraint equations in the primal problem are the same as the coefficients of the constraint equations in the dual problem *except that* the rows and columns are interchanged. That is, each $a_{ij}$ now becomes $a_{ji}$. In matrix notation, if

   $$A = [a_{ij}], \qquad \text{for } i = 1, 2, \ldots, m \text{ and } j = 1, 2, \ldots, n$$

   in the primal problem, then $A' = [a_{ji}]$ is associated with the dual problem.
8. The nonnegativity constraints apply to all variables in both the primal and the dual problems.
9. The optimal solution is identical for both the primal and the dual problems.

EXAMPLES

1. Given that the primal problem is the Acme Manufacturing situation:

$$\textit{Maximize: } R = 20X_1 + 15X_2$$

$$\textit{Subject to: } 5X_1 + 15X_2 \leq 60$$

$$3X_1 + 4X_2 \leq 24$$

$$12X_1 + 7X_2 \leq 84$$

$$X_1, X_2 \geq 0$$

then the dual problem is

$$\textit{Minimize: } Y_0 = 60Y_a + 24Y_b + 84Y_c$$

$$\textit{Subject to: } 5Y_a + 3Y_b + 12Y_c \geq 20$$

$$15Y_a + 4Y_b + 7Y_c \geq 15$$

$$Y_a, Y_b, Y_c \geq 0$$

And the optimal solution is: $X_1 = 6.22 \qquad X_2 = 1.33$

$$R = Y_0 = 144.35$$

$$Y_a = 0 \qquad Y_b = 1.47 \qquad Y_c = 1.30$$

Note that the $Y$'s are shadow prices. $Y_a = 0$ because units of input $a$ remain unused after the optimal solution has been implemented.

2. Given that the primal problem is

$$\textit{Minimize:}\ X_0 = 2X_1 + 5X_2$$

$$\textit{Subject to:}\ 5X_1 + 6X_2 \geq 12$$

$$-3X_1 + 4X_2 \geq 10$$

$$X_1 - 5X_2 \geq 8$$

$$2X_1 + X_2 \geq 3$$

$$X_1, X_2 \geq 0$$

then the dual problem is

$$\textit{Maximize:}\ Y_0 = 12Y_1 + 10Y_2 + 8Y_3 + 3Y_4$$

$$\textit{Subject to:}\ 5Y_1 - 3Y_2 + Y_3 + 2Y_4 \leq 2$$

$$6Y_1 + 4Y_2 - 5Y_3 + Y_4 \leq 5$$

$$Y_1, Y_2, Y_3, Y_4 \geq 0$$

## INPUT-OUTPUT ANALYSIS

The system of markets in the United States contains millions of separate and independent economic decision units. Each decision unit is interested primarily in its own welfare and survival, and seemingly pays little heed to the survival and welfare of any other decision unit. Nonetheless, as Adam Smith persuasively demonstrated more than two centuries ago,[2] the self-serving efforts of millions of independent economic decision-makers are somehow harnessed and drawn together into an economic system. Day in, day out, this economic system unfailingly provides approximately the correct quantities of food, clothing, shelter, and other goods that consumers wish to purchase. This is Smith's "invisible hand" at work, for no central planning agency wills this to take place. The individual decision-maker, intending only personal good, unwittingly does public good as well. How and why does the economic system hang together? What are the interrelationships between inputs and outputs that affect our everyday lives? The answers to these types of questions are provided by general equilibrium analysis.

Adam Smith was an early practitioner of general equilibrium analysis. This analysis explicitly includes and analyzes reactions and feedback effects among large numbers of variables. Nothing is held constant,[3] and it is assumed that all markets and all decision-makers are affected by one another's actions to some degree. In general equilibrium analysis, the price of oil affects the price of gasoline, but it also affects the price of automobiles, plastic drinking cups, and the temperature at which you choose to heat your home. The quantity and

[2] Adam Smith, *The Wealth of Nations*, Penguin Books, Baltimore, Md., 1970.

[3] In contrast to the *ceteris paribus* assumption that we made when we were using partial derivatives, we now make a *mutatis mutandis* assumption. All possible changes and interreactions are permissible.

quality of public transportation available affects the quantity of automobiles supplied and demanded, value of homes served by public transportation, and the location of industries and banks.

This section is devoted to input-output analysis, a general equilibrium approach to production. Input-output analysis is entirely empirical in nature. It describes the relationship among various inputs and various outputs. Demand conditions play no part in input-output models, because input-output analysis examines only the relationship between inputs to the productive process and the outputs that result. The prices and quantities at which we might produce and sell such inputs and outputs and such factors as price elasticity of demand are not considered.

The father of input-output analysis is the economist Wassily Leontief.[4] Leontief used input-output analysis to demonstrate that the production of one sector of the economy depends, to some degree, on the production of all other sectors of the economy. The input-output "tables" Leontief produced described in great detail the precise numeric relationships between inputs used and the outputs produced in the American economy. This set of relationships was stated in physical terms (for example, tons of steel or gallons of gasoline) rather than monetary terms. The price of a ton of steel was not considered.

Most input-output models make three basic assumptions. First, they assume that no two commodities are produced jointly. Each firm or market is assumed to produce only one homogeneous product. Second, all inputs are employed in rigidly fixed proportions in production. There is no law of diminishing returns because input proportions never vary. There are always constant returns to scale. Third, no external economies or diseconomies exist for any firm or market. The production of steel, for example, does not generate any pollution, nor do public schools confer any benefits on those who do not attend them.

Let the total production of any single industry during a particular period be represented by $X_i$. Industry $X_i$'s production can be used as inputs in other productive processes, or it can be used to satisfy final consumption demand. If there are $n$ different industries, then potentially $n$ different industries can use output $X_i$ as an input. This enables us to write

$$X_i = X_{i1} + X_{i2} + \cdots + X_{in} + d_i \tag{9.12}$$

where $X_i$ = output of industry $i$, $X_{ij}$ = output of industry $i$ used as an input in industry $j$, and $d_i$ = final demand for the finished goods and services of industry $i$.

We pointed out above that input-output analysis assumes that all production takes place under conditions of rigidly fixed proportions. Thus the amount of steel it takes to produce one car does not change, regardless of the number of cars produced. Let $a_{ij}$ represent a *technical coefficient of production.* Specifically, $a_{ij}$ tells us the constant number of units of input $j$ that are required

[4] The first exposition here is Wassily Leontief, "Quantitative Input-Output Relations in the Economic System of the United States," *Review of Economics and Statistics*, 18 (August 1936), 105–125.

to produce one unit of output $i$. We can therefore express the production of industry $i$ as follows:

$$X_i = \sum_{j=1}^{n} a_{ij}X_j + d_i \qquad i = 1, \ldots, n \tag{9.13}$$

where $X_i$ = output of industry $i$, $a_{ij}$ = number of units of input $j$ needed to produce one unit of output $i$, $X_j$ = output of industry $j$, and $d_i$ = final demand for the finished goods and services of industry $i$.

In an economy that has $n$ industries, there are $n \times n$ technical coefficients of production to consider, since each industry can potentially provide inputs to every other industry (including itself). Table 9.3 illustrates the possible technical coefficients of production. We can see that we can arrange these technical coefficients in the form of an $n \times n$ matrix $X = [a_{ij}]$.

We can now write a full system of linear equations that describes the input-output relationships for an economy composed of $n$ industries:

$$\begin{aligned}
X_1 &= a_{11}X_1 + a_{12}X_2 + \cdots + a_{1n}X_n + d_1 \\
X_2 &= a_{21}X_1 + a_{22}X_2 + \cdots + a_{2n}X_n + d_2 \\
&\vdots \\
X_n &= a_{n1}X_1 + a_{n2}X_2 + \cdots + a_{nn}X_n + d_n
\end{aligned} \tag{9.14}$$

The equations in (9.14) could equivalently be written in terms of the final demands for goods and services, the $d_i$'s. This version of the input-output model indicates where the final goods and services in the economy are produced:

$$\begin{aligned}
d_1 &= (1 - a_{11})X_1 - a_{12}X_2 - \cdots - a_{1n}X_n \\
d_2 &= -a_{21}X_1 + (1 - a_{22})X_2 - \cdots - a_{2n}X_n \\
&\vdots \\
d_i &= -a_{i1}X_1 - a_{i2}X_2 - \cdots + (1 - a_{ii})X_i - \cdots - a_{in}X_n \\
&\vdots \\
d_n &= -a_{n1}X_1 - a_{n2}X_2 - \cdots + (1 - a_{nn})X_n
\end{aligned} \tag{9.15}$$

Table 9.3 The technical coefficients of production in an economy with $n$ industries

| *Industry producing* | *Industry purchasing* 1 | 2 | 3 | $\cdots$ | $n$ |
|---|---|---|---|---|---|
| 1 | $a_{11}$ | $a_{12}$ | $a_{13}$ | $\cdots$ | $a_{1n}$ |
| 2 | $a_{21}$ | $a_{22}$ | $a_{23}$ | $\cdots$ | $a_{2n}$ |
| 3 | $a_{31}$ | $a_{32}$ | $a_{33}$ | $\cdots$ | $a_{3n}$ |
| $\vdots$ | $\vdots$ | $\vdots$ | $\vdots$ | | $\vdots$ |
| $n$ | $a_{n1}$ | $a_{n2}$ | $a_{n3}$ | | $a_{nn}$ |

In matrix notation, the system of linear equations found in (9.15) is expressed as

$$\begin{bmatrix} (1-a_{11}) & -a_{12} & \cdots & -a_{1n} \\ -a_{21} & (1-a_{22}) & \cdots & -a_{2n} \\ \vdots & \vdots & & \vdots \\ -a_{n1} & -a_{n2} & \cdots & (1-a_{nn}) \end{bmatrix} \begin{bmatrix} X_1 \\ X_2 \\ \vdots \\ X_n \end{bmatrix} = \begin{bmatrix} d_1 \\ d_2 \\ \vdots \\ d_n \end{bmatrix} \tag{9.16}$$

or

$$(I - A)X = d \tag{9.17}$$

In Equation (9.17), $I$ is an $n \times n$ identity matrix, $A$ is the technical coefficient matrix, $X$ is the $n$-industry variable matrix, and $d$ is the final demand matrix. We frequently refer to the matrix $(I - A)$ as a *Leontief matrix*. Using matrix inversion, *if* $I - A$ is nonsingular, then we can find $(I - A)^{-1}$. This means that the unique solution for the $X$ matrix is

$$X = (I - A)^{-1} d \tag{9.18}$$

EXAMPLE Table 9.4 lists the sources of inputs, and the destinations of outputs, in a hypothetical economy. We could represent Table 9.4 as a system of 11 simultaneous linear equations in 11 unknowns. Movements along a given row, from left to right, show the output of a particular industry, and where that output is sent. For example, Row 6 lists the destinations of the output produced by industry $F$. Two units of that output are sent to industry $A$, six units to industry $B$, and so forth. Column 7 reveals that two units of industry $D$'s output are devoted to the accumulation of inventories in industry $F$ itself. The total production of industry $F$ is found in column 12; it is equal to 46.

A movement down any column in Table 9.4 lists the inputs that each industry or sector receives from other industries or sectors. For example, column 5 indicates the inputs that industry $E$ receives from other industries and sectors. Thus industry $E$ uses five units of industry $A$'s output, three units of industry $B$'s output, five units of industry $C$'s output, and so forth.

The "processing sector" of an input-output table (rows 1 through 6 and columns 1 through 6 contains all those industries that produce salable goods and services, such as cars, furniture, and toothpaste. The processing sector of most input-output tables is highly developed and may contain as many as 500 industries.

Columns 7 through 11 contain the "final demand" sector. For example, household purchases of goods and services are recorded in column 11; they total 14 units from industry $A$, 17 units from industry $B$, and so forth. Rows 7 through 11 contain the "payments sector" of the input-output table. The payments sector shows the contribution of various owners of factor inputs (for example, households) to the production of each output. For example, households provide 19 units of their inputs, predominantly labor, to industry $A$, as recorded in row 11, column 1.

The input-output table shown in Table 9.4 also records total gross outlays (in row 12) and Total Gross Output (in column 12). The total gross outlay of

Table 9.4 Input-output table

| Industry producing (inputs[b]) | Industry purchasing (outputs[a]): Processing sector (1) A | (2) B | (3) C | (4) D | (5) E | (6) F | Final demand: (7) Gross inventory accumulation (+) | (8) Exports to foreign countries | (9) Government purchases | (10) Gross private capital formation | (11) Households | (12) Total gross output |
|---|---|---|---|---|---|---|---|---|---|---|---|---|
| Processing sector | | | | | | | | | | | | |
| 1. Industry *A* | 10 | 15 | 1 | 2 | 5 | 6 | 2 | 5 | 1 | 3 | 14 | 64 |
| 2. Industry *B* | 5 | 4 | 7 | 1 | 3 | 8 | 1 | 6 | 3 | 4 | 17 | 59 |
| 3. Industry *C* | 7 | 2 | 8 | 1 | 5 | 3 | 2 | 3 | 1 | 3 | 5 | 40 |
| 4. Industry *D* | 11 | 1 | 2 | 8 | 6 | 4 | 0 | 0 | 1 | 2 | 4 | 39 |
| 5. Industry *E* | 4 | 0 | 1 | 14 | 3 | 2 | 1 | 2 | 1 | 3 | 9 | 40 |
| 6. Industry *F* | 2 | 6 | 7 | 6 | 2 | 6 | 2 | 4 | 2 | 1 | 8 | 46 |
| Payments sector | | | | | | | | | | | | |
| 7. Gross inventory depletion (−) | 1 | 2 | 1 | 0 | 2 | 1 | 0 | 1 | 0 | 0 | 0 | 8 |
| 8. Imports | 2 | 1 | 3 | 0 | 3 | 2 | 0 | 0 | 0 | 0 | 2 | 13 |
| 9. Payments to government | 2 | 3 | 2 | 2 | 1 | 2 | 3 | 2 | 1 | 2 | 12 | 32 |
| 10. Depreciation allowances | 1 | 2 | 1 | 0 | 1 | 0 | 0 | 0 | 0 | 0 | 0 | 5 |
| 11. Households | 19 | 23 | 7 | 5 | 9 | 12 | 1 | 0 | 8 | 0 | 1 | 85 |
| 12. Total gross outlays | 64 | 59 | 40 | 39 | 40 | 46 | 12 | 23 | 18 | 18 | 72 | 431 |

[a] Sales to industries and sectors along the top of the table from the industry listed in each row at the left of the table.
[b] Purchases from industries and sectors at the left of the table by the industry listed at the top of each column.
*Source: The Elements of Input-Output Analysis*, by William Miernyk. Copyright 1965 by Random House, Inc. Reprinted by permission of Random House, Inc.

inputs and the total gross output of goods and services are not equivalent to gross national product. Gross national product is a concept that deliberately excludes intermediate outputs and inputs and concentrates only on the value of final goods and services. On the other hand, total gross outlay and total gross input involve repeated double counting. This is not bad, however, because the purpose of input-output analysis is to illustrate the input-output connections of the economy, not to provide a measure of the value of total inputs used or outputs produced.

We can use Table 9.4 to compare the technical coefficients of production that we discussed earlier. Each technical coefficient of production should tell us the number of units of input $j$ required to produce one unit of output $i$. Table 9.5 contains technical coefficients of production that were derived from the input-output matrix in Table 9.4. For example, industry $C$ receives a total of 40 units of inputs, one of which comes from the depletion of its own inventories. Seven of these 40 units come from industry $F$. Therefore the technical coefficient of production is $7/39 = 0.18$. This tells us that every unit of output produced by industry $C$ requires 0.18 unit of the output of Industry $F$. (Note that one must subtract inventory depletion from total gross outlay before computing the technical coefficient of production.)

Technical coefficients of production can be very useful to a researcher or forecaster if they are based on up-to-date data that accurately portray the actual productive processes being surveyed. For example, one can use technical coefficients of production to determine the probable effects of a decrease in the output of steel on the output of cars, on apartment construction, and even on Christmas toys.[5]

We can also trace the effects of public policies such as road building, increased defense expenditures,[6] and the like by means of technical coefficients of production. The U.S. Department of Commerce has long maintained a sophisticated input-output model to assist it in predicting the consequences of a wide range of public and private actions. Regional development authorities

[5] See Walter Isard and Robert E. Kuenne, "The Impact of Steel on the Greater New York–Philadelphia Industrial Region," *Review of Economics and Statistics*, 35 (November 1953), 289–301.
[6] Wassily Leontief and Marvin Hoffenberg, "The Economic Effects of Disarmament," *Scientific American*, 205 (April 1961), 3–11.

Table 9.5 Technical coefficients of production for the processing sector

| *Outputs produced by industries* | *Inputs purchased from industries* | | | | | |
|---|---|---|---|---|---|---|
| | *A* | *B* | *C* | *D* | *E* | *F* |
| *A* | 0.16 | 0.26 | 0.03 | 0.05 | 0.13 | 0.13 |
| *B* | 0.08 | 0.07 | 0.18 | 0.03 | 0.08 | 0.18 |
| *C* | 0.11 | 0.04 | 0.21 | 0.03 | 0.13 | 0.07 |
| *D* | 0.17 | 0.02 | 0.05 | 0.21 | 0.15 | 0.09 |
| *E* | 0.06 | 0.00 | 0.03 | 0.36 | 0.08 | 0.04 |
| *F* | 0.03 | 0.11 | 0.18 | 0.15 | 0.05 | 0.13 |

and larger corporations have also made extensive use of input-output models. It is clear that a well-designed input-output model could be of great assistance in predicting the probable economic effects of a strike in, say, the rubber industry that shut down all production there.

It is possible to derive input-output multipliers that show the total change in output that will occur as a result of a change in the output of one industry. According to Table 9.5, industry *D* receives 0.36 unit of output from industry *E* whenever industry *D* expands its output by one unit. Suppose that industry *E*'s output increases initially by one unit; this initially causes industry *D*'s output to rise by 0.36 unit.

However, observe in turn that when industry *D*'s output rises by one unit, industry *E*'s output rises by 0.15 unit. Thus a 0.36-unit increase in industry *D*'s output has a feedback effect that increases industry *E*'s output by $(0.36) \times (0.15) = 0.05$ unit. But this increase in industry *E*'s output once again requires additional inputs from industry *D*, and so forth. The original expansion in industry *E*'s output has set off a chain reaction of secondary increases in output. This multiplier process, which is not unlike the "national income multiplier" of Keynesian models, can be precisely quantified, so that we can isolate and analyze the final, terminal effects of a given action.

Input-output analysis is an applied matrix-algebra technique that requires substantial amounts of detailed information in order to be usable. The solution and manipulation of input-output matrices typically require the use of a computer because of the complexity of the calculations. This reflects the high degree of detail that input-output users typically want, rather than the innate characteristics of input-output analysis itself. Input-output analysis can be used to analyze very simple economic systems, such as the trading relationships between two towns or even the flow of students between two university departments. It is flexible enough to deal with a wide range of decision-making situations.

## PROBLEMS

1. Given the following linear-programming problem.

$$\textit{Maximize: } 3X_1 + 4X_2$$

$$\textit{Subject to: } 2X_1 + X_2 \leq 12$$

$$3X_1 + 2X_2 \leq 20$$

$$X_1, X_2 \geq 0$$

(a) What are the decision variables in the problem?
(b) Graph the problem.
(c) What quantities of $X_1$, $X_2$ maximize the objective function subject to the two constraints?
(d) What if the nonnegativity constraint ($X_1, X_2 \geq 0$) were removed? What difference would this make in the solution? Would such a solution be sensible?

2. O'Leary, Kowalski, and Schmidt (OK & S) run an accounting firm that performs tax audits and also completes tax returns for those who are willing to pay OK & S to do so. In a typical week, OK & S have 100 hours of staff time available for performing audits and doing tax returns. Of these hours, 60 are production hours and 40 are review hours. Each time an audit is performed, 10 hours of production time and 4 hours of review time are used. Each time a tax return is completed, 3 hours of production time and 2 hours of review time are used. An audit is priced at \$100, while a tax return is priced at \$30. OK & S wishes to maximize the sales revenues that they receive from performing audits and completing tax returns. (a) How many audits and how many tax returns should OK & S do? (b) How many hours of staff time will be devoted to each activity? (c) What is the total revenue that OK & S will generate by this solution? (d) Select any other feasible solution, and demonstrate that it generates less total revenue than the optimal solution.
3. Tony and Jim open a lemonade stand on their front sidewalk. They can make ordinary lemonade, or they can make a Lemon Fizz for their customers. The ingredients per quart for each of these drinks are as follows:

| *Lemonade* | *Lemon fizz* |
|---|---|
| 1 cup of sugar | $\frac{2}{3}$ cup of sugar |
| 2 lemons | 3 lemons |
| 1 quart of water | 1 quart of ginger ale |

The prices of the ingredients are as follows: Sugar is 15¢ per cup, lemons are 5¢ apiece, and ginger ale is 50¢ per quart bottle. Water is free. A total of 10 cups of sugar, 30 lemons, and 20 quarts of ginger ale are available. Tony and Jim believe that they can sell each 8-ounce glass of lemonade for 10¢, while each Lemon Fizz will sell for 25¢. They wish to maximize the profit that they realize from the sale of lemonade and fizzes. How much of each drink should Tony and Jim make? How much profit will they make?
4. Many courts in the United States have required specific school districts to undertake busing of school children in order to achieve racial balance in schools. In Gotham City, there are four schools, *A*, *B*, *C*, and *D*, each of which can accommodate 1000 students. There are a total of 3300 students in Gotham City. Of these students, 2000 are white, while 1300 are black. The Court has ordered that no school have more than 75% white students, nor less than 50% white students. The locations and race of each student are known and are given by $L_i^w$ (the location of white student *i*) and $L_i^b$ (the location of black student *i*). The school district in Gotham City wishes to accomplish this with a minimum of inefficiency and grief. (a) What objective function should the school board attempt to maximize or minimize? (b) What are the constraints that the school board must satisfy?
5. Indicate verbally how linear programming might be used in the following situations:
   (a) By the Defense Department when it is planning an antimissile defense

(b) By the Schlitz Brewing Company when it is deciding where to produce beer in its various American plants
(c) By the local zoo when it is planning the menu that will provide food for the animals
(d) By State University when it is scheduling scarce classrooms throughout a week
(e) By State Farm Insurance Company when it is deciding what type of computer it should rent or lease

6. Below is a simple input-output table for the economy of Polonia. Demonstrate the short-run and the long-run effects of a five-unit decrease in the output of industry *A* on all other industries in Polonia.

| *Industry* | *A* | *B* | *C* |
|---|---|---|---|
| *A* | 40 | 10 | 33 |
| *B* | 35 | 80 | 33 |
| *C* | 25 | 10 | 34 |

7. The economic planners of Polonia have just revised their input-output table, and the technical coefficients of production shown in the following table are one of the results of that revision. An enterprising young economist has pointed out, however, that such technical coefficients are not possible. Why?

| *Industry* | *A* | *B* | *C* |
|---|---|---|---|
| *A* | 0.50 | 0.40 | 0.13 |
| *B* | 0.15 | 0.36 | 0.71 |
| *C* | 0.45 | 0.48 | 0.68 |

8. Leontief-type input-output models frequently assume that each industry produces only one homogeneous commodity. In order to square this assumption with the real world, "composite commodities" are permitted such that one unit of the output of industry *A* may (for example) consist of two locomotives and three sticks of chewing gum. (a) Can you foresee any problems associated with such an assumption? (b) Are Green Stamps a real-world counterpart to such a composite commodity? Why or why not?
9. Input-output models do not formally incorporate prices or incomes. Is the absence of prices and incomes a crucial error? What problems might one encounter as a result of this omission?

# APPENDIX A

# TABLE OF INTEGRALS

1. $\int a\,dx = ax + C$

2. $\int af(x)\,dx = a \int f(x)\,dx$

3. $\int (f(x) + g(x))\,dx = \int f(x)\,dx + \int g(x)\,dx$

4. $\int u \frac{dv}{dx}\,dx = uv - \int v \frac{du}{dx}\,dx$

5. $\int x^n\,dx = \frac{x^{n+1}}{n+1} + C \qquad n \neq -1$

6. $\int b^{ax}\,dx = \frac{b^{ax}}{a \ln b} + C$

7. $\int e^x\,dx = e^x + C$

8. $\int e^{ax}\,dx = \frac{e^{ax}}{a} + C$

9. $\int xe^{ax}\,dx = \frac{e^{ax}}{a^2}(ax - 1) + C$

10. $\int \frac{dx}{x} = \ln |x| + C$

1. $\int \frac{dx}{a + bx} = \frac{1}{b} \ln |a + bx| + C$

12. $\int \ln x\,dx = x \ln x - x + C$

3. $\int a^x \ln a\,dx = a^x + C$

14. $\int \ln (a + bx)\,dx$
$= \frac{(a + bx)[\ln (a + bx) - 1]}{b} + C$

5. $\int \sin x\,dx = -\cos x + C$

16. $\int \cos x\,dx = \sin x + C$

7. $\int \tan x\,dx = \ln |\sec x| + C$

18. $\int \cot x\,dx = \ln |\sin x| + C$

9. $\int \sec x\,dx = \ln |\sec x + \tan x| + C$

20. $\int \csc x\,dx = \ln |\csc x - \cot x| + C$

# APPENDIX B

# A STANDARDIZED EXAMINATION

Economics majors at Illinois State University are required to take a course entitled Introduction to Mathematical Economics, which closely parallels the material presented in this book. The following final examination has been given (with minor changes in coefficients) to about 225 students over a space of five years. The questions have been collected from a wide variety of different sources. The total value of the test is 150 points. The mean test score at Illinois State University over the five-year period has been 125.5; the standard deviation of these scores has been 18.6.

1. Assume that consumption is a linear function of income. The marginal propensity to consume is 0.90. When income is zero, there is dissaving of \$180. What is the explicit consumption function? What is the multiplier for this problem?
2. Given the CES production function

   $$Q = \gamma[\delta K^{-\rho} + (1 - \delta)L^{-\rho}]^{-v/\rho}$$

   where $Q$ = output, $L$ = labor, $K$ = capital, and $\gamma$, $\delta$, $\rho$, $v$ are parameters. Find (a) $dQ$ and (*b*) the degree of homogeneity.
3. Given the demand curve $q = a - bP$, where $a$, $b > 0$ are parameters. What is the elasticity at each intercept? Prove your answers using the formula for elasticity.
4. The production function for a firm is

   $$Q = 12L + 20K - L^2 - 2K^2$$

   The cost to the firm of $L$ and $K$ is \$4 and \$8 per unit, respectively. The firm wants the total cost of inputs to be \$88. Find the greatest output possible subject to this cost constraint.
5. Assume that the demand per week for the Fuzzy TV Cable is 10 subscribers when the price is \$15 per unit, and 20 subscribers when the price is \$10. (a) Determine the demand equation, assuming that it is linear. (b) What is the elasticity at \$10? (c) What advice would you give to the Cable Company?
6. A vertically integrated firm producing fertilizer has a production function $Z = 2x^3y^2 + x^2y$, where $Z$ represents the output of fertilizer, $x$ the input

of sulfuric acid, and $y$ the input of chemical flux. Sulfuric acid is produced with labor $L$ and capital $K$ according to the following production function: $x = \ln L^2K^{-3}$. Chemical flux is produced according to the following production function: $y = e^{L^2K^3}$. What are the $\text{MP}_L$ and $\text{MP}_K$ in the production of fertilizer?

7. The Shishka Bobsled Company manufactures two types of sleds, the Lightning and the Alaskan models. Suppose that the joint-cost function for producing $L$ sleds of the Lightning model and $A$ sleds of the Alaskan model is $C = 0.06L^2 + 7L + 15A + 1000$, where $C$ is expressed in dollars. Determine the marginal costs for both the Lightning and the Alaskan models when $L = 50$ and $A = 100$. Explain what your results mean.
8. Blinko Company is the sole producer of artificial lightning bugs. Management has determined that the company's total revenue function is $\text{TR} = 100Q - Q^3$. Determine the point elasticity of demand for artificial lightning bugs when $Q = 5$.
9. Assume the following national-income model:

$$Y = C + I + G$$

$$C = \alpha + \beta(Y - T) \qquad \text{where } \alpha > 0,\ 0 < \beta < 1$$

$$I = \psi + \delta Y + \gamma i \qquad \text{where } \psi > 0,\ 0 < \delta < 1,\ \gamma < 0$$

$$G = G_0$$

$$i = i_0 \qquad \text{interest rate}$$

$$T = t_0 + t_1 y \qquad \text{where } t_0 \text{ and } t_1 > 0$$

(a) List all parameters, and endogenous and exogenous variables.
(b) Solve for the equilibrium income level using *Cramer's rule.*

10. Mr. Tonio Ling, president of the Ding-a-Ling Alarm Clock Company, has determined that the total cost function for the Pittsburgh subsidiary is $\text{TC} = x^2/4 + 3x + 400$, where $x$ is the number of units produced. At what level of output will average cost per unit be a minimum for Ding-a-Ling alarm clocks in the United States?
11. Find the extreme value(s) of

$$W = -x^3 + 3xz + 2y - y^2 - 3z^2$$

12. How much of goods $q_1$, $q_2$, and $q_3$ should a person consume so as to maximize utility, where the utility function is given by $U = 10q_1q_2q_3$, and where the price of $q_1$ is \$1, the price of $q_2$ is \$2, the price of $q_3$ is \$4, and the available budget is \$120?
13. Solve the following set of equations using inverse matrix algebra:

$$\begin{aligned} x_1 + \qquad 2x_3 + x_4 &= 4 \\ x_1 - x_2 + \qquad\qquad 2x_4 &= 12 \\ 2x_1 + x_2 + \qquad\qquad x_4 &= 12 \\ x_1 + 2x_2 + x_3 + x_4 &= 12 \end{aligned}$$

14. Find the values of $x_i$ using Cramer's rule.

$$x_2 - x_3 + 3x_4 + x_1 = -14$$

$$x_2 + 2x_3 - \quad 3x_1 = 12$$

$$2x_2 + 3x_3 + 6x_4 + x_1 = 1$$

$$x_2 + x_3 + x_4 + x_1 = 6$$

15. J. P. Jellybelly, president of Jellybelly Jelly Bean Corp., faces a production function, in the short run, of

$$Q = 3(7 - L)^5 + 18$$

At what level of labor input do diminishing marginal returns come into play?

16. Given the following demand and supply functions for products $A$, $B$, and $C$, find the equilibrium prices for $A$, $B$, and $C$ using Cramer's rule.

$$Q_{DA} = 8 - 2P_A + 3P_B - P_C$$

$$Q_{DB} = 4 - 4P_B + P_A + 3P_C$$

$$Q_{DC} = 6 - P_C + 3P_A + 3P_B$$

$$Q_{SA} = 10$$

$$Q_{SB} = 2P_B + 2$$

$$Q_{SC} = 8 + P_C$$

17. Suppose that $A$ and $B$ are the only two *firms* in the market selling the same product (we say that they are *duopolists*). The *industry's* demand function for the product is $P = 92 - q_A - q_B$, where $q_A$ and $q_B$ denote the output produced and sold by $A$ and $B$, respectively. For $A$ the cost function is $C_A = 10q_A$ and for $B$ it is $C_B = \frac{1}{2}q_B^2$. Suppose that the firms decide to enter into an agreement on output and price control by jointly acting as a monopoly. In this case we say they enter into *collusion*. [*Hint: Express profit* as a function of $q_A$ and $q_B$, and determine how they should allocate output so as to maximize the profit of the monopoly.]

18. Given the Cobb-Douglas production function $Q = AK^\alpha L^\beta$, where $A$, $\alpha$, $B$ are parameters, show that the *expansion path* of a firm is equal to a *constant*, implying that the optimal input ratio should be a constant. Remember that the expansion path of a firm describes the least-cost combinations required to produce varying levels of $Q$. Assume that the total cost of production is given by $C = P_K K + P_L L$, where $P_K$ and $P_L$ are constants.

19. The Sweet-Tooth Candy Company produces two delectable varieties of candy, $A$ and $B$, for which the average costs of production are constant at 70 and 80 cents per pound, respectively. The quantities $q_A$ and $q_B$ (in pounds) of $A$ and $B$ that can be sold each week are given by the joint-demand functions

$$q_A = 240(P_B - P_A) \quad \text{and} \quad q_B = 240(150 + P_A - 2P_B)$$

where $P_A$ and $P_B$ are the selling prices (in cents per pound) of $A$ and $B$, respectively. Determine the selling prices that will maximize the manufacturer's profit.

20. Suppose that a monopolist is practicing price discrimination by selling the same product in two separate markets at different prices. Let $q_A$ be the units sold in market $A$, where the demand function is $P_A = f(q_A)$, and let $q_B$ be the units sold in market $B$, where the demand function is $P_B = g(q_B)$. Assuming that all units are produced at one plant, let the cost function for producing $q = q_A + q_B$ units be $C = C(q)$. [*Hint*: Keep in mind that total revenue from market $A$ is solely a function of $q_A$, and total revenue from market $B$ is solely a function of $q_B$.] Set up and determine *only* the first-order conditions for the monopolist to maximize profits with respect to outputs $q_A$ and $q_B$. Explain your results.

21. Given that

$$A = \begin{bmatrix} 1 & -1 & 2 \\ 0 & 3 & 4 \end{bmatrix} \qquad B = \begin{bmatrix} 44 & 0 & -3 \\ -1 & -2 & 3 \end{bmatrix}$$

$$C = \begin{bmatrix} 2 & -3 & 0 & 1 \\ 5 & -1 & -4 & 2 \\ -1 & 0 & 0 & 3 \end{bmatrix} \qquad D = \begin{bmatrix} 2 \\ -1 \\ 3 \end{bmatrix}$$

find: (a) $A + B$, (b) $3A - 4B$, (c) $A'$, $D'$, (d) $D'D$, (e) $DD'$

Show the following:

(f) $(A + B)' = A' + B'$ (g) $(A + B)D = AD + BD$

22. Evaluate the following determinant.

$$\begin{vmatrix} 2 & 3 & -1 & 2 & 1 \\ 0 & 1 & -1 & 1 & 2 \\ 0 & 0 & -1 & 2 & 3 \\ 0 & 0 & 0 & 1 & 4 \\ 0 & 0 & 0 & 2 & 5 \end{vmatrix}$$

23. Find the inverse for the following matrix.

$$\begin{bmatrix} 1 & 1 & 1 \\ 0 & 1 & 1 \\ 0 & 0 & 1 \end{bmatrix}$$

24. Solve the following equations using Cramer's rule (*no* credit unless Cramer's rule is used).

$$x_1 + x_2 + x_3 = 0$$

$$x_1 + 3x_3 = 1$$

$$2x_2 + 2x_1 = 0$$

25. Find the extreme value(s) of

$$Z = 2x_1^2 + x_1x_2 + 4x_2^2 + x_1x_3 + x_3^2 + 2$$

26. Determine the values of $x_1$, $x_2$, and $x_3$ that maximize or minimize the function $Z = x_1^2 + x_2^2 + 7x_3^2 - 2x_1x_3 + 10$ subject to the constraint $x_1 + 2x_2 + 3x_3 = 0$.

# INDEX

*Proper Names*



*Subjects*